SWEDEN
Scale of Miles
0 25 50 75 100 125 150
Historic subdivision into Landskap (Shires)
Boundary Lines mark off the three main Subdivisions: Svealand, Götaland and Norrland; identical with Central, Southern and Northern Sweden.
LAPPLAND
NORRBOTTEN
VÄSTERBOTTEN
JÄMTLAND
ÅNGERMANLAND
MEDELPAD
HÄRJEDALEN
HÄLSINGLAND
DALARNE
GÄSTRIKLAND
UPPLAND
VÄRMLAND
VÄSTMANLAND
NÄRKE
SÖDERMANLAND
DAL
BOHUSLÄN
VÄSTERGÖTLAND
ÖSTERGÖTLAND
SMÅLAND
HALLAND
BLEKINGE
SKÅNE
GÖTTLAND
ÖLAND
Stockholm
Uppsala
Västerås
Örebro
Nyköping
Norrköping
Karlstad
Göteborg
Jönköping
Växjö
Kalmar
Halmstad
Hälsingborg
Malmö
Kristianstad
Karlskrona
Visby
Gävle
Falun
Söderhamn
Sundsvall
Härnösand
Östersund
Umeå
Luleå
Haparanda
Gällivare
Kirunavara
Oslo
Uddevalla
Trollhättan
Åmål
ATLANTIC OCEAN
NORWAY
FINLAND
GULF OF BOTHNIA
BALTIC SEA
Kattegat
Arctic Circle
Longitude East from Greenwich
Williams Engraving Co., N. Y.

A HISTORY OF SWEDEN

A HISTORY OF
SWEDEN

by

ANDREW A. STOMBERG

Professor of the Scandinavian Languages and Literature, University of Minnesota
Formerly Professor of History, Gustavus Adolphus College

Illustrated with Numerous Half-tone Illustrations and Line Drawings

NEW YORK
THE MACMILLAN COMPANY
1931

KRAUS REPRINT CO.
New York
1969

Set up and electrotyped. Published October, 1931.

L.C. Catalog Card Number 31-30744.

KRAUS REPRINT CO.
A U.S. Division of Kraus-Thomson Organization Limited

PRINTED IN THE UNITED STATES OF AMERICA

PREFACE

The noteworthy progress in practically all worth-while endeavours which the Swedish people has made, during the most recent decades especially, has served to arouse a deep interest in this northern nation and its institutions. This interest is very manifest among English-speaking peoples as well as among other races. A book in the English language which recites the history of Sweden from earliest times to the present day has therefore long been a desideratum. This volume is the result of a desire to be helpful in making available data which reveal "how it actually has happened."

It has been my constant aim to bring into relief those personages and events which seem to have actually counted for something in the long and painful struggle for human betterment. If it should appear to some that the agricultural class, the *bönder,* is given undue prominence in the following pages, it may justly be answered that the group has played so unique a part in the nation's history that it would be difficult to find a parallel in the records of any other country. One cannot properly write a history of Sweden without taking cognizance of the *bönder's* sterling worth and valuable contributions. Too much emphasis has not, I think, been placed upon the part that royalty has played in the life of the Swedish people. In the words of one of Sweden's foremost historians, Geijer: "The history of the Swedes is the history of their kings." While this statement is admittedly an exaggeration, any fair-minded man must certainly concede that Swedish kings have profoundly affected the lives and fortunes of their subjects. Most of them, men of outstanding intellectual endowments, have been impelled to worthy achievement by tremendous energy. The cooperation of the sturdy *bonde* class and patriotic and clear-visioned kings presents much of human interest and has been of profound significance to the nation.

It would be highly presumptuous to claim that all of this

work is the result of original research. While the author can truthfully say that he has done an extensive reading of primary sources in the field, he frankly admits that the excellent standard works on the history of Sweden in the Swedish language have been relied upon largely both for facts and interpretation. This will appear not only from the text, but from the references cited.

It has seemed desirable to retain the Swedish spelling of names of Swedish provinces even in cases where English forms have become familiar, as in the case of Skåne and Dalarna (Scania and Dalecarlia). Proper names sometimes appear in Anglicized form, especially where distinct English forms have been developed. The word *bonde* (plural *bönder*) is used throughout the text since no English word is an exact equivalent. The *bonde* was an independent land-owner, and hence the term peasant will not do. The word farmer connotes one who tills the soil, and the *bonde* not only did that, but he was member of a class which had won and always maintained the right of representation in the national legislative body, the Riksdag.

The list of friends to whom the author is indebted for assistance and encouragement is a long one. Special mention is gratefully made of the kindness of Archbishop Nathan Söderblom, primate of the state church of Sweden and pro-chancellor of the University of Uppsala. An invitation from him to give a series of lectures under the auspices of the Olaus Petri Foundation at that university gave opportunity to spend several months in research work in its wonderful library. The cooperation of Dr. Anders Grape, chief librarian, Oskar Lundberg, assistant librarian, and other members of the staff is remembered with pleasure and gratitude. Similarly the author is under obligation to Frederick Hjelmquist, chief librarian at Stockholm. The following friends have kindly read portions of the manuscript critically, checked errors, and offered valuable suggestions: Dr. Sune Lindquist, professor of Northern antiquities, University of Uppsala; Dr. Edward Thermænius, department of history, University of Lund; Dr. Gustaf Jacobson, instructor in history, Östermalm högre allmänna läroverk, Stockholm; Dr. George Landberg, instructor in history, University of Uppsala; Dr. Sten Engstrom, Stockholm; Dr. Conrad Peterson, professor of history, Gustavus Adolphus College, and Roy W. Swanson, editorial writer, The Pioneer Press, St. Paul. It would be manifestly unfair to charge these men with responsibility for errors that undoubtedly will be found in the text; for these the author alone should be blamed. Finally grateful acknowledgment is made of the helpful cooperation of Mrs. Axelia Kallin of Södertälje, Sweden, formerly assistant in the Department of Scandinavian, University of Minnesota, who typed most of the original draft of the manuscript and offered valuable suggestions. Miss Ruth Westerlund, instructor in Swedish in South High School, Minneapolis, and Miss Alice M. Johnson, assistant in the Scandinavian department, University of Minnesota, have been especially helpful in preparing the index. Professor Peterson of Gustavus Adolphus College and Professor Walter G. Johnson of Augsburg College have assisted greatly in reading the galley proofs, and Mr. Victor E. Fundell of Minneapolis has prepared some of the maps which appear in the text. To more than any one else I am indebted to my wife for constant help and encouragement in the preparation of this volume.

A. A. STOMBERG.

University of Minnesota,
May, 1931.

KEY TO THE PRONUNCIATION OF SWEDISH PROPER NOUNS

a, when long about like *a* in *far,* when short like the first *a* in *aha.*
e, almost like *a* in *day* or like *a* in *lane.*
i, when long like *ee* in *feel,* short like *i* in *ditto.*
o, when long like *oo* in *moon,* short like *o* in *oho.*
u, about like *u* in *value* without the y sound.
y, like the German *ü* as in *Lützen.*
å, when long like *o* in *hope,* short like *o* in *obey.*
ä, almost like *ai* in *air.*
ö, when long like *ö* in German *böse,* short like *ö* in *Götter.*

Most of the consonants are pronounced almost like the English letters; *g* before a hard vowel (a, o, u, and å) has the sound of *g* in *gå* when the syllable is stressed, and before other vowels somewhat like the English consonantal *y; k* before hard vowels in stressed syllables is sounded like the first *k* in *kodak* and before other vowels it approaches the sound of the English *ch. Sk* before hard vowels are like *sk* in *skate* and before soft vowels somewhat like *ch* in *chary.*

CONTENTS

MAPS AND ILLUSTRATIONS

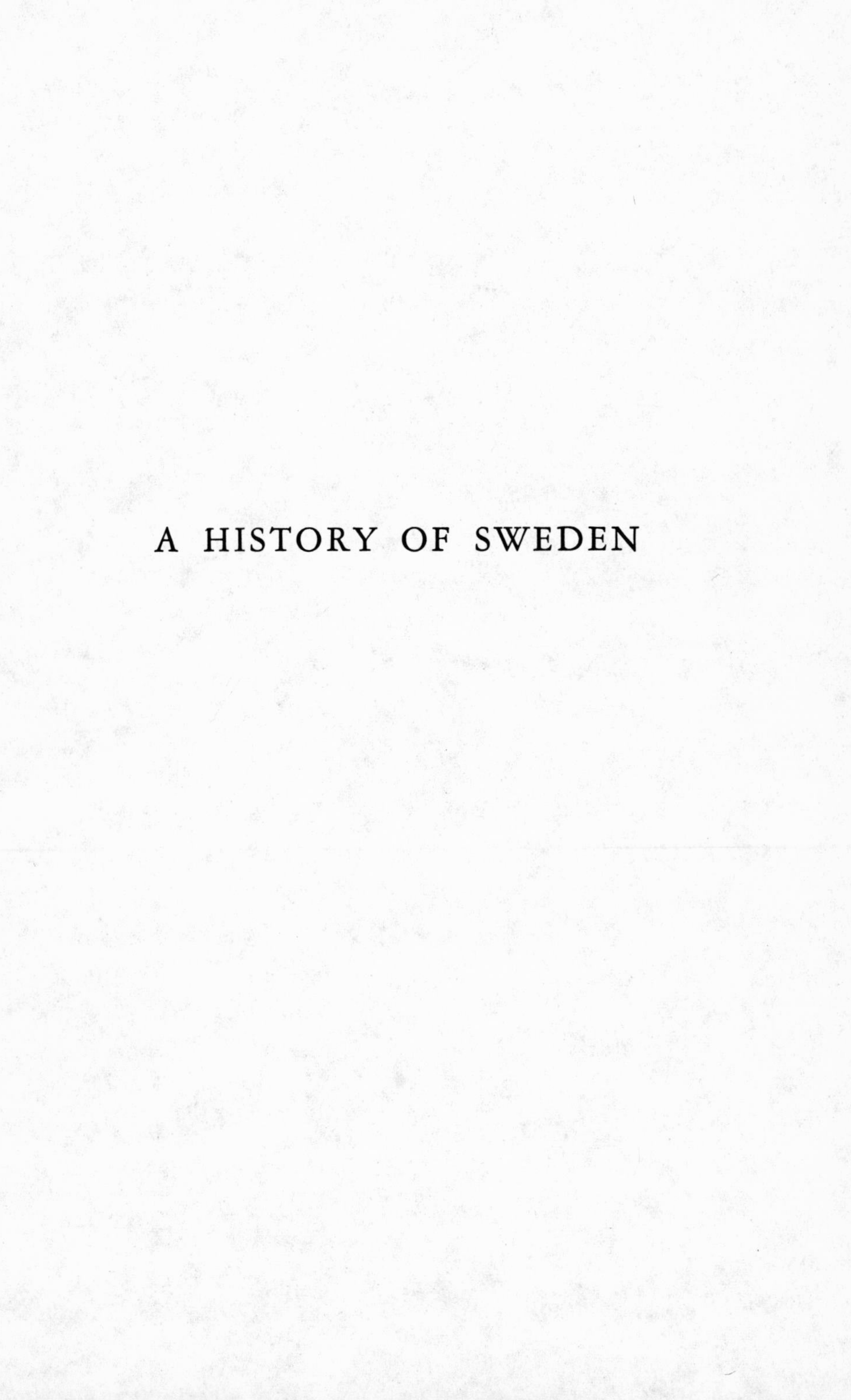

A HISTORY OF SWEDEN

A HISTORY OF SWEDEN

Introduction

LAND AND PEOPLE

Configuration.—The kingdom of Sweden comprises the eastern and southern part of the Scandinavian peninsula, together with Gottland, Öland, and the great number of smaller islands along its coast-line, and with its 173,075 square miles of territory constitutes one of the largest political divisions of Europe. Its area is about equal to that of France or Germany, and one and one-half as large as England and Ireland combined. In form the country is roughly rectangular and with a slight inclination lies due north and south; its southern terminus almost touches the fifty-fifth degree north latitude, while its extreme northern end rests on the sixty-ninth degree north latitude. With respect to area and form, Sweden and California present striking similarities. If a map of one be superimposed on the map of the other similarly scaled, it will be found that the boundary lines do not run very far apart. From north to south Sweden extends over nearly fourteen degrees of latitude, or one-seventh of the distance from the equator to the pole. If one might imagine that the entire strip of land which constitutes Sweden were swung halfway around, it would be found that the northern tip would, in the new position, rest on a line considerably south of Rome; to put it another way, it might be said that the length of Sweden from north to south is almost the same as the distance by a direct line from London to Algiers on the north African coast. The width of the country is considerably less than its length, the former being quite uniformly from two hundred and fifty to three hundred miles.

The greater part of Sweden is built of the most ancient rock recognized in geological history, and from this point of view the country is, therefore, one of the oldest lands on the globe.

The entire Scandinavian peninsula has been likened to a huge overturned boat which, it is true, has been badly battered and pounded, and a study of a relief map shows that this simile is somewhat apt. Approximately in the centre of the peninsula and for the greater part of its length, runs a ridge or mountain chain appropriately called the Keel (*Kölen*). On the Swedish or eastern side the land slopes gradually in terraced areas towards the sea. At quite regular intervals, deep valleys, the effect of erosion, extend from the highlands towards the Baltic, and at a point about one-third of the distance from the southern end the entire land seems to have been flattened as though pressed down by some tremendous weight.

Divisions.—In crossing Sweden, north to south, four main regions are traversed. The first, or the region of the highlands of upper Sweden, embraces the greater part of the country. It includes Norrland, a collective name for the provinces of Lappland, Norrbotten, Västerbotten, Jämtland, Härjedalen, Ångermanland, Medelpad, Hälsingland, and Gästrikland, and in addition the provinces of Dalarna and Värmland. This region is intersected by a great number of deep river valleys running almost west and east, between which lie vast mountain, forest, and moorland regions. The valleys and the coast regions have received large deposits of clay from the rivers and the sea, and thus constitute an agricultural section of considerable importance. South of this extensive northern section lies the district known as the lowlands of central Sweden, which includes the provinces of Uppland, Västmanland, Södermanland, Närke, Dalsland, Östergötland, the greater part of Västergötland, and Bohuslän. Although this district is only one-sixth the size of the highlands of upper Sweden, its large areas of fertile soil have in the past given it a pre-eminent importance. Several mountains of inconsiderable height cover a part of the area, and through it runs a belt of dense forests, which in earlier times lay as an almost insurmountable barrier to communication between its northern and southern sections, thus greatly delaying the realization of political unity between them. Having been submerged during the late Glacial Ice period, this area rose unevenly as the ice receded, and thus was formed one of the greatest lake regions in the world. Four of the lakes in this district, Vänern, Vättern, Mälaren, and Hjälmaren, are among the largest in Europe. By facilitating intercourse between the adjoining regions, these lakes and connecting rivers in earlier time played an important part in knitting together the different parts of this general area.

The third region is the Småland Highlands, which includes the main part of Småland, the southern part of Västergötland, and the parts of Halland, Blekinge, and Skåne which border on Småland. This region is in reality a prolongation of the continental plateau of upper Sweden from which it is cut off by the lowlands of central Sweden. In this section is found the same kind of river valleys as in the Norrland district, except that in this southern area they have been formed on a smaller scale, and the bed-rock is almost everywhere covered by a sandy moraine little adapted to agriculture. This region has the same extensive forests of pine and spruce, the same desolate peat-moss areas with stunted firs, the same succession of inconsiderable heights and shallow valleys that characterize a large part of the Norrland districts, but because of more favourable climatic conditions, agriculture has here always assumed a far greater importance than in the northern region. The district is dotted by a large number of shallow and irregular lakes and extensive marshy areas between which rise hills on which pine forests grow. A number of rivers flow radially from the Småland Highlands, most of them in a southeasterly or southwesterly direction, and at present furnish a great abundance of water-power for homes and industry.

The region lying farthest south, known as the Skåne Plains, is practically co-extensive with the province of that name. Its geological history and natural features differentiate it from the rest of Sweden. Geologically it has the same structure as Denmark and the Baltic provinces. This section has no high mountains, but merely ridges between which lie large and fertile areas. Because of its abundance of fertile soil and easy accessibility, this section has since time immemorial had a relatively large population and has played an exceptionally important part in the life of the North.

The Coastline.—The waters bordering upon Sweden are along the coast-line studded with islands of varying sizes and shapes; these are almost innumerable. The force of the winds which here often blow violently from the sea and ruthless despoliation by man have reduced almost to a minimum the forest-covered areas of the islands which lie along the western coast; most of the smaller islands here consist of rock alone. Along the eastern coast, on the other hand, are found densely wooded groups of islands, some mere specks in the sea, others large enough to form entire counties; two of them, Gottland and Öland, are the size of provinces. A group of these islands, almost countless in number, constitute the picturesque and justly famous Stockholm archipelago. The coast of Skåne differs in character from the rest of the Swedish coast, since here the bed-rock slopes gradually into the sea and very few islands border the coast-line.

Lakes and rivers.—Because of erosion and differences in the elevation and subsidence of the ground, great unevenness in land surfaces has resulted over the greater part of the country, and this, coupled with the unusually large precipitation caused by the moisture-laden currents of the Gulf Stream, has given to Sweden a relatively larger area of lakes and rivers than any other country in the world, Finland alone excepted. Lakes and rivers lie scattered over the country in such large numbers and with such delightful promiscuity that a noted traveller was once moved to remark: "When God in the beginning separated water from the dry land He forgot all about Sweden." Slightly more than one-twelfth of the surface consists of rivers and lakes, the latter sparkling with fresh crystal-blue water and lying amidst a picturesque setting of cliffs and forest land. Because of the terraced nature of the country, the rivers, most of which have their origin in the highlands towards Norway and flow in a southeasterly direction to the Gulf of Bothnia and the Baltic, have an abundance of waterfalls or swift currents, thus furnishing a potential water-power which, when fully utilized, can supply an abundance of electric energy for homes and industry. Few countries are in this respect as blessed as Sweden. In the total of estimated potential water-power, Sweden is surpassed by Norway alone among European countries; for the former it has been estimated at 8,000,000 horse-power at 70 per cent efficiency, for the latter at 9,500,000.

Lakes and water-courses are well distributed over the country, but are especially numerous in Norrland and in the lowlands of central Sweden. Fourteen of the rivers drain an area each of more than 3,800 square miles, or a total of 69 per cent of the entire area of the land. Thirty-one rivers drain from 386 to 2,440 square miles each or 16 per cent of the total. The largest basin is that of the Göta River, which empties into the North Sea at Gothenburg and has a drainage area of 18,640 square miles. The largest basin in the Norrland region is the Torne River, which drains a district of 15,440 square miles, a part, however, of this area being included in the area of Finland. The rivers with a drainage area of less than 386 square miles number not less than 70. The many rivers which have their sources in the highlands between Sweden and Norway are assured of a fairly even flow not only by an abundance of precipitation, but also by the huge natural reservoirs which erosion has produced. By reason of the many waterfalls and rapids resulting from the terraced or sloping nature of the surface over which they flow, Swedish rivers are for the most part unnavigable, but nowadays they afford excellent means for transporting the large quantities of timber that are brought to the sawmills and paper-pulp mills located near the coast. Several rivers in central Sweden have, however, by the construction of locks and canals, been made important arteries of internal trade and commerce. The most important canals are Södertälje, Göta, Trollhätte, Hjälmare, and Dalsland. The average annual precipitation for Sweden is 24.7 inches, the heaviest being along the Keel from about the sixty-fourth degree to the northern terminus (from 27.5 to 40 inches) and in the region bordering on the North Sea.

Climate.—Sweden lies in the same northern zone as Labrador and the Hudson Bay territory, fifteen per cent of its area being situated north of the Polar Circle, but because of the moderating influence of the warm and moisture-laden air currents which the Gulf Stream sends over the Scandinavian peninsula and of the winds which blow quite steadily from the south, it is climatically far more favourably situated than the corresponding belt on the American continent. In Stockholm the mean annual temperature is 42 degrees Fahrenheit, as compared to 50 in London, 51 in Paris, and 52.3 in New York. For Lund, situated in the extreme southern part of Sweden, the figure is 45 degrees, while for the corresponding latitude in Labrador it is approximately 23. Because of the great distances between the northern and southern sections, as well as differences in elevation, the mean annual temperature for different sections within the country itself varies greatly. For Kiruna, the important mining centre north of the Polar Circle, it is 28.1 degrees, or approximately 17 degrees lower than at Lund. While spring usually comes to southern Sweden in March, and is followed by a comparatively long summer season, the northern region, as a rule, sees the snow melt in the valleys as late as June, and its summer season is extremely brief. In Skåne the summer and winter days number respectively 142 and 72 days, in Stockholm 124 and 121, while for Haparanda, a city situated at the northern tip of the Gulf of Bothnia, the corresponding figures are 88 and 186; at Kiruna the summer season numbers on an average only 57 days. The brevity of the summer season in the northern section is, however, to a considerable extent atoned for by the abundance of sunshine which is poured over it as long as summer lasts. At Karesuando, in the extreme north, the sun remains constantly above the horizon from May 26th to July 18th, and even as far south as Stockholm the sun at midsummer sinks daily below the horizon for only five and one-half hours. Nature also seems to take care that the northern region should have the fullest possible benefit of this abundant sunshine, for most of the days here are cloudless during the summer season. The almost constant sunshine causes a remarkably luxuriant growth of certain kinds of plants.

Snow falls everywhere in Sweden every winter, but the average time during which it covers the ground varies greatly from province to province; in Skåne it remains in the open spaces 47 days, in the region north of the great lakes, 86 to 140 days, and in the valleys of Norrland, from 170 to 190 days, while on the mountains of the latter section it remains in certain places during the entire year and some large glaciers still exist.

The extremely low mortality rate of Sweden, often listed

by insurance companies in their comparison as the lowest, and so far the best that any nation can show, can be at least partly attributed to the bracing and healthful climate of the country. While the winters are cold, they are not extremely so, and the air is clear and crisp; in the summer there is never any excessive heat. Other factors which contribute to keep the death-rate low are an abundant supply of pure water and a high state of culture, one manifestation of which is a general cleanliness which never fails to win the praise of foreign visitors, excellent sanitary regulations, a highly efficient system of medical and hospital care, love of outdoor life, and popularity of both summer and winter outdoor sports.

Agriculture.—By reason of differences in climate and glacial deposits, Sweden exhibits great variations in soil conditions and vegetation. Approximately 12 per cent of her total area consists of arable or meadow-land, a very small per cent when compared with countries like Denmark or Belgium, but extremely favourable when compared with the neighbouring country, Norway. The proportion of arable land to the total area differs enormously in the southern and northern districts. Thus, while the Malmöhus district in Skåne, with an area of 1,725 square miles, shows about 80 per cent field and meadow-land, the province of Norrbotten, 38,278 square miles in area, shows only ⅖ of 1 per cent fields and 15 per cent grazing-land. In the provinces of central Sweden, as Uppland, Västmanland, Närke, Södermanland, Östergötland, and Västergötland, the arable land is from 30 to 40 per cent of the total area.

Despite the fact that natural conditions in the land have been less than moderately favourable to agriculture, the tilling of the soil has nevertheless, from the Middle Ages until comparatively recent times, been the chief pursuit of the Swedish people. In 1830 the agricultural population represented no less than 82 per cent of the nation, in 1870 this had dropped to 72.4 per cent, in 1900 to 55.4 per cent, in 1910 to 48.8 per cent, and in 1920 to 44.0 per cent, and this in spite of the fact that the total area under cultivation has about quadrupled in this period. Almost one-half of the cultivated land is devoted to the raising of oats, which is the chief cereal crop of the country. Barley, which in earlier times held first place, is now grown on comparatively small areas, principally in upper Norrland. Rye, which ripens as far north as the Polar Circle, comes next in importance. Wheat, mostly of the winter variety, can be raised only in central and southern Sweden. Potatoes are grown successfully in all sections of the country; in fact, the northern region offers certain advantages for their production, since here the crop is far less subject to destructive diseases than in districts farther south. The per capita production of potatoes in Sweden is only slightly less than the average for western Europe. In the production of sugar beets and the manufacture of sugar, the country has seen an enormous development in the last few decades. Skåne is the chief area for their cultivation, and the average yield per acre is here only slightly less than that of Belgium or Holland. While as a whole the Swedish land devoted to agriculture is not remarkably rich, good care and scientific methods have resulted in a yield which, considering the average, exceeds by a considerable margin that of more favoured France.

Next to agriculture, cattle-raising has since earliest times been the leading industry in Sweden. The prolific yield of practically all fodder crops in nearly all sections of the country has always been, and still remains, a most favourable factor in this occupation. Aside from the arable land which in later years has to an increasing degree been converted into pasture-land, there are vast stretches of forest and mountain areas, especially in the northern and central sections, which afford excellent pasturage. The value of the hay harvest is approximately one-third that of the total grain harvest of the country. The dairy industry has naturally, under these conditions, assumed large proportions, especially in later years. This development has been greatly facilitated by a number of epoch-making inventions by Swedish engineers, notably those of the cream separator by G. de Laval and the ice-method treatment of milk by J. G. Schwartz.

Forest areas and lumbering.—The main reason why Sweden in this mechanical age has turned so largely from agriculture to manufacturing industry is found in her vast resources of lumber and iron-ore. Between 55 and 60 per cent of the country's area is covered with forests, of which pine, spruce, birch, and oak predominate. Only one other European country, Finland, has, relatively, a more extensive forest area. For every one hundred inhabitants, Sweden has 966 acres of forest land, while Russia has 405, Germany 54, and the British Isles 7; the average for Europe being 183. Sweden's main forest areas are located in the moraine and peat-moss belt of the highlands of upper Sweden, where they cover about 40,000 square miles. Another extensive area of coniferous trees is found in the Småland Highland region, while the central area likewise has extensive forests. It is but natural that under modern industrial conditions with their demands for lumber and paper pulp, these vast belts of timber should have assumed great commercial importance. The total value of the output of sawmills and paper and paper-pulp factories in 1927 was approximately 875,000,000 crowns (a crown is worth about 27 cents). It is claimed that in technical and administrative efficiency the Swedish sawmill industry has no superior, while in volume of output it is surpassed only by the United States and Canada. Sweden's system of timber protection and reforestation is generally recognized as the most scientific and effective in the world. Its lumber is sold mainly to England, but considerable quantities are also exported to Mediterranean ports, to the Dutch West Indies, to Australia, and to Egypt. As an exporter of wood-pulp, Sweden holds first place among the nations. The many rivers with their tributaries, radiating into nearly every nook and corner of the forest region, afford easy and inexpensive means for transporting the timber to the sawmills or pulp and paper factories which are generally located on or near the coast, and thus easily accessible to ocean-going vessels.

Mining.—Except for iron the land has no minerals of importance, although in the seventeenth century Sweden was the world's largest producer of copper. This metal was found mainly in one small area near the city of Falun in Dalarna, which, according to estimate, has yielded half a million tons of copper since mining began. The income which the state derived from its monopoly of this mine at one time constituted its principal source of revenue. In the time of Gustavus Adolphus the income from copper amounted to $200,000, as figured in American money, while in the same period the customs duties of Sweden proper and its conquered territories yielded only $80,000. Without this income, Sweden could not have for a hundred years carried the enormous financial burdens which her rôle as one of the leading military powers of Europe imposed upon her. After the supply of copper-ore in this very circumscribed area was exhausted, the mining of the metal became relatively unimportant in the country as a whole.

The enormous iron-ore deposits of Sweden have been productive of wealth ever since the Middle Ages. The earliest document regarding the company which was formed for the purpose of exploiting the mineral wealth of Dalarna and known as *Stora Kopparberget* bears the date of June 16, 1288. The first royal privileges were granted in 1347. This company has had an uninterrupted existence to the present time and is therefore undoubtedly the world's oldest industrial organization. In the eighteenth century the country was the greatest producer of iron in the world, but although today it produces far more iron than in its days of leadership in the field, the total output now falls much below that of countries like the United States, Germany, France, and Belgium. The iron-ore deposits are found in two widely separated districts, the Bergslagen, which lies north of the great lakes of central Sweden, and the Kirunavara-Gellivare, situated north of the Polar Circle. The former field has been known and mined since mediæval times, but it is only with the building of railroads that the latter has become important. It has been estimated that of the present available supply of iron-ore in Europe not more than approximately 10 per cent is high grade, and that 92 per cent of this is found in Sweden. The value of Swedish iron-ore lies not only in the quantity mined but in the quality of the finished product. The best steel in the world is produced from Swedish ore, and considerable quantities of it are exported even to countries like the United States which have their own iron-ore deposits; here it is used in the manufacture of articles requiring the very finest material. Sweden uses considerable quantities of her iron-ore in her own constantly growing manufacturing industry, but the major portion is exported either in its crude state, as pig or wrought iron, or as Bessemer steel. Germany is the greatest buyer of Swedish ore, and next in order come

Great Britain, the United States, and France. The total value of the iron-ore mined in 1927 and the iron industry was $250,-290,000. Other metals besides iron, as zinc, sulphur, silver, and manganese, occur only in small quantities. Some coal is found, principally in southern Sweden, but it is of inferior grade. Silver was once mined in considerable quantities, principally at Sala in Västmanland, but the yield no longer makes this industry profitable. Some oil is being extracted from shale rocks, of which Sweden has abundant supplies, and it has been predicted that the production of oil will some day become an important industry in the country.

The Swedes have in recent decades turned rapidly to manufacturing pursuits, their principal output being agricultural implements, matches, electrical and dairying machines, locomotives, beacon-lights, telephones, and ball-bearings. This development has been greatly facilitated by the increased utilization of their vast water-power resources for electrical energy.

Transportation and communication.—In proportion to population, Sweden has the largest railway mileage among European countries, and her system of railroad transportation is supplemented by an extensive network of canals and more recently by motor-bus service, the latter having been, to a considerable extent, inaugurated and is being maintained by the state-owned railroads and the postal department. In the utilization of water-power for electrical energy, the country has perhaps advanced farther than any other country, fully one-half of its population in city, town, and country being now supplied with electricity for illumination, motive power, or heat. No other country in Europe has a larger mileage of electrified railroads. Railroads and motor transportation is supplemented to a considerable extent by the aforementioned canals and the coastwise trade is also considerable. Telephones are found in practically every home, even in the extremely isolated districts in northern Sweden. In 1926 the total number of telephones in the country was about 450,000, or approximately 75 for every 1000 inhabitants, as against 21 for Germany, 17 for Great Britain, 8 for France, and 3 for Italy. One system serves the entire country; the telegraph system is run jointly with the postal department.

Population.—The population is relatively small, amounting to only 6,087,923 in 1927. The average number of people to the square mile is 35, as compared to 665 in Belgium, 589 in the Netherlands, 207 in Denmark, and 21.2 in Norway. (The figures for Belgium, the Netherlands, Denmark, and Norway are for 1920.) In spite of the loss through emigration—according to estimates 1,370,000 emigrants in round numbers left Sweden in the period 1850-1916—the population has increased steadily during the later decades, so that in 1926 it was about 2,000,000 more than in 1863, an increase of 51 per cent. In the seventeenth century, when the country during some decades was rated the leading military power of Europe, her population was but slightly over one million. The rate of increase has for a long time been in excess of that of Europe as a whole and is due almost wholly to an exceptionally low deathrate, the mortality being for every age-group between fifteen and seventy-five less than the average for Europe. The birthrate has, however, shown a steady decline in late years and is now lower than in any country in Europe, not even France excepted.

Characteristics.—The Swedish people have, according to a process of computation which will be discussed more in detail later, lived in their present home for approximately 12,000 years, perhaps a longer uninterrupted residence in the present-day habitat than any other European people can rightfully claim. Immigration and a blending of the native stock with foreign elements have never reached such dimensions in the country that the original race type has been noticeably modified, with the result that the Swedes are recognized by anthropologists as the purest Nordics today. Mostly within historic time about 30,000 Finns, a few thousand Belgians (the Walloons), and a sprinkling of Germans, French, and Scotch have been added to the native population, but with the exception of the first-named group, which is confined almost entirely to the province of Norrbotten, they have all been thoroughly amalgamated. Most of the French and Scotch families which settled in Sweden, and many of the German, belonged to the cultured class and came to Sweden primarily for diplomatic or military service, or for the sake of business. In northern Sweden live the Lapps, numbering about 7,000. Their origin is unknown and, like the North American Indians, they seem quite incapable of adopting the ways of the so-called civilized man; in dealing with them the Swedish people have, as a rule, adopted a wise and humane "let-alone" policy. Aside from certain minor and necessary regulations, they are permitted to live their nomadic life as their ancestors did. This seems to be the greatest kindness which can be shown them, for when compelled to live like civilized men they succumb to disease.

In physical features the Swedes show marked conformity to the Teutonic type: high stature, fair features, blue eyes, physical strength, and mental capacity. An Arabian writer of the Viking period who met them in Russia was amazed at their stature, saying that they were as "tall as palm-trees" and ruddy in complexion. Measurements of Swedish conscripts indicate that in stature they are excelled by no people. Observations over a series of years show that the average height has in the last decades shown a slight increase. An unquenchable spirit of independence, daring enterprise, industry, honesty, humaneness, and a strong tendency towards idealistic thought may be cited as the outstanding good traits of the race. The spirit of independence of the Swede is the result partly of inherent Germanic virtues, partly of a favourable physical environment —nearness to the sea, wide areas, and plenty of elbow-room, the existence of a frontier somewhere in the country almost throughout the nation's long history—and partly of the fortunate appearance at critical times of great leaders in the cause of individual and national freedom. Subsequent chapters will have much to say about these leaders, whose influence helped to save the great middle class from sinking to the position of serfdom, and the nation from ever becoming subject to foreign domination. The courage of the people, which is apt at times to run into recklessness, has been fostered by the identical influences which have bred in them a spirit of independence. Their bold enterprises in Viking times, their heroic exploits in the Thirty Years' War, and subsequent participation in a long series of wars, their less spectacular, but none the less important and glorious, work on every sea and in many new lands as sailors and pioneers, have abundantly proved their courage and enterprise. The limitation of natural resources in their land has stimulated inherent inventive talents, and the list of epochal inventions by Swedes is impressive. These limitations of nature have also taught them the necessity of thrift and industry, virtues which foreign visitors to their land seldom fail to comment on and praise.

With its myriads of lakes and rivers, roaring waterfalls, silent, impressive forests, towering mountains and smiling valleys, glorious midnight sun and fantastic play of the Aurora Borealis, its ground covered with an unusually rich vegetation in summer and a blanket of sparkling white snow in winter, Sweden is a country of singular enchantment, and this has set its deep and abiding impress upon the people. The Swedes are pre-eminently lovers of nature—among no other people are proper names so commonly derived from natural objects as among them—and their poets are mainly lyrical in tone. Their singers, among whom Jenny Lind and Christina Nilsson may be mentioned as the noblest representatives, symbolize a high perfection in art. Their creative minds in the field of natural science form an impressive galaxy, Rudbeck, Linné, Scheele, Swedenborg, and Arrhenius being some of the most famous and honoured representatives.

The Swedish sense of right and feeling of humanitarianism have been exemplified not only in legislation to insure social justice, in which respect Sweden has perhaps advanced farther than any other nation, and in a number of splendid institutions and organizations for the protection of the weak and for the alleviation of suffering; but also in fair dealing with foreign peoples over whom the nation has in the past had dominion. Sweden governed Finland for approximately six hundred years, and while her rule was by no means free from selfishness and mistakes, conditions were, on the whole, no worse in the conquered land than in Sweden herself. Swedish law was introduced into the land, and the citizens of Finland were early given exactly the same privileges as the subjects of Sweden. There is in the story of Sweden's rule in Finland no such harrowing details of cruel exploitation of the weaker race as occur in the contemporary history of other colonial powers. As a colonial power in America—on a small scale and for a brief period, it is true—the nation manifested the same spirit of justice and humanity in dealing with the Indians. A study of social conditions at different periods reveals no such revolting oppression by masters in their dealings with their dependents as blacken the pages of most of the other nations' histories.

Love of knowledge and an intelligent interest in education are nowhere more in evidence than among the Swedes. The case is thus summed up by an authority on Swedish institutions: "In regard to a desire for knowledge and interest in education, the inhabitants of Sweden probably stand highest in the world. General education in the whole country is, with us, of an older date than anywhere else. The state grants a larger sum, in comparison to the number of inhabitants, to be spent on elementary education than is the case of any other country. One can practically say that there is no one in Sweden who cannot read."

Fundamentally the Swede is conservative in character, and is not found identified with revolutionary movements which employ violent means. Loyalty to the government under which he lives is one of his most marked characteristics. His conservatism is, however, not of the blind and immovable kind. It is a demonstrable fact that Sweden has advanced as far as any country in the world in what is called democracy, including the franchise for both men and women, representative government with a ministry or other governing or directing body responsive to the will of the majority, free speech, and liberty of conscience, but the change from the old aristocratic rule, or from arbitrary royal power, to the present organization has come about gradually and through peaceable means. Since the Middle Ages, Sweden has never passed through a bloody revolution.

On the reverse side of the medal may be seen such qualities as a certain stiffness of manner, and an inherent love of display and of titles. In spite of its democracy and culture, the nation has no generally accepted and common pronoun of address corresponding to the English "you." The Swede is prone to overestimate the advantages which foreign lands have to offer and by the same token reckon those of his own country too lightly. His quickness in acquiring a foreign language and adopting new customs is both a strength and a weakness. His predilection for thrift is often negatived by love of display and good living. The abundance of food in the typical Swedish home and the Swede's capacity for enjoying it are themes which foreign travellers in Sweden have seldom failed to dwell upon, often making themselves guilty of gross exaggerations. A great national failing has been drunkenness. At times it has become so great a curse that it has threatened to engulf the nation in ruin. As later pages will show, unwise legislation and systems of regulation can be cited as partly responsible for the extent of the evil in the past. Education, new social standards, and restrictive legislation have, however, combined to make the per capita consumption of intoxicating drinks almost as low in Sweden as in any other European country.

Chapter I

PREHISTORIC TIMES

Age of man in Sweden; Olof Rudbeck's claims.—"How long has man lived in Sweden?" and "What part did the country play in early development of culture?" are questions which in the past provoked lively discussion among both Swedish and non-Swedish scholars, and for the archæologists and historians of today they still hold much of intriguing interest. For the beginning of these discussions, one must go back almost three hundred years. After the rapid and unexpected rise of Sweden in the seventeenth century to a place among the great nations of Europe, the newly awakened national pride which filled the souls of all patriotic Swedes could be satisfied, it seemed, with nothing less than a historical demonstration that the country had played a unique rôle in the world even in the most remote antiquity and antedating the beginnings of culture in other lands. The most versatile and daring patriot and defender of the claim of his country's long and glorious past was the genial and brilliant professor at the University of Uppsala, Olof Rudbeck, who died in 1702. Rudbeck's early interest lay in the fields of natural science and anatomy, where he made discoveries which placed him among the foremost scientists of his age, but when later his interest shifted to the field of archæology he threw himself with passionate fervour into this, for him, fascinating study. For thirty years he laboured on a monumentally conceived but never completed work of four large volumes entitled *Atland,*[1] in which he made the bold and startling claim that Sweden was settled by Japhet, the son of Noah, and his descendants immediately after the Deluge, and that it is in Sweden that the traces of the world's earliest civi-

[1] Copies of Rudbeck's *Atland* are very rare except for Vol. IV, as no reprints have been made since soon after the first appearance of the work; a reprint of Vol. IV exists from as late a day as 1863. Copies of the first and subsequent editions are found complete in the library of the University of Uppsala and in the Royal Library in Stockholm.

lization must be sought. By a most ingenious marshalling of facts from archæology, philology, and classic writers, Rudbeck endeavoured to build up an impregnable defence for his sweep-

Olof Rudbeck explains his *Atland* to the scholars of the world
(contemporary copper plate)

ing claim. The more he read Greek writers and familiarized himself with their descriptions of the enchanted land of their imagination, "Atlantis," the more convinced he became that their account tallied exactly with what was known of early

Sweden. The two, he concluded, must be identical. What, then, had attracted the early members of the human race to Sweden? According to Rudbeck, it was her abundance of wild game and fish, her clear, invigorating air and absence of deadly malarial fevers, and a climate glorious alike in summer and winter. Rudbeck's enthusiastic and ingenious defence of his claim convinced some of the leading scholars of his own day and generation. It became, in fact, the patriotic duty of every one-hundred-per cent Swede to believe and vigorously defend Rudbeck's thesis, and scepticism on this point was severely condemned as rank treason. But while Rudbeck's theory was fantastic enough, the charge that he made the ridiculous claim that the original paradise lay in Sweden and that Adam and Eve were Swedes, which has given occasion for many a jocular remark, has no basis in fact; Rudbeck never claimed this, but some obscure followers of his did. His claim, it should be noted, did not, according to the generally accepted chronology of that day, ascribe any extraordinary age to Sweden, as the Deluge was supposed to have occurred about 2,000 years before the beginning of the Christian era.

The reaction; Dalin.—The pendulum of historical thought soon swung to the other extreme; a decided reaction to Rudbeck's sweeping claims naturally followed, and even the bitter defeats on the battle-fields which suddenly relegated Sweden to her former humble place among the European powers was reflected in a far more modest claim regarding the country's age and status in antiquity. The new theory held that man's life in Sweden did not even antedate the Christian era. The chief proponent and defender of this view was the Swedish historian, Olof von Dalin, who, about the middle of the eighteenth century, wrote an extended history of his country. Basing his deduction on the observed fact that the Scandinavian peninsula had been gradually rising at a rate which in his day was supposed to be definitely established, Dalin maintained that Sweden lay submerged under water until towards the end of the pre-Christian era, and, therefore, naturally could not have been the abode of man until comparatively late in time.[2] The scientific observation which Dalin and his followers accepted as

[2] Dalin, Olof von, *Svea Rikes historia*, Stockholm, 1763, I, Ch. 1.

conclusively destructive of Rudbeck's theory was soon proved to be grossly fallacious, and Sven Lagerbring, with whom real critical historical scholarship begins in Sweden, while rejecting the views of Rudbeck as the dreams of a too imaginative and patriotic soul, showed, on the other hand, that Dalin's theory also was utterly untenable.[3] While not able to follow Rudbeck in his extreme deductions, Lagerbring attributed a very great age to man in Sweden.

The spirited controversies which at one time raged between the Rudbeckians and anti-Rudbeckians might be passed over as merely another instance of utterly fruitless discussions, except as they served as a sort of mental gymnastics, were it not for the interesting fact that distinguished archæologists some decades ago came forward with a theory regarding Sweden's rôle in early civilization which seems strangely to hark back to the bold claims of the learned Uppsala professor.

Penka's hypothesis.—Foremost among these scholars was the Austrian anthropologist, Karl Penka, who advanced the startling theory that Sweden was the original habitat of the Aryans.[4] The claim implied, of course, that practically all the races which have played an important part in human history could look upon Sweden as their original home. From this centre, according to Penka, began the great dispersion of peoples which resulted in the formation of the various Aryan branches. Penka based his arguments partly on anthropological and partly on archæological data. Thus the people of Sweden, he says, have since time immemorial possessed, and still possess, the race type that is always associated with the ancient and unmixed Aryan type. The farther one proceeds from southern Scandinavia, he argues, the fainter become the traces of this type, and, reasoning from the analogy of plant and animal life, that the nearer one comes to the true type the nearer one also approaches the home of this type. Penka found in the gradual fading away of Aryan characteristics, approximately in proportion to the distance from Scandinavia, an added argu-

[3] Lagerbring, Sven, *Svea Rikes historia från de äldsta tider till de närvarande*, Stockholm, 1769.

[4] Penka, Karl, *Origines Ariacæ*, Vienna, 1883. The author further elaborated upon and defended his theory in *Die Herkunft der Arier*, Vienna, 1886. Indo-European and Aryan may be taken as synonymous in meaning; in our day many scholars prefer to use the latter designation in a restricted sense as applying to the eastern branch of the group.

ment in support of his theory. He also found supporting data in the similarity of the vegetable and animal kingdoms in primitive Sweden to what is known of the early Aryan flora and in the conformity of the civilization of early Scandinavia to that of the early Aryans; the historical fact that since earliest times Sweden has actually sent successive waves of emigration to different parts of the world gave greater plausibility to the theory.

Penka's views were accepted, though generally with some reservations and modifications, by many of the foremost archæologists.[5] Scandinavian scholars, however, were slow to give it credence. The interesting discussion seems to have ended in the quite general acceptance of the view that Penka's hypothesis in the main offered the best solution of the problem, and had more sound arguments to support it than any other theory, but that the region which must be conceived as having been the habitat of the early Aryans included not only Sweden but also Denmark, south Norway, and Germany between the Oder and the Elbe, and extending southward about as far as Brandenburg. One authority says on this point: "Serious difficulties are in the way of the localization of the Indo-European parent tribe or nation or group either in Asia or in any part of Europe outside of the Baltic Plain, Jutland, and Scandinavia—it is almost certain that southern Scandinavia, Jutland, and the lands between the lower Elbe and the Oder contain the cradle of the Indo-European family of languages." [6]

While the discussion involving Sweden and adjoining lands and their relation to the question of the original home of the Aryans was still going on, the science of geology stepped in to offer its evidence and make necessary a decided modification of Penka's theory. The investigations of this science conclusively established the fact that Scandinavia and north Germany were covered by glacial ice at a time when the region farther south enjoyed a moderate climate. The Cro-Magnon race, which may be considered progenitors of the Aryans, was already living in

[5] Sayce, *Contemporary Review,* 56, 1889; Rendall, *The Cradle of the Aryans,* 1889; Brunier, J. W., *Die Heimat der Indogermanen,* 1896; Hirt, H., *Indo-Germanen,* Strassburg, 1905; Wilser, J. S. L., *Die Germanen,* Leipsic, 1904; Rossina, G. G., *Die Indo-Germanische frage beantvortet, Zeitschrift für ethnologie,* Vol. 34.

[6] Richard, Ernest, "Scandinavian Theory of the Indo-European Origins" in *Boas Anniversary Volume,* N. Y., 1906.

the latter area. As the glacial ice receded, groups of these peoples moved into the new regions. Sweden and the neighbouring territory could not, in view of these facts, have been the original home of the Aryans. This conclusion does not mean, however, that she played no important part in the early life of the race.

Montelius' conclusions.—According to Montelius, undoubtedly the leading archæologist of modern times, it was in the North, and more particularly in Sweden, that the specific

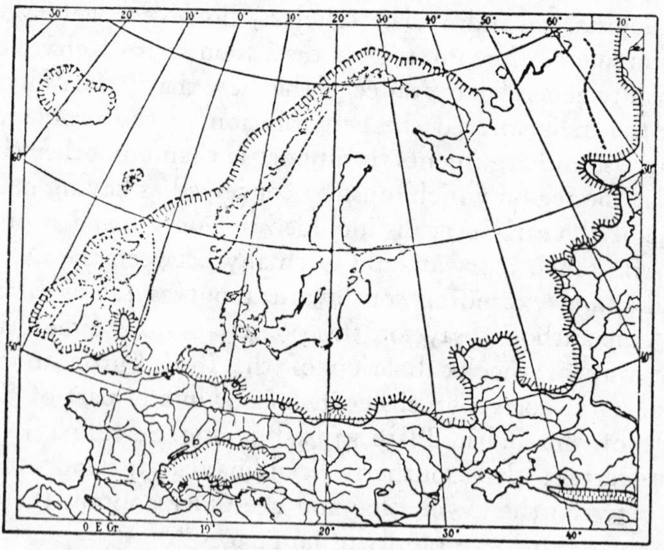

Glacial ice at its greatest extent

Teutonic race characteristics were developed, characteristics that have made the members of this group leaders in civilization. On this point this great authority says: "The people who immigrated to the North after the end of the glacial period cannot be called Teutons, but they were the forefathers of the Teutonic (Nordic) race. At this remote age, when our forefathers first began to settle Sweden, there was probably not much dissimilarity between the tribes that wandered about in different parts of central and southern Europe. Our forefathers have lived in Sweden since the end of the last glacial period and, consequently when they arrived there, the country which is now called Sweden was not at all inhabited. We Swedes possess a country which neither we nor our forefathers have taken from any other race. We Swedes have ourselves made our country, have cultivated the lands and made the roads. We have thus an unusually good 'title' to our land. Some scholars have supposed that the home of the Indo-Europeans was to be found in the countries around the south Baltic. My opinion is, however, that this supposition cannot be correct. Here in the Scandinavian North we have the home of the Teutonic race, but not that of the Indo-Europeans. All that I know of the remote ages, when the Indo-Europeans left their native land to spread over the earth, has convinced me that we cannot take upon ourselves the honour of our country's being the cradle of the Indo-European race. It is honour enough that the Teutons became Teutons in our country; a race that has inscribed its name on many pages of the history of civilization and which, I hope, will, even in the future, have a great mission in the mutual work of furthering the welfare of mankind." [7] The views here expressed may be said to state the position of most of the leading authorities in the field today. Among those who in recent works have discussed this subject and who reject the conclusions of Montelius, as well as the broader claims of Penka and his followers, may be mentioned Charpentier [8] and Karsten.[9]

Answer of geology.—If the ancestors of the present-day Swedes moved into their northern home at the end of the last glacial epoch, the question naturally arises: "How much time has elapsed since this happened?" An answer was given to this question in 1910, after one of the most ingenious and arduous feats of research that the thrilling story of scientific achievements records. The noted Swedish geologist, Gerard de Geer, concluding that the receding ice of the glacial drift must at each spring thaw have left successive layers of deposits, in their way corresponding to the rings of a tree, set out to count these annual markings. Seized with enthusiasm at the prospect that he might thus be able to give an answer to a most baffling question, de Geer and his assistants fell vigorously to work digging

[7] Montelius, Oscar, "The Emigration of our forefathers to the North," in *The Swedish Nation,* edited by Lundborg and Runnstrom, Uppsala, 1921.

[8] Charpentier, Jarl, *Jämförande indo-europeisk språkvetenskap,* Stockholm, 1926.

[9] Karsten, E., *Germanerna,* Stockholm, 1927.

in the soil or investigating its strata wherever a brick-yard, well, basement, or other excavation laid new layers open to inspection. In this way the soil was examined all the way from Skåne to the central part of Jämtland, a distance of approximately 800 miles, and in the neighbourhood of 5,000 rings or layers were counted; hence de Geer concluded that this marked the time required for the glacial ice to recede as far north as the latter point. It now remained for him to determine the number of years which have elapsed since Jämtland became free of ice. Fortunately for his investigation, a section was found near a lake which showed the annual layers of deposit, and not less than 7,000 were here counted. Hence de Geer came to the final conclusion that man moved into Sweden about 12,000 years ago; this, then, is the approximate age now ascribed to man in Sweden, an age far greater than any which Rudbeck ever dared to suggest.[10]

Nature of early records.—The written records which throw light on the people of Sweden and their culture are merely fragmentary until the thirteenth century A.D., but remarkably illuminating data regarding the earliest periods are furnished by an extraordinary wealth of archæological remains. A visit to the Historical Museum of Stockholm, where a great part of this material has been assembled and ingeniously classified, gives most convincing proof that already in the Stone Age Sweden had a considerable population, and that the men of that day were exceptionally well supplied with well-fashioned weapons, utensils, implements, and ornaments. The extent of the collection and variety of objects represented are due not merely to the great number of imperishable objects left in the soil by primitive man, but also to the fortunate and remarkable circumstance that as early as 1667 a law was enacted in Sweden providing for the establishment of an official state antiquarian, whose special function it should be to collect, study, and classify antiquities. This was one of the earliest provisions, if not the earliest, made by a state for the scientific study of prehistoric material. A law enacted in 1867 makes it more profitable for the individual who discovers archæologi-

[10] Geer, Gerard de, "A Geochronology of the Last 12,000 Years," in *Proceedings Congrès Géologique International*, Stockholm, 1910.

cal finds to turn these over to the state than to offer them for sale to private collections; another provision makes it mandatory upon the finders to report to the state antiquarian all discoveries of archæological material found in graves, building sites, or other fixed places as well as in all other cases where the finds are of silver or gold. As a result of this and subsequent supplementary laws, the collections of archæological data in the Stockholm museum are exceptionally complete. The number of Swedish archæological remains are said to reach the enormous total of 500,000.

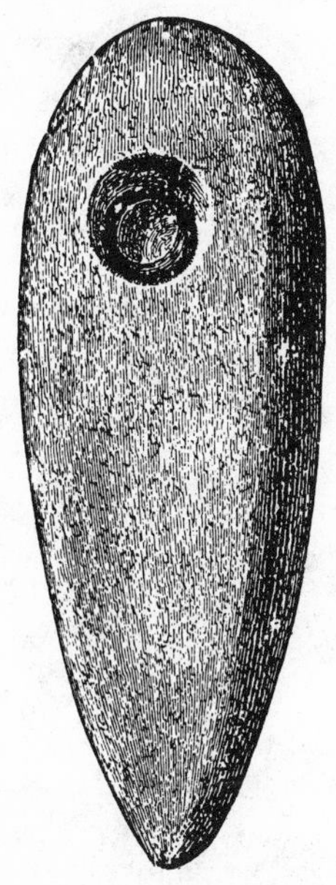

Stone axe with incompleted drilling. ½ size. Värmland

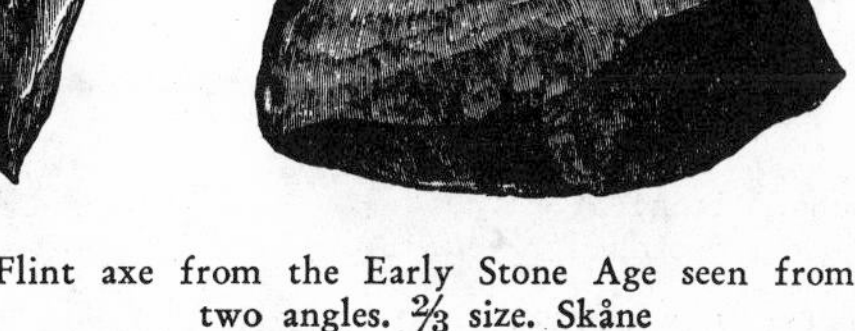

Flint axe from the Early Stone Age seen from two angles. ⅔ size. Skåne

The older Stone Age.—According to the ingenious computations of Montelius, the older Stone Age came to an end in Sweden about 5000 B.C. and the younger Stone Age about three thousand years later. From the former era remains are comparatively few, but sufficient to throw a good deal of light upon conditions of life in this age which, it should be remembered, must be counted in more years than the period from its close to the present time. While the remains unearthed in

Sweden from this period are not as many as those from the Danish "kitchen middens," the latter being large refuse piles which primitive man, still untrammelled by rules of sanitation or by a sense of the æsthetic fitness of things, built up by throwing the remains of meals, broken utensils, weapons, and the like into heaps which afterwards became covered with sand and débris, they are, nevertheless, considerable in number and variety and give much information regarding the status of man. The Danish finds include mussel and oyster shells, bones of fishes, birds, wild boars, bears, beaver, otter, bison, fox, wolf,

Flint axe from the Younger Stone Age. ⅓ size. Gottland

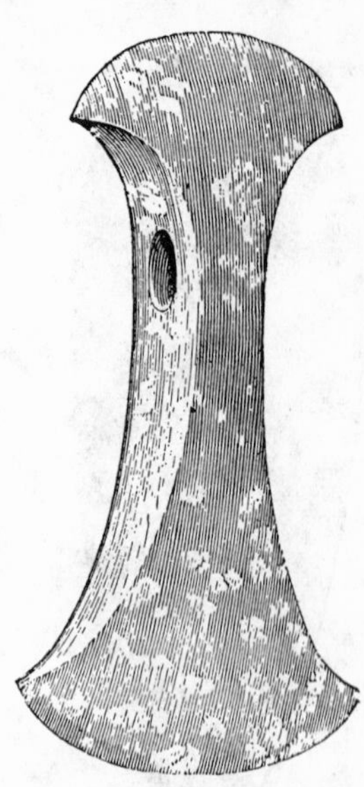

Flint axe from the Younger Stone Age. ½ size. Skåne

marten, wild cat, and the dog, which was the only domesticated animal. As for Sweden, the remains suggest that man subsisted solely by hunting and fishing, and this assumption is strengthened by the fact that no remains of grain have been found.

Life in the early Stone Age.—The great number of remains which sometimes have been found grouped in one locality point to some sort of community life. Settlements existed mainly along the coast-line in the southern and western part of the land, for it is principally in these parts that rough stone articles have been unearthed. Boats were evidently in use, since remains of deep-water fish, which hardly could have been caught without their aid, have been found. Even in this early period Sweden probably attracted hunters and fishermen by reason of her abundance of wild game and fish. Remains of crude fireplaces covered with ashes and charred fragments of wood and simple earthen vessels embedded in ash-heaps prove beyond a doubt that man already by this time had acquired his greatest power; namely the knowledge how to produce fire and use it in the preparation of food.[11] The oak predominated in the southern part of the country, but in a later period it was crowded out by the beech-tree, which still remains the predominant species in this region.

The younger Stone Age.—The younger Stone Age, in which the flint axes were polished, whereas in the earliest period

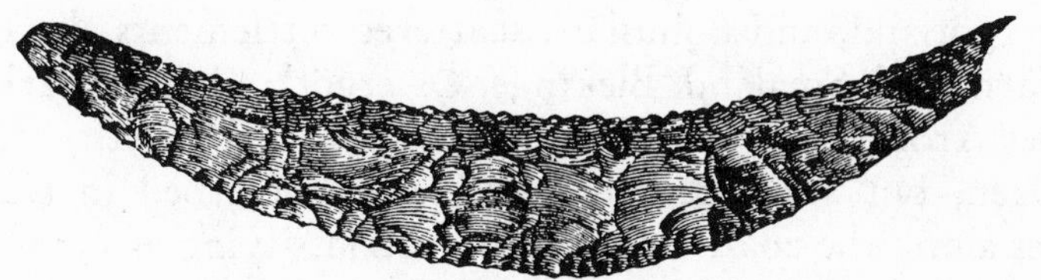

Saw of flint. ½ size. Skåne

they were given their form by chipping, shows such a remarkable advance in skill and culture that early historians and archæologists could find an explanation for the marked difference only in an assumption that with it a new and superior race had settled in the land. Thus Professor Sven Nilsson, one of the greatest among early archæologists, believed that the Lapps or Finns were the first inhabitants of the land, but that at the end of the early Stone Age they gave way before a new race.[12] Against this theory Montelius advances the seemingly unanswerable argument that save for the extreme north of Sweden all names of lakes, rivers, and mountains are Germanic in form.[13] A great number of short or brachycephalic skulls in graves from the younger Stone Age is indeed taken by Mon-

[11] Scandinavian mythology, it should be noted, relates how the gods, after they had created man, sent Heimdal to earth with fire and implements for producing it, and with grain which he was to teach men how to sow, cultivate, and reap.

[12] Nilsson, Sven, *Den skandinaviska Nordens urinvånare*, Stockholm, 1838-1843.

[13] Montelius' previously quoted chapter in *The Swedish Nation.*

telius to mean that members of a new race came into the land in this period, but he maintains that the long-headed or dolichocephalic race already in possession of the land was not submerged. An amalgamation of the two races took place in the southern territory, as well as in Denmark, but north of that the long-headed race remained unchanged. In central Europe the short-headed became dominant everywhere. Of the former home of the dolichocephalic race only the Scandinavian peninsula and southwestern France thus remains in possession of these people.[14] By proving that the oldest craniums found in Sweden belong to the long-skulled race, the noted anthropologist Fürst has given further evidence to substantiate the theory that the present race in Sweden were the original settlers in the land.[15] The large number of graves from this period point to a considerable population, which was densest in Skåne, Västergötland, and Bohuslän; scattered settlements also existed in Värmland, Småland, Blekinge, Östergötland, and Närke. No graves from this period have been found north of Lake Mälaren, but stone articles have been unearthed in scattered places along the coast-line even in districts lying as far north as Lappland.

The collection from the younger Stone Age in the Historical Museum of Stockholm proves in striking manner that the people of Sweden already in this period possessed a remarkable skill; it is, in fact, the opinion of archæologists that while Sweden is surpassed by some countries in the number of stone articles unearthed which were once shaped by man for his use, no people surpassed her in skilled workmanship and in artistic taste. The Swede's predilection for mechanical skill and willingness to take pains in order to produce fine articles, virtues for which he is known today, thus appear to be of a very ancient origin.

Most important finds from the younger Stone Age.—The most important find from the younger Stone Age was made in 1903 at Alvastra in the province of Östergötland. Here were found the remains of an ancient pole structure,

[14] Montelius, Oscar, *Sveriges historia*, 3d Ed., Stockholm, 1919, I, p. 13. Unless specifically stated, references to this standard work by different scholars are to the third edition. Reference is in each case to author and volume.

[15] Fürst, Carl M., article in *Fornvännen*, 1925.

similar to the Swiss pole dwellings. Among the well-preserved logs were embedded the stone remains of many fireplaces, quartz, and iron pyrites, cooking utensils, weapons, bones of

Distribution of graves from the Stone Age. Each cross represents one or more graves

bears, deer, cattle, sheep, and goats. No trace of the horse was found, but remains of this animal are known from a later part of the period. Domesticated animals had evidently been introduced from the Orient. That agriculture was now carried on is proved by the hollowed rocks used for grinding grain and similar to those still in use among certain savage tribes. Traces of kernels and heads of grain are still discernible in a few such primitive Swedish mills. Millet, rye, and wheat were the grains raised. The people had now established permanent abodes in fixed settlements, as only under such conditions could agriculture be possible. That nomadic life had ceased is further attested by the occurrence of the great number of graves which lie grouped together in certain localities. The occurrence of many graves in one area point to some sort of community life, and the great amount of labour expended in constructing them constitutes further evidence that life had assumed greater stability. Progress is also shown in the greater comforts which the people could enjoy. Clothes were made of skins, the sinews of animals serving as thread. No tools for making textile clothes have been discovered in Sweden from the period, as has been the case in central Europe, but undoubtedly linen and possibly also woollen cloth were already known; ornaments and amulets, consisting of pearls, amber, and perforated teeth of animals, were plentiful.

Types of graves; what they show.—Three types of graves exist from this period. The dolmens, belonging to its earlier part, are made of large perpendicularly raised stone slabs; they are roughly circular in form and covered with large boulders. The galley graves, which are larger than the dolmens, consist of 3 circular, oval, or rectangular vaults, with large stone slabs forming the walls and crypt, into which leads a passageway which was constructed like the main vault. The cist, or stone coffin, which occurs only from the later part of the period, was rectangular in form, with stone slabs thinner and more regular than in the case of the former types. Generally all three types of graves were covered by earthen mounds. The dolmen type has been found only in Bohuslän and the southern provinces. The galley graves lie closely together in Västergötland, especially near the town of Falköping, and the fact that two-thirds of all the graves of this type have been found in this one district suggests that already two or three thousand years before the beginning of the Christian era this locality was an important centre of population. The largest grave of the

Gallery grave. Västergötland

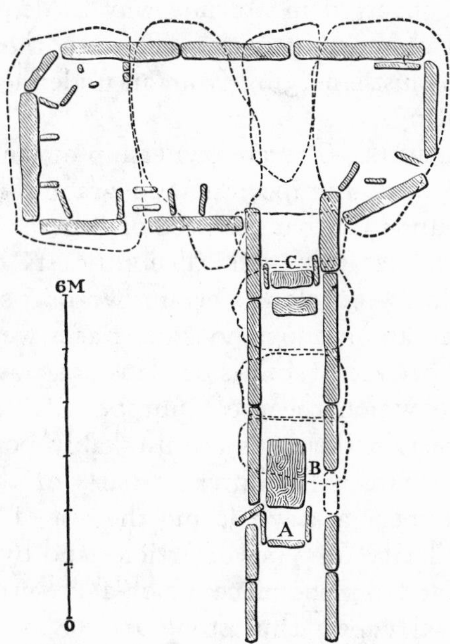

Interior arrangement of gallery grave

period, not only in this district but in Scandinavia, is approximately fifty-five feet long, nine feet wide, and with a passageway thirty-nine feet long. Since the cists belong to the later part of the era, when the population had evidently increased and spread farther over the land, they are found more widely distributed than the other two types, but none of this class has been found north of the province of Värmland. Remains of women and children, as well as of men, have been found in these burial places, indicating that they served as family graves. The care which was exercised in the burial of the dead points unmistakably to a belief in life of some sort after death, and this assumption is further strengthened by the great number and variety of weapons and ornaments, some of them unused, which were interred with the bodies. Vessels which evidently contained food and drink were usually placed beside the corpses. No doubt this was because the survivors wished to provide the dead with sustenance in the shadowy life of after-existence. The drilled holes which occur in some slabs undoubtedly were intended to contain sacrificial libations. The forces of nature were already conceived in a crude way as deities and a rudimentary form of worship is seen. Thor, as the terrifying god of thunder, was just emerging from an undefined natural force to a personal being.

Social relations.—Private ownership of land did not exist, for agriculture was unimportant and grazing land was available in such abundance that the need of controlling any definite area did not make itself felt. The interests of life centred around the family or clan. Certain words point to definite family relations, and monogamous marriages were undoubtedly the rule. Wars between families or clans had now become common, a fact to which the great number of weapons and the condition of certain skeletons unmistakably point. Communication existed between the different parts of the country and between the country as a whole and the rest of Europe. This is proved by similarity of types of articles and by the finding of stone articles far from the place which alone provided raw material for special types; thus stone articles, no matter where found in the land, were generally made of Skåne flint, which was far superior to other kinds of flint for the manufacture of weapons and implements. In 1830 there were unearthed in northern Sweden, more than six hundred miles from Skåne, seventy chisels and axes of flint from this province. Amber, a mineralized rosin of pine-trees, found originally only in southern Sweden, along the south Baltic coast, on the west coast of Jutland, and in east Prussia, frequently occurs far away from the original home. It was extensively used for ornaments and amulets and constituted the most valuable article which the North had to give in exchange for goods from the South. Similarity of types in stone articles and burial mounds suggest that communication existed between Sweden and England and between Sweden and the remote Orient.

While man in the Stone Age attained to a very remarkable skill in Sweden, it cannot be said that he reached the status of a civilized human being. The wonderful advance in material progress which the records of the past reveal was contingent upon the use of metals.

The Bronze Age.—Long before the end of the Stone Age the knowledge of a new metal—or rather compound of metals—came to Sweden. The Bronze Age had begun. There was no abrupt break between the Stone Age and the succeeding Bronze Age; the one merged imperceptibly into the other. By reason of the marked difference in the culture of the two ages, earlier archæologists assumed, almost as a matter of course, that a new race had come into the land with the latter, and that this explains the great transformation which took place. All the evidence of modern research disproves this, however. The situation, says Montelius, is analogous to the appearance of a mountain range; when seen from afar, the different peaks seem to stand out in isolation, but seen at close range the foot-hills and intervening lower mountains appear. In the same way, a closer view of the Stone and Bronze Ages, and a fuller knowledge of the culture of each, show that there was no abrupt leap from one to the other.[16]

The ingenious and patient investigations of Montelius, extending over a lifetime, with evidence for his deductions gathered from all parts of Europe, led to the conclusion that the approximate date for the beginning of the Bronze Age in

[16] Montelius, *Sveriges historia,* 2d Ed., Vol. I.

Sweden should be set at 2000 B.C. and its end at 500 B.C. Knowledge of bronze, a compound of copper and tin, came, as before intimated, from the South and was probably carried to the North by traders.

Importation of metals.—The metals were imported. Sweden's copper resources lay north of the district which had

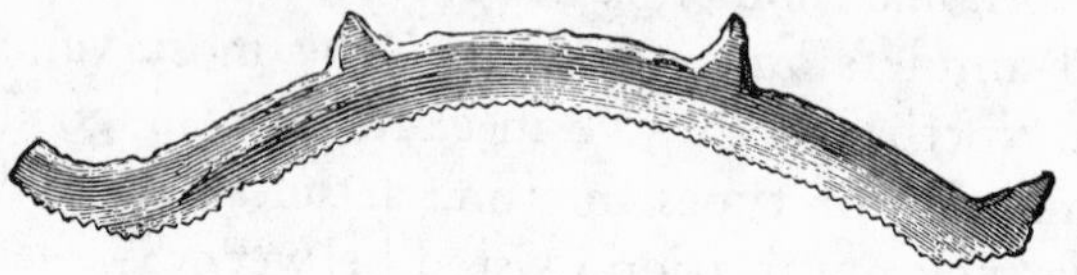

Bronze axe. ½ size. Dalarna

been settled thus early and were then unknown, and tin has never been found in the country. Copper came mainly from the region of the Danube, and tin principally from England. The highways over which the new materials and influences reached the North can be quite definitely traced, both by the numerous finds of amber along the rivers of central Europe and

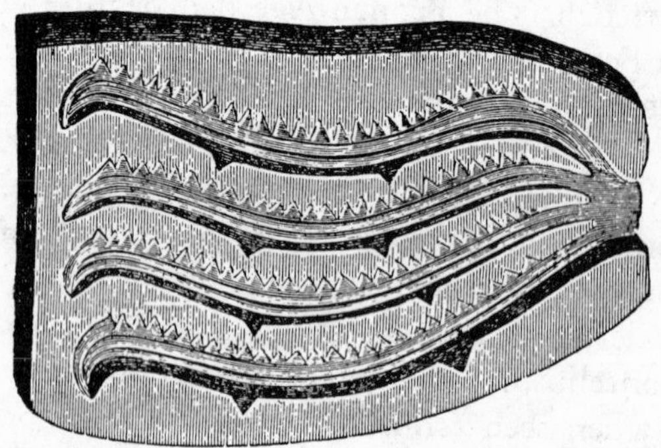

Mould for making four bronze saws at one time. An example of ancient "mass production." ½ size. Skåne

even as far away as Greece and Egypt, and by similarity of type in Swedish and foreign bronze articles. Much of the amber found in the region from which the copper came has been shown, on chemical analysis, to be Scandinavian in origin; included in this are hundreds of amber beads found in the Acropolis of ancient Mycenæ—a startling proof of the distance that articles were carried in those early days.

A striking similarity of graves in Sweden and England in the early part of the Bronze Age similarly point to close commercial and cultural relations between these countries in the period. Along a broad belt extending from the Göta River on the west coast of Sweden to the interior as far as the western part of Östergötland, twenty-five cists have been found which conform closely in type to certain English graves of the same period; these also occur in the western part of Continental Europe, but nowhere else. Archæologists have held that this phenomenon can be explained only on the assumption of a close commercial relation between the districts in question. Boats were necessary for trade and other communications which evidently assumed considerable importance in this period; that the people of the Scandinavian North knew how to build vessels which were serviceable for long journeys is graphically revealed by a large number of rock tracings found mainly in the province of Bohuslän, but also in considerable numbers in all the coast provinces of southern Sweden.

Swedish skill in bronze manufacture.—Many Swedish bronze articles bear unmistakable evidence of having been made outside of the country, Italy supplying the larger part. The greater number of weapons, implements, ornaments, and other bronze articles discovered in Sweden are, however, of domestic manufacture, which is proved in several ways. Thus moulds used in their manufacture and samples of defective articles which evidently were cast aside have been found in considerable numbers. The fact that some types are distinctly peculiar to Sweden gives added weight to the claim that there was a domestic manufacture. It would, no doubt, be correct to say that the earlier bronze articles which show conformity to the common type of the earlier bronze period in central Europe were imported, and that during the rest of the era the Swedes themselves supplied the "home market"; it may be further asserted that in this production they, as well as the Danes, exhibited an artistic skill and deftness in workmanship which was excelled by no part of Europe. Swords, shields, knives, axes, utensils, ornaments, and other articles show an elegance in design and execution which suggests the Greek sense of beauty. The North developed the making of bronze articles into a fine art just as ancient Mycenæ had done. The designs were, as a rule, borrowed from the South, but in the North these were improved and embellished in conformity with the ideals of the race. On this point Montelius says: "The results to which these

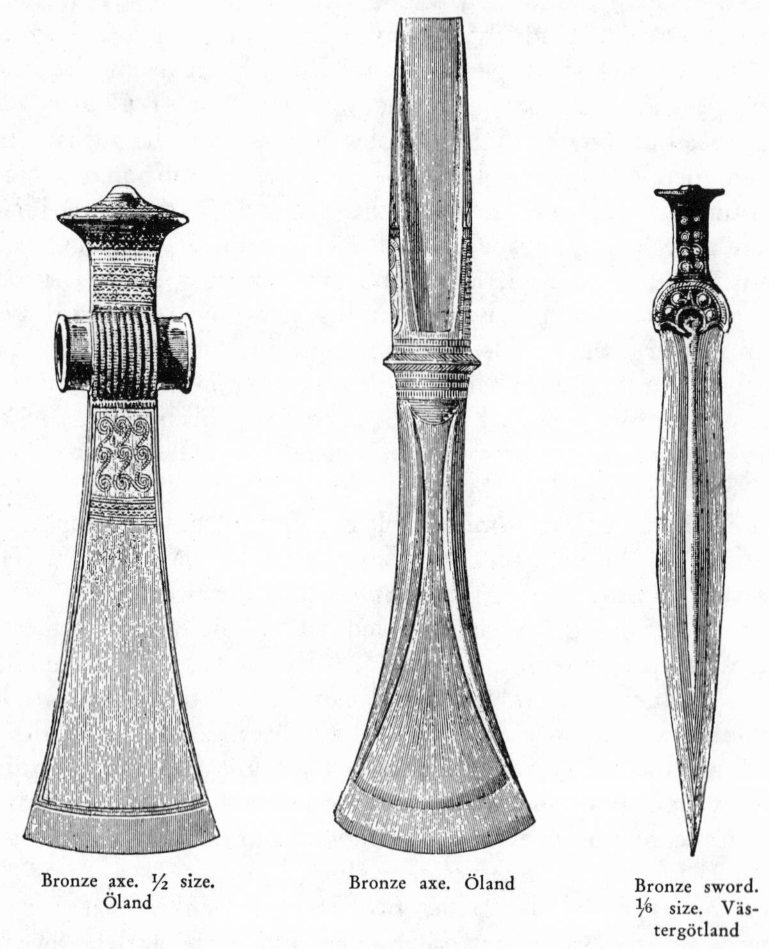

Bronze axe. ½ size. Öland

Bronze axe. Öland

Bronze sword. ⅙ size. Västergötland

investigations lead us are so much the more surprising as they prove that in artistic genius and skill in making bronze articles the Northmen must be considered not only as having equalled, but even as having surpassed, nearly all contemporary races in Europe." After enumerating certain specimens of Swedish domestic production, he continues: "In the best days of the Classic Period, when iron had already for centuries been in common use among her people, Hellas would need to feel no shame for such work. It is for this reason that we feel pride as we behold in this work the creation of Northmen and that, too, from an era much earlier than the days of Pericles." [17] A Continental scholar pays this tribute to Scandinavian skill in this and the earlier periods: "The Scandinavians, having for the fabrication of their axe-heads only materials like flint and rock that were very hard to work, produced marvels of work-

Bronze shield. 1/8 size. Halland

manship, copied in shape, it is true, from similar objects coming from the South. Without entering into the question of the origin and affiliation, which have been treated by Scandinavian and other writers, we must recognize the exceptional brilliance from more than one point of view of the Scandinavian Bronze Age as a mysterious phenomenon. The artists of the Bronze Age were the descendants of those incomparable flint workers who went before them." [18]

[17] Montelius, *Sveriges historia*, I, p. 124.
[18] Pittard, Eugene, *Race and History*, New York, 1926, p. 209.

Advance in culture.—The beauty and variety of the Swedish bronze articles prove beyond a doubt that a great advance in culture and well-being was made in the period; this

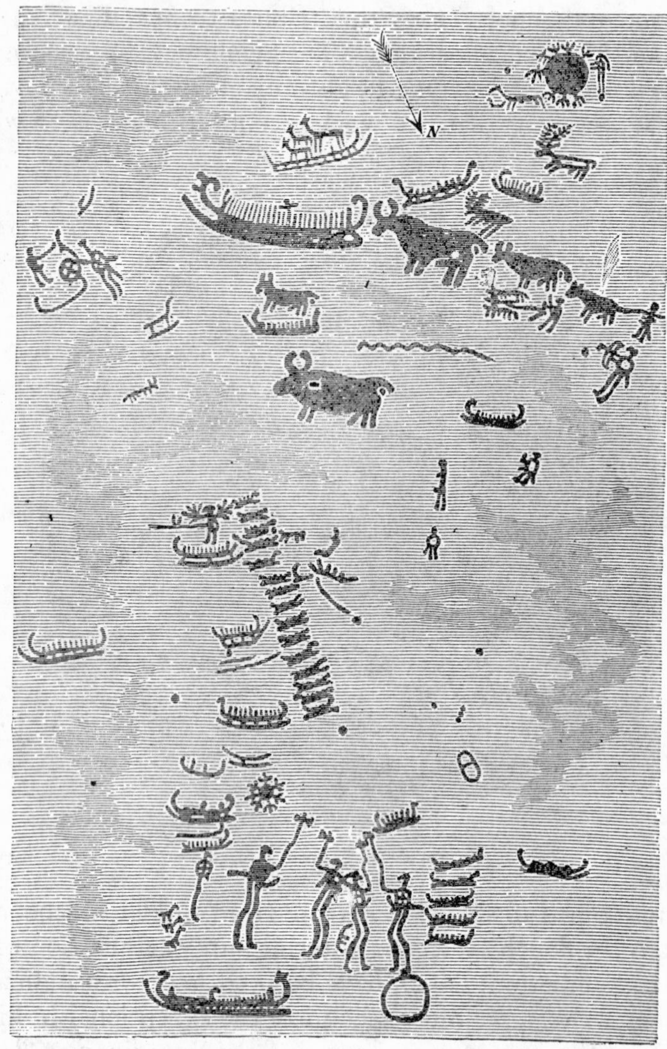

Rock inscriptions, Bohuslän

evidence is amply supplemented and supported by the rock tracings to which allusion has already been made. These are pictures or signs that have been cut into level or perpendicular rock surfaces, either to commemorate historical events or to illustrate religious rites. They occur in many parts of Europe, but are nowhere as numerous as in Sweden. The figures frequently reveal boats, which no doubt were used either for trade

Rock inscription. Wagon and oxen. Bohuslän

or war. In some instances a number of boats are grouped together, thus undoubtedly depicting some sort of national expedition. This again suggests the existence of a political organization of some kind. The more important islands of Denmark,

Rock inscription. Wagon and horses. Skåne

as well as Skåne, Västergötland, and Östergötland, probably formed separate kingdoms; a king was, no doubt, ruling in Uppland at this early date. Pictures of wagons, ploughs, and harrows indicate that agriculture had become important, and the great number of cattle carved in the rocks suggest that cattle-raising was an important occupation. From the evidence of bronze articles and rock tracings, it becomes clear that houses were built larger and much better than during the Stone Age. In shape they were much like the few clay urns of the period which have been discovered in Sweden; *i.e.*, oval structures of wood, smeared with clay and with an entrance in one of the side walls. The desire to find protection against the severe cold of winter was, no doubt, responsible for the lowness of the houses and for the small entrances and other openings, a factor which helped to give an added tinge of gloom and seriousness to life in the North. Utensils were mainly of wood; in Denmark some fine specimens of these have been preserved to our day. Some remains of woollen cloth have been found in Sweden, among them an entire artistically woven mantle found in a peat bog on Gerum Mountain in Västergötland. But it is especially the remarkable Danish finds which reveal the texture and style of clothing in this period. In one Danish grave were found a woollen mantle of coarse texture and a woollen petticoat of the same fabric. In another grave was discovered a woman's dress well preserved and almost complete, showing parts and styles not very unlike the dress of a later—but not the latest—period. Awls, needles, pincers, safety-pins, knives, bracelets, necklaces, spears, swords, hammers, and axes have been unearthed in very large quantities.

Religion.—Articles shaped by man and rock carvings suggest the existence in the Bronze Age of some kind of religious belief. The sun was worshipped as a deity. Sacrificial vessels, beautifully made and ornamented with four-spoked wheels, the symbol of the sun as the highest divinity, were brought from the South, and figures of such wheels also appear in the rock inscriptions. At some stage within the period, cremation became a common practice, the underlying idea being, no doubt, that in this way the soul would immediately be set free from its earthly prison. Illustrative of this is a story told by an Arabian writer in the ninth century of the Christian era. While on a sojourn in Russia, he saw how the Swedes whom he met there burned the body of one of their comrades, and on expressing surprise at this novel procedure he was told: "You

Arabians are certainly a foolish people. You take the man who is dearest to you and place him in the ground where worms and other crawling beings may consume him; we, on the other hand, burn him at once so that he may enter paradise immediately."[19] That the fear of spirits was strong and that amulets and other magic means were used for warding them off is strikingly revealed by a number of finds from the period. The best illustration of this is furnished by a grave near Copenhagen which, on this point, may be considered typical for Sweden also. Here were found by the side of the cremated remains of

Rock inscription. Men and horses. Bohuslän

a human body a leather pouch containing an amber bead, a shell from the Mediterranean Sea, wooden dice, a part of a serpent, the claws of a bird, the jaw of a squirrel, pebbles, small forceps, two bronze knives, and the flint part of a spear, enclosed in a piece of intestine. In another grave lay the teeth of a horse, bones of a weasel, claws of the lynx, parts of the windpipe of a bird, fragments of a serpent's skeleton, a twig of the maple-tree, two pieces of sulphur, a bit of charcoal, two bronze pieces, besides a miscellaneous assortment of other articles evidently believed to give protection against the forces of evil. The gods had assumed a more individual and human character in the minds of men, and were thus not merely vague representations of natural phenomena. They were still terrible and awe-inspiring beings, however, whom man believed he must propitiate by sacrifice and worship of some kind. Rock carvings

[19] Montelius, *Sveriges historia,* I, p. 146.

found in several provinces suggest that some kind of religious sacrifice took place, and many tracings of boats undoubtedly symbolized the journey on which the soul went after death.

All civilized peoples are today living in the Iron Age, and the Scandinavian historians have therefore adopted a purely arbitrary division when they place the termination of the age at the middle of the eleventh century of the Christian era; the justification for the division lies in the fact that historical evidence up to this point consists mainly of archæological remains, whereas from this time on written records begin to furnish most of the data for the history of the people.

The Iron Age.—Like bronze, iron came to the North as a gift from the South. It was from the Etruscans of Italy that the Germanic world of northern Europe received knowledge of this useful metal. Very slowly did it come to be known and used by the Germanic peoples, partly because it required new processes of manufacturing, partly because the races which had become familiar with its use were naturally loath to make the barbarians the beneficiaries of their knowledge. Nevertheless the spread of iron northward was not as slow as formerly was supposed, for, instead of assuming that several thousand years were required for the complete transition from bronze to iron, scholars now are certain that only about five hundred years lie between its first appearance and its adoption into general use in the North. Relatively few finds have been made from the early part of the period, since the material was then scarce in Sweden, only the kind of iron known as bog-iron being used. The earlier iron articles in Sweden were made from imported raw material, but soon the Swedes themselves learned the process of smelting and thus could use the plentiful material which their own country supplied. That they did this is proved by the many small and primitive kilns from this period which have been discovered. These were crudely made by merely placing boulders or rocks close together in a circle on the ground. Here fires could be made of sufficient intensity to melt the ore. The method was in use in some part of Sweden as late as the nineteenth century.[20] When these kilns, simple as they were,

[20] Grimberg, Carl, *Svenska folkets underbara öden,* Stockholm, 1916, I, p. 39.

came into general use, Sweden became independent of other countries for her supply of iron.

Iron was at first more precious than bronze, interesting proof of which is found in the fact that iron articles from the early part of the period are mainly for ornamental purposes. In time, however, iron became cheaper and more common. This is seen in articles of a later period when the visible parts of articles were bronze but all the rest iron. Many finds show that the people of the North in this age possessed the same technical skill and artistic taste which in the earlier age had given the country a remarkable wealth of fine ornaments, weapons, shields, utensils, and the like. The objects, as a rule, exhibit greater simplicity than those of the preceding age and are better adapted to practical use. The common man could now have a larger share in the things which enabled him to be more comfortable. Civilization had become more plebeian.

The North; the Celts and the Greeks.—In the early Iron Age the Germanic tribes were confined to a comparatively small area, including Denmark, central and south Sweden, and a narrow strip of north Germany between the rivers Elbe and Oder, or approximately the same region which, according to archæologists, had constituted their habitat soon after the recession of the glacial ice. To the south and west of them lived the Celts, for whom the Bronze Age denoted the era of greatest expansion and highest culture. Undoubtedly the Germanic peoples, including the Scandinavians, were greatly influenced by them. It was largely because of this influence that the Germanic gods like Thor, Loke, and Odin assumed more personal characteristics. Some of the more important mythological conceptions of later Germany and Scandinavia undoubtedly had their source in Celtic beliefs.[21]

It is in the early Iron Age that the first reference to the North is met with in classic writers. To the early Greeks and Romans the Far North was as much a *terra incognita* as interior Africa was to the modern world a century ago, and this in spite of the fact that some exchange had been going on between the North and the South since the Stone Age. Phœnician merchants may have visited Denmark and the Baltic shores, and

[21] Svensén, Emil, *Svenska folkets historia*, Stockholm, 1915, I, p. 174.

Greeks, on errands of trade, perhaps reached the same region at an early date. Some knowledge of the North must therefore gradually have percolated through to the people of the South. In Book X of Homer's *Odyssey,* dating from the ninth or eighth century B.C., mention is made of giants and cannibals who lived in a land where "day was so long that those who brought in the cattle at night could call to those who drove them out in the morning, for the paths of day and night lie close together." Later Herodotus, about 450 B.C., says that he has heard of a people in the North who sleep six months out of the year, but adds that he does not believe this to be true. Still later, Greek writers mention the Hyperboreans in the land of bliss, living north of chilly Boreas, who throw themselves in the sea when they are old and satiated with life.[22]

Pytheas.—More trustworthy information regarding the North was brought to the Greeks by Pytheas of Marseilles, who, as far as known, is the first writer who mentions Scandinavia, although not under that name. With skill as a sailor, Pytheas combined scientific interest and knowledge. His native city, founded by Greeks from Asia Minor, had about 300 B.C., by a victorious war against Carthage, won the right for its ships to pass unmolested through the Straits of Gibraltar into the Atlantic. Pytheas used this opportunity to make one or possibly two long voyages to the North, presumably in search of codfish, tin, and amber. This was, however, not the only purpose of his expeditions; he wanted to explore and gain further knowledge of the unknown regions of the North. His purpose and exploits make him, as far as known, the first explorer in the history of the race who had a scientific interest. According to Pytheas' account, as given in fragmentary forms by later Greek writers, he reached the islands lying north of England and here he heard of a land where the sun does not set. He then set out for this strange land which was reached after six days. This land was called Thule, a name assumed by some authorities to be Celtic in origin and meaning "the North." Undoubtedly it was Norway that Pytheas had reached. Its people, he relates, subsisted on fruits, roots, vegetables, and a kind of grain called "kevchons," supposedly millet, which was not threshed in the

[22] Bugge, A., *Norges historie,* Kristiania, 1909, I, p. 64.

open, as is the rule in regions farther south, but, on account of dampness and cold, had to be brought into sheds and threshed there. The people brewed a drink from grain and honey which evidently was identical with what later was known as mead.

First contacts with Rome; the Cimbri and the Teutones.—The Bronze Age and the early part of the Iron Age denoted, as already stated, the high-water mark of Celtic expansion and power in Europe. Towards the end of the pre-Christian era the Germanic peoples began a career of aggression and conquest which in time was to wrest from the Celts the greater part of their extensive territory and relegate them to a secondary place so far as power was concerned. One of the earliest, if not the earliest, of the attacks upon them by Germanic peoples was made by tribes from the North. This came in the second century B.C. when the Cimbri and a kindred tribe, the Teutones, the former dwelling on the Cimbrian peninsula, or Jutland, which long was known by the former name, and the latter probably having their homes south of them, invaded the Roman lands. Perhaps because of an inundation of their lands by the ocean, they had been forced to abandon their homes and then set out, men, women, and children, for the South, evidently in the expectation of finding a favourable place where they might locate. Before long they came into conflict with the Celts, who in the first encounter suffered defeat; a Roman army which tried to check their advance was likewise defeated at ancient Noricum. The road to Italy now lay open to the victors and Rome itself was in imminent danger, but the Cimbri, taking counsel of their gods, through the casting of lots, failed to act according to any deliberate plan. Instead of pressing on to Rome, they next turned westward. When the Romans, who are supposed to have had an army of 80,000 men, again tried to stop them, the Cimbri a second time inflicted defeat upon the Roman legions. Instead of marching directly towards the imperial city, they tried to advance now in one, now in another direction, only to meet formidable obstacles in their path, either in the form of armies or of natural barriers. Finally they turned south again to join the Teutones, who, having gone their separate way, had ultimately reached the region where later Rouen in Normandy was founded. Together the two tribes now marched southward, but parted company again in order to reach Rome by different routes. This made their defeat easier for the Romans. In the year 102 B.C. the Teutones were annihilated at the battle of Aquæ Sextiæ by a Roman army under the command of the experienced and cruel Marius, and the following year the Cimbri were similarly crushed at Vercellæ, located between Turin and Milan. The survivors became captives of war and were sold as slaves. Tragic indeed was the end to which the two brave peoples had come. Their energy had been put forth to no advantage because they had lacked a definite purpose. "Already at this point," says Schück,[23] "they showed themselves true ancestors of the Germanic peoples of the migration period and of the Northmen of Viking times—they had the same bravery, restless tendency to roam about, and incapacity for political calculation; and the result was the same: an expenditure of energy which ended with the destruction of the people."

Roman cultural influences penetrate the land.—Cæsar's conquest of Gaul and Britain near the middle of the first century before the Christian era gave new impetus to the

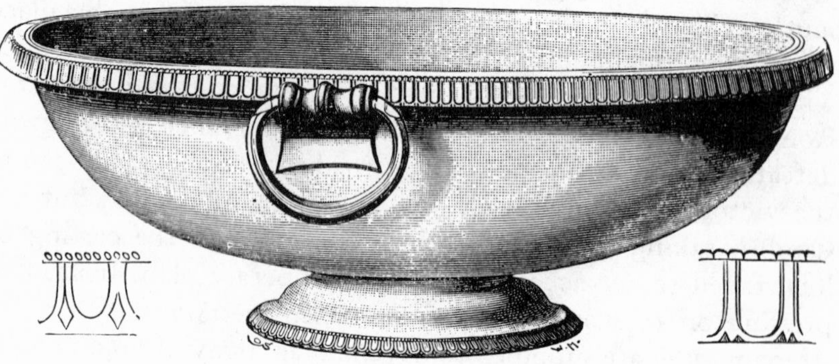

Roman bronze bowl. ¼ size. Gottland

trade which during the preceding centuries had been going on between the lands of the South and the amber regions on the North Sea and the Baltic; in the wake of this trade followed a great advance northward of Roman influences. The North escaped military conquest by the Romans, however, as the

[23] Schück, Henrik, *Svenska folkets historia*, Lund, 1919, I, p. 88.

crushing defeat which the Romans suffered at the hands of the Germans at Teutonburger Wald in the year 9 A.D. checked their advance in that direction.

Roman bronze statue of Venus. ½ size. Öland

By the beginning of the Christian era the Germans had greatly extended their territory towards the South. Migration and military conquests had both played an important part in this process of expansion. The centre of the Germanic world had shifted from the southern part of the Scandinavian peninsula, Denmark, and the islands of the Baltic to the region embraced by present-day Germany. It was through this Germanic world that the Roman influence percolated through to the Scandinavian countries. The extent of this influence is seen most clearly in the remarkably rich finds in Scandinavia of Roman coins, weapons, utensils, and ornaments from the earlier period of the Iron Age. These articles were carried thither over the important trade routes of the time, the Oder and the Vistula, and to a less extent by way of the Rhine. Approximately 7,000 Roman coins dating from the first two centuries of the Christian era have been found in Scandinavia; 5,000 on the island of Gottland, most of these in or near Visby, 600 on Öland and Bornholm, 650 in Skåne, less than 100 on the mainland of Sweden outside of the aforesaid province, 600 in Denmark, and only a few in Norway.[24] These coins, as well as large collections of coins from a later period, show great wear, proving that they were in active circulation. Many Swedish coins bear the impress of Roman dies. Besides the coins and other articles of gold there have been found a number of Roman vases and other objects, and these all point to a considerable Roman influence. Thus a bronze vase which was unearthed in Skåne bears the name of its Roman maker, and several of the same type have been found in other places in Scandinavia. More remarkable still is a vase found in 1828 in Hälsingland, a remote northern district. According to its inscription the vase was made by Lucius Ansius Epaphroditus. This takes on an added interest when it becomes known that several vessels by the same maker have been unearthed in the ruins of Herculaneum and Pompeii, as well as in other parts of Italy, in central and northern France, Scotland, England, and Denmark. Another Roman vase found in 1818 near the city of Västerås was, according to its Latin inscription, consecrated to Apollo Grannus. A large number of gold bracelets discovered in different parts of Sweden are either of Roman manufacture or show unmistakable Roman influence in form and ornamentation. Richly ornamented swords, helmets, spears, bridles, and

[24] Montelius, *Sveriges historia*, I, p. 181.

trappings for war horses show a preponderance of influence towards military life. Roman statuettes, goblets, metal mirrors, and similar articles, rich in ornamentation, give evidence of the increasing luxury that Rome brought to the distant North. Also into the more practical occupations there came a new wealth of articles—shears, razors, planes, distaffs, dippers,

A Northern chief in the fourth century A.D.

spoons, and other tableware—which are either of Roman make or reveal Roman influence in design and embellishment.

The remarkable power of peat bogs to preserve, under certain conditions, even perishable objects as cloth and wood through thousands of years has made it possible to reconstruct with great accuracy the parts and materials which entered into the garb of a Northern chieftain of this period. Remains found in graves in Denmark at Thorsbjerg and Nydam are especially well preserved and give interesting data. These are supplemented by helmets found in graves at Vendel, near Uppsala, on which occur images of several warriors. The clothing was made principally of wool, which was finer in texture and more skilfully woven than in the previous period. The most important garment was the long coat or jacket with sleeves extending to the elbows, breeches held by a belt and fastened below the knees to short stockings; over the body was thrown a mantle of wool, and sandals were worn on the feet, the latter undoubtedly due to influence of the South.

Remains of houses, especially numerous on Gottland and Öland, indicate that these were oblong in shape, the corners generally rounded on the outside, the entrance in one of the end walls. In size houses varied from 60 to 120 feet in length and from 30 to 60 feet in width and they were built extremely low. The walls were thick and made of rough stones and clay. Ceilings and board floors were lacking. The fireplace was generally set in the centre of the room, with an opening in the roof to permit the smoke to escape. Doors were equipped with crude and cumbersome locks. In the ruins of houses from this age have been found Roman coins from the second century, board for dice-playing (*spelbricka*), dice, cubes, keys, distaffs, stone mills for grinding grain, kernels of rye, spoons, drinking horns, tumblers of glass, and clay vessels. Many skulls showing trepanning indicate that delicate surgical operations were performed.[25]

To what extent foreign, mainly Roman influences and trade with the regions southward were responsible for new ideas and increase of wealth noticeable in the first centuries of our era cannot, of course, be accurately determined. Certainly the industry and inventive skill of the Swedes must have counted for something in this forward movement, but the assumption that foreign influence was by far the most important factor has been supported with increasing strength as the earth has yielded her archæological treasures. The great number of Roman coins unearthed in the North point unmistakably to an extensive trade, and the discovery in Sweden of small Roman scales, such as were used in trade transactions for weigh-

[25] Fürst, Carl M., *När de döde vittna*, Stockholm, 1920.

ing gold, gives further evidence of such trade. No coins of domestic make have been found from this period in any of the Scandinavian countries.

Communication; boats.—The trade within the country must have been inconsiderable and was hampered greatly by lack of roads, or by the miserable condition of the few that did exist. Most of the land was covered with dense forests and surfaces were marshy and low. A good deal of travel and transportation of goods therefore had to be done on horseback. Bits, reins, and spurs have frequently been unearthed. The difficulty of transportation was, however, not so serious a drawback as might be imagined, since settlements were confined mainly to the proximity of the sea and inland waters; here the Northmen were excellently equipped for travel, since boats were used—perhaps the invention of some unknown and unsung genius—which were so seaworthy, strong, and speedy that the same type is, in the main, in use today, particularly along the coast of Norway. The type is best known by two boats discovered in 1863 in a peat bog at Nydam in Jutland. One of these boats had been built of oak, and was 80 feet long, almost 10 feet wide amidship, with the bottom plank made from one piece of timber more than 45 feet long. Its form was symmetrical, both ends being pointed so that either of them could serve as the prow, a great advantage in shallow waters or narrow rivers, where it might be difficult to effect a turn. It had been equipped for fourteen pairs of oars. The oars were ingeniously arranged to permit the rowers to shift about easily when retracing the course. The dimensions, form, and arrangement of the vessel therefore tally in almost every detail with Tacitus' description of the boats of the Suiones or Swedes which will be discussed later (p. 65). Recently two boats have been discovered at Galtabäck, Halland. They conform in type to the Nydam boat and are probably older.[26] Rock tracings in Gottland and in Häggeby in Uppland show outlines of boats which conform very nearly to the Nydam type. The Nydam and other boats of the period contained a diverse collection of articles. The condition of the articles shows that a wild orgy of wanton

[26] Enquist, A., *Skeppsfyndet vid Galtabäck*, in *Kulturhistoriska studier och uppteckningar*, Halmstad, 1929.

destruction of property had evidently taken place: clothes had been torn, weapons broken, swords bent, the bodies of horses hacked and mutilated, and the bottom planks broken. Archæologists were at first puzzled by this, but the explanation, given first in 1865 by the Danish archæologist, Worsaæ, that a great battle had taken place and that the victors had offered the spoils of war as sacrifices to their gods, seems now to have found general acceptance. Finds other than those in peat bogs reveal the same practice. Burial places, particularly of important men, were marked by stone monuments or so-called "*bautastenar*" of which there are no less than 150 in one field at Grubbestad in Bohuslän, the highest one rising almost fifteen feet above ground. Such fields of granite memorials frequently meet the eyes of the traveller through a Swedish countryside. Though as a rule they bear no inscriptions, they are, nevertheless, solemnly impressive in their silent and faithful watch over those who, underneath, have so long rested in their peaceful slumbers. Only a few isolated rocks in this period bear chiselled runes, a remarkable innovation in written characters, which now makes its appearance in the North.

The runes.—Very divergent, and in some cases fanciful, opinions regarding the origin and age of the runes have been advanced and earnestly defended by a great array of facts. Rudbeck maintained that they antedate the Christian era in Sweden, and in this view he found many supporters, an extremist being Johan Göranson [27] who maintained that they had originated in Sweden two thousand two hundred years before Christ and thence had spread to all lands. In time, however, the pendulum of opinion swung to the other extreme and then the claim was made that runes were hardly known in pagan times. The scholarly investigations of runologists like Wimmer in Denmark, S. Bugge and Magnus Olsen in Norway, and Otto von Friesen in Sweden have, however, in our day cleared up most of the controverted points. According to the generally accepted theory, the invention of signs for the expression of common ideas—undoubtedly the greatest invention human genius ever has achieved—originated in Syria. Through the

[27] Göranson was a follower of Rudbeck. His work on runes, published in 1750, bears the title: *Bautil, det är Alle Svea och Götha Rikens Runstenar.*

Phœnicians the knowledge came to the Greeks, who modified and supplemented these signs so as to make them far more adequate to the needs of varied expression. From the Greeks the knowledge of letters passed to the Romans. The Germanic tribes which lived in specially close association with the Romans were the Goths and the Heruli, and these now constructed a

ᚠ ᚢ ᚦ ᚨ ᚱ ᚲ ᚷ ᚹ : ᚺ ᚾ ᛁ ᛃ ᛇ ᛈ ᛉ ᛊ : ᛏ ᛒ ᛖ ᛗ ᛚ ᛜ ᛟ ᛞ
f u th a r k g w h n i j ẹ p -ʀ s t b e m l ng o d

The Germanic runes

new alphabet by modifying the Greek and Latin script. They next transmitted the knowledge of these new signs to their kinsmen in the North, as well as to Germany and, through the Anglo-Saxon invasion, to England.[28] The similarity of many of the runes to Greek and Latin letters is especially striking in the so-called "younger runes" of sixteen characters which were in use only in Scandinavia. The reduction in number was achieved by making certain characters express a combination of sounds. For reasons which runologists have been unable to explain, the runes do not follow the order of the Greek and Latin alphabet; the first in the series of letters are f, u, th, a, r, k.

ᚠ ᚢ ᚦ ᚬ ᚱ ᚴ : ᚼ ᚾ ᛁ ᛅ ᛋ : ᛏ ᛒ ᛚ ᛘ ᛦ
f u th o r k h n i a s t b l m -r

The Scandinavian runes

The deviation of the lines of the runes from the classic alphabet is evidently due to the fact that the former was cut into wood—generally the beech—bone, or rock, on which straight lines could more easily be chiselled than curved lines. In Sweden approximately 2,000 rocks bearing runic inscriptions have been found, but this, of course, serves as no certain index to the extent to which the runes were used; most of them were undoubtedly carved on pieces of wood [29] which have naturally disappeared in the course of centuries. The deciphering of the older runes was made possible by the discovery in Den-

[28] Bugge, *Norges historie*, I, p. 134.

[29] Swedish *bok*, beech and *stav*, staff, hence the Swedish *bokstav*, letter, and the English *book*.

mark of a gold-inlaid horn on which was inscribed a sentence. A gold ornament discovered near Vadstena in 1774 is the best representative of this earlier type found in Sweden. This has been invaluable to the runologist in clarifying the meaning of this early script. At first the ability to write and understand

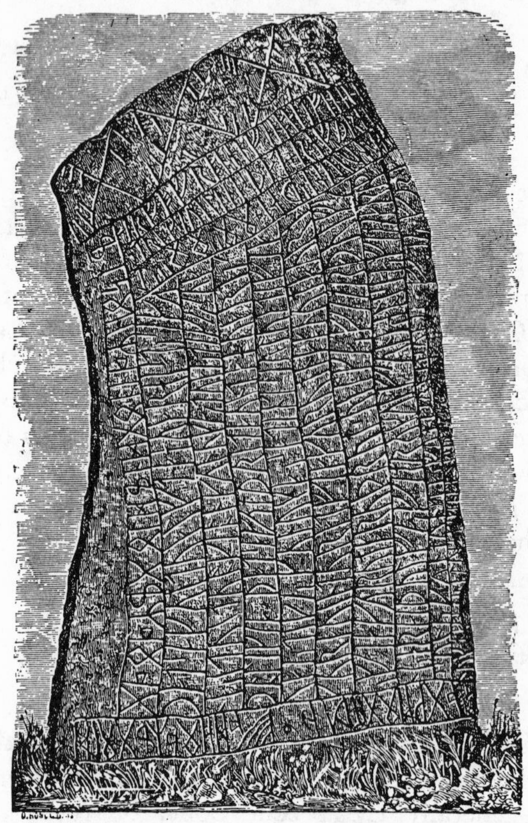

The *Röksten,* the longest runic text known. Östergötland

runes was, no doubt, limited to a few men belonging to the higher classes. This explains the belief that there was magic power in runes (etymologically the word rune is explained as meaning mystery), reference to which occurs often in the Icelandic sagas—as Odin hanging in the tree of Yggdrasil to learn runes, Heimdal teaching runes of victory, of eloquence, of the healing art, and others to men; Segerdrifva admonishes Sigurd Fafnesbane to learn wonder-working runes and to inscribe them on his sword, horn, and the backs of his hands, if he would win victory and escape dangers.

The longest runic text.—The longest runic text—over 170 words—ever discovered in any land is the one inscribed on a rock by the church of Rök in Östergötland, hence known as *Rökstenen.* It is a slab standing eight feet above ground, is four and one-half feet wide, with runes inscribed on every surface. Because of abbreviations, grouping of signs without regular spacing, transpositions, and other difficulties, the text baffled all runologists until Sophus Bugge of Norway was able partly to clear up the mystery; other points have been cleared up by the leading runologist of our day, von Friesen of Uppsala, but some points still remain obscure. The text makes mention of Theodoric, a northern chief, and probably a namesake of the famous Gothic king of the Ostrogoths in Italy.

Principally, no doubt, because of the labour involved in cutting the letters in wood and rock, the runic writers were extremely chary of words—the contrast to our age of stenographers and type-writers is apparent—and the runic texts therefore do not give any great amount of information of a historical value. To some extent they supplement the evidence of Roman remains in the North. In some cases they contain historical evidence of specific value. To this evidence of rune stones and archæological material is added the testimony of Roman and early Germanic writers, thus making possible a fairly detailed picture of the period. The runic writings, however, prove that the language of the time in the North was Teutonic, and, aside from the extensive changes which naturally have taken place during the centuries, the same as now spoken in the Scandinavian lands. With some variation the same speech was common in that day to Sweden, Denmark, and Norway.

Chapter II

IN THE TWILIGHT OF EARLY HISTORICAL WRITERS

After Pytheas, centuries elapsed before mention was again, so far as known, made of the North in written records. With the military conquest of Cæsar in the first century before the Christian era, some knowledge of it must, however, have filtered through to Rome and there stirred up interest in the great *terra incognita*. Occasionally mention of the Northern lands now begins to appear in the writings of Roman authors. The first in which the name Scandinavia occurs is Pomponius Mela, who about 43 A.D. wrote a geography in which he told of an enormous arm of the sea, which is called Codanus (this, it has been assumed, refers to the Cattegat), in which lies an island, Codanonia, inhabited by Teutons. The generally accepted view of scholars is that Codanonia is a corrupted form of the name Scandinavia, and occurred through a mistake in transcribing.

Roman and Germanic writers on the North.—Pliny the Elder, who perished in the destruction of Pompeii and Herculaneum in 79 A.D., is the first writer who uses the word Scandinavia. Codanus, he says, has many islands, among which the best known is Scandinavia, the size of which is unknown. The Scandinavia mentioned here is probably identical with Skåne. Pliny also mentions a number of other islands like the Orkneys and the Hebrides, and, lying on the north, farthest from the others, Thule and Nerigon, the former, no doubt, referring to the northern and the latter to the southwestern part of Norway.[1] The earliest mention of the Swedes by name is found in Tacitus' celebrated work, *Germania,* an account of a number of Germanic tribes, which was written in 98 A.D. Tacitus was neither a geographer nor a traveller, but his account is based on careful studies of the documentary material available and

[1] Bugge, *Norges historie,* I, pp. 73-74.

on oral statements. His wide information and remarkable trustworthiness are attested by the fact that his great work has come through the test of modern historical criticism with increased prestige as a historical document. Tacitus speaks of a great bay, "the Swedish Sea," between the Cimbrian peninsula and the land of the Ostyrians, and in this, he says, "lies a land inhabited by the Suiones"; the name is the Latinized form for Svear or Swedes. Tacitus next proceeds to make some significant statements regarding the organization of the Suiones, which are noted elsewhere (p. 65). According to the distinguished authority on Old Norse, the late Professor Adolf Noreen, of Uppsala, the name Suiones means etymologically "those who are their own" or "we ourselves"—both expressions undoubtedly connoting a sense of independence. Von Friesen believes that the etymological meaning of the name is "kinsmen." [2]

The next classic writer to mention Scandinavia was the Alexandrine geographer, Ptolemy, who lived in the second century A.D. He states that east of the Cimbrian peninsula lie the Skandeian Islands, the largest being called Skandia. Among the tribes which he enumerates as dwelling on this island only "*gautai*," or Goths, are recognized; he is thus the first one to assign this group to Sweden. After Ptolemy there follows another lapse of at least two centuries before a Roman writer again makes any mention of Scandinavia; this writer was Prokopius, whose death occurred probably in 562. He had served as secretary to the Byzantine general, Belisarius, and had accompanied him in a campaign against the Goths. He was therefore well informed about the Goths and the Heruli concerning whom he wrote. Prokopius gives a fairly detailed account of the Scandinavian peninsula and some of the customs of its people, notably the yuletide celebration as an expression of joy at the return of the sun. The first historian of Germanic

[2] Friesen, Otto Von, *Om det svenska rikets uppkomst,* in *Verdandis Småskrifter* No. 200. In a recent discussion Elis Wadstein rejects these derivations of the name Sweden. He finds its root in an old Germanic word *swīn,* meaning "land that has become dry or is covered by shallow water." This word enters into several present-day place names, especially north of Lake Mälaren in the neighbourhood of the city of Enköping. Large sections of land here lay under water in early times. The region had early a comparatively large population of *Svear.* Wadstein believes that the word *Suiones* was originally applied to the people of this section because of the nature of the land on which they lived and then in time came to be applied to the entire group. *Suiones* would, according to this theory, mean "those dwelling on lowlands or on ground formerly covered by water." Wadstein, Elis, *Sveriges namn, Fornvännen,* part 4, 1930.

descent to mention Sweden was Jordanes, a contemporary of Prokopius, who wrote a history of his own people, the Goths. As will appear later, his account has had an important bearing upon the views of early Swedish historians with respect to the age and early culture of man in their country; he has also served as an authority on certain important phases of European history. Paul the Deacon, who in the latter half of the eighth century wrote the history of the Lombards, also supplies some data which have a bearing on Swedish history.

The migration of nations: character and effects.—The great movement known as the migration of nations signified in its ultimate results one of the most important events in the history of the European peoples. In its far-reaching effects upon civilization it may be said to have been comparable to the Protestant Reformation of the sixteenth century or to the revolution wrought by the triumph of liberal ideas in the nineteenth century. When the migration period, after much shifting of peoples, accompanied by expeditions and wars without number, drew to a close in the eighth century, the once mighty Roman Empire had succumbed before the fierce attacks of the barbarians, and on territory once ruled with an iron hand by the Roman colossus, Germanic kingdoms had been built or were in process of building. The period is marked by an unusual unrest among practically all Germanic peoples, due to a combination of circumstances, chief of which were attacks by the fierce Huns, crowding due to growth of population, and the discovery that Rome, the proud state, was not strong enough to defend her rich cities and vast areas of fertile territory; once this discovery was made, the starving and harassed barbarians pressed relentlessly upon the empire and gave it no peace. Unable to defend her extended frontiers by the aid of her own legions, Rome resorted to the dangerous expedient of engaging barbarians to fight against other barbarian foes, but these *fœderati* proved in most cases unreliable allies. The story of Sweden at this point touches very closely upon the history of the empire, inasmuch as the most important Germanic peoples taking part in the great migration movement and in the final downfall of Rome had traditions of a Swedish origin. The credibility of the story of the emigration of these people from

Sweden, once taken for granted by Swedish historians, was for a long time rejected; the statements of early historians were looked upon as extremely fanciful and untrustworthy, but it has come to pass that in our day leading authorities accept much of the interesting narratives as historically reliable.

Tribes of alleged Swedish origin in the migrations.—The Germanic race with traditions of a Swedish origin taking the most important rôle in the great migration period was the Goths. In his work on the Goths, Jordanes [3] speaks of the island of Scandza lying in front of the river Vistula in which dwells a race which is said to have continual light in midsummer time for forty days and nights, and which likewise has no clear light in the winter season for the same length of time. By reason of this alternation of light and darkness, joy and sorrow, these people are like no other race in their blessings and tribulations. He then goes on to say: "Now from this island of Scandza, as from a hive of races or a womb of nations, the Goths are said to have come forth long ago, under their king, Berig by name." That Scandza is identical with Sweden is a view accepted by scholars.

At the time when the Goths first appear in the light of history, they dwelt in the region of the Vistula, but later they occupied an extensive territory on the lower Danube, while at the beginning of the third century A.D. they had, in their wanderings, reached the Black Sea region. In the reign of Constantine, the Roman territory along the eastern frontier was no longer safe from attack by them. About the year 370 the tribe separated into two branches, the West Goths and the East Goths, the former settling in the district known as Dacia, and the latter, under their great king, Ermanarich—the Jormanrek of the Icelandic Saga—establishing, about 300 A.D., a kingdom of vast extent which is said to have extended from the region of the Black Sea clear to the Baltic. In this period lived the great bishop of the Goths, Ulfilas, who created a new alphabet from the models of Greek and Latin characters and whose claim to fame rests primarily on his translation of the greater part of the New Testament into the language of his people. The

[3] *De Origine Actibusque Getarum, Monumenta Germania Historica, Auctores Antiquissime,* Berlin, 1882; translated into English and published under the title "*The Origin and Deeds of the Goths,*" by C. C. Mierow, Princeton, 1908.

greater part of a copy of this most important work is still extant and is known as the Mæso-Gothic Bible of Ulfilas, or Codex Argenteus, now the invaluable prize of the library of the University of Uppsala. It constitutes an important key to the early Germanic languages and thus serves somewhat the same purpose in this field as the famous Rosetta Stone to the study of the Egyptian hieroglyphics.

The Ostrogoths.—The Ostrogoths or East Gothes were finally crushed by the fierce Huns, and the conquered people suffered humiliating subjection under their cruel conquerors. After the overwhelming defeat which the Huns suffered in the momentous battle of the Catalaunian Fields (451) the Ostrogoths settled in Pannonia, in the present-day Hungary, as *fœderati* of the Romans, but peace was maintained between the two peoples only through the payment by the emperors of liberal amounts of tribute money. After the fall of Rome in 476, the most famous king among the Germanic peoples in the period before Charlemagne, Theodoric, the Ostrogoth, also known as the Great, led his people into Italy, defeated Odoacer, who some time earlier had seized the city, and established a kingdom which included practically all of the Italian peninsula, part of the region across the Adriatic, and the islands west of Italy. Under the vigorous rule of Theodoric, this kingdom was not only the mightiest European state in its day, but in a fuller measure than any contemporary state gave security to its subjects and realized the ideals of justice. After the steady hand of Theodoric had been removed by death, dissensions arose which so weakened the once mighty state that it succumbed to the attacks of the Byzantine general, Belisarius, whose chief, the Emperor Justinian, had conceived the idea of again uniting the severed East and West sections of the old Roman Empire. After this defeat the East Goths gradually became merged with other peoples and lost their identity as a separate race.[4]

The West Goths.—Their kinsmen, the West Goths, had, after being sorely harassed by the Huns, forced their way into

[4] A gripping account of the heroic but unsuccessful struggle of the Ostrogoths against the Byzantine Greeks is found in Felix Dahn's historical novel, *A Struggle about Rome*. While in his strictly historical work Dahn expresses doubt regarding the credibility of the story of an original emigration of the Ostrogoths from Sweden, he accepts it and uses it with telling effect in the concluding chapter of his novel.

Roman territory and at the battle of Adrianople (378) inflicted a crushing defeat on the Roman legions, an event which may be looked upon as the first important step towards the final downfall of the Eternal City. They were now permitted to settle in the Balkans and in a part of the region included in present-day Hungary. While sojourning here their relations to Rome alternated between friendship and alliance, based on money considerations, and hostility, with its accompaniment of bitter warfare. Under their leader Alaric, the West Goths, or Visigoths, a name by which they are generally known, in 410 made their historic attack upon Rome, which was captured and sacked. After the death of Alaric they again entered the service of the empire and as its *fœderati* rendered invaluable service to civilization by playing a decisive rôle in the battle of the Catalaunian Fields where the Huns suffered a crushing defeat. Later the Visigoths crossed the empire into Spain, where they established a kingdom which lasted until 711. As in the case of the Ostrogoths in Italy, the Visigoths were soon merged with other peoples and completely lost their identity as a separate racial group.

The Heruli.—Another Germanic tribe of alleged Scandinavian origin were the Heruli, who in the second century A.D. dwelt alongside the Goths in southwestern Europe. In enumerating the different tribes that dwelt in Scandza, Jordanes mentions the Suetidi, who, according to the opinion of most authorities in the field, are the same as the Suiones or Swedes, and says that they excel the rest in stature. He then continues: "However, the Dani, who trace their origin to the same stock, drove from their homes the Heruli, who lay claim to pre-eminence among all the nations of Scandza for their tallness." [5] At first these Heruli evidently lived in Denmark, but were driven out by the Danes, who, according to Jordanes, were of the same tribe as the Suiones and thus had their original home in the region of Lake Mälaren. Prokopius relates that in the beginning of the sixth century they dwelt near the Danube, but when trouble arose between them and kindred tribes, the Longobards and the Gepidæ, they fled across the Danube, whereupon a part of them received permission from Rome to

[5] Mierow translation.

settle in Illyria. According to Prokopius, the other group marched to the North, to Thule, where homes were found by the side of the Goths. Some time thereafter, the group which had settled in Illyria slew their king and thereupon sent some of their leading men to Thule to get a new king. There they found many of royal birth and they chose the one that pleased them best. On their journey southward their new king died, and so the emissaries returned to Thule for another ruler. In the meantime their kinsmen, who had remained at home, believing it unwise to ignore the Roman emperor in so important a matter, sent emissaries to him asking that he provide them with a ruler. The emperor complied, selecting a man of Herulian descent, who long had dwelt in Constantinople, but as soon as the group which had visited the North returned with their prince the Roman appointee found himself deserted and he returned to Constantinople. It has long been the theory of Swedish historians that the Heruli who returned to settle in the North located in the province of Blekinge, and this assumption has been given striking confirmation by later archæological discoveries. This is also in harmony with Snorre Sturlesson's account of the invasion of Sweden by Odin and the other gods.[6] The Heruli who remained on the Continent led a restless existence, being at times allies of the empire and later its enemies. Odoacer, who overthrew Rome in 476, was called the king of the Heruli and these constituted an important contingent of his army. It is no doubt this fact which Tegnér, the great national poet of Sweden, has in mind when in his poem *Svea* he speaks of his Swedish forbears as "the conquerors of Rome" (*Roms besegrare*). The supposition has been expressed by scholars,[7] that it was principally the Heruli who, through their rôle of tradesmen, brought the knowledge of runes to the Germanic peoples.

The Longobards.—The theory of the Swedish descent of a third race, the Lombards or Longobards, rests upon the statement of the aforementioned Paul the Deacon, who wrote the history of his people; added weight is given his testimony by

[6] Montelius, *Sveriges historia,* I, p. 233.

[7] Bugge, Sophus, *Inledningen till Norges Indskrifter med de aeldre Runer,* Kristiania, 1891, and Friesen, Otto Von, *Röstenen i Bohuslän,* 1924.

the fact that his statements in general bear the stamp of historical veracity. He begins his account of the Lombards by calling attention to the salubriousness of the northern climate, in contrast to the disease-breeding climate of the South; from the fact that so few die in the North comes over-population and the necessity for emigration. "In like manner," he continues, "also the race of Winili—that is, of the Longobards—which afterwards ruled prosperously in Italy have sprung from a German people and from the island which is called Scandinavia." [8] It has been assumed that their early Scandinavian home was on Gottland.[9] Like the rest of the Germanic tribes, the Lombards moved about a great deal within the confines of the empire, and after the fall of the Ostrogothic kingdom in Italy in the middle of the sixth century they established a new kingdom in the northern part of the Italian peninsula which continued an important power until it fell before the attacks of Charlemagne. Reminiscent of their rule in Italy is the name of one of the peninsula's most important provinces, Lombardy. The Burgundians, another tribe to play an important part in the migration period, probably lived originally on the island of Bornholm, from which their name was derived. They ultimately settled on land included in present-day France, and the name Burgundy remains as a reminder of the important rôle they must have played in that kingdom.

The credibility of the evidence of their northern origin.—The trustworthiness of the claim of these early writers that the aforesaid tribes had a Swedish origin has been questioned, and radically divergent views have been held by historians. Some decades ago they were generally inclined to reject the accounts as unreliable, but later the pendulum of historical thought has swung decidedly over to the other side. The greatest authorities in the field of early Germanic history—Hodgkin, Ludwig Schmidt, Kossina, Alexander Bugge, Schück, and von Friesen—accept the statements of Jordanes, Prokopius, Paul the Deacon, and other early Germanic writers as offering

[8] Paul the Deacon's *History of the Longobards,* translated by W. E. Foulke, Philadelphia, 1907.

[9] Schmidt, Ludwig, *Geschichte der deutschen Stämme,* Berlin, 1910-1918, I: 4, p. 429.

the most plausible and trustworthy account of the early history of these people.[10]

It is, in the first place, significant that so many of these tribes had almost similar traditions of a descent from the North, and certainly the burden of proof rests upon those who would discredit these. The straightforward and apparently honest way in which Jordanes, Prokopius, and Paul the Deacon tell their stories adds greatly to their plausibility. It is known that these men had close contacts with the people of whom they wrote and thus enjoyed good opportunities of getting information concerning their history. Archæologists have later entered the discussion and they have given weighty evidence in support of these accounts; the philologists have been able to give further supporting facts. As the latter in their studies have penetrated more and more deeply into the meaning of the old Icelandic heroic songs and Germanic legends, the close relationship which exists between these has become strikingly evident. The assumption that the Germanic tribes in question had a Scandinavian origin is thus strengthened. Archæology has, however, offered the most convincing proof. As stated before (p. 48), Swedish soil has yielded a mass of articles from the Roman period, consisting largely of gold coins and ornaments, but it is a most significant fact that the number of articles found in Sweden from a given period bears a direct relation to the fortunes of the Goths on the eastern frontier in that particular period. Certain Roman emperors paid large sums as tribute money to the Goths, and it is coins from the reign of these very emperors which are most numerous among the finds unearthed in Sweden. The fact that these coins do not show much wear proves that they came directly into the land and not by the slow processes of trade. Supplementary evidence of a most striking and convincing character has been offered by an examination of early burial mounds on Gottland and Bornholm and in south and west Sweden. These examinations, conducted by the brilliant Swedish archæologist, Stjerna,[11] reveal

[10] Hodgkin, Thomas, *Italy and Her Invaders*, Oxford, 1880; Schmidt, *Geschichte der deutschen Stämme;* Kossina, G., *Die deutsche Vorgeschichte,* Leipsic, 1921; Bugge, A., *Norges Historie;* Schück, *Svenska folkets historia;* Friesen, Otto Von, *Emigration from Sweden,* in Lundborg and Runnström, *The Swedish Nation.*

[11] Stjerna, Knut, *Essays on Beowulf,* London, 1912, pp. 64-69.

a large decrease in the number of graves in the identical periods when, according to story and legend, a considerable migration movement was going on from the alleged Scandinavian homes of the Goths and other Germanic tribes in the North to their kinsmen on the Continent. Stjerna believes that this falling off in the number of graves was due to a decided decrease in the population through emigration. This decrease in the population is indicated by other circumstances and, as noted elsewhere (p. 67), had an important bearing upon events in Sweden.

The beginning of the Swedish state; Tacitus.—Tacitus' *Germania* [12] gives a hint where the nucleus of the early Swedish state is to be sought. The Suiones, he says, are powerful through the possession of weapons and ships; the latter are not driven by sails but by oars which may be shifted from side to side as circumstances may require. Their boats are unique also in the respect that they have a prow at both extremities, enabling the rowers to reverse their course speedily without the necessity of turning. Among the Suiones property is honoured and one man rules "with no restrictions, with no uncertain claim to obedience. The right to carry arms is not found among them as among other Germanic tribes, but weapons are in the custody of a slave, for the sea makes a sudden attack of enemies impossible, and weapons in the hands of idle men are dangerous and demoralizing." The tenor of his account seems to indicate that this centralized state was not a new thing when he wrote. It is a significant fact that in the case of no other people does Tacitus mention a similar organization; royal power was, on the contrary, weak among the other Germanic tribes. The account of Tacitus and especially his statement regarding the concentration of authority in one man seems to make the conclusion inescapable that already in his day a strongly centralized government existed in Sweden. From this it may be concluded that the nucleus of the present Swedish state existed already two thousand years ago, thus giving to Sweden the distinction of being the oldest among the present European states. Not only was Sweden the first to receive a state organization which has endured to the present day, but the nature of this

[12] Tacitus, *Germania,* A. M. Church and W. J. Brodribb translation, London, 1868.

organization has undergone no radical changes through violent revolutions; it has changed gradually in conformity to the requirements of new standards set by education and new political ideas.

The period 400-800 was thus an era during which the Swedes expended a tremendous amount of energy in military enterprises at home and abroad. At the same time the process of enlarging and consolidating the Swedish state led to important results. Another phase of development in this era deserves special mention; namely, the remarkable culture which flourished, as evidenced by archæological finds. It was in a sense a "golden age" in the land. The various contacts with other nations through migrations evidently had a remarkably stimulating influence upon Swedish artistic skill. Not only coins but rings and bars of gold were imported from the South. The Swedish goldsmiths, as the finds reveal, were superior artisans and from their skilled hands came the splendid gold necklaces and other articles which in the period excel anything found abroad. While the remains unearthed in the mounds of Old Uppsala are not numerous, some of the reclaimed objects are remarkably fine. The burial mounds at Vendel have, however, yielded the most impressive evidence of a remarkable love of luxury and great golden wealth. These graves, from a period extending over four or five centuries and especially rich in finds from the fifth and sixth centuries, have yielded fine gold ornamented helmets, shields, saddles, stirrups, and bits, besides swords, spears, and utensils. These finds constitute one of the most valuable possessions of the Historical Museum in Stockholm. During the "Vendel period" Sweden is richer in valuable and artistic objects than the other Scandinavian lands, and no people anywhere surpass them in delicacy of touch and sense of beauty. The era as a whole also saw a marked growth of population and an improvement in living standards.[13]

The organized Swedish state of Tacitus' time comprised only a small part of the present kingdom. Its centre was at Uppsala; southwards it extended to Lake Mälaren and across this body of water to Södermanland, while westward it reached

[13] Stolpe, H. J., and Arne, T. J., *Gravfältet vid Vendel*, 1902; Lindquist, S., *Ottarshögen vid Vendel*, *Fornvännen*, 1917; Lindquist, S., *Gamla Uppsala Forminnen*, Stockholm, 1929.

as far as Västmanland. This section then lay much lower than now (p. 2), was intersected by a large number of arms of the sea, and had many lakes which since have disappeared. By making intercourse easy these many water-courses were an important factor in hastening the consolidation of the various sections of the district. To the south of the Suiones or Svear lay the region of the Götar or Goths, Västergötland and Östergötland. Between the peoples of these two sections a bitter struggle for supremacy began in the beginning of the sixth century, which ended with victory for the Svear, who thus came to give a name to the entire country (*Svea Rike*, contracted to *Sverige*—Sweden). The defeat of the Goths by the Svear was no doubt due to the fact that they had become seriously weakened in man power by the departure of hosts of men for the wars which the Goths on the Continent were waging against Rome. Most of the details of the century-long struggle are hidden in obscurity, but it is certain that the conflict was exceedingly bitter. Written documents give merely hints of what actually happened. The most important of these are the Anglo-Saxon poem *Beowulf* and Snorre Sturlesson's *Ynglingasaga*.

Were the Geats Swedes or Danes?—According to *Beowulf*, written in England in the beginning of the eighth century on the basis of Scandinavian sagas and poems, which in turn belong to the sixth and seventh centuries, there existed in that period at least three kingdoms in the North, those of the Danes, the Geats, and the Svear (Swedes). The opinion that the Geats were the Goths of Sweden—the inhabitants of Västergötland and Östergötland—and not the Jutes of Denmark, as was once quite generally supposed, seems to have the preponderance of weighty arguments in its favour.[14] The territorial limits of these kingdoms are not indicated, but the Danish realm was in all probability approximately the same as

[14] Among scholars who have taken this view may be mentioned Björkman, E., *Englische Studien*, 1908, p. 39; Stjerna, Knut, *Essays on Beowulf*; Klaeber, F., *Beowulf*, Boston, 1922. A recent brilliant defender of this position is Elias Wessén in his *De nordiska folkstammarna i Beowulf*, Stockholm, 1927. Among the scholars who have held the view that the Geats were identical with the Jutes, or inhabitants of Jutland, may be mentioned Kier, Chr., *Beowulf*, Cophenhagen, 1915; Fahlbeck, P., *Beowulfs kvädet som källa för nordisk fornhistoria*," in *Kungliga Vitterhets Historie och Antikvitets Akademiens Handlingar*, Ny följd 13:13, 1923; Weibull, C., *Om det svenska och det danska rikets uppkomst* in *Historisk tidskrift för Skåneland*, No. 7.

at a later period; namely, Skåne, the Danish islands proper, and Jutland.

The Beowulf story.—The Beowulf poem relates how a certain monster, Grendel by name, at night stole into the hall of Hrodgar, king of the Danes, and seized and killed many of his men. Hrodgar was entirely helpless against the attacks of the dread enemy. In the course of time the report of Grendel's bloody deeds reached Beowulf, a kinsman of Hygelac, king of the Geats, and he set out with a few trusty retainers to bring assistance to the Danish king. When Grendel appears in the king's hall and seizes and kills one of the Geats, Beowulf, who with some of his men lay concealed in the hall, boldly attacks the monster, severs an arm from his body, and compels him to flee. The following night Grendel's mother appears on the scene to exact vengeance for the mutilation of her son and she succeeds in carrying away one of Hrodgar's most trusted retainers. Beowulf now went in pursuit of the monsters. Discovering their hiding-place in a morass, he dashed in and a furious fight ensued, from which Beowulf finally emerged as victor. Great was the rejoicing in the land of the Danes. The last part of the story is laid fifty years later when Beowulf has become king of the Geats and already approaches the sunset of his life. A cruel monster now begins to harass his land, but the aged hero attacks it valiantly and again is victorious. He succumbs, however, to the wounds which had been inflicted upon him in the encounter.

War of Svear and Geats.—Besides the story of the deeds of Beowulf, the poem contains accounts of other men and their deeds, and here a nearer approach is made to historic realities. Thus it goes on to say that when Hredel, king of the Geats, died and his son Hraedcyn succeeded him on the throne, war broke out between the Geats and the Svear, the latter precipitating the struggle by attacking their neighbours. After inflicting great damage, the Svear returned home. Hraedcyn, assisted by his brother, Hygelac, retaliated by attacking the Svear, and the wife of their king, Ongentheow, was taken prisoner. In a counter-attack, Ongentheow rescued the queen, killed Hraedcyn, and surrounded his troops, who were threatened with death in the morning. Again the fortunes of war shifted when the followers of Hygelac attacked the Svear, who hastily fled to their fastnesses, pursued by the Geats. Ongentheow soon thereafter lost his life in a fight and peace reigned between the two peoples. Added prestige was given to Hygelac by the support given him by his nephew, Beowulf, who after his mighty exploits in Denmark joined the king of the Geats. His victories had made Hygelac ambitious to enter upon still greater exploits, and about 516 he undertook a marauding expedition into the Frankish land. That this expedition actually was undertaken is confirmed by Gregory of Tours, a French bishop and chronicler of the sixth century,[15] who also fixes the date. Possibly the expedition was undertaken to assist Theodoric the Great, king of the Ostrogoths in Italy, who at this time was seeking assistance against the Merovingian kings.[16] The expedition ended disastrously, however, as Hygelac and his followers were slain and his fleet destroyed. This expedition may be considered the first in the long series of Viking expeditions. Beowulf saved himself by swimming back to his own land. Hoerdred succeeded his father Hygelac as king, and Beowulf rendered him royal service as he had done to the father. A series of encounters between the Svear and the Geats followed and the downfall of the latter is clearly foreshadowed.

That back of the fanciful dates of the poem historical persons and actual events appear has become convincingly clear to scholars. The kings mentioned, no doubt belonged to dynasties which actually ruled their respective groups, although the names in the Anglo-Saxon poem have become quite unrecognizable. Ongentheow is undoubtedly the same as Egil of the *Ynglingasaga.* Othtere, his son, is Ottar, and Onela, Othtere's brother, is Ale. Besides the historical confirmation of certain episodes of the poem furnished by Gregory of Tours, the presumption of a historical basis is furnished by Saxo (p. 125), and the *Ynglingasaga.*[17] From the viewpoint of Swedish history, the important data furnished by the Beowulf poem are those which bear upon the struggles between the two

[15] *Historia Francorum, Monumenta Germaniæ Scriptores Rerum Merivingicarum I,* Hanover, 1885.

[16] Wessén, E., *De nordiska folkstammarna i Beowulf,* pp. 59-61.

[17] For an excellent summary of the whole question see Klaeber's Introduction to his edition of *Beowulf.*

important groups in Sweden, the Svear or Swedes and the Geats or Goths.

Snorre's *Ynglingasaga* is based principally upon a poem written in the latter part of the ninth century by Thjodolf of Hvin for the purpose of showing the long and glorious ancestry of Ragnvald, cousin of Harold Fairhair of Norway. As the family ruled over a small principality in Norway and was then obscure, Thjodolf ingeniously seeks to glorify his hero by connecting the latter's ancestry with the ancient family of the Uppsala kings; the poem thus throws some light on rulers and events of the period in Sweden.

Testimony of the Ynglingasaga.—Snorre starts out by recounting the story of the coming of Odin and the other gods to Sweden and their settlement in the Uppsala region, after which a list of the kings who ruled in the land is given and their wars described. Among these kings were Aun, Egil, and Adils, who, he says, were buried at Uppsala. A fourth king, Ottar, is also given prominent mention. It was therefore assumed already at an early date that the famous mounds at Old Uppsala, located about two miles from the present city of Uppsala, are ancient burial grounds. This supposition was given strong confirmation when two of these mounds were opened, the so-called Odin's mound in 1846 and 1847, Thor's mound in 1874. The third burial-place, Frey's mound, was opened in 1846 and 1925, but the examinations have not at either time been carried far enough to give definite results.

In the case of the first mound, cremated remains of human beings, besides bits of gold ornaments and other articles, were found which indicated that a man of high station had been buried there. The remains indicate that the mound had been built about the year 500 A.D. Thor's mound was found to contain remains very similar to those of Odin's mound and to date from the sixth century. The partial examination of Frey's mound indicates that it was built after Thor's mound had been completed. These dates coincide with the dates given for the deaths of the three kings in question.[18] Snorre also states that Ottar went on an expedition to Vendel in Jutland where he fell in battle, his body being laid on a mound, a prey to wild

[18] Lindquist, S., *Gamla Uppsala Fornminnen.*

beasts. But not far from Uppsala lies a place which also bears the name of Vendel, and here is a mound, which in tradition has long been known as the Ottar mound, having approximately the same dimensions as those of Old Uppsala. The supposition that this mound is in reality the king's burial-place is supported by the strongest evidence. The remains which have been uncovered in a great number of graves in proximity to the Ottar mound (p. 66), prove beyond the shadow of a

Iron helmet with bronze ornaments. Vendel

doubt that kings at one time resided at Vendel. The manner of burial indicates that these kings belonged to the same family as those buried at Old Uppsala.

The legendary kings.—Snorre's account of Aun, Egil, and Adils is embellished with many fictitious elements. Thus it relates how Aun, by sacrificing nine of his sons in succession to Odin, was granted such a long life that he finally became so weak that, like a suckling infant, he was compelled to lie in bed and drink milk from the small end of a horn. Neither *Beowulf* nor *Ynglingasaga* has anything of importance to relate about

Egil and Ottar, but hints are given that they took part in many battles; if the encounters were with the Goths or with the Danes is not clear. With Adils is associated one of the most popular Scandinavian tales of the Middle Ages. On a plundering expedition to Saxony the king took prisoner a young maiden, Yrsa by name, whose beauty was widely celebrated. She became his wife, but after returning to his home Adils was compelled to flee before King Helge of Denmark, who suddenly fell upon the land with a great army. Yrsa was now carried away to Denmark where she became the wife of her captor. Their son was Rolf Krake. When later Yrsa was told that she was a daughter of Helge she returned to Adils. Later Rolf Krake became king of Denmark. Towards the end of his life Adils was compelled to meet Ale of Norway in a battle fought on the ice of Lake Vänern and here the Norwegian king fell. *Ynglingasaga,* as well as other sagas, give the impression that Adils was a mighty ruler, and since he ruled at the time when the power of the Goths, according to hints given by *Beowulf,* was nearly broken, there is good reason for supposing that the triumph of the Swedes or Svear over the Goths or Geats became definite during his reign. The time can be quite definitely established as the last half of the sixth century. The next king who figures somewhat prominently in the sagas is Anund, whose accession to the throne has been placed at about the year 600. Peace prevailed during his reign. The king built roads in all parts of Sweden and laid new tracts in the wilderness under cultivation. A royal estate was created in every principal country and some of these seem to have retained their status as royal property down to our own times.[19] Anund was succeeded by Ingjald Illråde, whom historians have looked upon as the successful, albeit unscrupulous, welder of many petty Swedish states into a strong kingdom. His foster-father had, according to Snorre, given him a wolf's heart to eat, and this had made him more cruel than other men. To the funeral feast at Uppsala, in honour of his father, Ingjald invited seven of the petty kings who were his neighbours. Six of these accepted the invitation, and when they had taken their places at the banquet-table the host raised his goblet and made the solemn vow that he

[19] Nerman, B., *Det svenska rikets uppkomst,* Stockholm, 1926, p. 218.

Iron knob of shield ornamented with gilded bronze. Two views. Vendel would double the area of his kingdom in every direction or die in the attempt. In spite of the ominous warning which this ought to have conveyed to the guests, they remained at Ingjald's court, entering into the spirit of the festivities with such abandon that they became helpless from drink. During the night the building was surrounded by Ingjald's retainers and was set on fire, no one of those within being permitted to escape. Ingjald then proceeded to incorporate all the lands of the slain kings with his own dominions. Another account in Snorre says that Ingjald in all killed as many as twelve petty kings.

Snorre, no doubt, paints Ingjald with much blacker colours than his character and deeds warrant. The Icelander received his information from persons who had every reason to hate the king and who, naturally, pictured him as the very incarnation of wickedness. Ingjald, no doubt, was an ambitious and aggressive ruler, who had conceived the idea of building up a large state by the consolidation of several petty states, and like most state-builders, especially in the turbulent period in which he lived, he was not very scrupulous as to the means to be employed.

Ingjald's summons to the unfortunate petty kings gives a good idea of the extent of the territory which now was subject to the rule of the Svear. According to Snorre, he sent men to all of Svithiod (the land of the Svear), bringing invitations to the seven kings who ruled in the land; "all of Svithiod," we are further told, included Västergötland, Uppland, part of Västmanland, Södermanland, and Närke.

Retribution speedily came to Ingjald for his evil deeds when a hostile force under Ivar Vidfamne (wide-embracing) who belonged to the royal house of the Sköldungs in Denmark, invaded his land with an army. Hemmed in on every side and realizing that to offer battle would mean certain defeat, Ingjald and his evil-minded daughter, Åsa, lured their men to drink until they were in a stupor, when they set fire to the hall and all perished. These events are supposed to have happened about the middle of the seventh century.

Ivar Vidfamne and Olof Trätälja.—Ivar Vidfamne now ruled over a vast kingdom which included the land of the

Svear and the Danes, a great part of Saxony (Saxland), "all the land in the East, and a fifth of England." Snorre then goes on to relate how Ingjald's son Olof, who was sojourning in Västergötland at the time of his father's death, went to Närke as soon as Ivar had established his rule in the land. The Svear, unwilling to permit any of Ingjald's family to remain among them, compelled him to take his departure, whereupon he went to the region north of Lake Vänern where he began to clear the land. For this reason the Svear called him Olof Trätälja (wood-cutter). He married a Norwegian maid, and from her country came many settlers to the new colony; a still larger accession came, however, from those who were compelled to flee before Ivar Vidfamne and sought refuge with Olof. The new colony later was called Värmland. As the population grew, famine came upon the land. The people then charged Olof with responsibility for this, saying that he had failed to make proper sacrifices to the gods, and the unfortunate king was put to death. Another Icelandic saga gives a different version of Olof's story, saying that he became king in Uppsala, where he ruled after his father and died at a ripe old age. The best historical evidence seems, however, to support Snorre's account rather than the older Icelandic saga. The assertion that Olof and his men were the original settlers of Värmland is, however, unfounded; ground had been broken there already in the Stone Age.

Snorre has very little information about events in Sweden during a couple of centuries after Ivar Vidfamne's death in the latter half of the seventh century. In other narratives, notably those of Saxo Grammaticus, who as early as the latter part of the twelfth and the first part of the thirteenth century wrote the history of the Danes, a vivid account is given of a terrible battle fought at Bråvalla in the province of Östergötland. The great conflict grew out of a quarrel between Harold Hildetand, grandson of Ivar Vidfamne, and Sigurd Ring, each of whom commanded an enormous host. Sigurd was a kinsman of Harold and by him had been set to rule over Svithiod. When irreconcilable differences between them made war inevitable, both began to make great preparations for the impending struggle, hosts of armed men being summoned from far and near, and the boldest and most powerful warriors of the North placing themselves at the head of the opposing armies. No details of gory carnage are lacking in the account of the battle which Saxo gives. The battle ended with the defeat and death of the aged and decrepit Harold, after which Sigurd ruled over all his former domains. Historians have not been able to establish the truthfulness of this story, and many of its details are contradictory. Back of the legend lies, no doubt, the actual occurrence of a bitter struggle between the Svear and the Goths, in which also the Danes may have been involved. Recent archæological researches on the legendary site of the battle have brought to light most interesting and conclusive evidence that a great conflict had actually taken place there at some time.

Chapter III

THE VIKING EXPEDITIONS

The migration of nations may be viewed as a prelude to another great movement of peoples which affected European civilization profoundly; namely, the Viking expeditions. The Scandinavians alone were now the aggressors, and against their attacks practically all the states of Europe—Germanic, Celtic, Slavic, and Greek—were compelled to defend themselves. Roughly speaking, this movement began in the latter part of the eighth century and came to its close towards the middle of the eleventh. There were, of course, isolated expeditions by Scandinavian corsairs before the great movement began, one of which has already been noted (p. 69), and others occurred after the end of the period, but these were merely sporadic events.

Character of the expeditions.—The numerous Viking expeditions were a manifestation of tremendous vitality, aggressiveness, and a genius for organization on the part of the Northmen, and, when judged by their main results, they must be considered as constructive in character. The extent to which they touched and influenced different parts of Europe, reaching even America in the West and Asia in the East, has never failed to arouse amazement. "Leaving their Northern homes in the ninth century," says an English historian,[1] "they had by the end of the twelfth penetrated into nearly every country in Europe. So close were their political and family relations with all the countries of the West, from Iceland to Constantinople, from Russia to Spain, during the tenth, eleventh, and twelfth centuries, that a history of the Northmen is little short of a history of Europe during these ages."

Early historians have been in the habit of stressing the cruelty of the Vikings and the destructive character of their

[1] Johnson, A. H., *The Normans in Europe*, London, 1903.

raids. While it is undeniable that the Scandinavian Vikings many times grievously violated the fundamental principles of justice and humanity, it can justly be said that this feature has been greatly magnified and the constructive character of the great movement unduly minimized. If the Vikings made themselves guilty of revolting cruelties, they were at least no worse than corsairs of other lands even in much later times. "The standards of right and wrong of the Northmen of the tenth century," says a recent excellent work in this field,[2] "as regards property, were but little different from those displayed by high class Englishmen six hundred years later; the former attacked all foreign lands which failed to buy them off, while Sir Francis Drake and his school restricted their depredations to the commerce and the territory of Roman Catholic Spain in the Old World and the New. The earlier freebooters had all the courage and daring of the later ones, and perhaps were no more cruel and lawless than they; both classes were the products of the times in which they lived."

The term "Viking expedition" came to be synonymous with cruelty and wanton destruction largely because those who in former days wrote accounts of the raids generally derived their material from the very individuals who had the greatest reason for hating these unbidden visitors from the North; namely, the monks. The early Vikings took a special delight in robbing monasteries and in killing monks; this was, no doubt, for the simple reason that in these monasteries they could make their easiest and richest hauls; the inoffensive and peaceable dwellers within the cloister walls also aroused the special contempt of these fierce pagan warriors. The monks were, however, practically the only contemporary individuals who wrote some kind of historical accounts, and in painting the picture of the Vikings they naturally did not refrain from using lurid colours. A more dispassionate historical scholarship and the accumulation of evidence of various kinds have shown that while the Viking expeditions were at first undertaken mainly for plunder and, in their early stages especially, were attended by revolting acts of cruelty, they nearly always ended as great constructive enterprises, resulting in the firmer organization

[2] Williams, Mary W., *Social Scandinavia in the Viking Age*, New York, 1920, p. 249.

of states and in the expansion of trade and commerce. The latter was a perfectly natural phase and one that everyone who knows the character of the Northern people would expect; their entire history for thousands of years gives unimpeachable and impressive evidence that the will to build, rather than the desire to tear down and destroy, is one of their fundamental traits.

Difficulty in determining the Swedish part in the expeditions.—In endeavouring to determine what rôle the Swedes played in the Viking movement the historian finds himself confronted by many perplexities. Their exploits in the Baltic lands, Russia, and the Black Sea region seem quite clear and well authenticated, but how important their part was in other sections is not easily determined and will perhaps forever remain largely a matter of surmise. The traditional view has held that the Viking raids and settlements in the West, as in England, Ireland, Iceland, and the smaller islands, as well as in France, were Danish and Norwegian enterprises, except as some straggling Swedes may have participated, and that, on the other hand, the expeditions towards the East and Southeast were exclusively Swedish affairs. The facts in the case are evidently not so simple as this theory assumes. A number of runic inscriptions, archæological finds, various saga accounts, as well as geographical and political considerations, point to an important part by Swedes also in the western field, and conversely it may be taken for granted that Danes and Norwegians took at least some part in the expeditions into Russia and to the Black Sea region.

One difficulty in determining the Swedish part in the Viking movement arises from the changes which have taken place in the territorial limits of the Scandinavian lands. Thus Skåne and Blekinge, two provinces which furnished an exceptionally large number of men for Viking expeditions, were at that time Danish possessions, whereas they have now been a part of the Swedish realm for over two hundred and fifty years; similarly Bohuslän, which perhaps was a more important centre of Viking organization and supplied more men, comparatively, than any other district in Scandinavia, was at that time a part of the Norwegian realm, whereas it is now Swedish and has been for

The shaded areas, now a part of Sweden were then incorporated with Norway or Denmark.

Sweden in Viking times

many hundred years. Swedish historians have, as a rule, discussed the question of the nationality of this or that Viking group or leader with calmness; they have claimed as Swedes only those who evidently came from the parts included in their land at the time. Danish and Norwegian historians have been considerably more disturbed by this problem of "national origins."

Causes of the Viking expeditions.—Back of the extraordinary outpouring of men and truly amazing energy and power which they manifest lay the inherent love of adventure which in all ages has been a fundamental trait of the Northmen. As a classic example of this may be cited the story of Harold Hardrule, who once sailed northward merely that he might ascertain just what would happen if he pressed on far enough; the history of explorations in every period and in every part of the world gives ample evidence that where adventure beckons the son of the Northland is quite certain to put in an appearance.

Love of adventure.—A restless disposition has naturally been associated with this spirit of adventure. The Scandinavian has been disposed to magnify the difficulties of existence in the homeland and to dream of life in other climes as far brighter and happier than the Northland can offer. The South has always held a lure for him—until he has tried it. The pagan religion of the Vikings was undoubtedly also a mighty factor in giving energy and character to the raiding enterprises; it helped to steel their nerves against danger, for what use was there in shrinking from it? The Fates, they firmly believed, had determined the span of each individual's life, and until that was completed no situation could bring death to him; furthermore, the joys of Valhalla were vouchsafed only to the courageous man who died the heroic death of the battle-field.

The consolidation of states.—Viewing the more external circumstances which played a part in launching the great movement, the principle of primogeniture and the process of consolidating petty states into larger kingdoms appear important. By the aforesaid principle only the elder son of the family inherited the ancestral estate—a measure devised to prevent the breaking up of a property into many parts, with its consequent disintegration and weakness. It generally meant that younger sons must shift for themselves. The prospect of acquiring estates in other lands then came with an especially strong lure to these dispossessed young men. The effect of the consolidation of states were very similar, except that here the interests involved were greater; rather than accept a humiliating subordinate place under their conqueror, the subdued petty kings and their retainers generally chose to lead expeditions into other lands where opportunities were to be had to carve out new states for themselves. While, no doubt, important factors, love of adventure, principles of heredity, and the consolidation of states are, however, not sufficient to explain the genesis and growing dimensions of the Viking movement.

Overpopulation.—In his monumental work on the Viking period, the noted Danish historian, Steenstrup,[3] maintains that the main cause of the Viking exodus was overpopulation. This contention might seem strange in view of the fact that Sweden and Norway then had vast areas of territory upon which lived a meagre population. Bugge[4] conjectures that the population of Norway in the Viking period was only one-tenth to one-ninth of that of the present day; that is, from 200,000 to 300,000. Basing his estimates on the amount of tithes paid in the period 1320-1322, thus three or four hundred years later than the period under consideration, Hildebrand[5] comes to the conclusion that the population of the six dioceses of Sweden was 384,280 at that time. There are many gaps in these reports, but the figures are sufficient to indicate that the population in the fourteenth century was not over half a million. In the Viking period it must have been considerably less. Montelius says on this point: "How great the population of Svithiod was at the end of heathen times we do not know, of course; but we may reasonably suppose that it was not a fifth part so large as that of Sweden today."[6] It must, however, be borne in mind that the cultivated areas, a thousand years ago, being confined mainly to the river valleys and regions near the coast, were very much smaller than they are today, and even on these areas the yield fell far below present harvests, since methods of cultivation were then exceedingly crude. Even in summers, when climatic conditions were favourable, the population, no doubt, found it exceedingly difficult to procure the necessary sustenance, and when, as frequently happened, cold and frost caused a bad harvest, the pinch of hunger was felt almost immediately. The pressure of population had, however,

[3] Steenstrup, J. C. H., *Normannerne,* 4 vols., Copenhagen, 1876.
[4] Bugge, *Norges Historie,* I, p. 221.
[5] Hildebrand, H., *Sveriges medeltid,* Stockholm, 1879, I, pp. 58-62.
[6] Montelius, Oscar, *Sweden in Heathen Times,* London, 1888, p. 145.

according to Steenstrup, become more than ordinarily acute in the period preceding the Viking expeditions, because polygamy and concubinage had become common among the wealthier men of the North. While polygamy as known in the Orient is not associated with a high birth-rate, it did, in fact, among the physically vigorous Northmen mean a large excess of births over deaths,[7] and contemporary accounts very frequently speak of unusually large families. With a large brood of children to be taken care of, the question of sustenance became more than ordinarily perplexing to more than one pater familias; disputes regarding inheritance also became frequent and tormenting. In the matter of worldly affairs, men of this period were, as a rule, far removed from weak sentimentalism; on the contrary, they were cold and calculating. Callous of heart and fully determined to preserve the family estate intact, the fathers sent their sons, with the exception of the first-born, into the world to shift for themselves. Foreign lands, always richer than their own, then beckoned with their greater opportunities, and the practice of going abroad to carve out a fortune became more and more common. As experiences revealed how easy and direct this way to wealth really was, others were tempted to follow in the paths of those who had gone before.

Weakness of other European states.—In enumerating the causes of the Viking expeditions, one should not lose sight of the fact that the states outside of Scandinavia were weak and poorly prepared to meet attacks from the outside. The remarkable endurance and undaunted courage of the Vikings have been celebrated in song and story, and assuredly they possessed these virtues in a pre-eminent degree, but it is also clear that their way to victory was made much easier by the hopeless dissensions which in this age afflicted the nations of Europe outside of Scandinavia. With the exception of the empire of Charlemagne, there was not a country in Europe that was not torn by internal dissensions and ill prepared to ward off attacks by foreign enemies; after the death of the great emperor in 814, this state also began to disintegrate. Especially were the lands ruled by the Celts, as Ireland, and the islands north of England, rendered practically helpless before an aggressive

[7] Steenstrup, *Normannerne*, I, p. 224.

enemy by their own chronic and bitter internal squabbles. The Scandinavians, on the other hand, had the wisdom and the will to work unitedly—they had in a pre-eminent degree what in modern parlance is called "team play." In some countries, as in England, the national weakness and helplessness were not so much due to internal dissensions as to the loss of the former military spirit, but the results were the same—they fell easy prey to an attacking party which was held together by the mind of one leader and struck with almost machinelike precision. Once the Scandinavian Vikings had discovered that the other European states were by no means as strong as they had believed, and that the wealth which they so eagerly coveted was by no means unattainable, their boldness grew rapidly and their attacks became increasingly frequent. The different stages through which a Viking settlement in a conquered land passed were nearly always the same; at first the Northmen landed unexpectedly near a town or abbey, plundered and burned, and then were off again before the natives could organize their defence or marshal their forces for pursuit. The story of the Viking expeditions frequently suggests that the Northmen were wonderfully well informed about changing conditions of the various countries; in lands where they could expect determined resistance they did not put in an appearance, but where a weak king had come to rule or the country's power of resistance had for any other reason waned, they were quite certain to appear in force. As they won greater advantages and the wealth of the land was revealed to them, they came again in larger numbers, stayed longer, and finally took up their permanent abodes in the land.

Land and naval forces.—The Viking attacks naturally resulted in arousing the national spirit of the nations attacked and led to the strengthening of the latter's defences, and to meet this situation the invaders found it expedient to merge their own forces into larger units; thus the formidable fleets and armies of the Vikings which are often mentioned by chroniclers, generally with gross exaggeration of their size and formidable strength, came into existence. The composition and organization of these fighting forces gave the Northmen a tremendous advantage at a time when the other peoples of Europe were utterly deficient in military organization. The Viking host was made up of free men, physically strong and mentally alert, who voluntarily had placed themselves under the command of a leader whom they followed only as long as he proved worthy. They were governed by definite rules which had the binding force of custom, and one of these was loyalty to the leader who ruled rather by virtue of superior intelligence and courage than by arbitrary authority. The Northern corsairs perhaps derived their greatest advantage from the superiority of their boats. Some historians have even gone so far as to claim

A Viking boat

the possession of this superior type of boat is one of the main causes underlying the entire movement.[8] The superiority of ruling nations has almost always been contingent upon sea power. The Viking boats were of the same type as those described by Tacitus. The type is best known by the famous Gökstad boat which was discovered buried in the sand near Sandefjord in Norway and now constitutes one of the great treasures of the museum of the University of Oslo. Whence the type came or who the ingenious inventor was is unknown, but that this splendid vessel was Scandinavian in origin is

[8] Svensén, E., *Svenska historien,* Vol. I.

certain. These craft enabled the Northmen to make swift and comparatively safe journeys across the sea, to launch sudden attacks, and return before resistance or pursuit could be organized. The Scandinavians were perhaps the first people to make themselves independent of the coast-line in navigation, passing, as they did, across the seas and even across the Atlantic without fear.

As the Northmen lived in close association with nature the laws of which they had a remarkable understanding, they knew how to take advantage of tides, of favourable winds, and of the terrain. As dwellers in a region of deep and extensive forests, they knew how to find safety in the wooded regions near by after an attack; these regions also afforded them a good hiding-place before surprise attacks were made. Contemporary accounts also attribute to the Vikings superiority in military strategy. In advancing to battle, their armies generally proceeded in wedge-shaped formation in order to divide the forces of the enemy; so effective did this method prove that they believed that Odin himself had invented it and had taught it to men in their own countries. The Northmen seem already to have known how to construct crude forts. It was their practice as they advanced into a foreign country to build many forts so that they might be able the more effectually to hold the conquered territory.

Strategy.—Their attacks upon the fortified places of the enemy, whether these took the form of regular sieges or of sudden onslaughts by the aid of towers and battering-rams, also revealed great skill. In rapidity of motion and ability to bewilder and elude pursuers, they had no equals and they did not disdain a resort to deceit in order to bewilder the enemy. Thus Rollo, the founder of Normandy, in besieging a Frankish citadel, built a fort of his own, inside the open doors of which the Vikings lay in simulated sleep. On seeing them thus apparently off their guard, the Franks were beguiled into entering, only to be set upon and overpowered. Saxo relates how Frode, King of Denmark, after an unsuccessful siege of a fortified place, caused the report to be spread that he was dead. A great mock funeral was arranged, the Danish army giving vociferous expression to its despair and grief, and when the besieged thereupon relaxed their watchfulness they were overwhelmed in a surprise attack.

Their physical strength and endurance also helped to give superiority to the Vikings. Not only did they spring from a physically strong race, but they kept fit by vigorous exercise and by a life in the open. That the people of the North in Viking times took much interest in what today would be called physical development and followed a rational system of exercise is attested by many statements in the sagas.[9]

Extent of Viking settlements.—It may be difficult in our day to realize clearly how far from their northern home the Scandinavian Vikings roamed in their journeys and how many were the regions which became dotted with their settlements. Their dispersion on the face of the earth about the year 1000 may be illustrated by the experiences of a Swedish chief who, one may imagine, one fine day in the springtime sets out on a long itinerary. Leaving his native land, he crosses the North Sea, visits several places in England, thereupon proceeds to Ireland, and after a time turns northward to Scotland, the Orkneys, and Shetland islands; finding that he has plenty of time on his hands and that the journey offers many interesting experiences, he goes on westward to Iceland, is urged to go still farther west to Greenland—the name sounds so attractive—continues westward on a still more adventurous journey to a land that has just been discovered and is called Vinland. Having now had his fill of adventure in the West, he returns to Europe, visits the northwestern section of France, goes on to Italy and Greece, (only occasionally could the Vikings get through the Strait of Gibraltar, which was guarded by the Arabs), finally reaching Constantinople; longing for home, he travels clear across Russia by river and land routes, circles the Baltic along the coast of Courland, Esthonia, Livonia, and Finland, and finally, after some years, reaches home where by his own fireside he sits in the long winter evenings telling his amazed friends how on this long journey he had all along the route found his own people, the Northmen, living in scattered settlements and had frequently heard his own tongue, the Norræna (Old Norse) spoken.

[9] Williams, *Social Scandinavia*, p. 327.

The Vikings in the West.—The year 787 is generally taken as marking the beginning of the Viking period, although isolated expeditions with more or less hostile intention had gone out from Scandinavia since earliest times. In the above year three pirate ships came from Hoerethaland to England and are said to be "the first ships of Danish men" who sought the island, but whether these ships came from Denmark or Norway is one of those perplexing questions to which Danish and Norwegian historians have given different answers. The party attacked Dorchester and after securing some plunder sailed away. From this time on the corsairs or "Danes," as they are called by the Anglo-Saxon chroniclers, whether their homes were in Denmark, Norway, or Sweden, came in increasing numbers and with growing frequency until after a heroic struggle King Alfred was compelled by the treaty of Wedmore in 878 to cede a great part of his kingdom—roughly speaking, the northwestern part of the island, by reason of its cession to the Danes known as the Danelaw—to the victors.

In England.—Although suffering some occasional setbacks, the Scandinavian power increased in England until, at the beginning of the eleventh century, it reached its zenith under Canute the Great. Canute ruled over all of England, Ireland, and the other islands, north and west, and over Denmark, but after his death, in 1035, royal power in England soon passed to the Anglo-Saxons again; this was, however, only for a short time; the Norman conquest of 1066 in reality vested power in a people which, although an amalgamation of the Scandinavians and native Celts of France, had maintained Scandinavian ideals of organization and law. The territory settled by the Northmen in England constituted about one-half of the land, and perhaps contained one-third of the population at one time. The extent of their settlements and influence is illustrated by the great number of place-names of clearly Scandinavian origin. According to the great Danish archæologist, Warsaae,[10] about fourteen hundred places in England have Scandinavian names, of which the most common endings are -by, -holme, -force, beck, -dale, and -ness. In commerce, trade, legal institutions, and especially in the im-

[10] Warsaae, J. J. A., *The Danes in England, Ireland, and Scotland,* London, 1852.

petus given to the building of a fleet and the organization of the army for defence, the Viking influence upon England was momentous.[11]

In Ireland.—In Ireland the Vikings had firmly entrenched themselves by 834. Their great leader was Turgeis, who made extensive conquests in northern Ireland and aimed to lay the entire country under his rule. His career was, however, cut short when he fell into the hands of the Irish, who forthwith put him to death. After his death the Scandinavian invasions became so frequent that "there was not a point without a fleet of Northmen." Olof the White, a Norwegian king and the greatest Viking leader in Ireland after Turgeis, established a large Norse kingdom on the island. Dublin, Waterford, and Limerick were founded by the Norwegians and served as important strongholds.[12] The Emerald Island seems to have held a special attraction for the Northmen, presumably because there was much wealth in its cloisters and its fields were uncommonly attractive; a chronic dissension among the Irish which seriously weakened their power of resistance contributed to the frequency of the Viking attacks.[13]

In Scotland and neighbouring islands; Iceland.—In Scotland the Scandinavian element also became strong, as proved by the fact that many important place-names are of Scandinavian origin. The number and influence of the Vikings on the Isle of Man are shown not only by the frequent occurrence of place-names of Scandinavian origin, but also by the survival down to our own day of certain unique Scandinavian methods of procedure in the enactment of laws. The Hebrides, Orkneys, Faroes, and Shetland islands virtually became Norse in language and customs. Iceland, which had been discovered between 850 and 860 by Gardar Svavarson, a native of Sweden (some accounts attribute the discovery of Iceland to Naddodr, a Norwegian, and others to the Irish), became the refuge of the stiff-necked and liberty-loving lords who, having suffered defeat in their struggle against the aggressive and unscrupulous Harold Fairhair, of Norway, rather than humble themselves

[11] An excellent brief statement of the influence of the Northmen in England is found in Mawer, Allan, *The Vikings*, London, 1913.

[12] Bugge, A., *The Norsemen in Ireland*, Christiania, 1900.

[13] Keary, C. F., *The Vikings in Western Christendom*, London, 1891.

before him and submit to his rule, left in large numbers for Iceland, where they set up a unique republic and developed a culture which still evokes the admiration of scholars everywhere. From Iceland as a base, explorations and journeys were made westward to Greenland and America, and settlements, with a population aggregating at one time perhaps as many as three thousand souls, existed along the coast of the former; on the sites of these settlements there still remain a number of foundations of houses, an old stone church, as well as other reminiscences of these early Scandinavian habitations in the land. The discovery of the mainland of North America by Leif, son of Eric the Red, in the year 1000, led to attempts to establish settlements in the New World, but these were not successful. Columbus is said to have visited Iceland in the year 1477 and it has been conjectured that traditions of these early discoveries which he may have heard there explains his unshakable conviction that land would be found if he only pressed on far enough westward. This assumption does not seem plausible; if Columbus had been guided by these traditions he would, it seems, have taken a northern instead of a southern route on his own momentous voyage; his conviction that land would be found towards the West no doubt had largely been formed by a study of a map of the famous Italian geographer, Toscanelli, a copy of which he carried with him on his eventful journey.[14]

The Swedish part in the Viking expeditions towards the West.—The people of the districts which in Viking times constituted Sweden, an area considerably smaller than the present-day country (p. 79-80), evidently did not appear in distinct groups and under their own leaders in the great expeditions westward, but as archæological evidence has thrown more light on the subject the assumption that the Swedes played a far more important part in these western journeys than was formerly supposed has received strong confirmation. Even if nothing directly were known of Swedish participation in the expeditions westward, it could, *a priori*, be assumed that they had some part in them. According to Tacitus, as already noted, the Svear were already in his day pre-eminent by

[14] Fiske, John, *Discovery of America*, Boston, 1892, Vol. I.

reason of their military and political organization, and the *Ynglingasaga* of Snorre Sturlesson as well as *Beowulf* indicate that the inhabitants of Sweden were numerous and aggressive in the days of which they write. The rock inscriptions are especially numerous along the coast country of Sweden, and these point to an early knowledge of the sea and to a military organization by the inhabitants of the land. During the period of the earlier migrations it was from Sweden far more than from Norway and Denmark that the exodus of peoples had proceeded. In the early centuries the Swedes appear as the leading and most aggressive element among the Scandinavian peoples; and they were the first, it appears, to enter upon the scene as Vikings (p. 69); under such circumstances it would seem strange if they, too, had not been attracted to the inviting western lands. It might, however, be objected that even under these conditions other circumstances might have served to bar them from the West. Aside from their enterprises in Russia and the Black Sea region, no factors are known, however, which are likely to have kept them away from "the Western Sea." This was to them almost as accessible as it was to the other Scandinavian groups; even those who lived inland in Sweden could without great difficulty find their way by river courses to the great waters that washed their western coast.

The claim that the Swedes in this restless period played an important part in the expeditions to England and neighbouring lands rests, however, not on mere assumption, but on the apparently incontestable evidence of archæological finds, especially rune stones and coins. Memorial stones containing short runic texts to the effect that the men in whose honour they have been raised had journeyed to the Western land are especially numerous in the provinces of Gästrikland, Uppland, Västmanland, Södermanland, Östergötland, Småland, and Västergötland.[15] Only a few typical ones can be noted here. The wall of the ancient church of Old Uppsala, built above the foundation of the most celebrated pagan temple of the North, contains a rock bearing a runic inscription saying that "Sigurd Englandsfarer" had caused this stone to be raised over his father. Concerning many others, it is specifically stated that they died

[15] Montelius, *Sveriges historia*, I, p. 324.

in England. In the parish of Häggeby, Uppland, is a rune stone placed there by two sons on the grave of their father "who in the West sat in the 'Tingmannaled'"; this is interpreted by Montelius as referring to the great army organization of Canute the Great, which was composed of prominent Northmen. In the parish of Yttergården in Uppland is another runic stone bearing the inscription: "But Ulf has thrice collected tribute money in England, the first sum was that paid by Toste, then it was paid by Torkel, and lastly by Knut (Canute)."[16] The payment by Canute is taken by von Friesen to refer to the sum which the great king was compelled to pay in 1018 to his Scandinavian auxiliaries before he was firmly secure in the possession of the English throne. Torkel and Toste von Friesen identifies as Torkel the Tall, and Skoglar Toste, mentioned by Snorre Sturlesson as great Viking chiefs, the former a jarl of the Jomsvikings and the latter a Swedish leader and father of Sigrid the Haughty. In the parish of Vallentuna, in Uppland, a runic stone was unearthed in 1909 which contains the inscriptions: "And Dan, Huskarl, and Sven caused this stone to be raised in memory of Ulfrik, their grandfather. In England he had collected two money tributes." It may be taken for granted that only the leaders were honoured by having rune stones erected to their memory; those who thus have had their deeds commemorated undoubtedly represent a quite imposing number of less important men who have been honoured by no such memorials.

The assumption that a great number of Swedes took part in campaigns to different parts of England and other lands in the Western Sea is further confirmed by statements of Adam of Bremen, as well as by the early chronicle accounts. In one of these it is asserted that in the army which captured York were Danes, Swedes (Svear), and Goths (Götar).[17] These accounts are further substantiated by a great number of finds of weapons and shields that have been unearthed in England, the forms and ornamentation of which point unmistakably to a Swedish origin. The strongest evidence is offered, however, by the great number of Anglo-Saxon coins which have been found in Swedish soil. The collection of such coins in the Historical

[16] Friesen, Otto von, *Historiska runinshrifter, Fornvännen,* 1909.
[17] Von Friesen, *Fornvännen,* 1909.

Museum in Stockholm, more than 30,000 in all, exceeds even that of the British Museum itself. These coins date from the reigns of the very kings who are known to have paid large sums in tribute money to the Northmen, and they have all been unearthed in Sweden, mainly on the east coast, and principally on Gottland. Trade cannot explain the presence of this large collection, since Sweden's trade in those days touched mainly the lands to the east. On this point Schück has the following to say: "The Swedes were mercenary troops, who therefore got the lion's share of the tribute money, which explains the existence of these large quantities of money in Sweden when Denmark has very few of these coins. In the last campaign of Canute, his army contained as many Swedes as Danes. At the same time the Swedes served as mercenary soldiers in Russia and Constantinople, as will later appear. The energy that could have been used in the service of their own land was sold (*hyrdes ut*) to others and Sweden's only gain was the hoard of gold which, avariciously, was interred in the ground." [18] Coins have also been found in Sweden which were struck by Scandinavian kings in Ireland, and some ornaments found in Sweden have either been brought from Ireland in this period or were made after Irish models.

The lands eastward.—A close communication between the Scandinavian countries and the lands on the other side of the Baltic existed, it may be assumed, almost from the very beginning of settlements in the North. In the younger Stone Age, or about 2000 B.C., the influx from the Scandinavian lands, particularly from Sweden, to Finland assumed considerable proportions, as archæological remains clearly show. Ginds from the era, especially in the southwestern part of Finland, have the same type as contemporary Swedish stone weapons and implements, and they reveal that in this region dwelt a people with a comparatively high culture.

In Finland.—The waters that separate Sweden from Finland were narrow and it would have been strange if the Swedes had not crossed over them in quest of new areas for settlement. When, therefore, near the beginning of the Christian era the Finns came to settle in this land—who they were and whence

[18] Schück, *Svenska folkets historia*, I, p. 221.

they came is hidden in obscurity—the Swedes had evidently taken possession of considerable areas already. The great number of early Germanic words which are found in the Finnish language suggests that the early intercourse between the two peoples was, on the whole, peaceable.[19]

Hints of Swedish expeditions to the East are frequently given in the *Ynglingasaga* and these, no doubt, have some historical basis. In Rimbert's *Life of Anskar,*[20] we read that shortly before the arrival of Christian missionaries in Sweden in 830 the Swedish king, Olof, had gone on a military expedition into Kurland and had made this district a Swedish *syssla,* or land subject to pay taxes to the Swedes. The stronghold of the Swedes was Säborg on the site where Riga afterwards was built. The islands which lie along the coast, as Ösel, Dagö, Runö, Nuckö, Ragö, and Odensholm, had mainly a Swedish population already before the Viking age. The beginning of the Viking period was to see a pronounced augmentation of the tide of Swedish emigration into Finland and to the Baltic lands south of it, a fact which clearly appears from the evidence of rune stones and place-names. The noble national epic of Finland, *Kalevala,* according to more recent investigation, shows evidence of having been composed in a mixed Swedish-Finnish population in southwestern Finland and Esthonia.[21] As was natural, the Swedish invaders turned mainly to the region around Lake Ladoga the fertility and cleared areas of which attracted them far more than the unbroken and inhospitable stretches of Finland proper or the islands of the Baltic.

In Russia.—The main portion of Russia east and south of Lake Ladoga was in this period inhabited by a heterogeneous mass of tribes, most of them Slavic or Turkish. Most of them were barbarians of a very low type, while some had, through trade contacts with other peoples, acquired some degree of culture; they all were afflicted with the malady which seems chronic among Slavs: inability to understand and develop a

[19] This question is fully discussed in: Nordenstreng, Rolf, *Vikingafärderna,* Stockholm, 1926, p. 143; Montelius, *När kommo svenskarna till Finland,* in *Finsk tidskrift,* T. XLIV, pp. 81-105; Wiklund, K. B., *När kommo svenskarna till Finland,* 1901, and *Ibid., Die ältesten germanischen lehnwörter in Finnischen,* 1917.

[20] An English translation of this work by Charles H. Robinson has appeared under the title *Anskar, the Apostle of the North,* London, 1921.

[21] Krohn, Kaarle, *Kalevalarunornas historia,* Helsingfors, 1903.

political organization. Here was an inviting field for the aggressive and adventure-loving Swedes. According to the Russian chronicler, Nestor,[22] a monk of Kiev, they did not have to force their way into these regions but came in response to an invitation. In his chronicle, written in the beginning of the tenth century, Nestor relates how the Varangians came across the sea and collected tax from the various tribes in the interior. In the year 6370 (862 A.D.), these tribes drove the Varangians across the sea, paid no tax, and began to rule the country. But the administration of justice failed among them, tribe rose against tribe, division and contention prevailed among them, and they began to make war on one another. And, according to Nestor, they said to one another: "Let us choose a prince who can rule over us and judge what is right. And they went across the sea to the Varangians, to the Rus, for thus these Varangians are called—Rus, just as others are called Svear, others Norman, others Anglians, and others Goths, and they said, 'Our land is large and fertile, but there is no order in it; come, then, and rule over us! And three brothers were chosen with their followers and they took with them the whole of Rus and they came. And the eldest, Rurik, fixed his abode at Novgorod, the other, Sineous, at Belo-Ozero, and the third, Truvor, at Izborsk, south of Lake Peipus. And the Russian land—namely, Novgorod—received its name from these Varangians." Nestor then goes on to tell how Rurik, through the death of his brothers, after two years became ruler of all the Slavic tribes of the district.

The question of the identity of the Varangians and Rus of Nestor has stirred up much learned discussion among historians. Especially have certain Russian scholars conceived it to be their patriotic duty to refute the claim that the people who laid the foundation of Russia were Swedes. Outside of this group, however, the view that the tribes credited by Nestor with being the founders of a state in Russia were Swedes is accepted by practically every historian. Especially did the scholarly work of the

[22] Apparently no English translation of Nestor's chronicle has ever been published. A German translation by Schözer which appeared in 1802 carried the account only to 980. A French text by Louis Leger was published in 1884, under the title *Chronique dite de Nestor*. Most recent is a Swedish translation by A. Norrbäck, *Nestorkrönikan*, Stockholm, 1919.

Danish historian, Thomsen,[23] give a body blow to the Russian so-called "anti-Normans," who derided the contention that the Varangians and Rus were Swedish groups. The discussion has naturally revolved around the meaning of these names. In a full and scholarly presentation, Thomsen shows that the former is a Scandinavian word, into which the word "var," oath, enters, and interprets it to mean "one who enjoys security through an oath." Classic and other early writers, he shows, used the word only as a designation for Scandinavians.

Who were the Rus?—The word "Rus" has come to the Slavs through the Esthonians who called Swedes *Rots* (Finnish *Routsi*), and this again is derived from the name Roden (Roslagen), a word applied to the coast district of Uppland, Södermanland, and Östergötland, which lay nearest to the sea, since this area was divided into sections, each one of which was under compulsion to supply a certain number of rowers (Swedish *ro*—to row). That the word Rus meant Swedes is corroborated by other than etymological facts. Thus Bishop Prudentius of Troyes relates that in 839 a deputation came from the Greek emperor to Emperor Louis the Pious, and travelling with it were some men who said that they were Rus and that their king had sent them to the emperor because of the friendship he felt for him. The Greek emperor, in a letter to Louis, asked that the Rus be given safe conduct through the land. Louis then made inquiry regarding the nativity of these people and was informed that they came from Sweden. They had evidently come for the purpose of securing from the Frankish emperor certain trade advantages, which points, as Schück suggests,[24] to a highly developed social organization in Sweden at the time; otherwise the country would not have entered into negotiations with the two greatest rulers of the time, the Byzantine emperor and the emperor of the Franks. Further proof of the identity of Rus and Swedes is found in a treaty of 911 which Oleg, a successor of Rurik, concluded with the emperor at Constantinople, after he had attacked the emperor with 80,000 men and inflicted great losses upon the city. The treaty was signed in behalf of the Russian tribe by fifteen

[23] Thomsen, Wilhelm, *The Relation between Ancient Russia and Scandinavia, and the Origin of the Russian State,* Oxford and London, 1877.

[24] Schück, *Svenska folkets historia,* I, p. 197.

men and without any exception their names are Swedish, not a single Slavic name occurring among them.[25]

Additional evidence that the Rus were Swedes has been supplied by Greek and Arabian writers. Thus Ibn Dunstah, an Arabian, who lived in the tenth century, gives an account of the appearance, military organization, and customs of the Rus, as he saw them in Russia, which seems to leave no doubt of their identity with the Swedes. Another Arab, Ibn Fadhlan, who, as a representative of the Turkish caliph in the second decade of the tenth century, visited the region of the Volga and there often saw the Rus that had come to those parts for purposes of trade, describes their appearance and customs, emphasizing particularly the gruesome details of the burial of one of their chiefs and their tall stature. His description tallies with other contemporary accounts of the Northmen.

But if Nestor's statement regarding the founding of Russia by the Rus may be taken as creditable testimony, and the contention that the Rus were Swedes is furthermore accepted as proved, it would, no doubt, be a mistake to assume that the events happened exactly as he describes them. Rurik and his brothers, together with their followers, had most likely emigrated from Sweden at an earlier date and settled in the region of Ladoga, and it was from this place that they now proceeded in response to a call for help to the land of the Slavs.

Swedish organization in Russia.—It was an enormous territory over which the Swedes thus became masters, covering, as it did, all of northern Russia. Everywhere in the conquered territory the Swedes erected forts, by means of which they could exercise control over the surrounding regions; their numerical weakness made such strongholds essential, if they were to continue in control. The number of fortified places was so great that the Swedes called the land *Gårdarike* (the land of fortified places). The Swedish element predominated in Novgorod, or *Holmgård,* as it was usually called by the Swedes, as late as the twelfth century, and it was, in fact, up to that time looked upon as a Swedish city. Striking evidence of the preponderating Swedish influence in Russia is the fact that during the two centuries after Rurik the greater part of the men

[25] Schück, *Svenska folkets historia,* I, p. 223.

whose names appear in Russian history bear Scandinavian names.

In every fortress which they built in Russia the Swedes placed one of their chiefs with a force of Swedish retainers. That their control was vigorous and successful is suggested by the fact that Nestor's chronicle makes no mention of any insurrectionary moves by the Slavs. What was known as Russia remained, until the eleventh century, a Swedish dependency from which taxes—very small amounts, it is true—were collected.

Undoubtedly the Rus venture into Russia was largely prompted by the thought that thereby Constantinople, the wealth and splendour of which was a tempting bait to lure the daring Vikings, could more easily be reached. This was, no doubt, also the purpose of a military expedition which two men, Askold and Dir, two of Rurik's followers, made into the neighbourhood of Constantinople in 862, after they had first taken and fortified Kiev, which ranked next to Novgorod as a great Swedish stronghold. In the year 865 their fleet was ready for the attack on the great and wealthy city. A swift descent upon Constantinople put that city in immediate peril, but it was saved by a sudden storm which destroyed the Swedish fleet. Very likely the city was compelled to pay a liberal sum as tribute to the invaders, and this naturally served to whet their appetite for more. A new attack was made in 907, this time led by Oleg, the successor of Rurik.

The Swedes at Kiev.—Some years earlier Oleg had attacked and taken Kiev, caused Askold and Dir to be put to death, after which he made this city instead of Novgorod the chief centre and stronghold of the Swedes in Russia. This was a fateful move, one of those unfortunate decisions which, it might with good reason be maintained, has had a profound bearing upon European history. With the capital so far removed from their homeland, and submerged as never before by the Slavic population, the Swedes were bound soon to become Slavized. With the centre at Novgorod, the new state might conceivably have been made Swedish in ideals and character; certainly the advantages were here on the side of the Swedes rather than with the Slavs. What happened emphasizes still more the inability of Scandinavians to use an exceptional opportunity for building a great empire. Oleg was a powerful ruler and extended and consolidated his dominions in every

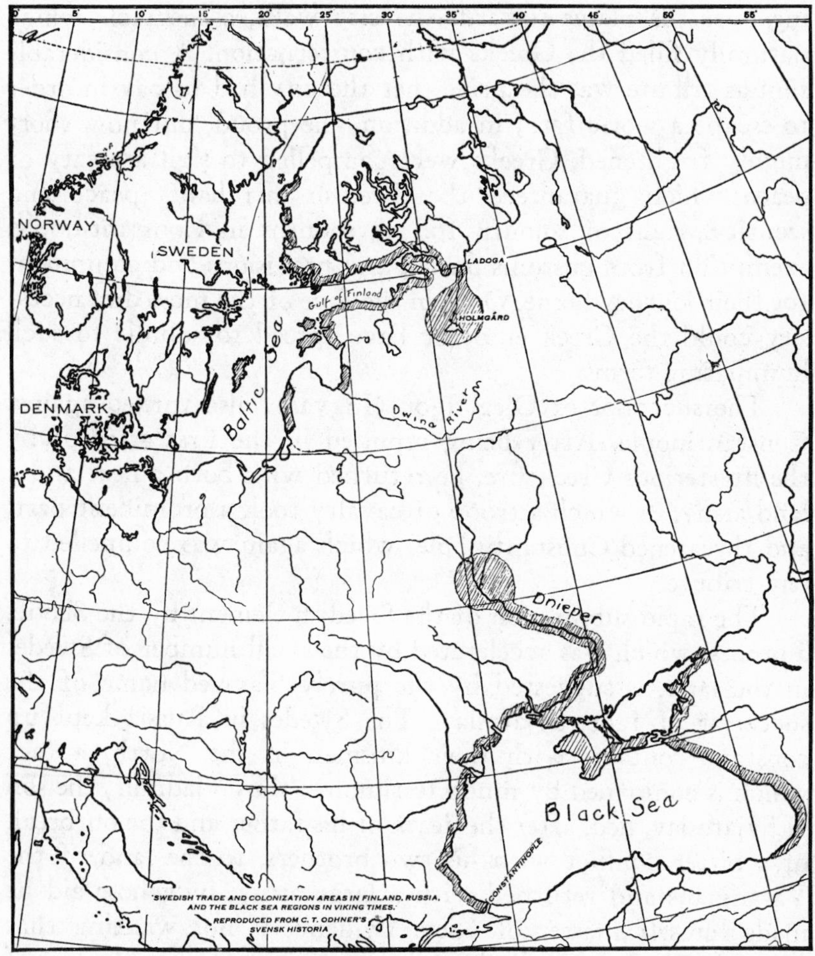

Swedish trade and colonization areas in Finland, Russia, and the Black Sea region in Viking times indicated by shaded portions

direction. According to Nestor, he made use of a clever and daring strategy in attacking Constantinople which has become a classic in the story of Viking deeds. With a fleet of two thousand ships he entered the Black Sea and plundered the cities on its shores even as far as the outskirts of Constantinople, but since the Greeks had placed barriers across the Golden Horn, thus closing the way by that route, he ordered all his boats to be hauled up on land and equipped with wheels and sails. When a favourable wind set in, the fleet got under way and came rolling over the plains towards the city walls, a spectacle which naturally filled the Greeks with consternation. A considerable sum as tribute was the prize that the city had to pay in order to escape a worse fate; in addition, the proud, but now thoroughly frightened, Greeks were compelled to sign a treaty of peace which guaranteed the Swedish merchants peace and security, right of sojourn for six months in Constantinople, exemption from customs duties, and provisions and equipment for their journey home. Only in the face of the most dire necessity could the Greek emperor have agreed to submit to such humiliating terms.

The successor of Oleg, Igor (Ingvar), also turned against Constantinople. After being repulsed in the first attempt by the mysterious Greek fire, he returned with both a fleet and a land army, in which a troop of cavalry took a prominent part, and threatened Constantinople, which again was compelled to pay tribute.

The rapid submersion of the Swedish element by the Slavic, a process which was accelerated by the small number of Swedes in the land, is suggested by the purely Slavized name of the successor of Igor, Svjatoslav. The Swedes in Russia kept up constant contacts with their kinsmen in the North, a fact which is confirmed by much testimony; thus Vladimir, the son of Svjatoslav, fled, after the death of his father and the outbreak of a bitter conflict with his two brothers, to the land of the Varangians and returned with a large army, by whose aid he made himself master of Kiev. Evidence is not wanting that even as late as Vladimir's time—the concluding years of the tenth century—the ruling class in Russia spoke the Northern tongue. Vladimir himself married the daughter of the Jarl of Polotsk, Rogvold (Ragnvald), who had come "from across the sea." Part of the Varangians who had accompanied Vladimir were rewarded by fiefs in Russia and others went to Greece where they entered the service of the emperor.

Duration of Swedish influence in Russia.—The story of Olof Tryggvasson, the heroic King of Norway, also shows the close contacts which at this time existed between Russia and the North. His mother was compelled to flee from Norway with her young son, and the statement that she aimed to find safety with the boy's uncle, Sigurd, who was a powerful man in Vladimir's kingdom, is significant. When Jaroslav, son of Vladimir, and Governor of Novgorod, in 1015 started a revolt against his father, it is said that he "secured Varangian auxiliaries from across the sea," and later, when he was hard pressed by his brother, Svjatopold, he intended to "seek security among the Varangians on the other side of the sea." This Jaroslav had as a wife Ingegerd, the daughter of Olof Skötkonung, the first Christian king of Sweden, and when she went to Russia she was accompanied by Ragnvald, Jarl of Västergötland, who received the fort of Aldeigjuborg as a fief from the Russian ruler. As a visitor at the court of Jaroslav is also mentioned Harald Sigurdson, half-brother of Olof, the Saint of Norway, who for some years was chief of Jaroslav's defence troops and prior to his return to Norway to become king married his daughter.

During the reign of Jaroslav (1015-1054) the contact between Russia and the North was perhaps closer than at any other time, but at the end of this period it rapidly tapers off to near the vanishing-point. But as late as 1118 the historian, Thielmar, of Marseilles, asserts that the majority of the inhabitants of Kiev were Danes, *i.e.*, Northmen. Such confusion of terms was common. There were undoubtedly in the Varangian contingents a great number of Danes and Norwegians who had joined these groups, attracted by the prospects of rich plunder. The vast majority of the Varangians were, however, Swedes.[26] While Kiev more and more lost its Swedish character, Novgorod retained a strong Scandinavian element and kept up its close contacts with the North. As late as the twelfth century the merchants of Gottland had their own factory and guildhall in the city. The contacts, based largely on commercial interests, were, however, broken when the Hanseatic League forced the Swedes from the Russian markets; not until the fourteenth century, however, did Novgorod cease entirely to

[26] Nordenstreng, *Vikingafärderna*, p. 169.

be a Swedish centre. The lure of Constantinople had drawn the Swedish contingent farther and farther to the South, where it grew constantly smaller and weaker, finally to be submerged totally. A great opportunity for Swedish expansion and consolidation had irretrievably been lost.

The Swedes at Constantinople.—No records reveal at what date the Northmen, either individually or in small groups, first reached Constantinople, but it was probably in the early part of the period of the migration of nations. With the establishment of the Swedish stronghold at Kiev, it naturally followed that the number of those who drifted down to Constantinople grew considerably, especially as the Byzantine emperors were glad to employ such vigorous and trustworthy warriors in their service. The Northmen are not mentioned, however, by Byzantine writers as forming distinct organizations in the capital until the year 1037. At that time they are described as constituting separate groups as regiments employed to guard the emperor. The majority constituting these regiments were undoubtedly drawn from the descendants of Swedes in Russia, but a considerable number of men came directly not only from Sweden but from Norway and Denmark; in fact the first man of whom it is said that he served as the emperor's body-guard was an Icelander, Torkel Thjestarsson. Finding themselves surrounded by intrigue and bitterly contending factions, the Byzantine rulers found that their greatest security lay in organizing a body-guard from those Northmen, the famous "Varangian guards," who stood aside from the petty local squabbles and who by reason of inherent race characteristics were naturally and strongly disposed to be faithful to the master to whom they had sworn fealty. The Varangians thus came to form a distinct army organization and enjoyed special privileges. In the palace they were near the emperor night and day, and on military expeditions they always remained close to him and guarded his person. They received the keys to the cities into which the emperor entered and kept them until his departure.

Runic and archæological remains.—The number of runes and other remains bearing upon the Swedish migrations to Russia and regions further south is very impressive, and yearly new evidence is brought to light by archæological investigations. These finds have been particularly numerous in Uppland, Södermanland, and Östergötland, thus the very districts which, from other evidence, appear to have been the ones which sent the greatest number of emigrants to the East. As typical of such rune stones may be mentioned one in the parish of Ed in Uppland, placed there in memory of Ragnvald, "who in Greece was chief of the army," *i.e.*, chief of the Varangians, or another one at Fjukeby, near Uppsala, which a father has raised in memory of his sons, one of whom guided the ship until it reached the harbors of Greece and who died at home. Others mention journeys to Gårdarike, or Holmgård. An interesting runic inscription is the one cut into the sides of a Grecian marble lion which once stood by the harbour of Piræus but in 1687 was carried by the Venetians to their city and placed near its arsenal. On its sides are runic texts enclosed in serpentine rings; because many characters in the inscriptions have been effaced, scholars have been baffled in their attempts to decipher the words. They are, however, in practical agreement that the characters were written in memory of a Swede from Uppland who fell in the service of the Greek emperor.

Until lately, no Scandinavian rune stones have been found in Russia, a fact which has occasioned some surprise. Probably this finds its explanation in the circumstance that rocks were not, as a rule, available there, and that the invasion fell mainly in the period when the use of runes was being discontinued in the North. In 1905 there was, however, unearthed on the island of Berezanj, near the point where the river Dnieper empties into the Black Sea, a rock containing a runic statement; the brief text reads: "Grane built this monument over his comrade Karl." Whence Grane and Karl had come and whither they were bound is not known, but the form of the rock and its inscription suggest that the men hailed from Gottland. Evidently the two were on a journey to or from Greece when Karl died and his comrade buried him and marked his grave with this memorial.[27]

The number of weapons and ornaments found in Russia and the Baltic lands which either have come from Sweden or show

[27] Arne, T. J., *Fornvännen*, 1914.

conformity to Swedish type is large, and as the collection grows and scholars become more and more able to decipher its meaning, the evidence of a large Swedish exodus into Russia becomes increasingly convincing and impressive. This evidence is supplemented by the discovery at various times of no less than 24,000 whole and 14,000 fragmentary Arabic coins in Sweden. These, no doubt, were brought to the country mainly through the extensive trade relations which Sweden established with countries to the south and east.

Effects of Viking expeditions upon Sweden.—The effects of Swedish participation in the Viking expeditions were far-reaching. The formation of an orderly government in Russia, which could serve as the nucleus for the subsequent mighty state, was an event of prime importance in world history. By this achievement and through the aid which they gave the rulers of Constantinople, both as their personal body-guards and as leaders of military exploits against the enemies of the Byzantine state, the Swedes in a measure helped to postpone the evil day when Constantinople fell into the hands of the Turks. The postponement of this tragedy gave the young civilization of the West time to strike deeper roots before it here also had to resist Turkish attacks. The entire region east and south of the Baltic as far as the Black Sea and the Caspian Sea profited by the extensive trade which the Swedes established. Through Swedish influence and Swedish dominion vast sections in this extensive territory came to enjoy greater security and added opportunities for peaceful occupation. The Scandinavian ideals of independence were, to a certain extent, made known to them. In turn Scandinavian literature was, no doubt, greatly enriched by these contacts, but to what extent this was the case cannot be determined. Schück has made the very plausible suggestion that Swedish contacts with the South and the Orient brought to the North a great many classic legends and stories, and that here is to be found the genesis of many of the best sagas appearing in Icelandic literature. Through the travels of the Swedish merchants these tales of heroic deeds were transmitted to Norway, Iceland, Denmark, and even to northern Germany. The stories of Hervor and Hildren, Orvar-Odd and Hjalmar, Rolf Götrikson and Theodoric of Verona (Diedrich of Bern), and others reveal, according to Schück, a Grecian substratum, and this might have been instrumental in giving them the forms under which they became known by the Swedes in Miklagård. Sweden herself was the chief beneficiary of the expeditions, since the new contacts brought her more definitely than before into great currents of European thought.

CHAPTER IV

LIFE IN THE VIKING PERIOD

Over no period of history of the Northern countries has there come to rest so much of poetic glamour as over the Viking age. The reason for this is obvious; it was in very fact a period of stirring adventure and of heroic deeds, a period in which the people of the North played a part in world history so important that it far transcended everything that their numerical strength or material resources could lead one to expect; later came the patriots—poets and historians—who, wishing to stir the men of their generation to loftier thinking and greater deeds, idealized the Viking, or saga, period and exalted its heroes as fitting models to be admired and emulated.

The land.—At the end of the Viking period the Swedish territorial area was, as before indicated, very much smaller than it is in our day. In view of the fact that water-courses did not in these early times serve as barriers between districts, but, on the contrary, helped to bring them into greater proximity with one another, it seems but natural that the provinces of Skåne, Blekinge, and Halland, through easy communications across Öresund and Cattegat, had become a part of Denmark. These provinces were furthermore separated from the Swedish districts north of them by great forest areas which served as most effective barriers against all intercommunication. The region on the west coast and south of the Christiania (Oslo) Fjord was most accessible to Norway, with the result that the province in this area, Bohuslän, came to belong to this country, whose territory thus extended as far south as the Göta River. Only along a narrow strip near this river did Swedish territory touch upon the North Sea. The Swedish land therefore extended approximately from the Baltic in the east to the province of Värmland in the west and from Uppland and Dalarna in the north to Småland in the south. The region north of this territory bore the general designation Hälsingland and here a considerable population had found homes several centuries before the Viking period. The main area of Sweden was divided into two quite distinct sections by wide stretches of dense forests which, north of the great lakes, Vättern and Vänern, extended clear across the country. The region north of the forest land continued to be known as *Svealand* and the one south of it as *Götaland*. Within these areas lay in turn large sections which were almost entirely isolated from the rest of the country by great forests. Gottland was practically an independent state under Swedish protection. There is, of course, no basis upon which to estimate the amount of cultivated land in this period, but it can be taken for granted that it was only a small fraction of the present area. Large areas which now are dry land were then submerged or were covered with bogs and morasses.

The important territorial divisions were the "lands" or provinces which, however, in many cases were not identical with these divisions as they exist today. Västergötland, Östergötland, Värmland, Gästrikland, Dalarna, and Södermanland had approximately the same limits as now and constituted units of judicial, and to some extent of political, administration. In the southern district the units were several in number, as Värend, Finveden, and Njudungen; north of these were Ydre, Kind, Tjust, and Möre, which later came to be known collectively as Småland. The Uppland region was divided into Tiundaland, Attundaland, and Fjädrundaland. At times the provinces were virtually independent, or sovereign states, to use a modern term. These "lands" were the important units of administration. Within each of them Things or judicial assemblies convened at regular intervals, administered justice, and deliberated upon other matters pertaining to the district, somewhat after the fashion of the later New England town-meetings. At the head stood the lawman, whose function it was to keep the law, as determined by custom, in his memory, and to quote it whenever required; he also gave opinions as to what justice demanded in case new situations arose. Subdivisions of the "land" were the *hundare* or hundred in Svealand and the *härad* in Götaland. These were identical in meaning and served as units for the local administration of justice and of government. In some of the outlying districts the local units were known by still other names.

Classes of society.—The two classes of society were the free and the unfree, or slaves. It is worthy of special note that the Swedish law did not recognize any different classes or gradations in the former group; the *wergeld,* or man-money, was the same for all subjects of a given province; fundamentally there was no difference between the king and the *bönder*. Inequality was, however, bound to come by reason of differences in wealth and intelligence; in time, membership by birth in a family that had become powerful gave a certain pre-eminence. In fact no social equality prevailed, but at the same time no barriers existed which the bold and aggressive could not surmount in the endeavour to pass from a lower to a higher class. The name jarl connoted the incumbent of an office rather than a hereditary title and does not often occur; when used it is in the sense of regent or protector. Royal families had undoubtedly existed since early times in several of the provinces, and although they had lost their political power during the process of consolidation which had resulted in the formation of the kingdom, descent from these families still constituted a distinct social and political asset. The royal families were never numerous and the Viking expeditions, as well as civil wars, were as a rule disastrous to their power and prestige.

The king.—The king represented the unity of the country, but aside from that his functions and authority were quite uncertain. The extent of his power was almost entirely dependent upon his own aggressiveness and personal influence. Rimbert,[1] the biographer of St. Anskar, says: "Among the Swedes the good custom prevails that decision in every public matter depends more upon the united will of the people than upon the authority of the king," which agrees precisely with the words of Adam of Bremen,[2] "the Swedes have kings from an old family (*av gammal ätt och stam*), but their power depends on what the people think (*på folkets mening*). The king must accept what the people jointly have decided, unless his opinion

[1] Rimbert, *Life of Anskar.*

[2] Adam of Bremen, *Beskrifning af Sverige, Danmark och Norge,* Peringskiöld translation, Stockholm, 1748.

seems better; then they follow him, even though hesitatingly. Therefore they proudly proclaim that at home they are all alike. In war they render the king, or the man whom the king has placed at the head, the most complete and unquestioned obedience." It thus appears that the king's authority sprang mainly from the exigencies of war; a military campaign, they realized, could not be "won by a debating society." The old Scandinavian freemen derived a tremendous advantage in warfare from the realization that, especially in military campaigns, centralization of authority was essential to success. Certain religious functions were, no doubt, also attached to the royal office; the king should at certain times render sacrifices to the gods in behalf of the people. Another duty of the king, which had found voice but incidentally and timidly, but later grew into his most clearly recognized function, was the maintenance and safeguarding of peace within the land, which in turn involved the punishment of criminals. His own person was declared inviolate, and a crime against his person drew a heavier penalty than against the ordinary man. He held his power by right of election by the free men of the land assembled at the rocks of Mora near Uppsala; following the election it was incumbent upon the new king to make his royal journey through the land to receive the homage of the people.

The bönder.—The class which included the majority of the freemen, the *bönder,* had several gradations, and only those known as *odalbönder* enjoyed complete freedom and were invested with full rights of citizenship. They possessed the estate on which they lived by the undisputed right of inheritance. This class constituted the backbone of the nation, had a well-developed class consciousness, and generally knew how to defend its rights, as many episodes in the subsequent story will reveal. Beneath the *odalbönder* on the social and economic scale stood those freemen who had only a conditional title to the land on which they lived, or who farmed the land of someone else according to definite stipulations. Towards the close of the Viking period the *bönder* of Denmark and Norway suffered serious setbacks before the encroachments of wealthier freeholders or through the selfish and unscrupulous tactics of kings or earls whom Viking raids had made wealthy and powerful;

while this tendency was noticeable also in Sweden, the strong position which the *bönder* had held here since earlier times was not seriously impaired. Whereas in the other countries the name *bonde* came to carry with it a suggestion of contempt and stigma, in Sweden it continued to imply dignity and honour.

Clan and family.—Membership in the clan (*ätt*) was essential to the enjoyment of the prerogatives of a free man; if a man was not born to membership, it was necessary for him to go through a certain ceremony of adoption. In the clan were centred practically all the obligations and privileges of the freemen. It exacted penalty for murder or less serious crimes committed against any of its members, and land held by the individual could not be sold except by the consent of the clan, since the latter must protect itself against any diminution of its strength and influence. As the population became more stabilized in permanent settlements and the industrial organization assumed somewhat new forms, the clan disintegrated gradually, but during the Viking period it remained quite unimpaired. The smallest unit under the clan was the family, with the father at the head; his authority was unlimited, extending even to the right of decision whether the new-born babe was to live or be set out in the forest and exposed to the elements and to wild beasts. A verdict that the latter be done was, however, looked upon as brutal. The ceremony of conferring a name on a child through the sprinkling of water was performed by the father. In the first year of its life the child was left almost entirely to the care of the mother and maid-servants, but as it grew older the father took a hand in its education. The children of kings and other rich men were generally sent away from home to be educated by some *bonde* who was known for his wisdom. In that way the children would be removed from the bad influence of sycophantic servants and constant reminders that they were born to wealth and high station.

The slaves.—On the lowest social scale stood the slaves, whose status was recognized by all the old provincial laws, but more distinctly so in the old district of the Goths than of the Svear; this fact suggests that the institution of slavery was more common among the former than among the latter. The status of the slave came by descent from slave parents, but the class was greatly augmented, especially during the Viking times, by captives of war. A freeman might also be forced to join the ranks of the slaves through inability to pay his debts; sometimes an unsuccessful game of chance, when the gambler's own person had been the stake, might place the stigma of slavery upon a man. Few slaves, however, derived their status from debts or games of chance, nor did they, when such was the cause of their misfortune, long remain in servitude. The slave was the absolute property of his master, his *wergeld* being merely equivalent to the price he would command in the market. The master was obliged to make reparation for any misdemeanour on the part of his slave, just as he had to do for depredations on the part of his cattle. The master might even kill or maim his slave with impunity so long as he publicly announced his deed upon the day it was committed.[3] The relative number of slaves was always small in Sweden, because of an especially strong innate feeling of repulsion on the part of the people against the system, as well as to physical environment and certain social factors which facilitated escape from bondage. The institution disappeared in Sweden at an earlier period than in almost any other country, for by the beginning of the fourteenth century there is no longer any evidence of its existence in the land (p. 158).

Occupations: agriculture.—The principal occupations were agriculture and cattle-raising. The saga literature, although replete with stories tending to glorify the warriors of the period, gives many hints of the honourable service which the tiller of the soil was thought to render, and genuine praise of the repose and satisfaction that belong to rural life is not entirely wanting. Still better evidence of the importance which agriculture held is, however, given by the old provincial laws. One provision says that the same solemn inviolability which applied to the house in which a man dwelt with his family also applied to the fields. Stealing grain from a neighbour's fields or causing damage to them in any way was punishable with excessively heavy fines.[4]

[3] Williams, *Social Scandinavia*, p. 39.
[4] Hildebrand, *Sveriges medeltid*, I, p. 177.

The common grains raised were oats, barley, rye, and, to a very limited extent, wheat and hops. Flax and hemp for the manufacture of coarse cloth were also raised in considerable quantities. The tiller of the soil had his garden in which he raised cabbage, beans, peas, turnips, and some other less known vegetables. Most home-owners had bees, and honey entered into the diet of the time to a degree which now can hardly be imagined.

Adam of Bremen thus speaks of agriculture in Sweden: [5] "Sweden is the most bountiful land in the world; its fields are fat and rich with grain and honey; besides which this land surpasses all others in cattle-raising . . . therefore one may not say that the Swedes need any possessions, for they have a supply of everything, and yet are free from the vanity which fills us," but the reality was hardly in accord with this idealized picture. Agriculture was, in fact, carried on with extreme difficulty because implements were crude and the land cold and soggy. Furrows had to be dug close together for drainage. Frosts in the summer season were probably more common than in our day. The modern method of increasing the annual harvest by a system of rotation of crops was not then understood.

As a rule the agricultural class lived in village communities, a system which added greatly to the griefs of the farming class, since each man's portion of land was divided into a number of detached patches. Beyond the scattered patches belonging to the residents of the village lay generally large areas of community or state land, which in case of need might afford pasturage to the cattle of the village community. Cattle-raising was, in fact, a more important industry than the cultivation of the soil. Cows grazed in every part of the country which had been settled and swine were raised in great numbers in the southern section. By providing milk, meat, and hides, the cattle herds were the main reliance of the population against starvation. Hay grew abundantly and was cured by placing the newly cut grass upon special scaffolding so that the wind could pass freely through it, a method still employed in the central and northern sections of the country. Swedish horses were known for their

[5] Peringskiöld translation, p. 16.

great endurance, and, according to Jordanes, a considerable export of them was going on already in the sixth century. Olaus Magnus, one of the last of the Catholic churchmen in Sweden, in a noted work on his native land, speaks in praise of the Swedish horses, especially those from the island of Öland. Sheep were everywhere raised because of the necessity of securing wool. Poultry was another item which provided food, "and no *bonde* was so poor that he did not have at least a rooster and two hens." [6]

Hunting.—A thousand years ago the Scandinavian peninsula was a hunter's paradise. The vast extent of forest and mountain lands served as a splendid refuge for all kinds of wild animals whose lives were very little jeopardized by hunters; bows and arrows, clubs, spears, and knives were the only weapons employed. Nevertheless, hunting provided a considerable portion of the food required. In spite of the limitations under which it was carried on, hunting assumed such proportions that, already in this period, deer were threatened with extermination. The Scandinavians were expert in training hunting dogs, and even established an extensive and profitable export trade in trained falcons. In the making of traps for the capture of elk, deer, wolves, and other animals they became very skilled. A great number of laws were in force from earlier times which fixed penalties for poaching on other people's lands—permitted under certain conditions—and made definite provisions in regard to ownership of the quarry in cases where disputes might arise. Besides hunting on one's own or; on certain conditions, on a neighbour's lands, the Nimrods of that day could also betake themselves to the community lands, as these were open to the whole population, except that for certain game, such as squirrels and hares, whose furs were especially valuable, certain months of the year constituted closed seasons. The great enemy of every community was the wolf, and this animal was hunted all over the land with the same vindictive energy which animates the Lapp today in his pursuit of the beasts that tear and kill his reindeer. The wolf's ferocity made it advisable for men to be armed when travelling over the forest roads; this was one reason why people so jealously

[6] Hildebrand, *Sveriges medeltid,* I, p. 197.

guarded their right to carry arms.[7] The common species of animals hunted were the deer, reindeer, elk, wild boar, wolf, marten, otter, hare, bear, and fox. Naturally, hunting was also looked upon as a manly sport and as a means of recreation.

Fishing.—Fishing as a means of livelihood has ancient traditions in the Northland. In Viking days the lakes and streams of Sweden teemed with edible fish of every kind and along the coast there was always opportunity for deep-sea fishing. The salmon catch seems to have been most important. Fishing was so profitable and was engaged in by so many people that a whole series of regulations came to prevail regarding open and closed seasons, tackle, fees, and the like. According to Olaus Magnus, fish-hatcheries were established at a very early time.

Trade and Commerce.—The Northmen showed a remarkable interest and aptitude for trade and commerce. "Commercially they were to their time what the Phœnicians were to the Eurasian lands of a thousand years earlier," is the well-substantiated statement on this point by one authority.[8] A brisk trade was carried on within the country itself by pedlars, usually travelling about on horseback with their wares slung across the back of the beast, somewhat after the fashion of the pack-mule transportation on the American continent in early days; other traders followed the water-courses in boats.

The foreign trade of the Viking period there took the Swedes far beyond the confines of Scandinavia. There not only profit but honour served as a strong lure. Swedish commercial enterprise was directed mainly towards Russia and the Baltic regions, but beyond them it extended even to Arabia, Persia, and Greece. During this period Sweden was a real land of traders in very much the same sense as England is known in our day. Adam of Bremen says that ships from Denmark and from the lands of the Slavs, Sembrians, and Scythians usually assembled in the harbour of Birka on Lake Mälaren and that the whole country was filled with foreign wares.[9] The Swedes were the middlemen who negotiated the exchange of goods of the Orient and Greece with western Europe. They occupied a most favourable position for doing this, since all the trade routes, ex-

[7] Hildebrand, *Sveriges medeltid*, I, p. 204.
[8] Williams, *Social Scandinavia*, p. 215.
[9] Peringskiöld translation.

cept that over the Baltic and the Volga to the Caspian Sea, both held by the Swedes, had been closed, or were rendered very insecure by Arabs and pirates. Birka was the great centre of this extensive trade. The place developed a considerable degree of self-government and the "right of Björkö" (*Björkörätten*),[10] embodying regulations regarding the government of the city and duties and obligations of merchants, came to serve as a sort of norm for trading centres everywhere in the North. Slesvig-Hedeby in Denmark was another city which had great influence in giving form to city government in the period.[11] More than 30,000 so-called "Kufic" or Arabic coins most of them struck in the ninth and tenth centuries of our era, have been unearthed in Sweden (p. 104), and were, no doubt, received in payment for goods. No less than 47,000 German coins from the period before the thirteenth century have been found, of which 28,800 have come from Gottland. The evidence of an extensive trade furnished by this multitude of coins is further substantiated by many rune stones which tell of men who went to distant places for the purpose of trade.

The articles sought for import were principally spices, silks, embroidered goods, jewels, and costly rugs. In payment, amber, horses, and pelts were exported. With the coins came also an abundance of silver ornaments, some of which have been preserved to the present. At the important meeting-places of merchants, cities soon grew up, and among these were, besides the aforesaid Birka, Sigtuna and Tälje (Södertälje) on Lake Mälaren, Kalmar on the east coast of the Baltic, Skara and Falköping in the centre of Västergötland, and Lödöse near the site of present-day Gothenburg. In reviewing the extent of Swedish commerce in this period, Schück makes this comment: "No era in the history of Sweden, not even the Thirty Years' War period, has exhibited so much activity as the days of the Vikings. Both the Orient and the Occident lay open to our warriors and to our merchants." [12]

[10] Björkö is an island on which Birka was situated.

[11] For an account of the whole subject of trade and city development by the Swedes in this era see Schück, A., *Det svenska stadsväsendets uppkomst*, Uppsala, 1926.

[12] Schück, H., and Warburg, K., *Illustrerad svensk litteraturhistoria*, 2nd Ed., Stockholm, 1911-1916, I, p. 58.

Village communities.—With few exceptions, the people lived in village communities, and Montelius is of the opinion that most of the villages of that day still exist in the original locations and with the old names retained. Private property in land had been established already in prehistoric times, and by the beginning of the Viking period most of the land was held by such ownership. Just how title originally was acquired by the individual is not clear, but the process was perhaps not very unlike the "staking of claims" of pioneer days in America. Land tracts were generally laid out in rectangular areas, and frontage on water was eagerly sought. As the quality of soil in a given village-holding generally was not uniform, some parts being rich, others rocky and unfruitful, some marshy, others dry and barren, some mountain-land, others meadow-land or fields, the area was subdivided into very small tracts which were distributed among the individuals in such a way that there would be equity in the value of their individual holdings. This was, of course, the system common to all European countries until comparatively recent times. The problem of unscrambling this mess was, as will appear later, one of the perplexing questions which arose to torment economists and legislators alike in the nineteenth century (p. 596, 617).

Dwellings and other structures.—In examining a plot showing the lay-out of a typical *bonde's* home a thousand years ago, the modern man is struck by the great number of buildings which are on each plot. The substantial farmer might have as many as thirty or forty different houses on his place and the number perhaps rarely fell below fifteen or twenty, even for the farmer of average means. The Uppland law of a somewhat later period prescribed a minimum of seven buildings for a new parsonage.[13] On the average-sized homestead, there would at least be the following separate buildings: living quarters, dining-room, sleeping apartment, kitchen, pantry, bath-house, women's bower, store-house, and guest-room, in addition to barns, stables, and granaries. The well-to-do farmer also had sheds, smithy, boat-house, and fish-houses. All structures lay close to the buildings used by the family and with these formed a rectangular square. The sagas give many

[13] Montelius, *Sveriges historia*, I, p. 368.

hints regarding the forms of the houses of the period; it is quite evident that they conformed very closely to types still seen in Iceland. The main building or *stofa,* which contained the living quarters, was generally rectangular in form, and the long walls rarely higher than six feet. It was built of unhewn logs, with the crevices filled with clay; poorer houses evidently were built by means of a network of willows, smeared over with clay. On the site of ancient Birka have been unearthed

The interior of a guest room in Scandinavia in Viking times

the remains of a building which evidently has been ravaged by fire. The big slabs of clay show marks of the logs and even of the traces of the hands of the men who applied the clay. The entrance to the main building was through a vestibule at one of the end walls. If windows were found at all, they were placed in the roof, which was supported by rows of pillars. No houses had ceilings, one reason for this naturally being that they would have excluded the little light that might stream through the windows and prevented the escape of smoke from the fireplace. An ordinary house had one fireplace in the centre of the clay floor, but in larger structures two or even three would be found necessary. No chimneys were built, the smoke finding its way through an aperture in the roof. This was generally of straw, turf, or wooden shingles. The walls were bare of decoration, except for the weapons which were sometimes hung on them; on festive occasions, however, it was customary to adorn them with fine pelts and fabrics.

House furnishings.—Pieces of furniture were exceedingly few and, except for the chairs, which generally were elegantly carved, simple and crude. Rough seats placed along the walls, simple beds, one long, rough table, and some chests completed the furnishings of even a rich man's home. In the middle of one of the long walls was a seat, higher and more elegantly made than the rest, which served as the master's place of honour. Chests were generally strong so as to make a reliable deposit-box for the housewife's jewelry, but in time of danger even this was not a safe hiding-place, and valuables were then usually buried in the ground. Many things could then happen to prevent a return of the wealth to the owners and much of it was lost until it came to light again in later decades. Sometimes treasures were buried with the bodies of departed relatives, in the belief that these material things would serve a good purpose in the land of the dead. The persistent belief that the ground where such treasures were hidden would sometimes be lit up at night by light emanating from the ground, has, according to Montelius, been the cause of much senseless despoiling of old graves by persons deceived by reflections of moonbeams and by phosphorescent light.

The kitchen utensils were very few, but many of them were beautiful in design. Spoons were generally made of wood or bone. Forks were unknown. In the Edda song, *Rigsthula,* one gets a glimpse of home life in the period:

> Then Mother brought a broidered cloth
> Of linen bright, and the board she covered;
> And then she took the loaves so thin
> And laid them, white from the wheat, on the cloth,
> Then forth she brought the vessel full,
> With silver covered, and set before them,
> Meat all browned, and well-cooked birds;
> In the pitcher was wine, of plate were the cups,
> So drank they and talked till the day was gone.[14]

[14] Bellows, H. A., *The Poetic Edda,* New York, 1923.

This is, of course, the picture of a well-to-do home. The poor man's home was, in Sweden as everywhere else, cramped and squalid.

Old accounts give astonishingly elaborate bills of fare: fish, meats, and poultry, well spiced, formed important articles of diet. Other foods were cheese, rice, rutabagas, cabbage, peas, apples, raisins, honey, and nuts. Meals generally required a long time, usually two hours for each, and the different courses, especially in the better homes, were often interlarded with conversation, stories, or even with lectures.

Hospitality.—One of the conspicuous virtues of the Swedes in the period under consideration was hospitality. Remarkable consideration was shown strangers and guests. "Hospitality is characteristic of all Northmen, but especially of the Swedes," says Adam of Bremen; "to refuse shelter to a traveller is the greatest disgrace among them; yea, they even argue with one another as to who has the first claim to entertain a guest. All that charity enjoins they show such a guest, and when he has dwelt among them as many days as he himself deems proper, they commend him to their friends from one place to another."[15]

Dress.—The ordinary materials of clothing were wool, linen, skins, and furs. Silk was imported and was considered a great luxury. In the *Rigsthula* is told how "the mother wrapt the new-born jarl in silk." Many finds exhibit beautiful embroidery work. The woollen and linen cloth was of native production, as shown by the large number of remains of implements used in its manufacture. Distaffs were used, the spinning-wheel being perhaps as yet unknown. The man's garments comprised about the same parts as now: shirt, breeches, stockings, shoes, coat, mantle, and cap or hat. Even men's dress sometimes showed brilliant colours. Women's dress naturally was more colourful and varied in form than men's. The sagas speak of the luxury and magnificence which the Northern women of the period displayed in dress.

In the *Rigsthula* occurs this passage:

> The lady sat, at her arms she looked,
> She smoothed the cloth, and fitted the sleeves;

[15] Persingskiöld translation, p. 17.

Gay was her cap, on her breasts were clasps,
Broad was her train, of blue was her gown,
Her brows were bright, her breast was shining,
Whiter her neck than new-fallen snow.

Brooches, buckles of silver, bracelets, and finger rings of gold and silver, chains, pendants, and beads were especially numerous and magnificent in design. Many articles of this kind had been made in Sweden. The women paid much attention to their personal adornment, especially, it seems, to the dressing of their hair. Bleaching was resorted to by brunettes, since blond hair was considered the ideal of beauty. The bleaching material was made of lye from wood ashes in combination with fats.[16]

Position of woman.—Woman enjoyed a favourable status; nowhere in contemporary Europe did she enjoy as much independence as in the North. This was due partly to the survival of old Germanic ideals, partly to the equality of the sexes, with respect to their training and mode of life, which made for comradeship. The responsibilities which naturally devolved upon wife, sister, or mother through the frequent absences of the men on extensive journeys was also a factor in giving woman her favourable station. Not only did the women as a rule enjoy the same training as the men, but they were their comrades in work as well as in amusements. While they thus entered upon activities which, according to the standards in other lands, in mediæval times, seemed masculine and shocking, they seemed to a great degree to have retained their womanly qualities of tenderness, self-sacrifice, and devotion. In time of danger they were given special protection; they were to leave a burning house before anyone else, and were the first to be removed from a sinking vessel. The wrongs committed against the honour of a girl were avenged by the male relatives or severely punished according to provision of the laws. Women were in general placed upon the same basis as men before the law, except in the matter of inheritance and divorce, where the discriminations against them, however, were more apparent than real.[17] While this picture, no doubt, in the

[16] Williams, *Social Scandinavia,* p. 80.
[17] *Ibid.*, p. 111.

main correctly portrays the ideal as well as the reality, there are in the sagas many instances of women who were callous, shrewish, and selfish.

As the young people mingled freely in work and amusements, they themselves generally had an important part in the business of choosing life mates, but even so, romantic love apparently was not a great factor. Many instances are indeed told of sons and daughters, especially the latter, who refused to abide by the wishes of the stern parent with respect to marriage, but as a general rule matrimony was a business proposition in which especially the father of the prospective bridegroom was interested. A suitor usually had to prove before marriage that he could support the young woman according to the standards to which she was accustomed. The amount of the dowry to be paid by the bride's father and of the gift to be settled by the groom upon the bride was discussed in a purely business-like fashion. Betrothals took place under forms which were almost as sacred and binding as the marriage ceremony itself. The latter consisted of pledges by the contracting parties similar to the promises made at betrothals; sometimes Thor's hammer figured in the ceremony as an emblem of consecration. Great feasting and merry-making, lasting for several days, followed the nuptials. In taking up her abode in her new home the bride was invested with a bunch of keys, the insignia of her authority and dignity as mistress of the household. Women could easily obtain divorce and yet retain their property; this, no doubt, was one reason for their comparative freedom and authority in the home.

Recreations and amusements.—To the present generation, so amply blessed with books, magazines, newspapers, and organizations of every conceivable kind, not to mention telephones, automobiles, theatrical performances, motion pictures, phonographs, and radios, as aids in keeping dull care away, it must indeed seem at first glance as if a generation which had none of these must have found existence exceedingly drab and cheerless. The Northern latitude of the Scandinavian countries, with their long winter season and correspondingly short summers, must, so it would seem, have added its part to cast a gloom over the land such as was unknown to the South. Undoubtedly the Northmen themselves felt that they were sort of step-children of Nature and their yearning for the Southland was one important factor in the migration movement and the Viking expeditions. It would, however, be a serious mistake to assume that life in Sweden, a thousand years ago, was nothing but dull monotony and unrelieved gloom. The great mass of the Swedish nation, it should be remembered, belonged to the same social class and social barriers were few. Life moved along in accordance with very free forms, and social interchange was easy and common. Welcome diversion was, no doubt, offered by attendance upon the multitude of social and religious meetings which were held. Weddings, birthday parties, funeral feasts, banquets in honour of persons starting out on, or returning from, a long journey, religious festivals, especially at Yuletide or in spring, midsummer, and autumn, and festive processions, judicial assembly meetings, market days—all followed upon one another in rapid succession and gave frequent and pleasant interludes between the usual humdrum duties of life. That the people of that generation were splendid entertainers is attested by a great many facts. Parties were generally lengthy affairs, weddings, as stated, sometimes lasting several days. There was usually no dearth of food. Many a long winter evening was made to pass more rapidly by stories of dramatic interest, which were told by some traveller who had just returned, or were sung or recited by a *skald* or minstrel. There were many forms of indoor amusements and sports, such as debates on the relative merits of prominent men, contests in rhyming, the telling of stories, which developed into a fine art, music on the violin, fife, lyre, horn, and especially the harp. Singing filled a great part of their lives; it was generally entered into with great earnestness and volume of voice. Dancing, somewhat on the order of the æsthetically attractive and much admired modern Swedish folk dances, was no doubt also indulged in, as is evident from the fact that towards the end of the eleventh century the clergy opposed it as objectionable. "But," as a writer observes, "there is no reason to believe that even the worst of these dances were actually any more objectionable than some of the fashionable dances of the present day." [18]

[18] Williams, *Social Scandinavia*, p. 324.

Chess-playing, checkers, and throwing dice were favourite indoor pastimes.

In summer there was the enjoyment derived from gardens. That this form of enjoyment played an unusual part is shown by the frequency with which ballads bestow praise upon the pleasures of the bowers. It was, however, in the great outdoors that the best entertainment was found, not only in summer, but in winter as well. Hardly a market or a Thing was held that did not also see some athletic contests on fields especially set aside for this purpose. Sometimes special athletic meets, lasting several days, were staged in these places. These meetings assumed so much importance that they have been compared to the Olympiads of Greece.[19]

While it is true that this statement refers mainly to Iceland, the description, no doubt, applies to Sweden as well. It was an age when physical strength and prowess were glorified and contests generally were marked by extreme roughness and even brutality. Wrestling, rope-pulling, swimming, ball-playing—with balls of tough wood—were the most common. So popular were the ball games that even great structures were erected to permit games also in winter-time. Otherwise skiing, skating, and coasting were the usual winter sports. Hunting, while engaged in primarily, no doubt, for the sake of food, came to be looked upon as perhaps the chief delight of the men.

Government.—Genius for law and order has undoubtedly been one of the strongest and most salutary endowments of the people of the North. "With law shall our land be built and settled; with lawlessness wasted and spoilt," says the old saga,[20] and this expresses one of the fundamental conceptions of the Scandinavians. Their organization of strong states at home at an early period and their contributions to orderly government in Iceland, England, Normandy, and Russia constitute convincing and striking proof of this. By the end of the Viking period, the process of consolidation had proceeded so far that Sweden, Denmark, and Norway could be considered as separate sovereign states, but the old divisions of minor districts in the

[19] Bååth, A. U., *Nordiskt forntidsliv*, Stockholm, 1890, p. 134.
[20] Dasent, George Webber, *Saga of Burnt Njal*, New York, 1906, p. 1.

first-named were largely retained as a convenient unit of administration.

Language and literature.—The language spoken by the Scandinavian peoples in the Viking period was, according to the evidence given by rune stones and sagas, the same throughout the North, save for variations of dialects. In all sections the people spoke the Norraena tongue, and the differences in dialects between two different Scandinavian countries like Sweden and Norway were no greater than might be the variations in separate districts within the same country. At the end of the period, differentiations—due mainly to the processes of consolidation which had taken place within the countries of the North, and partly to contacts with different parts of the outside world—had, however, taken place and one could now speak of three separate languages, Swedish, Danish, and Norwegian, to which should, perhaps, be added Icelandic. This unity of language during the centuries when the vast and remarkable saga literature, the greatest intellectual and ethical product of the Middle Ages, took form in oral tradition, makes the assumption almost inevitable that this literary wealth was a common possession of the three countries. That was the opinion of all scholars in the age of Romanticism in the early part of the nineteenth century; a strong sense of Scandinavian solidarity found expression in the writers of the period. To this literature of the saga age the name "Gothic" was applied. Tegnér's *Frithiofs Saga* is the most remarkable expression of this sentiment. Tegnér's brilliant verses have since their first appearance been acclaimed as the grand national epic of Sweden, but both the hero, Frithiof, and the heroine, Ingeborg, were Norwegians. To a generation so strongly imbued with the idea of Scandinavian solidarity as that of the first decades of the nineteenth century, there was nothing contradictory in this. This theory of Scandinavian literary solidarity was, however, in time vehemently attacked by the Norwegian scholar, Rudolf Keyser, who claimed that the rich saga literature was strictly a Norwegian possession, which, by a most fortunate circumstance, the Icelanders had preserved.[21] This view caused one of the liveliest literary controversies that have ever flared up in the North and

[21] Keyser, R., *Efterladte skrifter*, Kristiania, 1866, I.

put a severe strain on the amicable relations between the three kindred peoples. The Danes, especially, resented vigorously the attempt to deprive them of the honour of having had a share in the creation of the great saga literature. They could, furthermore, make out a strong case for their side, since their earliest historian, Saxo Grammaticus, a cleric, who, in spite of his calling, had a great admiration for the pagan culture of his country, wrote down all the legends that he had heard at home as well as legends which visiting Icelanders had related to him. Saxo's writings prove that the lays of gods and heroes contained in the saga literature were known in Denmark even before they were put down in writing by the Icelanders. Sweden, however, had no Icelandic poets and no Saxo to preserve her mediæval heritage. It thus appeared that this period, intellectually so brilliant in Norway, Iceland, and Denmark, was strangely barren in Sweden. Many facts can be cited which seem to prove that intellectual life did not languish among the Swedes any more than among their neighbours. It is, in the first place, hardly conceivable that the Swedes, who in other matters were certainly as alert and enterprising as their kinsmen, should in this period have assumed an utterly apathetic attitude towards heroic legends and songs and therefore have been without a literature similar to that of Norway, Denmark, or Iceland. Secondly, there is the evidence furnished by hundreds of Swedish rune stones, which either in their brief texts or in their serpentine rings and illustrations, show that the stories contained in the Icelandic manuscripts, like the Sigurd saga, the stories of Thor, Balder, Frey, and Loke, were not only known in Sweden long before they came from Iceland through written documents, but in fact were very popular. This evidence is further supported by statements in the sagas themselves. Thus in the Saga of Diedrich of Bern, the author, whose identity is unknown, after first remarking in the preface that the story will tell of Diedrich of Bern, Sigurd, Fafnesbane, and others, continues, "But the Danes and the Swedes have many stories about these, some in poetic form, with which they entertain distinguished men. Many of the poems recited were composed long ago."

The investigations of Schück in Sweden and of Kaarle

Krohn in Finland have proved another point which has a significant bearing here. They have shown that the important stories that make up the Icelandic Poetic Edda had their counterparts in Finland and the Baltic lands even before the end of the Viking period, and hence before the Icelandic literature became known. This influence naturally came from Sweden, the people of which, as already told, were numerous in these lands as settlers and merchants. Schück's investigations in this field have led him to express this conviction, "We therefore take for granted that Swedish literature in Viking times was just as rich in sagas and songs as the Norwegian and the Danish." [22]

Religion.—In religion as in literature the people of the three Scandinavian countries showed great homogeneity; only in some slight variation in cult or in the degree of importance ascribed to certain gods was there a difference between separate sections. The genesis of the Scandinavian religious beliefs lies in the most remote past and, as in the case of other pagan religions, first took the form of nature worship. Early pictorial representations on Swedish rock inscriptions indicate that the sun was early looked upon as a god. Many of the Scandinavian religious beliefs were, no doubt, a heritage from the Celts, whose high culture and great influence in the Bronze Age have been noted. Many of their religious beliefs the Scandinavians shared in common with other Teutonic peoples, but Scandinavian mythology became far more complete than the common Teutonic, by the addition of several gods and goddesses, as well as by the addition of several new religious conceptions. One explanation for this is, no doubt, to be found in the Northmen's inherent love of nature and exceptionally strong tendency towards a personification of natural forces; their greater wealth of mythological ideas was in a larger measure, however, due to their wide acquaintance with a number of different peoples and religions. Through the many contacts established with the rest of Europe in the migration, and particularly in the Viking period, they must very early have received some knowledge of the Christian religion, and its influence seems

[22] A full and convincing discussion on this entire subject is found in Schück and Warburg, *Illustrerad svensk litteraturhistoria*, I, 3d Ed., Stockholm, 1926.

unmistakable in such personalities as Balder ("The White Christ"), and Loke (Satan), and in conceptions like Ragnarök, or the destruction of the world and the end of the gods.

To the early Scandinavians, as to all other primitive peoples, an explanation of the phenomena of nature was possible only through a belief that a personal living force was present in it. To take one example: with his knowledge of physics, the modern man explains the phenomena of the echo by the theory of sound waves, but the early Northman, ignorant of any such physical agents, assumed that a dwarf stood in the distance and mocked the speaker by repeating what had been said; only in this way could he explain the phenomenon. To the children of this early age nature was a living thing, and forests, lakes, rivers, waterfalls, the gardens, and the fields were peopled with spirits which affected the life of the individual either for good or for evil. The three Norns spun the web of men's lives even before they were born and sent to each one a *fylgia* or *haminja*, a "guardian angel," to follow him through life. The modern man, harassed by business and social cares, always dodging the multitude of things which, on, above, or below the earth, threaten to slay him, sometimes looks back to those remote times as indeed "the good old times," but he forgets that men in the past, too, had their tribulations, for they were constantly haunted by superstitious fears of witches, giants, werewolves, and other evil spirits; much of their time was evidently spent in trying to ward off the stealthy attacks of these enemies. Scandinavian mythology differed from the Greek, however, in so far as it conceived of the gods as genial friends of man whom they sought to protect against evil. Thus while in Greek mythology Prometheus is bound and the vulture set to devour his vitals because he has dared to steal fire from Zeus and give it to men, in Scandinavian mythology, the gods, after having created man and placed him on the earth, sent to him Heimdal with fire and the devices for making it, grain and the skill to raise it, and runes of eloquence, runes of victory, runes of the healing art, and the like.

Gods and goddesses.—Thor was the most popular god and received the most reverent worship. He was conceived as a regular *bonde* type, mighty in physical strength, fearless and honest, but somewhat naïve. Riding on his chariot after his goats,[23] he hurls his hammer, *Mjolnir,* the symbol of thunder, and kills the frost or flood giants that meditate evil against gods and men. He is the god of agriculture in the sense that his thunderbolt brings the refreshing showers and keeps the heat, frost, or flood giants away. Evidence of Thor's popularity in Sweden is found in a very large number of personal and place-names. Montelius mentions no less than twenty-four common names and thirty place-names in Sweden where his name enters as a component part.[24] The more common names are Tord, Tore, Torbjörn, Torger, Torgny, Torgrim, Torsten, Haldor, Tora, Torberg, Torfrid, Torgärd, and Bergtora; more common place-names are Torshälla and Torlunda in Uppland, Västmanland, Södermanland, Halland, Västergötland, Östergötland, and Öland; Torsby in Södermanland, Dalarna, Värmland, Dalsland, Bohuslän, Västergötland, Östergötland, and Småland; and Torsåker, Torsjö, Torsbro, Torsås and Thorsborg in Västergötland. His image was often placed in temples or carved on pillars by the high seats of the house; diminutive hammers, symbolic of Thor's hammer and an emblem of divinity, were carried by the pagan Swedes just as Christians carry their emblem of the cross. The hammer is often found cut into rune stones raised over the dead. The name Thursday is also a tribute of Thor's popularity. In the same way Tuesday, Sw. *tisdag,* after Tyr, Wednesday, Sw. *onsdag,* after Odin (Wodin), Friday, Sw. *fredag,* after Frigga; Swedish *lördag,* Saturday, is derived from old Norse *laugrdag,* and means bathing or wash day.

Odin, "the All Father," came into prominence much later than Thor; his name was generally associated with the legendary migration of the Swedes from the South into the North. His name does not occur as frequently as Thor's in personal and place-names. Montelius enumerates twenty-nine place-names and adds that the masculine *Odinkar* and the feminine *Odindisa* are the only known personal names.[25] This god was represented as a one-eyed man of about fifty, with a wide, flowing mantle and broad-brimmed hat; one eye had been given to the giant

[23] Cf. old Swedish, *asækia, as*-god, and *ækia*-ride, and modern Swedish, *åska,* thunder.
[24] Montelius, *Sveriges historia,* I, p. 391.
[25] *Ibid.*, p. 393.

Mimir in return for the privilege of a drink from the fountain of wisdom. As the sun god, his one eye no doubt represented the orb of day. Odin was primarily the god of war, although his spirit was dominant in several fields of activity, and his wonderful spear, Gungnir, which always struck its mark when thrown and then returned to its owner, symbolized his martial character. His horse, Sleipnir, equipped with eight legs and swift as the wind, travelled over land and water and through the air, and was symbolic of the swift course of the sun. His two ravens, Hugin (mind) and Munin (memory) flew out into the world every morning and returned at night with tidings of what had happened. To his splendid and spacious hall, Valhalla, provided with 640 doors, wide enough to enable 960 men to walk abreast through each, Valkyrs brought most of the brave men who fell in battle, and here they lived a life of perfect bliss, doing the things they loved to do on earth, but in a fuller measure, fighting, feasting, and boasting of their deeds. The boar Sährimner was slaughtered for food, but always came back to life again. Odin disdained the coarse food of the heroes; his only nourishment was mead. Frigga, the stately wife of Odin, shared many of the secrets that he knew but discreetly kept her own counsel. She typified the Scandinavian ideal of feminine beauty in the saga period—and in later periods—tall in stature, with golden hair, rosy cheeks, and blue eyes. She was pre-eminently the goddess of the household, and, as symbolical of this, carried a bunch of keys in her girdle.

Frey, as the special god of sunshine, refreshing showers, and harvest, was worshipped quite generally in Scandinavia, but, no doubt, more so in Sweden than anywhere else. Frey was so popular in Sweden that he was called by Snorre *Sveaguden* or "the god of the Swedes." [26] Thus at Christmas, or Yuletide, a festival which fell about a month later than the Christian holiday, Frey was honoured in a great feast, symbolic of the people's rejoicing since the powers of darkness have been checked. A boar was killed and roasted as a sacrifice to Frey, and with hands on its head the heroes vowed that they would perform great deeds during the coming year. As the god of the harvest,

[26] Schück, *Svenska folkets historia,* I, p. 263.

Frey was also the god of peace, and as such was loved by women because he did not slay their husbands.

Balder, the god of piety and goodness, in whose hall, Breidablick, nothing evil could dwell, shows more clearly than any other god the influence of Christianity upon Scandinavian mythological conceptions. He was the peace-maker and when, through the evil machinations of Loke, he fell mortally wounded, the era of happiness and strength came to an end for the gods. The worship of Balder, perhaps quite common, and occurring at midsummer-time, is not mentioned in any of the pagan writings except in the original Frithiof's saga; this suggested one of the finest cantos of Tegnér's great epic. Njord was the god of the peaceful commerce of the sea, and his realm, Noatun, very fittingly means "home of ships." He was so wealthy that he could always give aid when this was invoked. Loke was the most baffling of the gods. Although a god, and even a foster-brother of Odin, he was constantly bent on evil and his heinous crimes brought destruction to gods and men alike. Loke is clever, affable, and popular at first, a sort of Don Juan character, but evil always follows in his footsteps. Among other gods and goddesses may be mentioned Tyr, god of battle; Uller, the beautiful god of winter and of the hunt; Forsete, god of justice, whose judgments are so fair and wise that all parties to a controversy must acquiesce in his verdict; Brage, god of poetry; Heimdal, the watchful guard of the bridge Bifrost (the rainbow), which connected the abodes of gods and men with the lower worlds, and whose keenness of perception was so great that he could see one hundred miles in every direction and hear the grass grow; Idun, wife of Brage and keeper of the apples of youth, which kept the gods young and vigorous; Freya, goddess of love; and Gerda, the beautiful daughter of a giant, who was wooed and won by Frey.

Cult.—The pagan community in the North had no special priesthood, but each head of a household was supposed to perform the sacrificial ceremonies; in the large communal worship and sacrifices the king was high priest; in fact, the prestige and leadership of the old kings of Uppsala rested largely upon their office as chief priests in the leading temple of the Svear. Temples were probably not common, but the gods were worshipped in groves under the open sky; *bönder* often built their own temples. Adam of Bremen [27] states that every ninth year a great religious meeting was held at Uppsala in which all the provinces participated and at which it was obligatory for every one to be present and to bring gifts to the god. The picture that he gives of the sacrifices not only of animals but also of human beings is most gruesome in its details. Such human sacrifices are mentioned by others as well. Throughout the country are found places where huge rocks—generally nine, a sacred number—are placed in a circle and these, it has been conjectured, denote ancient places of sacrifice.

The ethical principles of the Viking period, as they are expressed chiefly in the great Eddic poem, *Havamal,* are the results of rich experience and deep reflection. They express in a striking and forceful way what is implied by the modern phrase, "good common sense." All mundane things are transitory and only one thing, an honoured name, remains after a man has passed away; this is a central idea. "Cattle die, kinsmen die, but one thing I know never dies, the verdict that is passed over dead men," says *Havamal.* The virtues most emphatically emphasized by *Havamal* are hospitality; temperance ("not as good as men say, is ale for the sons of men; the more you drink, the less you know whither your sense departed"); moderation in eating ("Cattle remember when they shall leave the field, but a glutton doesn't know the measure of his own stomach"); wisdom; taciturnity; respect for old age; and humility in prosperity. The chief failing of woman is inconstancy ("Thus it is to put faith in woman; it is like driving a two-year untamed colt on the smooth ice; like sailing the stormy sea in a rudderless ship, or like a lame man on skiis hunting reindeer on the mountain-side"), but man has no reason for boasting since he is false ("Then we speak the fairest, when we think the falsest").

[27] Peringskiöld translation, p. 21.

Chapter V

CHRISTIANITY AND THE NEW RELIGIOUS AND POLITICAL ORDER

Early contacts with Christianity.—The geographical location of the Scandinavian North was, no doubt, the main reason for the comparatively late arrival of Christian missionaries among its people; it took time to extend missionary activity to what then was looked upon by many as the periphery of the civilized world. The propaganda of Continental Christians, as well as the many contacts which the Viking expeditions established between the North and the rest of Europe, made it inevitable, however, that men ultimately should come also to the Northland to preach the gospel of the new faith. That the peoples who had to meet the savage Viking attacks and in whose churches the Christians on Sunday prayed "from the fury of the Northmen, good Lord deliver us," had early conceived of the Christian gospel of peace as an effective means for taming the wild spirits of these corsairs, also seems plausible.

The strong hold which the pagan cult had on the people and the assurances of the bliss of Valhalla to all those who met the death of heroes on the battle-field, made Northmen of the ninth century loath to give up the ancient faith. It was, however, being gradually undermined; the scepticism which Tegnér attributes to Frithiof was, no doubt, quite typical of the period in which he is supposed to have lived; namely, the eighth century. Very early some knowledge of the Christian faith must have trickled through to the North; it came through Christian slaves, the victims of Viking raids in foreign lands, and through merchants who had journeyed far on errands of business and had reached Christian lands. The silent influence which was making its way slowly into the country can be read in the common symbols on ornaments and rocks; a figure of a wheel as a pagan representation of the sun as a divinity before the Christian era occurs frequently, but not during the first five centuries after Christ. After about 500 A.D. it appears again, but now as the Christian symbol of divinity.[1] The circumstances attending the coming of the first missionary to the land give strong foundation for the assumption that the new faith was not entirely unknown in Sweden even before the Christian missions began.

In the year 822 Pope Paschal I commissioned Ebo, Archbishop of Rheims, to establish Christian missions in the North. Ebo himself went to Denmark, where many accepted Christian baptism. When later Harald, an exiled Danish king or prince, sought aid of Louis the Pious, this was promised on condition that he and his household accept the Christian faith. Harald accepted this condition, and, on his return to Denmark, he was accompanied by Anskar, a young monk, a native of Picardy in France, who had become headmaster of the school at the cloister of Corvey. A burning desire to offer himself to the cause of Christian missions had long possessed his ardent soul. Anskar stayed in Denmark but a short time when civil war forced him to return to Corvey. Soon thereafter, according to Rimbert, men came from Sweden to the court of Louis who said that many in their country desired to hear about the new religion. Their king, whose name was said to be Björn, would not, they assured the emperor, oppose or harass Christian teachers. Probably Björn was anxious to enter into some trade agreement with the Frankish emperor, and as he was aware of the latter's piety and zeal, he sought to gain his good-will by suggesting a Christian mission to Sweden.

Anskar's first visit to Sweden.—The emperor rejoiced at this unexpected opportunity to further the Christian cause, and inquired of Anskar whether he was willing to undertake the mission. The young monk's heart leaped with joy at this providential opportunity to do something for his Master, and in company with another monk, Witmar, he set out from Corvey in 829. They took passage on a merchant ship bound for Sweden, but before they had reached half-way their vessel was attacked by Vikings and Anskar lost the costly articles which Louis had sent as presents to Björn; lost also was the

[1] Montelius, *Sveriges historia,* I, p. 423.

supply of religious books which had been taken along. Anskar himself narrowly escaped death, but managed to reach shore, and, heedless of the advice of his companions to turn back, he and Witmar trudged through the dark and seemingly endless forests until they came to Birka, at that time the most important commercial centre of Sweden (p. 115). King Björn gave friendly reception to Anskar, and Rimbert adds that the joy of the Christian believers on being permitted to hear the Gospel preached was unspeakable. A few converts were made, among them being one of the great chiefs of the land. After staying in Sweden a year and a half, Anskar and Witmar returned to their home. The emperor now established a special archbishopric for the North, with its seat at Hamburg—later transferred to Bremen—and appointed Anskar to serve as its first incumbent. Together with Ebo, he also became papal legate to the people of the North. Another monk, Gautbert, was next sent to Sweden. He also was favourably received by king and people, but his excessive missionary zeal, after some years, provoked a popular uprising which drove him from the land and broke up the congregation at Birka. Anskar later sent another monk, Ardgar, to Sweden, but he soon left the country, probably because of persecutions.

Second visit.—Anskar then decided to return to Sweden himself and in order, this time, to be able to gain greater prestige than on the former visit he went with official commissions from the rulers of Denmark and Germany. The king at the time, Olof, was duly impressed by these commissions and arranged to have a popular assembly decide whether or not the visitors should be permitted to preach the Christian doctrines. According to a story, which has its parallel in other countries as well, the assembly was persuaded to give its permission by the pleas of a wise old man, who said that men have been in the dark as to whence they come and whither they go at death, and if this stranger could tell them anything which might help to clear up the mystery he ought to be heard; one more god, thought the old man, might be an advantage, in the event that the old gods were no longer able to help. Churches were now built, and after the work had been placed on a firm foundation, Anskar returned home, leaving another monk, Erimbert, to continue the work. The welfare of the Swedish mission was always close to Anskar's heart, and until his death in 865 he showed his interest by sending several missionaries to the country. His successor on the archiepiscopal seat, Rimbert, shared this interest and went on a visit to the congregations in Sweden. This gave new impetus to missionary activity there, but after Rimbert's death in 888, there followed a period of almost fifty years during which the Bremen archdiocese exhibited no interest in the North. When Unne, one of Anskar's successors, arrived at Birka, probably in 936, he found that the people had reverted to paganism. A new congregation was, however, founded by him, but although it appears that for some decades after Unne's death Christian missionaries preached at Birka there is no evidence that the influence of this mission ever extended to any other part of Sweden. Soon thereafter Birka itself was ravaged, or perhaps destroyed, by corsairs from the Baltic lands. A number of graves which evidently contain the remains of early Christians have in our day been found on this ancient site; the bodies have not been cremated and covered by mounds, but enclosed in wooden coffins, a fact which suggests Christian influence, since the new religion always condemned the practice of burning the bodies of the dead. A great number of crosses and other symbols likewise indicate that the new faith had made some headway.

While written records fail to throw any light on the first appearance of Christian teachers in other parts of Sweden, archæological finds point to a decided Christian influence in the provinces of Skåne, Västergötland, and Bohuslän in the tenth century. From this period there are very few graves in this section which reveal pagan forms. This is quite in contrast to the situation in other parts of the country. Montelius sees in this circumstance strong evidence that Christianity had already become so great an influence in this district that the ancient pagan burial forms had been changed. Since this part of Sweden had the closest and most frequent contacts with the rest of Europe, such early Christian influence here is just what might be expected. After the victory of Canute the Great in England and his conversion to Christianity, it was inevitable that for political, if for no other reasons, Christianity should make rapid headway in Sweden. As previously noted (p. 93), a large contingent in Canute's army were Swedes, who after victory had been won in England returned home in large numbers, bringing with them not only English money, but new cultural influences. Some Swedish rune stones in honour of these returned warriors indicate that they had become Christians while in England. Similarly, a great number of Christianized warriors returned to Sweden after the Norman conquest of England and thus gave added strength to its Christian group.

Strength of English influence.—The centre of Christian culture in Sweden had also shifted now from the Lake Mälaren region to Västergötland, which had closer contacts with England. Ecclesiastical terms were borrowed from the English, and the earliest Swedish calendar of saints extant—in Vallentuna Church in Uppland—reveals that, aside from the universally accepted saints, the ones worshipped in Sweden were nearly all English, as Cuthbert, Edward, Guthlac, Ealfege, Wilfred, Dunstan, Botulf, Alban, and Oswald.[2] For a time, therefore, Sweden received her cultural influences from England, and these were undoubtedly of a far more enduring character than those received from the Continent through Anskar and his successors. The first English missionary to Sweden was probably St. David, a monk of the Cluniac order, who came to the land some time after 1020. At first he laboured in the southern part of the country, but later transferred his activity to the province of Västmanland, the apostle of which he, in a special sense, became. The most important of the many missionaries who, with the beginning of the eleventh century, came from England, was St. Sigfrid, whose activity was confined to Västergötland and Småland, where he is said to have built the first church at Växiö.

First Christian king in Sweden.—A great victory was won by the new faith when in 1008 the king, Olof Skötkonung, accepted Christianity and was baptized by St. Sigfrid at Husaby, situated on Kinnekulle, a picturesque mountain in the northern part of Västergötland. The powerful jarl of this province had some time before accepted the Christian faith. Both Olof and his son Anund were zealous supporters of the

[2] Schück, *Svenska folkets historia,* I, p. 269.

Church; Olof's zeal was, however, restrained by a decision of his subjects at a Thing that while he might build a church and have Christian worship, he must abstain from trying to force the new religion on any one. A new bishopric, the first in Sweden, was established at Skara, in the heart of Västergötland, about 1013, and its first incumbent was a certain Turgot,

The Cathedral of Uppsala. The building was begun in the thirteenth century and given its present form in the nineteenth century; example of the Gothic style of architecture

probably a Swede. The Englishman, St. Eskil, laboured in Södermanland, where he suffered the death of a martyr when he appeared at a Thing and preached against heathen sacrifices. To the same period belongs St. Stephen, who went into the northern part of Sweden to preach the new faith. At the end of the eleventh or in the first part of the twelfth century, two bishops of Skara, Rikulf and Hervard, were English-born. In 1152 another Englishman, Nicholas Breakspeare, visited Sweden as a papal legate for the purpose of establishing an archbishopric, but finding that the Svear and the Götar could not agree on a location, he left the decision to the Archbishop of Lund. Soon afterwards the archiepiscopal seat was located at Uppsala, which thus became the ecclesiastical centre of Sweden.[3]

Towards the middle of the eleventh century the incumbent of the Bremen diocese seems to have had a new flare-up of interest in the missionary cause in Sweden and several bishops were, according to Adam of Bremen, sent there, among them two by the name of Adalvard. One became the third bishop of Skara, and the other was assigned to Sigtuna. The latter was a very zealous man and sought to have the pagan temple at Uppsala destroyed, but was unsuccessful.

Slow progress of Christianity.—Christianity at first made exceedingly slow progress in Sweden, but by the middle of the eleventh century many converts had been made, as shown by a great number of rune stones of the period upon which have been inscribed the symbol of the cross or the pious prayer, "May God and the Mother of God help his soul."[4] The reasons for the slow progress of Christianity in Sweden—and in Norway and Denmark as well—were many. The missionaries of foreign birth, no matter how excellent they were as men, or how admirable their zeal and courage, were looked upon with suspicion and disfavour. The new religion also set up ethical standards which a war-loving people like the Northmen of that era were disposed to rebel against. The heroic exploits of warfare had been exalted among them as a sure guarantee that the joys of Valhalla would come to them at death; to become followers of the lowly and peace-loving Nazarene seemed but an evidence of effeminate weakness. As a Christian the Swede could not go out and take other people's property, even if he was strong enough to do so; he could not with a good conscience exact vengeance for a real or fancied wrong, neither could he set aside his wife on a frivolous charge, nor calmly take his own life when he felt that he had lived his full period

[3] An illuminating and interesting account of early English missionary activity in the Scandinavian countries is given in Henry Goddard Leach's *Angevin Britain an! Scandinavia*, Harvard University Press, 1921.

[4] Montelius, *Sveriges historia*, I, p. 433.

of usefulness. The pagan defenders could not without reason contend that the many demands of the new religion would become grievous burdens. Another reason for the slow progress of Christianity in Sweden is found in the innate conservatism of her people and their utter unwillingness, in this as in other matters, to be hurried along by coercion from without. On

The Cathedral of Lund; example of the Romanesque style of architecture

the other side were the factors which favoured the progress of the new religion, and ultimately—after about two hundred and fifty years, reckoned from the coming of Anskar—gained for it, outwardly at least, a complete victory in the land. The superiority of the Christian religion, both as an explanation of the profound mysteries of existence and as a moral force, must have been apparent to a people as capable mentally as the Swedes. By reason of her excellent organization, the Church also became a great force for unity, and soon the kings realized that their efforts to bind the different sections together could be furthered most effectively by an alliance with this new power. For political, if for no other reasons, kings began to give the Church their strong support.

Olof Skötkonung and Norway.—Prior to his baptism, Olof Skötkonung had taken part with Denmark in an attack upon the famous King of Norway, Olof Tryggvasson, who on a visit to England had embraced the new faith. The preliminaries to this conflict are touched upon in one of the well-known tales from mediæval Scandinavian history. The Norwegian king, it says, had proposed to Sigrid the Haughty, the mother of Swedish Olof, in the expectation that he could thus add her dominions to his own. His apparently well-meant suggestion that she embrace the Christian faith was met with a curt refusal, for Sigrid was an unregenerate heathen, whereupon the pious king struck the proud queen with his glove, exclaiming, "Why should I marry you, you heathen dog?" Sigrid answered with anger, "This will likely mean your death." Later she married Sven Forkbeard of Denmark and thereupon inspired the formation of an alliance between him and her son against her erstwhile Norwegian suitor. The decisive encounter between the allies and Olof Tryggvasson came in the naval battle of Svolder in the year 1000, one of the memorable events of mediæval Scandinavian history. The forces of the Norwegian king were defeated and he himself perished. The Swedish part of the spoils of victory consisted of Bohuslän and a considerable part of the Norwegian coast region west of Jämtland.

It was not long after Svolder that trouble arose again between Sweden and Norway. In the latter country, Olof the Fat—or Olof the Saint, to use the more euphonious appellation, which was applied to him after his death—became king in 1015, and he forthwith seized the districts which had become Sweden's part of the spoils after Svolder. These border quarrels interfered, however, with the commerce of the *bönder* of Västergötland, who found it difficult to buy salt and herring from the Norwegians, and since these *bönder* had no special interest in the plan of their king for the reconquest of the Norwegian districts, they said they wanted peace. In spite of this warning, Olof Skötkonung persisted stubbornly in his belligerent course, and when therefore the thingmen at Uppsala and the Jarl of Västergötland, as well as messengers from the Norwegian king, appeared before him to plead for peace, he became very abusive and uttered threats against his people. Then, as Snorre relates, arose Thorgny, the Lawman of Uppland, an old man of commanding stature and with a beard flowing down to his girdle, and spoke fearlessly to the king. "We *bönder*," he said, "now desire that you make peace with Olof the Fat, King of Norway, and give him your daughter Ingegerd in marriage. . . . If you will not do as we say, we will proceed against you and kill you, because we will tolerate no disturbance, nor permit any war on your part. Thus it has been with our fathers before us. They threw five kings into the water at Mora Thing because they were full of insolence as you now are insolent towards us. State quickly what your decision is." The story relates that Olof acquiesced, although with malicious thoughts in his heart of a later reckoning with his stiff-necked subjects. By later historians this story has been attacked as apocryphal; it cannot well be assumed, even if the substance of the story is correct, that Thorgny spoke exactly the words which Snorre puts into his mouth. His courageous defiance, as depicted by the story, may, however, be taken as typical of the spirit of independence which made itself felt in the land at the time.

The Stenkil dynasty.—The successors of Olof Skötkonung were men of less importance, and about 1060 the last member of his family to occupy the royal office at Uppsala died. The royal dignity now went by election to Stenkil, a well-born and influential man of Västergötland. His election meant a victory for the Christian religion rather than for his province. According to Adam of Bremen, Stenkil had early befriended the Christian missionaries in his province. At the time of his election he was the foremost man of his province, in which Christianity now was more firmly entrenched than anywhere else in the land. "The most Christian king" was the title given him at his death by the Church. Stenkil's ascent to the throne meant war between the new faith and expiring paganism, but the details of this struggle are hidden in deepest obscurity. The only thing which certain facts enable one to surmise is that Stenkil was a tolerant and fair-minded ruler and that he did not believe that the cause of Christianity could be advanced by the use of force. His death is supposed to have occurred in 1066. With his passing follows a long period of civil wars, with several pretenders gaining a following and plunging the country into many bloody wars, the story of which contains a multitude of contradictory details. That the Christians in this disturbed period were often hard pressed is suggested by the statement of Adam of Bremen that the bishops who were ordered by the Archbishop of Bremen to proceed to Sweden "remained at home, fearing persecutions," thus leaving it to the Bishop of Skåne (then a part of Denmark) to exercise supervision of ecclesiastical affairs in Sweden. The sons of Stenkil, Halsten and Inge the Elder, alleged to have ruled about 1080, are said to have been zealous Christians; especially of the latter it is told that at one of the Things he issued an ultimatum to the Svear that they must accept Christianity. They replied in a spirit of defiance, saying that such coercion was a violation of their ancient rights; and then countered by making a demand that the king make sacrifices according to old custom or else relinquish the royal dignity. As Inge persisted in his demand, the people hurled stones at him and drove him from the Thing. A brother-in-law of Inge now offered to make sacrifices according to old pagan custom and therefore was accepted as king; later he was defeated and killed by Inge. After this Christianity made great headway in the land.

The Sverker dynasty.—The dynasty of Stenkil came to an end in 1125 and thereupon followed another period of civil wars. The Svear elected a king, and when, without previously asking the permission of its people, he entered Västergötland and demanded the homage due a king, he was straightway killed. Soon thereafter Sverker, a noted man who had married the widow of a former king, Inge the Younger, was elected. Sverker was a peace-loving man, whose chief concern was the strengthening of the Church. Monks of the Cistercian order came to Sweden by invitation of the king and queen. The first cloisters in the land were built at Alvastra in Östergötland, Nydala in Småland, and Varnhem in Västergötland. The Church of Sweden was at this time brought definitely into closer relation to the Roman Catholic hierarchy, when in 1152 Nicholas, Cardinal of Albano, came to the country as a legate of the Pope and met the leading men of the country at a meeting at Linköping. As an evidence of their allegiance to the Church of Rome, the Swedes here agreed to pay the Peter's Pence.

St. Erik.—Sverker was assassinated about the year 1156 by one of his servants, and thereupon, according to the chronicle, the Svear elected Erik, a rich and good *bonde,* to be their king, and with him begins a new dynasty. Very little is known of his ancestry, but his father is said to have had the English-sounding name of Jedvard.[5] He was strongly attached to the Christian faith, and under the guidance of Henry, an Englishman by birth, who served as the first Bishop of Uppsala, he laboured successfully for the further strengthening of Christianity, especially among the Svear. Many churches were built and preachers appointed. Erik was not satisfied with a mere outward conformity to the tenets of Christianity; through the influence of the new religion he hoped to bring about a purification of the people's morals. Erik likewise sought to improve the status of women and make marriage an honoured institution by giving her a legal right to a part of the family property.

The Swedes and the Crusades.—At this time all Christendom had for more than a generation resounded with the crusaders' call, and such a call, holding as it did a promise of adventure as well as of pious service, was certain to find open ears and receptive minds wherever men of Northland blood dwelt. Many of the chief leaders of the movement were descendants of the Northmen who had settled in Normandy, but from the other parts as well, where Northmen had settled, recruits flocked in large numbers. Here were opportunities for adventure and plunder no less than the Viking expeditions had offered, but now the enterprise had the sanction of the Church and was lauded as extremely pious.[6] Especially from Norway did a number of individuals and groups proceed to the Holy Land, but quite contrary to their general practice of roaming about and seeking the most distant fields, the Swedes concluded this time that they could find an inviting area for their operations much nearer home.

In the lands across the Baltic—that is, in Finland and in the coast districts south of it—still dwelt pagans who in a measure had taken over the rôle of corsairs, so effectively filled by Scan-

[5] Tunberg, S., *Sveriges historia,* II, p. 47.

[6] An account of the Scandinavian part in the crusading movement may be found in Riant's *Skandiavernas Korstog og Andagtsreiser til Palestina,* Kjöbenhavn, 1868.

dinavians in an earlier period. Against these people the zealous Erik now led an expedition, landing in southwestern Finland and forcing the Finns at the point of the sword, after the fashion of Emperor Charlemagne, to accept Christianity and submit to baptism. Groups of Swedes were left in the country to found settlements, and a number of ecclesiastics, among them Bishop Henry, remained to carry forward the religious work. Henry was soon afterwards slain by a native; subsequently he became honoured as the patron saint of Finland. Erik met his death at Uppsala, when a Danish prince, Magnus Henrikson, treacherously attacked the city. The pious king was attending mass when news of the enemy's approach was brought to him, but he would not cease his godly meditations until the services were at an end. In the encounter which followed, the Swedish king was killed, whereupon, according to one of the most commonly believed of Swedish legends, accepted without question by generation after generation of believers, a spring immediately welled forth from the place where his blood had flowed. Erik's body was interred in the cathedral at Old Uppsala, but when the archbishoprical seat later was moved to the new city of Uppsala, the bones were interred in the cathedral which had been built there. The metal casket containing the relict still remains in the stately temple as one of its chief objects of interest.

The credibility of the Erik legends has in our day stirred up lively polemics among Swedish historians, some of whom have endeavoured to show that Erik, who, after his death, came to be invested by the people with all good qualities, and honoured as the patron saint of Sweden, had in reality done nothing to deserve any special homage. The outcome of this controversy seems to be a well-founded conviction that, whereas the writer of the Erik legend permitted his imagination a rather free scope, and thus made use of many embellishments, the essential points in the account may be accepted as historically authentic. Although Erik's name has gone down in Swedish history with the attribute, "the Saint," this designation never rested on any act of canonization by the Church. The murderer of Erik ruled Sweden for a brief period, but fell in battle against Karl Sverkerson, son of the former king,

Sverker. He was the first ruler in Swedish history to bear the honoured name Karl. From his reign dates the definite establishment in 1164 of Old Uppsala as the seat of a new archbishopric, with Stephen as its first incumbent. The papal commission for the new archbishopric came as a result of earnest entreaties by Karl Sverkerson, Bishop Stephen, and Jarl Ulv, the king's chief officer. The commission stipulated that the archbishopric at Lund should exercise primacy over Uppsala, but this never amounted to more than a merely nominal authority. The inauguration of the new archbishopric at Uppsala was an event of prime importance to Sweden, as this became a strong influence in knitting the different parts of the country more firmly together.

Development under Knut.—Karl Sverkerson was killed by Knut, son of Erik the Saint, who long had sought to gain the Swedish throne for himself. As king, Knut assumed an attitude of great friendliness towards the Church. Liberal donations were made to cloisters, and one new order, the order of St. John, was founded. Knut appears to have been a strong ruler, who understood how to make the royal officeholder respected and obeyed in the land. Certain novelties were introduced, the most important being the coinage of money, minted from silver, which it has been surmised came from the country's own mines. Some aspects of Knut's foreign policy also are known. The intrepid claimant to the Norwegian throne at this time, Sverre, whose story forms one of the great epics of Norwegian history, found a friendly refuge in Sweden and later married Knut's sister. This helped to establish still more friendly relations between the two neighbouring countries. By negotiating a commercial treaty with Henry the Lion of Germany, the Swedish king also established closer economic relations between that country and his own and this in turn led to a marked advance in city building and development of industrial life in Sweden. This treaty resulted in a great influx of Germans; as the sequel will show, this threatened, later, to make the German element dominant in the land. As a defence against the attacks of the Karelians and the Esthonians, whose raids had grown increasingly daring and whose depredations probably account for the destruction of Sigtuna, an important town on an island in Lake Mälaren, Knut built, according to tradition, some sort of defences at the point where the stream connecting Lake Mälaren and the Baltic is the narrowest—that is, where Stockholm is now located; thus he may with reason be considered the founder of this city. War was also begun in Knut's reign against the pagan people in Esthonia, Livonia, and neighbouring districts, but Denmark's suspicions were then aroused that Sweden aimed to seize some of this territory. As Denmark herself had designs on it, she resented the intrusion of her neighbour. Here, then, was the real beginning of those unfortunate national antagonisms which filled centuries with ruinous wars. At the death of Knut, which occurred about 1196, Sverker the Younger, son of Karl Sverkerson, was elevated to the royal dignity although the former king left sons.

Rule of the Folkungs.—The rejection of their claims in favour of Sverker finds its explanation in the fact that the latter was the son-in-law of the mighty Birger Brosa who served as jarl under the former king, and was head of the Folkungs, the most powerful family in Sweden at the time.[7] To gain the support of the Church, Sverker conceded to her the right of ecclesiastical jurisdiction, *i.e.* the right of a clergyman or monk accused of crime to be tried by a court made up by the Church herself. As a further concession he stipulated that all Church property was henceforth to be exempt from taxes. In spite of the ecclesiastical support which these concessions brought him, Sverker became so hard pressed, when a war with the dispossessed sons of Knut broke out, that he was compelled to seek aid in Denmark. The king of Denmark at the time, Valdemar the Victorious, was engaged in constant wars in order to establish Danish suzerainty over all the lands of the south and eastern shores of the Baltic. The prospect of having a grateful and dependent friend on the Swedish throne was very pleasing to Valdemar and he fitted out a large military force to aid Sverker. At the head of this, Sverker now returned to take up the struggle against his enemies at home, led by Erik, son of the late King Knut. The ensuing battle, fought at Lena in Västergötland, was one of the bloodiest in Swedish history, and

[7] The jarl (English earl) as a rule commanded the military forces of the land or of certain districts.

ended in a crushing defeat of Sverker's forces. The defeated king now appealed directly to the Pope for assistance, this being the first instance of such an appeal from Sweden. The Roman Pontiff at the time, Innocent III, in whose person papal authority perhaps reached its climax and whose arrogance and power Philip Augustus of France, John of England, and the German emperor had been made to feel to their utter discomfiture, was not averse to taking a hand in Swedish affairs and playing the part of king-maker. But the papal letter to the bishops of Sweden in this matter did not help Sverker. On a new invasion of Sweden at the head of a small Danish force, Sverker met defeat and death. Erik now received the undivided support of all factions and was crowned king. For the first time in Swedish history the Uppsala archbishop officiated at the coronation; this was in itself an evidence that the Church and Erik now had become reconciled. Innocent sanctioned the coronation and confirmed the king's right to Finland.

On the death of Erik in the year 1216, a son of former King Sverker came to power, since Erik's only son, Erik Eriksson, was born after his father's death. The question of succession was practically decided by the archbishop in conjunction with the bishops, one of whom at this time assumes the title of chancellor; this is the first time the office is mentioned in Swedish records. The new king, John by name, paid his debt of gratitude to the Church by renewing and extending the privileges of the clergy. With the death of John in 1222, the family of Erik came to power again, in the person of Erik Eriksson. As he was still a minor, the government was entrusted to a small group of prominent men, mostly ecclesiastics, designated as the King's Council; the institution was not unknown in other countries at this time, but now for the first time it makes its appearance in Sweden.

Birger Jarl and the Church.—The young king found himself more and more dependent upon the powerful Folkung family, whose foremost representative, Birger, married his sister and later held the office of jarl. Erik, being at times hard beset by enemies, found it convenient to extend still further the privileges of the Church. Thus the bishops were given the right to retain fines collected in their dioceses for various violations of the law, especially in cases of perjury and adultery. Sweden now took her place definitely in the great ecclesiastical system which had been built up by Rome. In the year 1247 a Roman cardinal, William of Sabina, came to Sweden as the legate of the Pope, and in the following year he met with Birger Jarl, the Swedish bishops, and certain other prominent men at Skeninge. This meeting, the records of which are still extant, accepted the law of celibacy as binding upon the Swedish clergy and made the canon law their norm. The decrees of this important meeting were later followed by a papal bull instituting a chapter (*domkapitel*), in every bishopric, to consist of a number of priests of different grades in the diocese, in whose hands was placed the power to elect the bishop. The ecclesiastics were furthermore forbidden to swear fealty to temporal rulers. Birger Jarl, the dominant personality in the government at the time, and a man who was not disposed to acquiesce meekly in any measures that would result in stripping the temporal ruler of power and make him a mere obedient servant of the Church, must have looked with deep concern at this extension of ecclesiastical influence.

In his position as regent during the minority of Erik, Birger Jarl was called upon to make a decision in another matter which was fraught with far-reaching consequences; his decision can be said to have affected Swedish policies and Swedish cultural development profoundly during the centuries which have since passed. It so happened that the Christians in Finland were hard pressed by neighbouring pagan tribes, and the Pope, being greatly concerned about their plight, besought the Swedes to intervene for their protection. The Swedish bishops were exhorted to preach a crusade against the apostates and barbarians. Moved by the plea of the Pope, and at the same time anxious to save the Baltic lands from becoming a prey to the Karelians or the Russians, Birger Jarl sent a force to the scene of trouble, but met defeat. Death and desolation were now the fate of the exposed Christian settlements in Finland and the other Baltic lands. Further help from Sweden was therefore absolutely necessary if the centres of Swedish and Christian culture in these lands were to escape utter destruction. For a clear-minded and fearless man like Birger Jarl there was no hesitancy as to the course that must be taken, and in 1249 he went with soldiers to Finland, penetrated deep into the land, and subdued the pagan natives, the Tavasts, who now accepted Christianity. Birger now built a strong fort at Tavastehus as a defence against further attacks. From this time on, Sweden controlled the greater part of Finland.

Birger as ruler.—While Birger Jarl, as the power behind the throne during Erik's reign, had led his country in the successful execution of momentous decisions, it was after the death of this king that his genius for government found its fullest opportunity to assert itself and to establish for him the undoubted right to be considered, next to Engelbrekt Engelbrektsson, the greatest personality in mediæval Swedish history. His genius, as well as services already performed, made his right to the throne unquestioned, but the influential men in whose hands lay the power of election were jealous of his fame and prestige. Not daring to set him aside entirely, they elected his young son Valdemar as king. As an excuse for thus passing him by in favour of his son, they said that Birger was not of royal birth and therefore ineligible. Though little pleased with the arrangement, the great jarl was willing to abide by it, fully realizing that, as long as he lived, the essential thing, power, would rest in his hands, and not in those of his young and worthless son. It appears, however, that he did not come into undisputed possession of power without a bitter struggle, caused by the claims of descendants of other royal lines and by factions which were antagonistic to him because of his earlier policies and acts. The details of this struggle are not fully known, but significant statements in the Erik Chronicle indicate that Birger took cruel revenge upon his defeated enemies, and ugly insinuations of breach of faith on his part are not lacking. That Birger was for a time hard pressed seems clear also from the concessions which he made to the Church, evidently in order to win her support. Valdemar was crowned by a bishop and thus placed under special protection of the Church; in a communication to the Pope, Birger promised in the king's name to respect all the privileges that had been granted the Church prior to this time. He was, however, not the man to become a pliant tool in the hands of the Roman

Pontiff. While the records give no definite information regarding his subsequent relations to the Church, it appears quite evident that he did not respect the promise previously given of complete immunity for the clergy, but insisted on certain military service in return for fiefs which ecclesiastics held under the king. This position was, of course, not in accord with the policy of the Church.

Economic development and alliances.—Birger Jarl's constructive statesmanship had as its exalted aim the building of a nation which enjoyed justice and prosperity within and was secure against foreign aggressions. The former he would achieve by developing the rich natural resources of the country, fostering trade and commerce, and enacting laws giving citizens the safeguards of justice and protection, the latter by establishing good relations between the three Scandinavian countries. Birger's influence succeeded in bringing about the beginning of a friendly co-operation between Sweden and Norway. This was further cemented by the marriage of his daughter, Rikissa, to the heir of the Norwegian throne, Håkan Håkanson. Friendly approaches were next made to Denmark. The rulers of the three countries met near the Göta River in 1254 in order to confer about the matters which had disturbed the good relations of their lands and to endeavour to come to a friendly understanding on all points. Both the Norwegians and the Danes harboured deep-rooted suspicions, however, with regard to Birger's real purpose, and this naturally made a friendly accord difficult. Two years later came, nevertheless, the formal ratification of a treaty between Denmark and Sweden. Strained relations existed between Denmark and Norway, however, and Birger again sought to bring about a reconciliation between them. Later generations must look back upon these plans of Birger as an evidence of remarkable wisdom and foresight. As long as he ruled, Birger maintained amicable relations with Norway; such relations with Denmark became hardly possible, because of the chaotic condition into which bitter factional struggles plunged that country.

The Swedes and the Germans.—A reason for Birger's desire to bring the three Scandinavian countries into friendly accord with one another was the menace which German trade in the Baltic held for them. The enormous expansion east and northeast in this period of the German people is one of the remarkable facts of mediæval history. With good reason it may be suggested that the Northmen, and especially the Swedes, were at one time in a far more favourable position than the Germans for gaining possession of these territories and building up a lucrative trade. The Scandinavians lost their opportunity by failing to work aggressively according to any definite plan, instead dissipating their strength in rather meaningless, albeit daring and brilliant, ventures in different parts of the world. The Germans, on the other hand, had advanced consistently and, as it seemed, deliberately in accordance to a plan. With Lübeck at the head, the German cities now built up a formidable trade organization, the Hanseatic League, which threatened to establish a complete monopoly in commerce and trade in the North. Visby on Gottland, at that time completely German, although on Swedish soil, was with incredible rapidity becoming the great mart of the North. It is a proof of Birger's sagacity that, instead of trying to block the German merchants from doing business in his realm, he sought commercial treaties with them for the purpose of building up a profitable trade in his country. His subjects, who little realized what profits could be derived from trade, would, he believed, soon take their cue from the Germans and themselves begin to develop their rich natural resources and build up a lucrative trade. In the year 1251 a commercial treaty was ratified by Sweden and Lübeck; this granted the Lübeck merchants toll exemption on goods imported into Sweden; citizens of Lübeck who wished to settle in Sweden must place themselves under Swedish jurisdiction and law and become Swedish citizens; and Swedish traders in Lübeck should in return then enjoy the same trade privileges as German merchants in Sweden. A similar agreement was made with Hamburg, and, according to a letter which Henry III of England sent to Birger, the latter had on two occasions sent representatives to the English court, presumably with a commercial treaty in mind. Tradition has also made Birger the founder of Stockholm; in a sense this is perhaps giving him credit which he does not deserve, since a small fort was possibly built on the site before his time, but it is justified in so far as he made it a commercial centre of importance.

New Laws.—In this period, Swedish kings had no clear power to proclaim laws, but Birger issued important decrees relating to the security and rights of Swedish subjects. These were the famous enactments insuring security in the home, at the Thing, in churches, and guaranteeing protection to woman. Thus attack upon a man while he was in his own home or in attendance at church or Thing, or on his way to or from them, was forbidden and violations of the decree made an offense against the king himself as the representative of the law; he would exert himself to the end that law-breakers be apprehended and punishment meted out. There was thus in Birger's decrees a recognition of the responsibility of the ruler as the personification of society itself, to prevent or punish crime. The law relating to woman forbade the not uncommon practice of abducting them and forcing them into marriage. Birger is also remembered as the author of a new inheritance law for women. Before this period, daughters had enjoyed the right of inheritance only in case they had no brothers; it was now stipulated that a sister should be entitled to half as much as a brother in the division of an estate, a provision which remained in force down to 1845.

Magnus Ladulås.—Birger died in 1266 and troubles soon began. His worthless eldest son, Valdemar, was forced to vacate the throne in favour of a younger brother, Magnus, the only one of Birger's sons who had inherited the strong qualities of the father. Like his father, the new king was above everything else a law-maker and administrator, and from his reign date a number of new legal enactments and institutions that reflect the great economic, political, and social changes which Sweden was at this time undergoing.

Political and social changes.—The personnel of the King's Council was now for the first time clearly defined; henceforth it consisted of a certain number of bishops, lawmen, and other lords, from among whom the chief officers, the marshal, the steward (*drots*), and the chancellor were selected. The latter served as a sort of secretary to the king, and wrote the royal documents. Meetings to which a large number of lords (*stormän*) were invited, and known as *herredager* or diets, now came to be held with some regularity. A system of military service was introduced, the old organization, designed primarily for naval service, being no longer adequate. With the introduction of heavy armour, cavalry had become the effective and indispensable arm in all warfare, but the heavy cost involved in fitting out a man with horse and trappings had kept the royal forces in Sweden down to a minimum. Magnus therefore decreed that men who served in the cavalry or fitted out man and horse for such service, should enjoy immunity from taxes. This exemption was a privilege which soon became hereditary in certain families, and a distinct class, the nobility, was thus created. By stipulating that none of the taxes ordinarily paid to the crown should be levied on any of the property which had come into the possession of the Church, Magnus added greatly to her privileges. It was during his reign also that knighthood became a distinct and honoured institution in the land.

Protection for the bönder.—While favourably disposed towards his rich and powerful subjects, and ready to give them new dignities and privileges, Magnus set himself squarely against any encroachments upon the rights of the *bönder* by the powerful lords. The latter had fallen into the pernicious habit of going about with their retinues and helping themselves to lodging in the homes of the *bönder*, taking food and fodder from their stores without making any payment in return. The king now issued a drastic rule against this practice. In order that there might no longer be any excuse for such enforced hospitality, a man was to be appointed in each village to provide food and other necessities to travellers in return for pay. It was because of this solicitude for the *bönder's* security that the honourable sobriquet *Ladulås* (barn-lock) has always been attached to Magnus's name.

Civil Wars.—The story of the three decades following the death of Magnus in 1290 is filled with the most gruesome details of ambitions and bitter rivalries of brothers, base treachery, civil wars, and cruel murders. The only outstanding individual in this dark period is Torgils Knutsson, the marshal under Magnus Ladulås, who served Birger, his son, and successor as he had served the father, with great ability. A Swedish army was, under his direction, sent to Eastern Finland, where disturbances had occurred near the Russian boundary. A certain district was occupied by the Swedes here and a fortress, Viborg, was built. Some years later Torgils led a considerable Swedish force to the region situated near the mouth of the river Neva, where a second fortress, Landskrona, was erected. Soon the Russians made an attack, with the result that the Swedes lost practically all their recent gains in this section. Their losses were later retrieved and more territory gained, so that Swedish suzerainty was acknowledged over the greater part of Finland. Not by force alone, but by a liberal and humane policy, giving the people practically the same privileges the Swedes themselves enjoyed under their laws, was Finland bound to Sweden by strong ties. Evil days came when the king's brothers, jealous of Torgils' influence, poisoned Birger's mind with base insinuations against him. Foolishly believing, or pretending to believe, the outrageous charges against the aged statesman, Birger caused his arrest and later permitted a decree of death against him to be carried out. Birger's brothers also involved Sweden in a series of disputes with the kings of Norway and Denmark. The dismal period ended in 1319 with the election of Magnus Eriksson, grandson of Magnus Ladulås, to the throne. His mother was the only daughter of the Norwegian king, Håkan Hålägg, who died just prior to the election of Magnus in Sweden. By hereditary right he was, therefore, also King of Norway.

Chapter VI

MONARCHY AT WAR WITH ENEMIES ABROAD AND AT HOME: MAGNUS ERIKSSON

Magnus Eriksson was a mere child when Fate placed the royal sceptres of both Sweden and Norway in his hands. In Sweden the Royal Council and the steward, Matts Kettilmundsson, were therefore vested with power to govern during the king's minority. Prior to Magnus's election by the Swedes, the relations between their country and Norway under a joint king had been defined by the Agreement of Oslo, which stipulated that the two countries should be governed by their respective councils until the king reached the age of maturity. He should first be brought to Norway for a year's stay, and thereafter his time was to be divided equally between the two countries; the retainers and councillors of one country should accompany him only as far as the boundary of the other; this stipulation was, however, modified to the extent that those Norwegians who desired to serve Magnus also in Sweden or wished to serve his mother, should have a right to enter this land. Mutual distrust had evidently struck deep roots already in both nations.

Many of the older historians looked upon the Oslo agreement as some sort of act of union, the first definite step towards the merging of the two countries, but it is evident that it had no such purpose. It was merely an arrangement whereby the two councils should be bound to a definite course during the king's minority; it was not intended to be binding upon him after he had ascended the throne. The signers of the Oslo agreement, representing both countries, evidently did not touch upon the question of the king's status as joint ruler of the two countries, or upon the mutual relations of these after he had reached the age of maturity.

Dazzling prospects of the young king.—The prospects before the young king seemed dazzling indeed; in possession of the crowns of both Norway and Sweden, and placed in a most advantageous position for eventually bringing the two countries together in a firm union; with Denmark in what seemed a state of hopeless dissolution and thus with fair prospects that at least parts of that country would be added to his wide domains; such were the brilliant possibilities which appeared to lie before this boy, whom, it seemed, Fortune had favoured above other mortals. Few individuals have, however, as did Magnus, in a long life filled with bitter strife and grievous disappointments, learned through experience that Dame Fortune is indeed a fickle lady. He grew to be an honourable and well-meaning man, but he did not have the acumen nor the power of decision to cope with the tremendous difficulties which rose in his way. It was his great misfortune, too, that practically during all of his life he was compelled to contend against two of the most skilful, as well as unscrupulous, men of his generation, Valdemar Atterdag of Denmark and Albrecht of Mecklenburg, and that he found opposed to him in Sweden a group of utterly selfish and ambitious lords, who at all times were ready to follow a "rule or ruin" policy.

The Council of Regency tries to safeguard Sweden's interests.—As the Swedish Royal Council was aristocratic in its composition and policies, its position as a Council of Regency during the king's minority naturally meant a further strengthening of the nobility, with consequent encroachment, on the one hand, upon the rights of the people, and upon royal authority on the other. The Council was, however, at first made up of high grade and, for the most part, patriotic men, and its first acts revealed a firm determination to safeguard the interests of the country. Thus the treaty of Nöteborg was concluded with the grand-duchy of Novgorod in 1323, the first political agreement with the Russians; by its terms the eastern boundaries were fixed. The Council also acted with commendable firmness and great wisdom in checkmating the ambitious and intriguing Duchess Ingeborg, mother of Magnus, who in some respects was a remarkable woman, "married at twelve, a mother at fifteen, and a widow at seventeen," but her reckless schemes threatened to involve Sweden in serious trouble. After the death of her husband she had cut quite a wide swath in her native Norway and was determined not to be brushed aside in Sweden. Here she became the leader of a group of reckless and unscrupulous men, the most notorious among them being a Danish nobleman, Knut Porse, whom she later married; soon she was travelling a path that led straight towards treason and insurrection. She first concluded a treaty in behalf of Magnus with Henry the Lion of Mecklenburg, a bitter enemy of Denmark, by the terms of which the German prince was to furnish her with military aid for an invasion of Skåne, which was to be detached from Denmark and added to Sweden. The duchess also gave her daughter Euphemia in marriage to Albrecht, the son of Henry, a union which, as the sequel will show, was destined to have a far-reaching and most unfortunate bearing upon Swedish affairs. The Swedish Council was, however, determined to maintain friendly relations with Denmark and disapproved of the mischief-breeding plots of Ingeborg and Porse, and as a result civil war broke out in the country, which ended with a compromise, according to which the duchess gave up most of her possessions. With that Ingeborg and Porse disappeared from the scene. Other acts are also recorded to the credit of the Regency. The privileges of the Church were not extended and the transfer of further grants to her was limited by restrictions and subjected to careful supervision; the temporal lords, although receiving friendly treatment, were brought under new restrictions, especially in regard to the size of their retinues; a special commission was established to guard against illegal tax exemptions. One patriotic scheme promoted by the Council deserves special mention, since it seemed modern in conception and purpose; it aimed at the colonization of the fertile parts of the country along the Gulf of Bothnia. Here a large area was opened to settlement and land was made free to whosoever was willing to cultivate it, and settlers on these lands were granted exemption from taxes during the king's minority.

Magnus becomes king.—Magnus was declared of age when he was sixteen (1332). Three years later he married the beautiful and sensible Blanche of Namur, against whom the bitter enemies of the royal couple in a later period did not hesitate to make the most cruel and unjust charges. The young king came to the helm with very definite convictions regarding the power and prestige that should belong to royalty. The glorious times of his grandfather, Magnus Ladulås, and of his great-grandfather, Birger Jarl, must have served to stir his imagination and fill his mind with the determination to be a great ruler; the age, too, in which he lived saw a strengthening of royal power in many parts of Europe, and Magnus was by no means insensible to these influences. According to Swedish custom, the king, soon after becoming of age, went on his royal journey (*Eriksgata*) through the different provinces to receive the oath of fealty of his subjects after he himself had sworn to abide by the ancient laws of the land. The most important provision of his royal charter abolished the last vestige of slavery in Sweden (1335). The institution had, in fact, become most uncommon towards the end of the thirteenth century. In Norway and Iceland it had disappeared at even an earlier date. It should be noted, too, that contrary to the situation in other lands, the abolition of slavery was not followed in Sweden by bondage (serfdom).

The beginning of Magnus Eriksson's troubles.—Magnus was soon to discover that although his position seemed glorious enough, it was indeed extremely perilous, and that troubles were piling up before him on the path which he had set out to travel. Financial troubles were a chronic affliction of his reign. He found as soon as he assumed charge of affairs that the Council of Regency had saddled a heavy debt upon the country through loans with which to pay the indemnities to Ingeborg and her unworthy friends in return for their strongholds. More serious still were the obligations assumed by the king in regard to Skåne. In the period of confusion through which Denmark had just passed, this province, one of the richest parts of Denmark at the time, had come under the control of Count John of Holstein, against whose shameful rule the people of Skåne soon rose in rebellion. Realizing that, unaided, they would be unable to defend themselves against Holstein, they had invoked the assistance of Magnus. The suspicion that the Swedes had themselves encouraged them to make this appeal is not entirely without foundation. Be that as it may, Magnus promised to send aid to the people of Skåne, whereupon Count John, forseeing the difficulty of holding the province for himself, and without giving any thought to Denmark's rights in the matter, sold not only Skåne but the neighbouring province, Blekinge, to Magnus for 34,000 silver marks (approximately 1,150,000 crowns, according to present money standards), to be paid in instalments.

Even if the sale of the provinces had been a perfectly legitimate transaction, the great sum involved would have caused serious embarrassment to Magnus; the fact that he was trading in stolen property naturally made the situation worse for him. As Sweden was already heavily in debt and royal incomes in those days, when payments were generally made in kind, were exceedingly meagre and uncertain, the king soon found himself in desperate financial straits and was compelled to resort to the dangerous expedient of borrowing great sums from the Church and laying heavy taxes on the *bönder*. At this critical juncture another factor enters to add grievously to Magnus's troubles; Valdemar Atterdag had become King of Denmark. After forty years of chaos in the land, this sagacious and unscrupulous man had seized power and established order, and the Danes could again see light; hence the appellation which they gave the ruler, *Atterdag* (day again). Valdemar was naturally determined that his kingdom should remain intact. He therefore had no intention of relinquishing any claims to Skåne and Blekinge, but troubles with enemies at home compelled him to postpone action against Sweden in order to get possession of the province again. As a preliminary step to a contemplated action against Magnus, Valdemar secured the support of the shifty Duke of Mecklenburg, brother-in-law of Magnus, and made certain trade concessions to the powerful north German cities in order to assure himself of their assistance when needed. Magnus countered by granting certain concessions to the Dutch, and neither king overlooked the advantage which might come from papal sanction of their respective claims; the Pope, however, had nothing to gain in this affair and cleverly dodged the issue. In order to gain further time and arrive at a more opportune moment for action, Valdemar next made a compact with Magnus by which he sanctioned the transfer of the provinces to Sweden. The respite given him by this agreement Magnus devoted to affairs in Norway. In 1343 he arranged that his younger son, Håkan, should become King of Norway as soon as he had reached the age of maturity. As his elder son, Erik, was in the next year elected to be Magnus's successor in Sweden, the union of the two countries was thus headed for dissolution. With an array of enemies against him, like Valdemar, Duke of Mecklenburg, his own Swedish lords, and many Swedish ecclesiastics, Magnus was sorely embarrassed. Now another person began a bitter attack upon him. This was the pious lady, St. Birgitta. Just what the king's standards of morality were is not known, but it is very evident from the charges which St. Birgitta made against him that they fell far short of her ideals. St. Birgitta had many good intentions, and through her monastic order and endeavors to increase sobriety and piety among Christians, she accomplished great good, but it is quite evident that she was most ambitious, passionate, and partial, and so her strictures on King Magnus cannot be taken very seriously. St. Birgitta spent much time in Rome and it is likely that she did not stand entirely aloof from the influences which at last added the Pope to the list of Magnus's numerous enemies.

The Black Death.—It was in the reign of Magnus that the frightful scourge, the Black Death, swept over Europe and took its terrible toll of life. It was brought to the North by an English ship, which sailors had found drifting about without a crew outside of Bergen in Norway and had brought into port. Its cargo was unloaded, but soon those who had been on board were stricken with the dread disease. From Norway it soon reached Sweden, and it is estimated that here one-third of the population became its grim toll. So fearful were its ravages that entire districts were left without a living soul. As a ghastly example of the thoroughness with which the plague depopulated the land, may be cited the tale of a hunter who, generations afterwards, while on a hunting trip, happened to shoot his arrow into a thicket. On going to pick it up, he discovered the moss-covered stone walls of an old church which after the desolation of the plague had become entirely forgotten and in time overgrown by weeds and trees. In the province of Uppland only one-sixth of the population remained after the scourge had passed and in a parish of Värmland only three persons survived. In Västergötland about four hundred and fifty priests succumbed to the disease. Magnus had taken whatever precautions were in those days believed effective against pestilences; he had ordered his subjects, "men, women, and children, to come barefooted to the parish church, confess their sins, march in procession around the church, hear mass, and lay their gifts to the poor on the altar." By thus bringing the people together, he simply helped to spread the disease.

Evil plans of the lords.—The blow which his bitter and unscrupulous enemies had long been ready to deliver soon fell upon the sorely afflicted king. Not only the *bönder,* but the lords and clergy, were bitter against him because of the heavy taxes he had been compelled to levy. The dissatisfied elements had found a tool ready to their purpose in the king's eldest son, Erik, who now raised the standard of revolt against his father. In the settlement regarding the royal succession in Norway he had been passed by in favour of his younger brother; in Sweden also he had been left without a part in the government, and this had, it seems, made him bitter. His own excuse for starting the revolt was his father's alleged subserviency to evil councillors, especially to one Bengt Algotsson. The latter, it seems, was in fact a man of noble descent and great ability. He had impressed the king that justice and necessity demanded an effective check upon the nobility and the clergy, and it was perhaps his influence which had induced Magnus in 1352 to revoke all grants to churches, decree that all ecclesiastical property was subject to taxation, and take measures for checking the further transfer of taxable lands to the nobility. This was a challenge which the lords, especially, were not slow to accept. The disgruntled Erik now came handy to their purpose. The favourable moment for the contemplated revolt seemed to have arrived in 1356, when the Pope joined the ranks of Magnus's opponents. In his desperate financial plight, Magnus had some years before secured some good-sized loans from the Roman Curia, and when payments were not made on time the Pope sent insistent demands for liquidation. Possibly Valdemar, who naturally watched the increasing perplexities of the Swedish king with genuine satisfaction, did not stand entirely outside the intrigues which in many places were going on against Magnus; that he had given gratuitous advice to Erik is certain. With so formidable an alliance against him, Magnus was soon compelled to yield on every point. About half of his kingdom was ceded to Erik and fortified places in the territory which was to remain under Magnus should never, it was stipulated, be given as fiefs to any one but him or his sons. The area ceded to Erik became virtually an independent kingdom. The settlement denoted a decisive victory for the lords. Having begun to yield, Magnus was soon forced to make new concessions, and his position became more hopeless still when in 1358 a papal bull of excommunication was issued against him.

Relations to Valdemar of Denmark.—The king and queen now made a strange and unexpected move; they visited Valdemar at Copenhagen and here a new alliance was concluded. One of its provisions stipulated that Håkan, son of Magnus and Blanche, was to marry Valdemar's daughter, Margaret. As the sequel will show, this stipulation was to have a momentous bearing upon the Scandinavian North for several centuries. Valdemar now, on behalf of his new ally, invaded Skåne and regained a large part of it, but then he turned back in anger because the stipulated compensation was not forthcoming. Magnus again made a shift and reached an accord with his rebellious son, Erik; father and son were now united in a common purpose to restore the unity of Sweden. Two weeks later Erik was stricken with the plague, thus cruelly dashing to the ground all the hopes which Magnus had built upon this alliance. At the request of the Council, the king in 1359 issued a call for a general assembly to consider the deplorable conditions which existed in the country. This was to meet at Kalmar, and besides the nobility and the clergy there should also be sent "representatives from the cities and four *bönder* from each lawman's district." The inclusion of the commons has been praised as a feature of genuine statesmanship, as a means for the king to meet the opposition of the nobles. This is, however, exaggerated; the step is more likely to have been a mere attempt to enhance the representative and solemn character of the meeting, which was finally held, though not in Kalmar but in Söderköping. To the keen disappointment of Valdemar, to whom nothing could be more welcome than civil war in Sweden, a complete accord was, outwardly at least, reached by Magnus and the nobles. The time had now come for the Danish king to act vigorously, and with consummate skill he drew to his side the support of all those who had a grudge against the Swedish king. He found that Duke Albrecht of Mecklenburg was quite willing to betray his Swedish brother-in-law. In 1360 Valdemar was ready to take military action, but of this there was no need, for his skilful intrigues achieved his purpose without resort to arms. Not aware of Duke Albrecht's treachery, Magnus appointed him one of the arbitrators to decide the matters at issue between the two kings. The Swedish king was now induced, by deception or strong persuasion, to surrender the important stronghold, Hälsingborg; as a result Skåne passed into Valdemar's hands and for three hundred years more the province was to remain Danish.

Valdemar's attack on Visby.—Valdemar was now ready to strike another blow at Sweden. The city of Visby had become the chief commercial mart of the North and here enormous wealth, according to the standards of the day, had been accumulated. Thirteen ruins of stately Gothic temples today bear witness to the city's former opulence and splendour. If he had possession of this stronghold, Valdemar could advance a long step farther towards his real goal, Danish control of the Baltic; Sweden herself would then be compelled to yield to Danish power. An attack upon the strong-walled city was therefore resolved upon and this was made suddenly so that the unfortunate inhabitants had little chance to organize their defence. Many of them lost their lives defending the city, others failed afterwards to locate the treasures which they had hastened to conceal before the attack, and this circumstance accounts partly for the great hoard of coins and other valuables which in our day have been unearthed in or near Visby. The city fell into Valdemar's hands and was compelled to pay an enormous ransom. From this blow the city never fully recovered. In attacking and plundering Visby, Valdemar had, however, struck a blow not merely at Sweden, but at the Hanseatic League which was a more formidable foe. An alliance between Sweden and the League was the natural outcome of the overt act. The representatives of Magnus overstepped their authority, however, and made guarantees to the League which, if complied with, would have placed Sweden's industrial and political independence in jeopardy. The king therefore felt compelled to repudiate them. The Swedish nobles who were responsible for these dangerous concessions took great umbrage at this and chose his son, Håkan, who had been elected King of Norway, to become King of Sweden also. Håkan soon perceived, however, that the lords were merely intent upon securing power for themselves in order that they might exploit the land more ruthlessly, and he hastened therefore to make peace with his father. The alliance with the Hanseatic League failed to give the promised help; the war against Valdemar was unsuccessful.

Alliance of Magnus and Valdemar.—Magnus now gave another exhibition of his ability in shifting position; he again visited Valdemar in Copenhagen and made a new alliance with him, which was further cemented by the marriage of Håkan and Margaret. Magnus now proceeded vigorously against the lords and harried some of them out of the country. No compromise was any longer possible, and rather than yield the lords took a most fateful step which shows how desperately determined they were that the king should not get the upper hand.

The lords offer the crown to Albrecht of Mecklenburg.—They offered the crown to Albrecht of Mecklenburg, a youth of twenty and son of the intriguing self-seeker, Duke Albrecht, whose treachery had prevented Magnus from acquiring Blekinge and Skåne. The dire consequences of Ingeborg's unfortunate intrigues in 1321 now manifested themselves. The selection of his son served well the purposes of the crafty old mischief-maker, Duke Albrecht. The possibility of Valdemar's intervention in behalf of Magnus was practically the only contingency which the lords had to fear, but the Danish king blandly announced to the world that he was preparing to go on an extended trip abroad. In the struggle which ensued between Magnus and the Mecklenburgers, in alliance with the Swedish lords, the king was defeated and taken prisoner. Albrecht now began to exercise the power of king. The success of the campaign in his behalf had as a further consequence that a great number of Germans came into the land who seem to have expected complete control there before long. The *bönder* sympathized with Magnus, and this was particularly true of those living in Västergötland, but neither he nor Håkan understood, as did Engelbrekt, Sten Sture the Younger, and Gustavus Vasa later, how to arouse and organize the common people in defence of the nation and its ancient rights. Håkan next tried to secure his father's release by enlisting the aid of Valdemar, who had returned from his foreign journey. A new agreement for joint action was made and with combined forces Håkan and Valdemar invaded Sweden. They met with complete success at every point, but instead of helping his ally, Valdemar now treacherously concluded the treaty of Ålholm (1366) with Duke Albrecht for the dismemberment of Sweden. This was undoubtedly the blackest in the long list of Valdemar's acts of duplicity. He was to have all of Gottland, including Visby, considerable parts of the Swedish territory on the west coast, with the stronghold of Älvsborg, "and besides all the forts and fiefs which had been in his possession on Whitsunday the same year."

Ambitious plans of Mecklenburgers.—The heinousness of these terms did not bother the duke, who showed great solicitude for his son. Another of his sons, Henry, was married to Valdemar's eldest daughter, Ingeborg, and thus it seemed likely that Denmark would later, as Sweden was now, become a Mecklenburg possession. It therefore mattered little to him just then what was Swedish and what Danish territory. Duke Albrecht next came to Sweden in order to get the acquiescence of the Swedish lords to the shameful agreement, but he was not long in discovering that while these could go far in sacrificing national interests for their own advantage they were absolutely set against his and Valdemar's scheme for the dismemberment of their country. Instead of acquiescing, they forced the duke to join with the Hanseatic League in a new aggressive action against Valdemar. Their combined strength compelled Valdemar to confirm the League in its trade monopoly in Denmark, but after this point had been gained and the German merchants could proceed to pluck the fruits of their victory, Sweden and Mecklenburg were left to their own devices; it was no more to the advantage of the German merchants to have a strong Sweden than a strong Denmark in the North.

Opposition to Albrecht.—Albrecht of Mecklenburg's position as king was, from the first, encompassed by danger. With the connivance of the lords, the Germans had secured important strongholds or fiefs in all parts of Sweden, but when these foreigners straightway proceeded to put into force the principles of servitude common to their own country, but utterly abhorrent and foreign to the Swedes, the anger of the common people became intense and a great national uprising, supported by a new attack by Håkan, began to brew. In this extremity Albrecht was forced by the lords to issue a royal charter (1371), the first of its kind in Swedish history. In this Albrecht surrendered practically all power to the nobles. The charter specified that all forts were to be placed in the hands of the Council, which was to have the sole power in the appointment of new members, and in all things the king was to abide by its advice. No doubt the German king made a wry face when he signed the provisions, "the Council shall with the advice of the king appoint only native men as commanders to the castles and forts," and "with implicit faith I entrust myself to the Council, with castles and lands." The principle here laid down by the lords that only native men should be favoured by appointments was henceforth to play an important part in the affairs of Sweden; over it some of the hottest contests raged, and it was the one point upon which the great mass of Swedes, with stubborn determination, stood firm.

Magnus was released from his prison after paying a huge ransom, and followed his son to Norway, where his tempestuous career came to an end in 1374 when he perished in a shipwreck. Both in Sweden and Norway his memory lived among the *bönder* as "the honest and good King Magnus." It had been his fatal misfortune that he lacked ability to cope with and surmount the tremendous difficulties which a combination of circumstances constantly piled in his way.

The crafty plotters, Duke Albrecht and Valdemar, once again indulged in their clever play of politics. In 1371 an agreement was reached between them, according to which Albrecht relinquished all the territory which he held in Denmark in return for Valdemar's pledge that in the event of his death without a male heir the Danish crown should go to Duke Albrecht the Younger, grandson of the duke. The prospects thus became appreciably brighter for the ambitious house of Mecklenburg to secure possession of Denmark, as it had already secured Sweden. When Valdemar died in 1375, Duke Albrecht made haste to claim the Danish throne for his son, but for the first time another personality here entered with decisive force and talent—a personality that was to thwart all the clever schemes of Mecklenburgers and Swedish lords alike and give a new direction to the course of Scandinavian affairs. This interesting individual was Margaret, the second daughter of Valdemar and the wife of King Håkan of Norway. With consummate skill she handled the complicated situation in Denmark so that her only son in her marriage with Håkan, Olof, was elected king there, thus thwarting the Mecklenburg plans completely. An attempt by the duke to secure the assistance of the Swedish lords against her to dislodge her met with no success; some years later he died. When Håkan died, Olof was proclaimed king in Norway, and after his premature death in 1387 Margaret was able to induce the leading men of both Denmark and Norway to elect her as regent.

A lord in his glory; Bo Jonsson Grip.—Meanwhile young Albrecht was finding his rôle as King of Sweden most distressing and humiliating. The real ruler of the land was Bo Jonsson Grip, a Swedish nobleman of boundless ambition and unusual energy, who had an insatiable desire for offices and landed estates. His most important office was that of steward, and the number of estates to which he finally secured title has been estimated at more than two thousand. To none of these did the king's authority extend to collect taxes or maintain order. But while Bo Jonsson had been a leader in the insurrection which had brought Albrecht into the land, he feared the effects of the influx of Germans into the land. Bo Jonsson was a Swedish patriot to the extent at least that he wanted native men to have control in the land. Albrecht fumed and fretted, but dared not make a move against his powerful subject. When, however, Bo Jonsson in 1386 went the way of all flesh, the king thought the time for self-assertion had arrived, especially as the dead statesman's last will and testament had proved to be a direct challenge to the German king—Bo Jonsson's fiefs and his entire estate were left for administration to a group of prominent men from which Albrecht and his German henchmen were carefully and completely excluded. The king cited all those named by Bo Jonsson as executives of his property to appear before him and show satisfactory evidence of their competence in the matter. This most unusual display of energy came as both a surprise and a challenge to the executors, as well as the Swedish lords, who felt their entire class threatened. They were not slow to accept the challenge.

Margaret offered the crown.—A civil war broke out, and when the king began to gain ground the lords, rather than yield, offered the crown to Margaret of Denmark. In so doing, they made concessions to her which certainly went as far as Albrecht ever had asked. Their fear of the growing power of the Germans, and hope that Margaret would have enough to do in Denmark and Norway, no doubt explains this action. They, no doubt, reasoned that Margaret was merely a woman who could be easily controlled, and furthermore she was young and, besides, a foreigner; she might be expected to stay away from Sweden, leaving the lords to rule according to their own pleasure. This reasoning proved entirely wrong, as will appear later. The Swedish offer fitted nicely into Margaret's plans. Practically all the royal forests and castles which the nobles controlled were surrendered to her and she in turn pledged herself to rule Sweden according to Swedish law. Albrecht now proceeded to Mecklenburg to muster an army, and soon returned with a large German force. Margaret accompanied her forces in Sweden, but the actual military leadership did not rest in her hands. According to a mediæval Danish ballad, Albrecht took pains to show his contempt for his feminine antagonist by calling her "king trouserless," and sending her a whetstone a yard long with the advice that she had better use it for sharpening her sewing needles and scissors; included among his gifts was a coarse banner of homespun cloth. The decisive battle between the two was fought near Falköping in the year 1389.

Margaret's army was made up of Swedes, Danes, and Norwegians, while Albrecht's army was made up chiefly of Germans. After a fierce struggle, Albrecht's army was routed, the king himself being taken prisoner.

Society during the period of the Folkung kings.—The process of consolidation under a common king had, by the beginning of the fourteenth century, resulted in the partial obliteration of the former provincial lines and the idea of Sweden as a nation had become clearer and more potent. Whereas the provincial divisions partly disappeared, social differentiations became more pronounced in this period. The old equality disappeared with the creation of secular and spiritual lords whose privileges enabled them constantly to widen the gulf which separated them from the common people. A new class also appeared; namely, the merchants in the cities, which now gained considerable importance and strength through growth of trade and development of industry. This was the burgher class and consisted mainly of Germans, who came by invitation of the rulers to help in the development of the resources of the country or were otherwise attracted to it by the opportunities it offered to the trader and the skilled workman. The language itself received a considerable addition of German words. A legal document of 1297 was signed on behalf of the city of Stockholm by a mayor who was German and by ten of the leading citizens of whom perhaps only one was a Swede. Birger Jarl had especially encouraged emigration from Germany, as he felt that only in this way could skilled workmen and able traders be procured, but he evidently hoped that the newcomers would be speedily nationalized. Towards the end of the period, emigration from Germany increased and alarm evidently began to be felt that the foreigners would secure a preponderance of power and influence. This feeling is revealed in the provision of the city law of Magnus Eriksson that not more than half of the mayors and councillors in the cities might be Germans. These provisions were largely ineffective, however, and towards the end of the period it appeared probable that Visby, Kalmar, and Stockholm would become independent of Sweden and organize themselves as German commercial cities under Hanseatic leadership. Ultimately the German element became thoroughly amalgamated with the Swedish people, but only after a hard struggle which extended far into the next period. While for a long time constituting a menace to the unity of Sweden, it must be said that the German element played a very important part in the economic development of the country.

Town and country.—While a new class was formed, another one, the slaves, disappeared entirely in this period. Social differentiations were increased by the organization of guilds; these naturally followed the development of industry and were an innovation introduced by the Germans. With the new industrial order came also restrictions upon trade. Prior to this the *bönder* had often had the right to trade, usually in the products of their own fields, as a side line, but by a series of royal orders this privilege was now taken away from them and all trade confined to the cities. The government of the cities usually consisted of six mayors and thirty councillors. The royal bailiff represented the king in the city government and looked after his interests. As the population of the country was small —estimated at about 315,000 persons after the terrible ravages of the Black Death—and mainly rural, there was no city of any considerable size. By far the most important was Visby, which derived its importance from its strategic position with reference to the trade between Russia and the east Baltic lands and the Scandinavian countries.

Government.—The national government also underwent considerable changes in this period. At first the kings held their power both by virtue of heredity and right of election, a choice being made by the people, at the "stone" of Mora, in Uppland, the selection being confined to members of royal families, but gradually the principle of election became the more important factor in the choice of rulers. This development took place in spite of energetic efforts of kings to make the royal dignity hereditary in their own family. The growing influence of the aristocracy and of the Church, both institutions naturally profiting by the elective principle, of course ran contrary to the king's wishes and thwarted their efforts. Many of the evils which came to plague the country had their source in the success of the secular and spiritual lords in maintaining their right to elect kings.

As the different provinces were consolidated under a common king, the latter naturally took over many of the duties and responsibilities which before had belonged to the rulers of the separate districts and hence the need of added subordinate officials and of a more complete government organization came to be felt. The conscientious ruler who really wished to govern well was compelled to travel almost incessantly from place to place in his wide domains to supervise the administration of his subordinates and confer with leaders and communities of the various districts, but even with the best of intentions and though endowed with great physical strength, he must leave most of the work undone, or entrust it to others. As one consequence of this situation, two new officials appear; namely, the steward and the marshal. At first these officials stood next to the king in power and dignity, but in the beginning the powers and functions of the two offices were not clearly differentiated. They had charge of the royal castles and fortresses, collected revenues from the royal estates, and supervised the administration of justice. Their power naturally depended largely upon the character and ability of the incumbents. Strong and aggressive rulers sometimes preferred to get along without either of these officials or they made merely temporary appointments. The king had, however, a great many other officials, such as captains of the fortresses and subordinate and local bailiffs or sheriffs. The powers of the first-named grew vastly when they received their domains as fiefs, and in the same degree they became increasingly independent and ready, on occasion, to defy the king.

The old Things, or assemblies, whose functions were partly judicial and partly legislative, still met at fairly regular intervals, but they lost more and more of their old importance in legislation. If the king wished to ascertain the opinions of the lords on different questions, he used to summon them to diets representative either of a province or of the whole realm. As has been seen, the ruler came in time to confer more confidentially or in detail with a smaller group of men, who became known as the King's Council (p. 206). The archbishop, several bishops, and even other ecclesiastics, the chief officers of the king, a few lawmen, and a certain number of lords generally made up this branch of the government which in time was to attain to power inferior only to that wielded by the king, and sometimes transcending his. From the time of Magnus Eriksson the King's Council was generally known as the National (or Swedish) Council.

The provincial laws.—Since early times every Swedish province had its own district laws, but these were merely a collection of customs and precedents, often expressed in the pithy form of maxims. They did not exist in writing, but were handed down from generation to generation by oral tradition. Special dignity and influence devolved upon the lawmen because they, above all other men, remembered precedents and rules and could quote them as occasion arose at the Things. Through the influence largely of the canonical law of the Church, these laws were in the thirteenth century brought into more systematic order and reduced to writing. Provisions that no longer had any meaning because of changed conditions were eliminated; thus the ones bearing upon the cult of the old pagan religion could now be excluded. The eldest and best known of these provincial codes is that of Västergötland, which appeared complete in written form at the end of the thirteenth century. The principal labour connected with its codification was done by the lawmen of the province, Eskil, brother of Birger Jarl, in the period 1215-1227. The law is very specific in its provisions and couched in quaint and vigorous language. The law of Uppland, codified at the end of the thirteenth century, contained a more modern legal conception than the law of Västergötland or the other provincial laws. It came to have a great influence on later legal principles and practice. The law of Östergötland is also considered a masterpiece of legal literature. Of the law of Småland, from the end of the thirteenth century, only the part relating to the Church is extant. The law of Skåne exists in two editions, one in the vernacular and one in Latin. At first the kings evidently took no part in the revision of these laws or in the work of reducing them to writing, but Birger Jarl and his son, Magnus Ladulås, took consid-

A page from the Law of Västergötland. Thirteenth century

erable interest in the matter. From their time on, the king's sanction was supposed to be given to laws before they received binding force. This royal interest in the laws of the land culminated in the reign of Magnus Eriksson, when a commission was appointed by the king to codify a law the provisions of which should be binding upon all subjects in the different provinces of the country. The desire for such a common law sprang from the growing sense of solidarity in the nation and from the fact that the growing commerce of the country found itself greatly hampered by differences in the laws of the different sections. At the same time a common law for the whole country gave a strong impetus to the further amalgamation of the different provinces. The people no longer felt primarily as citizens of Västergötland, or Uppland, or of any other province, but as citizens of Sweden.

The law which was evolved by the aforesaid commission, known as Magnus Eriksson's common law, was built largely upon the codes of Östergötland and Uppland, and contains the usual present-day divisions of civil law and criminal law. Like early Germanic laws in general, it gives very minute provisions for penalties, which, in conformity with the spirit of the time, were exceedingly severe. The law provides that the king is to secure power by election and not through heredity. After prescribing that he shall love God and his Church, defend justice and punish wrong, deprive no one of life or property without due process of law, and rule the kingdom with native men and not foreigners, the law states specifically that the king shall levy no new tax, except in certain defined cases, especially when his country is attacked by a foreign foe; in such a case, a commission of every province, consisting of the bishop, six lords, and six of the common people shall decide what assistance shall be rendered him. After the king has taken this oath, he shall undertake his royal journey and, lastly, be crowned by the archbishop—"because of the dignity of both." [1]

The Church.—The zeal of her members, superiority in organization, and unity of leadership had given an influence to the Church at this time which made her servants equal in importance to any class in the land. Sweden had definitely been

[1] Schlyter, C. J., *Sveriges gamla lagar,* Lund, 1862, X.

made a part of the great ecclesiastical organization of the period, paid the stipulated revenues to the papacy, and granted special favours to the Church, but from the beginning the menace of the aggressive fiscal policy of the Church seems to have been understood in the land. Here efforts were made to check the policy of granting property to the Church and giving a privileged and unique status to her servants. Only to a limited degree were these efforts productive of results. The archbishop was elected by a consistory and the secular ruler was not supposed to interfere in his choice nor in the election of bishops. A tremendous difference had already come to exist in the grades and emoluments of the ecclesiastics. Thus while the lower clergy, as a rule, had to eke out their existence on a mere pittance, the higher clergy enjoyed princely incomes. It has been estimated that the Bishop of Linköping in 1282 enjoyed emoluments which in purchasing power as reckoned today amounted to more than 200,000 crowns.[2] The wealth and property of the Church increased enormously, her income in 1282 having been estimated at about 5,300,000 crowns, as reckoned by the purchasing value of coin money in that day.

St. Birgitta.—The most remarkable and famous individual in the spiritual and cultural life of Sweden in the Middle Ages was the aforementioned St. Birgitta, the first among her people to win European fame and the only Swede ever to be officially canonized by the Church. She was born in Uppland, probably in 1303, her family being one of the richest and most aristocratic in the land. Her professions of piety and her many good deeds to the contrary notwithstanding, she always was extremely dictatorial and vainglorious. At the early age of seven, she began to have visions in which Christ and the Holy Mother appeared and spoke to her. She was married at the age of thirteen to a man who, like herself, delighted in pious meditations. When her husband died in early manhood, Birgitta was filled with indescribable grief and heavenly visions now began to come to her with increasing frequency. These she told in her native tongue to her father confessor, who then wrote them in Latin. Thus, as Schück remarks, "the sickly brooding of a sorrowing widow gave the North its foremost saint." The pious

[2] Schück, *Svenska folkets historia*, I: 2, p. 112.

Birgitta now became filled with a burning desire to reform the wicked world, and she denounced King Magnus unmercifully because of his alleged iniquities. Even the Pope did not escape her castigations. Being desirous of founding a monastic order, St. Birgitta proceeded to Rome at the time when the Black Death was spreading over Europe and was taking its fearful

St. Birgitta receives a revelation. Painting in the Tolfta Church, Uppland

toll of lives in the southern and central parts of the Continent; she had no fear, however. At Rome she found the city in desolation. It was torn by factions, robbers infested the streets, and Christendom was disgraced by the spectacle of the Pope living a licentious life in France. Fearlessly she attacked the iniquity and had the satisfaction ultimately of seeing the successor of Peter visit the Holy City again. In 1370 a papal bull gave her the coveted permission to found a monastic order after the model of the order of St. Augustine. The first monastery of the new order was built at Vadstena and splendid gifts came to it from King Magnus and his queen, as well as from the prominent lords of the country. Life in the Birgittine cloisters was governed by very strict rules and the order undoubtedly exerted a profound and wholesome influence. Monasteries were ultimately built by the order in England, Germany, Poland, Netherlands, Norway, Denmark, Spain, and Italy. St. Birgitta saw the glory of the heavens, felt the all-conquering love of Christ, perceived the grandeur of a pure and spiritual life as against worldly-mindedness and sordidness, and her colourful and ecstatic descriptions of her experiences, as given in her *Revelations*, appealed to all Europe. They have been either wholly or partly translated into most of the European tongues, and even into Arabic. The pious woman died in Rome in 1373 and the folowing year her earthly remains were brought to Vadstena for their final resting-place.

Chapter VII

THE MEDIÆVAL SCANDINAVIAN UNION WHICH FAILED

Margaret of Denmark was, as before intimated, one of the most remarkable personalities to appear in the Scandinavian North during the entire mediæval period. Her ability to curb opposing wills and lead or force them into channels along with her own rested upon a combination of qualities, such as sagacity, resourcefulness, and courage, that amounted to genius. Born in 1353, the youngest child of Valdemar Atterdag and Helwig of Sönderjylland (a Danish duchy) she had at the age of six been betrothed by her parents to Håkan of Norway, and their marriage had been solemnized when she was ten. Brought to Norway at the age of thirteen, she had for a time been under the tutelage of one of St. Birgitta's daughters. Her only child, Olof, was born in 1370. After the death of her father in 1375 she succeeded, as already told, in thwarting the well-laid plans of Albrecht of Mecklenburg, by which this crafty prince sought to acquire Denmark for his grandson, and induced the Danes to elect her infant son as their king. When her husband died five years later, Olof was proclaimed king (by hereditary right) in Norway also. As regent in the name of her son, Margaret now ruled both Denmark and Norway, and when the Swedish lords opened negotiations with her with a view to securing her help against King Albrecht, she had the satisfaction of seeing her plans for merging the three Scandinavian countries under one sceptre progress towards realization more rapidly than she at first had ever dared to hope. But just then a terrible tragedy, which in an instant seemed to shatter all her plans and hopes, fell upon her; the son around whose person all the ambitious and daring projects of her fertile mind had revolved, the prince of nobler birth, so it was said, than any of his European contemporaries, died suddenly in

1387. It was a terrible blow, for not only was the mother-heart stricken, but the very foundations upon which she had been rearing her splendid structure seemed all at once to have crumbled completely. The Mecklenburgers could now press their claim again and with better right than ever before. But Margaret was not one who for a moment would let personal grief paralyze her energy. Within a short time after Olof's death, she had induced the Danish Estates to pass a new act designating her regent of the land until such time as they should choose to elect a king. She then hastened to Norway where the situation involved greater difficulties, since in that country the principle of heredity in the royal succession was firmly established, but here, too, her influence soon overcame all hesitancy. After being elected regent of Norway, she was recognized by the Swedish opponents of Albrecht as "Sweden's plenipotent mistress and rightful master" (*Sveriges fullmäktiga fru och rätta husbonde*). After that she resolutely pursued her plans for making royal power secure in her own family. Such was her influence that, setting aside all other claims to the throne, Norway proclaimed her grand-nephew, Erik of Pomerania, king in 1389. As his duchy was an insignificant German state, this choice would cause no apprehension that the "balance of power" would be disturbed, and, since Erik was a mere boy, Margaret could assure the Norwegians that he would receive a purely Norwegian-Danish education. Both Sweden and Denmark a few years later followed Norway's example by electing Erik to be their king. After the battle of Falköping, the adherents of Albrecht continued for several years to defy Margaret. Stockholm was in their hands and refused to open its gates; Visby also fell into their power and became the rendezvous of pirates who swept up and down the Baltic, driving peaceful commerce everywhere from its waters. Not until 1398 did Stockholm yield to the inevitable and join the rest of the country in acknowledging Margaret as ruler.

Margaret's union plans; the Kalmar agreement.—Just what Margaret's plans were for the government and future status of the three Scandinavian countries under one sceptre is not clear, but she was evidently anxious to work out some scheme of union with as little delay as possible which would receive the sanction of the three kingdoms. Representatives of Sweden, Denmark, and Norway were therefore summoned to meet at Kalmar, a fortified town in the southeastern part of Sweden, in June 1397, to witness the coronation of Erik and confer on the question of joint rule. The result of the deliberations of a special committee was the submission to the assembly of the remarkable act of union, the original of which is still in existence and kept in the Royal Records Office in Copenhagen. Its main provisions were: 1. The three countries shall always live in peace with one another, and in all future times have the same king; 2. When a king dies, leaving sons, then one of these shall be elected his successor, but if a king dies childless then the worthiest man shall be elected; 3. If one of the three countries must wage a defensive war, the other two shall give it aid; 4. Negotiations with foreign powers shall be conducted by the king in consultation with the councillors present where he happens to be sojourning; 5. Each country shall be governed by its own laws and no law or right shall be transferred by the ruler from one country to the other; 6. An outlaw in one country shall not find refuge in any of the other two. Historians have seen in this document an evidence of a clearly conceived and far-reaching plan of Margaret and her advisers for bringing about a political union of three countries, and their ultimate amalgamation into one large political entity. Such an idea was by no means new, and the possibility for its realization, although remote, was not a merely fantastic dream. Canute the Great had no doubt harboured similar plans in his mind for a Scandinavian union, and this idea had, it may safely be surmised, stirred the minds of many in the days of Magnus Eriksson and Valdemar. War with non-Scandinavian peoples could not be avoided, but the wrangling, the warfare, and the bitter hatreds between the Scandinavian countries undoubtedly seemed to many utterly senseless and unnecessary. The feelings of the *bönder,* as they had been voiced by Thorgny Lagman, may here be called to mind. The serious dangers which threatened the Scandinavian states jointly from the jealousy and encroachments of the Hanseatic League, Mecklenburg, Holstein, and the Slavic tribes no doubt served at this time to arouse alarm and quicken a desire for unity in the North.

Was a permanent amalgamation possible?—Whatever Margaret's and her advisers' sentiments and intentions may have been, and no matter how external conditions favoured the project of a Scandinavian union, the obstacles in the way were, after all, well-nigh insurmountable. On the physical side was the huge dimensions of a state embracing all Scandinavia. The combined area would have been almost 450,000 square miles, aside from the Norwegian colonial possessions, or more than double that of present-day France; with the means of travel, as they existed in that generation, communication between the centre and the periphery would have been almost impossible. Denmark would naturally have been the leading state in this large empire, partly because she had taken the initiative and had, for a time at least, real statesmanship at the helm, partly because she was nearer to the Continent than Norway and Sweden, and hence was more closely in touch with its culture; her supremacy would, however, have rested chiefly on the fact that she had a population approximately equal to that of the other two countries combined (estimated for Denmark at 750,000, for Sweden at 450,000, and for Norway at 250,000). That the differentiation in language, customs, and law had already proceeded so far at this time that it formed an insuperable obstacle to a merging of the three peoples into one, can hardly be believed. The people of Skåne became thoroughly identified in language and political thought with the rest of the Swedish nation as late as the latter half of the seventeenth century, although, up to that time, they had been a part of the Danish nation (p. 431). Some writers have also cited the merging of the Svear and the Götar in the early centuries as an analogous case, but no doubt the amalgamation process could be far more rapid and easy at that early time before the national languages and institutions had assumed very fixed forms.

Margaret's attitude towards the Kalmar agreement.—The Kalmar union document was merely a sort of preliminary draft and it was intended that copies should be made and sent to the three countries for ratification, but this was never done. Something happened at the meeting which evidently was contrary to Margaret's wishes, but just what it was may only be surmised. The draft, as formulated, should have carried seventeen signatures, but only seven Swedes and three Danes actually affixed their names to it. The queen herself seems to have lost interest in the document and its provisions as soon as the meeting adjourned. The probability is that its assertion of such special national interest as the right of each country to be governed by its own separate laws and the provisions for an elective monarchy were sorely distasteful to her. As she perceived that national differences and interests could not be submerged by mutual agreement, she decided to gain her end by the more direct method of vigorous personal rule; in fact, she may have concluded that there might be an advantage in not being bound in her actions by any hard-and-fast rules. Margaret was far from being a visionary; like her father, she dealt with realities and took matters as they came. Except for the first article, which declared the three countries to be indissolubly united, a point around which affairs in the Scandinavian North were to revolve for more than a hundred and twenty-five years, the provisions of the Kalmar agreement therefore had no particular bearing upon the course of events.

Margaret's rule in Sweden.—The Swedish lords had, as before stated, invited Margaret because they felt certain that she would interfere little with their affairs, thus enabling them to continue serenely on their way usurping power and seizing property, but they were not long in discovering that they had utterly misjudged her. The conditions to which they had submitted at her election provided that all the taxable land which in Albrecht's time had fallen into their hands should revert to the crown; all sales of land through which the crown had suffered loss of revenue should be annulled without compensation in case fraud had been practised, or if the property had fallen into the hands of foreigners; all who had become tax-exempt since 1363 must produce legal documents as evidence of their right to exemption, and if these were not forthcoming taxes must be paid; no bailiff was henceforth to collect taxes without the orders of the ruler. All forts which had been built during the period of anarchy were to be demolished. No one was henceforth to be permitted, through military service, to make more than one specified estate tax-exempt, and this exemption was to be granted only through royal patents; as a further check on the noblemen, it was stipulated that they could not in the future legally purchase land from tax-paying *bönder*. Margaret lost no time in beginning proceedings against the great landholders and most of them found their rights to their property challenged and from 1396 until her death the process of royal confiscation went on unceasingly. The desire for land became a passion with Margaret, who pressed all claims against the lords with ruthless severity. She bought land, made loans, and foreclosed on mortgages, and in other ways acquired property. Enormous areas thus reverted to the crown. The power of the Swedish lords, the very men who had been so haughty and defiant in Magnus Eriksson's time, was broken completely. They now held none of the important offices in the administration. Margaret's resourcefulness in keeping them in check was most remarkable. Although she ruled severely, she was generally liked by the common people, and this was, no doubt, the principal reason for her success. While she generally, in her appointments of bailiffs or other officers, ignored the Swedes, it can hardly be said that this was due to any dislike of them. She felt, undoubtedly, that she could place more reliance on her people, the Danes. In spite of the enormous increase of the wealth of the crown during her reign, complaints that taxes were high were common; these complaints were, no doubt, justified, as she was compelled to wage war against the Holsteiners and this consumed much of her revenues. Still the common people of Sweden had no reason to look with longing for a return of the conditions which had existed under Albrecht of Mecklenburg.

Erik of Pomerania.—Margaret died in 1412, and Erik of Pomerania, now a man of thirty, assumed control of the government. Of mediocre ability, he had shown no talent for government. His mind had a decidedly Danish slant, which, in the eyes of the common people of Sweden, was very serious. It could be condoned in the case of a vigorous and, on the whole, fair-minded ruler like Margaret, but not in the case of a weakling like Erik. His selfishness and petulance boded ill for his reign. The common people of Sweden disliked him heartily from the start because of his aloofness; they were used to kings who went freely among them and listened to their complaints.

A bitter war between Denmark and Holstein, wherein the Swedes had no direct interest, kept the king away from the country except for brief visits, generally several years apart, but the oppressive burdens of taxes which were levied upon them to help pay for the costly struggle were constant reminders that the Swedes were being cruelly exploited in order to help others. Since Erik had appointed no one as steward to govern in his absence, Sweden was in this period virtually ruled by the royal bailiffs. Sometimes, indeed, it happened that a member of the Swedish Council was summoned to Denmark for consultation, but as a rule even important matters pertaining to Sweden were decided solely by the Danish Council.

Misrule of the royal bailiffs.—The rule of their bailiffs was extremely irritating to the Swedes. Many of these officials were Germans who had ideas about the manner in which *bönder* ought to be treated that were entirely at variance with Swedish ideals and practices. Many of the Danish bailiffs looked upon Sweden merely as a field for exploitation. To quote Schück on this point: [1] "Sweden was in this period—of course in a far more modest way—as attractive to penniless Danish noblemen as later America . . . was to Spanish nobles." Without royal supervision these bailiffs not only permitted tax-money in larger and larger amounts to find its way into their own spacious pockets, but they constantly found new objects on which to levy taxes. It is doubtless true that the oppression which the Swedish *bönder* were forced to endure at the hands of Erik's bailiffs was not any worse than that which Bo Jonsson had inflicted upon them, but he was at least not a foreigner and the money wrung from the people had remained in the country instead of going to support a foreigner in his dynastic wars. For the Swedes the union therefore came to mean simply a malicious scheme to establish Danish supremacy and extend the Danish state. The king's neglect of their interests and the nefarious conduct of his bailiffs naturally caused bitterness among them, and this was stirred to greater intensity by the favouritism which he showed Johannes Gerkesson, a notoriously dissolute and unscrupulous man, whom he appointed Arch-

[1] Schück, Henrik, *Engelbrekt*, in *Svenska Akademiens Handlingar*, Vol. 26, 1914. Published as a separate volume, Stockholm, 1915.

bishop of Uppsala, but whom the nation had good reason to hate and despise. Insurrectionary movements were the inevitable result of the situation. These had their inception in the province of Dalarna.

The first step in the break-up of the Union; the people of Dalarna.—Dalarna occupied at this time, as well as later, a place among the several Swedish provinces which was unique. Very likely there was not anywhere in a civilized country at the time a community where the spirit of independence was more dominant a force than here. The reasons for this situation can be quite definitely determined. The original settlement of the province evidently came much later here than in the provinces south of it, as shown by the fact that very few remains from the Stone and Bronze Ages have been found within its limits. In the course of time people from the Lake Mälaren district were attracted in large numbers to its fertile river valleys. With its isolated inland location, the province remained relatively unimportant until copper and iron-ore were discovered in its southern districts and the Germans came in large numbers to develop these resources. To the districts also flocked adventurers, fugitives from justice, highwaymen, and others of the same ilk who found life more congenial where a lax enforcement of law was the rule, and where opportunities for easy wealth beckoned. While these settlers, or their descendants, in course of time and under new conditions became as law-abiding as any in the land, a live spirit of independence and a ready disposition to rise in revolt against injustice remained as a heritage of primitive days. Mining became the chief industry, and since this industry was in the hands of a great number of individuals and the profits thus widely and quite evenly distributed, the district, as a whole, enjoyed a remarkable prosperity. Wealth had grown fast, largely because the mine-owners by special privileges enjoyed a favourable position with regard to taxation. Erik, however, seems to have refused to confirm the privileges of the chief iron district; thus the mine-owners saw themselves threatened by burdens that they feared would crush them to the ground. Into this district, the most congenial soil for the seeds of revolution, was sent a bailiff, Jösse Eriksson by name, who personified all the detested evils of the king's régime. He posed as a very pious man, and his liberal gifts to Vadstena Abbey, as well as to the cathedral of Västerås, won much praise. He was, in reality, a coarse and brutal person, and the statement of the chronicle that he seized practically all the property of the people, brutally strung up a number of men in a building filled with smoke, and compelled women to work as beasts of burden in the fields, is perhaps no exaggeration.

Engelbrekt Engelbrektsson.—Fortunately for the oppressed classes, a man now appeared to lead them in revolt against their oppressors who had the genius of true statesmanship. This was Engelbrekt Engelbrektsson, "the first Swede," as he has been called, and the first, and one of the greatest, in a long line of remarkable leaders in the cause of the common people of Sweden. While his public career fell within the brief period of only three years, his deeds were of such importance that they were to determine the direction of Swedish national thought and political development down to the present time. Engelbrekt (Swedish historians almost universally refer to the great hero by his baptismal name) was a descendant of one of the Germans who, in the time of Birger Jarl, had come to Sweden and located at Uppsala, and was born soon after 1380. His family had risen steadily in the economic and social scale, and the great leader stood somewhat midway between the status of the privileged noble and the *bonde*. His genius as a military leader and his sound insight into the political situation perhaps find their explanation partly in the fact that he had travelled extensively on the Continent and had been in contact with revolutionary movements there, especially with the Hussite revolt.[2] When an appeal for help came to him from the oppressed *bönder* and mine-owners Engelbrekt undertook the long and arduous journey to Copenhagen to lay complaints against the hated Jösse Eriksson before the king. Pretending that he was interested in seeing justice done and giving some evidence of a good disposition, Erik gave orders to the Swedish Council to investigate the charges. Secretly, however, he sent word to the Swedish councillors that they were to exonerate the bailiffs against whom the charges had been made.

[2] Schück, *Engelbrekt.*

The councillors did indeed make the investigation, but their report was a complete substantiation of Engelbrekt's charges. With this document in his possession, Engelbrekt again appeared before the king at Copenhagen, but this time he was met with abuse. In a fit of anger the king shouted: "You always complain; depart and never show yourself before my eyes again." "It is likely that I shall return once again," said Engelbrekt, as he left the royal presence. On his return to Dalarna, the flame of revolution was soon kindled.

The revolt.—Engelbrekt was chosen leader of a group of indignant *bönder* and mine-owners, who, on Midsummer Day, 1434, seized and destroyed the fort of Borgenäs, southwest of Falun. Soon they were joined by the people of all the Swedish provinces. The Swedish lords wished to assume a discreet watchful-waiting attitude. They met for an important conference at Vadstena, but Engelbrekt appeared unexpectedly among them with some of his armed followers and by threats forced them to join in a statement to the king that they no longer considered themselves bound by their oath of fealty to him. This, in effect, meant that Erik was deposed. Engelbrekt showed extraordinary skill as a military leader, and within three months the entire country was practically cleared of Danish and German bailiffs and the control of the government restored to the Swedes.

King Erik had in the meantime induced the Norwegian Council to send a letter of protest to the Swedes, charging that they had proceeded irregularly in deposing the king, since no statement of grievances had previously been submitted to him. The Swedish Council gave a carefully worded answer to this protest, in which Erik's numerous violations of the law of the land were especially emphasized and their right affirmed to withhold their obedience to a man who had violated his oath. As a further answer to the Norwegian Council, the Swedes proceeded to elect Engelbrekt administrator of Sweden. The election took place at a meeting at Arboga, in 1435, whither the citizens of the towns and the *bönder*, as well as the clergy and the nobility, sent representatives. This was the first representative meeting in Swedish history in which the commons clearly had a part, the earlier projected meeting of Magnus

Eriksson with similar representatives being of a more dubious character (p. 162). The nobles found it exceedingly distasteful to acquiesce in the elevation of an upstart like Engelbrekt to so high an office and managed to manipulate affairs in such a way that a second man was elected to rule jointly with him; in this way they hoped to detract from the great leader's power and prestige. The man elected to share power with Engelbrekt was Karl Knutsson (Bonde), whose tragic story will be told later. Engelbrekt laboured unceasingly and with the force and insight of true constructive statesmanship for the welfare of Sweden, and it was the tragic misfortune of the country that his career should soon be cut short by the dastardly deed of a murderer.

Assassination of Engelbrekt; estimate of his services.—Among the jealous lords who had opposed him was Bengt Stensson Natt och Dag, who harboured a personal grudge against him because of a fancied wrong. The matter had been adjusted in a way which Engelbrekt believed had removed all ground for bitterness, and on a journey from the interior of the country to Stockholm he sought lodging for the night near Bengt Stensson's home on Lake Hjälmaren. No sooner had Engelbrekt, who was a man of small stature and furthermore was ill at the time, stepped ashore than his enemy's son, Magnus Bengtsson, brutally attacked him with an axe and cruelly murdered him (1436).

Few leaders have in so short a time as Engelbrekt succeeded in rallying all the forces of a nation and in giving such direction to these forces that the entire subsequent life of the nation has been profoundly affected thereby. For only three years was he permitted to remain as the head of the nation, but in that brief time he laid solidly the foundation of Swedish independence, stirred the class consciousness of the *bönder,* and won for the common people a remarkable degree of political influence. By appealing directly to the mine-owners and *bönder* for support of the national cause, and leading them to victory, he taught them to understand their own ability to defend their rights, and this knowledge served them well afterwards. The confidence which their victories under Engelbrekt inspired enabled them to advance still farther in political wisdom and influence. Nor was the example which Engelbrekt had set lost upon later patriotic leaders of the nation's cause. He had shown what advantage could be derived from the support of the common people, especially the *bönder,* and the later national leaders, profiting by his experience, also naturally turned to them for help. Here, no doubt, is found the main reason for the unique position which the Swedish *bönder* have held ever since Engelbrekt's day. Engelbrekt also rendered a great service to the cause of national unity. Under him, for the first time, all the different provinces of the country fought side by side in a common cause and won success; having shared sacrifices and triumphs together, national interests came to mean more than purely provincial interests. To be a subject of Sweden meant more after this time than to be a citizen of any particular province.

It is an evidence of the broad-minded, scholarly attitude which has characterized Scandinavian historians in the last few decades that one of the best estimates of Engelbrekt Engelbrektsson's personality and influence has come from a distinguished Danish scholar, Erslev. In emphasizing the greatness of the Swedish leader, he says: [3] "Engelbrekt's career extended over barely three years, but during this brief period he accomplished more for his people than any one before or after him. The aristocracy had submitted to the rule by which Sweden was being exploited in behalf of another country, and had become reconciled to the rule of Erik's foreign bailiffs. Engelbrekt then aroused the *bönder* to battle for the country's liberties; they all followed him, and foreign rule came to an end in Sweden, never to appear again. By this mighty deed the Swedish *bonde* class secured a position which it utterly lacked in the other two Scandinavian countries. The slumbering spirit of nationalism was awakened, and the struggle for freedom brought unity of the Swedish people to the hitherto divided provinces, and to the contending classes."

National and Union parties.—New and bitter struggles began after the death of Engelbrekt. The nation now became definitely divided into two groups which may be designated as the Union Party and the National Party. The former was

[3] Erslev, Kr., *Erik av Pommern,* Copenhagen, 1901, p. 358.

made up of the higher ecclesiastics and members of the higher nobility, among which the families of Oxenstierna and Vasa, later so honourably associated with the cause of Swedish independence and national greatness, were the foremost. This party was quick to seize the opportunity given them by Engelbrekt's death to usurp power and help themselves forthwith to a great number of valuable fiefs. Engelbrekt had rid the country of a king who had favoured foreigners in the distribution of offices and fiefs, and, as far as the lords were concerned, the exit of Erik had meant good riddance; their main objective now was to keep the *bönder* in submission. The Union Party, therefore, favoured a union king, in conformity with plans of the Kalmar Union, since such a king would not be likely to have much time, and still less liking, for Swedish affairs; he could be counted on to remain away from the country most of the time and thus leave the lords free to rule very much as they pleased. While some among them undoubtedly had the sincere belief that a common king for the three Scandinavian countries would help to bring unity and concord among them, the great majority were undoubtedly, after Engelbrekt's death, actuated almost wholly by considerations of self-interest. To gain their purposes they committed acts which, from the Swedish viewpoint, constituted rank treason.

The National Party was composed of the common people of which the *bönder* naturally constituted the backbone. It also included many of the clergy and a very small but influential group from the nobility. The party, violently anti-union as it was, wanted a Swedish king who would rule according to the ancient law of the land. Its members were willing to sacrifice every political advantage which the Kalmar Union might give, in order to preserve the liberty of the masses of Sweden. The success of the Union would undoubtedly have meant the firm establishment of the feudal order, which the nobles favoured. The nation's love of freedom finds eloquent expression in the noble words of the "Hymn of Liberty" by Bishop Thomas of Strängnäs, written about the middle of the fifteenth century, and constituting, in the words of Schück,[4] the foremost creation of Swedish poetic talent during the

[4] Schück and Warburg, *Illustrerad svensk litteraturhistoria*, 3d Ed., I, p. 441.

Middle Ages. The ideals and sentiments of the National Party in Sweden also suggest similarities with contemporary events in France and the martyrdom of Joan of Arc.

Karl Knutsson and the National Party.—At the head of the National Party stood the knightly Karl Knutsson Bonde, the foremost representative of the ancient noble family, Bonde, which almost alone within the ranks of the higher nobility had taken sides for the national cause. It will be recalled that it was Karl Knutsson whom the manipulations of the lords had made joint ruler with Engelbrekt. At the death of his colleague he put himself at the head of the National Party, but unfortunately for himself and for the country he lacked almost completely Engelbrekt's brilliant powers of leadership. The personal magnetism and the eloquence which could stir the masses to action had been denied him and his military ability was mediocre. The well-founded suspicion that he was endeavouring, through the aid of the *bönder,* to seize the Swedish crown for himself also served to weaken his position; the jealousy of the other aristocratic families which were wealthier than the Bonde family caused him no end of trouble.

Christopher of Bavaria; the royal promise.—King Erik's shameful rule had caused Danes as well as Swedes to rise in revolt against him and drive him out of the land. He now became a pirate on the Baltic, an occupation for which he seemed better qualified than for the duties of kingship. In Sweden, royal power and dignity were conferred upon Christopher of Bavaria, a nephew of Erik, whom the Danish Council had already chosen King of Denmark. His election in Sweden by the Swedish Council was achieved through the use of discreditable tactics. Karl Knutsson was placated by the grant of Finland as a fief. The Swedish nobles took the precaution to exact a solemn declaration from Christopher, prior to his coronation as King of Sweden, by which he surrendered virtually all powers to them. In this declaration, the king promised that Swedish law and custom should prevail in the land, none but Swedes should be appointed members of the National Council, and the castles and fortresses should be placed, at the death of the king, in the hands of the archbishop, the steward, the lawman of Uppland, and three other men appointed by the Council; castles, fiefs, and crown lands should be transferred to none but Swedes, all such transfers to be made by authority of the Council; all the principal officers, as steward, chancellor, chamberlain, cupbearer, and other members of the royal household should be native men, and, finally, that the income of the crown from Sweden should not be used in the interest of any foreign power.

The lords found conditions very much to their liking under the lax and easy-going ruler, a youth of twenty-two, good-natured and indolent, who is said to have relished his Bavarian beer far more than the vexing affairs of state. He became exceedingly unpopular among the common people and was made the scapegoat for the lords' increasing oppression. Bad harvests caused widespread starvation among the people, who were compelled to grind bark and mix this as an ingredient in their bread. This gave him the nickname "The Bark-king." The most creditable fact to be noted in connection with Christopher's reign was the enactment of a new law (1442) for the entire land, based on the old common law of Magnus Ericksson. This remained the common law of the country until 1736.

Karl Knutsson's election.—After a brief rule of six years, Christopher died unexpectedly in 1448, and immediately the Swedish lords and the members of the Danish Council became deeply involved in schemes for the control of Sweden. Karl Knutsson speedily set out from Finland and appeared in Stockholm at the head of eight hundred knights and squires and presented himself as a candidate for the throne. His candidacy immediately won strong support, not only by reason of his knightly manners and his known sympathy for the popular cause, but also because a long drought which had afflicted the land was broken by refreshing rains just as he arrived in the capital, which was taken as a good omen. With great sagacity, Karl Knutsson had summoned a general assembly at Stockholm, in which representatives of the common people also took part. After very little deliberation, this assembly elected him king. Simultaneously the Danes elected Christian of Oldenburg as their king. Karl's forces wrested Gottland from the old pirate, King Erik, but through the treachery of Magnus Gren, a Swedish nobleman, it was delivered into the hands of Christian, and this treasonable act was soon followed by another on the part of the Swedish lords.

Struggle for the control of Norway.—Both Karl Knutsson and Christian now bestirred themselves in order to secure the Norwegian crown. Sympathies in Norway were far stronger for Karl Knutsson than for Christian, but a military force from Denmark soon compelled the Norwegian Council to summon an assembly for the purpose of electing a king; this was attended by one bishop, two clerics, one Danish knight, five councillors, and a few others, but no commons, unless some fishermen from the little coast village where the assembly was held should be so counted, and this unique assembly, in no wise representing the popular will, now proceeded to elect Christian king of the country. This seemingly farcical act can be said to have sealed the fate of Norway for four hundred years. Another Norwegian assembly elected Karl Knutsson, who entered Norway, received the homage of a great part of the population, and secured possession of practically the whole country, but in a few months all the advantages he had gained were lost through the treachery of the Swedish lords who, at a meeting held at Halmstad for the purpose of settling pending questions, went beyond their instructions and agreed with the Danes upon new articles for a union of the three countries. Karl Knutsson now stood practically alone, for he had failed to include the common people in the assembly which had been summoned to accept or reject the provisions of this agreement. He was therefore compelled to acquiesce in the Halmstad agreement. At a subsequent meeting, composed of twelve Swedes and an equal number of Danes, for the purpose of finding a solution to some of the questions still at issue between them, the former were startled by a Danish demand that the dowry of Christopher's widow, who had remarried and was now King Christian's spouse, be delivered to them. Made wiser by this time by experience, Karl Knutsson had taken the precaution to send only reliable men to this meeting and these men met the Danish demand with a firm refusal, fully justified by the law, because the Swedish Council had never approved the contract regarding the dowry as the law required; furthermore, the queen had remarried, an act which in itself nullified any arrangement which might have been made. Without any previous declaration of war, the Danes now began hostilities by invading both Värmland and the Kalmar region in Småland. On the Danish side the war was marked by extreme cruelty, large sections of the country being wantonly laid waste and a great part of the population killed. Now as never before began to be bred the unfortunate national hatred between the two kindred peoples that was to rest as a curse upon Swedes and Danes alike until well into the nineteenth century. Before this time the conflicts between the two countries had appeared mainly as the results of personal controversies between kings, which, after all, did not deeply concern the people in either land, but from now on a bitter national hatred and a deep suspicion became firmly lodged in the minds of the people in both lands. On a march through Skåne the Swedish troops showed that, in the plundering and burning of cities and in the perpetration of cruelties, they had nothing to learn from their kinsmen across the Sound. The archiepiscopal city of Lund, said at that time to have had twenty-four churches, was sacked. With an army consisting largely of German mercenaries, Christian invaded western Sweden, took Älvsborg, an important stronghold near the mouth of the Göta River, and compelled the people of Västergötland to swear allegiance to him. The army of Karl Knutsson contained many traitors, and Christian was kept well informed of every move or plan of the enemy.

Archbishop Jöns Oxenstierna.—The most dangerous of these traitors was the Swedish archbishop, Jöns Oxenstierna, a haughty, brutal, and unscrupulous ecclesiastic who, actuated mainly by jealousy, raised the standard of revolt against Karl. The latter was now compelled to flee from the country, and the Swedish nobles next elected Christian as king of the land. Fortune now seemed to smile on the Danish king, for soon after the Swedish crown had been placed on his head in Uppsala cathedral, he secured control also of Schleswig and Holstein, with the title of duke in the former and earl in the latter. The provinces were acquired by Christian through election, but he was compelled to satisfy other pretenders by huge sums of money, and the necessity of raising these, together with sums required for the costly wars which he was waging against German princes and the Hanseatic League, forced him to lay tax burdens upon the people which crushed them to the ground. As a result, he was bitterly reviled. His greed was, furthermore, insatiable, and he never lost an opportunity to secure financial profit.

The merciless exactions of Christian at last exhausted the patience of the *bönder* of Uppland, and in 1463 a force of from three to four thousand men marched upon Stockholm and forced the archbishop, who ruled in the absence of the king, to agree to a cancellation of the obnoxious taxes. When Christian was informed of this, he caused the archbishop to be arrested. When the Uppland *bönder* heard of the arrest they marched on Stockholm again. Christian's captains induced them to agree to a truce, but when the king arrived on the scene he treacherously attacked them and slaughtered about two thousand men in cold blood. He then returned to Denmark, but no sooner had he left Sweden than the land was ablaze with the fire of revolution. Christian returned in order to subdue the rebels, but he suffered a crushing defeat near Haraker Church in Västmanland. He then returned precipitately to Denmark, and Karl Knutsson was asked to return as king, the lords taking the precaution, however, to insist on a complete amnesty for themselves and exacting a promise that he would secure the release of the archbishop.

Karl's whirligig on the wheel of fortune.—Karl Knutsson was not destined to enjoy the sweets of victory very long. Archbishop Jöns, whose jealousy and dislike of the king knew no bounds, had promised Christian that he would rid Sweden of the hated enemy and he now raised the standard of revolt. After six months in power, Karl was forced to abdicate and again betake himself to Finland. Being again rid of Karl, the lords proceeded to divide the spoils by seizing valuable fiefs. The *bönder* were deeply stirred by their rapacious acts and among the people of Dalarna, now clearly convinced of the treachery of the archbishop, pamphlets were circulated in which his treasonable acts were laid bare and the terms "liar" and "traitor" freely used.

After much intrigue and bickering, Karl was again invited to return to Sweden, and in November 1467 he became king for the third time. A month later the bellicose archbishop died, but even with this implacable enemy gone Karl was not to find any peace. Christian was preparing a military action against Karl again and the rapacious Swedish lords were constantly stirring up trouble and harassing him. It cannot be wondered at that he felt weary of the struggle, especially as age was beginning to weigh upon him, but he found a worthy champion of his cause in Sten Sture, his nephew, who, although still young, had shown himself possessed of much of the political acumen and military leadership which had enabled Engelbrekt to save the country. This was the man whom Karl Knutsson before his death in 1470 had designated as his successor, giving him much sound advice, the fruits of his own rich and bitter experience. One of the points he emphasized was that Sten Sture ought never to aspire to the royal title, but content himself with the title of administrator (*riksföreståndare*).

Sten Sture the Elder.—Sten Sture the Elder was one of the truly great men of Swedish history, a man who, at a most critical time in the nation's history, gave constructive leadership of the highest order. The experiences of his uncle, the former king, in his relations both to the Swedish lords and to Christian, had revealed to him how utterly untrustworthy both were. Sten Sture realized fully how grievously Karl had erred when he failed to rally the common people to his standard and strike a decisive blow before it was too late. Like Engelbrekt before him, the administrator took the common people into his confidence, called on them for assistance, and again it was revealed that with the guidance of an able and patriotic leader they were able both to safeguard their own rights and successfully to defend the nation's rights against foreign aggression.

Battle of Brunkeberg; Swedish independence saved.—Not much time was allowed to pass after the death of Karl Knutsson before the Danish king made a determined effort to secure the Swedish crown. With an army of 5,000 Danes, he sailed to Stockholm, outside of which he effected a union with a contingent of Swedish adherents. This force engaged in battle with Sten Sture's army on a ridge known as Brunkeberg, situated just outside of the city walls, and suffered an overwhelming defeat (October 10, 1471). The moral effect of the battle was immediate and far-reaching. The Swedes suddenly realized that their cause was by no means hopeless, and the old Union Party disintegrated completely. The Danes, on the other hand, already tired of the war, were reluctant to follow Christian any longer in his endeavour to win the Swedish crown. Their conciliatory attitude smoothed the way to an agreement between the two nations in 1472, according to which they pledged themselves to maintain perpetual peace with one another; what was perhaps still more significant was the inclusion of a provision in the treaty that the two countries would assist each other in case of attack by some other state or rebellion threatened either of them. Later came other agreements, all aiming at an adjustment of their mutual interests in such a way that peace and good-will would prosper; a league of friendship was in process of formation. No credit belongs to Christian for these wise projects, for he constantly brooded on plans for revenge. The crushing defeat at Brunkeberg had taught him only one thing; the next time he attacked Sweden he must have a larger army, better military plans, and the support of a strong anti-Swedish alliance. Against Sweden he was constantly concocting most reprehensible schemes: Sweden was to be placed under interdict by the Pope, the country should be barred by the emperor from all trade with other lands, Russians should invade Sweden from the east, the force of James III of Scotland, Christian's son-in-law, from the Norwegian side, while Christian should attack on several fronts and with both fleet and army. With the country completely subdued, all Swedish lords should lose their property and be driven into exile, whereupon the *bönder* of Dalarna and the burghers of Stockholm were to be exterminated. The details of the dastardly plot were revealed to Sten Sture by one of Christian's servants soon after the king had passed away. Christian did not live long enough to enable him to carry these schemes into execution, and his son, to whom they descended as a political testament, did not have the inclination to take them seriously. We shall see, however, how they were resurrected in the grandson of Christian I, and with momentous consequences to Sweden and Denmark alike.

Sten Sture as administrator.—Until Christian's death in 1481, Sweden enjoyed tranquillity under the wise and able administration of Sten Sture, and this respite between wars was used to good advantage for the strengthening of law and order, reviving industry, which had naturally suffered grievously during the period of conflict, and promoting purely cultural interests. The administrator, thoroughly Swedish himself in interests and sympathies, looked steadily to the protection of the Swedish element in the land. Soon after the victory of Brunkeberg the charter of Stockholm was amended by striking out the old provision that half the members of the city council should be Germans. The statutes of the guilds were codified. The old legal institutions were given new vitality and force. Sten Sture himself travelled extensively through the land to meet the *bönder* at the Things in order to confer with them about their grievances and desires.

Founding of a national university.—The new national consciousness which had been aroused by Sten Sture's victory against the foreign enemy and by his wise administration expressed itself in various ways, most notably, however, in the founding of a national university at Uppsala. The young Swedes who, prior to this, desired an education beyond the merely elementary stages, had been compelled to go abroad. At an early time, these students generally attended the University of Paris, where, during a long period, they were so numerous that separate students' quarters were maintained for them. Several Swedish students attained considerable prominence at Paris, four serving as procurators for the English "nation," the group in which all the students from the North were matriculated; others became members of the faculty, and not less than four attained the dignity of rector.[5] Later the Swedish students preferred to go to Prague, and when disturbances broke out there between the German and Czech students they followed the former to the newly founded University of Leipsic. Still later, when the universities of Rostock and Greifswald were founded, the Swedish students flocked to these institutions, especially the former. A trip abroad and a sojourn at a foreign university during several years involved, however, an expense which only the richer families could meet, and the early suggestion of a university in Sweden arose largely from

[5] Annerstedt, C., *Uppsala Universitets historia,* Uppsala, 1877, I, p. 10.

the desire to make higher education accessible also for the less wealthy. The first suggestion for a Swedish nucleus of a university is said to have been made in 1417, but nothing came of it. The matter was discussed later in the century, but no definite steps were taken until Sten Sture's time. The quickened national spirit and the feeling of the leaders that Sweden ought to take her place more definitely than before in the ranks of the cultured nations of Europe spurred the leaders to action. The new national spirit needed a medium through which it could express itself and which likewise could be the means of awakening the national spirit still further. The matter was urgent since Christian of Denmark had already secured a charter for a Danish university (opened in 1479); to have the Swedish students trained in Denmark seemed to the Swedes both dangerous and humiliating. Finally a charter for the establishment of a Swedish university at Uppsala, after the model of Bologna, was granted by the Pope, in 1477, the archbishop at the time, Jakob Ulfsson, having been particularly active in securing the papal approval. The beginning of the institution was extremely unpretentious. Members of the ecclesiastical chapter served as teachers, for which they received no special compensation. The first special appropriation for the university appears to have been made in 1504, when the cathedral authorities voted a sum of 130 marks. The students lived together and lectures were given in various buildings in the vicinity of the cathedral. The lectures were almost entirely in the field of canonical law and theology.

The lords at their old game again.—Sten Sture was in time to learn that the irreconcilable opponents of a strongly centralized power in Sweden—namely, the Swedish nobles—were still aggressive and dangerous, and his situation was rendered more critical by the continued plotting of Danish leaders. Christian had left a son, Hans, who was twenty-six years of age at his father's death. He had some ability and was fully determined to secure the Swedish crown for himself. He had, in fact, under his father's short reign been elected heir to the Swedish throne, and now he included the words, "King of Sweden by election" in his title. The game of politics and intrigue now began again. In their anxiety to placate the Swedes and win their support for a union king, the Danes suggested a joint meeting for the purpose of reaching an agreement regarding the relations of the two countries. This took place at Kalmar (1482) and here both groups pledged themselves to maintain peace with each other under one and the same king, but the Swedes refused to proceed to an election on the ground that the Norwegians were not present. At a meeting at Halmstad in the following year, Danish, Swedish, and Norwegian delegates were in attendance, but this time the Swedes found an excuse for their refusal to join in the election because Sten Sture, who at this time had eye trouble, had been unable to attend. The Danes and Norwegians, however, reached an agreement known as the Halmstad Recess. This contained practically the same guarantees as the Swedes had wrung from former union kings; namely, that each country should be ruled by native men, no castle, fortress, or fief to be given to foreigners, membership in the Council to be given only to native lords, and the king, as well as the unprivileged class, to be excluded from the right to acquire tax-exempt land from the privileged class. The king was also to sanction the principle that his subjects were no longer bound by their oath of allegiance in case he deprived any man of liberty or property without due process of law. The Halmstad agreement was given such a form that it was taken for granted that the Swedish lords would accept it and acknowledge Hans as their king. Other baits were dangled before their eyes. Thus hints were dropped that Hans would help Sweden get possession of Gottland, then held by a rebellious Danish lord, and secure the withdrawal of the Pope's interdict, which rested over Sweden because of its failure to pay the dowry of the former queen (p. 193). Sten Sture, who knew of Christian's political testament to his son, and thus had special reason to feel alarm, was playing for time. Finally, the pressure which the scheming Swedish lords brought to bear upon him forced him to acknowledge Hans as king, but on condition that the latter should first make good his promise regarding Gottland. Neither Hans nor the Swedish Union Party dared to proceed with their plans for ousting Sten Sture from office, since a general assembly, which the administrator had prudently summoned, had clearly revealed that he could count on the support of his people. Hans was merely biding his time, and when Sten Sture became involved in a quarrel with his enemies of the Union Party he formed an alliance with Russia for an attack on Sweden. In 1495 a Russian attack upon Finland compelled Sten Sture to proceed to that country, when the Swedish lords used the occasion for starting a revolt against him. Sten Sture hurried home in order to meet the attack. His enemies had the effrontery to declare that since his presence was necessary to Finland—a truce with Russia had in the meantime been concluded but was not yet known in Sweden—he could naturally not be in Sweden also, and his official status had thus ceased. The administrator made the pointed reply to this statement that he held his commission from the people of Sweden, and he would relinquish his office only when they and the Council asked him to do so. The lords in turn issued a letter to the people of Sweden solemnly protesting against the report that they intended to bring a king into the land; they would, they declared, have no king, except one chosen according to the law of the land by the people themselves—but the very day after issuing this declaration, they dispatched a letter to Hans affirming their unswerving loyalty to him! Sten Sture used the next few months in travelling through Dalarna and neighbouring provinces in order to inform the people of the danger which threatened and to enlist their aid in meeting it. On returning to Stockholm, he was compelled to defend himself against the Swedish lords and against an attack of the Danish king who advanced with an army said to have amounted to 30,000 men. Against this formidable combination, the administrator was unable to defend himself successfully. He now acknowledged Hans as King of Sweden on condition that the latter would abide by the provision of the former recess limiting the power of a union king. On October 11, 1497, Hans entered Stockholm, and the three countries again had a joint ruler. His coronation at Uppsala was at first a joyous affair, since the lords expected the new ruler, from sheer gratitude, to be generous in conferring the dignity of knighthood upon them. Inasmuch as Sweden had been for so long a time without a king, who alone could confer such honours, there had been a lamentable dearth of knightly appointments. Sten Sture was, in fact, at the time the only one entitled to be called Sir and his wife Lady—an honour which by no means had served to increase their popularity with the jealous lords and still less with their equally jealous spouses. Hans satisfied about half a hundred of these eager candidates, leaving many hundreds in keen disappointment and with bitterness in their hearts. Through the connivance of the Swedish lords, promises were now made by the Swedish Council that on the death of Hans his son Christian would be acknowledged his successor in Sweden. As Hans violated his pledges even to the lords who had secured his election, so much resentment was aroused that his position became insecure, especially as revolts and military disasters in other areas had also caused great bitterness among the Danes. After a time Sten Sture was again elected administrator and war came once more to afflict the land. Stockholm capitulated to the national forces one day before Hans appeared outside the city with the entire Danish fleet.

Death of Sten Sture.—The king returned to Denmark and the war went on, but death soon removed Sten Sture from the scene (1503). His good friend, Hemming Gadh, a shrewd, resourceful, and eloquent man, in whom all the Swedish hatred and distrust of Denmark seems to have been focussed, kept his death a secret for three days by having one of his servants pose as the aged regent, while in the meantime he took measures which would insure the election of a dependable man as his successor. A Riksdag [6] was hastily summoned, and when this met, Svante Nilsson Sture, a kinsman of the deceased statesman, was made administrator. Like his predecessor, Svante Sture was genuinely patriotic, but lacked the statesmanship and military skill of the former leader. The war with Hans went on with varying success, finally turning definitely against the administrator and his party. At this juncture Svante Sture died (1512) and soon afterwards Hans also passed away; new leaders now came on the scene, and the war over the Kalmar Union enters its final and most bitter phase.

[6] This is the designation usually given the general assembly from this time on. It was the practice after this that the four orders—nobles, clergy, burghers, and *bönder*—constituted the Riksdag. The fact that Sweden had four orders instead of three, as in other lands, where the *bönder* were left out, is deserving of special mention in this connection.

The close of the mediæval period.—The close of the mediæval period found Sweden at the threshold of a new era in which radical, political, religious, and economic changes were to affect the country profoundly. National unity had been achieved through a slow process of development and after many vicissitudes of fortune. The merging of the peoples of the different provinces which constituted the Sweden of that day had been brought about mainly through the strength and aggressiveness of the Svear, but until towards the close of the mediæval period national spirit had been as a mere flickering flame. Not only had the factors which serve to create and stimulate national interest, as glorious traditions and a great culture, been largely wanting, but certain influences had been directly antagonistic to sentiments of nationality. Thus the Church, imbued as she was with the idea of universality, sought consciously in all countries to discourage the development of the idea of nationality and to oppose national boundary lines. It was but natural that the Danish and German union kings should be happiest when the Swedes cared least for their own country, and for its institutions and rights, and as far as they were able these kings discouraged all manifestations of national emotions. Most inimical to Swedish national life was undoubtedly the influence of the nobility. A considerable number of the nobles were firm supporters of the Kalmar Union, and while a high-minded desire for unity and peace undeniably to a degree determined this attitude, they were, it must be said, actuated mainly by selfish considerations.[7] A union king, as stated, generally meant that the ruler had his hands full with important matters other than that of looking after the lords and trying to check their propensities for plunder and usurpation of power; intermarriage between members of Swedish and Danish noble families had, moreover, served to extinguish sentiments of loyalty to the fatherland among the lords in Sweden.

Growth of national sentiment.—In spite of the efforts of Church, kings, and nobility to destroy or hinder further growth of a national spirit, the people of Sweden had towards the end of the period come to think of themselves as Swedes, possessed of a common fatherland, whose liberties they had a

[7] Tunberg, S., *Fredstanken i nordens medeltid, Nordens Årsbok,* 1925.

duty to preserve and whose honour was of no small concern to them. This was due partly to a natural and bitter resentment against the spiritual and temporal powers which ruthlessly exploited them, partly to the influence of the Engelbrekt insurrection. Two institutions whose beginnings belong to the period not only typified the growing national spirit, but were given generous support because they were Swedish and filled the Swedes with pride. These were the Order of St. Birgitta and the University of Uppsala. The prospect that a monastic order founded by one of their countrywomen would be a great international power for good in a world that evidently seemed sadly

A mediæval *bonde* home in the evening. The woman is spinning with distaff, the wool tied to her head; torches are carried in the mouth

degenerate, was a matter of special pride for the Swedish nation, and this sentiment was undoubtedly one of the main reasons why the order became the recipient of extraordinarily liberal gifts. The decision to found a university at Uppsala was due largely to a desire that future leaders of Sweden be given a training which would make them national in sentiment.

No great changes were made in the boundaries of Sweden during the Kalmar Union period and at its end the southern provinces, Skåne, Blekinge, and Halland, were still Danish, and Bohuslän, Härjedalen, and Jämtland belonged to Norway. The eastern Finnish boundary passed from a point near the mouth of the Neva River in a northerly direction to the White Sea. The regions round the Gulf of Bothnia were more definitely incorporated with the country and the Lapps in large sections submitted to Swedish rule. The island of Gottland was a prize for which many contended; from the end of the fifteenth century it was virtually held by the Danes. Stockholm had by this time come to be universally looked upon as the principal place of residence of the king, and centre of the government.

Land and government.—The country had remained an elective monarchy. The choice was made by a group of the most powerful men of the land, often acting through the Swedish Council. After Engelbrekt's time, the Riksdag sometimes came, in spite of constant opposition from the Council, to wield a preponderating influence in royal elections. In the period 1470-1497, no less than nineteen meetings of the Riksdag were held, and in the period 1501-1520 no less than thir-

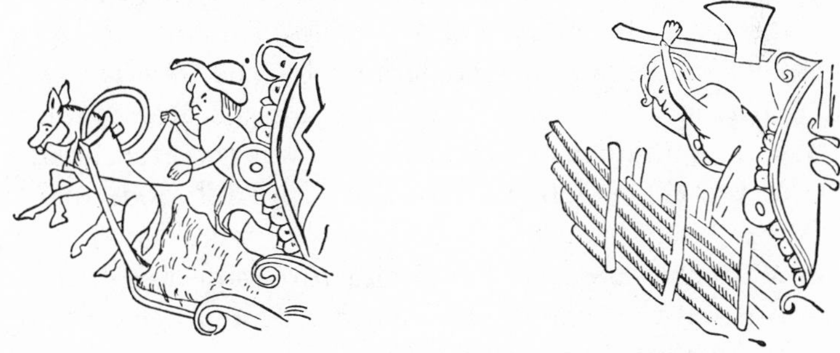

Hauling hay and building fence. From the work on the North by Olaus Magnus

teen. Its deliberations were marked by no definite order of procedure, no votes were taken, and the meetings served mainly to give the ruler an opportunity to lay certain propositions before the orders, hear objections, and in a general way notice how they reacted to his proposals. Often the ruler would confer with only the one estate which was most vitally interested in a given matter. Each *härad,* or "hundred," sent from two to six *bönder* to the Riksdag meetings, but the manner of their choice was determined by no definite principle. The personnel of the city representation was generally determined by the City Council. Theoretically, at least, every nobleman was entitled to membership in the Riksdag and the clerical representatives were identical with the clerical members of the Council. The nobility was not a closed corporation and theoretically at least the lowliest *bonde* could break into the charmed circle.

Not many, it is certain, could leap over the many hurdles which lay in the way, but in the case of one man born of the *bonde* class it is recorded that he became not only a nobleman but a member of the National Council. No doubt the man had a superabundance of energy and cleverness coupled with knavery, since the chronicler adds significantly that he was finally executed as a pirate.

The nobility.—An effective check had been placed upon the nobles by Margaret's rule of 1396 that no more land subject to taxation could henceforth be purchased by them and thus made tax-exempt. This proved a very effective means of protection for the *bönder* against the rapacious lords. Already at an earlier date the right to extend the privilege of tax-exemption in return for military services had come to be exercised by the king, who naturally was chary with the coveted writs, an attitude to which he was driven largely by the *bönders'* violent outcry against all tendencies to decrease the areas subject to taxation. The number of noble families was therefore relatively small; in the three rich provinces of Uppland, Södermanland, and Närke, only sixty-six noble families were listed in 1526 and in Västergötland and Värmland forty-one families. It has been estimated that the nobles owned only ten per cent of the land when the mediæval period closed. These checks upon them were a great benefit to the *bönder*, who at one time were at the very edge of serfdom when Margaret's great reckoning with the lords, and especially Engelbrekt's uprising, saved them from being pushed over the precipice.

The Council.—The different administrators who served at critical times were almost wholly the creations of the people, acting through their important organ, the Riksdag. Certain rich and powerful men were, as a matter of course, members of the Council, although the law prescribed that the temporal lords holding membership in it should not exceed twelve. Its authority was very indefinite and varied greatly with the character of the king or administrator. It was a weakness of the state that no definite official class had as yet been created which could attend to administrative affairs, but from their own group the members of the Council sought to produce a few officials for the chief administrative functions of the nation.

Only the chancellor, who served as a sort of secretary to the Council, became important in the period and came to have fairly definite tasks assigned him.

Swedish cities were advancing very slowly in population and wealth. The Hanseatic League was losing ground, but piracy flourished and hindered the development of Swedish trade and commerce. The German influence had waned steadily as the national spirit was stimulated, and it will be recalled that soon after Sten Sture the Elder's victory at Brunkeberg the rule that half of the members of the city Council of Stockholm should be Germans was abolished. In this city the Swedes seem to have maintained their right to fill half the places, but of the four burgomasters and twenty-eight councillors who in Kalmar swore fealty to Margaret only six were Swedes.

Baking bread. From the work on the North by Olaus Magnus

The Church.—It was one of the misfortunes of the Church that she became involved in the union struggles in the North. Both Swedes and Danes were constantly busy at Rome, in order to gain sympathy and support for their respective sides. At first Swedish stock had the highest rating at the Curia, but towards the end of the period the Danes became decidedly *personæ gratæ,* a fact which caused the Swedes much embarrassment and also made them more willing later to follow Gustavus Vasa in his anti-Catholic policies. As a matter of fact, the papacy took very little interest in affairs in Sweden except as they pertained to her financial contributions to Rome. Either the revenue collectors of the Church were able to build up a far more effective organization in Sweden than in Denmark or Norway, or the Swedes were more easily influenced, or perchance felt a clearer consciousness of sin than their kinsmen, since far greater sums were sent by them to the papal treasury at Rome than from the other two northern countries. Cost of

Hunting fowl and bear. From Olaus Magnus

collection, leaks, confiscation, and robbery by the Danish kings cut the part which ultimately reached Rome to forty per cent of the total collected from the Swedes, and still the papal share was large. The sale of indulgences was particularly brisk and profitable in Sweden, especially when the Italian, Marinus de Tregeno, came in 1460 as a sort of district agent with the entire North as his territory. Evidently he was a high-powered and unscrupulous salesman, and the chronicler declares ironically that he allowed poor and simple-minded people to go hungry from his door; he did not disdain any article in exchange for his indulgences, but accepted copper, tin, iron, old kettles—in fact, anything that could be converted into money.

In spite of the losses by confiscation and leaks, Marinus could, in the two years 1463-1464, send 15,000 Lübeck marks (a Lübeck mark was worth about 30 cents), to Rome, more than the entire income of the government in one year. Nearly all of this sum had been collected in Sweden. The indulgence seller *par excellence* was, however, Angelus Arcimboldus, another Italian who came to the North in 1518. He played for high political stakes in Sweden (p. 214), but by no means neglected the business which had brought him to the land. Christian II took a special delight in appropriating as much as possible of the sums which the papal agent had collected in indulgence money, and still the latter could in one shipment send 15,000 marks to his master.

Indulgence money constituted, however, only a fraction of the sums that flowed from Sweden in a steady stream to Rome. All kinds of dispensations, appointments, papal bulls, required money payments to the Curia. Thus a papal bull passed through from ten to fifteen sets of officials before it was valid and ready to accomplish its purpose, and all along its way the course had to be smoothed by fees and bribes. One of the archbishops was compelled to secure an age dispensation before he could assume his office, but this cost him 1,100 ducats and Sten Sture paid 800 ducats for a bull proclaiming a crusade against the Russians. While the large sums were collected from the higher clergy, these cleverly shifted the burdens upon the lower clergy and the common people. The annual income of the higher ecclesiastics was enormous. A Swedish historian, Forssell,[8] has computed that the bishops and consistories had an annual income of 170,000 marks or about twelve times the revenues of the state. In the meantime the Church as an organization grew enormously wealthy through donations and shrewd business transactions. The Black Death meant a regular windfall for her, as a vast number of estates were left ownerless or did not have enough labourers for their care, and these the Church bought for a pittance. It has been estimated that the Church was in possession of 13,700 estates when the mediæval period came to an end. While thus the Swedes were, according to the testimony furnished by their contributions

[8] Forssell, Hans, *Sveriges inre historia från Gustav I*, Stockholm, 1869-1875.

to the Church, rather exemplary members of the Church, on the whole the Popes found the Swedish *bönder* very hard to deal with. They insisted on the right to elect their own bishops, and by reason of their opposition the rule of celibacy did not become really effective in the land until the fourteenth century. On Gottland the priests were even allowed to marry, and their children could inherit property.

CHAPTER VIII

THE FINAL PHASE OF THE KALMAR UNION

Sten Sture the Younger.—As leader of the National Party in Sweden there now appeared a young, able, and ambitious man, whose soul was aflame with the desire to save his country from political extinction and its people from social and economic bondage; on the Union-Danish side appeared two leaders, also energetic and resourceful, but so selfish and conscienceless that their names have come to be associated with the most dishonourable deeds that Scandinavian history records. The leader of the Swedish cause was Sten Sture, called the Younger, and leading the attack upon him and upon his country were Gustaf Trolle who became Archbishop of Sweden soon after Sten Sture's election, and Christian II of Denmark, to whom the opprobrious title "the Tyrant" has always clung.

The young Sten Sture was a son of Svante Nilsson Sture and only nineteen years of age when, by his father's death, he was called to grapple with the stupendous difficulties and dangers that beset his country. He was well qualified to play his difficult rôle; clear-sighted, energetic, and not bothered too much by scruples, the younger Sture was a representative leader of the Renaissance type who might be said to have showed Gustavus Vasa the way.[1] His first act as administrator was to seize all the important castles and fortresses in the land, and with these in his power he could bid defiance to the lords who had made haste to elect another man as ruler. Their choice had fallen upon Erik Trolle, whose Danish sympathies were well known. Sten Sture turned directly to the people for support, and so vehement were the cries which they raised against Trolle, who, they said, "was of the Danish king," that the intriguing lords, with Archbishop Jakob Ulfsson at their head,

[1] Carlson, G., *Sten Sture d. y. Scandia, Tidskrift för historisk forskning,* I, 1929.

were compelled to acclaim Sten Sture protector. Chagrined at the outcome, the intriguing old archbishop resigned, giving as his reason old age and the desire to lead a peaceable and quiet life during his remaining days; he now lent his influence towards the election of Gustaf Trolle as his successor.

Gustaf Trolle as archbishop.—This Trolle was a son of the Erik whom the lords had desired as administrator. Their family was an ancient and powerful one and had long been a bitter rival of the Sture family, whose pre-eminence in the affairs of Sweden had aroused its intense jealousy. In the hope that by a conciliatory attitude peace could be established between the two families and thus the internal tranquillity of Sweden be promoted, Sten Sture exerted his influence at Rome in behalf of Gustaf Trolle's appointment, even assuming himself a great part of the expense connected with his candidacy. Sten Sture had, however, made it a condition of his support that before his consecration as archbishop, Trolle must render homage to him as regent. Only twenty-six years old when, through political manipulation, the highest ecclesiastical office of Sweden came to him, Trolle had up to this time carefully concealed the insane malice towards Sten Sture and his family which burned within his spiteful soul. His own family had always been forced to yield to the Stures, but now he saw the time at hand when old scores could be settled, and in his endeavour to destroy his rival he was ready to commit crimes which earned for him the title of "the Judas Iscariot of Swedish history." The treachery of Trolle was soon to manifest itself. While still sojourning at Rome, in the interest of his candidacy, he sent a very threatening letter to Sten Sture, and on his journey home he evidently took the occasion to visit the young Danish king, Christian II, and agree with him on plans for their united attack upon the Swedish protector. Instead of going to Stockholm, as he was under obligation to do to render homage to the regent, Trolle proceeded directly to Uppsala, whence in letters he began to fulminate against Sten Sture. The latter again assumed a conciliatory attitude, even expressing his willingness to make reparation, as far as he was able, for injuries done, and going in person to Uppsala to implore the archbishop to let bygones be bygones and to join him in an alliance by which the peace and security of Sweden could be preserved. Trolle met all these advances with contempt and new expressions of bitter malice. Soon thereafter he summoned some of the disgruntled lords to a secret meeting, and here it was decided to invite Christian into the land, and if further support were needed to make him king, it was agreed that the Russians should be urged to come to their assistance. Realizing that Trolle's hatred was implacable, and that traitorous plans were being hatched, Sten Sture laid siege to Trolle's fort on his estate, Stäket, and at the same time called a Riksdag to meet at Arboga. At this meeting a statement of the situation was prepared and the assembly adopted a resolution, pledging the people to a determined opposition to Christian and his party and approving Sture's measures against the archbishop. In their statement, all the members present declared that they acted in behalf of the nation, and were jointly responsible. The canny Bishop Brask of Linköping, mindful of the fact that a day of reckoning might come, slipped a strip of paper under his seal, on which he had written: "To this I am compelled and driven" (*Härtill är jag nödd och tvungen*). It was a foresight that soon was to do him a good turn (p. 219). When later Sten Sture demanded the surrender of the fortress of Stäket, the only answer was a derisive threat by Trolle that in a few months Christian would be on hand to give him assistance. This was by no means an empty threat, for some months later a Danish army of 4,000 men, under the command of an uncle of the archbishop, landed on Swedish soil and advanced into the country, pillaging and collecting tribute as it pressed forward. A Danish fleet entered the Stockholm archipelago, and soon the smoke of burning villages rose so high that it could be seen by the people in the beleaguered Stäket, where Trolle himself was leading the defense. Eye-witnesses later declared that they had never before seen the archbishop so happy. In the meantime, messages had been dispatched to Rome informing the Pope of Sten Sture's heinous crime in trying to lay unholy hands on the Swedish archbishop, and as a result the regent and his followers were excommunicated as heretics. At Vädla (now inside the city limits of Stockholm), Sten Sture met the Danish invaders and inflicted a crushing defeat upon them. Stäket surrendered some time later, and Gustaf Trolle was put under arrest and deposed as archbishop. Realizing how serious a matter it was to depose a high official of the Church, Sten Sture prevailed upon the Uppsala Consistory (*domkapitel*), to elect Arcimboldus, the indulgence seller, in Trolle's place. With the proper documents and commissions Arcimboldus set out for Rome to set the Swedish situation in its proper light before the Pope and secure papal confirmation of his election, but through the treachery of one of the members of his own group he fell into the hands of Christian, and the plans of Sten Sture and Arcimboldus were thus frustrated. The enemies of the Swedish regent continued to have the ear of the Pope, whose attitude was determined largely by political considerations. The only thing that the Roman Pontiff could see was on the one side the Swedes, weakened by serious divisions, and on the other the powerful and aggressive Christian, backed, as was commonly supposed, by the tremendous influence of Charles V. It therefore seemed certain to the Curia that Sten Sture was destined to meet defeat. He and his adherents were therefore excommunicated, all Sweden laid under interdict, and Christian of Denmark entrusted with the execution of the papal judgment.

Christian II.—The course of events in Sweden had so far been completely to Christian's liking. At the death of his father, Hans, in 1513, the Danish prince had immediately called upon the Councils of the three countries to acclaim him as their king, in conformity with earlier assurances, which, however, so far as Sweden was concerned, were not binding. At a later meeting at Copenhagen, attended by representatives of the Councils from the three countries, Christian was without hesitation acclaimed king by the Danes and the Norwegians, but the Swedish lords found themselves in a serious dilemma; they had the alternative, they said, of peace here and war at home, or war here and peace at home. Decision in regard to Christian's right to the Swedish crown was therefore deferred. That the matter would not be permitted to remain very long in this status must have been quite evident to all who knew the young king's character and ambitious schemes. He had already shown that he was not to be trifled with. As governor of Norway, Christian had shown exceptional administrative ability, having to his credit a number of highly beneficial economic reforms for which he had won the gratitude of the country. By official acts as well as by shockingly frank expressions of opinion, he had revealed a remarkable and praiseworthy disposition to favour the common people as against the great lords. His democratic leanings were the result largely of early environment and of training. In order that the young prince might receive the proper care and education, he had, as a young man, been placed in the home of a wealthy merchant of Copenhagen, but this mentor, like the rest of his class, hated the aristocracy intensely because of its arrogance, pride, and shameless selfishness, and Christian had come to share this feeling in the fullest measure. There were others for whom this Danish merchant, in common with the rest of his class, felt an intense distrust; namely, the Hanseatic traders and the Swedes, and here also Christian had evidently, as the sequel will show, been susceptible to influence. The Swedes, according to this merchant, were a most obstinate, rebellious, and ungrateful people, who deserved to be taught a severe lesson. Stately and courtly, most affable when in a good mood, a leader in sports and escapades, dashing in manners, and democratic in sentiment and actions, Christian had some of the genuine qualities of great leadership. Moreover, he was a friend of learning, an admirer of the great Erasmus, and he instituted reforms in Denmark which bore the impress of an enlightened and humane spirit. But unfortunately for Christian, these good qualities were counterbalanced by vices and weaknesses which made his reign an utter failure even in Denmark, and which filled his own life with a tragedy such as has come to few rulers in history. Moral standards he had none, and, according as it suited his whims or purposes, he was ready to violate the most solemn pledges. Suspicion and craftiness lurked behind the seemingly genial appearance, and when passion seized him he could become guilty of most inhuman cruelty. One may surmise, therefore, that Christian felt no scruples against taking the political testament of his grandfather (p. 197) as his guiding principle in his attitude towards Sweden.

Treachery of the Danish king.—The defeat of the Danish army at Vädla had not for a moment caused Christian to waver in his determination to crush Sweden and place its crown upon his head; it had merely proved to him that next time he must have a larger force and be prepared to strike a harder blow. In the summer of 1518 Christian came again, this time at the head of a large army, consisting mainly of mercenary soldiers, but this army also suffered defeat in a bloody encounter with a Swedish army chiefly made up of *bönder* under Sten Sture at Brännkyrka near Stockholm. Since after this defeat Christian found himself in a most perilous situation because of difficulty in procuring provisions, he now resorted to negotiations which reveal his utter lack of honour. He first invited Sten Sture to his headquarters for a personal interview, sending a number of Danish noblemen to the Swedish camp as an evidence of his good faith, and the high-minded Swedish leader, who found it difficult to believe in the utter perfidy of his enemy, was on the point of accepting his invitation when the burgomasters and members of the City Council of Stockholm, not as trustful as their chief, declared categorically that if he went they would immediately proceed to elect a new leader, as they knew that he would never return. The protector yielded to their entreaties and protests and declined to go. Christian then suggested that six Swedes be sent to his camp as hostages, and he would himself come to the Swedish headquarters for a conference. Sten Sture accepted this proffer and sent six men, one of them being a young man, Gustaf Eriksson Vasa. Immediately on getting on board Christian's ship, these men were put in chains and carried off to Copenhagen, where they were detained as prisoners. This shameful act of duplicity was to prove a colossal blunder on the part of the Danish king.

Christian's two unsuccessful campaigns had clearly shown him how difficult it was to subdue the Swedes under a leader like Sten Sture, and for the third campaign, which was now being prepared, he proposed to organize a far stronger force than ever before. Oppressive taxes were levied both in Denmark and Norway to provide means for strengthening the fleet and increasing the army. The king now aimed to strike at the very heart of Sweden. By January 1520 he was ready with his preparations and from Hälsingborg in southern Sweden he advanced with his army of 10,000 men through the interior of Sweden, with Stockholm as the objective, while the fleet shut off the capital from the sea. The Swedish army met the invaders near Lake Asunden in Västergötland and in the very beginning of the encounter came the great disaster to the Swedes. Sten Sture was wounded and rendered unable to continue in command.

Death of Sten Sture.—Depressed and thrown into confusion by the loss of their leader, the Swedes fell back, leaving the road to Stockholm open to the enemy. The wounded and fever-stricken Sten Sture hurried towards central Sweden in order to re-establish his lines, but on being informed of a Danish advance, he set out in the bitterly cold winter for Stockholm, travelling over Lake Mälaren by sled, in order to put the capital in a state of defense. While speeding over the wind-swept ice, and still far from the city, the intrepid leader died of his wounds (February 3, 1520).

With their leader gone, the Swedes gave way at almost every point and the Danish army advanced upon Stockholm. The Swedish *bönder* indeed fought valiantly and at Uppsala came near inflicting a crushing defeat on the enemy, but finally the tide of battle turned against them and what had promised to become a victory turned into a rout. The Swedish nobles, who had been held in line by the masterful hand of Sten Sture, now hastened to make their peace with Christian, and soon the Swedish Council acknowledged Christian king. In this hour of pusillanimity and confusion only four of Sten Sture's adherents in command of Swedish strongholds stuck faithfully to their posts, and two of these were women. One was Christina Gyllenstierna, widow of Sten Sture, who immediately after her husband's death had taken command of the defences of Stockholm, and the other, Anna Bielke, who led the defence of the castle of Kalmar. In spite of Lady Christina's resolute leadership, the capital soon fell into the hands of Christian (September 1520). With feminine intuition, as it were, Lady Christina had sensed the dastardly intentions of Christian, and of Trolle's bitter hatred she needed no further proof. Only after the king had signed the most solemn and sweeping declaration of amnesty for all who had opposed him, did she finally yield. The amnesty covered all hostile acts against Denmark since the time of Christian I, or against Jakob Ulfsson, Gustaf Trolle, or any other prelate, their servants, or their properties, and was to be binding upon both temporal and ecclesiastical courts; Christian also pledged himself to rule Sweden in conformity with Swedish law and with the provisions of all previous recesses. Sweden now seemed helpless, and the Kalmar Union was a reality again.

The Coronation Riksdag.—The victorious Christian next summoned a Coronation Riksdag at Stockhold for the latter part of October (1520). To this were invited the members of the Council, all the prominent nobles and prelates in the land, besides a great number of burghers and *bönder.* At the beginning of the session, Christian indulged in a bit of clumsy sophistry to prove his right to the Swedish throne: the ancient law, he maintained, prescribed that as King of Sweden "shall be elected a native man, preferably from among the king's sons, if there are any." The Swedes were now informed that since Christian was the only son of Hans they had no option in the matter, the hereditary principle automatically making him king of the country. Although succession by right of heredity was as yet unknown to Swedish law, the Swedish Council was now compelled to acquiesce in a declaration affirming Christian's right to the crown by virtue of the principle which he had proclaimed.

Christian was crowned king at Stockholm on November 4 by his worthy ally, Gustaf Trolle. Then followed a period of feasting and rejoicing in the city, but on the seventh, in the words of the chronicle, "a spectacle of a different kind began." On that day the prominent Swedes, members of the Council, the aldermen of Stockholm, and Christina Gyllenstierna were summoned to the palace where the king, attired in all the regalia of majesty, took his place on the royal throne. Before him now appeared Gustaf Trolle and, according to the hitherto accepted accounts, made formal charges of heresy against the adherents of the Sture party, at the same time reminding the king of his oath to defend the Church. (Later researches have cast some doubt on the claim that Trolle at this time presented charges of heresy. This may have come later at the instigation of Christian.) For the injury that he had suffered he now demanded reparations. Christian asked if a compromise could not be effected and a reconciliation made, to which Trolle gave the haughty answer that no reconciliation was possible. The sum demanded as reparation was next made known and amounted to 1,100,000 silver marks, a stupendous sum; for all of Skåne, Magnus Eriksson had agreed to pay 34,000 silver marks (p. 159), which amount, however, according to Trolle, might admit of some reductions. Immediately Christina Gyllenstierna stepped forward and presented the decrees of the meeting of Arboga of 1517, which showed that the measures against Trolle and his adherents had been official acts for which no individual could be held responsible. The prudent Bishop Brask now saved himself from all unpleasantness by opening his seal on the document and producing the little slip of paper which he, with such admirable forethought, had placed beneath it (p. 213). The existence of the document was unknown to both Christian and Trolle, and this unexpected turn of affairs made them temporarily confused; hasty consultations followed, the results of which were soon to appear. The next day a special jury of thirteen ecclesiastics with Trolle at the head, a most unseemly procedure, since this made him both accuser and judge, was appointed to try the accused on the charge of heresy; it was a foregone conclusion that the verdict would be "guilty," but the court did not specify what the punishment ought to be. The decree of guilty in an ecclesiastical court did not, however, carry with it the punishment of secular courts, and, furthermore, the Pope had already withdrawn the decree of heresy against the accused.

The Stockholm Massacre.—Two hours after the verdict of guilty had been rendered, two of the accused, Bishop Matthias of Strängnäs and Bishop Vincentius of Skara, were brought to the market-place and beheaded, and thereupon others were sent to the block in rapid succession. More than one hundred persons were thus executed, with revolting cruelty and without legal trial. The list of victims included practically all the leading burghers of Stockholm and several noblemen. Their bodies were thrown upon a pyre and burned and even the bodies of Sten Sture and his young son were disinterred and burned, while Christina Gyllenstierna and some of the other prominent women were thrown into prison. Thus had Christian with a bloody deed, which is known as the Stockholm Massacre, aimed to strike terror into the hearts of the stiff-necked Swedes. It is by reason of his bloody deeds at Stockholm that the epithet "the Tyrant" ever after clung to his name in Sweden. The turn next came to the provinces, even Finland not escaping; here Hemming Gadh, although he had turned traitor to Sten Sture because of some fancied wrong and had become a faithful tool of Christian, shared the fate of the other Swedish lords. The property of the victims was then confiscated by the king.

Responsibility for the massacre.—The responsibility for the Stockholm Massacre unquestionably rests with greatest weight upon the king himself. All the circumstances point to a deliberate plan on his part to get rid of the troublesome Swedish leaders and strike such terror into the hearts of his Swedish subjects that they forever after would remain humble and submissive. As he is reported to have said to the Dutch humanist, Erasmus: "Mild measures are of no use; the remedies that give the whole body a good shaking are the best and surest."[2] His attitude subsequent to the bloody scenes was that of a cynical prevaricator. First he tried to throw the blame on Gustaf Trolle, later on the court, which, he said, had consisted "of the wisest men in the land," and whose verdict he was in duty bound to execute. Later, when he found it necessary to absolve himself before the Pope of the crime of murdering two bishops, he lied brazenly and said the Swedish rebels had planned to blow him and his forces to pieces, and when his soldiers discovered this plot they became so infuriated that they cut the conspirators down. Finally, when this version was met with utter incredulity, he threw the blame upon one of his lieutenants, Didrik Slagheck, whom he later caused to be executed. Many of Christian's own men, it should be said, were filled with loathing at the dastardly deed. Trolle's guilt in the matter

[2] Bain, R. Nisbet, *Scandinavia,* Cambridge, 1905, p. 26.

cannot be fixed with definiteness. It is certain that he wished to ruin and humiliate his enemies, but the massacre was quite certainly not his suggestion and he was, no doubt, surprised at the king's violence.[3] For what had happened he showed, however, no regrets or qualms of conscience. Christian left Stockholm in December (1520), in the firm belief that the Swedes were now completely crushed, and that Sweden, the prize for which Danish rulers had been contending ever since Margaret's time, was at last secure in his hands. The first of the great objectives which he had set before him was, so it seemed, attained; the other two, the humiliation of the Hanseatic League and the creation of a great Scandinavian manufacturing concern and trade monopoly, with Copenhagen as the centre of great enterprises, remained. Brilliant indeed seemed the future of the young king.

The interim government.—When Christian left Sweden, after the Stockholm Massacre, he believed that the foundation of the Scandinavian Union had at last been laid securely, but within a year all his work was undone and he himself was an exile from his own land. For what happened, Christian had himself primarily to blame, for his conduct towards the country had been, and continued to be, marked by the commission of colossal blunders. The first of these is seen in his arrangement for the government of Sweden during his absence. As he feared that any individual or set of men, whether Danish or Swedish, to whom the government might be entrusted would very likely try to usurp power and start a revolutionary movement against him, he appointed as members of the interim government three cunning and unscrupulous men, who, he was convinced, would distrust one another and each in turn keep the ruler fully informed regarding the conduct of his colleagues.

[3] Professor Lauritz Weibull of the University of Lund has recently presented documents and made an interpretation of all the known facts in connection with the massacre which apportions the guilt quite differently from what nearly all Swedish and Danish historians have done. Weibull comes to the conclusion that the blame rests squarely on Trolle and that Christian was merely a weak tool in the hands of the irreconcilable and bitter Swedish archbishop and his friends. Weibull, L., *Stockholms blodbad* in *Scandia, Tidskrift för historisk forskning,* Stockholm, February, 1928. Weibull's position has since been severely criticised by several scholars. Sandström, Johan, *Kättardomen vid Stockholms blodbad, Historisk tidskrift utgiven* or *Svenska historiska föreningen,* 1928. Same author, *Några bidrag till Stockholms blodbads historia, Historisk tidskrift,* 1929; Ahnlund, Nils, *Kring Stockholms blodbad, Svensk Tidskrift,* 1928.

At the head stood Didrik Slagheck, a coarse, brutal man, who was suspected, and no doubt justly so, of being the king's chief adviser in perpetrating the Stockholm Massacre; the other two members were Gustaf Trolle and Jens Beldenak, the latter also a coarse and unscrupulous individual, whom the king had caused to be elected Bishop of Strängnäs. The character and records of these men filled the Swedes with fear and loathing. Great tact and strict attention to duties were required on the part of the new government if the people were to accommodate themselves submissively to the new régime, but these men were utterly incapable of manifesting any such virtues. When a serious situation confronted them, they failed to act with promptness, and, like the consummate knaves they all were, they spent most of the time in bitter wrangling among themselves.

One of Christian's most serious blunders was a journey to the Netherlands, which he undertook immediately upon his return from Sweden, primarily for the purpose of entering into negotiations with the Dutch regarding the creation of a great trade company, the ostensible purpose of which was, however, the elimination of the Hanseatic League from the Baltic trade. Frank, brutal, and tactless as he was, the king could not keep his plans secret and they soon became known, with the result that the powerful Hansa was more than ever ready to join in an attack upon him. He committed another blunder when, for reasons of economy, he soon after his return from Sweden dismissed all his mercenary soldiers, and thus no longer had an effective fighting force at his command. But the blunder which in its consequences far outweighed all others was his treachery in carrying young Gustaf Eriksson Vasa away as a prisoner to Denmark (p. 216), thus in all likelihood saving him from being present at the Stockholm meeting; his prominence and his decided and well-known national sympathies would most likely have made him one of the first victims of Christian's vindictiveness.

Even before Christian on his journey from Stockholm towards his own land had crossed the boundary-line between Sweden and Denmark, he heard the news that an insurrection had started in Dalarna, but he imagined that it was merely a local disturbance, which his interim government could easily handle. He therefore contented himself with setting a price on the leader's head and then with a light heart proceeded on his way. The leader of the insurrection was Gustaf Eriksson Vasa, or, as he is usually designated in English texts, Gustavus Vasa.

Early days of Gustavus Vasa.—Gustavus Vasa, the Hero King, who "built his Sweden from foundation to rafters," the founder of a dynasty which, because of the brilliant intellectual powers that characterized nearly all of its members, has been rated as being one among the four great families in history, belonged to an old noble family which, with only a few exceptions, had in the past been aligned with the Union or Danish Party in Sweden. On his father's side he was related to the Sture family. Born in either 1496 or 1497—the records are not in agreement on this point—on Lindholmen's estate in Uppland, Gustavus had spent his boyhood days in a decidedly anti-Danish and anti-Union environment. An old legend relates that he was placed under the care of a Danish schoolmaster, Ivar by name, at Uppsala, and on one occasion, becoming for some reason angry with the master, he defiantly shouted, "When I am grown, I will go to Dalarna, get the Dalecarlians with me, and we will whack the Jutes (Danes), on the nose." As Master Ivar naturally punished this insolent talk by a vigorous application of the cane, Gustavus plunged his dagger through his Greek text, exclaiming, "You and your school may go to the devil," whereupon he speedily and discreetly took his departure. At the court of Sten Sture, whither he had been sent to acquire courtly manners, the old Dane-hater Hemming Gadh became his eloquent and willing preceptor in everything anti-Danish. His early distrust of the Danes had naturally been strongly confirmed by Christian's treachery in carrying him away to Denmark and keeping him a prisoner there. During this enforced stay in Denmark his distrust and dislike of its people had received plenty of nourishment, for he had been compelled to listen to the boasts of his keepers that they soon would humble the stiff-necked Swedes; especially exasperating to him was their great glee because of the ease with which they had managed to deceive the simpleton Swedes. Gustavus managed to escape in disguise to Lübeck—going part of the way as an ox-driver—and here he was well received and befriended by influential men, including the burgomaster of that city; when soon thereafter the Danish jailkeeper demanded his surrender, the Lübeck officials turned a deaf ear to all such demands. Christian's anti-Hanseatic plans and his negotiations with the Dutch were by this time, mainly because of the king's own indiscretions, well known in Lübeck and it did not suit the purpose of the shrewd city fathers of Lübeck to accommodate him in any way. It would, on the contrary, be distinctly to their advantage if Gustavus could return to Sweden and there help to stir up trouble for Christian. They therefore gave him both their assistance and their blessing when he set out on a dangerous journey for the homeland, which he reached safely. Landing near Kalmar, in May 1520, "alone with his courage and his sword," he made his way into this fortified place, one of the two which still held out against Christian, and sought to stir up the defenders to a more determined resistance. But these were for the most part Germans, who met Gustavus's plans with threats to kill him. Pressing on farther into the interior, Gustavus next sought to arouse the country folk, but met with no encouragement; in Småland the *bönder* said they were satisfied with Christian, for he had provided them with salt and herring, and they sped Gustavus farther on his way by shooting arrows at him. Virtually a hunted fugitive by this time, Gustavus had reached his ancestral estate Rävsnäs near Stockholm, when news of the Stockholm Massacre came to him and now for the first time he learned that his father and his brother-in-law had been executed and that a price was fixed on his own head.

Gustavus a fugitive in Dalarna.—In the guise of a common labourer, carrying an axe on his shoulder, Gustavus now set out for Dalarna, in the firm belief that the people who had heeded the calls of Engelbrekt and the Stures and had rallied to the defence of the nation's freedom, held out the only hope that now remained for the salvation of Sweden. The story of the adventures of the young hero while in this picturesque province, seeking to arouse its people and dodging Christian's alert bailiffs, is perhaps better known to later generations of Swedes than any other chapter in their country's history. The story relates how Gustavus first came in disguise to his old schoolmate from Uppsala, Anders Persson, in Rankhyttan, but here a servant-girl chanced to perceive a gold-embroidered collar sticking out from beneath the young labourer's coarse homespun coat. She forthwith told her master of this strange combination in the young man's attire, and the fugitive's identity was soon revealed. Fearing to harbour Gustavus, Anders Persson urged him to be on his way, and next he came to Arent Persson at Ornäs. As he felt confidence in Arent, Gustavus made known his identity to him. Lured by the prospect of gaining the reward offered for the capture of the fugitive, and hoping in other ways to profit by Christian's favour, Arent simulated great friendship for his guest, but at the first opportunity drove to the home of the Danish bailiff and revealed to him the whereabouts of Gustavus. Arent's resolute wife, Barbro,[4] however, suspecting her husband of treasonable designs, speedily aroused Gustavus and with a horse and sled which the determined lady had made ready he made his escape over frozen Lake Runn. Arent, the story adds, never forgave his wife for thus having thwarted him. The fugitive now came to the priest Jon in Svärdsjö, and here he helped the men thresh grain. Jon was a reliable friend, but he committed the indiscretion one day of holding a towel for Gustavus while the latter was making his ablutions, which strange deference to a labourer aroused the curiosity of one of his maid-servants whose tongue was naturally set wagging by the incident, and fearing detection the faithful priest sent his friend to Sven in Isala, a royal forest warden. The Danish spies were, however, now hot on his trail. Once, as he was standing by the fireplace warming himself, Danish soldiers entered and inquired whether the fugitive had been seen. Fearing that their suspicions would be directed towards Gustavus, the quick-witted wife of Sven struck him a resounding blow on his back with her bread-spade, saying, "Why do you stand

[4] At Rättvik, one of the picturesque communities on Lake Siljan in Dalarna, a noble monument has in recent years been raised in commemoration of those who are alleged to have befriended Gustavus. The name of Barbro has an honoured place in this list; it is unnecessary to state that her husband's name is not included on the honour roll.

here gaping at strangers? Have you never seen human beings before? Get out of here and betake yourself to the threshing-loft." Naturally the wife of a commoner would never dare thus to treat the scion of one of Sweden's distinguished noble families, thought the pursuers, and forthwith departed. As Sven began to fear that his friend was not safe in Isala, he hid Gustavus in a load of straw and drove towards the region of Lake Siljan. Danish soldiers who swarmed about overtook Sven and suspecting a trick ran their spears through the load; Gustavus was wounded. As they drove on, Sven soon noticed that blood began to trickle down upon the snow and he therefore took his knife and cut a gash in his horse's foot; when the soldiers came up again and wanted to know whence the blood came, the driver disarmed their suspicions by pointing to the bleeding foot of his horse. Sven delivered Gustavus to some reliable friends who kept him concealed three days under a fallen pine. But as soon as the Danish soldiers had betaken themselves to other regions to continue their search, Gustavus came out in the open and began to exhort the *bönder* of Rättvik to rise in revolt against the Danish oppressor. With characteristic native caution the *bönder* said they would take no action until they had ascertained the sentiments of their neighbours; their attitude towards Gustavus, however, was friendly. Gustavus next proceeded to Mora, one of the most populous centres of Dalarna, and since the Danes were again in hot pursuit he was compelled to hide himself in a cellar under the house of Matts Larsson in Utmeland. One day the soldiers entered in order to search the house, but the quick-witted wife of Matts, who was busy brewing the Christmas ale, hurriedly rolled a large brewing-vat over the cellar trapdoor, and again Gustavus escaped.

It seems a pity that historical criticism could not permit these delightful stories, part of the treasured heritage, as it were, of the Swedish people, to escape the withering glare of its searchlight; sceptical historians have, however, pointed to the suspicious fact that Peder Swart, Bishop of Västerås, and chaplain of Gustavus Vasa, who at the king's own suggestion wrote a chronicle of his reign,[5] has not a word to say about some of these adventures. Another circumstance that is bound

[5] Peder Swart, *Konung Gustaf I's Krönika,* edited by Nils Edén, Stockholm, 1912.

to arouse doubts regarding the credibility of the tales is the fact that in some instances the same episode is laid in different localities and occurs in varied connections. Furthermore it should be noted that most of the traditions were not committed to writing until the latter part of the seventeenth century or almost a century and a half after the events were supposed actually to have happened, which naturally raises the suspicion that in the course of time many embellishments were added to the original stories. That the life of Gustavus was beset with many dangers and that he more than once had miraculous escapes may be taken for granted, and it may, after all, be assumed that in the main his adventures among the people of Dalarna were somewhat as related in the legends.[6]

The war of liberation begins.—At last Gustavus felt it safe to appear openly before the people and appeal to them to join in a revolt against Christian. As the sturdy *bönder* of Mora

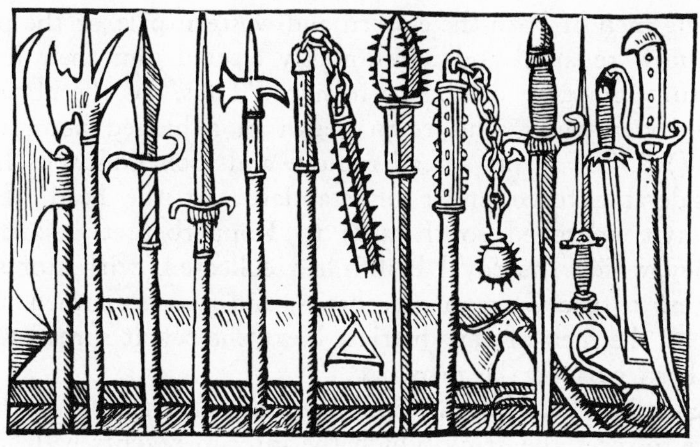

Weapons used in the wars of Gustavus Vasa

one day in the Christmas season emerged from church, the young patriot gathered them around him and with a soul afire with shame and indignation spoke to them of the country's dangers and dishonour, and offered to lead them against the foreign oppressor. The *bönder* answered that they were tired

[6] For a critical analysis of the legends of Gustavus Vasa in Dalarna, see Sixten Samuelsson, *Källorna för Gustaf Vasas äventyr i Dalarna*, in *Föreningen Heimdals Småskrifter*, No. 10.

of war and would not violate their oath to Christian. Utterly disheartened and despairing of his country's future, Gustavus Vasa thereupon set out alone on skis through the dreary regions northwest of Mora, intending to find a haven in Norway. Slowly he worked his way over the trackless waste of snow—which in commemoration of Gustavus's lonely journey, has now come to serve as the course for Sweden's greatest annual ski derby—and was already within sight of the Norwegian mountains when he was overtaken by two of the speediest ski-runners of Mora and urged to return to lead its people against Christian. This change of heart in the men of Mora had come soon after the departure of Gustavus, for then messengers from the southern provinces had brought the alarming intelligence that Christian intended on his royal journey to raise gallows at every sheriff's estate, and that new and unjust taxes would be levied. Joyfully and with renewed courage in his heart, Gustavus returned to Mora, whither the leading men of both the eastern and western part of the province now repaired and unanimously elected him their leader, solemnly pledging obedience to him. "Thus," as the chronicle quaintly remarks, "his reign began in a blessed hour (*salig stund*)." The revolt spread rapidly and soon Gustavus had a considerable force under his standard. At the head of this Gustavus marched southwards to Kopparberget, seized the money which the royal bailiff had collected, with stores belonging to the German merchants, and was acclaimed leader also by the men of this district. Next the revolt spread to the southern part of the province.

Swedish victories.—Soon Gustavus ventured with his force to meet the army which the interim regents had hastily raised and sent into Dalarna. The two armies met at Brunbäck's Ferry on the Dal River. On beholding the Swedish host under command of a miner, Peder Svensson by name, the Danish leader, Jens Beldenak, is said to have asked how many soldiers this region could muster. When informed that it could place 30,000 men in the field, Beldenak expressed his surprise at this and asked how they could procure food. "For the most part," was the answer, "they drink nothing but water, and when necessity requires they content themselves with bark-bread." "People who can live on bark and water," exclaimed the astonished Dane, "can be subdued neither by the devil nor, still less, by any man! Brethren, let us speedily betake ourselves hence." When the Swedes saw the Danes retreat, they set out in pursuit and inflicted terrific losses upon them. Gustavus, who during the Brunbäck's Ferry campaign had been absent in Hälsingland and Gästrikland to exhort its inhabitants to join in the revolt, now returned and was able to enter Västmanland at the head of an army of 15,000 men, and with this force he attacked the important fortified town of Västerås, which fell into his hands. Soon Gustavus was master of all the provinces north of Mälaren, and now made an attempt to bring about a reconciliation with Gustaf Trolle. The only reply of the old intriguer to these overtures was an insolent threat against Gustavus and a surprise attack upon Uppsala in an endeavour to seize him. This failed and Gustavus was soon ready to begin the siege of Stockholm, this being now the only place of any importance to hold out against him. He was, however, poorly equipped for such a siege. Unlike the earlier defenders of the Swedish national cause, Gustavus had no private fortune or great fiefs to draw upon, and the few lords who were still alive after the Stockholm Massacre and had joined his ranks were fugitives from justice like himself; naturally with a man like Gustaf Trolle at its head, the Church would give him no substantial assistance. The army had consisted mainly of undisciplined *bönder* and miners, armed with axes, bows, and arrows; when they had won a battle they imagined that their cause had safely triumphed and so rushed off to their homes again.

Assistance from Lübeck and Danzig.—Gustavus had neither large guns nor a fleet with which to press the siege of a fortified city. His position was, however, steadily strengthened by the accession of new forces to his ranks; several hitherto hostile lords and Bishop Brask joined the ranks of his supporters, and the provinces south of Lake Mälaren joined with the others in electing him regent (*riksföreståndare*) of Sweden, August 1521. For the siege of Stockholm Gustavus next year received assistance from Lübeck and Danzig, both of whom had been roused to opposition against Christian by his ambitious plans for a Scandinavian trade monopoly (p. 222). An offensive and defensive alliance between the two cities was signed, and in line with their defensive measures against the Danish king they sent a sum of money, a fleet, and 4,400 men to the aid of Gustavus Vasa. Equipped with fire-arms instead of bows and arrows, these foreign soldiers were looked upon as a specially valuable addition to the fighting forces of Sweden.

While the long siege of Stockholm was being pressed, Christian—who in the meantime had returned from his trip to the Netherlands—was mustering new forces for an attack upon Sweden, but as this involved large expenses he was compelled to resort to extraordinary taxes upon the Danish nobles and ecclesiastics. These men were already aroused to bitterness against the king because of his new laws aiming to ameliorate the conditions of the common people, and the renewed exactions brought their patience speedily to an end. They now invited his uncle, Frederick of Holstein, to come into the land and accept the royal office. The revolt and resulting confusion in Denmark seemed to offer a propitious opportunity to Gustavus for seizing Skåne, Blekinge, and Halland, which, as Bishop Brask had told him, according to the evidence of mediæval documents, once legally had belonged to Sweden and to which Denmark had no rightful claim.[7] A military force was actually sent by Gustavus into the first-named province, but the plans for the addition of these valuable provinces to Sweden could not as yet be realized.

Even with the formidable revolt against him, Christian's position was by no means hopeless, since the common people of Denmark were loyal to him, and Copenhagen and Malmö could be depended upon to stand by him, but at this critical moment in his career Christian collapsed completely and precipitately left the country for the Netherlands. Here he hoped to raise an army for the recovery of his lost kingdom, but the story of his life after this is merely the recital of one of the greatest tragedies of history. After sojourning in the Netherlands for many years, constantly planning to win back his former domains, he finally, in 1531, was ready to come with

[7] Hildebrand, E., *Sveriges historia,* IV, p. 43.

an armed force to Norway, prepared to advance upon Sweden and Denmark, but he was soon checked by Swedish and Danish-Lübeck forces. He now agreed to proceed to Copenhagen under safe conduct for a conference with King Frederick. In violation of all solemn assurances, he was, however, made a prisoner, and for the rest of his life, twenty-seven years, he was forced to languish in prison.

Gustavus elected king.—The flight of Christian by no means relieved the Swedes, for Danish claims to the Swedish throne were now renewed by Frederick. In order, however, to serve notice upon the Danes that further meddling on their part in Swedish affairs would be utterly unprofitable, the Swedes at a Riksdag at Strängnäs, June 1523, elected Gustavus king of the Swedish realm. The Lübeckers had likewise strongly pressed for this action, as it was to their interest to have a government in the land which could guarantee payment of the loans extended and be in a position to grant them trade concessions. The Strängnäs Riksdag also deposed Archbishop Trolle a second time. The struggles about the Kalmar Union were over and Sweden had definitely taken her place among the sovereign states of Europe.

Notifying the European rulers.—Not long after his election, Gustavus issued a circular letter to the people of Sweden, in which he gave noble expression to his intention to rule as a "kindly, good, and loyal lord" and in accordance with the ancient rights of the people. The rulers of the leading European states were likewise, through a lengthy document, informed of the action of the Swedish nation and of the reasons which had impelled it to take such action. The document constitutes a severe indictment of Christian and his rule.[8] On Midsummer Eve the same year, 1523, the gates of Stockholm were finally opened to Gustavus and he made his triumphal entry into the capital. This was, it has been assumed, the first occasion upon which the Swedish banner in blue and yellow was carried at the head of a procession. It was a devastated and miserable city which Gustavus now entered. Its tax-payers, numbering about 1,200 in 1519, had by 1523 dwindled to about 308, and the rehabilitation of the city became one of the first serious

[8] *Gustaf I:s Registratur I,* Stockholm, 1861-1867, pp. 65-78.

Stockholm as it appeared in 1524

concerns of the king. Royal orders were issued to certain citizens to take up their abode within its walls and industry and commerce were favoured by various measures.

Difficulties of the young king.—At this stage of his career, Gustavus might have felt elated over the wonderful success which seemingly had crowned his every effort. Three years before he had been an outlaw in his own country, hunted as a beast of the forest; alone and without means he had begun what might have seemed a hopeless struggle for the freedom and honour of his country against, apparently, one of the most powerful kings of Europe, and now the former fugitive had by the insistent and unanimous voice of the nation been called to occupy the royal throne and every part of Sweden gave him unquestioned loyalty. But if the young king had moments of elation, these were evidently not of long duration, for the difficulties and responsibilities that confronted him at the beginning were sufficient to keep him properly humble. He was a young man of twenty-seven, and lacked the experience in administration and statesmanship which the tremendously difficult position demanded. Search as he might, he could find hardly a man among his countrymen who possessed knowledge and experience in statecraft and whom he could trust. Local government had completely collapsed; courts had ceased to function, laws were openly flouted, and taxes could not be collected because the necessary machinery for collecting them was lacking; everything was in a chaotic state. At first the king had to bend every energy in order to get reliable bailiffs to serve him and bring order into the confused and hopeless finances of the country. So destitute was the country of trained men for state service that at first Gustavus was compelled to employ Germans like Wulf Gyler, Berent von Mehlen, and John van Hoja either as secretaries or on diplomatic or military missions. Naturally his own subjects soon began to mutter because of this preference given to foreigners. "Had Gustavus not called them to arms to drive out the foreigners?" they pointedly asked. Gustavus's only defense was that he could not get native men who were qualified for the service required, but his own people were not so easily convinced that this was true.

Jealousies.—Gustavus had, it is true, been the unanimous choice at Strängnäs, but if he felt any elation over that fact, it was considerably repressed by the knowledge that many groups and individuals were filled with bitter jealousy because this unprecedented honour had come to one of the Vasa family. There were other families more ancient and more distinguished than the Vasa; in fact, the latter family had not distinguished itself previously either by patriotic service or by a great degree of intelligence on the part of its members. The heads of most of the noble families had perished in the Stockholm Massacre, but young men, most of them of the same age as Gustavus, had taken their places. The Trolle family was now utterly discredited through the ignoble and anti-Swedish attitude of the former archbishop, but for the Sture family, with its splendid record of noble service, the people naturally felt the warmest affection. Christina Gyllenstierna's attitude was to give Gustavus no little concern, and that she on more than one occasion connived with the enemies of the young king cannot well be doubted.

Danish plans.—In addition to all his other troubles, the Swedish-Danish relations caused Gustavus much irritation, Frederick having been unseemly slow in recognizing Gustavus as king of Sweden. Some time after the Strängnäs election there even came an appeal to the Swedish Council from the Danish king and Council urging the election of Frederick as king of Sweden because of the blessing which a common ruler would bring to them all. Later Frederick advanced the excuse that the action taken at Strängnäs was not known to him when this communication was sent, but this statement has the ring of insincerity. The emphatic "No" of the Swedish Council in answer to the Danish suggestion evidently revealed to Frederick how futile were all hopes for the restoration of the Union. Gustavus watched the new Danish Government with the deepest suspicion. His failure to win the three southern provinces for Sweden and the defiance which one of Christian II's former lieutenants, Sören Norby, who had seized Gottland, manifested meant a serious loss of prestige to him and could easily have resulted in a dangerous and probably successful revolt had an able leader appeared among the malcontents; but no such leader appeared. There was to be no repetition of the story of Magnus Eriksson, Karl Knutsson, and Sten Sture the Elder.

Inertia of the bönder.—The *bönder,* the class for whom these men had fought, had now won new power and influence; they had in a sense superseded the great lords, and Gustavus, whom their loyal support had enabled to win victory, was soon to discover that the great unprivileged class was just about as ready to look to its own narrow interests when power seemed to rest with it as the other classes had been. They were suspicious, intolerant of any interference with what they considered their rights, and afflicted with seemingly hopeless inertia. Especially were they violently opposed to paying any new taxes, and whenever they could evade levies altogether they did so. It was reported that in 1521 there were one thousand *bönder* in the Kalmar district alone who had paid no taxes for ten years, and this delinquency was, no doubt, typical of the situation in general. To add to his troubles, Gustavus was soon to discover that the *bönder* had received an exalted notion regarding the place they were to occupy in the new régime. Since they had made Gustavus king, they naturally had the right, so they imagined, to tell him how the country ought to be ruled, but Gustavus had ideas regarding the rights and duties of a Swedish monarch that were greatly at variance with the *bönder's* antiquated notions. The former was determined to build on a new foundation, the latter were satisfied with the old structure as long as they could have peace and escape heavy taxes. Although Gustavus and the *bönder* had many a bitter tussle before the latter fell into line with the king's new policies, they, no doubt, at all times felt a genuine respect for each other.

Strength of Gustavus.—Gustavus had indeed tremendous difficulties to contend with, but he also had qualities which admirably fitted him for the difficult duties of the royal office. Endowed with giant physical strength and vitality and with remarkable quickness of perception, he was able to perform a prodigious amount of work, travel almost unceasingly, and make his plans rapidly. The incomparably best weapon in his hand against intrigue, indifference, and ignorance was the potent word. It would be hard to find among all the rulers of history one as able and resourceful as Gustavus to "conduct a campaign of education" or "make a fight for public opinion." His speeches were given in vigorous, pithy Swedish that could not fail to carry conviction, but it was especially as a letter-writer that he was far more effective than the leader of great battalions. His sincerity, his terse style, homely similes, quaint phrases, and remarkable lucidity of thought still make a study of his letters and documents a really delightful experience. One chronicler calls him "the most eloquent among men, who formulated his sentences so gracefully that everyone would a hundred times sooner hear him speak than any one else. Words flowed so easily that no impediment could be observed." [9]

Subjection to Lübeck.—The problem which first pressed for solution was the financial. The merchants of Lübeck had given money and a fleet to the king in order that he might be able to carry on the siege of Stockholm, and now in the hour of his victory they insistently demanded payment. Vainly did Gustavus play for an extension of time; the canny merchants hinted that if they could not get what they wanted from Gustavus, they knew very well where satisfactory terms could be secured—a plain hint that their support might be thrown to Denmark—and Gustavus then made a virtue of necessity and yielded to their hard demands. Five days after his election to the royal office Gustavus and the Swedish Council signed an agreement which virtually made Lübeck and its allied cities the absolute masters of Sweden's economic life. The Hanseatic cities were, according to this agreement, to have the right to import their wares to Sweden toll-free and in the case of certain articles of luxury, on which profits were the greatest, they had the right to trade directly with the citizens. Subjects of other countries should forever be excluded from the Swedish trade. Furthermore, the Swedish Government was not to interfere and regulate prices, none but citizens of the commercial cities were to have the right to become citizens of Stockholm or Kalmar; the Sound and other Danish channels were to be closed to Swedish commerce. Through these privi-

[9] Edén, Nils, *Gustav Vasas valda brev*, Stockholm, 1904.

leges the Hanseatic League secured a strangle-hold on Sweden's commerce.[10] Although he bitterly felt the humiliation of these concessions and foresaw their disastrous economic consequences to his country, Gustavus did not dare to reveal his real feelings; he even felt constrained to thank the German merchants for their kind consideration towards him and his country; he craved, he said, their good counsel for a wise rule in Sweden, to which the Council of Lübeck modestly replied that its advice would hardly be necessary, but if at any time there should come a request from him for guidance the city fathers would always counsel wisely according as it was given them to see the light. So humble was Gustavus that in Lübeck he was called "an angel," an appellation which was soon to be replaced by another of an equal number of letters but connoting an entirely different being. These trade privileges, of which mention has been made, were, however, not the only reimbursement that the merchant cities exacted from bankrupt Sweden; a few months after Gustavus's election, their representatives appeared in Stockholm and presented a bill for their aid in the siege of the city. This amounted to 116,472 marks, which already a year later, in spite of some payments by Sweden, had grown to 120,817 (120,000 marks is reckoned to have been equivalent to about 480,000 crowns in present value, or about $130,000. The extreme poverty of Sweden at the time is revealed by the fact that Gustavus was driven almost to distraction in attempting to raise this small amount). The debt to Lübeck was to harass Gustavus during the early part of his reign and was to have a most important bearing upon the king's policies and acts.

[10] Falk, A., *Gustaf Vasas utrikespoletik med avseende på handeln,* Stockholm, 1907, Ch. 2.

Chapter IX

THE REFORMATION AND THE NEW RELIGIOUS, ECONOMIC, AND POLITICAL ORDER

The status of the Catholic Church.—The Catholic Church had through her teachings and ministrations satisfied the religious cravings of the Swedish people to such an extent during the Middle Ages that it cannot be said that there existed any deep-rooted or widespread dissatisfaction with her as a spiritual power. Many of the shameful abuses which in other countries had brought reproach upon the Church and caused the people to rise in revolt against her authority were practically unknown in Sweden, partly because, being both poverty-stricken and remote from Rome, the country never became a very inviting field for ecclesiastical exploitation, and partly because the Swedes' ineradicable mistrust of foreigners and insistence that their land be ruled by native Swedish men only—a principle for which, as has been seen, they had all through the Middle Ages fought with stubborn determination —had resulted in excluding from the country those grasping churchmen who sought benefices, no matter in what land so long as these conferred wealth and power upon the incumbents. Some of the native churchmen had by no means been models of modesty and self-denial, but just as the people had somewhat complacently endured Bo Jonsson Grip because he was a Swede, and drove out the less grasping but foreign Albrecht of Mecklenburg, so they exercised some extra degree of tolerance for these sinful ecclesiastics because they, after all, were native men. While the Swedish clergy as a rule were ignorant, and drunkenness, gluttony, and licentiousness were common vices among them, the age was tolerant in Sweden as elsewhere in these matters. A reformation from within might therefore have been achieved, but this was as little likely to happen in Sweden as in the other countries which broke away from

Rome, mainly because the leaders in the ancient Church were unwilling to make needed reforms. In Sweden the Catholic Church was in a peculiarly unfortunate situation when the attacks upon her began and ill prepared to defend herself. The very extent of her wealth was a source of great weakness here as elsewhere. By the various devices by which wealth passed into the possession of the Church, such as gifts, tithes, tax-exemption, foreclosures, and grants of fiefs, almost 14,000 estates, as before stated (p. 209), not counting the lands set aside for the parsonages, or more than one-eighth of the total estates of the country, had come into her possession by the end of the Middle Ages. In some of the more fertile provinces the percentage of Church estates was much higher than the average for the country, as in Östergötland, 34 per cent, Västergötland, 29.3 per cent, Uppland, 21 per cent, Småland, 19.3 per cent.[1] Naturally the possession of this wealth had aroused much jealousy and ill-feeling and exposed the Church to the danger of attacks by those who for one reason or another wanted to secure a part of it. The ecclesiastical organization of Rome in Sweden had been most unfortunate and unwise, and had, just before the attacks on her began, done more to forfeit the love of the Swedes for the ancient Church than any other factor. The name of the recent head of the Church, Gustaf Trolle, was anathema to every patriotic Swede, and when the Pope, in the mistaken belief that victory must ultimately rest with Christian and Trolle, had persisted in supporting the Danish king and the hated archbishop, the indignation of the people naturally turned vehemently against him. There also lingered among the people a recollection of Christian's charges that the Swedish prelates had been the ones chiefly responsible for the Stockholm Massacre.

The Church is leaderless.—The Church was now entirely leaderless in Sweden. Trolle was an outlaw, the Bishops of Skara and Strängnäs had been executed in the Stockholm Massacre, the Bishops of Västerås and Åbo had both died in 1522, and the Bishop of Växio was old and helpless. The only ecclesiastic who could be expected to appear as an intrepid and forceful champion of the old organization was Bishop Brask

[1] Forssell, *Sveriges inre historia från Gustaf I*, p. 228.

of Linköping, but although he was an experienced and shrewd statesman, he was not the man to arouse the people in support of an unpopular cause. Matters were now made worse for the Church by new blunders at Rome. Gustavus had early become involved in a spirited controversy with the Curia regarding the filling of the many vacancies in the Swedish dioceses; native Swedish bishops and a new archbishop who would support the national cause, one "whose mind would go along with his," was the king's *sine qua non*. As a successor to Trolle, the Chapter of Uppsala had elected the learned and experienced Johannes Magni and the Pope's confirmation of this election had been requested. In his communication to the Pope in this matter, the king gave a full list of Trolle's crimes, but Rome ignored this document completely and instead requested Frederick of Denmark to assist Trolle in his attempt to regain the archiepiscopal dignity in Sweden. Letters were also dispatched from Rome to Sweden insisting on obedience, an act which stirred Gustavus to make another protest to both the Pope and the College of Cardinals. The Swedish emissary who carried these letters to Rome had instructions to impress still further upon the Pope that Sweden insisted on native men for ecclesiastical office who were in sympathy with the national cause, for only in this way could peace be maintained. The reply of Rome was startling: it announced that a young Italian, Francesco de Potenza, had been appointed Bishop of Skara. The idea of an Italian prelate in this, the oldest bishopric of Sweden, and one of the most ancient cultural centres of the land, seemed utterly shocking to Gustavus and other patriots; this was, they felt, the climax of papal insults. The answer of Gustavus to this challenge was characteristically vigorous and to the point; never, he declared, would a foreigner be permitted to occupy a Swedish bishopric and His Holiness need not think that Sweden would submit to such an indignity. As far as Gustavus was concerned, he would be willing, he averred, to shed his blood in resisting any such schemes. At the same time as Gustavus sent this vigorous message, he asked for confirmation of the newly elected Bishop of Åbo and for remission of papal taxes on account of the poverty of this diocese. To this communication was added the significant remark that if confirmation were denied or delayed, Gustavus would have his bishops confirmed by the "Chief High Priest, Christ." The only concession which the Curia would make was the appointment of Johannes Magni to take charge of the archiepiscopal office until Trolle's case should be investigated and a decision reached regarding his status; on the question of remission of papal levies, the answer was curtly negative. With this episode all negotiations between Sweden and the Pope came to an end. While this did not have the character of a diplomatic break, it justifies the assertion that Sweden was the first country of western Europe to cut loose from papal suzerainty.

Laurentius Andreæ.—In his early controversy with Rome, Gustavus enjoyed the counsel of Laurentius Andreæ, a shrewd, learned, and daring theologian, who in 1523 had become his secretary. The king soon found that here was a man whose thoughts on ecclesiastical affairs agreed with his own. Laurentius had studied in Uppsala, Rostock, and Leipsic, and had thrice visited Rome, whose corruption had bred in his mind certain ideas regarding the character and organization of the Church which appeared to Gustavus as most remarkable and just. The fact that the country was now in a desperate financial plight, no doubt helped to make clear to the king that Laurentius was surely right. The latter held that the Church is a congregation of Christian believers; its property, therefore, naturally belongs to those who constitute the organization; that is, to believers, or the people, and this property could rightly be used in the manner which best served the people's welfare, as for national defence, or to help avert a national disaster. This, of course, implied the right of confiscation by the king or Riksdag, for they embodied the will of the people.

Olaus Petri.—Prior to the first meeting between Gustavus and Laurentius, the latter had met a man, many years younger, who came to exert a profound influence upon him. This was Olaus Petri, the greatest man in the Swedish Reformation movement and withal one of the ablest and noblest among all the sixteenth-century reformers. In learning, eloquence, piety, and boldness, coupled with moderation and insight, he undoubtedly resembled Luther more closely than any of the contemporary religious leaders. He was born in Örebro in 1497, the son of a blacksmith. On going abroad to complete his education, he repaired to Wittenberg, which just then had gained fame because of Luther's teachings, and here he spent three years, becoming a personal friend of Luther and his co-labourer, Philip Melanchthon; their teachings he embraced whole-heartedly. After his return to his native country in 1519, he won the favour of Matthias, Bishop of Strängnäs, who made him deacon. Soon thereafter, Mäster Olof, as he was called, began to explain the Scriptures to the young students of the cathedral schools of Strängnäs, and this soon attracted the attention of Laurentius Andreæ whose heretical ideas regarding the nature of the Church naturally paved the way to a close friendship between the two men. Thus it was at Strängnäs that the doctrines of the Reformation were first heard in Sweden, and that these doctrines created quite a stir appears from the fact that the wide-awake and belligerent Bishop Brask soon felt it necessary to issue a protest against the new teachings. Whether Gustavus during his sojourn in Lübeck had become acquainted with the doctrines of Luther or had in any way become interested in the new religious movement which just then was gaining momentum is not known. Gustavus's first acquaintance with Olaus Petri very probably went back to the meeting of Strängnäs when he was elected king. The chronicle of Peder Swart relates that one day the king chanced to hear certain young men preaching doctrines that were new to him, and on questioning Laurentius Andreæ if there could be anything to these notions, he was told of Dr. Martinus, who had clipped the wings of the Pope, the cardinals, and the great bishops, and had made it clear that these men could not produce one single word from Holy Writ which could show that their worldly dominions and jurisdiction rested on God's commands. Coming from an authority which Gustavus considered the greatest of all, the word of God, the king became convinced and at the same time delighted, for here was unquestionable evidence that the Pope had no inalienable rights to the property of the Church. Olaus Petri was soon invited by the king to come to Stockholm and here he was made secretary to the City Council, and at the same time assigned to preach in the city's municipal church.

One of the most interesting aspects of the Reformation

in Sweden is the extensive and effective use to which the printing-press was put in the great controversy. The new doctrines soon stirred up a bitter struggle in the land and this raged for many years on all fronts, but it was a bloodless war in which the heavy artillery on both sides consisted of printing-presses and the projectiles of tracts, letters, decrees, books, translations, charges, and counter-charges. No country, it may safely be asserted, used, in proportion to population, as much printers' ink in trying to settle the great questions which in this period held the people's attention, as did Sweden. One of the chief assets of Gustavus, as has already been pointed out, was his exceptional power as a writer and speaker, and to Olaus Petri this power had been granted to a perhaps still greater degree. During a period of four years (1526-1530) he published no less than sixteen books, a list which appears the more impressive when it is observed that in all previous centuries only six works had been printed in Sweden. Olaus Petri created the literary language of Sweden, and this he did so well that even today his writings are admired as models of simplicity and elegant vigour. "He wrote the language of the people; he is the first author who wrote for the great, untutored masses, the first who made it his chief object to teach the Swedish people to read and think, and in this he succeeded; he made literature a treasure-house of ideas and sentiments to which even the common people were given access." [2] In his *Chronicle* Olaus Petri manifested qualities as a historian which placed him several centuries ahead of his time; he was never chauvinistic and exercised calm historic criticism.

Translation of the New Testament.—Outranking all his other literary labours in importance was the translation of the New Testament, published in 1526, and, according to the most recent views of scholars, his work alone. In this translation he was guided both by Luther's German text and Erasmus's Greek edition; the merits of both being embodied in it. The Swedes could now read the Bible in their own language and in words and idioms that were easily intelligible to them; they could now judge for themselves whether the reformers preached the truth or not. Before, so it has been surmised, there was prac-

[2] Schuck and Warburg, *Illustrerad svensk litteraturhistoria,* I, p. 270.

tically no one in all Sweden who had ever read the Sermon on the Mount or heard it quoted. The first Swedish hymn-book, published by Olaus Petri in the same year which saw the publication of his translation of the New Testament, constituted another of the great reformer's important contributions to the new religious life which was beginning to stir in the hearts of the Swedish people. In a series of pamphlets and other brief works, Petri undertook in masterly and simple style to make clear the doctrines of the Lutheran faith and their bearing upon the various relations of the individual as a member of family, society, and church. His emphasis upon the Christian's duty to take an active part in worldly affairs and find satisfaction in its enjoyments was most significant. "We must not," he says, "flee from the world as monks and nuns, for God gives us Christian liberty that we may as free men use food, drink, clothes, cities, time, and other such external things as it may please us to do. God desires us to exercise this freedom." [3]

The king needs money.—Although the Church possessed a large part of the wealth of the country, she carried a relatively small part of its financial burdens. Gustavus had, however, very early in his career begun to look to the Church as a possible source whence added income might be secured for the state, and through his acquaintance with Laurentius Andreæ and Olaus Petri his attention had been directed to the scriptural justification of a confiscation of property belonging to the ecclesiastics.

At this particular time the king was the more tempted to try to compel the Church to disgorge some of her wealth, because his creditors, the merchants of Lübeck, were making existence miserable for him by their insistent demand for at least part payment on the Swedish debt. But this was, after all, hardly more than an incident. With his clear realization of Sweden's weakness both in local administration and national defence, Gustavus understood clearly that order and prosperity could be found only in an effective machinery of government in which officials were rendered obedient to the ruler by being paid out of the royal treasury, and that safety against foreign enemies lay principally in the possession of a

[3] *Om Klosterlefverne* in *Olaus Petris Samlade Skrifter*, I.

strong army and navy. Such a program was, so far as Sweden was concerned, but an empty dream as long as the king was poverty-stricken. "The strong king," as Gustavus summed up the case, "is the rich king." While the Church enjoyed immunity from taxes, she had by no means withdrawn support entirely from national enterprises. Gustavus had received a contribution from her in 1522 to assist in the War of Liberation. The next year, when the Lübeckers had been more insistent than usual in clamouring for payment, and the soldiers likewise insisted on their pay, some money and valuables had been taken from the Church as "loans"; in 1524 another contribution was desired to defray the expense of a military expedition to Gottland. After that the Church was disturbed by one demand after the other upon her, and it was no longer a question of voluntary contributions, but regular levies were collected by the king's bailiffs. The bishops began to feel nervous, because of the king's infringing on their alleged rights, and opposition to him began to gain momentum. The financial predicament of Gustavus was, it is evident, increased by the "high cost of living" which afflicted all countries at the time, caused in large measure, no doubt, by the influx of gold and silver from the mines of Spanish America.

First revolt against Gustavus.—The first serious protest against the king's fiscal policy came in 1525, when the people living near Lake Siljan in Dalarna wrote insolent letters to the king, threatening to withdraw their allegiance. To this step the *bönder* had been inveigled by Peder Jakobsson Sunnanväder and Martin Knut Ericsson or "Mäster Knut" as he was called, the former having some time previously been elected Bishop of Västerås and the latter serving as curate in the same city; on well-founded suspicion of treason against him, Gustavus had later caused the election of Peder Jakobsson Sunnanväder to be declared void and Knut had been deposed. Conniving with these men in their opposition to Gustavus were some monks who had been driven from their cloisters. Betaking themselves to Dalarna, these men had persistently spread lies concerning Gustavus. Adherents of the Sture party and the Danish adventurer, Sören Norby, were evidently implicated in the plans against Gustavus. The malcontents complained in their letters of high prices and heavy taxes; the latter, they said, were so oppressive that it was impossible for the people to pay them, that they must instead "put the key in the door and go whithersoever God may give them mercy to go." Gustavus did not fail to answer, and in his statement, couched in most conciliatory phrases, he endeavoured to explain that the blame for the high prices could not justly be placed on him since they were due to world conditions over which he had no control. Soon thereafter the situation in the land became so threatening—"the country was rocking on its foundations," as Bishop Brask said—that Gustavus with characteristic promptness and daring now took the course which he often afterwards entered upon in case letter-writing proved unavailing: he called a meeting of the Riksdag.

At such a meeting, declared Gustavus, the representatives of the people must investigate the charges against him and then say whether they wanted him to remain king or preferred that he take his leave. It was, he continued, by their urgent appeals that he had been constrained to accept the crown; they had taken the oath of allegiance to him, but he was willing to put the crown aside and not for his sake ought the people to be compelled to endure more grief. In a second letter to the king, the malcontents resented the imputation of disloyalty, but advanced new charges. "May God forgive His Highness," the letter said, "for the poverty and anguish he has brought upon us and because we never did get the truth from him." The letter continued by reminding Gustavus of the days when he, a wanderer through their forests as an outlaw, could get help from neither German nor Dane, but only from "poor Swedes"; now, however, when their help had made him king, he despised them, brought Danes and Germans into the country and these got the money, while the Swedes got blows and stripes, or were subdued by threats of prison walls or chains. No more formidable list of crimes had ever been cited against Christian II himself than the charges which were now flung in Gustavus's face. The denunciation closed with the threat that unless he mended his ways they could no longer keep their oath of allegiance to him.

At a Riksdag meeting at Västerås in May 1525, matters

took the course which Gustavus had expected: the Estates by vote declared their confidence in him, refused positively to accept his resignation, and pledged their full support against intriguers and malcontents. Being now certain of the sentiment of the Riksdag, Gustavus dispatched another soothing letter to the people of Dalarna, and since they felt in better humour after their wrath against their king had been poured out, they were content to let matters rest. The restraint of Gustavus had been dictated by caution, for just then the fortress of Kalmar had fallen into the hands of rebels, of whom the shifty von Mehlen was the leader, and Gustavus had been forced to retake it by a military force. With this rebellion subdued, he could again proceed to Dalarna, where at Tuna he met the people at a Thing and a complete reconciliation was effected. Peder Sunnanväder and "Mäster Knut" were later captured and beheaded in Stockholm.

Second rebellion against Gustavus.—The desperate financial plight of Sweden soon forced Gustavus to tax the Church again. In spite of Bishop Brask's violent protests, a levy of two-thirds of the tithes of all parish churches was laid in 1526, in order that payment might be made on the Lübeck account. That same year Gustavus advanced another step when he challenged the legality of a deed granted by Sten Sture the Elder to a monastery at Mariefred. This was a well-understood hint that further attacks upon monastic property would soon follow. The murmur of discontent which now arose caused Gustavus to justify his course by making an attack on the old ecclesiastics. "There are too many lazy and useless priests and monks in the country," he told the people of Uppsala in 1526; "the monasteries are stuffed full with monks who are little better than the pests which consume the best grain of the land." For the learned and efficient men he said he had use, but not for "useless bread-sacks." The pressure from Lübeck forced Gustavus in 1526 to make new efforts to raise money, and this time he asked for two-thirds of the income of the clergy for the current year. A compromise was effected by which the Church paid him a lump sum. The dissatisfaction of the clergy kindled the fire of another revolt, and as before the scene was Dalarna (1527). A leader for the rebels now appeared in the person of the so-called *Daljunkern* (The Swain of Dalarna), a handsome and exceedingly clever and resourceful young man of the labouring class, whom the enemies of Gustavus had put through a course of training for his rôle. He now came forward and claimed the Swedish crown, by virtue of his being the son of the beloved Sten Sture the Younger. The young man was a consummate actor and glib of tongue and won a large following. When he spoke of "his dear father," he wept copiously, and the people were so touched by his show of grief that they wept with him. It was again the region around Lake Siljan, with the exception of Rättvik, that joined the revolt; the southern district remained neutral or supported the king, who again resorted to his trusty weapons, written communications. In statement after statement, all in pithy and vigorous language, Gustavus explained, denied, pleaded. As to the charge of "Luthery," he said he knew nothing. The only thing that he had done was to order that the Word and the Gospel be preached and that priests be not permitted to deceive the common people. It was a surprise to him, he confessed, that the worthy men of Dalarna should concern themselves about things which they never could understand anyway; let the learned men of the land, he advised, settle these matters. Again Gustavus felt that he stood before a great decision, and as was his custom in such a situation he summoned the Riksdag in order to lay the entire matter before the Estates and secure their support. Västerås was designated as the meeting-place.

The great decision by the Riksdag of Västerås, 1527.— The Riksdag of Västerås, which convened in June 1527, is one of the important mileposts in Swedish history, for it marked the complete triumph of the king and the Lutheran party, and laid solid the foundation for a monarchy which in point of strength and effectiveness was for many generations to have no superior in Europe. The meeting itself was full of dramatic incidents. Besides nobles, clergy, and burghers, the writ had summoned from each judicial district five or six prominent (*märkeliga*) *bönder* "who were experienced and were capable of following the deliberation (*giva akt på vad som hades för händer*)." Because of the importance of the meeting, the names of the delegates were recorded, and this is the first Swedish Riksdag at which this was done. More than one hundred *bönder* and a few mine-owners attended, their group being but slightly smaller than that of the nobility.

Gustavus was too systematic a man and realized too fully what was at stake for himself and the country not to have all his plans carefully laid in advance of the session. His secretary, the shrewd and trustworthy Laurentius Andreæ had undoubtedly collaborated with him in preparing a statement to be laid before the Estates and had given good advice as to the proper procedure to follow. On the opening day a detailed account was read in which the king gave a clear and frank exposition of the wretched condition of the country, refuted in vigorous terms the innumerable false and malicious accusations that had been made against him, and concluded by showing how utterly inadequate the income of the crown was for defraying the necessary expenses of the state. The total income, the statement revealed, was 24,000 marks, while the irreducible expenditures were 60,000 marks. In modern parlance, Gustavus here submitted a financial statement to his people and proposed a "balancing of the budget." To the delegates it was perfectly plain what Gustavus was driving at, and the redoubtable Bishop Brask therefore hastened to inform the assembly that the Church could not relinquish any of her property without the permission of the Pope. Some of the nobles also showed a disposition to be refractory. At this Gustavus's quick temper flared up, and he broke into a bitter invective against his unreasonable and ungrateful subjects. His words are thus quoted by Peder Swart: "If the people do not get rain, they blame me, and likewise if they do not get sunshine; if they experience hard years, hunger, and pestilence, or whatever it may be, then I must take the blame, as if they knew not that I am a human being and not God. You would rejoice to see the axe lodged in my head, but none of you dares to have his hands on its handle. You have chosen me to be your king, but who would under such circumstances be your king? Not the worst in hell. So let me tell you frankly that I will not be your king any longer, and you may choose any good man that you prefer in my place. . . . Pay me the value of the clods of earth I have here, and what I have spent of my own fortune upon the kingdom, and I promise you that I'll depart and never, so long as I live, return to this noisy, degenerate, and ungrateful land." With that the king burst into tears and rushed from the room to a castle near by, where he remained three days.

Great confusion arose in the assembly when Gustavus had finished his address. Ture Jönsson, a rich nobleman, who led the opposition to the king, the chronicler relates, walked home after the session with drummers walking before him and beating a merry tune, while he himself kept mumbling, "Tut, tut, tut! Never will they make a heathen and a heretic out of me this year." On the second day the younger men of the nobility began to yield in their opposition and the *bönder* were clamouring loudly for a speedy acquiescence in the king's program; Peder Swart, who has given a graphic account of these exciting days, says that in this the *bönder* were actuated by their eagerness to return home. The burghers were from the beginning unanimously with the king. Finally Bishop Magnus of Strängnäs exhorted the assembly to yield, for, as he said, "A child can see whither it would lead us if we renounce Gustavus and choose another king. It is well enough that the churchmen are protected, but this should not be done in such a manner that insolvency is brought upon the nation." On the third day the attitude of the *bönder* and the burghers became so threatening that the opposition to the king was forced to yield. Gustavus took his own good time before he again put in an appearance among the delegates. Message after message was sent to him, urging him "for God's sake" to come back, and when on the fourth day, certain that the fact of his indispensability had now had time to sink deep into their consciousness, he reappeared among the Estates, the forces of opposition were utterly demoralized and without delay the measures which he desired were passed.

The Västerås Recess.—These were embodied in the epochal document known as the *Recess of Västerås.* Its main provisions were that the surplus revenues of the bishops, cathedral chapters, and land-owning monasteries should be transferred to the crown, and that likewise the palaces and castles held by the bishops should revert to the state; the nobility might redeem from the religious houses all the land which had been devoted to pious uses since 1454 and to which they could establish valid claims. Two provisions to the effect that bishops and other ecclesiastics were never again to apply to Rome for confirmation, and that the Peter's Pence was henceforth to go to the king and not to the Pope, are not included in the authentic Swedish copies of the important enactment. They are quoted in a Latin statement probably intended for Bishop Brask and through him intended for Catholics to whom would thus be revealed the revolutionary and impious conduct of Gustavus Vasa. Whether at this time the king definitely was resolved on a break, or felt it expedient to keep a line of retreat open, is not entirely clear, but at all events he did not consider it expedient to insert the revolutionary provisions in the official statement.[4] By the Västerås Ordinantia it was ordained that in temporal matters the clergy were to be amenable to the temporal courts alone. As far as doctrines were concerned, the whole matter was covered by the simple statement that the word of God should be preached plainly and in its purity. (It may be noted here that none of the fundamental declarations of faith of the Lutheran Church were adopted in Sweden until the meeting of Uppsala in 1593.)

Results of the Västerås meeting.—With the Västerås Recess the fate of the Catholic Church in Sweden was sealed. While the definite break did not come until 1531 with the election of Laurentius Petri to the archbishoprical dignity, the Västerås meeting, to all intents and purposes, severed all connections between Sweden and Rome. Sweden, together with Denmark, were the first Lutheran lands, and next to Finland the former still shows the largest percentage of adherents to the Lutheran faith. An idea of the wealth that the Church was compelled to surrender is gained from an estimate of her property which Gustavus acquired for the state by virtue of the Västerås decrees and other subsequent measures. In the first place, the estates held by the Church, estimated, as above stated (p. 209), at about 13,700, reverted to the state. The addition to the annual revenue of the crown through rents and cancellation of tithes has been placed at 40,000 marks, or one-

[4] Sjödin, Lars, *Västerås möte 1527, Historisk tidskrift,* 1927 and 1928.

fifth of the regular and extraordinary taxes. The value of the silver taken from the churches cannot be determined, as complete accounts were not kept; that the amount was large is certain. The incomes of most of the ecclesiastics were in most cases reduced, Gustavus taking particular care that the greater part of the princely incomes which some ecclesiastics enjoyed should be lopped off. In the case of the most poorly paid clergy, some increases were granted. The sweeping provisions of the Västerås Recess were followed by supplementary regulations, known as the Västerås Ordinantia, for the appointments and remuneration of the bishops and parish priests, and defining their jurisdiction.

The victory of Gustavus at Västerås had been complete; he had been given almost unlimited authority not only regarding property but also in the matter of Church doctrines. What the outer organization of the Church and the character of her teachings would be was therefore largely contingent upon him. Gustavus was naturally very cautious, had a due regard for realities, and was not the man who would press for rapid and radical changes. Above everything else, he desired that the new doctrines should be tested by the Holy Scriptures and not by Church decrees or old traditions.

The incumbency of the archiepiscopal office was also a matter for serious consideration at the Västerås meeting. In 1523 the dignity had been conferred on Johannes Magni, a learned, well-meaning, and pliant man, who had followed Gustavus in his anti-papal policies as long as he believed that only a reformation within the Church was contemplated, but had held back when he perceived whither the king was leading him.

Laurentius Petri, archbishop.—Gustavus soon began to feel that he needed a man of greater courage and more resourcefulness in the office, and therefore sent the aged archbishop as ambassador to Poland, hoping that he would remain there. Magni congratulated himself on his most fortunate escape and took care never to return to his native land. The choice for the high office later (1531) fell upon Laurentius Petri, the learned and mild-mannered brother of Olaus, and he was consecrated by Petrus Magni, Bishop of Västerås. Inasmuch as Petrus had been consecrated at Rome according to canonical forms in 1524, the apostolic succession was thus maintained unbroken in Sweden.[5] The bellicose champion of Catholicism, Bishop Brask, was, after the Västerås meeting, a broken man. The failure of this undaunted and consistent champion of the old order of things in Sweden contains much that is pathetic. No one can question his honest and ardent devotion, not only to his Church but to his own country, Sweden. His active mind had conceived projects which in many ways placed him hundreds of years ahead of his contemporaries. Thus the original project for a system of canals across Sweden came from his active mind. He was never a trimmer, and now he went honourably down to defeat, fighting to the end for what he conceived to be right. Realizing the hopelessness of the struggle, and with a feeling of helplessness and the weariness of an aged man, Brask decided to leave Sweden. Under pretext that he wished to make a trip of inspection to Gottland, he went on a journey thither, and during this he escaped to Danzig, where he later found refuge in a cloister near the city and lived the rest of his days in retirement. He died in 1538.

End of the second rebellion.—After the king's victory at Västerås, he could again turn his attention to the trouble-makers in Dalarna. The Sture pretender had not only deceived many in this province who had given him their support, but in addition he was encouraged and aided by such powerful personages as Archbishop Olof of Norway and Vincent Lunge, the latter being in this period virtually the ruler of Norway. He had also gained the good-will of Lady Inger in Östråt, a proud and ambitious Norwegian noblewoman, and this worthy dame had been made most happy when her daughter was betrothed to the handsome and dashing cavalier. Mother and daughter lived in happy anticipation of the glory that would be theirs when the palace at Stockholm should welcome them as its occupants. Again Gustavus opened the attack by a bombardment of letters. The impostor was never able to muster any strong force and finally found it prudent to escape to Germany, where he was captured and, at the request of Gustavus, be-

[5] Since England was the only other Protestant country thus to retain the succession unbroken, interesting suggestions for a closer union of the national churches of Sweden and England have in late decades been seriously discussed.

headed, after he had made a clean breast of his duplicity. In due time the king went to Dalarna at the head of an armed force, and now its people were to discover that words were not his only weapons in a fight and that he did not hesitate to use drastic measures if the exigencies of the situation seemed to require it. The people were summoned to a meeting and here they were massed together, after which a cordon of men was thrown around them and menacing cannon turned upon the terrified crowd. The people were ordered to assume a kneeling attitude and were next made to listen to statements of their insolence and treason by the king; thereupon the royal officers, who in the exercise of their duty as tax-collectors had received much abuse and blows, were directed to go in among the people and pick out the ring-leaders. These were tried on the spot and speedily beheaded.

The execution of the decrees of Västerås was immediately undertaken and carried out with great energy, and this, as a matter of course, stirred up an intense bitterness, for at the moment when the old ties which for centuries had bound people and clergy together were severed, the delinquencies of which the latter might have been guilty were naturally forgotten and a wave of indignation swept over many regions.

Further definition of doctrines; revolts.—In order to allay this discontent and likewise to secure a more definite expression regarding doctrines and liturgical services, Gustavus summoned a meeting of churchmen at Örebro in 1529. The decisions of this meeting, which may be considered as norms for religious faith and practices in the land, were conceived in a distinctly liberal spirit. No drastic changes were attempted, the word of God should be preached in its purity, opportunities were to be provided pastors, especially in the rural districts, to receive instruction in the doctrines of the new faith, unnecessary holidays should be abolished, ancient ceremonies like the burning of incense, use of holy water, worship of saints, and fasting were declared to have no magic power and should be considered as permissible and helpful only in so far as they were the outer expressions of heartfelt desire for greater purity of soul. The decrees simply asserted the idea that the essential fact of Christian life is faith; if that is right, it will naturally tend to result in good deeds. The Örebro resolutions unmistakably bear the stamp of Olaus Petri's tolerant mind. The moderate and enlightened principles, however, met the fate which in periods of excitement and bitter strife usually awaits reasonable men and their propositions. On the one hand, they were fiercely assailed by zealous Lutherans as weak and cowardly concessions to old Catholic traditions and heresies, and on the other they aroused the violent opposition of the conservative element, who saw in them a complete surrender to the Lutheran party. The discontent and excitement which this provoked caused a new revolt against the king, this time with its centre in Västergötland and Småland. This uprising speedily grew into such dimensions that Gustavus, together with his program of religious reform, at one time seemed inevitably doomed. The leader of the revolt was Ture Jönsson, the influential and proud lord, who at the Västerås Riksdag had been one of the defiant opponents of Gustavus. Associated with him was the Bishop of Skara and a number of priests who had preached opposition to the king; these priests had been particularly active in preaching sedition among the *bönder* of Småland. The trouble started when the people of northern Småland met and renounced their allegiance to the king. According to the plans of the malcontents, a meeting was next to be held at Larf in Västergötland by lords and *bönder* and a decision reached to make common cause with the Småland rebels.

Gustavus was not caught napping, however, for by this time he had organized a well-functioning "intelligence department," with trusted agents in every part of the country, and the leaders in the revolt and their plans were fully reported to him. Again Gustavus resorted to one of his most trusted weapons, the printed word. The standing army which he was building up and making a model of efficiency was his best persuader, but this was resorted to only when other means had failed to bring conviction. The country and more particularly the rebellious districts were literally showered with letters, in which the king's attitude was ably explained and justified. Moreover, he had instructed his agents to grant concessions and make promises of favours which were so liberal in scope that it is impossible to believe that the king ever had serious intentions of abiding by them. The people of Dalarna, having vivid recollections of what had previously happened to them when they opposed Gustavus, were now loyal and even sent letters to the leaders in Västergötland, warning them of the serious risks they were running. The *bönder* of Uppland did likewise. Ture Jönsson experienced the mortification of seeing two of his own sons desert him and join Gustavus. When the meeting at Larf got under way, the old intriguer and marplot was destined to receive his worst shock, for after he had made a bitter denunciation of Gustavus, depicting in lurid colours all the iniquity of the king, an attack which he expected would be followed immediately by a declaration repudiating Gustavus, he was dumbfounded at finding the *bönder* shouting loudly that they were satisfied with Gustavus and intended to remain faithful to him. At this, in the words of the chronicle, Ture Jönsson and the other lords became "so benumbed that they knew not what to do." Their plight was made still worse when they fell to quarreling among themselves about the division of the anticipated spoils. At the same time the people of Värmland declared that they would support the king to the bitter end. The revolt, which shortly before had threatened to engulf Gustavus in disaster, ended with a compromise, the agents of the king signing an agreement with the lords granting full amnesty to all who submitted and at the same time pledging that "Lutheran heresy and the evil practices that go with it" would be suppressed. Gustavus approved the agreement, shrewdly adding the proviso, however, that in carrying out its provisions he "would do whatever seemed best for the country."

Subsequent revolts against Gustavus.—Back of most of Gustavus's troubles lay the debt to Lübeck and the monopoly of Swedish trade which that city had wrested from the Swedish king at the time when dire necessity forced his hand. Under these trade privileges Swedish commerce could not develop nor Swedish cities grow, and by the toll exemption the crown was deprived of large sums which otherwise would have been collected as revenue. All appeals to the merchants of Lübeck that they slacken their strangle-hold on the Swedes fell on deaf ears.

Gustavus then began to negotiate with the Dutch in order to induce them to enter the Swedish trade and thus give some relief from the Lübeck monopoly. In 1528 the first Dutch ship arrived in Sweden with a rich cargo. The king likewise intended to develop a commercial port on the west coast of Sweden and with that as a point of vantage carry on independent trade, and Lödöse, near the mouth of the Göta River, assumed some importance as a trading centre during this period. Swedish relations with Lübeck therefore became increasingly strained. Gustavus on his part maintained that Lübeck had granted him several years' extension of time for making payment, but the Lübeck representatives denied that this had been done. A payment of 11,000 marks, besides various supplies, as iron, butter, and hides, was made at one time, but the debt nevertheless grew. At last, in 1529, an agreement regarding the debt was reached; it was placed at 68,681 marks, besides 8,689 marks in addition for interest and debasement of coins. In order to meet the installments due on this amount, Gustavus found it necessary to resort to new measures of taxation and now seized the largest bell in every church, chapel, or monastery located in the cities as well as in rural districts; the parishes could, however, forestall seizure by paying the tax in copper or silver. Tender memories were associated with these bells, their tolling having been a cherished part of the impressive ceremonies of festival and Sabbath days, and the threat to take them and melt them down stirred up deep indignation. A revolt against the king soon threatened his power again. The dissatisfaction was greatest in Dalarna, where some of the king's bailiffs, while discharging their duties, were severely beaten. The Dalacarlians were so puffed up with ideas of their own importance that they took it upon themselves to issue summons for a Riksdag of their own. The watchful agents of Gustavus were quick to seize the writs, and the assembly, in the words of the chronicle, "froze up."

Encounter of king with people.—The king next summoned the people to meet him at Uppsala, where on the famous mounds at Old Uppsala, a memorable verbal encounter between ruler and people took place. Gustavus explained the reason for the new levies, and thereupon demanded a statement of the reasons for his subjects' persistence in making obstinate resistance. Then the people, "according to their custom, began to use their mouths," until the king became angry, saying that he would rather they strike him than scold him. "Why not begin with the latter immediately?" he asked. The crowd then became reasonable and an amicable settlement was made. The king was more than willing to meet his subjects half-way and not run the risk of extreme measures, for a new and serious danger had suddenly appeared; Christian II had finally received aid from the emperor, Charles V, for his contemplated expedition to regain his lost crowns and was ready to invade Sweden from the Norwegian side. In his camp were the former archbishop, Gustaf Trolle, Ture Jönsson, and other Swedish malcontents. Surely it was not a time when Gustavus could afford to quarrel with his own people. He took vigorous measures to defend his country and Christian's advance into Sweden was soon effectively checked, the ex-monarch being forced to fall back into Norway, and here he was compelled to surrender to a Danish force. Sweden, it may be noted, had no part in the dishonourable betrayal by which Christian became a prisoner and was made to spend the rest of his life in confinement. The danger from Christian being thus safely passed, Gustavus could again give attention to the Dalecarlian revolt, but now he came to the land of the rebels in no conciliatory mood. He marched into the province with an armed force, summoned twelve *bönder* from each parish to meet him at Kopparberget, and here came the king's great reckoning with the stiff-necked people of the province. The summoned men were huddled together in a square with soldiers lined up all around them, and now the king and members of the Council took turns in recounting their wicked deeds. "Did they actually take the king to be a clown who was to give a performance for their benefit every year?" "Did not the king have the right to cross the boundary into their province without asking safe conduct of the mine-owners and those who lived north of Långheden?" These and similar questions were hurled at them by the angry ruler, and he ended by asserting that this must be their final performance; he would either have an obedient section in Dalarna or he would make of it a waste land, "where neither the barking of a dog nor the crowing of a cock would henceforth be heard." The terrified people confessed their sins and promised in the future to show obedience. After this several of the ring-leaders were arrested and three years later they were executed. It was one of the tragedies of Gustavus's life that in this case he felt compelled to send to the block some of the very men who had been the first to befriend and assist him when he came, a fugitive, to their region in 1520. "Thus the glorious history of Dalarna was quenched in blood" (*släcktes i blod*), as one of Sweden's greatest historians [6] says.

[6] Geijer, E. G., *Svenska folkets historia*, Stockholm, 1832-1836.

Chapter X

THE FOUNDATION OF SWEDEN AS A MODERN STATE IS SOLIDLY LAID

Gustavus's fight for economic independence.—The Hanseatic League had been unwilling to relinquish even the slightest part of the trade privileges which the Swedish king had been under the necessity of granting in order that the war against the Danes might be brought to a successful close. Because of a combination of circumstances, such as the new maritime conditions which the discovery of America had produced, the growth of Dutch and English trade, and the strengthening of royal power in the Scandinavian north, its trade monopoly was, however, fast crumbling. Gustavus had, as stated (p. 257), favoured the Dutch, trying thereby to turn some of the Swedish trade to them and thus to get some relief from the hated Hanseatic monopoly, and he was cautiously watching the situation for an opportunity to get rid of its strangle-hold completely.

The Count's War.—The opportunity came with the outbreak of the conflict known as "The Count's War" in 1535. At the head of affairs in Lübeck now stood the ambitious and eloquent Jörgen Wullenwever, a man who had more ability to arouse people's minds by agitation than to lead cities and states in important political or military enterprises. He dreamed of a restoration of the hegemony of Lübeck under his guidance, and watched for an opportunity to strike a mighty blow for the city. This opportunity came, he thought, when civil war broke out in Denmark. That country was still an elective monarchy, and as no definite provisions had been made during the lifetime of the former king regarding the successor, a bitter scramble for the throne ensued when Frederick I died in 1533. The nearest claimant to the throne was the late king's son, Christian, Duke of Holstein, but as his sympathies for the doctrines of the Lutheran reformers were well known, the powerful bishops decided to take matters into their own hands and govern the land at least until the old Catholic system, which in Denmark, as well as in Sweden, had at the time been forced to meet bitter attacks, could be restored to its former power and prestige. Wullenwever, who was well informed of Denmark's weakness at this time, now made an alliance with Copenhagen and Malmö, in order to restore Christian II to power. The aristocracy of Denmark naturally resisted to the utmost all attempts to bring back a king whose democratic sympathies had more than a decade earlier caused them to rise in revolt against him and drive him out of the land, and hence they rallied to the support of the Duke of Holstein. Sweden also aligned herself on this side, mainly because of the opportunity it gave her to settle all scores with the Hanseatic city. The head of the Catholic party in the conflict, with which were aligned the common people of Denmark, was Count Christopher of Oldenburg, hence the name of the ensuing conflict, "The Count's War." Lübeck was strongly Lutheran and, moreover, had formerly been an implacable enemy of Christian II; its support of him in this struggle had a purely political and selfish basis. The count's forces won some victories at first, but the strategy of Gustavus and of Christian's Holstein general, Johan Rantzau, combined with the effectiveness of the united Swedish-Danish fleet, in the end brought victory to the Swedish-Holstein-Danish aristocracy alliance. In a battle of this war on the island of Fyen, Gustaf Trolle was wounded and died a few days later in Holstein captivity. Peace was concluded in February 1536 between Lübeck and Christian of Denmark; Sweden was not invited to the peace meeting, Christian assuming even the authority to act in her behalf and agreeing to arbitrate between her and Lübeck. Gustavus naturally felt incensed when he was informed of this gratuitous service, but after a time an agreement was concluded between Sweden and Lübeck directly, according to which Swedish ports were to be opened to other merchants besides the Hanseatic members, the latter continuing, however, to enjoy some advantages; the Swedes were to have freedom to pass through the Sound and the channels separating the Danish islands from Jutland, and all money claims against Sweden were to be cancelled. While Lübeck never ratified the agreement, but continued to insist on her privileges, in reality the outcome was equivalent to Sweden's liberation from her former economic oppression. Gustavus had won a complete victory in this conflict, but Holland, not Sweden, was to be the chief gainer by the overthrow of the Hanseatic League.

Gustavus breaks with his old advisers; the German régime.—After nearly two decades of discussion and bitter conflict, the question of religion and ecclesiastical property had been settled almost exactly in accordance with Gustavus's wishes, but serious difficulties were still to be encountered on the path which he had chosen to travel. In 1540 came a break between the king and the able and loyal supporters of his early days on the throne, Laurentius Andreæ and Olaus Petri. The latter especially had become increasingly disinclined to follow the king on a path where violence, duplicity, and various sharp practices of the "practical" statesmen were by no means tabooed. The use to which the confiscated Church property ought to be put was also a point on which he and his sovereign differed radically. Olaus Petri had hoped that the king would use the enormous wealth which had come into his hands [1] for the support of churches and schools, and for the promotion of other cultural enterprises; the property had, according to him, been primarily given for these purposes and no one had a right to divert it to other uses. But Gustavus had little sympathy for so idealistic a program. A well organized and large army and a good fleet, as certain means of defence of the nation against foreign aggression, had become a sort of obsession with him and he was willing to spend money quite freely for military needs, but what could be saved after these expenses had been met the thrifty king preferred to put aside in the royal strong-box. Gustavus became more and more impatient of criticism and opposition, and as both Laurentius and Olaus had a habit of speaking rather freely to him, a break between them and the ruler was inevitable. A group of Germans now came to take the place of the former Swedish advisers of the king. Most promi-

[1] It should, of course, be understood that the property was not the king's personal wealth. As king he was merely the personification of the nation. However, a considerable number of estates had, in fact, become the king's private property.

nent among these were the German jurist, Konrad von Pyhy, an adventurer whose antecedents were for the most part unknown, and George Norman, a learned and honest man, who had come to Sweden to serve as tutor to the king's sons, but soon had been entrusted with important commissions in public affairs. On the heels of these two men came many other Germans, and with them a number of ideas regarding the way in which a country ought to be governed which were foreign and utterly repugnant to the Swedes. The dominant idea of the new régime was the duty of the subject to show complete submission to his sovereign. Startling proof that new men and ideas were in control was soon given when Laurentius Andreæ and Olaus Petri were both arrested and brought to trial on the charge of treason. The formal accusation, written in German and later translated into Swedish, charged the two men with responsibility for nearly all the troubles which had afflicted the king since the beginning of his reign, and culminated in the specific charge that they had been cognizant of a conspiracy against Gustavus but had failed to divulge their knowledge to him. Their plea that the knowledge had come to them through the confessional and was thus confidential and privileged information, was not accepted as an exonerating fact. The sentence of death was pronounced against the two reformers, but this was commuted by the king, who evidently never intended that the extreme penalty should be inflicted. Instead of the death penalty, the alleged culprits were sentenced to pay large fines, which in the case of Olaus Petri were assumed by his parishioners.

A bureaucratic government.—A number of novel ideas with respect to the management of ecclesiastical and secular affairs began temporarily to assert themselves. The whole complicated machinery of a full-fledged bureaucracy, with various gradations of officials, supervisors, censors, assessors, marshals, secret council, was set up, with hardly any detail lacking, in the paper project at least. With this followed all the usual iniquities of such a system of government as interference with the lives of the individuals, spying and harassment of law-abiding citizens; in reality there was perhaps very little actual oppression, but the evident tendencies of the government aroused alarm. The fact that German was the official language of this outlandish system naturally served to intensify the suspicion and anger in the land. The suggestion which these German bureaucrats advanced from time to time that the Swedish monarchy was a hereditary institution naturally created the suspicion that a move to deprive the people of one of their most ancient and cherished rights—the right to elect their ruler—would soon be made. The situation seemed to assume a more sinister aspect when the clergy were told that they must not fail, in their sermons, to emphasize the duty of subjects to obey their ruler. As a final episode in this series of irritating acts, came an inspection trip which George Norman undertook through Östergötland, Västergötland, and Småland, ostensibly for the purpose of ascertaining how the old and new provisions of the government were being obeyed, but in reality in order that he might make an inventory of the valuables still in the possession of churches, such as communion plates and cups, money, and other treasures. That the latter was the real object of the trip became evident when soon afterwards the churches in these provinces were so completely stripped of their valuables that in many places only that which was absolutely required for the celebration of the sacrament of Holy Communion was left.

The resentment caused by this despoilment led to a new revolt, the last one against which Gustavus during his long reign had to contend, but the one which most nearly succeeded in wrecking his policies and his hopes. This time Småland was the seething centre of the revolt. In this province, and especially in the border country towards Blekinge where a vast forest area lay, lived a wild and lawless element which had made life insecure for every one of the king's officials who had ventured thither to collect taxes or apprehend criminals. Some of the king's bailiffs, it is claimed, had been killed while on official errands, and their severed heads carried from place to place as a reminder to other officials of what would likely happen to them if they had the temerity to show themselves and try to interfere with the people's alleged rights. It was also a curse of the district that it had a number of petty nobles who, in their mad desire to rise to wealth and power on a par with the greater lords, had ground down their dependents by most cruel exactions. The king and Council decided to make a searching inquiry into the conduct of the people of Småland, and in due time serious charges were made against them. Trials were next held in the eastern part of the district, many were found guilty and fines were collected, after which the people acknowledged their crimes and asked forgiveness. The net result of the inquisition was, however, that the number of those who as refugees had resorted to the forests, where they lived as outlaws, grew rapidly, and many of the king's bailiffs were murdered.

Nils Dacke.—Finally the outlaws received a leader, Nils Dacke by name, a *bonde* who had fled to the forest region after having killed a bailiff, for which crime so exorbitant a sum of money had been exacted as a fine that he had become utterly impoverished. Dacke had a native talent for leadership and understood well how to fan the flames of discontent. It must be admitted that the statement he issued, depicting the injustice which the *bönder* were suffering, has a ring of truthfulness and reveals most wretched conditions among the people. Soon Dacke was at the head of a force of 10,000 *bönder*, and the commander of the king's forces in the district was compelled to beat a hasty retreat (1542); Gustavus now found it necessary to proceed in person to the scene of trouble, and here he found the situation so alarming that he deemed it wise and prudent to make a truce with Dacke, by the terms of which the proud rebel agreed to serve the king, assist him in suppressing any subsequent uprising, and help in the abolition of the evils which had incited the revolt. It was a humiliating experience for the king thus to be compelled to treat with one of his rebellious subjects, and to submit to humiliating terms; by the same token, it was a proud day for Dacke when mighty King Gustavus had to bow to him, the outlaw.

The king reasons with the people.—The breathing-spell which this truce afforded Gustavus he used to good advantage; never did his letters to his subjects have so clear and appealing a ring as the ones that now issued from his pen. Evidently the writing of the documents had not been entrusted to his German advisers, for they are replete with terse, ringing, Swedish phrases. "We understand," he says, "that the people have risen in revolt because they wish to have the old order of things restored." With this as a text, the king, with the skill of an old master in dialectics, draws a graphic picture of Sweden as it was before his day. The humiliation of the country under the Union rulers, its shame and despoliation under "unkind King Christian," its bondage and exploitation under Lübeck; these were scenes from that very past for the return of which the people said they were yearning that were unfolded before their eyes and which, when drawn by the consummate word painter, became hideous and terrifying spectres. As a school-master endeavours to give his immature pupils the most elementary facts in order that they may be able to follow his reasoning, Gustavus explained in plain language and with infinite care just what changes had been made by him in the government, and how and why these changes had increased the cost of the government, but he also showed how the returns to the people in added security and "service" had far outweighed the increase in public taxes. As a parting shot to the disgruntled ecclesiastics, who throughout his reign, and not least, in the Dacke rebellion, had been active in fomenting sedition, Gustavus with pretended naïveté remarked, "Since Sweden is an ancient and glorious monarchy and not a state made up of bishops or priests, the king has believed that bishops ought to serve in the office which God has entrusted to them; namely, celebrate mass, teach and preach the Holy Word of God and his Gospel to the common men, and be less concerned about worldly might and power." [2]

In the meantime Dacke acted as an independent sovereign prince in Småland, appointed bailiffs, summoned judicial assemblies, and cancelled tax levies. These were proud days for the *bonde* chief, since Duke Albrecht of Mecklenburg, a descendant of the former King of Sweden by that name, who entertained the fantastic hope that opportunity might now come to him to seize the Swedish crown for himself, conferred the rank of nobility on Dacke, and no less a person than Emperor Charles V sent greetings, with a pledge of support. Behind Dacke stood now in solid phalanx practically all the disgruntled individuals who during the two preceding decades had

[2] Hildebrand, *Sveriges historia,* IV, p. 275.

for some reason or other stored up bitter grievances against the Swedish king; the only ones missing from the ranks of his enemies being Lübeck, Denmark, and the people of Dalarna; the two former showed themselves utterly unresponsive to every suggestion that they make common cause with the enemies of the Swedish king, and the latter had learned their lesson. The wisdom of not opposing Gustavus was clear to them now.

The end of Dacke.—The dizzy heights to which fate had hoisted Dacke had, however, turned his head, and arrogance and cruelty began more and more to dominate his behaviour. He caused one of the most prominent *bönder* with whom he had a controversy to be slain and others who had incurred his ill-will were imprisoned. The soothing tone of the king's letters, furthermore, served greatly to allay the hostility of the people towards him. They now could understand the reasons for his royal acts. As Dacke began to play the rôle of a tyrannical and wilful ruler more obnoxiously, they thought, than Gustavus had ever done, the people grew tired of him.

After the king's forces had inflicted a severe defeat on those of Dacke, the latter found himself deserted by many of his followers and soon he was hunted as a fugitive by the king's men. He was before long betrayed by his own followers as he was endeavouring to escape into Blekinge and met his death by an arrow piercing his back as he was trying to run away from his pursuers. The long and bitter struggle in Småland, ending in a complete victory for the king, decided the important issue that the separate provinces must subordinate themselves to the strong centralized government which Gustavus had built. From this time on, Småland as well as Dalarna knew full well who was the real ruler in Sweden. The extent and violence of the Dacke rebellion had also had their salutary effect upon the king, as it had served to open his eyes to the wisdom of proceeding with greater moderation. He understood that it was a serious mistake to endeavour to force a new system of government precipitately on an entire nation, and the realization that his German advisers were largely responsible for his turning to a more bureaucratic and oppressive régime caused him to lose confidence in them and on some pretext or other the departments were soon cleared of them. With them went the greater part of the complicated scheme of local and national administration of finance and industry, which they had tried to fasten upon the country. After the brief but stormy excursion into strange channels, where the ship nearly foundered on the breakers, a return had been made to the well-known and tried courses and good Swedish men, with the king as the unquestioned master, again manned the vessel.

The Swedish throne becomes hereditary.—With the formidable Dacke revolt finally suppressed, and peace restored in the rebellious province, Gustavus, in full harmony with his usual course of summoning the Estates of the land to a meeting whenever a momentous issue called for settlement, issued a call to a Riksdag at Västerås. For the first time in the history of the country, representatives of the lower clergy were also summoned. Like the fair and fearless leader that he was, Gustavus always urged that those who were known to be most bitter against him might be present at the meetings called by him, in order that they might be given an opportunity to state their grievances. The bailiffs in Småland were therefore on this occasion instructed to make sure that two pastors were sent from every hundred "and the worse Papists they are who are sent, the better we shall like it, so that once and for all time they may hear and understand what reason or proofs God provides and against which they are striving so hard and rise in opposition," wrote the king. The representatives summoned from Småland dared not absent themselves even if they were so disposed, and at the meeting they were put in a most uncomfortable position. At its very beginning they were placed, as it were, before the bar, and subjected to a searching inquiry by delegates from other provinces regarding the reasons for their going on their recent rampage. Humbly they admitted that no good excuse could be advanced for their rebellion and that the king's chastisement of them had been amply deserved.

The one momentous decision which this assembly made, one that may justly be considered a mighty factor in Sweden's subsequent rapid march towards extraordinary strength and prestige, declared the Swedish crown hereditary in the Vasa family. That the country was ready to set aside the principle of an elective monarchy, a principle which had had the firm sanction of custom since time immemorial and had been given solemn legal sanction by the laws of Magnus Eriksson and King Christoffer, in itself constitutes the most impressive evidence of the strong position Gustavus now held and of the gratitude and confidence with which the Swedish people had come to accept his rule. Its immediate effect was to strengthen Gustavus in his own land. Plain and emphatic notice was thereby served on all pretenders, all malcontents who were flitting about from country to country seeking to bring about coalitions against the Swedish king, and trying to make foreign statesmen believe that he was a despised and hated tyrant whom his subjects loathed, as well as upon all noble families at home who were jealous of the king and still harboured hopes that one of their respective groups might displace him, that the Vasa right to the Swedish throne was definitely settled and that it was a waste of time and energy to try to change this fact.

Relations to foreign powers.—The manner in which the Count's War ended had naturally bred in Gustavus a deep distrust of Denmark, and this suspicion took firmer root in his mind during the years immediately following. One of his chief grievances against the neighbour was the hospitality which the latter always had been ready to extend to Swedish or German rebels who had escaped from Sweden. More than once the situation became so bad that hostilities seemed imminent.

Denmark.—In the fear that Denmark might be induced to join Lübeck, which was constantly worrying Sweden by stressing her privileges in the land, Gustavus was especially anxious to come to a friendly agreement with his neighbour. Both he and Christian had reason to fear that the emperor, Charles V, in his anxiety to defend the Catholic faith and assist Christian II, contemplated hostilities against them.[3] At a personal conference of the two monarchs at Brömsebro, near the Blekinge boundary (1541), an offensive and defensive alliance to be binding for fifty years was concluded. According to its terms, each contracting party was to help the other in case of insurrection or foreign aggression, and all controversies between the

[3] Landberg, George, *De nordiska rikena under Brömsebro förbundet,* Uppsala, 1925.

two countries were to be settled by arbitration. The agreement is an evidence of the wisdom of the two kings who sought to find security and strength in alliance and who, as long as they lived, averted war between their respective nations. Unfortunately these agreements became a dead letter when these rulers passed from the scene. The deep-rooted mutual distrust which existed between the two rulers, a distrust which was fully shared by their respective Councils, soon again drove the two nations far apart.

France.—The fear of Charles V also had the effect of bringing the Scandinavian countries into alliance with France, whose king, Francis I, was the bitter rival and foe of the emperor. On the Swedish side the negotiations with France were carried on by a delegation at the head of which stood the German-born Chancellor Pyhy, who on this occasion posed as an extraordinarily important personage, displaying a splendour and distributing such largesse that he made away with a great deal of the money which Gustavus, with the practice of the strictest economy, had managed to store away in his strongbox. This first alliance in a long series of similar agreements between the two countries was concluded at Montiers sur Saulx in 1542, between "the king of the Goths and the king of the Gauls," and here the contracting parties mutually agreed in case of war to come to each other's assistance with a force amounting to anywhere from 6,000 to 25,000 men, the number depending on the exigencies of the situation, and with fifty ships. The terms of this alliance were almost entirely ignored by Gustavus, who was not slow to perceive that compliance with them would bring no advantage to his country but meant merely that its resources would be employed to assist Francis in his attack upon the Netherlands. The Swedish king could feel the more satisfied with this attitude when, later, Christian III, having concluded a similar alliance with Francis, threw himself into a hazardous war venture, only to find himself shamefully left in the lurch by his shifty ally.

New quarrels with Denmark.—Sweden's relations to Denmark continued to be strained. The Danish king gave deep offence to the Swedes when he ordered the three crowns of Sweden to be stamped on Danish seals and coins, explaining that this was intended merely as a reminiscence of the Kalmar Union, which explanation, however, failed to placate Gustavus. After the death of Christian III (January 1559), and the accession of Frederick II to the Danish throne, there began a lively exchange of abusive letters between the two Scandinavian kings; these, when read today, may seem very amusing, but in that day they were taken with tragic seriousness. On the Danish side appeared a poetic chronicle which roundly scored Gustavus for his iniquities. Moved to extreme anger, Gustavus, as a retaliatory measure, ordered Peder Swart to repay the compliment by writing a poem in which ridicule and abuse were heaped upon the Danes and their king, and all the deviltry which Denmark had tried to perpetrate against Sweden from Margaret's day to their own time was vividly recounted in great detail. For good measure, Gustavus also caused to be printed and distributed a collection of ancient and bitter Swedish diatribes against the Danes. Gustavus went too far, it must be admitted, but it must also be conceded that the Danes had provoked him grievously. They found it difficult to acquiesce in Sweden's sudden growth in strength and influence and their jealousy led to insulting words and unfriendly acts.[4] It should be remembered also that Denmark was at this time ruled largely by Holstein nobles who despised the Swedish *bönder* and their plebeian king.

Russia.—The danger of a war with Russia also rested as a dark cloud on the horizon for a couple of decades in this reign. Mutual fear and distrust were mainly responsible for this situation. Unlike most of his successors on the Swedish throne, Gustavus felt a wholesome respect for the strength of his Muscovite neighbour, and was always anxious to avoid hostilities with him. A settlement of pending troubles was made in 1557 between Gustavus and the Governor of Novgorod, the czar, Ivan the Terrible, refusing to deal with the Swedish king, since

[4] Danish and Swedish historians have set an example of toleration and fair-mindedness which the historians of other nations would do well to emulate. It matters very little whether one reads a Danish or a Swedish history on this and later conflicts between the two countries; the facts given and their interpretation are about the same in either case. It is claimed that today the historical text-books used in the common schools of Denmark could well be used in the Swedish schools without giving offence, and vice versa. When other countries assume such an attitude in their teaching of historical facts, peace and good-will may perhaps have a better chance than now to become dominant factors in this distracted world.

the latter had been a cattle-buyer (an allusion to Gustavus's alleged service as an ox-driver on his escape from Denmark), a fastidiousness on the part of one of the worst monsters known to history which appears grotesque in the extreme. It stipulated that a truce was to prevail between the two countries for forty years, and that pending boundary disputes should be settled by subsequent agreements.

It was not in Finland but in Livonia that the conflicting interests of Sweden and Russia were to have their first clash. Here the old commonwealth of the Order of the Sword was tottering to its fall. When, therefore, the czar in 1556 sent a force into the unhappy land to plunder it in regular Tatar style, Gustavus's son, John, now Governor of Finland, sensing an opportunity to make some gain for his country, opened negotiations with the Master of the Order and agreed to make him a loan of money in return for the surrender of certain Livonian fortresses to Sweden. Gustavus's usual caution did not forsake him, however, and he vetoed the proposition. A serious storm was now brewing over the question of Livonia, as Poland and Denmark both came forward with claims in the hope of getting as much of the spoils as possible. This situation filled Gustavus with anxiety. He foresaw the dangers which interference in the affairs of the Baltic land involved, but at the same time he wanted his country to make some gains when the spoils were divided. Before the storm broke, however, the aged king had died (1560).

The great administrator.—Gustavus conceived himself as a ruler ordained by God to lead his people out of the slough of despond in which injustice, ignorance, inertia, poverty, and national humiliation made their lot miserable, to a fairer land where justice, enlightenment, industry, prosperity, and security from enemies both within and without the land would bring them a degree of well-being that they had never before enjoyed. Endowed as he was with tremendous energy and a clear understanding, and guided by the most exalted conception of his own responsibility, he became what might be termed the ideal paternalistic ruler. It would be no exaggeration to say that in the entire history of the modern age it would be difficult to find a sovereign who more nearly than the great Swedish state-builder approached the ideal expressed by the phrase, "The father of his country."

Personal rule.—It was the first and foremost aspiration of Gustavus that his country be given an effective administration. The first requisite for this, the effective check of the arbitrary rule of the feudal lords, he achieved through the vigorous enforcement of the principle that important fiefs could at any time be recalled by the crown. Many of the powers which the noblemen formerly had enjoyed on their estates were now taken away from them and entrusted to the royal bailiffs. The lords were thus soon disabused of the ideas that they could exercise well-nigh absolute authority on their respective estates. It is significant of the extension of royal jurisdiction and power that the number of bailiffs increased from fifty to one hundred and sixty in Gustavus's reign. Royal orders literally hailed down over these functionaries and wherever a recipient failed to comply, scathing reprimands or summary dismissal were quite certain to follow. Through constant travel over his extensive domains, and by meeting freely with all classes and conditions of men, the king sought to ascertain how his officials were conducting themselves. When his oldest son Erik sought permission to go to England to woo Elizabeth, and in the same connection hinted at the possibility of a union of his and her countries, Gustavus wrote to him: "The kingdom of Sweden gives its ruler sufficient labour and cares; I received it in my youth, and behold, after forty years, my solicitude for it sends me with grey hairs to my grave. I have brought order into its administration, item by item, and these may be counted by the hundreds." One of the king's main causes of worry and irritation was the difficulty of getting bailiffs upon whom he could depend. Many of them were coarse and brutal men who inflicted more hardships upon the *bönder* than formerly the feudal lords had done, and in order to secure a more effective check upon them larger administrative divisions were formed, over which were placed governors who in turn became directly responsible to the king.

As far as conditions of the times permitted, system was brought into the fiscal administration. As a first step towards this, taxes were made more equitable. Before this time the *bönder* had generally been taxed alike, irrespective of the size of their holdings, but according to a new system inaugurated in 1539 taxes would be made proportionate to the area held by the individuals. The following year a sort of assessors' list of property was made and definite instructions issued to the bailiffs regarding the correct principles to be followed in making assessments and collections.

With infinite care and patience Gustavus pored over the reports of his officials, heard complaints, and issued orders. He

A *bonde* and his wife. From the work on the North by Olaus Magnus

was entirely untrammelled by customs and former decrees and many times he nonchalantly reversed his former orders and took a new position. Especially galling to his methodical mind was the jumble which he often found in his bailiffs' reports. Their books, he once complained, were like "shadows in moonlight." "The dumb swine" could not keep anything in order, "but roll around and wallow in the nation's money; that they could do." As a result of the king's solicitude and watchfulness, the resources of the state grew enormously. Not only had almost 14,000 estates been added to the crown holdings, but the royal coffers were full and two-thirds of the tithes now went regularly to the crown. While thus the king's mind was constantly directed to the welfare of his country, he at the same time had a thrifty regard for his own personal fortune and interests. It has been claimed that at his death Gustavus left a fortune in the form of coin and silver bars valued at about 21,000,000 crowns, purchasing power of coins and metals at that time being considered, and besides this 5,000 of the sequestered Church estates had become the personal property of the king. The income from these estates was, however, devoted largely to public enterprises.[5]

People became accustomed to ask the king's advice on every matter: what kind of boards and nails to use in constructing a house or a boat; where to find a good boat-builder; where goods might be sold most profitably; and a thousand and one other things. Gustavus might have become a cruel and unbearable tyrant, but from this calamity he and his people were saved by his live consciousness of duty. There was danger, too, that the multitude of cares and annoyances would paralyze his energies and make him sour and petulant, but from this fate he was rescued by his sense of humour. An official who let several requests for a report go unheeded was finally asked the reason for his delinquency: "Had he dropped into a mountain and was he held prisoner there, or had some old woman bewitched him so that he had lost both memory and reason, or were his fingers paralyzed, his mouth sealed, or his hands tied, so that he could neither speak nor write?" asked the angry king. Gustavus was a statesman of high order, but often unscrupulous and arbitrary. He knew, however, when it was the part of wisdom to yield and he seldom failed to act with promptness at the opportune moment.

Military reorganization.—Constantly mindful of the fact that Sweden's former misfortunes and humiliation were caused mainly by the lack of an adequate military force, it became a cardinal principle of Gustavus's administration that a national army must be created. He realized that mercenary soldiers were, at the best, wholly unsatisfactory and therefore dismissed those whom he had secured for his service and established regiments composed of his own people. Many men would, he believed, be better off in military service than in the wild and wretched life they were leading, and not only would the country as a whole benefit through the added se-

[5] Hildebrand, *Sveriges historia,* IV, pp. 318-319.

curity which a national army would provide, but through the discipline which would be imposed upon a considerable part of the populace many individuals would be especially benefitted. Gustavus therefore introduced an innovation in military organization which his successors were to extend further and thus lay the basis for the later remarkable efficiency of the Swedish army. Realizing the evils which inevitably seemed to spring from military life by reason of long periods of idleness in army camps, Gustavus proposed that soldiers who in peace time were not employed as servants by landholders should be provided with their own patch of land, on which they could live during the long intervals between military manœuvres or actual campaigns. This proposal was partly realized during his reign. Several model farms were, furthermore, established in different sections of the country, one for each two or three parishes, upon which soldiers were to live and work under guidance of the king's officials and were to teach the *bönder* correct principles of farming. Several castles were built, as at Vadstena, Uppsala, and Vaxholm, and others, as at Kalmar and Älvsborg, were strengthened. At the king's death. the fighting force of Sweden was estimated at 15,000 men, a small but most efficient army. In addition to this force, there were a certain number of auxiliaries available which the lords were under obligations to furnish. A new fleet was built, and in 1560 Sweden had 6 large, 19 medium size, and 28 small war vessels.

Agriculture.—The population of the country, not counting Finland, was estimated at approximately 500,000 in 1560. Great areas were uninhabited and covered by dense forests. Roads were miserable, practically all travel over the land being done on horseback, and long journeys could hardly be undertaken except in winter-time when lakes, bogs, and rivers were frozen over. Agriculture sustained at least 90 per cent of the populace, cattle-raising being relatively more important than in later periods. No industry existed, except as in each home nearly all the articles needed were manufactured by the household members themselves. Cities were few and insignificant, the most important, Stockholm, having 7,000 people and Uppsala 2,500. Ignorance and laziness made agriculture most

Agriculture in the time of Gustavus Vasa

Threshing the grain in the time of Gustavus Vasa

Primitive mining

unprofitable and Gustavus was unceasing in his efforts to instruct his people how they might get their fields into better condition by digging ditches, cutting down forests, ploughing correctly, drying the grain properly, and bringing it into sheds in proper time. He even, on some occasions, specified on what particular day hay ought to be placed under roof. No more hay or grain should be cut at one time, he ordered, than could be properly cared for in one or two days. In families where there were several sons they were told that they must not remain as lazy drones on the old homestead; instead they should go out into the uncultivated areas and break new ground. Failure to obey the king's orders was made punishable by fines, and in aggravated cases of negligence Gustavus did not hesitate to either confiscate farms and add them to the royal holdings or else order his bailiff to send men to work these and charge the cost to the delinquent owners. He likewise tried to improve the cattle stock, cows being imported from Holland and Jutland, sheep from England, and horses from Denmark and Holland. Rules were prescribed for fishing, not even the detail of how the fish ought to be salted being neglected. To the complaints of the farmers that they were suffering want, Gustavus seldom lent a sympathetic ear, as he held that they had themselves to blame for their plight. The mining industry was stimulated to new activity by the importation of German miners and smiths, and the establishment of smelters on several of the king's estates. Roads were built through the mining region to facilitate transportation.

Trade and commerce.—The significance of the success of the Hanseatic cities and of the growing prominence of Holland and England through the development of their foreign commerce was not lost on Gustavus and no phase of the nation's economic life held his interest so firmly as trade and shipping. At one time he requested from the city council of Stockholm a complete inventory of all articles imported and exported, and on the basis of this information he took measures to increase exports and decrease imports. Once the merchants of Västergötland were summoned to Stockholm for a conference with the king regarding the most efficient methods for extending their trade and throughout his reign he took occasion, upon his various journeys through the country, to discuss this subject with the traders and merchants of the respective localities. Hitherto, averred Gustavus, Swedish merchants had simply brought losses and ruin upon themselves by flocking like half-witted fools with their wares to the same markets on the Baltic, where they madly underbid one another, and he therefore admonished them to extend their trading operations to the North Sea, Atlantic ports, and Russia. For imported goods they fought, as the king said, "like hungry swine," and thereby simply boosted the price of foreign wares, and he remonstrated vigorously against this practice and urged that only useful articles be imported.

A project was even considered for a buying and selling organization with a capital of 100,000 marks, in order thus the more efficiently to be able to handle the trade in various articles in England, France, Flanders, and Germany. The king also suggested that the state ought to have regular trade representatives in such centres as Frankfort, Hamburg, Riga, Danzig, Moscow, and Novgorod, whose duty it would be to work for the extension of Swedish commerce. Retail trade at home had suffered, had, in fact, become a veritable scourge to the people, since everyone wanted to go about peddling wares. Such practice was forbidden by Gustavus, itinerant merchants being permitted only in the sparsely settled northern communities. Cities were ordered to specialize in the manufacture and sale of certain goods and all unemployed were to betake themselves to the country districts so that the *bönder* might have sufficient help available. No unnecessary cities should be built, and the king even went so far as to order the citizens of one city to abandon their community and take up their abode in another city since, as he said, two trading centres near each other hurt both. Gustavus's watchful interest did not neglect any matter that might affect the prosperity and well-being of his citizens, and in 1557 he ordered that two men be appointed in the various city districts to watch over sanitation and enforce rules of cleanliness. Swine, cows, and other cattle were not to be kept within the city walls, gutters were to be cleaned twice a week, and for this purpose each householder was ordered to have a barrel of water ready at all times.

Customs.—Customs were crude and vulgar, and eating and drinking were indulged in immoderately. The principle of blood feud and "man money" still persisted in many parts of the country and brawls and murder were common. The homes of the *bönder* were generally built in a quadrangle, made of unhewn logs with clay or dung smeared into the cracks and partitions; moss covered the roofs on which goats were wont to graze in summer. Only one small window, covered with a membrane or a pane of glass, admitted scant light to the damp and low living-rooms, where even chickens, pigs, and calves not infrequently were kept in winter. Homes were largely thus until about a century ago. In spite of all their crudities, the people nevertheless won the admiration of foreigners who happened to sojourn among them. One who visited Sweden about two decades after the death of Gustavus, speaks of them as "a plain, healthy, and defiant people, among whom there is a certain degree of wealth." The stock was sound and under efficient leadership the hardy and liberty-loving Swedes were capable of great deeds.

The king's lack of cultural interests.—The great administrator was least happy in his relations to the Church and cultural interests. He sought to bring order out of the chaos which the Reformation created in the ecclesiastical organization by appointing commissioners to those dioceses which had become vacant, but these found it impossible to secure proper men as pastors, largely because of the king's niggardly policy towards the servants of the Church. It has been estimated that the income of the higher ecclesiastics was at his death only one-seventh of what it had been during the Middle Ages and while a lopping off of some princely salaries was highly salutary the step did not greatly benefit the under-paid lower clergy. The king manifested a strange indifference towards education, and appropriations for schools were cut down. The University of Uppsala was practically defunct and Swedish students who wished to receive a thorough training were compelled to go to Rostock or some other foreign university. Two Swedish scholars gained European renown in this period; namely, the brothers Johannes and Olaus Magnus, but for both the king felt nothing but contempt, and harassed them both by petty persecutions. Olaus published his *Carta Marina* containing illuminative and interesting maps and descriptions of the North and likewise a richly illustrated history of the Northern peoples.[6] His brother Johannes wrote an erudite work on the history of the Goths and the Svear. These works added greatly to the fame of Swedish scholarship throughout Europe. Gustavus's only cultural and æsthetic interest was art,

A school in the olden times. From Olaus Magnus

especially as it revealed itself in the architecture and ornamentation of his castles. He instituted a court orchestra and at court there were likewise employed many jewelers, glass-blowers, and workers in gold.

Last years of Gustavus.—As the long and eventful reign of Gustavus Vasa was drawing to a close, dark shadows gathered more and more menacingly over him. The repose and joy to which a long life of heroic and incalculably valuable service entitled him were denied him. His eldest son, Erik, destined, by the enactment of the law making Sweden a hereditary monarchy, to succeed him on the throne, had early given evidence of those weaknesses and idiosyncrasies which later were to bring tragedy to himself and others and humiliation to the country; John, the second son, was wilful and given to futile speculations. From childhood these two brothers had disliked

[6] *Historia de Gentibus Septentrionalibus,* published in Rome in 1555.

and distrusted one another. A third son, Magnus, eighteen years old at his father's death, was mentally weak, and became violently insane soon after the father had passed away. A favourite daughter of the king, Cecelia, became involved in an ugly scandal, and this caused him more poignant grief in his declining years than anything else.

In time the aged monarch's strength began to wane rapidly, and he complained of weariness. He had a premonition that his days were soon numbered, and the urgent need of action by the Riksdag on several matters, including certain provisions of his will and appropriation for Prince Erik's projected trip to England to pay suit to Queen Elizabeth, prompted Gustavus in the summer of 1560 to summon the Estates to Stockholm.

Farewell address.—On June 25th there occurred a scene in the Riksdag assembly which in impressiveness and touching pathos has few, if any, counterparts in Swedish history. On this day the aged and venerable king, with his sons at his side, appeared before the representatives of the nation and spoke a solemn farewell to his people. As he spoke reminiscently of the events of his life, his voice faltered with emotion. "My career," an old account quotes him as saying, "has been like that of David, whom the Lord chose from among the lowly and gave victory against the great and the mighty. If any good has been done during my reign, let the people thank God for this, and if, on the other hand, there has been any failure or injustice in my government, I ask your forgiveness, and God shall be my witness that this has not happened through malice or obstinacy, but because of human frailty and because I have not been able to do any better." Perhaps no words attributed to Gustavus have been quoted as often by Swedish historians as the concluding sentence of this memorable address: "I know that in many things I have been a harsh king, but the time will come when the people of Sweden would gladly dig me from the sod again, if they only were able to do so." Historical criticism has proved quite conclusively that these words were not uttered by the king, but were spoken later, in the sermon which Peder Swart preached at the royal funeral at Uppsala, and were an expression of his estimate of the dead monarch.

The precise wording of the king's farewell address is not known. Towards the end of the century, an old secretary, who had taken part in the memorable meeting, wrote of its incidents, and quoted the address from memory, as well as from Peder Swart's sermon. With this as a basis, Olof Celsius included, in a history of Sweden which he wrote, an address [7] which purports to be spoken by the king, and subsequent historians merely assumed that Gustavus had actually spoken the words attributed to him. The king's last will and testament, which next was ratified, bequeathed, according to the terms of a previous enactment of the Riksdag, the crown to his eldest son, Erik, while John received Finland as a dukedom, Magnus was given a part of Östergötland and Småland, and the youngest son, Charles, received parts of Södermanland, Västmanland, and Närke as a dukedom. The creation of these dukedoms proved to be a serious mistake, and the cause of much subsequent evil. The young queen, Catharine Stenbock, and the king's daughters were by the will to receive large sums of money.

The end came to the king on September 29, 1560, and the interment took place in the cathedral at Uppsala on December 21st. Over his grave in the stately temple was later raised an elaborate marble monument, made in Antwerp, which to the Swedish people still remains a sacred shrine.

Gustavus's personality and family.—Gustavus Vasa is described in his mature years as a stately individual of medium size, with keen, penetrating blue eyes, ruddy complexion, flaxen hair, and a long, flowing beard. By nature he was jovial and delighted in the companionship of congenial souls, loved music, in which he was himself quite proficient, and wholesome frolic. People who were associated with him marvelled at his extraordinary memory; he knew the roads over which he had not travelled for thirty years and persons with whom he had once come in contact were decades later recognized by him and called by their right names when he chanced to meet them again. In his acts he was generally actuated by the highest motives of public interest, and keenly felt an overpowering

[7] The address is printed in Hildebrand and Grimsberg, *Ur källorna till Sveriges historia*, I. A discussion of its authenticity is found in Emil Hildebrand's *Gustaf Vasas sista tal till ständerna* in *Historisk tidskrift*, 1899.

Gustavus Vasa

sense of responsibility to God and to the Swedish nation. A quick temper which often got beyond control, a tendency to suspect everyone of evil designs, intolerance and harshness against those who dared to oppose him, and a thriftiness which often tended upon penury were the main weaknesses in his otherwise sturdy personality. In his private life he set a noble example of rectitude; in the whole list of calumnies that his enemies and traducers cited against him, there was never even a hint of licentiousness or scandal; he was a good husband and a kind, perhaps too indulgent, father. Gustavus was thrice married; to his first wife, Catharine of Saxe-Lauenburg, he was united in marriage in 1531. This was a political marriage pure and simple, the king being then mainly concerned about gaining added security for his dynasty by an alliance with a German Protestant royal family. Catharine was a weak person and subject to despondency, and the union was most unhappy. To this marriage one son was born, the later ill-fated King Erik, who evidently had inherited some of the unfortunate qualities of the mother. Catharine died in 1535, and the following year the king married Margareta Leijonhuvud, a daughter of one of the ancient aristocratic families of Sweden. Margareta was a noble-minded and wise queen, who in the fullest measure won the love and affection of her subjects. To the king she became a real helpmate, and their domestic life was most happy. Margareta became the mother of five sons and five daughters; two of the sons, John and Karl, were to play an important part in their country's history. The queen died in 1551 and in 1552 Gustavus married a sixteen-year-old girl, Catharine Stenbock, niece of his former queen, an act which scandalized many of his subjects, not only because of the disparity in their ages, but mainly because their close consanguinity prevented ecclesiastical sanction. The marriage was happy, but childless; Catharine survived her husband by sixty-one years.

Chapter XI

THROUGH DISSENSION AND WEAKNESS TO UNITY AND STRENGTH

Personality of Erik.—Sweden was soon after the death of the great Gustavus to discover that the royal sceptre had passed from the steady grasp of a giant into the trembling hands of a weak man. Erik, who now by virtue of the law of succession became king, was a strange contradiction of good and bad qualities; the latter, unfortunately, soon gained almost complete mastery of him. He had been carefully instructed in the subjects which then were considered especially important, namely, languages and theology. It had been one of Gustavus's chief concerns that the prince receive careful instruction, as well as practical experience, in statesmanship. He had absorbed the ideas of the humanists and spoke French, German, and Latin as well as he did his mother tongue, and he had a great love for music and song. His good qualities were, however, heavily outweighed by vanity, licentiousness, cruelty, and suspicion. He had a clear understanding of the requisites of a Swedish monarch under the conditions which then prevailed, but he was not sufficiently strong and well balanced to play the rôle.

The beginning of Erik's reign was marked by two acts which in themselves were justifiable and which public interest demanded; namely, the creation of a sort of Supreme Court (*konungens nämnd*), and a radical curtailment of the privileges which the dying father had granted to Dukes John, Magnus, and Charles. The court was to hear and judge cases which came up to it through appeals from lower courts, and in certain cases it had the right of original jurisdiction. Thus it was designed to simplify legal processes and insure a greater measure of justice, but its control fell almost at once into the hands of unprincipled men, and it thus became a dangerous instrument of injustice.

The radical curtailment of the broad powers which the former king had given his younger sons when they were created dukes was effected by resolutions adopted at a Riksdag at Arboga in 1561, and hence known as the Articles of Arboga.

Erik XIV. Contemporary painting

According to these articles, the subjects of the dukes were compelled to swear fealty directly to the king, and in case of war they were to be subject directly to the king's command, who was furthermore to be supreme in the matter of appointments, foreign relations, and appeals. About all the privileges that remained to the dukes was the right to collect the specified revenues in their respective domains. In itself the Arboga Act seemed dictated by wise statesmanship, but it was largely personal and petty jealousy which impelled Erik to press for its adoption.

The evil genius of the reign.—The people of Sweden were soon to learn that the sombre days of Gustavus Vasa, when thrift and simple living was the rule in the palace of the king, as well as in the humble cottage of the labourer, had passed. Erik's coronation, which was staged as soon as the necessary arrangements could be made, was featured by so many pageants and vulgar festivities running through many days, with unlimited quantities of food and drink served to the hungry populace, that a great part of the money which the thrifty Gustavus had hoarded for the future needs of the country was speedily squandered. At the coronation, barons and counts were created for the first time in Sweden, Erik's purpose being merely the frivolous desire to add more lustre to his royal dignity. The first recipients of the honours were compelled, however, to content themselves with little more than titles, only the counts receiving small fiefs.

Being a man of flaccid mind, and having many evil propensities, Erik naturally fell under the influence of other minds stronger and more dominant than his own. The man who became the evil genius of his reign was a vulgar and utterly unscrupulous individual by the name of Göran Persson. He was the son of a former Catholic priest who, under the influence of the Reformation doctrines, had flouted the rule of celibacy and had entered the marriage relation. Göran had studied for a time at Wittenberg and on returning to Sweden received employment in the chancery of Gustavus. Very likely because of the moral delinquencies of the young secretary, Gustavus had conceived a strong dislike for him and soon dismissed him from office, but he was, at the same time, admitted into the circle of Erik's intimate and dissolute friends. With the accession of Erik to the throne, this boon companion in dissipation became chancellor and procurator, a new office, carrying with it the functions of a public prosecutor. His lowly origin naturally made Göran an object of the bitter hate and unrestrained contempt of the proud nobility, and Göran Persson reciprocated this feeling with an intensity that could mean nothing but bitter warfare between him and the privileged class. The mind of Erik, naturally inclined to be suspicious, was a fertile field in which to sow the seeds of suspicion against the prominent nobles; it was already one of Erik's fixed notions that the old families were consumed with jealousy of the Vasa family and were constantly watching for an opportunity to contrive its undoing.

Erik's marriage plans.—Erik was inordinately vain, and his soaring vanity now demanded that he marry a princess belonging to one of the illustrious and powerful royal families of Europe. His first choice of a mate was no less a person than Elizabeth of England, and Duke John had been sent to London to prepare the way for a union of his royal brother to the great English queen. The results of John's mission were nil, and Erik next decided to go to London himself, and in person lay siege to the impregnable citadel of Elizabeth's affections. An alliance between Sweden and England seemed to the young prince a dazzling prospect. Soon after Erik had started on his London journey, Gustavus died and the prince turned back; thus ended the English marriage project. Elizabeth evidently never gave serious attention to the suit of the Swedish prince,[1] and no doubt treated it as a joke. Later Erik wooed Mary, Queen of Scots, but almost at the same time he entered into negotiations with Philip of Hesse with a view to marrying his daughter; still later he sought the hand of a princess of Lorraine. Largely by reason of the multiplicity and rather indiscriminate character of these marriage plans, which, of course, became a precious morsel for international gossip mongers, Erik found the path leading to matrimony far from smooth; in fact it seemed blocked altogether, and the suspicion, cleverly and maliciously fed by Göran Persson, that his enemies in Sweden, the great noble families, in their anxiety that the king remain unmarried and thus leave no heir to the throne, were secretly thwarting his marriage schemes now became a mad obsession with him. He therefore sought consent from the

[1] Recently a suggestion has been made that Erik was in reality the "mad prince" of Shakespeare's "Hamlet." It is not unlikely that Erik's wooing of Elizabeth gave rise to a good deal of court gossip in London about the "crazy" Swedish prince and it is by no means impossible that this gossip came to the ears of the great bard.

Council to marry whomsoever he might choose, and to this the Council finally agreed, adding the wish, however, that the king would not make his selection of a queen below the rank of the nobility.

The fight for the Baltic lands.—Gustavus Vasa could truthfully say in a letter to his subjects near the close of his reign that Sweden had ceased to be a country for foreign exploitation and adventures and that security and peace reigned in the land. Provocations to war had often come in the later years of the great king's reign, and only his prudent caution had saved the country from devastating conflicts with foreign powers. The storms which so long had threatened were, however, to break over the land in Erik's unhappy reign. As Gustavus's reign was drawing to a close, a delegation from the Esthonian city of Reval, then threatened by Russia, Poland, and Denmark, arrived in Sweden to solicit aid against the city's enemies. Poland had secured a part of Livonia as a fief, and now, when the city of Reval, including a great part of the province of Esthonia, placed itself under the Swedish protectorate, serious conflicts between Poland and Sweden were inevitable. As Governor of Finland, Duke John, who was closely in touch with the situation in the Baltic lands, was especially anxious to secure a part of the spoils for himself, and for that reason had been ready to enter upon an adventurous enterprise. While Gustavus lived he had, however, been held in check, but now he entered into an alliance with the Polish king, Sigismund, the terms of which provided that John should marry his sister, Catharine Jagellonica, and in return for a large sum of money secure possession of certain fortified places in Livonia. Perceiving clearly the dangerous consequences of John's projects and feeling deep resentment at his determination to pursue his own independent course in foreign affairs, Erik commanded his brother to scrap all these plans, including the marriage to the fair and good Catharine. The duke obstinately persisted in his course, married Catharine, and received the specified forts in return for the sum agreed upon. John's course naturally served still further to arouse the anger of Erik, and when a little later a confession, wrung from one of the duke's messengers, intimated that the latter meditated a rebellion against the king, John was forthwith summoned to appear in Sweden within three weeks to stand trial. He failed to heed these summons, and thereupon the king prevailed upon the Riksdag to declare him guilty of high treason, which carried a death sentence and the confiscation of all property as penalty. A military force was then sent to Finland and John and Catharine were made prisoners, brought to Sweden, and incarcerated in the castle of Gripsholm on Lake Mälaren.

War with Denmark.—The strained relations which existed between Sweden and Denmark during the last years of Gustavus have already been noted, but, as intimated, the dogs of war had been held in leash by Gustavus and Christian. Unfortunate changes in both countries now united in bringing the two nations into a conflict, which, with some interruptions, was to go on for one hundred and fifty years, and to bring in its wake growing hatreds, harrowing misery, and ultimately weakness and humiliation for both. The unfortunate changes alluded to were the accession of Erik to the throne in Sweden and of Frederick II to that of Denmark a year earlier. The specific causes for the war which now broke out, known as the Seven Years' War, seemed trivial indeed, but back of them lay the ancient antagonism of the two nations, which now was accentuated by the intense bitterness which the two royal cousins felt for each other. Like Erik, the Danish king was young, inexperienced, and puffed up with inordinate pride, and in his mind had been conceived plans for the speedy subjection of Sweden, followed by the incorporation of part of it with Denmark, and possibly a re-establishment of a union of the three Scandinavian kingdoms under Danish sovereignty. As another disturbing factor, had come conflicting interests in the province of Esthonia. This province had been Danish in the time of Valdemar the Victorious, which was one reason why the prospect that it would fall into the hands of Sweden was most distasteful and disturbing to the Danes; when therefore Erik sought to hinder them from trading with Narva, the chief port of the province, their cup of resentment began to run over. The conflict was precipitated by Frederick's high-handed act in arresting the members of a Swedish embassy which was passing through Denmark on the way to Hesse, where just then Erik was angling for a bride, and in dispatching a Danish squadron into the Baltic to prevent the carrying of war-material to and from Sweden. Erik promptly retaliated by sending his fleet on a cruise on the Baltic "to see what the Danish fleet would do if they met." The two squadrons did meet off Bornholm, and an engagement began which ended with a victory for the Swedes.

Character of the war.—Poland and Lübeck now joined Denmark in an alliance against Sweden, which escaped isolation and complete cutting off of food supplies from the outside only because the other Hanseatic cities and Pomerania refused to join in the attack on her. The war was fought on both land and sea, and was marked by intense bitterness and heartless cruelty, Danes and Swedes vieing with one another in committing depredations. The provinces of Blekinge and Halland especially suffered terrible ravages at the hands of the latter, while the Danes tried to even up scores by pillaging and plundering in Västergötland and Småland. Early in the war a detachment of the Danish army, which throughout the war was made up mainly of German mercenaries, captured Älvsborg, Sweden's only harbour on the North Sea. This loss was keenly felt by the Swedes. A Swedish army gained possession of Jämtland and Härjedalen and penetrated into Norway. The land forces of Sweden found it hard, however, to gain and retain any advantage. Erik was by no means deficient as a military strategist,[2] but the Danish forces were commanded by a general of more than ordinary ability, the Holsteiner, Daniel Rantzau. On the sea, victory as a rule inclined to the Swedes, whose fleet under command of the able Klas Kristerson Horn finally succeeded in gaining mastery of the Baltic, thus enabling the country to get much-needed food supplies from Germany. To the horrors of war were now added the ravages of the plague, whose progress and malignity naturally were increased by starvation and the hardships of camp life. The war in Livonia proceeded without much interest or energy being displayed on either side. Russia, under Czar Ivan the Terrible, seemed to Erik a far greater menace to Sweden than

[2] Stillé, A., *De ledande ideerna i krigsföringen i Norden, 1563-1570* in *Lunds universitets Årskrift,* 1918.

Poland, and he was ready to make great concessions in order to appease her. He even agreed to comply with the czar's shameful request that John's wife Catharine be delivered to him, the uncouth autocrat professing an ardent desire to possess the beautiful princess as his wife, but very likely having in mind some diplomatic gain from Poland through the advantage which possession of her would give him. The fact that Erik could agree to this proposal, even though he had little intention of abiding by his promise, is an evidence of his moral delinquency.

The Sture murders.—Erik was now advancing rapidly into the night of insanity. His various matrimonial projects had all ended in failure. At this point his suspicion turned with insane bitterness against the Sture family, and Göran Persson did his share to keep this hatred at fever-heat. The head of the Sture family at this time was Count Svante Sture, a brother-in-law of Gustavus Vasa through the latter's second marriage, and his two sons Erik and Nils were both in the service of the king. Nils, an able young man of twenty, had already rendered his sovereign loyal and valuable service both in diplomacy and warfare, but he was nevertheless on his return to Stockholm from a diplomatic mission arrested and subjected to the most humiliating treatment. The Sture family naturally resented keenly this insult to one of its members, and Erik, frightened by the outburst of indignation which his conduct had caused, tried to make amends by sending Nils on a mission to Lorraine to carry on pending negotiations for the marriage of Erik and the daughter of the Duke of Lorraine. In the meantime Göran Persson had been busy trying to unearth evidence of a widespread conspiracy, and for a consummate knave like him this offered no particular difficulty; he felt no scruples against manufacturing evidence if it could not be procured in any other way. A Riksdag was then summoned to Uppsala in May 1567, before which several prominent nobles, including the members of the Sture family, were summoned to stand trial on the charge of conspiracy. Only about twenty heeded these summons. In the meantime Svante Sture and his son Erik, together with some other nobles, had been thrown into prison at Uppsala, a fate which also befell Nils when about the same time he returned from Lorraine, and this in spite of the fact that he reported favourably regarding the king's marriage project. Erik acted all this time like an insane man, alternating between cringing fear and abject pleas for forgiveness on account of the injustice he had done, while back of it all always lurked an unreasonable suspicion and a vindictive hatred.

Immediately following a hasty visit to Svante Sture in the latter's cell, when he fell on his knees and abjectly begged Svante's forgiveness, which was freely assured him, Erik went on a stroll, but soon returning, he rushed like a madman into Nils Sture's cell and with his own hand plunged a dagger into the prisoner's body, then commanded a soldier to complete the act of murder. Rushing madly from the castle into the neighbouring forest, he gave orders to the men who accompanied him that all the other prisoners except one should be dispatched. Svante Sture and his son Erik and two other lords were cruelly put to death. Before the dastardly deed became known, Göran Persson prevailed upon the Riksdag to pronounce a death sentence against the slain men, after which the assembly was dismissed. Three days later Erik was found wandering about the country in the garb of a *bonde*, and it was with difficulty that Karin Månsdotter, the corporal's daughter who had completely won his favour and had become his mistress, could calm his mind and induce him to return to Stockholm. For a year following the murder of the Stures, he was in a demented state. (Medical experts have on the basis of the records established that Erik suffered from the malady now known as dementia præcox.) The affairs of the government were conducted by a group of noblemen. In some lucid interval, when remorse overpowered him, Erik tried to make amends for his crime and even set his brother John at liberty. For a time it seemed that reason had returned to him and his marriage to Karin Månsdotter was now solemnized, whereupon she was crowned queen at Uppsala. The spectacle of the daughter of a lowly corporal on the Swedish throne of course scandalized the aristocrats of the country.

Deposition of the king.—As Erik's violent insanity showed signs of returning, threatening new acts of violence, and Göran Persson became increasingly brutal and menacing, a conspiracy, with Dukes John and Charles at the head, was formed which easily prevailed against the king, who was made a prisoner and forced to renounce his crown (1568). Göran Persson, being justly held responsible for many of Erik's worst crimes, was speedily convicted of treason and executed. Erik was first kept in confinement at the palace in Stockholm, but after being transferred several times from stronghold to stronghold finally found abode in Örbyhus Castle in Uppland. Several conspiracies to secure his release were in the following years unearthed, and finally John, who without any further enactments or ceremonies had assumed the duties of king, secured the sanction of the Council to a suggestion that the prisoner should be put out of the way in case plots for his deliverance from prison were revealed. In judging John's conduct towards his unfortunate brother, a conduct which seems revolting in its heartlessness, it might be well to remember that even several of the bishops of Sweden had previously recommended that Erik be put out of the way in order that by this act a new carnival of crimes and civil war be forestalled. Karin Månsdotter, who, all through the sad days both before and after her royal husband's deposition, had showed a singular steadfastness and nobility of mind and who was the one person in the whole world who always enjoyed the trust of Erik, was at first permitted to share the prison with her husband, but after some time she and her children were removed to an estate in Finland which John provided for them. She lived forty-four years after a cruel fate had dispossessed her of the royal crown, and died in 1612, leaving a cherished memory of kindness and good deeds. Erik died in 1577, presumably from the effect of poison mixed in his food.

The nobility gains more power.—The recognition of John as king had met no obstacles when a Riksdag met soon after the arrest of Erik. Not a vote had been cast in favour of permitting the unfortunate Erik to retain the crown and his line was declared forever to have forfeited all rights to the throne. As a reward for the assistance which Duke Charles, in spite of his youth—he was only eighteen—had given in the campaign against Erik, he was now relieved of the limitations imposed on him by the Articles of Arboga. The aristocratic group had also assisted John with all the resources at its command, and was now determined upon receiving substantial rewards for its services. Deprived of its leading men by the Stockholm Massacre, the noble class had been unable, had it been so disposed, to encroach upon the royal power at the time when Gustavus was seriously embarrassed by the revolts of the *bönder,* and by the time that a new generation of nobles had grown up the king was so firmly entrenched and ruled with so firm a hand that the futility of any efforts to restore a part of aristocratic prestige and privilege at the expense of royal power and dignity must have been apparent to every one. In the reign of Erik the nobles had been compelled to meet continually the brutal attacks upon them by their inveterate foe, Göran Persson. Now that this unrelenting and resourceful enemy was out of the way, and they had a king who owed his throne to them, the nobles saw their opportunity to regain their lost prestige. Among the nobles were several men who, by reason of learning, shrewdness, and an aggressive spirit, could ably and successfully champion the cause of their class. The extent of aristocratic power and the victory the noble class gained in the beginning of John's reign are clearly revealed by the letter of privileges which the king issued near the close of his reign; this contained the important provision that aristocratic privileges were thereafter to be hereditary and not contingent upon the rendering of military service to the state, the number of men and horses which the nobles must supply in war was reduced, the customary royal incomes from fiefs were granted in perpetuity to counts and barons. Members of the National Council and the knights were granted the right to collect and use the royal share of fines imposed upon their subjects; important offices were to be the exclusive prerogative of the nobles, who in matters that concerned their honour were to be judged by none but members of their own class, and the usual restrictions in regard to domestic trade were not to be binding upon the nobility. As a final favour, John created several new counts and barons and bestowed upon them great fiefs, which were to descend from father to son by hereditary rights. The counts and barons were also given right of jurisdiction over the people of their fiefs, these retaining, however, the right of appeal to king or Council.

End of the war.—The confusion attending the change of rulers in Sweden had enabled the Danish forces under Rantzau to press into the interior of the country as far as Motala. Both the warring nations were, however, inexpressibly weary of the senseless struggle and ready to consider terms of peace. Under the mediation of Emperor Maximilian parleys were held at Stettin and a treaty ending the war signed December 13, 1570. Älvsborg was retroceded to Sweden, which in return restored Jämtland and Härjedalen to Denmark and agreed to pay 150,000 riksdaler (600,000 crowns, in purchasing power equivalent today to about 3,500,000 crowns). Sweden also gave up all claims to Halland, Skåne, Blekinge, and Gottland, Denmark in turn relinquishing her claim to Sweden. The question of the royal seals (p. 270) was to be the subject of later arbitration. The war thus meant no gain for either of the belligerents and its net result can be said to have been a marked augmentation of nation animosities.

At the time of Erik's surrender to his brother, a Russian embassy was tarrying in Stockholm, waiting to get possession of Catharine Jagellonica (p. 293) and conduct her to Ivan, but instead of the pleasure of welcoming this fair and good woman to his presence, the czar now received a communication from her husband, now king, informing him of the change which had taken place in Sweden and asking for a conference by representatives of the two nations in order to consider, and, if possible, to adjust their difficulties. The czar, fearing for the safety of his commissioners in Stockholm, tried to mollify John by resorting to a brazen lie: he had understood, he said, that John was dead, and had therefore wanted to save the beautiful Catharine from being confined in a Swedish prison. Swedish representatives who later were sent to Russia by invitation of Ivan in order to carry on further negotiations were subjected to the most cruel and humiliating treatment, and the only result of the mission was an exchange of letters between John and Ivan, in which each tried to outdo the other in broadsides of vile epithets. War followed these preliminary verbal skirmishes, and Esthonia and Livonia were overrun by the Russian hordes, who, as usual, were guilty of unspeakable atrocities. At last only Reval remained in the hands of the Swedes. Matters took on a brighter hue for them, however, when Stephen Bathory, King of Poland and brother-in-law of John (he had married a sister of Catharine Jagellonica), joined Sweden in the war. The situation brightened still more when Pontus de la Gardie, a Frenchman who had previously served in the Danish army, but later had entered the Swedish service, was placed at the head of a dependable force of Swedes and Finns and in a series of daring and successful campaigns took possession of all Esthonia, as well as a great part of Ingria. Russia now signed a truce with both Poland and Sweden, the latter retaining possession of Esthonia and Ingria. Late in John's reign (1590) the war on the eastern frontier flared up again, and Ingria was retaken by Russia.

Mismanagement in administration.—Throughout John's reign, Sweden was in turmoil, due partly to the wars, which constituted a heritage from Erik's unfortunate reign, partly to the king's utter lack of administrative ability or practical sense, and to his ill-advised although well-meaning projects for religious unity. One conspiracy followed the other in rapid succession, most of them for the ostensible purpose of restoring Erik to power, but in reality having as their real impelling force a deep and widespread dissatisfaction with John's administration.

Gustavus Vasa's government had approximated the ideal of a paternalistic régime as closely as the reign of any ruler of a modern state. When controlled by an honest sovereign of superior ability like Gustavus, whose prodigious energy and capacity for work, practical good sense, and fearlessness made themselves felt in every department, such a government could function most satisfactorily for the common good, but when control passed to the hands of a man like John, almost totally lacking as he was in practically all the qualities which had made his father a great king, the results were disastrous. Such administrative functions as the checking of incomes and expenditures and performing other duties connected with the fiscal administration fell into the hands of secretaries who generally were deficient in both honesty and insight. In money affairs, John was like a child. Huge building projects were started by him before he had any clear conception whence the money was to come. His was an æsthetic soul, which found its chief delight in building fine churches and splendid palaces. The royal palace was crowded with unnecessary functionaries, the number being in 1573 no less than 1,040, and the annual expenditures for the court consumed no less than one-sixth of the revenues of the state. Every year the deficit of the royal treasury was alarmingly great: against a total expenditure of 895,648 daler in 1573 could be placed only 442,513 daler in revenue. In his despair John finally resorted to the expedient so common to weak and spendthrift rulers; namely, the debasement of the metal money of the realm. As usual the cure simply aggravated the evil. So widespread and bitter was the dissatisfaction due to John's weak administration that one conspiracy which involved some of the most prominent nobles in Sweden aimed at nothing less than the re-establishment of the elective monarchy in Sweden, with the lords as the real rulers, as had been the case before the days of Gustavus Vasa. The conspirators intended to issue a statement that the Vasa family had forfeited its right to the Swedish throne and should therefore be excluded from the government; such, at least, was the sinister plan which the French minister to Denmark, Dançay, reveals in reports to his government. According to this story, Dançay was one day visited by two of the Swedish lords who laid the above plan before him, justifying it by declaring that the Vasa family was hopeless; Gustavus Vasa's father had been crazy, Gustavus himself had had his peculiar vagaries, and all his sons were much worse than the father.[3] The conspiracy did not progress very far before its existence became known, and it was then nipped in the bud, but the Swedish lords had cleverly managed to keep in the background and thus escaped punishment.

John's dream of religious unity.—John's great redeeming quality was his love of the æsthetic and his abhorrence of senseless strife, especially in matters of faith. He ardently believed that religious ceremonies ought above everything else to be made beautiful and impressive, and his whole being re-

[3] Hildebrand, *Sveriges historia*, V, p. 159.

belled against the barrenness and emptiness which in his opinion characterized the worship of the new faith in Sweden. These feelings are perfectly intelligible, for although the Reformation in Sweden under the influence of men like Olaus Petri had been marked by a greater degree of tolerance than in most countries, many churches had been stripped of their ornaments and made ugly-looking through the spoliation by the bailiffs of Gustavus Vasa. Public worship had for the most part ceased to be edifying and the new pastors were often ignorant and incompetent men. John's interests tended mainly towards theology and religious questions, and it was therefore but natural that the great question of religious unity should absorb much of his attention. While theologians in the divided Protestant camps were quibbling over petty dogmatic points or hurling the deadly weapons of invective and insinuation against each other, many reasonable and peace-loving men had begun to wonder whether believers could not find, back of the non-essentials, some fundamental religious truths on which they could all agree. An exponent on the scholastic and theological side of this noble ideal was the Belgian theologian, George Cassander, who in a work had suggested that by going back to the early Church fathers Christians could get a correct idea of how Christ's teachings were to be interpreted. Catholics and Protestants could on this basis, he believed, find it possible to unite in a common faith again. This now became the ideal of John, who in his long imprisonment had spent the time in earnest reading of theological works, especially the writings of the Church fathers. By the king's side, as his aid and adviser in theological questions, stood one of his secretaries, Peter Fecht, who had returned to his native country from his theological studies in German universities thoroughly in sympathy with Cassander's unionistic plans. Jointly the king and Fecht now wrote an order of service, known as the Ordinantia of 1575, which was laid before a meeting of clergy and approved by them. In almost every detail the Ordinantia sought to carry out Cassander's ideal of a *via media*. Toleration was one of its great pleas. Thus it says regarding the priestly office: "We are not lords having authority over the faith of our neighbours, but servants and stewards of God's secrets; therefore we should not despair of the salvation of any, nor hastily judge anyone." As a next step towards a union of the faiths, John and Fecht wrote a new liturgy, which because of the colour of the initial letters of some paragraphs in the original edition, became known as the Red Book. In spirit it conformed closely to the Catholic "*Missala Romanun*," and embodied the cult of the old Church, as defined by the Council of Trent, but intermingled with the provision of this Ordinantia were a number of precepts taken from earlier Swedish liturgies. It was a mixture of many heterogeneous elements that could not wholly satisfy either Protestant or Catholic.

Negotiations with Rome.—The great concession to Catholic thought and cult which the liturgy revealed aroused the hope in Rome that John, and through him Sweden, could be brought back into the fold again. The king's well-known dislike of certain features of Lutheran faith and cult gave added foundation to this hope. The Curia could naturally count on the queen as a strong ally in these plans, the more so since her beauty, nobility of character, and piety had given her a strong influence over her husband. The first contact between the king and Rome was, in fact, established through her mediation. It so happened that she had turned to one of the high cardinals of the Church for light on a certain controverted question in religion, and both John and the Pope, at this time Gregory XIII, were soon drawn into the correspondence which the query of the queen had started. This, in turn, led to the dispatch of a Polish Jesuit to the Swedish court, in the hope that the king's mind might by the exercise of proper influence be made to incline still more towards Catholicism. Finding John open-minded and sympathetic, the Jesuit recommended to his superiors that other men be sent to the Swedish court to continue the good work which he had begun. This suggestion was favourably acted upon at Rome and a Norwegian ecclesiastic, Laurentius Nicolai, and a Dutch priest, Florentius Feyt, were dispatched to Sweden. In accordance with the instructions which they carried with them, they were to establish a school or "kollegium" at Stockholm and there simulate a straight-laced Lutheranism until they had won the confidence of their disciples; having proceeded thus far, they were tactfully to sow the seeds of doubt regarding the faith of the Reformers. The school was opened according to plan, and since it was held in an old Franciscan cloister Nicolai became known as "Klosterlasse." [4] It did not take long, however, before those who had a keen scent for dogmatic heresies became suspicious and were on the trail of the zealous teachers. The king's new liturgy from the first met with the violent opposition of leading churchmen and this became the more formidable as Duke Charles became the staunch and aggressive ally of this group; he absolutely forbade the use of the new liturgy in his duchy, an assumption of authority which can hardly be justified on any other grounds than the desire to defend and perpetuate the ecclesiastical system which his great father had given to his country. The liturgy was, however, defended by the new archbishop, Laurentius Petri Gothus, a learned and highly cultured man, who, like John, desired to elevate the tone of religious life in Sweden and who likewise abhorred strife. Most reluctantly the clergy outside of Charles's duchy gave their approval to the Red Book.

Influenced largely by Klosterlasse, and quite likely also by his queen, John next sent Pontus de la Gardie and Peter Fecht on an important diplomatic mission to Italy; they were to suggest an alliance between Spain, the emperor, the Pope, and Sweden in order to give the latter security against Denmark and Russia, but as the main part of their mission they were to make certain suggestions regarding the eventual return of Sweden to Catholicism. Fecht met his death by drowning while on the journey, but de la Gardie reached Rome, and carried out his instructions faithfully.

Antonio Possevino.—To the leaders of the Catholic reaction, the message which he brought seemed to offer an extraordinary opportunity for winning a great victory for the old faith, and the secretary of the Order of Jesuits, Antonio Possevino, a learned and experienced man, undoubtedly the ablest and most versatile diplomat in the service of the Church at the time, was next sent to Sweden. In order not to arouse

[4] *Kloster*—cloister—*Lasse*, a corruption of the Swedish name Lars, and implying a plebeian.

suspicion and opposition prematurely, he had instructions to pose in Stockholm as a diplomatic agent of the emperor, whom he visited on his way to Sweden. In several secret conferences between the king and the papal nuncio, during which the question of a political alliance between Sweden, Spain, and Poland was also a topic for discussion, the former laid bare his thoughts and aspirations relative to religion and unity of faith, and the latter with all the consummate skill which he possessed sought to win the king completely for the Catholic Church. Possevino in his report to his superior[5] relates how one day John in a moment of religious ecstasy embraced him, exclaiming, "Thus do I embrace you and the Holy Church for all eternity"; the next day the king, after confession according to the practice of the old Church, received holy communion at the hands of Possevino. But John was not so easily to be brought back, a weak penitent, into the ancient faith as Possevino at first imagined. He was indeed willing to return to Rome and do everything in his power to bring his people with him, but only on the basis of a give-and-take policy. In a letter to Pope Gregory, under date of March 8, 1578, he presented twelve petitions, the granting of which was expected before the king would embrace Catholicism. The most important of these were: the right to use the vernacular in the Church service; distribution of the wine as well as the bread to the laity in the Lord's Supper; right of the clergy to marry; a promise that the body of Gustavus Vasa be not removed from the Uppsala cathedral; and the abolition of holy water and other parts of the Catholic cult. Some of these petitions had earlier been presented to the Pope, but no answer had been given by him. Possevino now went in person to Rome, carrying with him John's new letter, in order to urge an answer. The Pontiff's answer, which came in due time, was a grievous disappointment to John; it denied every one of his petitions except one exempting the king from the obligation to return the confiscated Church property. On this point the Pope yielded, but with some reservations. "If I cannot get all, I can do nothing," was John's comment on receipt of the Pope's reply.

[5] The correspondence and documents from these interesting negotiations are printed in Theiner's *Schweden und seine Stellung zum heiligen Stuhl unter Johan III, Sigismund III, und Karl IX*, Augsburg, 1838.

Failure of the negotiations.—Other epistles passed between the king and the Pope, but all efforts to come to an agreement stranded on the latter's absolute refusal to yield any further point, and John's equally unqualified refusal to yield on at least three points: the use of the Swedish language in religious worship, the right of the clergy to marry, and the distribution of the wine as well as the bread to all laymen in the sacrament of the Lord's Supper. Possevino later came to Sweden for a second visit, but now found the king indifferent to any project for a return to Rome. John's interest was now centred in the endeavour to enforce the use of his Red Book in the church service. One victory Possevino had, however, won in Sweden, the consequences of which were to be far-reaching, for it was mainly through his influence that the crown prince, Sigismund, was completely won to Catholicism.[6]

Soon after Possevino's departure after his first visit, another diplomatic agent arrived in Stockholm, and this visit not only flattered John's vanity tremendously, but opened up prospects for the realization of a most ambitious scheme on his part. The new visitor was Francisco de Eraso, legate of Philip II of Spain, who came to propose an alliance between his country and Sweden, according to the terms of which the latter, in return for a subsidy, should assist Spain in its war in the Netherlands. Great schemes were also discussed by Eraso and John regarding an attack on Denmark, which it was hoped would result in adding the Danish islands and Jutland to the domains of Spain, and Skåne, Blekinge, and Halland to Sweden.[7] The matter never went beyond a preliminary agreement between the king and Eraso, and no money was received from the Spanish monarch. After some time, Eraso fell completely from grace at the Swedish court, and the negotiations became a closed issue. Having failed in his negotiations with Rome and Spain, John now redoubled his efforts to force his Red Book upon all congregations, but the opposition could now muster a determined force. At the head of this opposition stood Abraham Angermannus, rector of the Stockholm City School, who

[6] Hammargren, J. A., *Den liturgiska striden under Johan III*, Uppsala, 1898.
[7] Hildebrand, E., *Johan III och Filip II* in *Historisk tidskrift*, 1886.

represented the extreme narrow and orthodox type of Lutheran theology, and in his fight against the king manifested a coarseness and bitterness which were highly inconsistent with his office and with the cause for which he was pleading. As the professors of the University of Uppsala had taken a leading part in the fight against the Red Book, this institution was closed by order of the king, who now endeavoured to build up another school in Stockholm, but this project failed. The most effective opposition to the Red Book continued to come, however, from Duke Charles, who not only in utter defiance of the king forbade its use in his dukedom, but at the same time gave a secure haven to all those opponents of the liturgy elsewhere who were solely harassed by John.

A strange alliance.—King John was to enter upon one more ambitious and ill-conceived enterprise before he died, and this was to end, like his projects for religious unity, in disillusionment and bitter disappointment, involve his country in dangerous entanglements, and stir up controversies and wars which were to drag their weary way through many decades. By reason of his marriage to Catharine and the political alliance with Poland, John had come to have both a large money claim against that country and a personal interest in the queen's inheritance. It was therefore most important to him that whosoever was ruler of Poland was his dependable friend, and in three different royal elections in this torn and distracted country John had interfered in order to safeguard his own interests. When in 1586 a vacancy on the Polish throne again occurred, overtures were speedily made to John by interested individuals in Poland with a view to securing the election of Sigismund to the hazardous, but nevertheless much coveted, royal office. The young prince was not averse to enter upon the risky venture.

A close dynastic and political union of two states so utterly different in language, traditions, forms of government, and religion—Poland was now a leader in the Catholic reaction and Sweden was fast becoming the leading champion of an uncompromising Lutheran orthodoxy—must have appeared rather anomalous, and the task of finding a common basis for such a union must have seemed rather difficult, but John made haste to assure his Council he could suggest articles of agreement which would be acceptable to Poland and at the same time would safeguard Sweden's interests. The Swedish Council interposed no serious objections to the project for an alliance of the two powers which might serve as a counterpoise against Russia; possibly the great lords were further inclined to favour the union by the consideration that it would eventually take their king away from their own land and their own opportunity for grasping more power would be improved. In due time these articles were presented and are known as the Constitution of Kalmar. As for Sweden, they provided that the two countries should be on a basis of equality; no Swedish territory should ever be ceded to Poland, the Swedes should remain in untrammelled possession of their ancient rights, and no heretical religion was to be brought into their country. As a final clincher to these safeguards, it was further stipulated that the Pope should under no circumstances absolve the king from these obligations. John was willing to go so far in his endeavour to safeguard all Swedish interests that the draft even contained a proviso that the Swedish language should not be debased by the admixture of foreign words or phrases. In the absence of the king, the Constitution continued, Swedish affairs were to be managed by a Council of seven members, of which one was to be appointed by Duke Charles. John assumed sole responsibility for these provisions, but there is reason for suspecting that some of the powerful lords did not stand entirely outside of the affair; this scheme opened up splendid prospects for them to gain more power, since royalty, under the contemplated union, would naturally be greatly weakened. These negotiations were kept secret from Duke Charles, who did not know of Sigismund's candidacy until several months had passed. He then tried to dissuade his nephew from entering on the dangerous venture, but since the latter was determined to go forward with his plans, Charles curtly wished him good luck. Possibly even then the clear-sighted and strong-willed duke had resolved that, as far as he could help it, neither blessing nor good fortune would attend upon his royal kinsman.

A Swedish prince on the Polish throne.—Meanwhile negotiations concerning the same matter were going on in Poland, and here the Swedes had been confronted with the unreasonable and unacceptable demand that their country must first cede its conquests in Esthonia to Poland before Sigismund could be elected to the vacant throne. The Swedes were finally induced to make some vague promises of an eventual surrender of Esthonia, and in due time Sigismund was elected king by the Poles. The Polish act of election also laid down specific conditions for Sigismund's guidance as King of Poland, which in some details were at variance with the Constitution of Kalmar.

When the first news of Sigismund's election reached the Swedish court, it brought joy to the fond royal father—Catharine had died some years previously—but as the details of the conditions which had been affixed to it became known his joy turned to dismay and bitter resentment, and he declared categorically that his son would not be permitted to accept the proffered crown. As the Polish delegation, which in the meantime had arrived at Stockholm for the purpose of escorting Sigismund to their country, threatened to leave in a huff and serious complications with Poland over the matter seemed imminent, John at last gave his reluctant consent to the arrangement, giving Sigismund the parting admonition, however, that he must not under any circumstances cede any part of Esthonia to Poland.

John longs for the return of Sigismund.—From this time on, Sigismund's path was strewn with thorns, and John's soul was henceforth to his dying day to be tormented by loneliness and grief. The Poles would not let their king-elect enter their kingdom until he had agreed to the cession of Esthonia, but as Sigismund, mindful of his father's parting injunction, thereupon threatened to return home, they finally agreed that a decision regarding this territory should wait till a later date. At the same time Sigismund gave the Swedish councillors in his party private assurance that whatever concessions he had made were merely a blind promise and that he would never give up Esthonia.

Two years had barely passed after Sigismund's election to

the Polish throne before the lonely and grief-stricken John suggested a meeting between him and his son in Esthonia. At the same time, and in all probability with the full knowledge and connivance of John, Sigismund began to lay plans for getting rid of the Polish crown, with the result that a situation arose which had all the features of a tragicomedy. The father and the son were both determined to be done with the Polish venture, while the Swedish Council, fearing that if Sigismund now deserted the Poles this would involve their country in a war which its desperate financial situation, aggravated by failure of crops, rendered it unable to wage, was still more determined that the royal father and son must keep their pledge to the Poles. Officers in the army gave notice of their determination to mutiny if war were brought upon the country by Sigismund's contemplated French leave from Poland. In the face of these threats, John and Sigismund, who in 1589 met at Reval, were compelled to yield, and with bitterness in their hearts each one went his way. John now turned with vindictive fury against the members of his Council, whom he blamed for the unhappy outcome, and the rest of his years he spent in persistent efforts to humiliate and impoverish them as well as other members of the nobility, whom he suspected of being in league with the Council. Back of this vindictiveness was, however, not only the chagrin which he felt because of the Polish affair; Duke Charles had now made his peace with his brother and was spurring on the king in his attacks upon the privileged order. This shrewd prince had clearly seen that Sweden was headed directly towards a rule by aristocrats, such as had made the reigns of Magnus Eriksson and Albrecht of Mecklenburg synonymous with wretchedness and humiliation, and he had, in spite of irreconcilable differences in their character and ideas, joined the king in an unrelenting war upon the ambitious and grasping lords. In the years following, the latter were more than once to feel the iron grip of this stern and unyielding foe of aristocratic usurpation.

Death of John.—In the midst of the crumbling of all the grand edifices which he had conceived and endeavoured to build, John died in 1592, a tragic failure in everything that he had undertaken. A lover of learning and a patron of the arts, he had closed the doors of Uppsala University and had retarded the nation's cultural development; a dreamer and an ardent apostle of unity of faith, he had caused his own people to be rent by bitter controversies regarding theological questions; a champion of a union with Poland in the hope that thereby his own country would gain greater security, he had inaugurated a bitter quarrel between two great nations which was to bring many wars and cruel losses to both.

The situation which confronted Sweden at the death of John was fraught with grave dangers to the country. The religious and political institutions of the country seemed to be placed in serious jeopardy; in fact Protestantism throughout the world was endangered by the situation which John's death had created. By the Swedish law of succession, making the crown hereditary in the Vasa family, Sigismund was now clearly entitled to royal power and dignity in the land. Insecure as he at first had felt on the Polish throne, the hard-pressed king had sought support from the Catholic Church, and by this time Jesuits were his constant advisers. Easily influenced by stronger wills than his own, and by nature inclined to fanaticism, he had become an ardent defender of the ancient faith and the Catholic reaction had no more zealous champion than he. His position as King of Poland—then one of the greatest powers in Europe in spite of unfortunate internal division and strife—and his own ardent religious zeal, had made him the leading figure in the counter-Reformation movement outside the ranks of the ecclesiastics themselves.

Dangers to the Lutheran faith in Sweden.—Sweden's return to Catholicism, which, under the new alignments, did not seem a very remote possibility, would mean an immense strategical gain for Catholicism. The Dutch were fighting desperately against powerful Catholic Spain, and although the latter's attack upon England had in 1588 ended with the defeat of the Armada, Spanish plans for crushing the island foe were by no means abandoned. With Sweden as a Catholic nation and in alliance with Spain, the latter would secure a needed naval base in the North from which England could be successfully attacked. A Catholic Sweden would, in all probability, mean that Denmark also would be won for the old faith again. It must be remembered that the ultimate victory of Protestantism in the Scandinavian lands was by no means definitely assured at the time when Sigismund became king. Especially among the common people, sympathy for the old Church was still strong. Unfortunately for Sigismund and for the Catholic cause, and fortunately for Sweden and for Protestantism, the latter had in Duke Charles a leader against whom the young king was no match. While Sigismund was dull, vacillating, and inexperienced, Charles had inherited the tremendous energy of his father, acted with rapidity and decision, had a clear sense of realities, was not overly scrupulous as to means, and, like his father before him, realized clearly the advantage which an appeal to the people for support would bring him and his cause.

The meeting at Uppsala.—Charles lost no time in taking the proper measure, so as to be able to meet the emergency which necessarily would arise when Sigismund arrived to claim his crown. First of all, he effected a reconciliation with the great lords, and thereupon summoned an assembly of prominent men to meet at Uppsala for the purpose of formulating, before the king's arrival, some definite program on which the nation could unite. The meeting was held in March 1593, and was attended by more than three hundred of the leading churchmen of the country, many of whom had suffered persecution under John, because of their opposition to the Red Book. The temper of the meeting was made evident when in the very beginning Nicolaus Bothniensis, a young professor of theology at Uppsala University, who because of his opposition to John's ecclesiastical policy had been ousted from his position and thrown into prison, was elected chairman. The delegates soon were in complete accord in declaring the word of God "the true norm for man's faith" and in accepting the Augsburg Confession as the correct interpretation of the Bible. With uplifted arms the members then took a solemn vow that, if necessary, they would unto death stand united on the foundation of these principles. "Now," exclaimed the chairman, "Sweden has become as one man, and we all have one Lord and one God." Next came the turn of the Red Book, which now found no defender and was forthwith rejected. Some difficulty was encountered in securing the approval of Duke Charles to the decision, as he felt aggrieved at not being consulted, and was furthermore angered because a paragraph in the resolution condemning the Calvinists, for whom he was known to have sympathies, had been inserted. Finally he consented, however, that this group might remain on the proscribed list. "Include them all," he broke out in anger, "and the devil, too, for he also is one of my enemies." The same meeting also took measures for reopening the University of Uppsala and elected Abraham Angermannus archbishop. "It is scarcely possible," says an English ecclesiastic, John Wordsworth,[8] "to exaggerate the importance of this Council as a turning-point in the history of Sweden. . . . There are very few, if any, parallels to be found to it in the religious history of mankind."

Even prior to Sigismund's departure from Poland for his journey to Sweden to receive his new crown, the Uppsala resolutions were placed before him for approval, but he naturally refused to accommodate the Swedes in this matter; the most Catholic prince could hardly be expected to subscribe to a document which declared that the Augsburg Confession contains the true and faithful interpretation of Holy Writ. In September 1593 he arrived in Stockholm, where Duke Charles and the new archbishop, Angermannus, were on hand to receive him. Very likely they were the last persons in the world whom Sigismund had any desire to meet, but the amenities of diplomatic procedure were properly observed. Accompanying the king and serving as his confidential adviser was Germanico Malaspina, papal nuncio, and one of the shrewdest diplomats of the Catholic Church. At Danzig he had received a large sum of money from the papal treasury to be used in the campaign for winning Sweden back to Catholicism. With the money had also gone elaborate instructions regarding the most effective method of procedure.

Sigismund subscribes to the Augsburg Confession.—Soon after Sigismund's arrival in Sweden, the demand was formally made upon him that he approve the Uppsala resolutions, send Malaspina away, and reopen the University of

[8] Wordsworth, J., *The National Church of Sweden,* London, 1911.

Uppsala. As before, Sigismund bluntly refused to affix his signature to the decrees, and as the Swedish Council stood firm, the king, properly coached by Malaspina, began to argue and equivocate, at last announcing that he would comply with its demands, but not until he had been crowned king and the people had taken the oath of allegiance to him. To this the Council returned the curt answer that he must sanction the Uppsala decrees before they would swear fealty to him, or else make up his mind that he would never be crowned King of Sweden. Sigismund next tried to divide his enemies by creating a schism between Duke Charles and the Council, but in this he failed, the latter's only answer being a demand for further securities that the Constitution of Kalmar would be respected. An attempt was now made by Sigismund to win the *bönder* to his side, but they made it plainly known that they were heart and soul for Duke Charles. Meanwhile the members of the Riksdag were gathered at Uppsala for John's obsequies, and here the final negotiations took place. Each order of the assembly met separately and took a solemn oath not to yield to the king on any point, and this exhibition of unity—and a well-timed statement by Duke Charles that if Sigismund did not yield within a definite time, his coronation would never take place—had its effect. Sigismund now capitulated and took the oath to abide by the Uppsala decrees, rule the land according to the ancient laws of Sweden, and employ none but Lutherans in the service of the state. He had, however, before the ceremony, submitted a secret written protest to Malaspina, in which he solemnly declared that his oath had been wrested from him by threats of revolution, and that he did not consider himself bound by it.[9] The outcome of this remarkable conflict naturally caused bitter disapointment in the Catholic world, not least in Rome.

No sooner had Sigismund returned to Stockholm than he violated his oath by appointing Catholic governors for Stockholm, Uppland, and Norrland, and instituting Catholic service in the capital. In the summer of 1594 he returned to Poland. In Sweden the government was left in confusion by Sigismund's departure. The king had entrusted it to Duke Charles

[9] Hjärne, H., *Sigismunds svenska resor,* Stockholm, 1884.

and the Council jointly, their authority to last during the king's absence, but at the same time he appointed governors for the provinces who were instructed to take orders directly from him in Poland.

Civil War.—A strong-willed and aggressive man like Duke Charles could not acquiesce in such a division of power, and he soon secured from the Council an appointment as regent (*riksföreståndare*). Against this action Sigismund naturally protested, and as his protest had a very menacing tone, the members of the Council began to waver in their support of the duke. The latter, however, was not seriously alarmed by the signs of defection among the lords, for he knew that he could count on the unswerving loyalty and support of the common people. At a Riksdag at Söderköping in 1595 the lower Estates forced the adoption of measures which firmly fixed his status as protector, and those who would not acquiesce in this arrangement were declared traitors. The same Riksdag likewise resolved that all Catholic priests must leave the country, the Catholic laymen being permitted to remain as long as they refrained from agitation against the Lutheran faith and against the Swedish government. Duke Charles also prevailed upon the members of the Riksdag to enter into a solemn pact that they would individually and collectively stand firm in the defence of the Uppsala Decrees and of a continued rule of Sweden in conformity with the ancient law of the land. The important enactments of the Söderköping meeting were printed, and copies were, in accordance with the precedent established in the case of the Uppsala decrees, sent to all parts of the country for approval by the people. Although not a great master of the spoken and written word like his father, Charles employed the printing-press more extensively than had ever been done before in bringing his views and desires before the people; when this weapon did not seem effective enough, he set out on extended journeys throughout the land and addressed the people publicly very much after the fashion of modern statesmen or would-be statesmen.

The anomalous situation in Sweden inevitably led to serious conflicts between the irreconcilable factions. Sigismund made plain his intention to rule Sweden from Poland, and re-establish Catholicism in the former; Charles, on the other hand, was inflexible in his determination that Catholicism should not again secure a foothold in the land. That Charles was actuated largely by ambition cannot well be denied, and that he was unscrupulous and harsh in his methods is equally undeniable, but it must seem evident that his interests were intimately bound up with the true interests of Sweden. The religious ideals of Sigismund were diametrically opposed to those which the majority of the Swedish people cherished and on the political side the king's policies were utterly inconsistent with ancient Swedish law and tradition. Charles saw clearly how absurd and impossible was the arrangement by which Sweden was to have a Catholic king and be ruled jointly with a country so strange to her as Poland, and if in his fight against Sigismund he was unscrupulous and resorted to sharp practices, he could find plenty of reasons for justifying this, since Sigismund had amply demonstrated that he could not be trusted and that, largely under the influence of confidential advisers, who were past masters in the art of duplicity, he was preparing for an attack on the country's most sacred rights. The conviction that not only Sweden but all the Protestant nations were in jeopardy helped, naturally, to stir Charles to aggressive action.

Flight of the councillors.—Meanwhile the members of the Swedish Council found themselves between the devil and the deep sea. They knew that on the main point the duke was right, and that the great majority of the nation stood by him; but, on the other hand, they disliked and feared him and, furthermore, they felt bound by their oath of allegiance to Sigismund, even if they disapproved of many of his acts. In Finland, Klas Fleming, Sigismund's governor, defiantly refused to take orders from the duke, and remained loyal to his royal master, and Charles was determined to punish him for this. When the Council refused to approve a war on Fleming, Charles threatened to call the Estates and resign from his office. The call was issued for a meeting to be held at Arboga, but Sigismund vetoed the project, and entrusted the government to the Council alone. The die had now been cast, and Duke Charles was not slow in taking his measures. In defiance of the king's orders and protests, and without the Council's approval or co-operation, Charles went forward with his plans, and the meeting was held in due time, this being the first time in the history of the country that a Riksdag acted independently of the Council. The *bönder* stood behind Charles in solid phalanxes and again gave solemn pledges that they would support Charles against Sigismund to the bitter end. Foreseeing the hopelessness of further resistance to the duke's policy, all the members of the Council save one had remained away from the meeting. Soon they took their departure hastily for Poland, to make common cause with Sigismund, and civil war began. Charles displayed an extraordinary energy in arousing the people and preparing effectively for the struggle which he had foreseen as inevitable. In the summer of 1598 Sigismund landed at Kalmar at the head of an army of 5,000 men, for the purpose of suppressing the revolt against him. This force was, however, entirely inadequate. The fugitive Swedish lords had proved themselves very poor advisers to their master in suggesting so small a force and assuring him that as soon as he landed in Sweden his numbers would be swelled by the accession of Swedish sympathizers, whereas if he came with a large army the whole nation would be stirred by fear to oppose him and rally to the support of Charles. Sigismund's invasion of Sweden may justly be considered a decisive event in European history. The entire Catholic world was watching the progress of the zealous king with great interest, for his success meant not only the winning of Sweden for the ancient faith, but the possession of a needed base in the North for attacks upon England and the Netherlands by the great Catholic power. An interesting detail of the military plans of Sigismund and his supporters was the projected capture of Älvsborg, the Swedish fortress on the North Sea coast, and its surrender to Spain for a naval base. Malaspina reported to the Curia what Sigismund's intentions were and asked dispensation for any promise that he might, in his endeavours to realize his plans, be compelled to make in violation of his religious faith or contrary to his own conscience. Duke Charles had quickly taken precautions to meet the danger. The nobility, most of the military officers, and even Archbishop Angermannus, to whom Charles's Calvinism was just as offensive as Sigismund's Catholicism, cast in their lot with the king, but Charles could with confidence count on the support of the *bönder*. In spite of Sigismund's blunder in bringing with him an inadequate force, his prospects of success seemed in the beginning considerably brighter than those of the duke, but a run of bad luck befell him and the superiority of Charles in strategy won a decided victory for the latter.

Battle of Stångebro and flight of the king.—Once Sigismund had the Swedish army completely surrounded and could undoubtedly, had he pressed his advantage, have forced it to surrender, but at the critical moment he hesitated, influenced, as his defenders claim, by the appeals of the Swedish lords in his camp not to precipitate a fight in which Swede would slay Swede. Instead of engaging in battle at the moment when the situation was entirely favourable to him, the king moved his army farther inland, and at Stångebro the two armies met in decisive conflict (September 25, 1598). The day ended with the king's defeat, as a result of which he promised to surrender the members of the Council who had joined his cause, summon a Riksdag, where the controversy between him and Charles could be heard and adjudicated by foreign arbitrators, send home his foreign troops, and proceed to Stockholm to take charge of the government, the duke on his part promising to dismiss his forces. The agreement also states expressly that in case any one of the signatories failed to abide by the agreement the Riksdag would have the legal right to resist him. The king now left Stegeborg ostensibly for the purpose of going to Stockholm to assume charge of the government, but suddenly he changed his course and proceeded to Kalmar, where he boarded a ship for Poland. "Although nobody chased him, he ran away from land and kingdom," as one of his contemporaries remarked, and Duke Charles voiced the surprise and consternation caused by the king's departure when he wrote, "We would sooner believe that the Day of Judgment had come than expect such a leave-taking." Back of Sigismund's unexpected departure lay his well-justified fear of Charles and the need of coping promptly with an alarming situation which had developed in his own country. He had by no means given up the idea of ultimately suppressing the Swedish revolt and bringing the country to obedience, but this project must wait. An opportune time for this never came to Sigismund, however, and he never saw his native country again. The men who, largely from a spirit of loyalty to their lawful king, had supported him were left in a bad plight by his desertion of them, helpless as they now were in the hands of the unrelenting and harsh Charles.

Charles was now declared hereditary ruling prince, and at a Riksdag in Stockholm, 1599, Sigismund was formally deposed as a papist, oath breaker, and enemy of the realm, but at the same time he was offered the opportunity to send his young son to Sweden to become king, but to this offer was attached the condition that the young prince must receive a Lutheran education, a condition with which it was a foregone conclusion Sigismund would not comply, and nothing further resulted from the negotiations.

Chapter XII

LAYING THE FOUNDATION FOR SWEDEN'S POLITICAL GREATNESS

The reckoning with the councillors.—Charles's first act after coming into possession of almost unlimited power was to mete out punishment to the recalcitrant lords. The forces arrayed against him had been particularly formidable in Finland, where many cruel excesses were committed; these were now subdued and the leaders executed. The turn for a reckoning next came to the members of the Swedish Council whom Sigismund ignobly had surrendered after the battle of Stångebro. Ignoring the agreement with Sigismund that an impartial foreign court should be appointed to judge in their case, an agreement which Charles maintained had been abrogated in its entirety by Sigismund's flight, Charles caused a special court to be appointed, and four of the unfortunate men were found guilty and executed, the duke remaining absolutely unmoved by all pleas for clemency. A fifth member later met the same fate.

On being offered the crown at a meeting of the Riksdag in Stockholm in 1602, Charles declined the honour, on the ground that Duke John, a younger brother of Sigismund, had a prior claim to it, but when the latter voluntarily renounced all his rights, the duke, at a meeting of the Riksdag at Norrköping (1604), took the title of king as Charles IX. At the same time the right to the crown by heredity was transferred to his line of the Vasa family, even to the inclusion of its female members. The Council was reorganized by the appointment of new members, and the offices of chancellor, chief justice (*drots*), marshal, admiral, and treasurer were restored. The spirit of extreme and bitter religious intolerance which belonged to the age and in Sweden had been intensified by the events of John's and Sigismund's reign was reflected in a drastic law adopted in

1604, to the effect that only members of the Lutheran faith were entitled to hold office in the land, and that all who fell away from this faith would forfeit their property and be banished from the country.

A worthy son of a great father.—Sweden was soon to feel that a stern and strong, but just, administrator was in control again. The inefficiency and dissensions which had made the

Charles IX

reigns of Erik and John so unhappy had left the country in a deplorable condition, and the first serious concern of Charles was the re-establishment of firm administration. Charles had to the fullest extent fallen heir to his father's love of economy, and the royal bailiffs soon discovered that the new king was an exceedingly stern master who watched them with an eagle eye. Strict supervision became the rule, and certain punishment was sure to be visited upon the official who had been convicted of fraud, this at times coming in the form of a sound beating administered by His Royal Highness in person. Many whose peculations and extortions were particularly severe were strung up on the gallows. "A pack of thieves" was the phrase which Charles often used in paying his compliments to his bailiffs. Judges were likewise made to feel that dishonesty in the discharge of duty was likely to be detected and most severely punished; on the other hand, Charles sought to give justice to the common man and to prevent his exploitation by greedy and consciencelss officials and great lords. He thus became the idol of the common people and is known in Swedish history as "the *bonde* king."

Not only by insisting on honesty and economy in the government, but also by causing new industries to be established, did Charles endeavour to heal the wounds inflicted by wars and maladministration. Good money came into circulation again. To Charles belongs credit for having founded the mining industry of Värmland, and the city of Karlstad, the principal city of the province, was begun by him. The mineral resources of far-away Norrland attracted his interest and plans for their exploitation were considered. The people were encouraged to establish themselves in new settlements, where there still was plenty of virgin land available. On the west coast, near the mouth of the Göta River, the foundation was laid for a new city, to be known as Göteborg (Gothenburg), and Dutch builders were invited into the land to help in its construction. In order to facilitate commerce, river channels were deepened and canals built near Eskilstuna and Gothenburg. While not as learned as his elder brothers, Erik and John, Charles had a genuine interest in education, and the University of Uppsala found in him a generous benefactor. His earnest and sincere efforts to secure an honest administration and to add to the well-being of the people were, however, to a very large extent frustrated by his own violent temper and unreasonable suspicion; every one, and especially members of the higher classes, felt insecure as long as he was king. The consciousness that despite his great services to the country and his good intentions to rule justly he was bitterly hated by many among his subjects cast dark shadows over his life, and especially over its later years.

New wars.—Charles was too aggressive a person to wait complacently at home for the attack which he well knew Sigismund was preparing to launch against Sweden. In 1600 he went to Livonia with a military force and took possession of the greater part of the province, but lost it again when he suffered a disastrous defeat at Kirkholm.

With Poland and Russia.—A revolution in Poland prevented Sigismund, however, from deriving any advantage from this setback to his enemy. A more serious conflict was in the meantime going on in Russia, now threatened with complete dissolution. The ancient Swedish dynasty of Rurik had come to an end in 1598 and several claimants now sought the Russian crown, a situation which had enabled the Poles to invade the country with a view to making important territorial gains. The fear that all of Russia might fall into their hands induced Charles to listen favourably to an appeal by Czar Vasily for help, and a compact was made between the two, by the terms of which Sweden was to support the czar with 5,000 men in return for the fortress and fief of Keksholm. In conformity with this compact, the Swedish commander, Jacob de la Gardie, advanced into Russia with a considerable force, effected a junction with the army of Vasily, and penetrated the land as far as Moscow, which was captured. When a Polish army approached this city, Vasily hastily deserted his Swedish allies who, being further weakened by the defection of a large contingent of mercenary troops, were compelled to evacuate Russia. As a consequence, Vasily was overthrown, and Sigismund's son Vladislav was proclaimed czar. This turn in affairs changed the status of Sweden in Russia from that of ally to active antagonist. Inasmuch as Russia's dismemberment seemed imminent, Charles now resolved to enter more actively into the conflict, in order to prevent Poland from taking the lion's share of the spoils. A force under de la Gardie again advanced into Russia and captured Keksholm and New Novgorod. These victories were followed by chimerical plans for establishing another Swedish dynasty in the land of the Muscovites. According to De la Gardie's project, Gustavus Adolphus, eldest son of Charles, or his brother, Charles Philip, was now to be elected czar. The matter was still pending when Charles died, and the final chapter in the remarkable episode was written in the reign of his successor (p. 331). No definite advantage was gained by Sweden in the Russian campaign, and this war was one of the three conflicts which Charles left as a grievous heritage to his son and successor.

With Denmark.—Charles also became involved in a war with Denmark, whose young and ambitious king, Christian IV, reopened the controversy regarding the right to carry the Swedish emblem on the Danish coat-of-arms, while Charles had countered by claiming the Finnish Lappmark—this included Upper Sweden and Norway to the Lofoten Islands—as part of the Swedish domain. The Danes were also disturbed by the plans of Charles for building a city on the west coast of Sweden. Such a city, they held, would seriously reduce the Sound tolls on Swedish trade. As long as the southern part of the Scandinavian peninsula belonged to Denmark, the waters between this and the island of Seeland were Danish territory, and the Danish kings were in the habit of collecting tolls on all commerce which passed through it. This not only gave a substantial revenue to the crown, but was of great strategic value to Denmark. The question of the Sound tolls was from this time on, for a hundred years or more, to be one of the main causes of friction between Sweden and Denmark. For the war with Denmark which now broke out—known as the "Kalmar War" because much of the fighting occurred near the city of that name—Sweden, still suffering from the effects of mismanagement and bitter civil strife in the preceding reigns, was badly prepared. Simultaneous wars with Poland and Russia made her situation the more desperate. The vast majority of the people were dependent upon agriculture for a living, and this industry gave exceedingly meagre returns. No great wealth was available for carrying on war and for defraying the expenses of an extensive diplomatic service. For Charles this was a period of intense suffering and deep gloom, especially as his health was failing fast. His violent temper, never before kept well under control, now broke forth almost daily in wild fury against his enemies at home and abroad. Through treachery on the part of the commander of the fortress of Kalmar, this strategic point was lost to Sweden, and the Danish king began, as so many of his predecessors on the Danish throne had done before him, to dream of a conquest of all Sweden. In the midst of his reverses and humiliations, Charles died, in 1611. The firm conviction that his son and successor, Gustavus Adolphus, would succeed where he himself had failed, was the one consolation of the unhappy man as his end approached. "*Ille faciet,*" "He shall do it," are said to have been his reassuring words as he looked upon his stalwart and keen-minded son.

In spite of his harshness and vindictiveness, Charles must be considered one of the great rulers of Sweden. At his death the country was at the threshold of a period of extraordinary power and greatness, which not even the genius of his famous son could have made possible had it not been for the clear insight and indomitable courage of the father. The only son of Gustavus Vasa who had the will and the strength to perpetuate the Swedish state as remodelled by his great father, he laid the foundation for his country's greatness during the subsequent one hundred years.

Elements of strength and of weakness in the Swedish state.—In the beginning of the seventeenth century, Sweden, including Finland, had a population of only a little more than one million people, or approximately one-fifth to one-sixth of its present number. The country had no great industries nor extensive foreign commerce. For the wars with Denmark, Poland, and Russia, which had broken out near the end of the reign of Charles, she was, as before stated, badly prepared. When, therefore, the country, in the beginning of the third decade of the century, is seen to have advanced to the proud, if precarious, position of a leading military and political power in Europe, and is carrying the leading rôle in a prolonged and bitter conflict in which the most vital interests of humanity are at stake, the explanation of this strange spectacle cannot be found in the country's material or numerical strength. The explanation is, indeed, found in several factors, and foremost among these was undoubtedly the possession of political rights and the spirit of liberty and unity which from earlier generations had been the heritage of the common people, especially of the *bönder,* and which the great popular leaders like Engelbrekt, the Stures, Gustavus Vasa, and Charles IX had enabled them to preserve and to keep alive. As perhaps in no other country during the Middle Ages, Sweden had seen a remarkable co-operation of the common people and the great leaders. The reorganization of the political, economic, and religious life of the nation under Gustavus Vasa had created a spirit of nationalism such as had not been felt before, and at the same time had given to the crown a control over the financial resources of the country which made the monarchy unusually strong and effective. The determined attacks which the Lutheran faith had been compelled to meet under John and Sigismund had served to weld the ranks of its adherents more firmly together and there is good ground for the assertion that no Protestant people was more firmly bound together in one faith at this time than the Swedes.

Advantages of hereditary monarchy.—It was not the least of Gustavus Vasa's services to his country that he prevailed upon the Swedish Riksdag to make royal power hereditary in his family. Although this act gave Sweden some weak kings, like Erik, John, and Sigismund, in general its effect was good, for thereby the monarchy was greatly strengthened, a fact which, after all, redounded to the good of the common people; it was always the lords who preferred the elective monarchy, and naturally so, since under that system they controlled elections and thereby were in a position, by shrewd bargaining and by imposing their own conditions on candidates, gradually to strip royalty of power and influence and usurp power for themselves. A glance at the diverging paths which Sweden and Denmark were to travel from this time on shows the salutary effects of the hereditary principle. While in Sweden the king assumed office with no other obligations than those imposed upon him by the ancient law of the land and the decrees of the Riksdag, in Denmark every king was compelled to make concessions to the lords, a process which in time meant a preponderance of power for them, a relatively weak king, and the exploitation and oppression of the common people. There were, of course, other causes for the unfortunate status into which the Danish *bönder* had fallen and which in time laid the yoke of serfdom upon them. The dissensions, mismanagement, and lack of strong national sentiment which affected most of the

European states at this time also worked to the decided advantage of a nation like the Swedish, firmly united as it now was and sustained by a conviction that it had, by the providence of God, been chosen for a great mission. Even with these factors in her favor it is impossible to conceive of Sweden advancing to the proud status of a great power, one of the greatest in Europe for many decades, without taking full cognizance of the genius of the young king, Gustavus Adolphus. He was to live through only the first part of the great conflict which was to decide the momentous issue of religious and political freedom, but in that time his extraordinary ability as soldier and statesman strengthened Sweden enormously, brought crushing defeat to the hitherto triumphant forces of reaction, and laid solid the foundation upon which liberty of conscience and free institutions could rest.

Personality of Gustavus Adolphus II.—Gustavus Adolphus was born December 9, 1594, in the palace at Stockholm, where Duke Charles and his wife had taken up their abode at the time. His mother was Christina of Holstein, a stern and resolute woman, and of one mind with her husband in insisting that the young prince should be made fit for the stern duties of royal office by a system of severe training. Already at the age of six he accompanied his father to Livonia, from which they returned in the dead of winter by a route which led north of the Gulf of Bothnia and through vast regions that were practically uninhabited. To his tutor, Johan Skytte, the son of a commoner, Gustavus ever remained deeply grateful, for this splendid teacher not only gave him thorough instruction in the various branches which constituted the curriculum of princes in those days, but also implanted in his mind sound political ideas and gave him most trustworthy guidance in later years. The tolerance, magnanimity, and self-control which were outstanding virtues of Gustavus in his years of youth and manhood were, no doubt, largely the fruits of Skytte's wise precepts. Religion, philosophy, mathematics, and languages were the subjects emphasized in the studies of the prince, and such was his proficiency in the latter field that as a young man he spoke Latin, German, Dutch, French, and Italian, understood Spanish and English, and had some knowledge of Russian and

Polish. For international law he evinced a keen and sympathetic interest. The chief works of the founder of this branch of study, the Dutch Hugo Grotius, were always to be found together with the Bible on a table in his tent when he was

Gustavus Adolphus II

engaged in his military campaigns. Despite his brilliant mind and extraordinary power in the acquisition of knowledge, the young man was by no means a recluse; one of the court attendants once complained that the prince spent so much time in company with the young ladies at the court that his more serious occupations were neglected. His keen and inquisitive mind sought information from every source, and from the mercenary soldiers, Germans, Scotch, English, Dutch, Italians, and even Spaniards, who had found their way into the Swedish army, he extracted a great amount of valuable information regarding their respective countries, which more than once afterwards, when he undertook to improve the machinery of his government and create a new military system, gave him many new and constructive ideas. From the age of ten, he regularly attended the meetings of the Council, and in his twelfth year began to attend the ceremonies at which his father received representatives of foreign governments in audience. At the age of sixteen the young prince for the first time addressed the members of the Riksdag, even then demonstrating in the fullest measure that he possessed the power of persuasive eloquence which had enabled Gustavus Vasa, many a time, to disarm the opposition and weld discordant elements into unity. While Gustavus Adolphus, in common with his father and grandfather, had an unusual ability as administrator, he had one brilliant endowment which they had both lacked; namely, genius for military affairs. Another faculty which the earlier rulers of the Vasa dynasty had lacked, the ability to win people's affection and stir their enthusiasm to the point where they were ready to make any sacrifice for a great cause, was his to the fullest degree.

A youthful infatuation of Gustavus Adolphus for Ebba Brahe, a beautiful lady-in-waiting at the court, came to grief when it encountered the unyielding opposition of his stern and practical mother, who was determined that her son should contract a marriage alliance with a princess of one of the powerful Protestant royal families. Her wishes were fulfilled when Gustavus married the beautiful Maria Eleanora, sister of the Elector of Brandenburg. She had an erratic and mean disposition, running in later years into the most peculiar vagaries, which, as will appear later, after the king's death caused the statesmen of Sweden no end of embarrassment and trouble. Just as the marriage failed to bring happiness to her royal spouse, it failed equally in bringing any political advantage to Sweden.

The question of the royal succession.—The right of succession to the Swedish throne had, by the resolution of Norrköping, in 1604 (p. 318) been vested in the family of

Charles IX, but according to earlier decisions the royal office could rightly be claimed by Duke John of Östergötland, a brother of Sigismund. While John had already renounced his rights, the binding force of this renunciation was open to question, as it had been made prior to his reaching the age of maturity, and Charles IX, who was extremely scrupulous in regard to the observance of certain legal forms, had felt so serious a doubt regarding the matter that in his will he had stipulated that his nephew should be acknowledged king in case he came forward to claim the throne. The situation held possibilities for further dynastic quarrels and civil war, but to the great good fortune of the country, Duke John, in a noble spirit of humility and self-effacement, declared his willingness to step aside in favour of Gustavus Adolphus. A definite decision regarding the succession was now reached at a Riksdag at Nyköping in December 1611. Here Duke John himself was present and nobly pleaded that undivided support should be given his royal cousin, whose handicap by reason of youth, he said, was more than counterbalanced by the wisdom with which God in his omnipotence had endowed him. There was now no obstacle to the definite acknowledgment of Gustavus as king and he was forthwith hailed as ruler of the realm. In appreciation of his act of renunciation, John's duchy was considerably enlarged, but inasmuch as the prince died only a few years later his domain soon again became directly subordinate to the crown.

The king's charter.—Such was the confidence and trust which Gustavus had already inspired that although now only seventeen years old he was without further delay declared of age and vested with the power and dignity of royalty. The charter, or royal assurance, which he next promulgated as the fundamental principle by which he would be guided in his rule, showed a great willingness to extend the privileges of the nobility. This concession on his part was due both to a desire to make amends for his father's cruel treatment of the nobles, and to a clearly conceived policy for binding this powerful estate firmly to the crown by the grant of extensive favours in return for which loyal and valuable service could be expected. The charter furthermore declared that the decrees of the Uppsala Meeting of 1593 were to be respected and enforced, but religious freedom should be enjoyed by foreign traders or soldiers who sojourned in Sweden as long as they remained quiet, and this concession was justified by the noble statement that "no ruler has the power to control another person's conscience." The charter further provided that the chief offices were to be filled by members of the privileged class, the judges to have the power to convict or acquit without royal interference, no one to lose his property without due process of law, imprisonment to be inflicted on no one unless the accuser was known, no new law was to be enacted or old law changed without the consent of Duke John, the Royal Council, and the Riksdag, and no new taxes, custom duties, or enlistments laid or enforced without the consent of the Council and of the people concerned. In conclusion, the king pledged himself not to declare war, conclude peace, enter into any alliance, or make a truce without the consent of the Council and the Estates. These concessions were not an evidence of weakness in the king; they were, on the contrary, a wisely conceived means by which he aimed to establish the closest and most harmonious relations between monarch and subjects, and insure the utmost unity in the support of every enterprise involving the welfare and security of the country. The events of his own and of later reigns were to reveal how wise and farsighted the king's policies in this respect had been.

The end of the Kalmar War.—The question of his right to the throne having been settled in his favour, and the policies by which the new reign would be guided clearly defined, Gustavus next turned his attention to the wars in which his country was involved. He was sincerely anxious to end the conflict with Denmark, and to that end both he and the Riksdag assumed a very conciliatory attitude towards that country. Christian still cherished the ambition, however, to add Sweden to his domains, and was not ready to make peace on terms that were acceptable to the Swedes, and so the war went on, both sides manifesting extreme bitterness and a determination to lay waste as much as possible of the enemy's territory. The advantage rested with the Danes, whom Gustavus only with the greatest difficulty could hinder from penetrating into the very heart of his country. In the summer campaign of 1612, the enemy succeeded in capturing Älvsborg, Sweden's important fortress on the west coast, and seized the island of Öland, while a Danish fleet threatened Vaxholm, the fortress which protected Stockholm against attack by sea. By this time, however, Christian found his resources exhausted, and when, therefore, James I of England offered his services as mediator, he was willing to listen favourably to a peace proposition. Peace was concluded by the treaty of Knäred (1613), by which Sweden renounced her claim to Lappmark and acknowledged Denmark's right to the three crowns on her national emblem; Denmark agreed to exempt Swedish vessels from the Sound tolls; and both countries agreed to restore conquered territory, with the important exception, however, that for Älvsborg, Sweden was to pay an indemnity of 1,000,000 riksdaler specie, payment to be made in six years, six Swedish counties to be held as security by Denmark until the indemnity was paid. The only important concession which Denmark made was her promise to exempt Sweden from the Sound tolls and this was, therefore, for Sweden a hard and humiliating peace. By relinquishing the claims to Finnmarken, she lost for all time the opportunity to extend her territory until her domains touched the Atlantic, and the Älvsborg indemnity proved almost ruinous to a nation of a million people whose material resources were exceedingly limited. An idea of the difficulty of paying such a sum may be gained from the fact that the indemnity was approximately equivalent to the value of the entire annual crops of the country. As extremely little money was in circulation in these early days, and no banks existed to facilitate the funding of debts, the Swedes, and more particularly Gustavus, were driven almost to distraction before the final installment was paid; the king was even compelled to send the royal silver to the mint, inasmuch as Christian refused to accept anything but specie payments. In the long run, Denmark was to gain no advantage from the hard peace she had imposed upon her neighbour, for the heavy indemnity served to intensify, as almost nothing else could, the feeling of bitter hatred of the Danes which for a long time had burned in the hearts of the Swedes. Scarcely an individual escaped making some contribution towards the detested debt. When some decades later the rôles had been reversed and Sweden was the victor, she was less disposed, because of the Kalmar indemnity, than perhaps she otherwise would have been to show mercy to her prostrate foe. A more immediate effect of the harsh peace terms was, however, that Sweden and the Netherlands were now drawn more closely together in an anti-Danish alliance.

The war in Russia.—While Gustavus Adolphus had been engaged in the war against Denmark, the Swedish general, Jacob de la Gardie, and his military assistants had won signal successes in Russia. The fortress of Nöteborg had been captured by the Swedes, and Ingria and a large part of northwestern Russia had come into their hands. De la Gardie had captured Novgorod some months before the death of Charles IX, and thereupon its Estates placed themselves under a Swedish protectorate and requested that one of the sons of the Swedish king should come and rule over them (p. 321). In conformity with this wish, Gustavus Adolphus was elected Grand Duke of Russia by a large and powerful faction, and when he became king in his own land the Russians elected his younger brother, Charles Philip. The prospects of establishing a new Swedish dynasty in Russia and the possibility thereby to exert a dominating influence in that distracted land loomed before the Swedes with all its promises of adventure and prestige. De la Gardie supported the daring venture in the conviction that it offered the surest safeguard for Sweden against Russia. To the queen mother and Charles Philip the plan seemed extremely hazardous, and as Gustavus Adolphus at the critical moment of the negotiations had to give all his attention to the Danish war then still raging, the Russian embassy which had been sent to Stockholm for carrying on further negotiations was compelled to mark time for months awaiting an answer. Whatever chance of success the scheme may have had if speedy and decisive action had been taken in Sweden at the right time was lost by procrastination, for in the meantime the sweep of a revived national sentiment in Russia lifted Michael Romanoff to the lofty place of Emperor of all the Russias (1613). Michael was thus the first of the dynasty which came to so tragic an end in 1917. The negotiations for the election of Charles Philip having failed, and the election of Michael Romanoff being an accomplished fact, it next became the chief concern of Gustavus Adolphus to conclude a treaty with Russia which would make Sweden safe on her eastern border. Twice he went himself to Russia in order to direct the military operations, and in these he gained considerable advantage. Finally by the treaty of Stolbova in 1617 the war came to an end, the Swedes receiving by the terms of the treaty the fief Keksholm, the fortress Nöteborg with the adjoining territory of Ingria, extensive trade privileges, and 20,000 rubles as a war indemnity; Sweden agreed to evacuate Novgorod and acknowledge Michael Romanoff as czar, and in turn Russia renounced her claim to Esthonia and Livonia. Russia was now excluded from the Baltic, and between Finland and Russia lay the great Lake Ladoga as a barrier. "I hope to God," said Gustavus in his address to the Swedish Riksdag in 1617, "that the Russians will find it difficult to skip over that little brook." The king then went on to depict in glowing colours the splendid prospects of Swedish trade with the Russians and with other races living beyond them, prospects which, however, were never realized, partly because of lack of capital in Sweden, partly because the English and the Dutch were firmly entrenched already in these marts.

Administrative reform.—The name of Gustavus Adolphus is indissolubly linked with military campaigns, but the administrative reforms that under his genial and brilliant leadership were instituted in Sweden would in themselves be sufficient to justify his claim to an exalted place among the great and wise rulers of history. Into all phases of administration and cultural life the creative mind of the king entered, eliminating much that was useless or mischievous, building new structures of government or merely laying foundations, and ever modifying and improving the institutions which his grandfather and father had created. With the unerring insight of genius he chose large-calibred men for the service of the state, and trained them to a state of efficiency which gave Sweden a corps of administrators and leaders such as no other country in that age could boast.

Axel Oxenstierna.—Head and shoulders above the men who constituted the advisers and servants of the king stood

Axel Oxenstierna, unquestionably the foremost statesman in the history of Sweden, next to Gustavus himself; in his clear insight into realities, and in his determination to keep steadily to one course in order to attain a desired goal, he was undeniably the stronger of the two. Born in 1583 in Uppland, Oxenstierna descended from a family that already in the Kalmar Union period had held a prominent place in Sweden. After studying at Wittenberg, Jena, and Rostock, theology being his favourite subject, he returned to Sweden and immediately entered the service of Charles IX. Already before the death of this ruler, Oxenstierna had won recognition as a great statesman. On his accession to the throne, Gustavus Adolphus appointed him chancellor, and while he by virtue of this office came to hold all the many threads of the country's foreign diplomacy in his hands, he also became the king's confidential and sagacious adviser in all matters pertaining to the internal administration of the country. Although the two men were quite different in temperament, the king impetuous and warm-hearted, the chancellor cool and reflective, they always worked together in unruffled harmony, united in their deep devotion to the interests of the fatherland. The relations between the two are aptly illustrated by a colloquy between them; once on becoming impatient with the judicial prudence of his chancellor, the king exclaimed, "If my heat did not put a little life into your coldness, we should all *freeze up*," to which Oxenstierna immediately gave the retort, "And if my coldness did not assuage Your Majesty's heat we should all *burn up*."

Other advisers.—A second man who rendered the king great services was his brother-in-law, John Casimir of the Palatinate, who had married the king's sister and with his family had taken up his permanent abode in Sweden when the turmoils which afflicted his own country had compelled him to flee from his native land. He was an honest man and had great capacity as an administrator of finance, in which domain he was to render Sweden conspicuous service. Other distinguished members of the king's group of advisers and aids were Johan Skytte, already mentioned as the king's tutor, who entered the diplomatic service of the country and closed his honourable career as Governor of Livonia; Gabriel Oxenstierna, the chancellor's brother; Bengt Oxenstierna (Resare-Bengt), the chancellor's cousin and an inveterate traveller in the Orient, trusted diplomatic agent of Sweden and, in the later years of life, Governor of Livonia and Ingria; Klas Fleming, the creator of the Swedish navy; in addition there were the great warriors, all apt disciples of Gustavus, as Jacob de la Gardie, Gustaf Horn, Åke Tott, Nils Brahe, Johan Banée, and Lennart Torstensson. As Sweden rose to a pre-eminent place in Europe and its far-flung dominion and interests called for diplomatic representatives of a high order, foreign diplomats in large numbers were attracted into her service; among these were Ludwig Cammerarius, who represented Sweden at the Hague, the Englishman James Spence, and the Dutchman Louis de Geer, the latter known as the builder of Sweden's industrial system on a new foundation.

Reorganization in the Riksdag.—The Swedish Riksdag, composed as it was of the four Estates, nobility, clergy, burgesses, and *bönder,* had played an exceptionally important part in the government of Sweden ever since Engelbrekt's time and more particularly in the days of Gustavus Vasa. Under Gustavus Adolphus it was, however, to attain to a position of dignity and power such as it had not known before, and this development was the more significant as in all other European countries, England alone excepted, the old system of government through the Estates was breaking down. Former Swedish rulers had, in conformity with the practice in other countries, called the Estates together in a somewhat arbitrary fashion and mainly for the purpose of getting their support for special enterprises or measures, and the organization, duties, and rights of the body had never been clearly defined. No check had been made on the rights of those in attendance to participate in the deliberations, and Polish spies had been in the habit of attending and reporting important actions to their home government. It had even happened that enemy spies had posed as Swedish patriots and helped the *bönder* to formulate replies to the royal propositions. Meetings of the Riksdag were before this time governed by no definite rules of procedure, and Oxenstierna said in presenting the royal plan for a reform: "Matters proceed in a more orderly fashion at the Things or parish meetings than at the Riksdag, where one can behold the members run about like cattle or drunken *bönder*." By the Ordinance of 1617, Gustavus Adolphus sought to make the Riksdag a really effective body through which the nation's will could express itself and royalty thereby receive guidance and support. In the first place, the division into four orders was given legal sanction. These Estates were henceforth to meet jointly and receive the royal propositions, upon which they then were to deliberate in their own separate chambers. Each order thereupon made its reply in writing to the king, and differences of opinion between him and the Estates were adjusted after proper discussion; if the orders differed among themselves, they must defend their respective opinions before the king, "who might accept that which seemeth to him best." In their deliberations, which were an expression of opinion and not mandatory on the king, each Estate had one vote. The most important of the orders, the nobility, was given a definite organization by the creation of the House of Knights (*Riddarhuset*). Through lists of properly accredited members, a check was made upon those entitled to attend the Riksdag sessions, thus preventing spies from gaining access. With these changes, the Swedish Riksdag became far more than a mere debating society; while the king, through the submission of the royal propositions, possessed the initiative in all legislation, and in the last analysis could make arbitrary decisions, except in matters fixed by his own charter and the ancient law of the land, the Estates had the right to object to any proposal or measure and practically every ruler from now on, until absolutism superseded this system, was guided in matters of vital interest by the expressed opinion of the Estates. From this time on it also became an accepted principle that the resolutions of the Riksdag did not need further ratification by a submission to the people directly; in the case of taxes, however, popular approval through public assemblages was generally sought by the kings.

The strife and confusion of the preceding decades had wrought havoc with the enforcement of law and one of the first sections of the royal charter provided for reforms in the administration of justice so as to provide greater security to citizens. This pledge was redeemed by the inauguration of a more effective control of legal procedure in the lower courts and the establishment of three courts of appeal, as well as of original jurisdiction, one known as the Svea Royal Court (*Svea Hovrätt*) at Stockholm, another as Åbo Royal Court (*Åbo Hovrätt*), with special jurisdiction in Finland, and a third with headquarters at Dorpat for the Baltic possessions. These courts, which had been suggested already in the time of Erik and John, took the places of the temporary tribunals which had been created for special cases, and their efficiency and prestige were secured by the appointment of men of recognized probity and legal knowledge as judges.

Departments of administration.—Practically all the important activities of the government in relation to the internal administration, as the collection of taxes, law enforcement, improvements of roads, and the like, had up to this time been looked upon mainly as the king's exclusive business and over which he should exercise personal supervision; in the case of Gustavus Vasa and Charles IX, this had, as has been seen, resulted in an extreme type of paternalism. The desire for regular departments of administration had, however, found early expression, without leading to any definite action until Gustavus Adolphus's time. The rapid growth of industry and commerce which had taken place meant a large increase in the public business, and a corps of officials with definite appointments, clearly defined duties, and subject to some kind of careful supervision therefore became an almost imperative necessity. Gustavus sought to meet this situation by instituting a system of colleges or departments. In the Chamber of Accounting (*räkningskammaren*), accounts were kept of all state revenues and expenditures for public enterprises. A most remarkable novelty was the preparation of a budget of income and outlays. It was as head of the fiscal administration that the king's brother-in-law, John Casimir, rendered his most valuable service to the country. In the country districts, governors (*ståthållare* or *landshövdingar;* in time the latter designation generally came to prevail) were appointed with power of supervision over the bailiffs, and this arrangement resulted in a more honest accounting of the money collected in the form of taxes. Foreign affairs were in the hands of the Chancery, composed of several councillors and secretaries. One of the purposes partly attained by the system of colleges was a greater co-ordination between the different departments of the government. As officials of these various departments, the king appointed members of the nobility, who thus came to enjoy extraordinary privileges. It was, however, significant of the spirit of the country, and especially of its rulers, that the ranks of the nobility were never rigidly closed against new accessions. The commoner of lowliest rank could, through ability and distinguished service, rise to a nobleman's estate. In fact such promotions were quite common occurrences.

The country's many wars in this period made extraordinary demands upon its treasury, and only by increasing the resources of the nation could these be met. The prosperity which countries like England and the Netherlands had attained, through industry, trade, and colonizing enterprises, had shown how such increase could be most speedily attained. Economic thought was, furthermore, at this time dominated by the postulate of mercantilism that a country's wealth is measured by its supply of ready money and that therefore a state, in order to be prosperous, must buy raw material cheaply, convert this through work-shops into valuable finished articles, and sell in foreign markets. Colonies, able to furnish raw materials and provide markets for the finished products, therefore came to be looked upon as essential to prosperity in a state.

Beginning of Swedish factory industry; Belgian workers.—Destitute as she was of all important manufacturing industry, Sweden saw her money flow out of the country to pay for luxuries, necessities, and munitions of war, and it therefore became one of the chief concerns of Gustavus Adolphus and Oxenstierna to build factories in their country and develop its trade. Sweden was rich in iron-ores and copper, its many waterfalls gave effective and cheap motive power for forge hammers, and the unlimited forests gave abundant charcoal; coal was not used in smelting at this time, and in iron production Sweden therefore had a great advantage over England, and especially over Germany, at that time her chief rival in the iron trade. In line with their plans for economic expansion, Gothenburg, which, as has been seen, had been begun by Charles IX, was laid out on its present location, and Belgian capitalists and workers invited to settle in the city. The most prominent of these capitalists and industrial leaders was Louis de Geer, who is rightly honoured as the founder of Sweden's important industrial enterprises. Through his influence more than five hundred Belgian families were induced to settle in Sweden. These were the Walloons. The Walloon type is still easily recognized among the people in the industrial centres where they originally settled. Mainly through their skill and enterprise, the Swedish iron industry was rapidly developed into hitherto undreamt-of dimensions. In the manufacturing of weapons, for example, Sweden's production assumed such proportions that the country could, in spite of the great demands of her own wars, export large quantities to foreign countries. In order to facilitate the extension of trade, trading companies were at this time organized in all the leading countries and here Sweden followed the example set by the other prosperous nations.

Trade companies.—In 1626 Gustavus issued a charter to the Swedish South Sea Company for the purpose of carrying on trade with "Asia, Africa, America, and Magellanica." This project had with much persuasive eloquence been laid before Gustavus and Oxensierna by the Dutch merchant, Usselinx. The nation's hopes of easy wealth through this enterprise rose to great heights, the king sharing in the optimistic expectations to the fullest extent. The clergy were even asked to urge their parishioners to buy stock in the company and to "remember the enterprise in their public and private prayers," for which there appeared so much the better reason as missionary work among savage peoples was stated as one of the objects of the business enterprise. The plan at first contemplated a settlement in the Danish West Indies, which were to be wrested from Spain, but this project was soon abandoned, and the region of the Delaware River was instead selected as the site of the first Swedish colony in the New World. As the great king became engrossed in other matters of momentous importance, the entire colonization scheme was permitted to slumber during the rest of his reign, and it was not until six years after his death that Oxenstierna revived it (p. 378). Other companies besides the South Sea Company were chartered for the purpose of handling the export of individual products in order to get the highest possible price for the same; thus the Swedish Copper Company was chartered for the more effective handling and sale of the valuable output of the copper mines of Dalarna, which at this time reached their maximum production. The importation of grain from Livonian and German ports was for a time handled directly by the state. In order that ruinous competition between cities be eliminated, an elaborate and unique system was devised for their regulation and development; thus the towns situated on the coast or on important rivers were designated as ports or shipping centres through which all trade with foreign ports must pass, while the inland towns and market-places handled the distribution for the interior of the land. All trading was strictly confined to the regularly designated centres. In order that sufficient labour might be made available for industry and city building, Swedish subjects were often compelled by royal edicts to take up their abode in industrial centres. The guilds, which had been especially favoured by Gustavus Vasa and Charles IX as an effective means for regulating industry and improving the skill of the workmen, were given new privileges by Gustavus Adolphus, especially through the extension of restrictions on admissions and at the same time there was instituted a more rigid supervision of manufacturing processes. In Sweden, as in other lands, the theory of mercantilism discouraged agriculture. "The welfare of the country depends on trade and navigation" was an axiom of Gustavus Adolphus. The drain which the many wars every year made on the man power of the country added immensely to the great handicap under which agriculture was carried on.

Taxes.—The extraordinary expenses which the wars made inevitable were met partly by regular taxes and incomes from trade monopolies and custom duties and partly by special tax levies. As Sweden came to control the commerce on practically every river that flowed into the Baltic, with the exception of the Vistula and the Niemen, and could therefore collect large sums on all vessels on these streams, custom duties became especially important, but far more profitable was the state's monopoly of the copper mines at Falun in Dalarna. Special levies, as a rule, took the form of consumption taxes on bread, meat, fish, wines, ale, and other articles sold at retail. The tax on bread was collected through a special excise on baking ovens, and was graduated according to their size. These taxes were naturally very unpopular and caused several riots until Gustavus removed the most obnoxious levies. The crown likewise secured great financial assistance from the nobility, which in a commendable spirit of patriotism gave up its right of exemption from taxes. This concession on its part was, however, only provisional and temporary.

Cultural development.—For the cultural development of the nation, Gustavus Adolphus manifested a genuine interest. It was not until his reign that the University of Uppsala was established on a secure foundation. In order to provide a dependable income for the institution and make possible an extension of its program, the king transferred to its use for all time more than three hundred estates. This gift made it possible to secure a number of able scholars, both Swedish and foreign, for the university, and the number of students was doubled in a few years. A part of the revenue of this great university is still derived from the "Gustavian Estates" (*Gustavianska arvegodsen*). The University of Dorpat, in the province of Livonia, one of the six Russian universities before the World War, was also founded by Gustavus Adolphus. Its charter was issued by the king a few months before his death.

To this reign also belongs the credit for having established the first gymnasia, or colleges, in Sweden. Their curricula included classical and modern languages, theology, history, mathematics, and the natural sciences. They stood half-way between the elementary or "trivial" schools, which earlier had been established in most of the cities, and the University of Uppsala. Bishop Johannes Rudbeck established the first gymnasium at the seat of his diocese, Västerås, and the example which he had set was soon followed in the other dioceses. The more elementary training in counting and writing was given in special schools, and it was made the duty of the pastors of every parish to see to it that every individual under their care was taught to read and given instruction in the fundamental truths of Christianity.

National defence.—The question of national defence was always uppermost in the minds of Gustavus and Oxenstierna. The hostility and suspicion of Denmark, the menace of the reorganized and united Russian state, and especially the threatening attitude of Poland, where Sigismund still persisted in claiming the Swedish throne by right of inheritance, and behind whom stood the formidable forces of the Catholic reaction, constituted a serious menace to Sweden's peace and security, but Gustavus was not the man to despair. "It is the consolation of old women," he said, "to whine and suffer; through wise counsel must one cure and eliminate the evil." His earlier military campaigns had revealed to him the defects of the old system of warfare. The nobility was, under the new social and administrative order, needed as never before for service in the civil departments of the state, and under the changed economic situation the system of the old feudal army had broken down almost completely. Mercenary troops were utterly unreliable and unsatisfactory, and the expense connected with their services was entirely too great. In order to avoid expense and trouble, these soldiers were usually dismissed as soon as peace had been made, thus exposing the country to the danger of new and unexpected attacks; to keep them in service after war had ended was very costly. Furthermore, mercenary soldiers became in "the piping times of peace" insufferable nuisances, because of their incessant demands for pay and their wild orgies.

Reorganization of the army.—Sweden had in the past been less dependent upon mercenaries than any other country; her battles had been fought for the most part by her own soldiers, made up to a large extent of citizens who came from farm and shop to fight for their land. It was a system of volunteer service which in spite of its drawbacks—difficulty of keeping the men in the field for any extended time being one of them—had on the whole provided Sweden with an efficient fighting force whenever an urgent need of one had arisen. Earlier rulers, and especially Gustavus Vasa and Charles IX, had given much thought to a new system of military service with this national volunteer system as the foundation. During Charles's reign the practice of calling a certain number of men from definite districts had been instituted, and this system was now further perfected by Gustavus Adolphus. The rural communities were divided into units of ten *bönder* and each of these units was obligated to furnish one soldier. In the selection of men for military service, proper regard was to be taken to physical fitness, the value of a man's service in other lines, parents' need of help at home, and the like. Each soldier was given a plot of land on which to live in time of peace, thus materially reducing the cost of maintaining the army and eliminating most of the troubles which came from having a standing army in time of peace. Thus was created a national fighting force whose members were trained to greatest efficiency by regular exercise. Their conduct in the field was regulated by the famous Articles of War of Gustavus Adolphus in which the humanitarian views and the wisdom of the great king found their noblest expression. These constituted something new in the domain of war since they purposed to establish strict discipline among the men and prevent unnecessary cruelties. Such crimes as assaults upon women, blasphemy, incendiarism, seizure of property without compensation were most severely punished. In Gustavus's army religious services were held regularly and efforts made to instill the idea into the minds of the soldiers that in fighting for a holy cause they were but instruments in the hands of God. The king understood how to infuse an earnest spirit of patriotism among his men, and their effectiveness in the field was tremendously enhanced by the unshakable conviction that they were fighting for the defence not only of their country but of rights which affected all humanity.

From the time of Julius Cæsar to Gustavus Adolphus, the methods of warfare and equipment underwent few great changes, but with the great Swedish king there came an almost complete revolution in military organization and methods. In this fact is found one of the main reasons for the extraordinary successes gained against overwhelming numbers by the Swedish armies during this and following reigns. For the old-time ponderous Spanish squares, often fifty-five men deep, Gustavus substituted detachments only three deep; mobility took the place of momentum. Lighter guns, capable of firing twice or three times faster than the old muskets and needing no special supports for the barrels, were introduced. The new Swedish field cannon could be moved by a pair of horses while the foe required up to twenty-eight horses to move their ponderous artillery pieces. One-third of the army in battle array was kept in reserve, ready to move rapidly into any place where help was most needed. A regular system was also provided for the proper provisioning of the army.[1]

[1] A full account of the military system of Gustavus Adolphus is found in Dodge, T. A., *Gustavus Adolphus*, Boston, 1895.

Chapter XIII

THE CHAMPION OF PROTESTANTISM

Growing religious antagonisms.—The Catholic reaction which, in John's and Sigismund's reigns, almost succeeded in bringing the Swedes into the Catholic fold again in the meantime went forward on the Continent with accelerating strength. Having purged herself of many of the abuses which had brought reproach upon her, the Catholic Church could once more, and with better reason than for centuries, come forward to claim the allegiance of the people of Europe, on the ground that she alone could satisfy their spiritual needs and restore the unity which the Reformation had so ruthlessly broken. In the face of the woeful schism which now divided the Protestant group into many and oftentimes bitterly antagonistic factions, united and aggressive Catholicism, aided by the Inquisition and the Order of the Jesuits, was rapidly winning back much of its lost ground. On both sides in the great struggle, selfish forces, dynastic ambitions, lust of conquest and plunder, and bitter jealousies played their part, but it nevertheless remains true that the main impelling forces in the struggle were those which sprang from religious convictions and feelings. As the uncompromising champion of Catholicism and the old order of things stood Spain, which since its defeat through the wrecking of the ill-fated Armada by England in 1588 had watched for an opportunity to strike the powerful foe another blow and had been angling for a naval base in the North from which the new attack could be launched. Just now the country was engaged in its cruel war against the heroic people of the Netherlands. In France the Protestants were almost crushed by the St. Bartholomew Massacre, and in Poland Sigismund was with fanatical zeal ready to place the resources of his powerful country in the service of the Catholic reaction. In Austria and the empire, the Jesuit influence secured complete control when the fanatical Ferdinand of Steiermark became emperor in 1619.

Beginning of the Thirty Years' War.—In 1608, a number of Protestant princes and free imperial cities had formed the Protestant Union, with the Elector Frederick of the Palatinate as its head, for the purpose of securing a defence against Catholic aggression, and the following year saw the formation of a counter alliance, the Catholic League, at the head of which stood the able and aggressive Maximilian of Bavaria. The Protestant Union was made practically impotent from the start by the jealousies and suspicions which divided its members. The leading Protestant prince of Germany—leading because of the wealth and population of his domain and the preponderance of Lutheran adherents among the people—John George of Saxony, claimed to be an orthodox Lutheran of the purest type, but he had a picayunish mind and was utterly incapable of playing any heroic rôle in this serious crisis. He was actuated by one fixed purpose: never to give offence to the emperor and thus bring the latter's wrath upon his head; he therefore refused steadfastly to support the Protestant Union. To his strict orthodoxy, the Calvinism of Frederick of the Palatinate, the head of the Union, was as objectionable as the Catholicism of the emperor.

War in Bohemia.—The irreconcilable differences between Protestants and Catholics made a conflict inevitable, and this began in Bohemia, where the great majority of the people had embraced the Lutheran faith. Bitter dissatisfaction was aroused among them when the emperor violated their cherished religious rights, and in May 1618 occurred the fateful fracas in the castle of Prague which kindled the conflagration of a war that was to wreak its destructive fury over Europe for thirty years. When the fanatical Ferdinand of Steiermark the following year became emperor, the Bohemians refused to accept him and instead elected Frederick of the Palatinate as their ruler.

Events in Bohemia had aroused special interest in Sweden, since the underlying motives of the Protestants here were akin to those which earlier had impelled the Swedes to rid themselves of Sigismund. While Gustavus had fully realized the hazard which Frederick was running in accepting the proffered crown, he had nevertheless approved his decision to heed the call of the Bohemian leaders. An appeal by Frederick for assistance, both by money and soldiers, struck a responsive chord in his heart, but his own troubles in Poland made it impossible for him to come to his aid. The diplomatic agents of the Swedish king were, however, busy in Frederick's behalf in Russia, Saxony, and Holland, but to no avail, and no effective help came from the Protestant princes of Germany. The disintegration of Bohemia was well-nigh complete and no help could well be expected from the Protestant rulers of other powers who thought chiefly of their own selfish interests. No one understood this situation better than Gustavus, for after visiting Berlin to woo the daughter of the Elector of Brandenburg, he had taken a trip incognito into southern and western Germany in order to gain first-hand information. The knowledge thus gained before long served him to good purpose. The story of Frederick's tragic failure and the discomfiture of the Bohemian Protestants is soon told. He was a well-meaning prince, but of mediocre ability and utterly incapable of leading his people to victory against the tremendous odds which faced them, and the expected assistance from his father-in-law, James I of England, did not materialize. The fate of the Protestants in Bohemia and Moravia was sealed by the battle of White Mountain in 1620, when Frederick's forces were crushed by the Imperialist army under the command of its veteran general, Tilly.

The efforts of Gustavus to secure a united action in behalf of Frederick of Bohemia proving unavailing, he next directed his attention to the Polish situation. Here the Swedes had sincerely endeavoured to come to terms with Sigismund, but these overtures had failed because of the latter's stubborn refusal to acknowledge the right of Gustavus to the Swedish throne. In the summer of 1621, Gustavus entered Livonia at the head of an army of 12,000 men, and the important city of Riga was captured, after which event a Swedish government was established in the province.

The desperate plight of King Frederick of Bohemia in the meantime moved his father-in-law to bestir himself in his behalf. His own troubles with a refractory Parliament prevented him from taking the field himself, but he was willing to furnish subsidies and regiments to some other strong Protestant prince who would be willing to undertake a military campaign for the relief of the Protestants in Bohemia. He therefore sent a representative, Robert Anstruther, to the Danish court to ascertain on what terms the ruler, Christian IV, would undertake the task, and another diplomat, James Spence, to Sweden to carry on similar negotiations with Gustavus Adolphus. The important and hazardous task of bringing relief to an oppressed people was, therefore, according to James's sagacious plan to be entrusted to the lowest bidder. The Danish king felt greatly flattered by the offer, and, poorly informed about German leaders and affairs as he was and desperately afraid lest Gustavus, of whom he was extremely envious, should plunge in ahead of him and pick all the fruits of victory, set his demands quite low; Spence, on the other hand, found Gustavus unwilling to enter upon the risky venture without first securing binding promises of adequate help; the king emphasized that Sweden's nearest objective was a victory over Poland, but that thereby the most efficient attack could also be launched against the emperor.

Christian of Denmark enters the war.—As a result of these negotiations, Christian, without proper military preparations and with vague and insecure promises of aid from abroad, plunged into the religious war, while Gustavus returned to his Polish campaign, fully determined to bring it to an end. The Swedish army had by this time been reorganized in conformity with the plan which his own genius had devised; now came the opportunity to test its efficiency and institute further changes according as actual experience suggested them. In order to strike Poland in its most vulnerable spot, the king this time transferred his military operations to its Prussian provinces, hoping thus to gain control of the important region of the Vistula. In this way he would also be nearer the scene of events in Germany. The Poles, under their able general, Konieopolski, offered heroic resistance to Gustavus, but, in the main, the latter gained his great objective by securing a base on the Vistula.

In the meantime, Christian of Denmark, having entered

the Thirty Years' War against the advice of his own councillors and without adequate support either by his allies or his own Danish subjects—because of the opposition of his Council, he entered the war not as King of Denmark but as Duke of Holstein—suffered a crushing defeat at Lutter. Soon all of Jutland was overrun by the combined forces of the emperor, commanded by the able but grim and enigmatical Wallenstein, and fearful was the devastation that was inflicted upon the unhappy country. The Imperialists were now jubilant, for certain victory seemed within easy reach. Wallenstein induced the emperor to invest him with the title, "Captain-General of the Oceanic and Baltic Seas," and negotiations were opened with the Duke of Gottorp for a naval station on the Baltic for the Spanish fleet. Complete supremacy over the Northern waters was now Wallenstein's objective, but interwoven with these plans were proposals for the launching of a mighty offensive against all the Protestant nations. In conjunction with the King of Spain, Wallenstein planned to build a great fleet on the Baltic, with which to support Sigismund in his fight against Gustavus and Philip II in his war on the Netherlands. As another link in the chain which he was forging around the Protestant North, he next sought to secure possession of Stralsund, which he is said to have vowed would be taken "even though it were fastened with chains to the very throne of God himself." Realizing the enormity of the danger which would threaten them both if this important stronghold fell into Wallenstein's hands, Christian and Gustavus hastened to send assistance to the city with the result that Wallenstein was compelled to raise the siege.

To Gustavus it had become clearly evident that Sweden could not escape being drawn into the great conflict. Wallenstein had sent 10,000 men, under the command of the Imperialist general, von Arnim, to assist the Poles against Sweden, which act was *de facto* a declaration of war. In the face of the overwhelming dangers that in this crisis threatened the North, Gustavus urgently felt the need of Swedish and Danish cooperation. He was willing to ignore all conflicting interests, forget all former quarrels and wars, and enter into a "real, generous, and royal association for their common protection."

Gustavus proposes co-operation of Sweden and Denmark.—Suggestions of an alliance were therefore made to Christian, but his envy of the Swedish king would not permit him to give these overtures friendly consideration. Finally, at the urgent solicitation of Gustavus, the two monarchs met at Ulvsbäck's parsonage in February 1629 for a personal interview. Christian appeared at the conference dejected and irritable, for behind him lay the frustration of all his ambitious hopes for a glorious part by himself and his country in the great conflict; Gustavus, on the other hand, with great military successes in Poland just achieved, spoke hopefully of the future and unfolded before Christian's eyes daring and brilliant plans for concerted attacks upon the common enemy, the emperor. At this suggestion Christian's bitterness got the mastery of him and angrily he asked, "What business does Your Majesty have for going into Germany, or in what has the emperor done aught against Your Majesty?" To this Gustavus gave heated answer, reciting many instances of imperial interferences and threats, and ended by saying to Christian, "Your Majesty may be convinced that whosoever commits such acts against us, be it emperor, king, or republic, or who the devil it may be, we will take each other by the ears so that the hairs will fly." As it was evident to Gustavus that Christian's envy and suspicion made further parleys useless, the meeting ended, and the two monarchs parted to go their separate ways. The only apparent result of the conference was a decision by Wallenstein, who better than any one of his contemporaries already had gauged the superior statesmanship and military genius of Gustavus Adolphus, that prudence dictated that peace with Denmark be speedily concluded. He therefore made peace proposals to that country, which, in view of its utter helplessness, were extraordinarily moderate in their demands. By the peace of Lübeck, Christian was eliminated from the conflict (1629). The success of the Catholics now appeared complete and the Protestants were made to feel that reaction was at full tide. By the Edict of Restitution, which the emperor published in March 1629, they were dispossessed of all Church domains which had come into their hands since the treaty of Passau, 1552. Without regard to the changes that had taken place in their religious complexion and organization, two archbishoprics, twelve bishoprics, and five hundred monasteries were to pass into Catholic hands.

Swedish alliances.—Failing in his attempt to attach Denmark as an ally to Sweden, in the conflict which he foresaw was inevitable, Gustavus set his great and efficient diplomatic organization in motion in order to secure alliances with other powers. In every place where he knew that hostility to the empire existed, an alliance, or at least a friendly understanding, was sought: among Protestant German princes, in England, Holland, France, and Siebenburgen, the latter at this time ruled by Bethlen Gabor, an implacable enemy of the emperor; even to Venice, Russia, and Constantinople the diplomatic agents of the Swedish king found their way. Through the influence of Cardinal Richelieu of France, the war between Sweden and Poland was brought to an end by the truce of Altmark in 1629. A cardinal of the Catholic Church, who had just crushed the Protestant Huguenots in France, Richelieu did not hesitate to encourage Gustavus to attack the emperor. Although a good son and servant of the Church, her interests were, in his mind, subordinate to the realization of his great plan for making France supreme in Europe, which in turn necessitated a clipping of the emperor's wings. He now saw a splendid opportunity to get some one else to fight France's battle against the latter. By the truce of Altmark, Sweden was to have possession of Livonia and retain the cities of Elbing, Braunsberg, Pilau, and Memel for six years; the custom duties of these places, as well as of Danzig, which now accrued to the Swedish treasury amounted in one year to 500,000 riksdaler, a sum approximately equal to the whole of the extraordinary grants voted by the Swedish Riksdag. In the Swedish-French negotiations for a campaign against the emperor that now followed, Richelieu promised subsidies to Gustavus for a campaign in Germany which the Swedish king, however, was unwilling to accept since it would have made him a pensioner under France and restricted him in Germany to an attack upon the emperor alone and not upon the Catholic League as well. With no ally except the city of Stralsund, Gustavus entered the war. Good fortune, however, prepared the way for his campaigns in Germany, since a short time prior to his arrival with his army the emperor had been forced by the remonstrances of the princes of the League, egged on by Richelieu, to dismiss Wallenstein from his service because of the latter's excessive cruelty and alleged disloyalty to his master.

The momentous decision.—In the winter of 1628-1629 Gustavus had had frequent and earnest conferences with his Council regarding his country's participation in the great struggle in Germany, and the opinion had been unanimously held that if the kingdom and its ancient freedom were to be preserved the nation must not hesitate in making a decision. "No country in Europe," said the king on one occasion, "enjoys more freedom than Sweden, but this menace—the Catholic-Imperial victories—comes closer to us every day and every day gathers new strength." The momentous decision to enter the war found no dissenting voice. "You have always advised this war," Gustavus could afterwards say to the representatives of the nation in justification of the extraordinary measures to which he was compelled to resort in order to push his campaigns with vigour. This unanimity of mind and purpose was a tremendous advantage to king and nation alike, standing in marked contrast to the divided counsels in Denmark, where Christian's decision to enter the war had been violently opposed by high and low. One thing was clear to king and Council in Sweden: the war must be fought offensively and on German soil. Gustavus had in a statement fully set forth the advantages of an offensive warfare, as against a "watchful waiting" policy until attacked in their own land, and when the vote was taken in the Riksdag all voted for carrying the war into Germany, the *bönder,* in giving their approval, adding the sage remark: "As the saying is, the goat gnaws where it is tethered, and it is better that we tie our horses in the pastures of the enemy than in our own." [1]

Reasons for Sweden's entry into the war.—With the preparations for the expedition completed, Gustavus Adolphus bade farewell to the Estates at a Riksdag in 1630. His eloquent presentation of the reasons which had impelled him to enter the great struggle and his stirring plea for a united nation in

[1] Almquist, H., *Svenska folkets historia,* II, Lund, 1922, p. 536.

support of the fatherland ended with the prophetic words: "And as happens that the crock goes to the well so often that it finally is broken, no doubt it will befall me who amidst many dangers have shed blood for Sweden but still is privileged to enjoy life that in the end I shall lose it." Well aware that his motives would be questioned, he solemnly affirmed before God Almighty that he had begun hostilities out of no lust for power, but in self-defence and in order to deliver his fellow Christians from oppression.[2]

The motives which induced Gustavus Adolphus to urge his nation to take the decisive step which was to lead it into the most important enterprise in its history and procure for him a secure place among the world's heroes and benefactors, have been very differently understood and interpreted by historical writers. On the purely Catholic side, his motives have quite naturally been conceived as those of an adventurer bent on conquest and self-aggrandizement like a Hannibal, a Cæsar, or a Napoleon. Even some German Protestants have looked upon him as the embodiment of a vaulting ambition to be a conqueror, as a man who sought to take advantage of Germany's weakness in order to win territory and power for his own beloved Sweden. Others behold in him the undaunted idealist and hero, who was willing for the great cause of religious and political liberty to pour out the blood of his nation, and himself make the supreme sacrifice. No doubt all of these sentiments and motives in some measure at least entered into his epochal decision. That Gustavus was ambitious and sought to extend the boundaries and the influence of his own kingdom cannot be doubted, but it can reasonably be assumed that this was part of his plans for safeguarding the Protestant religion and the ancient liberties of Sweden. He wanted to build a strong Sweden, but it is conceivable that in his mind the security of the Protestant faith in Europe could most directly and surely be achieved and preserved through a powerful Sweden. It was natural for him to believe, however, that the ability of Sweden to carry this great rôle was contingent upon her having a strong military organization and control of

[2] The address is found in translation in Robinson's *Readings in European History*, Boston, 1906, Vol. II, pp. 207-210.

strategic points in north Germany and the Baltic lands. It would, no doubt, be in accordance with historical truth to say that in the beginning the thoughts of Gustavus Adolphus were almost wholly of defence for his own land, but as extraordinary success crowned his enterprise in Germany, plans of conquest took shape in his mind; the latter are not necessarily an evidence of ambition and desire for self-aggrandizement, as it can well be conceived that his experiences taught him that the security of Sweden could best be preserved by the possession of territory across the Baltic.

The resources and the forces which Gustavus had at his command when the decision to enter the Thirty Years' War was made must at first sight seem entirely inadequate to the successful carrying on of a campaign against the formidable foe. The army with which he set sail for Germany at midsummer time in 1630 amounted to 13,000 men. Even in that day this seemed a pitiably small force with which to proceed against a mighty antagonist, but it probably constituted the most efficient fighting machine that the world up to that time had seen; its fighting strength was not to be measured by the number of individuals in the ranks. Gustavus felt strong in the consciousness that back of him stood a united nation, determined to make every sacrifice in order to insure the success of the Swedish army, and he was hopeful that, once the Swedes were in the conflict and by a decisive victory had broken the spell of imperial invincibility, some of the hesitant German Protestant princes would join him as allies. Above everything else, however, he felt strong in the conviction that he was fighting for a just cause and trusted to the effectiveness of his own military genius.

Getting a foothold in Germany.—It was one of the first postulates of the strategy of Gustavus in this war that he must secure control of the main rivers of Germany, partly in order to have safe means of communication with his own country and thus to insure a plentiful supply of provisions and munitions of war, and partly in order that a wedge thereby might be driven into the enemy's forces; the control of the rivers would also give him, through collection of river tolls, a much-needed increase to his resources. At strategic points he would build forts, and by a gradual advance press the antagonist back. In conformity with this plan the Oder River became his first objective. After entering Stettin, the capital of Pomerania, he compelled the aged and vacillating Duke Bogislav, in spite of all his pleas to be permitted to remain neutral, to enter into an alliance with him, by the terms of which the duke's military forces were placed under Swedish command. After the defences of Stettin had been strengthened and a great part of the province of Mecklenburg occupied, Gustavus set himself seriously to the task of clearing Pomerania of the imperial host. The situation was full of overwhelming dangers. His forces remained small, auxiliary forces from Sweden not having as yet arrived, and instead of showing a disposition to come to his assistance, the German Protestant princes had assumed an indifferent if not actually hostile attitude. Their unwillingness to come to a quick decision and join the invader can readily be understood; Gustavus was as yet an unknown quantity, and for all they knew he might be another Frederick or Christian IV, and the German princes had good reasons for remembering what direful things were certain to be visited upon those who in this war cast their lot with a loser.

Magdeburg.—Only one German principality, the free imperial city of Magdeburg, dared to declare itself for Gustavus, and thus hearten him for the great enterprise. Another encouragement came to him when, by the treaty of Bärwalde, an alliance was concluded between Sweden and France to run for five years, by the terms of which Gustavus, in return for a French subsidy of 300,000 livres for the year that had passed and thereafter 1,000,000 livres annually as long as the treaty remained in force, undertook to keep at least 36,000 men in the field. He also bound himself to leave unmolested the Catholic religion wherever he found it established.

Since Magdeburg was the strongest fortress in north Germany and commanded the passage of the Elbe at a strategically most important point, its possession became the immediate objective of both Gustavus and Tilly, the commander of the imperialist forces. The latter hastened to lay siege to the city, and its relief now became the one great concern of Gustavus's negotiations and strategy. Much was here at stake for the Swedish king, since if Magdeburg fell into Tilly's hands, the latter would not only hold a decided strategic advantage, but the fall of the city would give warning to others who might be disposed to give aid and comfort to Gustavus that they had better refrain from so doing.

In order to reach the beleaguered and hard-pressed city, Gustavus must, however, pass through Brandenburg and Saxony, but neither the Elector of Brandenburg, George William, his brother-in-law, nor John George, Elector of Saxony, both Protestant princes, would permit him to march through their respective lands. After such fruitless parleying and since haste was urgent if aid was to be brought to the beleaguered city, Gustavus moved his army to Berlin and with cannon pointed at the city compelled the elector to yield, open his forts to him, and permit a free passage through his electorate. John George, however, remained obdurate, refusing to make any concession to the Swedish king which would make it possible for the latter to advance with greater speed towards Magdeburg. He even called a meeting of Protestant German princes at Leipsic for the purpose of forming an alliance against Sweden, but due mainly to John George's own obstinacy the meeting ended in a fiasco. The elector nevertheless persisted in his refusal to permit the Swedish army to pass through his territory, and Gustavus dared not defy him and thus arouse him to actual hostilities. It therefore became necessary for the king to try to reach Magdeburg by a circuitous route, and the delay occasioned by this sealed the fate of the city. It fell into the hands of the imperialists and became the scene of slaughter and pillage which were indescribably brutal. The city became a heap of smouldering ruins, only its cathedral and about one hundred houses having escaped the flames. The charge that Tilly was responsible for the conflagration is, no doubt, baseless, for the destruction of the city meant that the fruits of victory were snatched out of his hands. The fall of Magdeburg was a terrible blow to Gustavus, and the weeks following the catastrophe, no doubt, were the darkest period in his German campaign. In a statement to the Protestant world he explained the circumstances which had led to the calamity and made clear the reasons for his own inability to save the city. His timorous brother-in-law in Berlin, fearing that the fate which had befallen Magdeburg had an ominous meaning for him, now refused to abide any longer by the terms of the agreement which he had signed, pledging support to the Swedes. Gustavus now demanded of his kinsman a straightforward answer within a few hours to the question whether he was for or against him. In this dilemma George William chose as the lesser of the two evils to abide by his alliance, and gave up two of his important fortresses to Gustavus. The latter next moved his army to the confluence of the Elbe and Havel rivers, where he built a strong camp, in the meantime waiting for an opportunity to come to grips with the enemy and strike a decisive blow. Disease was thinning the ranks of his army and working havoc with the morale of his men. With every day that passed in this period of comparative inactivity, the chance of winning a decisive advantage seemed to be slipping rapidly from him. At this juncture Tilly made a move which finally gave Gustavus his long-desired opportunity. In spite of the violent protests of John George, who had desperately sought permission to remain neutral, Tilly sent his army into Saxony and captured Leipsic, after first threatening that unless the city surrendered it would share the fate of Magdeburg. Angry beyond measure because of this base ingratitude towards one who claimed that he had endeavoured to pursue a strictly correct course, the elector sent frantic appeals to Gustavus Adolphus to hasten to his assistance. Gustavus at once moved his forces to Saxony and effected a junction with the elector's troops.

Battle of Breitenfeld.—At the news of the approach of the Swedish-Saxon army, Tilly took up an advantageous position at Breitenfeld, a village just north of Leipsic, and here on September 7, 1631, was fought the battle which put the strength of the two foes to the test and clearly revealed the advantage of the new system of warfare over the old. The fate of Protestantism hung in the balance. The Swedish army consisted of 26,000 men and the Saxon army of 18,000 men, the latter resplendent in new uniforms, its cavalry riding fine horses, while the Swedes appeared ragged and battle-scarred; they were, however, inured to warfare and had implicit faith in their leader. Tilly, now a man of seventy, victor of eighty battles, commanded a force of 32,000 men, old veterans from many a campaign who, by reason of an unbroken series of successes, were filled with an unshakable confidence of victory so long as they could follow their idolized leader.

The battle began with an attack by Tilly's impetuous cavalry leader, Pappenheim, who, unable to restrain his impatience any longer, hurled his forces against the right wing of the Swedish army. He was met by a murderous fire and his men were thrown back. He then tried to attack the Swedes from the rear and on their flank, but, thanks to the flexibility of the Swedish regiments, the Swedish lines were hastily reformed to meet the onslaught coming from another direction, and again Pappenheim was thrown back. Seven times his forces rushed madly at the Swedes, only to be hurled back at last and thrown into flight. With the left wing of his army already engaged, Tilly found it necessary to advance with the right against the Swedish left where the Saxons stood; at the first impact these fled pell-mell from the scene, with the elector leading the procession. The exposed left side of the Swedish army now was compelled to meet the formidable attack of a largely superior force, but here again the mobility of the Swedish detachments decided the outcome; new regiments were immediately rushed to the strategic points where they helped to keep the Swedish line from breaking, or gave the extra momentum necessary to overthrow the enemy's line. Tilly's attack had left a gap in his army, and when the quick eye of Gustavus Adolphus detected this, he sent part of his forces forward. They seized the enemy's cannon, and trained them against Tilly's own square; this proved too much for the hitherto unbeaten imperialist soldiers, who broke into wild flight, and only with the greatest difficulty did the aged general himself manage to escape capture. Surrounded by about seven hundred men, all that was left of his splendid army, he escaped from the field. No less than 7,000 of his soldiers fell in the battle and 5,000 became prisoners of war. The booty which fell into Swedish hands was immense, including enormous stores of provisions and, most valuable of all, the money chest of the League.

Few battles in history have caused as great a sensation

throughout the length and breadth of Europe as the battle of Breitenfeld, and its effect upon the situation was profound. The thirteen years which had passed since the great conflict began had brought nothing but defeats and humiliation to the Protestants, but now in a few hours their status was changed completely: the Swedish king stood in the heart of Germany with a victorious army and there was no army of either the Catholic League or the emperor to oppose him. No

The Exultant Messenger. Contemporary caricature showing the joy of the Imperialists before the battle of Breitenfeld

wonder that pious Catholics, according to an oft-quoted story, were amazed that "God had all of a sudden turned Lutheran." The prestige of the emperor had received a severe and permanent setback and the Protestants could take heart again. A shout of joy arose from them everywhere. "English Eliot, writing from his prison in the Tower, could speak of Gustavus Adolphus as the person whom fortune and virtue had reserved for the wonder of the world." [3] For the Swedish king it meant the rapid accession to his ranks of new allies, both princes and cities, and for the Protestants of Germany it meant the abrogation of the Edict of Restitution.

[3] Gardiner, S. R., *The Thirty Years' War*, New York, 1889, p. 140.

Gustavus Adolphus at the parting of the ways.—After Breitenfeld Gustavus Adolphus stood at the parting of the ways; he could either take advantage of the emperor's defenceless situation and press forward towards Vienna, in the hope that there he might forthwith be able to dictate terms of peace, or he could advance into southwestern Germany, where the Catholic League was in control, and relieve those brethren in the faith who had been made to suffer grievous persecution.

The Lame Messenger. Contemporary caricature showing the condition of the Imperialists after the battle of Breitenfeld

John George urged him to take the former course, suggesting that as for himself he should proceed against the strongholds of the League in the Southwest. Oxenstierna and Gustaf Horn, the latter one of the king's most trusted generals, urged the same course as the most effective way for bringing the emperor speedily to his knees, and even many years later the great chancellor declared that Gustavus's failure to follow this plan was the one great mistake of his career. Gustavus Adolphus, however, chose the other course, and to this he was impelled not only by the most urgent dictates of honour, but also by the firm conviction that in the end this would prove to be strategically the wiser choice. He had proclaimed that his aim in entering the war was the bringing of succour to the oppressed Protestants, and if he now ignored their appeals for help it would at once appear as if selfish gains were uppermost in his mind. He also detected in the suggestion of the elector a clever scheme on the part of this turn-coat ally; if John George could go into southwestern Germany, he would escape the necessity of incurring still further the ill-will of the emperor, and the opportunity to play the saviour of the oppressed brethren in the faith would bring him nearer the position of leadership among the German Protestants which he coveted. Historians and authorities on military strategy have generally held that Gustavus Adolphus's choice in this instance was another evidence of his keen insight and masterly strategy. Instead of heeding the advice of John George and his own friends, he sent the former against Silesia and Bohemia, thus making inevitable a complete break between him and the emperor.

For Gustavus Adolphus the march into southwestern Germany meant, however, not only an opportunity to bring the promised relief to the oppressed Protestants of this region, but it made possible the establishment of a new strategic base from which he could with greater prospect of success press Spain back, while at the same time keeping a watchful eye on France, whose intentions the king had good reasons for distrusting. Richelieu had hoped that the emperor be given a sound drubbing, but the very magnitude of Gustavus's victory aroused his fear that Sweden might become too strong and herself pluck the fruits of victory.

March through the "Priests' Lane."—The advance through the southland, known because of the multitude of ecclesiastics busy in the district endeavouring to root out Protestantism as the March through the Priests' Lane, was a veritable triumphal progress for Gustavus Adolphus, hailed as he was everywhere as a deliverer; to his Swedes from their northland homes, unaccustomed as they had always been to all forms of luxury, the wealth and splendour of the sunny South was a source of constant amazement. They revelled in their newfound prosperity and drank copious draughts of sparkling wine from their capacious helmets. Great stores of arms and provisions fell into their hands and books and manuscript collections of great value were sent to the University of Uppsala.

In his march into the Southwest, Gustavus Adolphus sought to undo the injustice of the Edict of Restitution by expelling priests from the Protestant communities which had been compelled to accept them, and Lutheran services were again instituted. The Catholics were, however, according to the terms of the treaty of Bärwalde, left in the possession of their religious rights. Winter quarters were established at Frankfort on the Main, and here the Swedish king was sought by princes and diplomats from nations both great and small. In the hands of Gustavus Adolphus were now gathered the threads of diplomacy from every section of Europe and Swedish power and prestige had reached its zenith.

As France coveted territory along the Rhine as her part of the spoils, it was difficult for Gustavus to maintain friendly relations with her. Richelieu sought to bring about peace between Gustavus Adolphus and those Catholic powers of the League with which France was in alliance, but as Gustavus refused to give up his conquests until the princes of the League had disarmed, a condition they would not accept, the negotiations were broken off by the latter and war was resumed. Gustavus Adolphus now resolved on pressing into southern Germany.

Tilly had in the meantime managed to put another large army in the field, and in trying to prevent the Swedish forces on their way southward from crossing the Lech River, the old warrior was mortally wounded, dying soon after in the city of Ingolstadt. The imperialist forces now retreated and the Swedes could proceed on their way. Gustavus's objective was now Bavaria, whose elector, Maximilian, was the head and brains of the Catholic League. Munich, its capital, was entered by the Swedes without the League or the emperor being able to offer any effectual resistance, and a large war indemnity was collected. Along the entire path of his march the king maintained strict discipline among his troops, a matter which struck the people, accustomed as they were to the pillaging and heartless cruelty which other armies passing that way had visited upon the unhappy land, with utter amazement.

Real Objective of Gustavus.—At Munich Gustavus Adolphus stood at the pinnacle of his power and fame. His little northland country had forced its way to a commanding place among the powerful nations of the earth; no man could in his wildest dreams, a few years before, have foreseen such a rapid exaltation of the hitherto obscure nation. A vast area extending from the Alps to the polar regions was now subject to its authority.

What plans revolved in the mind of Gustavus Adolphus at this stage of his career have been a matter of much conjecture. While his chief object in entering the war in Germany had been the bringing of aid to the oppressed Protestants, it, no doubt, had become more and more evident to him that an effective check upon the forces of reaction could be maintained only by a strong and aggressive confederation. To Gustavus Adolphus it was clear that Sweden should form the centre of such a "*Corpus Evangelicorum.*" Such a rôle would, however, make extraordinary demands on her people for men, and especially for money. The king had therefore at this time undoubtedly begun to give increasing thought to the question of compensation for his country's services and of guarantees for the future. Sweden, it had become increasingly apparent to him, must of necessity and for her own security possess important territorial areas and strongholds on the south and east coasts of the Baltic.

Wallenstein in command again.—While Gustavus marched in triumph through the southern regions of Germany, receiving the homage of the people, re-establishing Protestant worship, restoring peace and security to unruly districts, punishing the chief instigators of evil, and giving thought to his plans for the future security of Sweden and of the Protestant religion, a threatening storm was rising in his rear. Without an army of adequate size and without an able leader, his land exposed to the imminent danger of invasion, Emperor Ferdinand had been forced to humble himself and again call upon Wallenstein for aid. Reluctantly the deposed general had after his dismissal gone into retirement, certain, however, that the exigencies of war would soon call him again to lead the imperial armies. After Breitenfeld, Wallenstein had even opened negotiations with Gustavus Adolphus, suggesting that the two join hands, drive the emperor from Germany, and establish religious liberty in the country. These negotiations never advanced far, for the king found it impossible to trust an adventurer like the Bohemian nobleman. It is inconceivable that two men so strong-willed and ambitious as Gustavus Adolphus and Wallenstein could ever have worked together as allies. Upon the solicitation of the emperor, Wallenstein now agreed to resume command of the imperial forces, but the terms which he laid down as the price of his services made him virtually the military dictator of the empire. Such was his fame as a general who could provide well for his men by leading them to victory, after which they had full freedom to satisfy their lust for plunder, that the roisterous, adventure-loving mercenary soldiers at once flocked to his standards from every corner of Europe. His proud words that he need but "stamp his foot on the ground and an army will at once spring forth" was no idle boast.

Gathering clouds.—Soon a force of 40,000 men was under his command ready to place itself in Gustavus's way. As the latter found himself in danger of being isolated in the south, he speedily moved his army northward. It was especially important for the Swedish king to prevent a junction of Wallenstein's and Maximilian's forces. Gustavus failed to prevent this junction and he next took up a fortified position at Nurnberg, where soon the army under Wallenstein entrenched itself in a strong position. As the enemy was reported to have 60,000 men, Gustavus Adolphus, who had been compelled to place so many of his soldiers on garrison duty in widely scattered places that he had only 18,000 men under his immediate command, dared not leave his advantageous position to offer battle until reinforcements could arrive. Wallenstein then took up a strong position in the proximity of the Swedish camp and a grim struggle of endurance ensued. Starvation, disease, and desertions were after some weeks working havoc with both armies. In this gruesome conflict Gustavus Adolphus was the first to give way. He made an attempt to dislodge Wallenstein, but was repulsed after suffering heavy losses. He next moved northward, intending to invade the emperor's domains, but was forced to abandon this course when Wallenstein invaded Saxony. The Swedish army was now in imminent danger of having its line of retreat cut off, especially as the vacillating John George could not for a moment be relied upon to remain loyal to his Swedish ally. The fear that the elector might join Wallenstein caused Gustavus to hasten with all possible speed towards Saxony. In the meantime Wallenstein had taken up a position near Leipsic and Lützen, while Pappenheim, his dashing cavalry leader, had been sent to the region of lower Saxony to harass the enemy. On the way thither he was to capture Halle. The news that a considerable force had thus been detached from the main imperial army reached Gustavus Adolphus at Weissenfels, whither he had advanced slowly. He now immediately decided to move forward with all possible speed and attack the enemy before his forces could be completely reassembled and placed in battle formation. The success of this strategy was contingent upon the possibility of advancing rapidly, but unfortunately for the Swedes heavy rains had fallen, it being now late in October, and the roads had been made almost impassable. This obstacle, together with the necessity of throwing back a detachment of the imperial forces which attacked, seriously retarded the march of Gustavus's army. It was late in the afternoon of November 5th (1632) that the Swedish army approached Lützen, but because of the continued delays Gustavus Adolphus could not engage the foe that day, as he had expected.

The hours before Lützen.—The attack was therefore planned for early the following morning before Wallenstein had had time to bring all his scattered regiments together. He had sent urgent summons to his absent officers, and especially to Pappenheim, to cast every other matter aside and hurry with their troops, with the greatest possible speed, towards Lützen. Gustavus Adolphus spent the night in an army wagon in the company of a few of his trusted lieutenants. One may surmise that no hours of his career were so heavy under the weight of overwhelming anxiety as these. He was well aware that the forces of Wallenstein were rapidly being augmented during the night by the arrival of the summoned regiments. Especially did the knowledge that the intrepid Pappenheim was riding through the night with all speed at the head of his dauntless cavalry, in order to be on hand for the fray as early in the morning as possible, disturb him. Everything now depended on Gustavus's ability to begin the battle at the first streak of daylight, before the enemy had attained his full numerical strength. Unfortunately for his plans, a dense fog hung over Lützen and its environs on the morning of the fateful sixth of November, so that it was not until towards noon that the order to advance to the attack could be given.

Wallenstein had taken up his position on the north side of the road which leads from Lützen towards the east. This was paralleled by deep ditches which now served his soldiers as defences against the Swedish army drawn up in battle formation on the other side of the road. The plan of battle was on both sides very similar to that of Breitenfeld, Wallenstein's army being drawn up in large squares with heavy artillery in position to pour shots into the approaching enemy, while the Swedes were arranged in small divisions and had light artillery. As at Breitenfeld, Gustavus Adolphus depended on rapidity of motion, ability to concentrate troops where most needed, and superiority in men and weapons to decide the issue.

Death of the king.—When the fog finally lifted the king himself at the head of a regiment led the opening attack. Just then the fog descended on the scene again; he and a few of his men now became separated from the main body and soon were surrounded by imperialist soldiers. In the mêlée which followed, the king was shot and fell from his horse. The actual details of what happened next cannot be definitely known, as only a young attendant remained by the side of the king, and the account of the tragedy rests mainly on a later statement by the father of this young man. One detail of the story relates that as the king lay on the ground some of Wallenstein's soldiers came up, and when they asked who the wounded man was, Gustavus Adolphus himself replied, "I was the King of Sweden," whereupon they shot him through the head, stripped his body, and left it lying on the field among the dead and wounded. The first intimation of the tragedy came to the Swedish soldiers when they saw the king's horse run about the battle-field riderless. When next Duke Bernhard of Weimar, in conformity with arrangements made by Gustavus Adolphus before the battle, assumed command, they knew that what they had feared most of all had actually happened. Instead of yielding to the feeling of poignant grief and utter hopelessness which at once gripped the heart of every Swedish soldier, the men in the ranks demanded that they be sent against the enemy again in order that they might avenge the death of their beloved leader. Furiously the battle now raged all day, and, as the sun sank over the bloody scene, Wallenstein's forces broke and began the retreat towards Leipsic, from which place it was continued until the army reached Bohemia. Pappenheim, the intrepid cavalry leader, who had reached the scene soon after the battle began, had been anxious to encounter Gustavus himself, but was instead informed of his death. Shortly afterwards Pappenheim himself fell mortally wounded.

The body of Gustavus was found after the battle, terribly mutilated by shot and the hoofs of horses. The sad funeral procession homeward was soon begun, and everywhere multitudes gathered to do reverence to the memory of their great benefactor. Interment took place in the Riddarholm Church in Stockholm in June 1634. On the spot where the king is supposed to have fallen now rests a huge boulder, known as "Schwedenstein." By a peculiar fitness of things, this boulder was, according to the views of geologists, in prehistoric times carried by the glacial ice from Sweden and deposited on the spot which later became the sacred shrine of the Swedish nation. "By birth the *Schwedenstein* is also a good Swede, although a Swede who already in glacial time emigrated from his northland home." [4] The blood-drenched elkskin waistcoat which the king wore on the fatal day, plainly showing where it was pierced by shots and sabre, was carried to Vienna, where it was kept in the armory of that city, as one of the most cherished trophies of war. In 1926 it was, however, presented to Sweden by Austria as a token of her appreciation of the splendid care which Sweden had given thousands of Austrian children, who, in the years following the World War, were brought by the train-loads to the North and there fed and tenderly cared for.

[4] Schück, *Svenska folkets historia,* I, p. 5.

Chapter XIV

THE NATION CARRIES ON. QUEEN CHRISTINA DESERTS HER LAND AND FAITH

The news of Gustavus's death did not reach Stockholm until December 8th, a month and two days after the fateful event, and this in spite of the fact that couriers were dispatched immediately after the battle who were ordered to ride night and day and bring the sad tidings to the homeland. The grief that seized the nation when the news of the tragedy came was naturally intensely bitter; the commanding greatness of Gustavus Adolphus and the epochal importance of his career seem to have been well understood even by the people of his own generation and in his own country. Now that the great leader was gone, it seemed for a moment to his countrymen as if all hope for the future had suddenly faded. With this sense of loss of a brilliant military leader and statesman was the sense of a personal loss, for the king's kindness, piety, tolerance, and humanity had endeared him to all classes.

Tragic change in Sweden's position.—By the death of her king, Sweden suddenly found herself plunged from the high eminence, where the sun of victory had shone brightly, to the very depths of darkness, uncertainty, and despair, and it is not surprising that for a moment the nation reeled beneath the shock. The great enterprise upon which the king and country had entered, when the momentous decision to draw the sword in defence of the distressed Protestants in the empire was made, had assumed dimensions which no one had at first foreseen. Sweden now held the greater part of Germany in her hands, her armies—not purely Swedish any longer, since the contingents of German Protestants and mercenaries constituted a majority at times—were fighting on a wide front, and practically every German Protestant prince had either voluntarily or by compulsion joined the Swedish standards; besides this,

Sweden was in alliance with France, whose policies were directed by the crafty Richelieu, and his determination to gain substantial spoils for his country out of the war had become increasingly evident. From the side of Poland, danger again loomed menacingly, for its ruler now resurrected the old Polish claims to the Swedish throne and he was ready at any time, if weakness and confusion in Sweden seemed to vouchsafe success, to make good his claim by military intervention. In this crisis a mere child of six, the only legitimate child of Gustavus Adolphus, Christina, was by the right of inheritance designated as the great king's successor. Probably the most impressive fact in the entire history of the Swedish nation is the extraordinary unanimity with which men of all ranks now joined in the solemn resolve to "carry on"; the nation did not give a moment's serious thought to the advisability or necessity of withdrawing from the struggle. From Per Brahe, one of the leading members of the Swedish Council, we have a graphic account of what happened when the message of the king's death arrived and struck its members as a clap of thunder. "We who were present," he wrote, "took high-minded counsel with one another before we parted, solemnly pledging ourselves to stand united in life and death for the safety and defence of our fatherland, and not only with vigour and unanimity of spirit keep everything intact at home, but also to the end, and in conformity with our departed leader's plans and intentions, pursue the war against the emperor and all his followers in order that an honourable peace might be attained."

Oxenstierna assumes leadership; his strength and weakness.—It was not the least of Gustavus's elements of greatness that he had been able to infuse his own faith and courage into the hearts of his countrymen and to train a group of statesmen, administrators, and generals to carry out his plans in their respective fields. Head and shoulders above the rest stood the chancellor, Oxenstierna, who, such was the universal recognition of his genius and probity, was immediately and without any opposition appointed "legate-plenipotentiary of the Swedish crown in the Roman Empire and with all our armies" by the Swedish Council. As a statesman he was the peer of his former master, but it was inevitable that the jealous and self-seeking German princes would not be so ready to subordinate their minds and interests to one who did not hold the royal title as they *nolens volens* had been when they had dealings with the great king. Nor was the chancellor a military man by training as the king had been, and difficulties in securing obedience and proper co-operation on the part of the generals could be anticipated. The chancellor suffered under the further handicap of rather austere manners; the personal charm and magnetism, coupled with a boundless enthusiasm, which had belonged to Gustavus Adolphus and had fired the Swedes with a never subsiding zeal to carry forward the great struggle as though it were the holiest of causes, was not a gift with which Oxenstierna had been endowed. But the chancellor never for a moment wavered in his determination to complete the task which Gustavus had begun. As no one else, he knew what his great master's plans had been. Compelled abroad to move in a sphere where open or secret hostility placed obstacles in his way at every step, finding at times nothing but faint-heartedness and divided counsel at home, Oxenstierna, through the sixteen gruelling years that after Gustavus's death were to drag their weary and bloody course over Germany before peace was made, held with unflinching determination to the course which he believed would bring victory to his country. Endowed with clear vision and a keen insight into human nature, Oxenstierna was able to read the intentions of his opponents and take his measures accordingly to thwart their designs. Like Gustavus Adolphus, he was a master of the spoken and written word, and many of his important victories were in the main won by his letters and addresses. His perseverance was indomitable; baffled and defeated on one point, he kept his poise and forthwith tried other means to gain the same end. The game of diplomacy, with its bluff, prevarication, and easy shifting of base was by no means unfamiliar to him, but an unbiassed opinion must assert that, as a diplomat and statesman, he was far more honourable than the contemporaries with whom he was compelled to match his wits. These were not long in finding out that in Oxenstierna they had a man of superior astuteness to deal with. Richelieu declared him to be "an inexhaustible source of well-matured counsels," and no greater tribute could have been paid him than the statement attributed to the French statesman, Mazarin: "If all the diplomats of Europe were in a boat together, they would unhesitatingly entrust the rudder to Oxenstierna." [1]

Axel Oxenstierna. Contemporary copper plate

At first Oxenstierna endeavoured to realize the plans of Gustavus Adolphus for a *Corpus Evangelicorum,* with Sweden at the head, and he therefore concentrated his energies on win-

[1] Bain, *Scandinavia,* p. 210.

ning everything possible to Sweden and to the Protestants. After the crushing defeat of Nördlingen (p. 373) he found it necessary, however, to modify his program. Sweden must, he now insisted, receive compensation for her sacrifices in the war in the form of land cessions in northern Germany, and wrest from the enemy an acknowledgment of the rights of the Protestants to enjoy freedom of conscience. This was the "irreducible minimum" which Oxenstierna was resolved on getting before peace would be made. Parallel with this program was another, embodying many and wisely conceived proposals for a complete economic and political rehabilitation of Sweden.

Fully realizing the extreme difficulties and dangers which confronted the Swedes in Germany, Oxenstierna remained in that country for two years after the death of Gustavus, in order the better to be able to keep all the threads of diplomacy firmly in his hands, and during all this time the Swedish Council was in charge of the government at home. The right of Gustavus's daughter, Christina, to the throne was reaffirmed by the Riksdag as a warning to Vladislav, King of Poland, and son of Sigismund, the latter having died in the early part of 1632, that the Swedish people would vigorously oppose his claim to their throne in case he decided to press it.

Situation in Germany.—At the time when Gustavus Adolphus fell, Sweden had approximately 120,000 men under its own and its allies' standards, but as a large part of this force consisted of Germans who were commanded by German princes, the latter having in most cases but unwillingly subordinated themselves to the Swedish king, the Swedish leaders could not have implicit confidence that all divisions would remain loyal to their cause. The general attitude of the most important of these princes, John George of Saxony and George William of Brandenburg, towards the Swedish king had been clearly revealed in the events that had transpired. It was but natural that Oxenstierna, not having the prestige of royal dignity and power, should find far greater difficulty in enlisting their cooperation than Gustavus Adolphus had done. After the fateful sixth of November, Richelieu, moreover, had begun to show plainly what was in his mind; namely, the establishment of French domination in German affairs and seizure of German territory along the Rhine. The first important act of Oxenstierna after assuming full control in Germany was the summoning of representatives of the south German Protestant states and cities to a meeting at Heilbronn in March 1633. With superior skill in diplomacy, he here succeeded in bringing about the formation of a Protestant league with himself as director; the powers vested in him were extraordinary. The members of the league solemnly pledged themselves to stand together, "risk life and property" until liberty had been secured, the Evangelical group in Germany made secure in its rights, and Sweden put in possession of compensation for her sacrifices in the war. In order to achieve these purposes, the necessary military forces should be raised and maintained by the league. It was a proud moment in the life of Oxenstierna when thus he stood as the undisputed leader of German affairs and the German princes themselves surrendered all powers into his hands, but no one knew better than he on how flimsy a foundation the seemingly imposing structure rested. The weakness of his position was soon made distressingly evident to him when a serious mutiny broke out in the Swedish army, caused by the inability of his government to provide the promised compensation for men and officers. In order to appease the latter, the chancellor was forced to distribute fiefs to them in Germany, from lands at the time subject to the Swedish crown, to the value of 5,000,000 riksdaler.

In this critical period of readjustment and uncertainty the Imperialists might, by a bold and decisive stroke, have given short shrift to the Swedes and their allies in Germany, had they attacked vigorously, but fortunately for the Protestant group, Wallenstein had after Lützen remained inactive on his Bohemian estates, unwilling to enter upon any further military enterprise in behalf of the emperor, but instead active in carrying on negotiations with Swedes, Frenchmen, and Saxons against his imperial master. Finally, with the connivance of the emperor, he was assassinated in 1634, just as he was making ready to flee to the Swedish camp for safety. Strangely enough, Wallenstein had wished to fall heir to Gustavus Adolphus's rôle; that is, drive the emperor out of Germany and establish religious peace within its domains. "Are we not arch-fools to break our heads for others when we who have their armies under our control also have the power to establish peace?" he once said, and in speaking in praise of the late Swedish king, he gave voice to the wish that at the head of his own and the Swedish troops he might be able to realize the plans of his fallen antagonist regarding Germany.[2] After the assassination of Wallenstein the command of the Imperialist army fell to the cruel General Gallas and military operations were resumed.

Defeat at Nördlingen.—When the Swedes under the command of Bernhard of Weimar and Gustaf Horn, one of the ablest of the Swedish generals, attempted to relieve Nördlingen, a city of southern Germany, they suffered a crushing defeat, Horn himself falling into the enemy's hands. (In reality the army was not Swedish, since not a single Swedish regiment took part in the battle. The outcome was nevertheless looked upon as a severe setback to Sweden.) How terrible this disaster appeared to Oxenstierna is revealed by the statement which he made in later life that he had spent only two sleepless nights in his lifetime, the first after he received news of Gustavus's death, the second when he was informed of the defeat of Nördlingen. "The nimbus of invincibility" with which the armies of Sweden had hitherto been invested instantly vanished. South Germany at once fell into the hands of the enemy, and the Heilbronn League immediately went to pieces. The defeat of Nördlingen meant that south Germany would remain Catholic, and it gave France its opportunity gradually to supersede Sweden as leader in the prosecution of the war. The weather-vane Elector of Saxony, entirely unmindful of Sweden's ready response to his appeal for help when a few years previously his land was overrun and despoiled by the enemy, concluded the treaty of Prague with the emperor (1635), to which the other German princes were asked to accede. According to the terms of this treaty, the execution of the Edict of Restitution should be postponed forty years, and the Swedes be paid a sum of money whereupon they were to be told to betake themselves from Germany. If they refused to heed this advice, they were to be driven out. With panicky fear the German princes now has-

[2] Hildebrand, E., *Wallenstein och hans förbindelser med svenskarna,* in *Historisk tidskrift,* 1883.

tened to make peace with the emperor, and at the end of the year 1635 Hesse-Cassel was Sweden's only ally in Germany. To add to her danger, Poland and Denmark both began to assume a threatening attitude. It therefore became vitally important for Oxenstierna to reach at least a temporary settlement with them.

Diplomatic victories.—In one of the greatest triumphs of his diplomacy, a twenty-six years' truce (the treaty of Stuhmsdorf), was concluded with Poland by which that country renewed its acknowledgment of Sweden's right to Livonia, and Sweden in turn agreed to evacuate the territory held by her in Prussia; the question of Vladislav's claim to the Swedish throne was left to a future settlement. Frightened by the situation which confronted their country, the Swedish councillors, however, made one sacrifice which stirred the chancellor to vehement anger: they relinquished the right to collect the Prussian tolls. How serious a loss this was appears from the statement that these tolls alone had provided nine times more revenue than the combined Swedish and Finnish tolls. The truce of Stuhmsdorf also roused the hope of the Swedes, now thoroughly weary of the struggle, that the war in Germany might likewise be brought to a close, and Oxenstierna made overtures to the emperor with that in mind, but these were met with scorn. Nothing then remained for the people of Sweden but to make new sacrifices in blood and property.

The enormous expense which the war piled on Sweden, and which French subsidies, tolls collected in her foreign possessions, and income from copper and other monopolies but partly helped to defray, rested with crushing weight upon a people whose economic wealth had always been meagre. It therefore became one of the main objects of the Swedish Government, under the guidance of Oxenstierna, to develop the resources of the country to a fuller extent than ever before. Its achievements in this direction, while falling far short of anticipations, reflect extraordinary credit upon it.

Legislative and administrative reforms.—The improvement of legislative procedure and economic and legal administration inaugurated by the reform act of 1617 (p. 335), was intended by Gustavus Adolphus to be but the preliminary step to further improvements, and shortly before his death he and Oxenstierna had conferred together about supplementary legislation. Soon after Gustavus's death suggestions embodying their ideas were laid before the Riksdag by the chancellor and received its sanction in 1634. In strict conformity with this legislation the government was divided into five departments or colleges—namely, justice, war, admiralty, chancery, and treasury—with their respective presidents constituting the chief officials of the country and during the queen's minority functioning as a council of regency. Later a new court for central Sweden and a college to have charge of the important mining industry were added. The members of the Council automatically held membership in one or more of the colleges and from now on it became a practice that they resided in Stockholm in order that they might be able to give full time to the duties of office. A most interesting and significant feature of the new organization was its specific and strict provisions for annual financial reports by all officials who collected or distributed public funds, and for a system of audit. The checking-up system was, however, not to apply merely to those who collected or expended money; every one having public duties to perform was placed under obligation to give an account of his stewardship.[3] The division of the country into administrative districts (*län*), with a governor (*landshövding*) over each was carried to completion. Governors vested with wide powers, but subject to strict control by the central government, were also appointed for Stockholm and the conquered territories. This act gave Sweden an organization for national as well as for local administration which in completeness of detail and in effectiveness in insuring order and security was far superior to anything that other states in this period could boast. A distinct official class or bureaucracy was one of the results of the act, and, since all the important offices came to be held by members of the nobility, the government became extremely aristocratic in character. Oxenstierna was thoroughly imbued with the idea of the superiority of the noble class as a ruling body and was willing to extend great favours to his own privileged order, but in return he expected honest and effi-

[3] Carlsson, A., *Den svenska centralförvaltningen*, 1521-1809. Stockholm, 1913, pp. 22-25.

cient service. However, while this administration, under the watchful eye of the great chancellor, became exceedingly efficient, the vesting of extraordinary power in "the rich, the well-born, and the able" threatened the ancient privileges of the *bönder* with extinction, a danger which they at the time fully realized and were determined to defend themselves against. The story of the social struggle which later arose, because of the conflicting interests of nobility and *bönder*, constitutes one of the stirring chapters of Swedish history.

Finances.—From this period dates also the inauguration of a regular budget system. According to a plan submitted by Oxenstierna, a statement was prepared by the Council in 1636 definitely showing the estimated income, grouped according to sources, and likewise giving amounts required for the various state activities. In the matter of an orderly and detailed budget, as well as in the matter of proper audit of accounts, Sweden may at this time be said to have been in advance of both France and England, the other two countries which had made the greatest progress in fiscal administration. The practice of fixing definite salaries for the servants of the state also had its beginning in this period. In 1644, when Christina was declared of age and took her place at the head of the government, it was estimated that approximately 56 per cent of the state's revenues were consumed by wars and the national defence.

Plans for increasing wealth and revenues.—The financial situation became more and more desperate as the war cost kept mounting and as Swedish credit suffered through military reverses. In order to get at least temporary relief, the Council, therefore, in 1639 began to sell certain portions of the crown lands and to mortgage the taxes levied on the property of the *bönder* against loans from the nobility, a most dangerous expedient, since the commons, while still retaining the title to their lands, were constantly menaced by the rapacity of the individual who now had the right to their tax money. With this practice another step had been taken towards a system of injustice and oppression which later led to a bitter social struggle. As the public exchequer in increasing degree evinced a tendency to show a deficit, new schemes, some of them quite chimerical and fantastic, were born, all designed as cures for the chronic malady. Thus a great number of new enterprises were sponsored for the purpose of securing added revenues, and in many instances these were financed by the government. Fabulous expectations of mineral wealth grew apace. "We also could attain to wealth if God would only give us good sense, initiative, and diligence, and if we abstained from drunkenness, but then we must also develop aright the Indies which God has given us right here in Sweden," said the chancellor on one occasion. The newly established department of mines undertook not only to increase the output of the existing iron, copper, and silver mines in central Sweden, but also to explore and develop new fields. Most extravagant expectations of wealth were raised by reports which from time to time came to the government officials telling of new discoveries of ore and precious metals, especially in the north of Sweden. In Värmland was found "a great mountain containing Swedish diamonds, some as large as the head of a mouse, others treble that size," and from another place it was reported that "a silver vein several miles long had been discovered." (A Swedish mile is equal to approximately seven English miles.) The chief promoters of the ambitious plans for the development of a great mining and smelting industry in the remote regions of Lappland were three brothers, William, Abraham, and James Momma, or Reenstierna, the family name after they had been raised to the rank of nobility. They were descendants of an old family from Aix-la-Chapelle, and they had emigrated to Sweden, lured thither by reports of great mineral wealth and possibilities for industrial expansion. Abraham explored Lappland from end to end, with the result that he afterwards maintained that here a new Liége could be built if only skilled labourers could be secured. This latter was a problem, however, as the *bönder* in the district were, in his opinion, strange individuals, who preferred to lie in their huts and sleep all winter, not caring to earn any money and actually looking with suspicion upon all plans for creating an industry in their district. The *bönder* in turn complained that the new enterprises would only increase the population and cause a shortage of food. Oxenstierna was for a time, it seems, inclined to put some faith in the reports of the existence of enormous natural wealth in the northern part of the land and in the possibility of a great industrial development there, but very soon all such dazzling hopes proved to be utterly vain; the statesman discovered soon enough that he must have recourse to more prosaic but also more dependable means for providing revenue for the state.[4] A great number of smelters were built in the ancient iron districts, and the export of iron rose steadily in volume. Woollen, paper, and textile mills, tanneries, and plants for the manufacture of glass and salt were established to supply domestic needs and in some cases for the export trade. The necessary labourers for these industries were secured mainly through the immigration of Walloon families, who were encouraged by the government to settle in the land. Certain cities were favoured by special trade privileges in order that they might be able to develop a greater foreign commerce.

The New Sweden colony.—The need of markets for the surplus products of the land revived old plans for the establishment of colonies and in the spring of 1638 the first contingent of settlers for a new colony in America arrived on two ships, "Kalmar Nyckel" and "Gripen" and cast anchor where the city of Wilmington, Delaware, now is located.[5] Oxenstierna's instructions to the governor of the colony, Johan Printz, antedating the famous Charter of William Penn by a generation or more, are remarkable by reason of their liberal provisions and humane spirit.[6] A large tract of land within the present states of Pennsylvania, Delaware, and New Jersey, and including the area on which the city of Philadelphia is now situated, was purchased from the Indians, with whom, by fair dealing, the Swedish settlers always maintained the most amicable relations. Quite in contrast, therefore, to contemporary colonies in the New World, these colonies on the Delaware were never threatened by Indian attacks. Several settlements were made on the acquired land and the new arrivals soon became favourably known because of their industry and thrift. The education of the children received special attention in the colony, and the

[4] Sondén, Per, *Bröderna Momma-Reenstierna* in *Historisk tidskrift*, 1911.

[5] A detailed and authentic account of the founding of the New Sweden colony is found in Dr. Amandus Johnson's *The Swedish Settlements on the Delaware*, 1638-1664, 2 vols., Philadelphia, 1911.

[6] Johnson, Amandus, *Instructions for Johan Prinz*, Philadelphia, 1930.

noble churches built by the poor and struggling Swedish settlers, which to this day stand in Philadelphia, Wilmington, Penn's Neck, Swedesboro, and Norristown, still testify to their religious interests. The institution of slavery never struck root in the soil of this colony as long as it belonged to the Swedes; all the people of the colony were free men. Missionary work among the Indians was also undertaken, and a translation of Luther's Catechism into one of the Indian dialects was made. The painter, Gustaf Hesselius, who was born in Sweden in 1682 but emigrated to America where he lived for the most part in Philadelphia, has been called "America's first important artist." His painting, "Christ Institutes the Holy Sacrament," was the first to be executed in the colonies as a result of a contract for the embellishment of a public building. Adolph Ulrikbert-Müller who was born in Stockholm in 1751 likewise became a famous artist in the colonies. His portrait of George Washington is especially worthy of note. The colony never became numerically strong, and soon was seized by the Dutch, only to pass in a few years into the hands of the English. Contact with Sweden was, however, kept up, at first through the coming of additional shiploads of immigrants and later almost entirely by clergymen, who were sent over to minister to the spiritual wants of the people. The Swedish language naturally gave way in time to English, but as late as the early part of the nineteenth century sermons were occasionally preached in Swedish, and the last clergyman who left Sweden to serve the colony died in 1831, thus only eighteen years prior to the arrival of Rev. L. P. Esbjörn, with whom organized religious work among the nineteenth century immigrants from Sweden began. During the stirring days of the Revolutionary War period, the descendants of the early Swedish colonists played a conspicuous part in the affairs of the thirteen colonies, one of them, John Hanson, at one time holding the important position of president of the Continental Congress under the Articles of Confederation; to him is also given main credit for the momentous act by which the Northwest Territory became the domain of the thirteen colonies jointly.[7] Another descendant of

[7] Grosvenor, G., "Maryland Pilgrimages," in *National Geographical Magazine,* February, 1927, p. 171.

the Swedish colonists, John Morton, was a member of the Pennsylvania delegation which passed a draft for the Declaration of Independence and he cast the deciding vote in that delegation in favour of its adoption. This act placed Pennsylvania in favour of the great act and brought to an end the deadlock which had arisen among the colonies on the question of independence.

As a further means for increasing and organizing the trade of Sweden, a commercial college, first suggested in 1637 and considered later at different times, finally became a reality in 1651. Its purpose was to regulate, control, and encourage the trade of the country.

Communications.—In this period of intense activity, determined attempts were made to build good roads. These were sorely needed in order that communication between the different sections of the country might be facilitated and markets made more accessible, but although several highways were built they were entirely inadequate to so large a country, and travel and transport of goods continued to be exceedingly difficult and time-wasting. Thus a trip from Kalmar to Stockholm, or from Gothenburg to Uppsala, required on an average twenty days. In the summertime progress was generally slower because of the long stretches of wet or muddy roads through interminable forests, and travellers were compelled to endure violent shaking and pounding as they rode along the rough highways in wagons the main virtue of which was their sturdiness. A winter trip was usually more speedy and comfortable, as the roads through the forests would then most likely be smooth, short-cuts could be taken over lakes and along rivers, and the traveller could be bedded down in warm furs. Taverns were built along the highways, and most of these were in duty bound to provide vehicles and horses for the traveller in return for a definitely fixed pay.

The great and stirring events of the period had naturally stimulated a widespread interest among all classes in what was happening in the world, and a regular system of mail transportation and delivery was instituted and a Swedish newspaper printed for the first time in 1645. This was known as "*Ordinari Post Tijdende.*" By order of the government it was published weekly by the postmaster of Stockholm, who was likewise head of the country's postal system; in that capacity it was his duty to secure correspondents abroad, who would send news items, and also to procure news from subordinate postmasters throughout his own land.

Education.—Oxenstierna and the Council manifested great interest in education and many new schools were founded, some of which gave instruction in the more advanced branches, but many of which were designed to teach the children of the common people the rudiments of knowledge. The greatest pedagogue of that day, the famous Moravian, Johan Amos Comenius, came to Sweden at the invitation of the chancellor in order to assist in the establishment of new schools and the preparation of a series of new textbooks. New gymnasia were established at Skara, Växiö, and Viborg in Finland, and from this time on the question of a general scheme of education to serve all the people began to be seriously discussed. The elementary schools which had already been established were improved, and many noblemen started primary-grade schools on their estates. Instruction in the elementary branches was as a rule given by the cantor of the village church. The ability to read was already at this time common in certain districts.[8] As the first chancellor of the University of Uppsala, serving in that capacity from 1622 to his death in 1645, the learned Johan Skytte, the teacher of Gustavus Adolphus, gave constant evidence of a genuine zeal for higher education, and under his long administration the economic resources of the institution were largely increased, new courses added, the teaching staff increased, and methods of instruction improved. In the later years of his life, Oxenstierna served as chancellor of the university and he likewise interested himself deeply in all projects for the growth and development of the university. In 1637 he visited it in person and made a thorough inspection of all its departments and activities, after which he issued new instructions to the professors, urging among other things that they make their methods and aims more practical in character. A university was established for Finland in 1649 with Åbo as its location, and elementary and secondary schools opened

[8] Hildebrand, E., *Sveriges historia,* VII. p. 92.

in several communities in that country. A translation of the Bible into the Finnish language was completed in 1642.

The military situation in Germany.—At the head of the Swedish armies in Germany after Nördlingen stood Johan Banér, an intrepid and energetic warrior, who had been trained in the military school of Gustavus Adolphus and had proved an apt pupil. With the death of Gustavus and the entry of France, the conflict had assumed an entirely new character. The strict discipline and high ideals of Gustavus were soon but a memory, and the struggle degenerated into a shameless scramble for plunder and territorial gains. The Swedish soldiers, who, under the strict régime of Gustavus Adolphus's famous articles of war, had given most remarkable evidence of restraint and humaneness, unheard of before their day, were now little better than the rest. War is not a good training school for developing any of the finer sentiments, and the longer these soldiers remained in the field the more their moral sensibilities became blunted, especially as the French and mercenary soldiers who now came to take an increasingly important part in the war set a very bad example of cruelty and exploitation. The defenceless people of Germany, utterly without national unity, were made to pay the ghastly cost.

Banér.—Against tremendous odds and with the utmost difficulty, Banér managed to keep a firm hold on Pomerania, and in the fall of 1638 he inflicted a crushing defeat upon the Saxons and Imperialists in the battle of Wittstock. When next year he entrenched himself at Torgau, he was in imminent danger of being surrounded by an Imperialist army of 60,000, but by a brilliant and daring move, said to be one of the most brilliantly conceived and executed manœuvres in military history, he succeeded in evading the enemy and saved from annihilation his little army of 14,000 men.

The empire was now well-nigh exhausted, and from this time on it began to weaken steadily under the incessant hammering of Swedish and French forces. Time and again Banér invaded the Imperial territory, venturing at one time even as far as Regensburg, where the emperor himself came very near falling into his hands. When he had returned to Saxony, after a march into the very heart of the enemy's territory, the great general, broken in health and spirit, fell ill and died (1641).

Torstensson.—The chief command was now intrusted to Lennart Torstensson, another of the great military strategists who had been trained by Gustavus. He was Banér's equal as a general, and superior to him in ability to maintain discipline and bring into relief some of the idealistic principles that earlier in the struggle had animated the soldiers. The political situation also had now changed to Sweden's distinct advantage: Saxony had been rendered powerless by defeats, and in Brandenburg, Frederick William, "the Great Elector," who had succeeded his father in 1641, had entered into a truce with the Swedes, shrewdly foreseeing that victory would ultimately rest with them, and fully determined to come in at the war's end as one of the chief beneficiaries of the great adjustment that must follow. From France came new subsidies. With his army reorganized, Torstensson now invaded Silesia, after which, turning westward again, he forced the Imperialists to give battle at Breitenfeld, on almost the same spot where eleven years before the momentous victory of Gustavus Adolphus had been won. Here Swedish superiority in military affairs again won a signal victory, the Imperial army suffering a defeat almost as crushing as Tilly's in 1631. This victory restored the military supremacy of Sweden, and from now on she became the aggressor almost all along the entire battlefront. In the spring of 1643 Torstensson invaded Moravia, intending to strike at Vienna itself, thus planning to do what some of Gustavus's advisers had urged him to do after the first battle of Breitenfeld, but at this juncture the general received orders from Oxenstierna to attack Denmark instead.

The Danish War.—These orders probably caused no surprise to Torstensson, for the relations between Sweden and Denmark had become increasingly strained. The attitude of Christian IV during this entire period had found expression in his question to Gustavus on the occasion of their meeting at Ulvsbäck's parsonage in the year 1629, "What business have you in Germany?" The glorious and unexpected victories of Sweden in Germany, her conquest of Baltic territory, and the almost certain prospect that a large part of these areas would at the conclusion of the war remain as a part of the Swedish domain, had not only aroused the bitter jealousy of the Danish king, but had filled him with genuine fear that Denmark herself would be overwhelmed by the triumphant neighbour and her territory incorporated with Sweden. While Christian is said to have shed tears when he heard the news of Gustavus's death, it is quite certain that this intelligence likewise brought a sense of infinite relief. But Oxenstierna felt a far greater distrust for Denmark and its king than Gustavus ever had done and watched her every move with suspicion and growing resentment. He had a long memory for the suffering and humiliation imposed by Denmark upon Sweden after the Kalmar War, and all his experiences after the conclusion of that conflict had bred in him a distrust of the Danes which nothing could allay. Certainly Christian had done nothing to allay this feeling; on the contrary he had constantly pursued a policy towards Sweden which the chancellor found most irritating. Christian was, however, incurring serious risks, for his military resources could not at this time by any means be compared to the Swedish. Already the year following the battle of Lützen, Christian appeared in the rôle of mediator in the conflict, thereby gaining some advantage for himself and securing the election of his son Frederick as Archbishop of Bremen. A secret compact was thereupon made between Christian and the emperor, which was intended to be preliminary to a general peace treaty to be drawn up by the two, and later acted on by a congress of rulers under Danish leadership. To the Swedes, who knew of these regulations, this seemed the more reprehensible, as Denmark was taking advantage of their weakness and embarrassment just then, a situation which they were convinced would be only temporary. They became further irritated when Christian refused to extend exemption from Sound tolls, guaranteed by the treaty of Knäred, to territories which Sweden had acquired since that treaty was signed, and furthermore laid obstacles in the way of Sweden's shipments of armaments through the Sound. Ugly rumors came to Oxenstierna, telling of a secret alliance between Denmark and Poland, and of a projected marriage between Christian's son, Valdemar, and a daughter of the Russian czar. These reports naturally did not help to allay his suspicions. When finally a peace congress was summoned to meet at Osnabrück under Danish mediation, for which the Danish representatives received instructions not to agree to any cessions of land to Sweden in Pomerania or anywhere along the Baltic coast, the measure of Swedish resentment seemed to be overflowing.

Other exasperating annoyances of a peculiar character were added to the already long list of grievances, and served as the final episode in Christian's policy of pin-pricks. The Swedes, and especially Oxenstierna, had been stirred to bitter resentment by Christian's meddling with the affairs of Maria Eleanora, widow of Gustavus Adolphus. After the death of her royal consort, this erratic woman had caused an endless amount of trouble and embarrassment, first by clinging to the insane notion that her husband's body should not be interred, pleading that as cruel fate had compelled them to live apart from each other so much while he was alive, the opportunity to behold his body, now that he was dead, ought not to be denied her; and later by a most reckless extravagance and most disgraceful display of contempt for everything Swedish. She made no secret of the fact that her sympathies were with her native Brandenburg, and this at a time when Sweden was at war with this power. It finally became necessary to separate her from her daughter—Gustavus himself had ordered that the daughter's education should not be intrusted to the mother—and she was placed under guard at the castle of Gripsholm. While confined here, she managed to open negotiations with the Danish minister to Sweden, with the result that Christian sent two ships to aid her in escaping from the land. Her flight made the situation extremely embarrassing for the Swedish statesmen. Christian's connivance at the queen's flight completed the evidence of Danish malice towards Sweden as far as Oxenstierna was concerned and the decision to begin war on the meddlesome neighbour was made. In May 1643, the Swedish Council approved the chancellor's proposal that Torstensson be instructed to invade Jutland. On receiving his orders, the Swedish commander opened negotiations for a truce with the enemy, and set out with his army for Denmark. The distance was covered with incredible speed. Christian and his people were utterly surprised when a foe which they confidently had believed was still far away, and so entangled in the Imperial lands that he could not extricate himself, suddenly appeared at their border. Although Christian had steadily pursued his dangerous policy of thwarting and irritating the Swedes, he had failed to prepare adequately for the war which his acts were certain to bring upon his country. Not only had he not put his military equipment in order, but he had failed to provide himself with a single ally. Holland might have joined him, but instead of winning the support of this strong nation by making proper concessions to it, he had incurred its anger by raising the Sound tolls on Dutch commerce. As a result, this country concluded an alliance with Sweden. Denmark herself was utterly unprepared for meeting a swift and vigorous attack such as Sweden was prepared to deliver. Jutland was therefore speedily overrun by one Swedish army, while another broke into Skåne and took possession of the greater part of this province. Torstensson now intended to transport his army by means of the allied Swedish-Dutch fleet to Seeland, but fortunately for Denmark there was one man in this crisis who did not lose his head, and that was Christian himself. Although now an old man of sixty-seven, the Danish king laboured with indefatigable energy to organize his defences by land and water. The Dutch fleet which was advancing was forced to turn back, and next Christian encountered the Swedish fleet between the island of Femern and the coast of Holstein (Kolberge Heide), where a terrific naval battle ensued (June 29, 1644). The conflict ended in a draw, but the Danish fleet succeeded in later blockading the Swedish ships in Kiel Bay. Taking advantage of a favourable wind, the Swedish fleet later managed to escape and unite with a new Dutch fleet which had arrived on the scene.

Treaty of Brömsebro.—In a new encounter between Femern and Laaland, the Danish fleet was annihilated, and Christian was forced to accept the proffered mediation of France and the Netherlands and conclude a peace with Sweden (treaty of Brömsebro, 1645), whereby Denmark ceded to Sweden the provinces of Jämtland and Härjedalen, the islands of Ösel and Gottland, and the province of Halland, the latter for only thirty years. Exemption from the Sound tolls was also extended to Sweden's Baltic possessions. The possession of Jämtland secured Sweden's control of all of Norrland; Halland's cession to Sweden really meant that the first steps had been taken towards the incorporation of the three Danish provinces on the peninsula with Sweden, and the surrender of Ösel and Gottland meant that control of the Baltic was definitely relinquished by Denmark in favour of Sweden.

The dying gasps of the Thirty Years' War.—With the Danish War at an end, the Swedes could return to the scene of conflict in Germany. Torstensson next fought his way to the very gates of Vienna, and the city would in all likelihood have fallen into his hands had not the plague decimated his ranks and compelled him to beat a hasty retreat. Utterly worn out by exertions and his body racked by disease—all through the campaigns of his later years he was carried about on a litter—Torstensson gave up the command to General Wrangel, who united his forces with those of the French general, Turenne. Together they invaded Austria, the emperor being now almost at the point of utter helplessness, unable to ward off attacks directed against the very heart of his empire. At the same time General Königsmark, at the head of a Swedish detachment, attacked Prague and managed to seize a part of the city. The Swedes here reaped a rich harvest in the form of spoils of war, chief among them being the famous Maeso-Gothic Bible of Bishop Ulfilas (p. 59). The encounter at Prague was practically the last military action of the war; by a strange twist of fate the frightful struggle which for thirty years had spread desolation over all of Europe, dragging almost every people into its vortex, ended in a sort of dying gasp in the very place where three decades before it had started as a seemingly unimportant local fracas. Utterly exhausted, the emperor finally bowed to the inevitable and agreed to the terms of the treaty of Westphalia.

Peace negotiations.—Negotiations had already been going on during five years between representatives of Sweden and the emperor at Osnabrück and between France and the emperor at Münster. Representatives from most of the German states and from Spain and Holland had also been in attendance to watch proceedings and, to the best of their ability, shape their course to the advantage of their respective countries. The deliberations had dragged on through interminable discussions, which took their tone largely from the trend of affairs on the battle-fields; the Imperialists becoming reasonable and yielding after defeats but stiff-necked and defiant as soon as news came of some military advantage gained by their forces. The power and influence of Sweden counted as the most important factor at the peace conference, but her position was considerably weakened by the inability of her two representatives to work together harmoniously for their country's interests. One of the Swedish commissioners, Johan Oxenstierna, son of the chancellor, was stubborn and vain, although an honest and patriotic man, and lacked the necessary astuteness and experience for so difficult a task; the other, Adler Salvius, the son of a commoner and disliked by the aristocratic Oxenstierna, a feeling which Salvius ardently reciprocated, was one of the most adroit diplomats of his day. He could always count on the support of Christina, who, envious of the Oxenstierna family and always resentful of the aged chancellor's influence, found great satisfaction in opposing anything that was favoured by the great statesman and his son. Sweden was in reality in better position to prolong the struggle than the emperor, and her prospects for securing favourable peace terms grew constantly brighter as the struggle went on, but Christina, moved, no doubt, in some degree by consideration of humanity, but mainly by the thought that the end of the war would mean a waning of the chancellor's prestige and power, kept on urging that negotiations be hastened and the struggle terminated. It meant little to her that thereby her country would sacrifice many advantages.

In Frederick William, Elector of Brandenburg, Sweden encountered another serious obstacle to a treaty which would give her ample compensation for her sacrifices in the war. He was firmly determined on increasing the limits of his own domains in Germany and therefore endeavoured in every way to circumvent the Swedes in their designs on German lands. After endless bickering and bargaining, the terms of the epoch-making treaty were finally given their permanent form and signed by the plenipotentiaries of the different nations.

Peace of Westphalia, 1648.—By the treaty Sweden received western Pomerania (Vor Pommern), with the islands of Rugen and Usedom, and in eastern Pomerania (Hinter Pommern), the cities of Stettin, Garz, Damm, and Gollnow, the island of Wollin, together with Wismar and the districts of Poel and Neukloster, the secularized bishoprics of Bremen and Verden, and the district of Wilshausen; she was also to receive 5,000,000 riksdaler as reimbursements for her expenses in the war. France received the coveted province of Lorraine. The Swedish delegates had firmly insisted upon a guarantee of religious freedom. They originally proposed that the year 1618 should be taken as the fixed point for determining rights to property; property taken by either Catholics or Protestants after that year to be retroceded. Instead of 1618, the year 1624 was finally agreed on. The Swedes also tried hard to procure the acknowledgment of full religious liberty in the Austrian crown lands, but only some concessions could, in this case, be gained. The rights under the religious peace of Augsburg were extended to other Protestant bodies besides the Lutheran, and in effect the settlement meant an acknowledgment of the principle of religious liberty.

Results of the war upon Sweden.—The outcome of the Thirty Years' War had a most momentous bearing upon Swedish life and policies. The hitherto insignificant state had suddenly become one of the leading powers of Europe and indisputably held the leadership among the Protestant nations. Her far-flung territory extended from the Weser River, with intermittent stretches of land along the south and east Baltic coast, almost to the White Sea, and she could collect tolls on traffic passing over nearly all rivers flowing into the Baltic. This pre-eminent position had been won, it is true, mainly by the genius of Gustavus Adolphus and of his statesmen and generals, but the remarkable unity of the Swedish people, their willingness to make every sacrifice asked of them, and their inflexible determination to carry the fight to a successful issue had been indispensable factors. It was a glorious position for the poor and hitherto obscure country to hold, but the new rôle brought with it many new tribulations and involved many serious dangers. The nation's loss of people and wealth had been enormous, the development of the country internally retarded, in spite of the government's efforts to build up industry. The government had, as stated, sold state land and mortgaged rents in order to secure revenues which were absolutely necessary for the further prosecution of the war, and for this policy there was a terrible price to pay in the form of bitter and long-continued class conflicts. With peace concluded Sweden now found herself with an enormous territory to defend, alien races to be governed and given the blessings of her own culture. Enemies on every side, Denmark, Russia, Poland, and Brandenburg, stirred by jealousy of the parvenu nation and fearing her aggressive policies and projects, were, hawk-like, watching her every move, ready to pounce upon her at any moment when she might show weakness. The task might not be an impossible one for her resources, but "there was not much margin for blundering" as an English historian, in discussing the position of Sweden after the peace had been made, aptly puts it.[9] Contact with the cultured lands of the South, and increase in the wealth of a few individuals through spoils of war and other means for securing wealth which the war had provided, meant an enrichment of Swedish culture. Interest in science, art, and education was greatly stimulated, but these benign influences were counterbalanced by the debasing and brutalizing influence of camp life and of sudden wealth in the hands of the coarse and the ignorant. Foreigners who visited Sweden soon after the conclusion of the war speak with amazement, sometimes with contempt, of the extravagant display in dress, the gluttony, and the drunkenness which then characterized social life in the land. The chasm which divided the social orders had also been greatly widened, the *bönder* especially having sunk deeper and deeper under the terrible economic burden and social stigma which weighed them down. Soon, however, they were to call for a reckoning and a readjustment in their status, and in that connection there flared up one of the most bitter social struggles in the nation's history. The Swedish state now stood at the parting of the ways:

[9] Bain, *Scandinavia*.

in one direction lay poverty and sacrifice, but also contentment, virtue, and rugged strength; in the other, wealth and power, luxury and dissipation, and, ultimately, weakness and woe.

Georg Stiernhielm.—Georg Stiernhielm (1598-1672), a robust son of the province of Dalarna, and honoured as the "father of Swedish poetry," warned his people in his great poem *Hercules* of the pitfalls which threatened, if they departed from the old and tried paths. The poem graphically tells how Lust, with her three sisters, Indolence, Sensuality, and Vanity, and a brother, Inebriation, appeared in enticing form to tempt the youth Hercules (Sweden) by glowing promises of the pleasures that awaited him if he followed her, but just as he was preparing to join the frivolous group, ready to travel with them on the path of sensuous pleasure, Dame Virtue, serious of mien and honest in speech, appeared and painted for him the misery which follows the fleeting hours of joy in lasciviousness and drunkenness. After this warning she extolled the greatness of the rewards which crown a life of sacrifice and right living.

Christina as a ruler.—As the only child of Gustavus and Maria Eleanora of Brandenburg, Christina had, by virtue of the law of succession, a clear claim to the Swedish throne. She was one of the most enigmatical individuals in all history. No doubt the strange contradictions in her personality were largely the result of heredity. From her brilliant father she had derived those personal charms, the keenness and quickness of perception, and the ardent love of intellectual pleasures that won for her the unstinted praise of the great scholars of her day; to her neurotic mother is, no doubt, to be traced her inconstancy of character, her callousness, and her contempt for the things that were most sacred to the people of her native land. Her ability to acquire scientific knowledge or to grasp the theoretical principles of government is by several contemporaries declared to have been extraordinary. Her love for art grew into a passion, and a great and splendid library which she assembled, with the old classics well represented in it, was one of her special delights. Nothing gave keener satisfaction to her inquiring soul than to hold conferences with the great scientists of her day and discuss with them the theories and discoveries in the field. The young professor at Uppsala, Rudbeck, who had many important discoveries in anatomy to his credit, and was brimful of new ideas in many fields of knowledge (p. 433), became in a sense her protégé and her purse was generously opened to support other searchers for knowledge. At her invitation, the noted philosopher, René Descartes, the founder of modern philosophy, came to Sweden and took up his abode in Stockholm in order that the queen might be instructed by him in the great truths of his science. The royal scholar and the great preceptor often, it is said, rose as early as five o'clock in the dark winter mornings in order to be less disturbed in their studies and meditations. Other foreign scholars came and Christina hoped by their aid to bring about a great cultural renaissance of her people. In the beginning of her reign, she took her official duties seriously, attending the meetings of the Council regularly in order to keep in touch with affairs both at home and abroad, and her part in the deliberations showed clear insight into government affairs as well as a determined will to make her power felt for the good of her people. She opposed and defied the nobility, whose monopoly of public offices, strengthened and extended by Oxenstierna's aristocratic tendencies, was cherished and guarded by the privileged class as an inalienable right, and when the aged chancellor protested vigorously against the appointment of Adler Salvius, a man of humble origin, she answered curtly, "I desire *capable* men in my service." Her resentment against the growing power and presumption of a small group of aristocrats may account partly for her reckless bestowal of new titles and fiefs on men who before had stood outside the charmed circle; in this way she would irritate and humiliate the arrogant members of the old families.

Character and ideals.—While the young queen thus in the beginning of her reign showed some evidence of an actual desire to give her country a good rule, certain evil tendencies in her character soon asserted themselves and brought dismay and humiliation to her people. Her most outstanding trait was an unbridled selfishness; it would be difficult to find, in all history, an individual in whom the ego ruled as supreme as in

Christina. Feelings of patriotism, a sense of obligation or of regard for the opinions of others, respect for the memory of her father—such considerations meant nothing to her, as against the gratification of her own bizarre desires. Sycophants were showered with favours as long as they would flatter her and serve her selfish interests, only to be trampled under foot with ruthless hatred and irony when her strange whims diverted her interest to someone else. For the religion of the land, in defence of which her father had given his life and the nation had poured out its blood and money until utterly exhausted, she felt nothing but contempt. More and more she felt a bitter dislike for her native land and for its poor and, in her opinion, uncouth people. The fact that this poor and uncouth people had made untold sacrifices in order to preserve the throne for her own Vasa dynasty counted for nothing in her callous soul. The exigencies of the situation demanded of the ruler a careful attention to the business of the state, especially since following the war a financial crisis that was unparalleled in its destructiveness afflicted Sweden, but the queen began to loathe the sight of official reports on the condition of the country and avoided so far as she could all conferences with her officials regarding ways and means for the proper government of the land. Soon her predominant feeling was a desire to be free from the irksome routine and escape from her tawdry surroundings into the world of luxury which she fancied as existing outside of her own poor land. Her prodigality at last knew no bounds.

Mismanagement.—Within ten years she created eighteen counts and about fifty barons. The number of noble families was more than doubled in her reign. In order to provide these privileged individuals with incomes that would enable them to live in splendour, as was befitting their new dignity, she sold or mortgaged so much crown property that it meant a loss of income to the state amounting to 1,200,000 riksdaler annually. At the death of her father the nobility were in possession of one-fourth of the land, but in 1654, when Christina renounced her crown, their holdings of the land in form of fiefs constituted one-half. In bestowing her gifts on individuals outside of the favoured few she soon began to manifest reckless extravagance; so reckless, in fact, that in certain instances grants of estates carried the provision that they were not valid in case said property had already been given by her to someone else. For part of this reckless transfer of property the regents during her minority were responsible, but for the greater part Christina alone was responsible. There is nothing in the records to indicate that the nobility ever hesitated to benefit by the queen's largesse or felt any conscientious scruples against accepting this valuable property as a gift. "When it rained blessings, everyone wished to be on hand," as one historian aptly puts it.[10]

The beginning of the bitter conflict of classes.—The bitter discontent of the lower orders, manifesting itself most vigorously as an intense resentment against the higher aristocracy, whose wealth and privileges threatened to remove the last vestige of economic and political independence on the part of the commons, resulted in a furious outbreak at a Riksdag held in 1650; the bitterness of social conflict that here had its inception makes this meeting one of the notable events in Swedish history. A series of crop failures and floods had furthermore added to the burdens of woe which oppressive taxes and the transfer of the crown's property to unworthy royal favourites had already placed upon the poor people. The Riksdag meeting of 1650 began in an atmosphere of bitter hatreds and rampant suspicions, but these feelings were not directed against the queen so much as against the nobles, who, well aware that the blow was about to descend upon their heads, were firmly united in their determination to ward it off and escape unscathed. Arrayed in a solid phalanx against the privileged class were the lower clergy, the burghers, and the *bönder*. The leaders of this group were Johannes Terserus, a learned theologian and professor at Uppsala, who later became Bishop of Linköping, and Nils Nilsson, Mayor of Stockholm. A full and clear-cut statement, mainly the handiwork of Terserus, was early laid before the Estates, and this gave not only a graphic account of the iniquities which had been practiced to the detriment of the people, but it also suggested pointedly, as a practical solution, that the property which had been bestowed upon the nobility should be returned to the state. The lower clergy

[10] Hildebrand, *Sveriges historia,* VII, p. 209.

who had their own pet grievances, such as social inferiority, paltry incomes, and a multitude of duties to be performed by them, while the incumbents of the higher ecclesiastical offices lived in luxury and ease, were naturally the best educated

Queen Christina. Painting by Bourbon

among those clamouring for a change, and they now made themselves the spokesmen of the group.

War of the classes.—The entire nation was now aroused by pamphlets which were distributed in practically every part of the land, and which violently attacked the unseemly privileges of the nobility. Preachers, forgetting their prescribed texts, thundered so fiercely and loudly against the iniquity of the higher classes that at last Christina found it necessary to warn them against the evils of political sermons. The struggle in the Riksdag took largely the form of a lively exchange of written statements, the lower orders naturally complaining that a vast amount of crown property had been bestowed on the noblemen and that other areas had, by dishonest practices, become included in the class of tax-exempt property, thus reducing the revenues of the state. Special taxes for war purposes, the statements continued, had been diverted to the use of the nobility, and the privilege of the noblemen to appoint clergy on their estates—an unjust right in itself—had been greatly abused. "We have heard," said the statement, "that in other countries the *bonde* is a serf. We fear that the same fate will befall us, who, however, are freeborn." [11] This document became the arsenal from which, in subsequent attacks on aristocratic privileges, the opposition helped themselves freely to ammunition. The nobility retorted with equally vehement statements; here they held unyieldingly to their privileges and protested vigorously against any encroachments upon their sacred rights. In this crisis the aged Oxenstierna appeared as a truly pathetic figure. He had honestly believed that the best interests of the state would be served by a strong noble class, and now he had the mortification of seeing that his policies had stirred up a tempest which threatened, with uncontrolled fury, to disrupt the nation. Although in sympathy with the demands of the lower orders, Christina could not, when the time for a definite decision came, make up her mind to enter upon a confiscation policy, as the lower orders had suggested. Instead, she managed by vague promises of a redress of grievances to get the matter postponed. Once brought forward, however, not even the royal fiat could render it quiescent.

Tired of wearing the royal crown.—One of Christina's vagaries took the form of a violent aversion to marriage. This caused serious anxiety to the members of the Council regarding the succession, and to set their troubled minds at ease she prevailed upon them to designate her cousin, Charles Gustavus,

[11] *Historiska handlingar till Skandinaviens historia,* Stockholm, 1879-1900, Vol. 22.

as her successor. Back of this act lay more than a mere desire to forestall controversy in the event of her death. Already at this time Christina had undoubtedly begun to give serious thought to the question of abdication. As early as 1651 she suggested such a course to a committee of the Riksdag, but refrained from pressing the matter further when a deputation of the Council, together with the Estates, with Oxenstierna at the head, waited on her and earnestly pleaded with her not to carry out such a strange resolve. Her determination to lay down her crown and quit Sweden became firmer, however, as the years passed and as the bitter discontent of her subjects grew and became each year more outspoken. Documents containing grave charges against her were circulated and were readily believed. The warnings of the 1650 Riksdag had gone unheeded, and mismanagement and profligacy became more flagrant at court than ever before. The expenditures for the royal court alone were in 1654 four times greater than ten years earlier. They consumed twelve per cent of the money expended for all government purposes; merely the German, French, and Italian musicians at the court cost annually 90,000 crowns, an enormous sum considering the higher purchasing value of money in those days. The queen's gifts were in value two and a half times greater than those of her father's entire reign and eight times those of the Council during her minority.

As discontent and troubles multiplied, Christina turned more and more from men who were in a position to give patriotic advice and render valuable assistance, to foreigners who undoubtedly were largely responsible for her flaunting of everything that she was expected to cherish and protect. Her confidential advisers were the French ambassador, Chanut, her French physician, Bourdelot, the Spanish ambassador, Pimentelli, the Danish adventurer and exile, Korfits Ulfeld, and a Polish exile, Radziejovski. The situation naturally seemed utterly scandalous to the Swedes. It is surmised that Chanut and the philosopher Descartes both had a part in turning her mind to Catholicism. In 1652 two Jesuits came to Stockholm with whom she discussed doctrinal questions. One day she surprised them with the statement that she was ready to embrace Catholicism. One of the Jesuits then proceeded with all haste to

Rome in order to bring confidential information to the Curia that a startling and most welcome accession might soon be expected to the ranks of the ancient Church. Not because of any deep conviction that the Catholic faith was more in accordance with truth than the Lutheran had Christina made her decision, but because the former appealed more strongly to her æsthetic sense. Furthermore, Christina dearly loved everything that was startling; nothing appealed to her so much as the theatrical. And what a spectacular move it would be, how the world would stand aghast at her strange deed, how the Catholic princes and potentates would acclaim her, the incomparable heroine, if she, the daughter of Gustavus Adolphus, the arch-enemy of the ancient faith, she, the ruler of the leading Protestant country in the world, would forswear her Lutheran religion and embrace Catholicism. The thought of such an unprecedented theatrical rôle evidently dazzled her.

The abdication.—The queen's determination to lay down the sceptre being at last absolutely fixed, a Riksdag was called to assemble at Uppsala in the summer of 1654 to receive her abdication and elect Charles Gustavus her cousin, as her successor. The session of the Riksdag was filled with dramatic incidents, for while the queen's decision to turn Catholic was not known as yet except to her few foreign advisers, her resolution to lay aside the royal regalia and leave the country filled her countrymen with utter dismay. The English ambassador at the Swedish court in this period, Whitelocke, has given a gripping account of the strange scenes that were enacted.[12] The earnest appeals of Oxenstierna, the Council, and the clergy failed utterly to create even a flicker of sentiment in her adamantine heart. If she was touched even for a fleeting moment it was when a plain *bonde,* dressed in homespun and with ponderous spiked shoes, advanced and spoke to her in plain and sincere words: "O Lord God, Madam, what do you mean to do? It troubles us to hear you speak of forsaking those that love you so well as we do.—Continue in your gears, good Madam, and be the forehorse as long as you live, and we will help you the best we can to bear your burden. Your father

[12] Whitelocke, Bulstrode, *A Journal of the Swedish Embassy,* London, 1855.

was an honest gentleman and a good king and very stirring in the world; we obeyed him and loved him as long as he lived, and you are his own child and have governed us very well, and we love you with all our hearts—as long as you live we are not willing to part with you, and therefore I pray, Madam, do not part with us." Then the *bonde,* without further ceremony, stepped up to the queen, seized her hand which he shook heartily and kissed it twice or thrice, then turning from her he pulled out a soiled handkerchief to wipe the tears from his eyes. It was a strange sight, at which the foreign diplomats who were present from Italy, Spain, France, and other countries marvelled, for in their countries a *bonde* would not even have gained admission to so august an assembly, let alone have the privilege and the courage to speak his mind freely. Nothing could, however, move the queen from her resolve, and in a formal act she transferred the regalia of the royal office to Charles Gustavus, after which she precipitately left the city. She had demanded and secured for herself a most liberal allowance from the Swedish state and when she left Stockholm she carried with her an enormous collection of paintings, books, jewels, and other valuables, some of which were her private property, most of it, however, the property of the state. Among other priceless treasures which followed her out of the land was the famous Codex Argenteus, or Bible of Ulfilas, which she either sold or gave away in Holland, and which only by a most fortunate circumstance was later restored to the library at Uppsala (p. 432). Feeling now as free and as jubilant as a released prisoner, Christina precipitately left her native land, going first to the Spanish Netherlands, where she stayed a year, and then proceeding towards Rome, which she had selected as her future home. At Innsbruck she publicly cast aside her Lutheran faith and was formally accepted into the Catholic Church, taking the new name of Christina Alexandra.

Christina's disappointments.—The story of her life after this is a tragic recital of disillusionments and disappointments. At first she was greeted by a boundless enthusiasm in the Catholic lands. The Pope had expected to find her a saint, but soon discovered that she was a horribly emancipated and bizarre woman, who, among other things, laughed openly at his cardinals. Her pretensions knew no bounds: thus if merely an archbishop and not a cardinal officiated at ceremonies at which she was present, she flew into a passion and made a disgraceful scene. From the scions of the proud Roman society she demanded obeisance as though she had been their queen. They endured her pretensions, smiled upon and flattered her, until they found that she had no money; then they knew her no more. Her financial plight was chronic and she became a plague to Pope and Catholic princes alike, who found it impossible to satisfy her incessant appeals for money. She became involved in several fantastic diplomatic schemes, only to receive rebuffs; twice she returned to Sweden, first after the death of Charles Gustavus in 1660, when she was angling to get the Swedish crown again. Instead of gaining this prize, she was compelled by the Riksdag to renew her renunciation of 1654 and when she came again in 1667, she was curtly told that permission would not be granted her to enter Stockholm if she persisted in celebrating Catholic mass. In anger she turned back at Norrköping and hurried with furious speed from the country. Only one man seems ever to have won her affection and respect; namely, Cardinal Azzolino, who helped to bring some order into her chaotic finances and in other ways brought repose to her soul. The court circles of Europe were more than once shocked by new tales of the eccentric doings of "the nomadic queen." Her steward Monaldesco was murdered by her order because she suspected him of treason; the appeals for mercy which the victim, as well as the captain of the guard and a friar, frantically directed to her made not the slightest impression on her callous soul. In only one respect did she live worthily, and that was in her devotion to art, literature, and science, for the enrichment of which she was willing to expend generously of her brilliant powers as well as of her funds. She died in 1689 and is buried at St. Peter's in Rome. "Just the same she is the daughter of the great Gustavus," mused Oxenstierna once, a few months after Christina's departure from Sweden. "*E donna*"—"She is a woman," the Pope is reported to have said laconically with a shrug of his shoulders, on the occasion of one of her strange actions, and that goes a long way in explaining her queer behaviour. She was a woman who had never learned to put the least restraint upon herself. The moralists can find in Christina a perfect example of the results of unbridled selfishness.

Chapter XV

THE RECKONING WITH POLAND AND DENMARK

Charles Gustavus.—While Christina by her renunciation of both the crown and the faith of her fatherland seemed to play the discreditable rôle of a traitor, much can be forgiven her, for by her abdication she gave way to a prince who, by reason of brilliant powers as a statesman and warrior, was to lift Sweden to the highest pinnacle of power and influence to which the country was ever to attain. The new ruler was one of the ablest in a long line of exceptionally talented and high-minded sovereigns, and had he not unfortunately become involved in a series of wars which occupied the greater part of his brief reign, but instead had kept to the task of bringing order into the economic and social life of the country, a task to which he first devoted himself with signal success, his reign would, no doubt, have gone down in Swedish history as one most fruitful of beneficent reforms.

The new king had been most carefully trained by his parents, John Casimir, Count Palatinate of Zweibrucken, and Catherine, a sister of Gustavus Adolphus, both of whom were sensible and high-minded people, to regard service to the state as his first great duty. The father had served honestly and with marked ability in the fiscal administration of Sweden, and through him the son had received an insight into the chaotic condition of the country's fiscal affairs as well as its causes. The love of economy which the father helped to foster in him had been further strengthened by his thrifty mother's example and admonition. In the larger field of politics and international affairs, Charles had had as guide and mentor no less an authority than Oxenstierna himself. When the time came for him to enter military life a high command in the army was offered him, but he declined this and instead became a man in the ranks under Torstensson. His promotion was rapid, due not only to royal favour, but mainly to proved ability, and the end of the Thirty Years' War found him at the head of all the Swedish armies in the field. As a member of the Swedish Commission at the Execution Congress of Nurnberg, following the treaty of Westphalia, he had found an exceptional opportunity for studying the intricacies of European diplomacy at close range.

The young prince had constantly been in an embarrassing position at home, distrusted and opposed as he generally was by Oxenstierna, who at first had suspected that he coveted the throne for himself. As a young man he had been a suitor for Christina's hand, and his love seems at one time to have kindled a spark of reciprocal feeling in her, but soon she made it known that she would never marry him or anyone else. When next the queen announced her intention to abdicate, designating Charles as her successor, and she at the earnest solicitation of the chancellor and the Council had been prevailed upon to desist from taking this drastic step, the prince's position had become more embarrassing than ever, since he was naturally suspected of being involved in all the opposition to the queen which was now beginning to seethe. He therefore discreetly withdrew to the island of Öland, where he lived in seclusion, far removed from the intrigues of the court, until Christina's abdication called him forth and placed him on the Swedish throne. He was then in his thirty-second year.

Shortly after becoming king, Charles Gustavus[1] married Hedvig Eleanor of Holstein-Gottorp, a union which politically was most unfortunate in so far as Denmark, always hostile to the young queen's native country, became more nervous than ever from fear that Sweden would now have a new and dependable ally against her. The situation which confronted Charles at his accession was truly appalling. The financial debacle of Christina's reign had left the country practically bankrupt, and as a result of the gross inequalities in taxes for the state the lower orders were arrayed against the nobility more bitterly than ever. All the factors which ordinarily are potent in kindling the flames of civil war seemed to be present. Endowed with insight and practical good sense, Charles understood from the beginning that radical measures were abso-

[1] In English known as Charles X.

lutely necessary to bring about a proper readjustment and that these must take the form of a decided curtailment of the privileges of the nobility. Possibly the fact that his own family had been constantly made to feel the envy and suspicion of the Swedish nobility made it somewhat easier for the king to make up his mind.

His firmness and wisdom.—He was, however, a big-calibred man who could rise superior to all personal feelings or party preferences. The aged Oxenstierna was showered with honours, an evidence of generosity and high-mindedness which the chancellor keenly appreciated and endeavoured to reciprocate by doing his utmost, as long as he lived, to help in bringing order out of the financial chaos. To the very last the great chancellor served his country unstintedly. In one of his conferences with the king he was suddenly stricken with a severe illness and died some days later in his seventy-first year (1654). Partly in appreciation of the father's services, but mainly as a recognition of his own splendid worth, Charles now appointed his son, Erik, chancellor, and the relations between the two young men became very similar to those which had bound Gustavus Adolphus and Axel Oxenstierna so closely together.

The first great task to which king and chancellor bent their energies was the economic readjustment. It was the firm conviction of Charles that Swedish power and prestige abroad could be maintained only by force of arms, but he also knew that the unity in counsel and spirit of sacrifice which were absolute prerequisites for the nation's military effectiveness, must be lacking as long as the lower orders were being ruthlessly exploited by the privileged classes. The ideal state, to Charles's mind, was a strong monarchy where the king stood united with the people against aristocratic privileges and injustice. Charles began his economic reform by sending away most of the servants and parasites who had previously infested the court, and ordering many of the councillors to proceed to the rural districts and there attend strictly to administrative duties. In conformity with the firmly established practice that every important action in which the nation's interest was involved must be taken in conjunction with the representatives of the four orders, he summoned a Riksdag the year after his accession to the throne. Two momentous decisions were made by this assembly: war was declared on Poland and the alienated crown property was ordered restored to the crown by the process of confiscation. The resolution to begin war against Poland was speedily passed, but the question of confiscation of the alienated crown lands provoked a struggle which became memorable in Swedish history.

Reckoning with the lords.—In contrast to what happened at the session of 1650, at which time the lower Estates led the fight against the privileged class, it was now the king himself who suggested and forced action against those who through Christina's reckless prodigality had come into possession of crown lands. He was, however, determined to extend the investigation beyond Christina's reign and subject the whole economic situation to a searching inquiry. An agreement was speedily reached in the Riksdag that all so-called indispensable lands should be returned, *i.e.* forest lands necessary for the mining industry, farms on which soldiers lived, lands furnishing fuel, building material, game, grain, and other articles for the royal household, and likewise all the territory in Norrland, Österbotten, Åland, Dalarna, and the greater part of the central and southern provinces, except Västergötland and Östergötland, which, according to a law of 1641, had been designated as crown land. Contrary to both old and new laws, Christina had with reckless abandon given away so much of these properties that little remained to the crown.

The beginning of the confiscatory policy.—The reasonableness of the king's suggestion that these classes of property should be restored was quite readily admitted by the nobility, but when next the king unexpectedly thrust a new proposition upon them this had much the same effect as an exploding bombshell. He proposed nothing less than a payment by the holders of all crown lands of an annual contribution of 200,000 silver dalers, until the income from the confiscated property yielded this amount, or else that they surrender one-fourth of all the land which had come into their possession since 1633. The income from this source was estimated at 600,000 silver dalers.[2] The nobles forthwith rejected the first proposition as a violation of the essential right of the aristocracy to be exempt from taxation; they would rather surrender a definite amount in order that the remaining part would be intact for all time. In the opposition to the proposition, a schism in the ranks of the privileged class itself now appeared, for the usurpations of

Charles X

the richer nobles and Christina's lavish favours upon them had aroused the bitter resentment not only of the unprivileged classes but still more so, if that were possible, of the less favoured members of their own order. These two antagonistic aristocratic groups now became the chief contestants in the fight which centred around a proposal for a graduated scale

[2] Silver and copper coins were both in circulation. By a royal order in 1643, it was stipulated that one of the former should be equivalent in value to two and a half of the latter. Values fluctuated, but in 1681 a silver daler had the approximate value of two crowns, or somewhat more than fifty cents.

in the process of relinquishments, it being suggested as a reasonable rule by the less favoured nobles that those who had received the larger gifts should be compelled to return a proportionately larger amount. The discussion on this point became very acrimonious and ended with a victory for the more exclusive and privileged group. The lower orders had stood aside while the two aristocratic factions figuratively had browbeaten one another; they felt secure in the conviction that their interests were safe in the hands of the king. They looked upon the measures already agreed upon as but the first step towards a radical curtailment of aristocratic wealth and privilege. When, therefore, the resolution already sanctioned by the nobility was found to contain a postscriptum that this settlement should be binding for all subsequent time, they refused point-blank to agree to it, the *bönder* declaring that if they did so they would run the risk of being beaten to death on their return home. The bitter social antagonisms which had assumed such menacing forms in the Riksdag meeting of 1650 again appeared. "There is danger," said the chancellor, "that the Riksdag may go to pieces, as has happened in Poland, but hitherto such a thing has been unheard of in Sweden." The king now took a hand in affairs and he did this in a manner which clearly revealed that a resolute man was at the helm again. When the Council, naturally the bulwark of the richer group, requested him to use his royal authority to squelch the lower orders, he simply countered by demanding that it furnish him with the arguments by which he would be able to convince the lower orders that right was on the side of the privileged class; he would not use his royal authority for the purpose of silencing anyone, nor could he favour, he said, one class more than the other. When one of the most zealous of the great lords still persisted in prating against the alleged unseemly behaviour of the lower orders, the king lost his temper, and, arising from his throne, exclaimed, "I can see what you are driving at. If you want to persist in this course, then I must take care that my own and the nation's rights are preserved." "This was," as a historian has said, "one of the proudest moments in the history of the Swedish monarchy." The firmness of the king and his words of warning, the import of which was well understood, broke all opposition, and the four orders now agreed to a proposition that a "Reduktion" Commission be created to have charge of the confiscation procedure in accordance with the act passed by the Riksdag.

Reasons for deciding on war with Poland.—The proposal to begin war on the old enemy, Poland, met with only slight opposition. It was a momentous decision, the consequences of which no one could even vaguely foretell. The reasons back of this sudden resolve to attack a nation with which Sweden at the time was at peace and which at the time did not threaten her have been much debated by historians and many different and at times diametrically opposite views have been expressed. Some historians have found justification for the resolve in the circumstance that once having begun to occupy territory across the seas, Sweden had no choice, if she wanted to protect herself, but to advance still farther. The evidence tends to show that this was the honest conviction of Charles. Sweden's conquests had stirred up jealousy and enmity on every hand, and only by showing her superiority as a military power was she able, so it was believed, to stay the hands of her enemies, who were ready to spring upon her. Later events certainly tended to prove that these assumptions were no mere fantastic notions. Others have seen in this war but the inevitable outcome of the young king's boundless ambition and unrestrained eagerness to display his brilliant military powers. To those who have taken this view, Charles has appeared as merely a military adventurer, who for the sake of his own glory was willing to plunge his country into a bloody war. Whatever may have been the motives, the effect of the attack on Poland was to stir up the smouldering fires of war over all of Europe and to intensify everywhere the bitter antagonism against Sweden; her rôle as a leading power of Europe became seriously jeopardized and only the genius of the young king saved the nation from catastrophe.

The situation was rendered tense by suspicions. Sweden had indeed some good reasons for beginning a war on Poland, for the latter's policy towards her had been exceedingly provocative. She had stubbornly persisted in her refusal to acknowledge the right of the Vasa family to the Swedish throne, and attempts to convert the existing truce into a permanent peace had failed because of Polish opposition. A Polish delegate was reported to have protested vigorously to Christina against the project to make Charles king, and in other ways this man had made himself so offensive that Oxenstierna had found it necessary to reprimand him. Later in that same year Sweden's legate to Poland reported that the Polish king, while willing to acknowledge Charles as king, nevertheless refused to relinquish his legal rights to the Swedish throne. The relations between the two countries were, however, not any more strained than they had been continuously since Sigismund's deposition in 1599, and an amicable settlement could have been made if the parties to the controversy had been the least inclined to seek a peaceable solution. The danger of a Polish attack was greatly minimized by the chronic internal dissensions which ultimately ruined the nation, and it was, no doubt, the realization of the weakness of the traditional foe rather than fear for the safety of his own country that prompted the Swedish king to begin war. At this very time, unfortunate Poland was passing through one of her worst social conflicts, and the king, John Casimir, second son of Sigismund, was unable to calm the storm; the state appeared to be completely falling to pieces. In 1654 Poles, Cossacks, Tatars, and Russians were all involved in struggles in the unhappy land. The Russians marched into Lithuania and threatened to take possession of all of Poland. The situation has been seized upon by the apologists of Charles as furnishing an explanation of, if not a justification for, the king's determination to attack Poland at this juncture. Other countries were rushing in to seize rich spoils for themselves and unless Sweden also made haste she would be left empty-handed. The Russian invasion also placed the Swedish possessions, Esthonia and Livonia, in imminent danger of being overrun by the enemy. It was a time when nations were involved in a wild scramble for territory, and the struggle for political and military advantage and power was little impelled by idealistic motives. The statement of an historian[3] that "he (Charles) contributed, more than any other contemporary diplomatist, to lower the political morality of his age" appears wholly unjustified. No doubt

[3] Bain, *Scandinavia,* p. 232.

the reign of Charles X showed marked imperialistic tendencies, but it should be pointed out that it is the only reign in the history of the country of which this can justly be said. It should be remembered, too, that Charles was a contemporary of such unscrupulous statesmen as Richelieu, Mazarin, Louis XIV, Frederick III of Denmark, and Frederick William, "the Great Elector" of Brandenburg.

Plans of the campaign.—The Swedish plans for the war in Poland contemplated an advance into the land by way of Russia and Livonia. Within a few weeks after war began, Charles had pressed forward with his army as far as Warsaw and John Casimir had been compelled to flee from his country. From Warsaw Charles advanced to Cracow, which after a most heroic defence was finally surrendered to the Swedes by the capable and patriotic Polish general, Czarniecki. The successes of the Swedes had, however, set the Elector of Brandenburg in motion. It was his intention at this juncture to seize West Prussia, but Charles turned northward with his army and forced him to conclude a treaty with Sweden, by the terms of which he agreed that East Prussia should be placed under Swedish suzerainty; the elector furthermore promised to send auxiliary troops to Charles.

Polish resistance.—At the very moment when the Swedish king felt absolutely secure in Poland, swift changes came and he soon found himself fighting desperately to extricate himself from a situation which threatened to involve him in utter ruin. Charles's sudden attack upon Poland and the imminent danger of national dissolution had caused a tremendous reaction among its people, and soon all sections and classes were afire with patriotic sentiment. A frenzied determination to drive out the invader now animated the Poles, and the conflict became a holy war against the heretic, in which the priests fanned the patriotic fervour of the people to fever-heat. John Casimir returned and Charles set out towards the south to break up the insurrection, but soon found himself involved in futile and senseless marches, now hither, now thither, in an effort to get a chance to give the enemy a knockout blow; the latter, however, kept discreetly out of his reach. By sudden attacks on the flanks and in the rear of the Swedish detachments, and by laying waste the country before the invaders, they harassed Charles until he was driven to utter distraction. The Swedish army melted away until only one-third of the original force remained, and had it not been for the superior military genius of the king, his dwindling divisions would inevitably have been compelled to surrender. In this dilemma, Charles was forced to secure the support of the Elector of Brandenburg, even though the cost of such support was great. That calculating ruler had with genuine satisfaction watched the mounting difficulties of the Swedish king, and was now willing to come to his assistance, but only in return for the promise of Charles to acquiesce in his seizure of Polish territory. Charles had no choice but to agree to pay the price, whereupon the Swedish and the Brandenburg forces were united. With an army of 18,000 men, Charles and the elector now advanced against the larger Polish-Tatar army, which had taken its position in an entrenched camp near Warsaw. A great battle, which raged for three days, ended in a complete victory for the allies, and in the flight and dissolution of the Polish army. The genius of the Swedish king as a military strategist was the main factor in achieving this victory. The results of the victory were, however, practically *nil* as far as Charles was concerned, for he was too weak to follow up his advantage, and the elector refused to advance farther south. In the meantime the defenceless Swedish possessions in Ingria, Carelia, and Livonia had been overrun by the Russians, who brought terrible misery upon the unfortunate inhabitants of these provinces. Charles's situation in Poland grew increasingly desperate and the world began to wonder how he would be able to extricate himself with honour from his most awkward predicament. Escape came to him when Denmark, thinking that the time was opportune for an attack upon his land, forthwith declared war. "I am saved," exclaimed Charles, when, to his infinite relief, news came to him of Denmark's belligerent move; now he had a good excuse for withdrawing from Poland. A three years' truce was concluded with Russia and the Swedish army was ready for a new venture.

Why Denmark declared war.—The fateful decision of Denmark to begin war against Sweden had been frivolously made when the latter appeared so inextricably involved in the Polish campaign that there seemed to be no possibility for her to defend her own territory. The long-awaited moment had come, so the Danish king, Frederick III, thought, for regaining what had been lost by the treaty of Brömsebro and thus wipe out all humiliations which had been suffered in the past. Frederick, who in 1648 had succeeded his father, Christian IV, after having first agreed to further curtailment of the royal power in favour of the nobility, was a well-meaning man of good education, but endowed with only mediocre ability; he was especially lacking in the insight and shrewdness which a statesman, particularly in those days of sharp practices in the diplomatic game, sorely needed. Unfortunately for both king and country, Denmark did not possess one statesman of ability at a time when such aggressive leaders as Charles X, the Great Elector, Cromwell, Mazarin, and Jan de Witt were pitting their keen wits against one another, generally with very little regard for the postulates of ethical standards. The Danish queen, Sophia Amalie, was ambitious and wilful, anxious that her husband should vindicate the authority of the crown against the nobility; she was suspected, no doubt justly, of being one of the most active individuals at the court in fomenting the war spirit.

When Charles had marshalled his forces prior to the beginning of the Polish campaign, the Danes had for a moment feared that they were the ones who must meet the attack, and they had therefore felt greatly relieved when he plunged into Poland instead. Swedish victories in this quarter, it was feared, however, would certainly work to the detriment of Denmark, and be followed by further Swedish embargoes on the eastern Baltic trade. The Dutch statesmen were also watching Sweden's progress with deep concern, and keeping closely in touch with Denmark, since occasion for their joint action against Charles might at any time arise. The national uprising in Poland and the increasing anti-Swedish sentiment of the Dutch had a decided influence in fostering the war spirit among the Danes, and when therefore a Dutch fleet appeared in the Baltic in the summer of 1656 they welcomed it with loud expressions of joy. A little later the two powers came to a formal agreement regarding their joint policy in opposition to Sweden. From other directions came encouragement to the Danes to strike at Sweden, now that the time seemed opportune. The czar, having already begun war on the latter country by invading Ingria, sent a legate to Denmark to promise co-operation, and the Spanish minister at Copenhagen, acting in behalf of the emperor, contributed his part to the game of intrigue by urg-

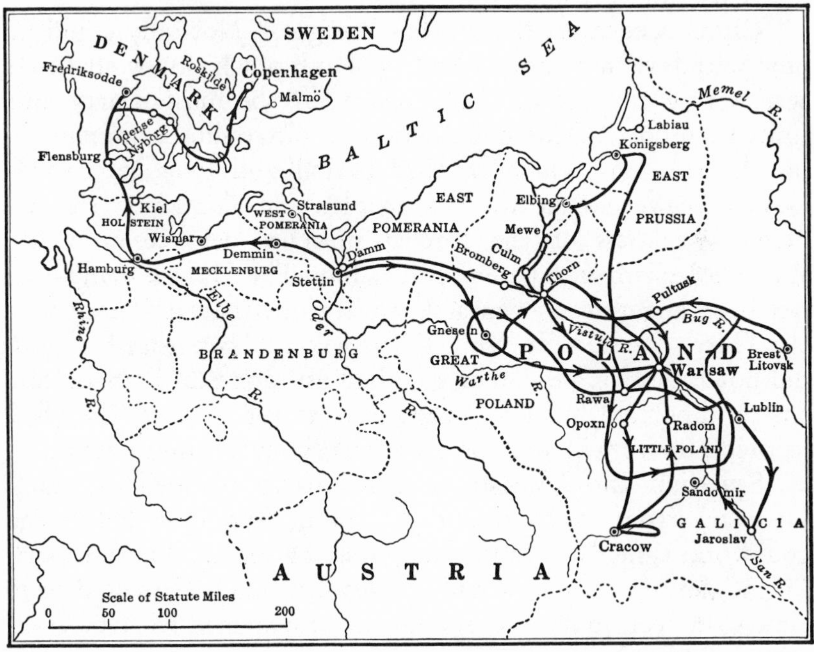

The campaigns of Charles X in Poland and Denmark

ing an attack upon Sweden. The victory of the combined Swedish-Brandenburg army at Warsaw had caused the Danish king to pause for a moment in his anti-Swedish moves, but as it became apparent that the victory had not materially improved Charles's position, his determination to attack the ancient foe became inflexible, even though the Swedish king, by guaranteeing the Dutch certain trade privileges in the Baltic, had managed to win them to his side. A promise by the emperor that he would send military aid removed all this hesitation from the mind of Frederick and on June 1, 1657, a declaration of war was issued. Being unprepared for war, and with no allies, but merely vague promises on which to depend, this was a fateful step for the nation to take. Under the circumstances, it was reckless, indeed, to attack the leading military nation of the day, at the head of which stood one of the ablest warriors of history; the Danes were soon to rue the day when they made their decision. The news of Denmark's resolve to enter the war did not come as a surprise to Charles, who already had his plans well matured.

Charles escapes from a bad tangle.—Not only could he now withdraw honourably from Poland, but he knew that in a war with Denmark he could count on the most hearty and united support of his own nation, a distressing commentary on the relations which in that period and long afterwards existed between two kindred peoples. He also knew the inherent weakness of the Danish military defences and the enemy's lack of competent leadership. The Danish army had not been engaged in even a skirmish since the early period of the Thirty Years' War, while Charles could boast that his army did not have a single soldier who had not gone through at least thirty important battles; "through constant victories they had learned how to win and had forgotten how to suffer defeat."

Swedish and Danish plans.—Charles planned to attack Denmark from the south and strike a decisive blow before she could find time to organize her forces, or the aid which Russia, Poland, and the emperor had promised to send her would have time to appear on the scene. The struggle opened with a serious strategic blunder by the Danes. Their fleet proceeded towards Danzig, intending to seize the Swedish fleet, which they assumed was stationed there in readiness to carry the Swedish king and army across the sea to their own country. Frederick himself accompanied the squadron in order to be present in person and witness the discomfiture of his antagonist, but when he arrived at Danzig he learned with consternation that the Swedish army had already left Poland and was marching overland towards the west, evidently intending to attack Denmark from the south. Certain that Charles would meet with serious delay in getting out of Poland, Frederick had sent the main part of his own forces westward to seize Bremen and take possession of Swedish territory in that section. In the meantime the Swedish army marched westward through Pomerania with unprecedented speed. After posting Swedish garrisons at strategic points in West Prussia, Charles left Bramberg on July 26, 1657, with the main army, and only three weeks after his departure from Prussia he was ready to lead his forces into Holstein. By the king's side was a group of generals who ranked among the greatest military leaders of the day, and accompanying him was also Korfits Ulfeld, the renegade Danish nobleman, son-in-law of Christian IV, who in order to wreak vengeance on his enemies in Denmark, especially the king, had turned traitor and joined the Swedish ranks. In possession of full information regarding Danish plans and disposition of military forces, Ulfeld was in a position to render valuable services to Charles. The Danish troops which could be assembled to meet the invader fled panic-stricken before the advance of the Swedish army, part of them taking refuge in Bremen and other contingents in Fredriksodde, the fortress which commanded the passage between Jutland and the Danish islands. All of Jutland was speedily occupied by the Swedes, Fredriksodde was now depended on to prevent the transport of Swedish troops from Jutland to the islands, but in a fierce attack by the invaders led by General Wrangel, a veteran of the Thirty Years' War, the place was taken, together with garrison, guns, and valuable stores. Thus one of the main obstacles to the Swedish advance towards Charles's objective, Copenhagen, had been removed. With the Danish realization that a national calamity had been suffered was mingled a feeling of intense anger and deep humiliation, since commander and officers, all members of the noble class, had shown shameless incompetency and cowardice in the defence of the fortress.

In spite of his temporary victory at Fredriksodde, the situation still gave Charles much anxiety. In January the emperor, the Elector of Brandenburg, and the King of Poland entered into a definite alliance against him and were preparing to send an army of 23,000 men to Denmark's assistance. Under these circumstances Charles yearned for nothing more than an opportunity to deliver a decisive blow at once. The Swedish army now entered upon a series of exploits that for sheer daring find few, if any, parallels in military history. After consulting with his staff, Charles on January 9, 1658, decided to transport his army over the ice from the mainland to the island of Fyen. The possibility of being able to make the passage by this route appeared extremely remote, but now nature came to his assistance. About the middle of the month intensely cold weather set in, and meteorological observations and measurements of the ice on the Little Belt, the sound between Jutland and Fyen, now became an important occupation of the Swedish generals.

Passage of the Little Belt.—January 30th being a clear and bitterly cold day, the entire Swedish army of 12,000 men boldly set out on a dangerous march over the broad expanse of ice beneath which moved a strong current, thus making the frozen surface extremely treacherous, and by daybreak Brandsö, a small island lying about midway between Jutland and Fyen, was reached. On Fyen the Swedes saw in the distance a Danish army drawn up in battle formation, but as Danish mobilization had not as yet been completed and the Danish commander, believing that the Swedes would not attempt the passage at this point, had concentrated his forces at the narrowest point of the Little Belt, he had only a force of 4,000 men with which to oppose the enemy. The latter did not hesitate to advance. At a point midway between Brandsö and Fyen, the Swedish horsemen dismounted where the ice was weakest and scattered over the ice as much as possible, each man leading his horse. Charles made the passage riding in a sled which he left as land was approached. No sooner had he mounted a horse and ridden towards the front than the ice under the sled broke and horse and sled disappeared in the deep. At another point the ice broke under two squadrons, which disappeared in the watery depths. At the sight of this the Swedish soldiers began to waver, but Charles quieted all fears by boldly riding to the very edge of the opening of the ice, after which he placed himself at the front of his forces as they advanced. The small Danish force was soon overcome and, with the exception of a few hundred men, became prisoners of war. In a short time all of Fyen fell into Swedish hands.

The utterly unexpected advance of the Swedish army had naturally caused consternation in Copenhagen, and already on February 3, Frederick opened negotiations with Charles through the English ambassador, Meadowe, with a view of agreeing on a truce. Charles answered that he was willing at any time to begin parleys for peace under the mediation of England and France, but to a truce he would not agree. As soon as Fyen was reached Charles had, in fact, decided on a new venture far more hazardous than even the one through which he and his army had just successfully passed; he now contemplated nothing less than the bringing of his entire army from Fyen over the intervening Great Belt to Seeland and to Copenhagen itself, which was utterly defenceless. To achieve this, it was decided to lay the course via the islands Langeland, Laaland, and Falster. Charles's daring engineer, Erik Dahlberg, whose diary is one of the important sources of information regarding the stirring episodes of these days, was untiring in taking measurements of the ice, and on February 4 he reported to his royal master that it would be strong enough to carry the army across. The king, according to Dahlberg's account, became jubilant at this news and exclaimed, "Now, brother Frederick, we'll talk to one another in good Swedish." Charles and Dahlberg now hastened to Wrangel's headquarters, but just then ominous signs of a coming thaw appeared. Wrangel opposed the venture with all his might as being utterly foolhardy, and when shortly the king left to retire for the night the general poured out his wrath on the head of Dahlberg because he had tempted the king with such an insane proposition. Charles, however, could not get the matter out of his mind and soon sent for Dahlberg to inquire further of him regarding the possibility of making the passage in safety. Dahlberg, whose unshakable confidence in the feasibility of the venture was based not on mere assumptions but on accurate scientific measurements and observations, replied that he knew that the ice would hold, even if 300,000 men were to march across; he stood ready to risk his own head on the venture.

Passage of the Great Belt.—Charles then gave orders for the army to march down onto the ice and advance on Langeland. The Frenchman Terlon who accompanied the Swedish army on this memorable march later declared it to have been "a terrible experience to march in the night over the frozen sea, where the tramping of the horses thawed the snow so that the water on the ice was a yard deep." On February 6 the longest and most dangerous stretch, that between Langeland and Laaland, fourteen kilometres long, was negotiated without any serious mishap, and soon the entire Swedish army stood on Seeland with the road open before it to Copenhagen. The Danish king, who, relying upon the promises of his allies and in the belief that Charles was caught in a quagmire in Poland, so rashly had rushed into the war, was now forced to sue for peace. Tactlessly and with reprehensible rudeness towards a beaten foe, Charles appointed the Danish traitor and arch-enemy of Frederick, Korfits Ulfeld, to serve on the Swedish commission to which was entrusted the task of formulating peace terms. In the first flush of victory Charles and his advisers intended to take drastic measures and incorporate all of Denmark with Sweden, thus bringing its status as an independent and sovereign state to an end, but the presence of both the English and French ambassadors in his camp was a warning that he must not go too far.

Treaty of Roskilde.—The formation of an alliance against Sweden by the emperor, Brandenburg, Poland, and Russia served to further accentuate this warning. The Swedes therefore felt it the part of wisdom to reduce their demands, but even at that they now made the greatest and most valuable territorial gain in their history (treaty of Roskilde, 1658). Denmark was forced to cede unconditionally to Sweden the provinces of Skåne, Halland, and Blekinge, the island of Bornholm, the districts of Bohuslän and Throndhjem in Norway, and besides agree to transfer to Sweden 2000 cavalry and 2000 infantry, renounce all anti-Swedish alliances, pledge herself to remain in steadfast friendship with Sweden, co-operate with her to prevent all hostile warships from passing through the Sound and the Belt, exempt Swedish vessels even when carrying foreign goods from tolls of every kind, and restore to Korfits Ulfeld all the estates and dignities of which he had been deprived. Finally it was stipulated that the Duke of Holstein should receive a small indemnity, according to a special agreement between him and the Danish king. These were hard terms for Denmark and it is not to be wondered at that one of the Danish commissioners exclaimed, as he was about to affix his signature to the document, "Oh, that I did not know how to write!" Events had thus led to a situation which no one some time before could have foreseen; two years earlier Charles had set out for Poland intending to settle old scores with that country, and here he found himself dictating a drastic peace to Sweden's neighbour in the South and wresting from her the very provinces concerning which there had been contention almost constantly since the time of Magnus Eriksson. With Skåne, Blekinge, and Halland added to Sweden her natural boundaries were attained. The value of the accession may be inferred from the fact that within these provinces now dwell one-fourth of the population of Sweden. Before the treaty of Roskilde she was almost entirely excluded from the North Sea and entirely so from the Sound. "A younger generation," says Geijer, "finds difficulty in picturing to itself the condition of its country when Blekinge, Skåne, Halland, and Bohuslän were not Swedish, when Sweden was excluded from the Sound and almost entirely so from the North Sea. It meant an entire age of darkness, weakness, and barbarism, and isolation from Europe; it meant that all of the early Swedish expeditions of conquest had taken their course eastward."

The ratification of the treaty of Roskilde was followed by a remarkable demonstration by the Danes in honour of their brave and victorious kinsmen. At the invitation of Frederick, Charles visited the Danish court in Fredericksborg Castle, although he was warned that treachery might be afoot, and splendid banquets were held at which Swedes and Danes vied with one another in heaping compliments upon the late antagonist. Even Dahlberg, to whom more than to any one else, with the exception of the king himself, must go the credit for the Swedish victory, was warmly greeted by Frederick. The high-spirited Danish queen, however, was not so polite. As Dahlberg relates in his diary: "She glared at me and surely did not wish me anything good."

Charles renews the war on Denmark.—Not a long time was to pass after the last toast had been drunk at Fredericksborg Castle in celebration of the signing of the Roskilde treaty before Europe was startled by the intelligence that Charles had a second time set his armies in motion against Denmark, evidently intending this time to go the full length and wipe the country from the map of Europe. For thus renewing the war and throwing himself upon an apparently defenceless nation with whom he had just concluded a treaty of peace, Charles has been severely blamed by Swedish and Danish historians alike; by the latter his act has been judged a shameful violation of a solemn pact, and as an evidence of a most sinister design against their country; by the former as being not only a dishonourable violation of a solemn pact, but also as a fatal diplomatic and military blunder.

Reasons for renewing the war.—It is, however, not very difficult to understand by what mental processes Charles was induced to decide on a new offensive against his recent foe. Even though the desire for peace made itself strongly felt among the people of Sweden after Roskilde, the situation forced Charles to continue on a war footing. Poland, Russia, Brandenburg, the emperor, and the Netherlands were still his active foes and he clearly realized that any sign of weakness by his country would be the signal for an attack likely to result in the seizure of Swedish territory on the other side of the Baltic. It was the king's intention, therefore, to strike at Brandenburg after the Danish affairs had been duly settled, but before he could leave Denmark with the assurance that the terms of the Roskilde treaty would be faithfully carried out he felt it absolutely necessary, for the purpose of keeping hostile fleets from the Baltic, to bind this country, through an alliance, more firmly to his own country. This move was primarily directed against the Dutch, who now protested vigorously to the Danes against their projected alliance with Sweden, insisting that they must abide by the terms of an alliance which now bound Denmark to the Netherlands. As a result of this protest the Danish commissioners who had met with Swedish representatives for the purpose of formulating terms for the projected alliance began to waver and seek evasions. Being in a nervous frame of mind and naturally suspicious, Charles watched with growing concern these various attempts at procrastination. His fear and suspicion grew apace when Frederick continued not only to keep his men under arms, but also to enlist additional men in the Netherlands, with the aid, as

Charles believed, of Dutch money. The terms of the Roskilde treaty relating to the Duke of Holstein, the father-in-law of Charles, were furthermore not carried out, the Danish commissioners placing all kinds of obstacles in the way of an adjustment. This merely served to stir the king's anger still more. In this excited frame of mind, Charles saw a serious conspiracy being forged against him. The Swedish commissioners therefore suddenly were given orders not to press the matter of an alliance any further, and Wrangel was instructed not to stir from Fyen and Fredriksodde until full satisfaction had been given the Duke of Holstein. But even then the king very likely did not intend to attack Denmark again.[4] The summer season was fast drawing to a close, and the most favourable moment for a contemplated military action against Brandenburg would soon have passed. Just then word came that the Dutch had decided to send a fleet to assist Brandenburg and Danzig against Sweden, which caused Charles to make a categorical demand upon Denmark that she place at least eight of her vessels at his disposal, a demand with which the Danish commissioners said they could not comply. In these days of nervous tension Denmark's former allies became increasingly threatening in their attitude and war with them seemed inevitable. With no prospect of assistance from France and England, Charles dared not enter a conflict with them so long as Denmark, in spite of all treaty obligations, stood ready, as he was convinced, to attack in his rear just as soon as his country became hard pressed. Many times before, Denmark had tried to take advantage of Sweden's weakness and preoccupation elsewhere, and it was natural that Swedish statesmen reasoned that she was capable of doing it again. The fateful decision to attack Denmark a second time, and by a swift and decisive campaign overwhelm her, was therefore taken by Charles and his advisers.

Heroism of the Danes.—Sweden's attack caused the same reaction in Denmark as had previously her attack on Poland in that country. National patriotism was fanned to fever-heat. King and nation were at once united in a firm resolve to stay the invader and at all cost preserve national independence.

[4] Carlson, F. F., *Sveriges historia under konungarne af pfalziska huset,* Stockholm, 1875-1895, I, p. 359.

For whatever weakness and blindness Frederick had evinced before, he now made amends by heroic courage and wise decisions. "I will die in my nest," were his defiant words to those who advised him to save himself by flight.

Without losing any time now and with tremendous energy, the citizens of Copenhagen built up the city's defences, and when on August 11 (1659), Charles stood before the Danish capital with his army he discovered that overwhelming difficulties would be encountered in any attempt to capture it. Contrary to the advice of Dahlberg, he decided to put off a storming of its defences until later. The Castle of Kronborg, which controlled the Sound, was taken by the Swedes and the capital closed in from every side. Famine soon made itself felt among its citizens, but relief came when a Dutch fleet, after six hours' bitter fighting, defeated the Swedish fleet in Öresund, and brought provisions and soldiers to the hard-pressed Danish capital. Charles was now compelled to raise the siege. From every side the enemies of Sweden advanced against him; Throndhjem was retaken by the Danes; Bornholm was lost through a revolt; rebellions broke out in Skåne; part of Prussia was retaken by a combined force of Poles, Brandenburgers, and Austrians; Holstein was attacked; and by the end of December all of Jutland was recovered for Denmark. Charles was, however, not the man to give way to discouragement. "I feel genuine admiration for the Swedish king," wrote Mazarin, "when I reflect that with six powerful enemies against him, he nevertheless does not take a step backward, but on the contrary, like the palms, merely rises higher when efforts are being made to bend him down." [5] Finally Charles determined upon an attack on the fortifications of Copenhagen, but his army was forced back with heavy losses. An English fleet, which arrived at the Sound to co-operate with Charles against the Dutch, gave him a small measure of encouragement, but troubles in England soon compelled this to return home and the loss of a large detachment of his army in a battle at Nyborg seriously added to his difficulties. From the depths of discouragement and hopelessness into which these reverses threw even a man of Charles's resolute courage, he was again lifted by

[5] Grimberg, *Svenska folkets underbara öden*, III, p. 596.

the change in the political situation of Europe. England became more and more hostile to Holland, and Mazarin, who above everything else preferred to see the armies of Sweden employed against the emperor, also lent his influence towards a settlement between the two northern countries. Charles now determined on a campaign against Norway in order to hasten Denmark's desire for a cessation of military operations and a renewal of peace on the basis of the treaty of Roskilde. For such a campaign he needed fresh levies and therefore called a Riksdag to meet at Gothenburg in January 1660. Soon after his arrival in that city the king was stricken with pneumonia. He continued his labour with his usual energy, however, until it became apparent that his condition was serious.

Death of the king.—With unflinching courage, the king, informed that his end was approaching, laboured almost up to the hour of his death, conferring with generals and statesmen about the war, drawing his will, and issuing instructions for the government of Sweden during the minority of his only child, Prince Charles, then only five years of age. On February 13, 1660, the king died, only thirty-seven years old.

What might have been achieved.—Some Swedish historians have deplored Charles's decision at the very beginning of the war to postpone the storming of Copenhagen, thus losing the opportunity to take the city. A success at that time, so they reason, would have resulted in welding Scandinavia together into one state, and this would have meant that this merged state would have held control of the Baltic, thus in all probability preventing the Muscovite power from ever pressing her way westward. Aside from all considerations of national sentiments, such a merger would undoubtedly have been a blessing whose good effect can hardly be conceived; the same statement would hold in regard to a merging with Denmark as the nucleus in the old Kalmar Union days. The wars and misery which had resulted from the antagonisms of the three Scandinavian countries form one of the tragic chapters of history. All Europe, and not only Norway, Sweden, and Denmark, have had to suffer from these antagonisms. To the objection that Denmark would not, if overcome by Charles, permanently have submitted to Sweden, even though temporarily subdued, these historians give answer by citing the case of Skåne, Blekinge, and Halland, which in a remarkably short time after their incorporation with Sweden became thoroughly Swedish in language and sentiment. There is no reason for believing that, although these provinces lay on the peninsula itself and contiguous to Sweden, they were in 1660 less Danish in character and sentiment than the rest of the Danish kingdom.

"Great as a statesman and warrior," says one of the leading authorities on this period,[6] "Charles X will, in spite of his faults, always be judged by an unbiased posterity as one of the best regents that ever occupied the throne of Sweden. The founder of a new dynasty—the Palatinate branch of the Vasa family—he, in more than one respect, opened up a new future to the Swedish kingdom. His fiery soul impelled him to begin new enterprises everywhere. By reason of his remarkable power, he set everything in commotion; surprised by death, time was not given him to bring any task to a finish. But with a strong hand he had, through the great changes wrought by his "reduktion," laid the foundation for the country's unity."

[6] Carlson, *Sveriges historia under konungarne of pfalziska huset*, I, p. 435.

CHAPTER XVI

FIGHTING IN SELF-DEFENCE

Without a great leader.—With the unexpected death of Charles, Sweden stood face to face with an overwhelming national disaster. At war with six nations, whose armies by this time had overrun practically all her outlying possessions and were ready to strike at the very heart of the homeland, she was almost at the end of her resources, and, what was worse still, there was no superior statesman like Oxenstierna to guide her along the dangerous pathway which must be travelled. As when Gustavus Adolphus fell in battle in 1632, the hereditary successor to the throne was now a child. One can therefore understand the pessimism of a Swedish councillor who in this dark hour wrote to a friend: "Never since the beginning of the world has a nation been in greater danger, nor a king's death been more untimely than this."[1]

In his will Charles had taken particular pains to insure the continuation of royal power in his family, and therefore had given his queen, Hedwig Eleanora, his brother, Duke Adolph John, and a trusted friend, Herman Fleming, the head of the "Reduktion" Commission, a prominent part in the Council of Regency which he had designated to rule the country during his son's minority. The duke and Fleming, however, were both objectionable to the nobility, the latter since he, more than anyone else, personified the detested confiscation measures which slowly but surely had compelled them to disgorge; the former, a peevish and arrogant man, who, not without reason, was suspected of sinister plans for the augmentation of his own power, had always been unpopular. In violation of Charles's dying wishes, the nobility, through superior skill in intrigue and sharp practices, succeeded in hav-

[1] Fåhræus, R., *Sveriges historia,* VIII, p. 3.

ing both Fleming and the duke excluded from the Council of Regency.

As Fleming was looked upon as the champion of the lower orders, his removal nearly precipitated a renewal of the bitter social conflict which had brought the nation to the brink of civil war. It was therefore necessary for the higher nobility, represented by the Swedish Council and the Council of Regency, to make haste in getting such action as would win for them the good-will and approval of the people. Nothing could at this period come as a more welcome boon than peace with all of Sweden's enemies, and hence negotiations looking to the end of the many wars became the all-important concern of the new government.

The wars end on all fronts.—The political situation was favourable to the Swedish statesmen; Poland faced a new royal election and was anxious for peace, while France exerted a strong pressure upon the emperor and Brandenburg to come to terms with their northern foe.

By the important Peace of Olivia (1660) between Sweden on the one hand and Poland, Brandenburg, and the emperor on the other, the conflict with these powers came to an end, John Casimir renouncing all claims to the Swedish throne and acknowledging Sweden's claim to Livonia. Thus the dynastic controversy between Sweden and Poland, which for almost a century had set the two nations against each other, was finally brought to a close. The Dutch, whose one great concern it was to prevent the Sound from becoming territorial water again, as it had been when Denmark controlled the land on both shores and as it would have become in case Sweden had secured possession of Denmark, were now satisfied that no great changes in the arrangements of the Roskilde peace terms would be made. They therefore withdrew from the war, leaving the Danes to continue the war alone. Deserted by her allies, her people weary of the war and utterly exhausted, Denmark was willing to bring hostilities to a close, and by the treaty of Copenhagen (1660), the treaty of Roskilde was reaffirmed, with the change that Sweden was to retrocede Throndhjem and Bornholm. The Swedes tried hard to retain a slice of Norway as far as the Glommen River, but in this they were blocked by the maritime powers, especially England, which were opposed to any further extension of Swedish territory along the North Sea.

Sweden at the time of her greatest expansion.—With the signing of the peace treaties terminating the wars of Charles X, Sweden reached her greatest territorial expansion

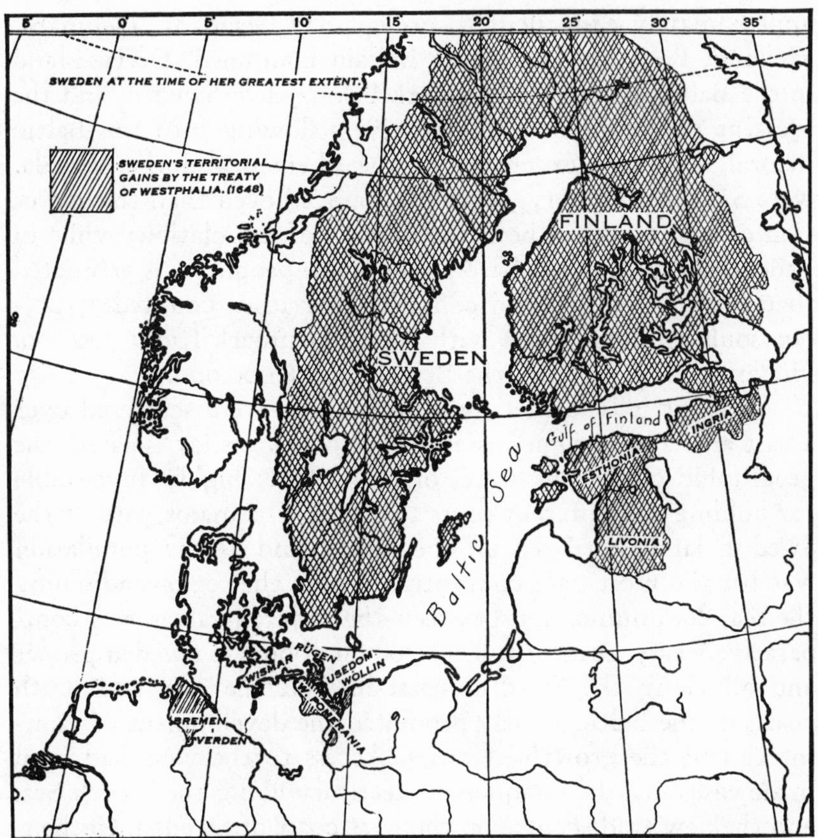

Swedish territory at the time of the country's greatest extension

and definitely assumed her place among the leading powers of Europe. Approximately a century and a half had elapsed since the nation started on its career of conquests, a period which had been filled with almost incessant warfare. Well-nigh superhuman exertions had been put forth by the nation. Territory to which Sweden since earliest times had claimed title, like Gottland, Jämtland, and Härjedalen, had been incorporated with the old domain, and provinces which had not before been Swedish soil, as Ingria, Livonia, Esthonia, Skåne, Blekinge, and Halland, had been added. In the time of Gustavus Vasa, the country and its possessions covered approximately 262,500 square miles of territory, to which by 1660 had been added 104,200 square miles, or a total of 366,700, approximately equivalent to present-day Germany, Denmark, Holland, Belgium, and Great Britain combined. Every island in the Baltic outside of Denmark belonged to Sweden, and the areas at the mouths of all the rivers flowing into the Baltic littoral, with the exception of the Niemen and the Vistula, were Swedish territory. More pronounced even than the accretion of territory had been the growth of population; while in 1560 the country had barely 1,000,000 people, it is estimated that in 1660 Sweden and conquered territory counted 2,500,000 souls, in comparison with which Denmark had 1,500,000, Holland 2,000,000, and the British Isles 8,000,000.

While it is true that Swedish subjects were scattered over a vast area and in some instances her provinces lay isolated, the geographic conditions were, on the whole, highly favourable for holding the different parts together. The major part of the Swedish lands bordered on the Baltic, and as the population was for the most part concentrated near the regions adjoining the sea, communication between the different areas was comparatively easy. A multitude of good harbours in Sweden proper and all along the Swedish coast-line on the east and south coasts of the Baltic greatly promoted the development of commerce and the growth of cities. Access to the west had been made easier by the conquest of territory along the North Sea, and the new trade centre on the west coast of Sweden, Gothenburg, greatly facilitated the extension of Swedish commerce in this direction.

Strength and weakness of Sweden's position.—This large territory had vast stretches of good agricultural land, and in favourable years Sweden found it unnecessary to import grain. The development of the rich copper and iron industry of central Sweden made possible a considerable export trade. The rich forest resources were also becoming, through export, an important source of income, its products going mainly to England and the Netherlands.

There were, however, inherent weaknesses in this new Sweden. Approximately one-half of the population consisted of Poles, Germans, Finns, Esthonians, Lapps, and various Slavic races, thus speaking other languages and having other political ideals and economic and social practices and customs than the Swedes themselves. To weld these heterogeneous elements into a compact homogeneous population was a gigantic task which foundered, as will appear, mainly upon violent opposition to the efforts of the Swedes to make their own laws and enlightened economic principles effective in the conquered territory; the Swedish ideal of a free people was anathema to the feudal barons of the Baltic lands, accustomed as these were to consider the great mass of the people as worthy of no better status than that of serfdom and who violently opposed any endeavours to better their lot. As far as the rank and file in the conquered territories were concerned, there was no insuperable obstacle to their being merged ultimately with the Swedish nationality, for sentiments of nationality counted for little in this period except with a few of the leading countries. There was, however, always the danger present that Russia and Poland, impelled by a desire to control the highways toward the sea, would seize Swedish territory and thus frustrate her attempt to consolidate her possessions, but the chronic and seemingly incurable ills which afflicted these countries seemed to minimize the danger from this direction. The German possessions presented a more serious problem. These consisted of detached strips of territory, and thus communion between them and Sweden, or between these individual districts themselves, was difficult; furthermore, the proximity to the large and growing German states, especially Brandenburg, which now, under the guidance of that remarkable line of aggressive and able rulers, the Hohenzollerns, was pursuing a consistent policy of expansion, made encroachment from that quarter inevitable.

Relations to Denmark.—In Denmark the feeling against Sweden was naturally now more hostile than ever and from this direction an attack might be expected at any time when a favourable opportunity presented itself. In surrendering Skåne,

Blekinge, and Halland, Denmark gave up approximately one-third of her territory, including some of the most fertile and most densely populated areas of the kingdom, but almost more serious than this loss was the changed status of the Sound; not lying any longer between Danish land strips, it had ceased to be a Danish highway upon which the kingdom could levy tolls on all commerce that passed over it. In spite of her losses, Denmark was in a sense, however, not so weak as she had been before, since as a result of the anger aroused against the nobility because of its pusillanimous conduct in the recent war, the king, aided by the citizens of Copenhagen, had been able to seize absolute power, thus giving to the nation the added strength which a centralized authority insured. Fortunately for Sweden, however, she escaped a Danish attack at this particular period when her own leadership was poorest; this because Denmark's great statesman of the period, Griffenfeldt, having in mind the blunders of his country in the past, was determined, before striking at Sweden again, to strengthen her position by favourable alliances and by the organization of the economic and military resources of the land. Even with his country organized for war, Griffenfeldt held back, realizing that the moment the conflict began power would pass from his hands to those of the military leaders.

The irreconcilable bitterness which one Scandinavian country felt against the other was well known to the statesmen of Europe. Louis XIV was especially anxious to utilize the situation to the advantage of his own country. In his wars against Austria and the Netherlands, he sought the aid of both Sweden and Denmark, certain that their rivalry would lead them to outbid one another in offering him aid in return for an alliance. With equal adroitness, Griffenfeldt sought to use this situation so as to bring about a Danish-French alliance, thus manœuvering his own country into the position formerly occupied by Sweden. At last the French king concluded, however, that Sweden promised to be the most useful of the two and decided to stand by his old ally. As a free passage through the Sound for their fleets and their commerce was the prime concern of both England and the Netherlands, a privilege that was never jeopardized as long as Denmark owned the land along one side and Sweden on the other, these countries now wished nothing better than the maintenance of the *status quo* in the North.

New acquisitions amalgamated with Sweden.—While the situation was fraught with danger and involved tremendous difficulties, the Swedish nation met the new responsibilities without flinching. With a commendable courage and wisdom, the statesmen went to their task, seeking to give the provinces acquired by the Roskilde treaty a new government. The development of their economic resources also received earnest attention. Already in 1662 the Swedish Council of Regency met with representatives of the conquered provinces and conferred with them regarding the needs and wishes of the new subjects. These representatives expressed the wish that their constituents be permitted to retain their old laws and privileges, a Swedish university be established among them, and the right to serve as officials and members of the Swedish Riksdag be accorded them. The Swedes gave favourable consideration to these proposals, and as a consequence Swedish law came to prevail by the side of the Danish, while the Swedish tax system and system of weights and measures were introduced, and in 1668 the promised university was ready to open its doors in the old cathedral city of Lund. Very generous provisions for the support of this university were provided by a grant of no less than 1,200 crown estates. Already at Roskilde, Charles had suggested a university in southern Sweden, as an important factor in binding the conquered territories more securely to the older sections of the country. At the meeting of the Swedish Riksdag in 1664, representatives from the former Danish provinces took their places by the side of the Swedish members. In order still further to hasten and facilitate the process of consolidation, highways were built to connect the old sections of Sweden with the acquired provinces.

Life under the Council of Regency.—The Council of Regency had made a promising beginning in handling the tremendously difficult task which circumstances had imposed upon it, but dissensions soon arose among its members which unfortunately ended in giving control to the least competent among them. As a result, the country before long faced a serious financial crisis and its peace and security were jeopardized by unwise political alliances. While the regents thus as a body manifested inability to cope successfully with the serious problems of state, individual members made partial atonement for this by their interest in cultural affairs. Foremost as a friend of education and as patron of the fine arts, stood the chancellor, Magnus Gabriel de la Gardie. Later as chancellor of Uppsala University he sought especially to foster the spirit of scientific research at that ancient institution, and in cooperation with the foremost scientist of Sweden in that day, Olof Rudbeck, who in 1661 was elected rector through de la Gardie's influence, he built anatomical and chemical laboratories, a botanical garden, and a library. From his own extensive library he made gifts to the university, some of incalculable value, including a large collection of Icelandic manuscripts and the Bible of Ulfilas. This unique work had, as already told, been carried away by Christina, who either sold it or gave it away in Holland, where de la Gardie secured possession of it by paying a price of 2000 gulden. Through his interest and watchfulness, other literary treasures were preserved when ignorance was on the point of destroying them. Thus the consistory of Uppsala once ordered the sale "by the pound" of a lot of papers to grocers and bookbinders, but the chancellor, suspecting that here was valuable library material, stopped the sale and made investigations. These revealed a number of irreplaceable and most valuable manuscripts. On the initiative of de la Gardie, a Collegium Antiquitatum was established in 1667, with a special commission to publish a Swedish dictionary, Icelandic manuscripts, and old historical documents which served to throw light on the early history of Sweden, to collect and publish runic inscriptions, undertake archæological researches, and preserve and classify the material acquired. The political greatness that had come to Sweden and the sentiments of pride and nationalism which this inspired, were revealed in the interesting attempt in this period, before alluded to (p. 17), to prove that her people had a great and glorious antiquity. A number of pre-eminent Swedish scholars, representing various lines of study, belonged to this epoch, and these always received encouragement and financial help from the enlightened and generous chancellor as well as from some of his like-minded colleagues.

Scholars.—The most prominent men of culture were Georg Stiernhielm (p. 391), who in his old age carried on important studies in linguistics and antiquities; Johan Locennius, one of the foremost of early authorities on Germanic legal institutions and a keen historian who built his historical works on a critical examination of original documents; Johannes Schefferus, an important contributor to the science of philology and the first archæologist of Sweden having a real scientific method and insight; Johan Hadorph, a scholar who took the initiative in the founding of a historical museum; Johan Stiernhöök, foremost authority on the origin and development of Swedish law, and originator of the scientific study of Germanic legal systems; Olof Rudbeck, the university rector whose fantastic theories regarding the early settlement of civilization of Sweden have already been noted (p. 17), made important contributions to anatomy—he was the first to discover the lymphatic glands and explain their function, and supplemented Harvey's theory of the circulation of the blood—to medicine, botany, in which science he was the forerunner of Linné, and mechanics. In the domain of knowledge he stood far above his contemporaries and his name lives in the annals of his university as one of its chief glories; Urban Hjärne, a great leader in his day in the science of medicine, vigorous and fearless in denouncing and exposing the witchcraft delusion which in this day as an epidemic seized the people of Sweden as well as other nationalities at this period. For the fine arts, Queen Hedwig Eleanora showed intelligent interest, and at court there were assembled some of the most famous architects and painters of the day. Architecture held first place among the fine arts, and at no time in the history of Sweden have so many magnificent castles and public buildings been constructed as in this era. Nicodemus Tessin the Elder and the Frenchman Jean de la Vallée were here the great masters. As examples of the aesthetic and creative genius of the former may be mentioned the royal palaces of Stockholm and Drottningholm; the Gustavianum in Uppsala and the cathedral at Västerås were remodelled by him. Creations of Vallée were the Hedwig Eleanora Church, the

Bonde Palace, and the Wrangel Palace in Stockholm, Skoloster near Uppsala, and the House of the Nobility (*Riddarhuset*), at the capital, besides a great number of other noble edifices. Other splendid palaces from this period were Brahe's Visingborg and de la Gardie's Läckö Castle on an island in Lake Vänern. Enormous were the sums that the members of the Regency, de la Gardie, Wrangel, and Brahe expended on their palaces. The great name among the painters of the time is that of David Ehrenstrahl, a German by birth, who is known principally by his decorations in some of the above-mentioned palaces.

Subsidy policy of the regents.—The respect and prestige which the regents had won by their successful peace negotiations, they soon lost through neglect and inefficiency, and as a result they soon found themselves confronted by bitter opposition and serious troubles at home and abroad. Dissensions among them caused laxity in the administration, which made any effective check upon the growing disorganization impossible. De la Gardie was reckless and extravagant, and furthermore leaned towards a policy of military adventure, while the treasurer of the realm, Gustaf Bonde, and, after his death in 1667, his successor, Johan Gyllenstierna, stood firmly for a policy of peace and rigid economy. De la Gardie emerged a victor from their controversy, which meant that the country's finances became more and more disorganized and chaotic. Schisms in the ranks of the nobility itself added to the troubles. The aggrandizement of the members of the regency and of some of the other members of the National Council had aroused the bitter opposition of the less favoured members of the nobility, who were now quite willing to make common cause with the non-noble orders in order to squelch the privileged few. As the financial confusion and inefficiency increased, new taxes were levied, and soon the *bönder,* who naturally were most heavily weighed down by the added levies, were discontented and again murmuring ominously.

For the purpose of improving the country's financial status, the regents, under the leadership of de la Gardie, now sought to trade the nation's prestige as a military power for money from foreign powers that had need of military assistance. The money thus received was termed subsidies. The traditional ally of Sweden was, of course, France, but the ruthless wars of Louis XIV against the Netherlands and the German states had created a strong feeling of resentment against the former ally.

Alliances.—This situation led in 1665 to an "agreement of friendship and trade" between Sweden and England, the latter at this time a bitter foe of the French king. France was in the meantime constantly angling for Sweden's friendship by holding out promises of support, while the Netherlands and England simultaneously sought a Swedish alliance. De la Gardie consistently fought for an alliance with France, but in this policy he was vehemently and ably opposed by a group led by Mattias Björneklo, a clear-sighted and fearless official, a subordinate to the treasurer, Bonde, whose ideas, it was understood, he represented. As was his practice when public affairs became badly involved and important decisions could not be avoided, de la Gardie left the capital and sought repose on one of his country estates. In the meantime the French party at the Swedish capital lost ground so completely that in January 1668 Sweden abandoned her traditional policy of friendship with France, and with England and the Dutch republic formed the Triple Alliance for the purpose of bringing about joint action against Louis XIV, thus checking his advance against the Netherlands. For its part in the enterprise, Sweden was to receive large subsidies to run until peace had been secured. While Sweden, in fact, received 480,000 riksdaler specie from her allies, she escaped the necessity of entering the war. Louis, soon after the consummation of the Triple Alliance, made peace with his enemies, prompted thereto, perhaps, by the fear that Sweden would soon be added to the forces arrayed against him. He was, however, determined to proceed with his hostile measures against the Dutch, whose Protestant faith and love of free political institutions had especially offended him, and his agents were constantly active in efforts to break up the Triple Alliance. In 1670, Charles II of England shamelessly deserted his allies and now the question whether to remain steadfast in support of the Dutch or again to become the ally of France was debated with greater vehemence than ever in Sweden. De la Gardie, as before, urged a French alliance, while the opposition, now led by Johan Gyllenstierna, favoured continued co-operation with the foes of the French king. The terms which the French offered in case Sweden would join her in an alliance were generous and the blandishments of the diplomatic agents of Louis irresistible, and in the end de la Gardie triumphed. By the treaty of Stockholm (April 4, 1672), Sweden and France agreed to take military action against the German princes in case these made any move to aid the Netherlands; in a secret article, the former agreed to place 16,000 men in the field against the German princes who might enter the war against the French, who in return promised to pay Sweden 400,000 ecus (an ecu was equivalent to $1.25) in time of peace and 600,000 ecus if war actually broke out. It was a shameless policy for the Swedish statesmen to enter upon and sordid self-interest was, with them, the determining factor. On the other hand, something can be said in explanation, if not in justification, of their course. England's desertion of the Triple Alliance had disgusted Swedish statesmen, and Dutch support of Denmark in the recent wars was not forgotten. The Swedes would gladly see the Dutch properly chastised, but certainly no Swedish statesman wished to see the brave little country overwhelmed by France. Furthermore, the responsible Swedish statesmen felt certain that their country would never be compelled to enter the war, but they were nevertheless willing to accept French money. Whatever the motives for the change in Sweden's attitude, the decision to join France was most unfortunate for the country. From being the recognized champion of the smaller Protestant states, Sweden was now relegated to the status of a mere satellite revolving around the orbit of the autocratic French king. The honoured place which the country had long held as the protector of the German Protestants was relinquished in favour of Brandenburg. To the bitter end, Johan Gyllenstierna fought against the French alliance, and with almost prophetic vision this clear-seeing statesman pointed to the disasters and the humiliation which it would inevitably bring to his country; the German princes would, he predicted, unite to drive the Swedes from their land, while England, again withdrawing from the French alliance, would make common cause with Denmark and Holland to drive them from the Baltic. Events were soon to prove Gyllenstierna's dire predictions fully justified.

A few months after his country had joined the unfortunate French alliance, Charles, now seventeen years old, was declared of age and crowned king. The regents now relinquished their power in favour of the young ruler and the Council, but since de la Gardie and other regents were also members of the latter

Charles XI

they continued to exert a deciding influence upon the government, especially as Charles at first evinced very little interest in affairs of state. The oppressive consciousness that the evils in the land were appalling and perhaps ineradicable, as well as his youth and shyness, deterred him at first from even attempting to take the control of affairs into his own hands.

Personality of Charles XI.—As a child the young king had been very frail, and the care of his health and development of his physical strength had therefore been the chief concern of his mother and the regents, who, according to the will of Charles X, had acted as his guardians. So jealously had they looked after the physical part of his training that, at the time of his accession, Charles was a robust young man, full of animal spirits, with hunting and military exercises as his chief delight. His mind, on the contrary, was deplorably lacking in general knowledge. He thus in one respect stood out in sharp contrast to his intellectually brilliant and learned predecessors on the Swedish throne. The haphazard methods of his mentors, absence of strict discipline in his training, and sycophancy of court retainers and statesmen had combined to aggravate the defects of his character; his temper became at times ungovernable and his obstinacy would not give way to any influence. On many occasions he showed merciless severity in dealing with his subjects. These defects were, however, counterbalanced by outstanding virtues, such as piety, moral austerity, and high-minded devotion to right and truth; that the king possessed these virtues was the more remarkable and praiseworthy, as he had grown up in an environment permeated by licentiousness and cold-blooded opportunism.

While Charles was giving his days to hunting, the country was fast drifting towards bankruptcy and utter confusion. Because of chronic mismanagement, the revenues of the state were now utterly inadequate, the fortresses and the navy had been permitted to deteriorate, soldiers, left without pay, had deserted wholesale in order to escape starvation, and government departments were closed because salaries were long overdue. As the storm approached, the members of the Council left the capital to find an escape from vexatious duties in the solitude of their country estates. "To get the Council to transact any business," declared the French minister at Stockholm, in speaking of conditions as he saw them, "is as hard as to elect two Popes and three Kings of Poland." [2] The financial plight of the nation at last aroused the king, who now brought pressure to bear upon the existing "Reduktion" Commission (p. 408), in order to speed up its work and bring money into the state coffers. His prodding actually resulted in bringing more property back to the crown in two years than all the years of the

[2] *Cambridge Modern History,* V, p. 574.

regents' administration had to their credit. As Charles, through bitter experience, now had become painfully aware that the members of the Council were utterly unreliable and incompetent, he turned more and more for help and advice to a few trusted personal friends in whom he could repose implicit confidence.

The German War.—The evils which Gyllenstierna had predicted as certain to follow in the wake of the French alliance soon manifested themselves. A shameless attack of Louis XIV upon the Netherlands led to the formation of a strong league against him, Brandenburg being among the members. Public sentiment in Denmark leaned strongly towards this coalition, but for a time Griffenfeldt's influence was strong enough to hold the country to a neutral course. The Danish statesman had suggested an alliance between his country and Sweden for aiding the Netherlands, but the able Danish diplomat, Jens Juel, who in 1671 had been sent to Stockholm to open negotiations in the matter, encountered nothing but a haughty demeanour and gratuitous insults at the Swedish capital. The new king of Denmark, Christian V, who in 1670 had succeeded his father, was a vainglorious and weak man, especially disposed to be jealous of Griffenfeldt's power and therefore ready to give willing ear to the latter's many bitter enemies, the Danish chauvinists. By this time de la Gardie was floundering about hopelessly, trying to find an escape from the uncomfortable situation into which his bungling diplomacy had brought the country. He did not wish to see the Netherlands destroyed, but, on the other hand, he found it difficult to evade the obligations to France which the Stockholm agreement had imposed upon Sweden. When Louis demanded that Swedish troops, according to the terms of said treaty, be sent against Brandenburg, de la Gardie issued orders for the transfer of Swedish regiments to Germany, but these instructions were disregarded; the chancellor never intended that they be taken seriously. A further promise by the French ambassador at Stockholm of 900,000 riksdaler in subsidies, to which was added the further inducement of liberal personal gifts to de la Gardie, Wrangel, and Sten Bielke, the latter also an influential member of the Council, finally brought the hesitation to an end, even though the French promises had been merely verbal and not even the time specified when the French subsidies were to be paid. Still de la Gardie hoped frantically that he might be able to avoid participation in the war, for he had a torturing premonition that with the Swedish army in the shape into which it had been permitted to fall, national disaster and humiliation must be the inevitable result of military action. Through diplomacy he tried to the best of his ability to avert the fateful step, but Louis was firm in his demand that the terms of the Stockholm treaty be observed. No alternative then remained for Sweden but to begin hostilities. The command of the army was entrusted to Wrangel, who, never a great military leader, was now by reason of poor health and old age utterly incompetent. The Swedish army moved into Germany, but France failing to pay the stipulated subsidies, desertions from Wrangel's army became so numerous that before long it had dwindled to about one-half its original size. The Elector of Brandenburg now urged his allies to join him in an attack on the Swedes, but the prestige of Sweden as a great military power was still sufficient to hold them back. The one, however, who was neither faint-hearted nor disposed to remain inactive was the elector himself; immediately he set out in search of the Swedish forces and, first at Rathenow and later at Fehrbellin, defeated them, and forced them to retire northward. The engagement of Fehrbellin especially was a serious blow to the military prestige which Sweden had long enjoyed. The engagement was a mere skirmish in which Sweden had been worsted with the loss of only 600 men, and that, too, in an encounter where 1,300 Swedes had met 5,000 Prussians, but nevertheless the outcome instantly gave courage to all her ancient enemies, including Denmark, which now declared war. The amiable Danish princess, Ulrika Eleanora, had, some time before, been betrothed to the young Swedish king, an event which quickened to life on both sides of the Sound the hope that thus would be strengthened the ties of friendship between the two nations and war averted, but the sentiments of the princess and the longing for peace were alike forgotten amidst the hue and cry for war and revenge which now resounded through Denmark.

Charles in control.—Arrogant in prosperity, de la Gardie became morose and despondent in defeat and remained on his country estate, permitting power to pass entirely out of his hands. To the young king the events had come as a terrible shock; his eyes were suddenly opened to the appalling fact that his nation had been driven close to the edge of a precipice, that its very existence as an independent state might be threatened. From this moment his life knew no surcease of labour or anxiety for his country. In a day he grew into the full stature of a man. Realizing how miserably his old advisers had failed him, he was convinced that next to the help of God he must place his main reliance on his own strength and his own counsel. It was indeed high time that some resolute will assumed leadership in the unhappy state, for everywhere the Swedish state appeared to be crumbling. Pomerania and Bremen were both overrun by the enemy. Charles made desperate efforts to bring his fleet into shape so that it might bring relief to his army detachments in the German provinces and prevent a junction of the Dutch and Danish naval forces in the Baltic, but hesitation and inaction among subordinates blocked his every effort; only upon his explicit command that the fleet proceed to search for the enemy on the Baltic did the officers bestir themselves and sally forth. The fleet was soon, however, crippled by a storm, and now disease among the men, caused by failure to provide proper provisions, came to render it still more helpless. By 1676 Sweden did not hold a single fortified place in Germany west of the Weser; her army of 15,000 men had not been able to hold back the combined forces of the allies amounting to 50,000 men. The Swedish soldiers had fought bravely and in accordance with their best traditions, but inferiority in numbers and lack of provisions were odds which counted too heavily against them. Charles laboured prodigiously during the winter of 1675-76 to repair the losses of his fleet and put it in good fighting trim again, since everything depended on its ability to prevent a Danish landing on the Swedish mainland. Fortunately for him and his country, Denmark failed to act promptly, the respite for Sweden being due mainly to Griffenfeldt's hopes that actual hostilities might still be averted by negotiations. He was, however, unable to stem the rising war tide in his own country. Soon he was himself engulfed by the frenzied clamour of the Danish war party, was accused of treason, found guilty and sentenced to death, this sentence being, however, commuted to life imprisonment. With Griffenfeldt removed from power, the noisy Danish war party had its way and warfare began in grim earnest.

Naval reverses.—In May 1676 the Swedish fleet, consisting of over fifty vessels, twenty of these being ships of the line, under the command of the brave, but in naval affairs inexperienced, Lorens Creutz, set out in search of the Danish fleet which had united with the Dutch squadron. The opposing fleets met near the southern point of Öland, and here the cup of Sweden's woes was filled almost to overflowing. Serious mistakes were made in manœuvring the Swedish ships, and when the Swedish flagship was blown up the rest of the Swedish fleet was thrown into confusion. Some of the Swedish vessels fell into the hands of the enemy while others managed to find their way into Swedish ports. Sweden's enemies were now undisputed masters of the Baltic and the Danish army under the command of Christian V in person now landed in Skåne, while another force invaded Västergötland by way of Norway. Soon practically all of Skåne was overrun by the enemy. The *bönder* of the province, most of them still Danish in sentiment, now started a savage guerrilla warfare against the Swedes, a conflict known as the War of the "Snapphanar" or "Nobblers." The many defeats which his forces had suffered on land and sea had left the young Swedish king utterly despondent, and for the time being his energies were completely paralyzed. In his highly excited state of mind, he suspected everyone of treason and saw nothing but inefficiency everywhere. His anger was at times so ungovernable that his behaviour seemed utterly irrational, and even his loyal supporters feared that his crown was in jeopardy. However, as the enemy pressed forward on every side, and Sweden seemed on the very brink of the precipice, he was suddenly aroused to heroic action. Immediately deciding to take advantage of Christian's blunder in sending a small detachment of his troops into Halland, Charles set out in pursuit, encountered the Danish forces at Fyllebro, near Halmstad, and inflicted a crushing defeat upon them. This victory, in itself trivial, had a momentous bearing upon subsequent events, for from this time on Charles had implicit faith in himself.

Johan Gyllenstierna.—There was, however, another reason for his sudden transformation at this time: Johan Gyllenstierna had joined him at headquarters. With open scorn and in vigorous, even profane, language he had laid bare to the king the whole wretched story of the regents' inefficiency and dishonesty. With the clear insight of genius, he had next proceeded to unfold to Charles his own ideas of what policies ought to guide Sweden's course in the future. They were that the country should at once cut loose from the French alliance and instead enter into a league of friendship with Denmark; above everything else, order and economy ought to be brought into the administration, the power of the higher nobles crushed, and power concentrated in the hands of the king, with the *bönder,* as of old, constituting the main reliance of monarchy. The country must, first of all, have its military forces brought to the highest degree of efficiency; finally, he averred, the king must trust to the strength, the patriotism, and the spirit of sacrifice of the Swedish people as the surest defence against foreign aggression. Charles was a willing listener, for these ideas were exactly in accord with what he himself had vaguely felt and thought. From this time on until his death a few years later Gyllenstierna was Charles's steadfast friend and sagacious adviser. Next to Axel Oxenstierna, Gyllenstierna was undoubtedly the greatest statesman, aside from the occupants of the throne, that has had a hand in shaping the destinies of Sweden. He was a giant physically, with an extraordinary appetite and capacity for bibulous refreshments, rough in manners, and plain of speech. His understanding of what the exigencies of the situation demanded revealed genius, and with indomitable will and high-minded devotion to king and country he sought to guide the nation on the path which might lead to peace and security.

Battle of Lund.—Believing that operations had ended for the year, the Danish king had, after the battle of Fyllebro, prepared to go into winter quarters near Lund. Charles's victory had, however, sent a thrill of patriotism and hope through the Swedish nation, resulting in large accessions to the army, and the king now decided to go in search of the Danes and offer battle. With this a long series of operations began, each army endeavouring to manœuvre into the most advantageous position. The Swedes were led farther and farther south where provisions began to fail them and disease and starvation daily took a terrible toll of men. For Charles there remained now only the two desperate alternatives of either retreating northward, thus relinquishing all hope of keeping Skåne and forfeiting the confidence of his own people, or of risking an attack on the strong position of the Danish army. He chose the latter alternative, and in the night between December 3 and 4 (1676) the Swedish army crossed the frozen Lydde River and made all possible speed to reach the Helgonabacke, an elevated spot north of Lund, before the Danes, for a time caught napping, but now making haste to reach the same spot, could occupy it. A spirited race began between the two armies and just as the sun rose over the snow-covered crest they met near the top of the hill.

At this critical moment Charles inspired his troops to advance with irresistible determination and courage, and the fine spirit of the Swedish troops, coupled with the king's masterly tactics and quickness in taking advantage of serious blunders committed by the Danish leaders, resulted in a sweeping Swedish victory. The Danish army was practically annihilated, and more than half of its combatants lay dead on the battlefield. The casualties among the Swedes were also enormous, amounting in their case, as well, to approximately fifty per cent. The battle was the bloodiest major engagement in which Swedish troops ever took part. The Danish military leadership had evinced glaring deficiencies, thus justifying Griffenfeldt's predictions. To Sweden the battle meant in the first place that the question of Skåne's union with Sweden was for all time settled, and, in the second place, it served to restore Sweden's military prestige throughout Europe. Hardly less important was its bearing upon conditions in Sweden itself. The king's many enemies at home suddenly subsided, and from this time on he held the reins firmly in his own hands. Every year throughout the remainder of his life, Charles observed the anniversary of the battle, not by pageantry and show, however, but in seclusion, spending the day in pious contemplation and thanksgiving.

The campaign of 1677 brought repeated defeats to the Swedish fleet, but a victory came to the army in the battle of Malmö, where Charles routed a Danish force of 12,000 men; with this defeat the Danish attempts at an invasion of Swedish territory came definitely to an end. In the meantime, Brandenburg had captured Stettin, Stralsund, and Greifswald, the principal Swedish strongholds in Pomerania. French armies had, however, been victorious on the battle-fields of Europe, and this, coupled with the advantages which Sweden had gained over Denmark, compelled the members of the anti-French coalition to sue for peace.

Peace treaties.—A general peace congress began its deliberations at Nimeguen in March 1677. The demands of her enemies that Pomerania, Verden, the cities of Landskrona, Helsingborg, and Marstrand should be relinquished by Sweden and that in addition she should lose her exemption from Sound tolls, was met by Charles's curt and emphatic rejoinder that he had no intention of giving up anything to which, by the terms of the treaties of Westphalia and Copenhagen, his country was entitled. Sweden's participation in the war had been of great assistance to France, since it had forced the league to withdraw from 50,000 to 60,000 men from the French border, but in the final settlement Louis showed, in the opinion of Charles and his advisers, a decided disinclination to protect the interests of his ally. He carried on a diplomatic game behind the backs of the Swedish representatives, promising their enemies the cession of such territory as Bremen and Stettin, with the greater part of Vor-Pommern; possibly Skåne was also involved. Guided by the clear-sighted and daring Gyllenstierna, Charles himself, through his agents at the peace conference, then began to carry on negotiations behind the back of the French king, in order to stiffen the opposition to him and thereby show him the need of Sweden's friendship. As Louis felt secure in the strong backing of England, and possibly also took to heart his obligations to Sweden, he now issued an ultimatum to the powers arrayed against him to the effect that no cession would be made of any Dutch territory seized by him until complete restitution had been made to Sweden. After much haggling, peace was finally concluded between France, the empire, and Sweden, by the terms of which the latter obtained full restitution of territory on the basis of the treaty of Westphalia. At the same time Louis offered to lend his good efforts to mediate between Sweden and Denmark; France and Sweden on the one hand and Brunswick-Lüneburg on the other came to an agreement through the treaty of Celle, by which the latter, a petty German state, which had joined the anti-French alliance, received three small strips of territory in the Swedish possession, Verden. This transfer was arranged by Louis without consulting Charles and the latter thought it the part of wisdom to acquiesce, but from this time on he disliked the French king more than ever. Deserted by all his former allies, the Elector of Brandenburg now sought by devious ways, such as the offer of a Brandenburg-French alliance, to gain Louis' acquiescence to the transfer of all of Pomerania to him, but the wily monarch, concluding that France had more to gain from the friendship of Sweden than that of Brandenburg, turned a deaf ear to all such proposals. Since French troops finally advanced towards Brandenburg to bring the elector to terms, the latter yielded, but not wishing to arouse the anger of the young and rising German state too much, Louis agreed in behalf of Sweden to permit the elector to retain the east side of the Oder River, besides Stettin, Damm, Gollow, and adjoining territory. Charles refused to sanction these provisions, and thereupon Louis by the treaty of St. Germain, June 29 (1679) took it upon himself to conclude the treaty with Brandenburg, at the same time giving this power a guarantee that its provisions would be observed. This high-handed act of treating Sweden as a vassal state was viewed by Charles as a monstrous insult, and from this time on his feelings were violently anti-French. In June of the same year negotiations had been opened directly between Sweden and Denmark with a view of bringing their conflict to a close. At the head of the Swedish delegation to the peace congress stood Johan Gyllenstierna, while the leader on the Danish side was the sagacious Jens Juel. The negotiations dragged their weary length until finally the French king, in accordance with his promise in the treaty of Nimeguen to act as arbitrator between the two countries, found a direct way to peace by ordering Denmark to restore all the Swedish territory which she had occupied. With this was coupled the threat that, if the Danes failed to comply, French troops would invade the country. Christian V was now compelled to relinquish every claim against Sweden, and on this basis Louis by the treaty of Fontainebleau now made peace with Denmark on behalf of Sweden, without ever even conferring with Charles or with any of his representatives. While Charles had every reason to feel satisfied with the terms, this additional evidence that Louis looked upon Sweden as simply a French understrapper naturally added new fuel to his already blazing resentment against the arrogant and self-willed French king.

The new Swedish-Danish Entente Cordiale.—The experience of both Danes and Swedes in the war had brought home to them the truth that by a waging war upon each other they were merely filling the imbecile rôle of the proverbial simpletons who pull chestnuts out of the fire for others. If not the first to realize this clearly, Gyllenstierna was at least the first statesman to denounce openly and frankly this criminal folly and seek to lead the two nations to an understanding by which both would gain strength and minimize the danger of devastating wars. Sweden's position as a great power, he held, could never be maintained so long as Denmark was an open or a secret enemy. "If the rulers of Sweden and Denmark," he said to the Danish envoys at the peace conference, "were in accord, they could accomplish great things and would have no need of being in the employ of others as their vassals. Then the control of the Baltic [3] would be their own affair, and each in turn could force his neighbour to listen to reason." With the power and prestige that unity of purpose and action would give them, the Scandinavian states could, in Gyllenstierna's opinion, act as mediators between the warring peoples of Europe and thus make easier the course of peace; with control of the Baltic, great material and economic profit would accrue to them both. These ideas, by no means new to the Danes, for both Hannibal Sehested and Griffenfeldt had previously voiced

[3] Holland and England always sought to keep alive hostilities between Denmark and Sweden, so that their fleets could more easily control the Baltic—Hjärne, H., *Karl XII*, Stockholm, 1902, p. 32.

them, struck a responsive chord in many a Danish heart. Since its disastrous participation in the Thirty Years' War, Denmark had been deserted by practically every ally which at one time or another had come to her with glib promises of support. Her wars of revenge against Sweden had brought nothing but grief and losses. These considerations appealed strongly to Christian V, who counselled his representative to enter into negotiations with the Swedes on the basis of Gyllenstierna's proposals. The upshot of it all was an agreement, the essential points of which stipulated that the two countries mutually agreed to support one another in case of attack; neither of the contracting parties should enter into any alliance without the other, or independently of the other carry on negotiations with foreign powers; neither should one state interfere in the domestic affairs of the other. Mutual trade concessions and guarantees of support were made, all for the purpose of making the North independent in maritime trade. In order finally to cement this League of Friendship the more solidly, it was stipulated that the marriage between Charles and the Danish princess, Ulrika Eleanora, which the war craze of the previous years had prevented, should now take place. It was with the joy which springs from the realization of a cherished ambition—namely, the binding of the two Scandinavian countries together in bonds of friendship—that Gyllenstierna the following year escorted the Danish princess from Copenhagen to Sweden, where in May 1680 her marriage to Charles took place.

The noble queen, Ulrika Eleanora.—To this noble princess also the occasion was one of genuine joy, for not only had she been united to the man whom she loved with the full strength of her warm nature, but she saw the fulfilment of her ardent hopes that the two kindred nations should learn to know one another better and become firm friends, and that she herself should be one of the strong links to bind them together. Throughout the bitter conflict, she had in her heart remained loyal to the Swedish king. Ulrika Eleanora was soon to learn, however, that there still remained many a cup of woe for her to drain. Charles's mother, the imperious Hedwig Eleanora, did what she could to make life bitter for her, since she feared that the young queen would supersede her in the king's affections. Many of her new subjects looked upon her as merely a Danish marplot, and, to add to her tragic fate, Charles himself, blinded by the insinuations and calumnies directed against her, long failed to see and appreciate her noble qualities. Not until shortly before her death did he realize the enormity of his and the nation's injustice towards her.

Death of Gyllenstierna.—With tragic suddenness, too, the young queen lost her firm supporter and most loyal friend,

Johan Gyllenstierna

for only two months after the royal wedding Gyllenstierna died. His death was an irreparable loss not only to the queen but to the nation. He had worn himself out in the service of his country, and now passed away at the age of forty-five. During the last years of his life he had performed the duties which generally devolved upon three such important officials as Minister of Foreign Relations, of War, and of the Interior. "He is a hero in war as well as in peace and can do anything," said the king once of him. By birth a member of the aristocratic party, he had become the most bitter opponent of its usurpation of power and privilege, and all efforts by the powerful interests to buy him off by splendid favours had been entirely unavailing. His own class had therefore come to look upon him as a renegade and its hatred of him was vitriolic in quality. This Gyllenstierna had freely returned in kind. Subsequent events were to show, however, that his denunciation of the aristocratic party was amply justified. The policies for which he had so severely criticized its leaders were soon to engulf the group in economic ruin and forever destroy its political and social prestige.

Chapter XVII

THE GREAT SOCIAL CONFLICT

At last Sweden had secured peace with all her enemies and could turn to the task of "binding up the nation's wounds." It was high time that this be done, for there was not a province outside of the original Swedish land that had not been overrun and laid waste by some hostile army. The regions that had escaped invasion were in almost as deplorable a condition as those which the enemy had visited, for here the burdens of taxation and conscription had rested with crushing weight upon the people.

Exhaustion of the country.—Once again the words spoken by Gustavus Vasa, "Sweden is a wasted and paralyzed land," were tragically true. The public debt was enormous, amounting to 44,000,000 silver daler (or approximately 46,206,000 crowns, the higher purchasing power of money of that day not considered), the treasury empty, and in many of the populous districts not a farthing in taxes could be collected. The distracted treasury officials were not only compelled to labour long periods at a time without being able to get money with which to pay their own salaries, but they were forever pursued and pestered by clamorous creditors of the crown; not even in their own homes could they find escape from them.

While the financial plight of the country, when the reign of Charles XI began, was strikingly similar to the situation at the time of Gustavus Vasa's election, there was still another similarity between the two periods: in both there was abundance of wealth in the land but it had fallen into the hands of a small group. In the earlier period it was the Church which enjoyed riches, now it was the nobility.

Wealth of the lords.—The landed property which the regents and other members of the higher nobility had, by devious methods, acquired was enormous. Thus Per Brahe derived income from approximately one thousand estates in Finland alone, while his principal Swedish fief, Visingsborg, was about 540 square miles in area; de la Gardie's principal fief, Läckö, included forty parishes with three hundred estates and his annual income from his land holdings amounted to about 500,000 crowns; in fact, the best part of the land provided princely incomes for a few lords who thereby were enabled to live in magnificence. Just as in 1527 the wealth of the Church had provoked an attack upon her, so the higher nobility now must meet a violent assault. And again it was the king who inspired and directed the attack.

The crown lands.—Since time immemorial, a part of the land had been set apart for the maintenance of the king and of religious rites. These estates were known as the "Uppsala estates" (*Uppsala öd*). The law of Magnus Eriksson (p. 174), stipulated that the king must retain them intact and permit no reduction either in their number or areas. Since land constituted the principal form of wealth in those days, it was natural that every vigorous ruler, having the common weal in mind, was anxious to increase the holdings of the state. Birger Jarl and Margaret had early typified this kind of ruler.

For the very patriotic purpose of safeguarding these holdings against the usurpation of grasping lords, new provisions had from time to time been made for reserving certain kinds of land exclusively for the crown. In spite of these safeguards, the mediæval Church had come into possession of the greater part of these former crown estates, only to lose them in the reckoning which Gustavus Vasa instituted. So successful was he in his confiscation policy that at his death the crown, as has been stated (p. 251), owned no less than 13,700 estates, or one-fifth of the total in the land, and 5,000 more than the combined holdings of the entire noble class. After his day the size of the holdings of the state varied quite regularly with the character and strength of the ruler; in periods of weakness in high places, as in the reigns of Erik XIV, John, and Christina, as well as of regencies during the minority of Christina and of Charles XI, the nobility managed to secure possession of great portions of the coveted lands. Not in every instance, however, was the royal grant of lands to the nobility an indication of royal weakness. Gustavus Adolphus himself was very liberal in bestowing estates on his nobles, but this was not due to weakness or indifference, but to a desire to build up a strong official class which in return for favours would render patriotic and able service to the state. The common people, especially the *bönder,* had naturally been keenly interested in the royal disposition of crown lands, for as the lands of the crown increased in area the income of the state grew, which was reflected in a decrease in their taxes. On the other hand, a shrinkage in the size of the state property soon made itself felt in the form of higher taxes. As a result, the king and the people had generally stood together in opposition to the feudal lords. It would, in fact, be difficult to find another nation where the alliance between king and common people had been as close as here and where the practical results had been so great.

The kings and the Riksdag.—It was in the assembly of the four Estates, the Riksdag, where king and people joined forces against the encroachments of the privileged few. The number of sessions of the Riksdag in a given reign was, therefore, somewhat in direct proportion to the strength of the sovereign and his determination to safeguard the rights of the common people. A conspicuous exception is the reign of Gustavus Adolphus, who freely bestowed lands, but at the same time summoned many Riksdags and was constantly mindful of the rights of the common people. Meetings of the Riksdag with all the four Estates present were held the following number of times in the different reigns from Gustavus Vasa to Charles XI: Gustavus Vasa, seven; Erik XIV, seven; John III, ten; Sigismund, four; Charles IX, seven; Gustavus Adolphus, eighteen; Charles X, four; Charles XI, twelve. The kings, however, frequently called meetings of one, two, or three of the orders in the Riksdag to consider matters in which they were specially interested. Such meetings of Estates (*ständemöten*) were summoned by the early Vasa kings as follows: Gustavus Vasa, thirty-four; Erik, two; John, seven; Sigismund, eight; Charles IX, three. It was but natural that Charles XI, who, more than any one of the other Swedish rulers, was a champion of the people's cause, should, immediately after peace had been secured, call the representatives of the four Estates together. In his summons, mention was made of the necessity for providing adequately for the national defence, but there was also the ominous hint that "several other pressing and highly important problems called for solution." These words, as the sequel was to show, gave ample latitude for proposals of the most revolutionary character. The Riksdag began its sessions on October 1, 1680. The situation was tense with feeling; bitter hate on the part of the many, fear on the part of the privileged few who had a premonition that for them a day of reckoning was drawing near. The king remained most of the time in seclusion, as was his custom, inaccessible to every one except the small group of trusted secretaries and advisers on whom he had come to lean; they alone knew beforehand the character of the royal proposals to the Estates. Despondent, taciturn, enigmatical, the young king, now twenty-five years of age, seemed to hold the destiny of the nation in his hand. But to the question, "What will he do?" there was no answer until the Riksdag began its deliberations.

When this Riksdag, which was destined to be the most important in the history of the nation, save that of Västerås in 1527, convened, it soon became evident that the king and his advisers had laid their plans carefully. In practically every detail these followed the suggestions which Gyllenstierna three months before, while on his death-bed, had made to the king. The dying moments of the great statesman had been cheered by the assurance that his advice would not go unheeded. "I am satisfied to die," these were among his last words, "for I know that Sweden will many years be governed in accordance with my principles." [1]

Arrogance of the lords.—The members of the aristocratic party, including the former regents, had nothing to expect but a determined attack upon them, since jealousy and a bitter feeling that rank injustice had been done ruled not only the lower orders but also the clergy and the less favoured individuals among the nobles; in fact, the most unrelenting enemies whom the great lords were compelled to face were

[1] Grimberg, *Svenska folkets underbara öden,* IV, p. 186.

the members of the aristocratic party, who themselves had been pushed aside and humiliated by the aggressive and unscrupulous few of their own class. Many of these wronged and dissatisfied nobles had grown old in the service of the state, but for their faithful service they had received but a pittance in compensation, while a few had grown enormously wealthy by exploiting the land. The acquisition of vast wealth had been followed by unblushing claims to social preference, so that grey-haired old noblemen of the less favoured class were compelled to occupy humble places both socially and in public service below certain young snobs whose only claim to precedence rested on their hereditary status. Thus a distinguished general who with honour had fought in the army of Lennart Torstensson was once challenged to a duel by a stripling earl because he had presumed to take a position ahead of him in a funeral procession; the only reply of the general was the scornful rejoinder that he had fought so long against the enemies of his country that his fingers no longer itched. Naturally the question of social pre-eminence had stirred up the feminine part of the aristocracy, and many a ticklish situation had arisen because the fair ladies, both young and old, fought desperately, though not with carnal weapons, for place and honour. Especially had the question of the order of seating at the table on state occasions caused much contention and heart-burning. The king shrewdly solved this vexatious matter by laying down the rule that married women should take the place to which their husband's rank entitled them, but unmarried women should be given preference at social functions in the order of age. The chronicler remarks that after that the competition for first place became less keen.

Leaders of the Riksdag.—When the Riksdag met, the king selected Klas Fleming to serve as marshal, or speaker, for the aristocratic order, a choice that was a clear portent of coming events. Fleming was the son of Herman Fleming, the chairman of the "Reduktion" Commission under Charles X, whom the Regency had summarily dismissed twenty years earlier (p. 425), and like the father he was a man of great ability and absolute probity. He was known to favour a drastic prosecution of the confiscation policy, which war and the lax government of the regents had interrupted. The chief actors in the conflict that, soon after the Riksdag had convened, flared up with great intensity were the brothers Hans and Axel Wachtmeister. Like Fleming they were members of a distinguished noble family and had been mainstays of Charles in his campaign in Skåne. They were firmly convinced that Gyllenstierna's proposals for a confiscation of feudal lands offered the only escape from national bankruptcy and the loss of ancient political rights. The chairman of the other orders, Archbishop Johan Baaz for the clergy, Olaf Thegner, Mayor of Stockholm, for the burghers, and Nils Larsson for the *bönder,* were also committed to the king's program and ready at any time to do his bidding. Weakened by schism in their own ranks, the powerful lords were rendered still more helpless in this crisis by the fact that they were old men and that none among them had the qualities of leadership which their predicament demanded. The king, choosing to remain in the background during the struggle, therefore felt quite certain of the outcome, but in order to be prepared for any eventualities that might arise he kept a military force of some five or six thousand men stationed conveniently near the capital.

Stormy sessions.—The meeting opened with a royal statement regarding the necessity for strengthening the national defence; the Estates, it suggested, should deliberate regarding the proper means for meeting this emergency. The discussion proceeded at first in a rather desultory manner, no one being anxious to come to real grips with the vexing question. Finally, Hans Wachtmeister suggested, casually, as it seemed, "if an accounting were made of the administration during the king's minority, means would undoubtedly be found so that little or no appropriation would hereafter be necessary. If matters shall proceed as hitherto, no appropriations will help, and we might just as well throw the money collected into the ocean." When some of the former regents interposed objection to having the question of an accounting by them and their colleagues discussed by the nobility, Fleming answered that no one need have any doubts regarding His Majesty's desire in the matter. To these words, which must have had an ominous sound in the ears of the regents, Wachtmeister added significantly the further statement, "The king cannot do everything alone, and certainly he will not be displeased if the Estates demand the right to see how the royal orders have been observed by the parties concerned." The result of the first verbal encounter was a vote by the order of nobles that the lower orders be consulted in the matter. That these would acquiesce in any proposition that involved an attack on the lords was a foregone conclusion. When a statement requesting the king to order an accounting by the regents was ready for final action, the *bönder* were represented by a committee who gave vociferous approval. Wachtmeister now advanced another step by suggesting that the king be asked to constitute a court with full legal jurisdiction "which could both render a verdict and execute it." A bitter exchange of words thereupon followed between Wachtmeister and Per Sparre, leader of the regents' party, on the question whether a court should be suggested to the king; finally the marshal of the aristocratic order ruled that nothing be said to the king about this. Thereupon the marshal and deputies of the four Estates waited on the king with their written request for an accounting, for which he thanked them graciously. When two days later the royal answer was received by the nobles, it was found to contain these ominous words, "Let the Estates therefore appoint among themselves certain persons from every order who as judges shall render a verdict and execute the same." Gravelike silence fell for a few moments over the assembly as these words were read, but, recovering his composure, Sparre finally found voice to say that "possibly His Majesty has not understood the intent of the statement," to which Fleming replied that the king had clearly understood the matter and now commanded that a court be instituted, "and such a decision by His Majesty," he added, "the Estates cannot oppose." That this remark went unchallenged, even received strong approval, reveals how thoroughly the Riksdag had yielded to the king and how short and easy the next step towards royal absolutism would be. The vote being taken on the question of a court, most of the representatives of the poorer nobles voted aye, and Per Sparre, speaking for the minority, was compelled to say, "We must be of the same opinion." The acquiescence of the lower orders was soon voted.

The first attack upon the higher nobility having thus been launched, a second was scheduled to follow in due time, according as the ever-watchful director behind the scenes gave the cue. This began in a sort of casual way when the *bönder* broached the question to the burghers and clergy whether there ought not to be inaugurated a confiscation of the lands of the entire noble estate. The upshot of the following discussions was a letter to the king suggesting measures for such confiscation. The nobles could, at this stage, have averted extreme measures had they been willing to make some concessions, but they stubbornly and blindly rejected all suggestions that they give up some of their property and privileges. Thus, instead of yielding on any point, they appealed to the king, urging him to use his royal fiat to put a stop to the bitter agitation against them. The king countered by referring the complaints and suggestions of the three lower orders to the order of the nobility itself, placing the responsibility squarely upon its members to give answer. After a heated discussion—in which certain speakers of the noble class dwelt long and eloquently upon the great services which the order of nobility had rendered the state, and in roseate colours depicted the idyllic status of the *bönder* and the burghers, freed as they were from all serious cares—the nobles resolved on an answer in writing to the king, refuting the charges against them and protesting against the projected confiscation of their property.

Hans Wachtmeister warned the nobles that the sooner they yielded to the demands of the *bönder* and the burghers, the better it would be for them, since in the end they would be forced to yield. The great fiefs, the counties, baronies, and other similar estates, he declared, must revert to the king. He next suggested that all who were in favour of this new "reduktion" should gather on one side of the hall and then proceed to the king, in order to lay the matter before him. To this Per Sparre replied, "We also can proceed to the king," whereupon he and his group left the hall in order to wait on His Majesty. On seeing them depart, Wachtmeister and his partisans returned to their seats. Calmly declaring that there was no opposition to the project in the group, inasmuch as those who had opposed the measure had appealed to the king, the marshal ruled that the proposition had been adopted without a dissenting voice. This was a sample of sharp parliamentary tactics which naturally brought forth a violent protest later by the absent members. On the marshal's announcement followed the appointment of a committee of thirty-six members, which was to formulate plans for the confiscation procedure and direct their execution. The lower and middle groups of the aristocratic order would, according to some assurances given, be left undisturbed in the possession of their property and privileges. With this understanding, these nobles at once voiced their approval of an attack upon their more favoured colleagues. The wedge which long had divided the nobility was now driven deeper than ever.

The confiscation decree of 1680 stipulated that all earldoms, baronies, former royal estates (*gamla kungsgårdar*), and certain fiefs that yielded more than 600 silver dalers annual rent (ground rent; the estates in question were those on which the annual fixed tax exceeded that amount. Two kinds of coin money were in use, copper and silver, the latter being reckoned at three times the value of the former and two times that of the present Swedish crown) should revert to the crown. Since it was chiefly the higher nobles that had come into possession of these particular fiefs, the execution of the decree was particularly ruinous to them. A large "Reduktion" Commission was next appointed to have charge of the administration of the confiscation.

Absolutism.—At the close of the meeting the king came with what appeared as merely a casual and innocent inquiry to the Estates. On the answer depended great issues, however. He wanted to have an answer to the question whether or not he was bound by the provisions of the Constitution [2] to rule with the advice of the Council. To this the Estates, probably without any comprehension of the implications of their answer, meekly replied that the king was subject only to the laws and statutes of Sweden and that with him alone rested the right

[2] The country had, of course, no Constitution in the sense of an organic act like the Constitution of the United States, but was governed according to customary law and important laws pertaining to the organization and functioning of the government as those of 1617 and 1634.

to decide what matters, if any, should be submitted to the Council.

With this important decision the fate of this old and honourable institution was sealed; after this it became a mere adjunct of royalty, and its changed status is reflected in the new designation, King's Council (*Konungens råd*) instead of, as before, National Council (*Rikets råd*). While thus Sweden adopted the absolute form of monarchy, she abided by this system a shorter time than any other country which had yielded to royal usurpation of power.

Fines of the nobles.—The commission, at first with Fleming, and after his death in 1685 with Fabian Wrede, likewise a firm and fearless man, as head, went to its task with ruthless severity, and before long the richest lords found themselves impoverished. The regents were first adjudged guilty of gross mismanagement during the king's minority, and the amount of the losses to the state through their malfeasance was estimated at 11,500,000 silver dalers. They were ordered to make restitution to the amount of 4,000,000 dalers. Later a still more radical step was taken when the many estates which during the Thirty Years' War and afterwards had been lost to the crown, through the mortgaging of their incomes, also were made subject to confiscation. Even beyond this, the king and his advisers were determined to extend the scope of the "reduktion" and at a Riksdag meeting in 1682 a number of smaller estates were included. The execution of the various "reduktion" decrees, which originally had been entrusted to a special committee, was, after some years, placed under a permanent department of state working under the direct control of the king. He worked at the task prodigiously, his working day sometimes starting at three or four in the morning and lasting till towards midnight, with a multitude of reports passing under his close scrutiny.

The validity of titles to thousands of estates held by the nobility was now questioned and the burden of proof always rested on the individual claiming the lands. If there was any flaw in the title, or the property was held in violation of any old principle of law or custom, it forthwith reverted to the crown. If the dispossessed owner could then save himself from loss by collecting anything from the individual who had sold him the property he was fortunate, indeed, but that was his lookout. Confiscation was applied to the conquered provinces where in some instances it was carried out with a more ruthless thoroughness than in Sweden itself.

Confiscation in the conquered lands.—In the Swedish German lands, checks were encountered in certain provisions of German law and custom and by the possibility that in extreme cases the aggrieved parties could appeal to the emperor for redress. In Pomerania it was enforced in a spirit of toleration and humanity, especially as long as the statesman Gustaf de la Gardie was in charge. In Esthonia these fiscal measures at first affected only the Swedish noblemen holding property there, but in time it weighed upon the native lords also. These complained with especial bitterness, saying that since they had voluntarily placed themselves under the rule of Sweden (p. 290), it was unfair to interfere with their domestic affairs. Here, too, the German feudal ideas were firmly entrenched and these clashed with the more humane Swedish ideas. Charles suggested to the Livonian lords that they voluntarily relinquish serfdom on their fiefs and that a limited "reduktion" be carried out. The stiff-necked Livonian potentates refused to acquiesce in any of these measures, instead offering to make some voluntary contributions. This aroused the ire of the king, who now decided to go ahead with his measures despite the truculent lords. The bitterness of the ensuing conflict was intensified by the brutal manner in which the Swedish governor, Hastfehr, carried out his orders. The Livonian opposition caused Charles to extend his fiscal measures in the province even to the period before the Swedish conquest. Under the leadership of Johan Reinhold Patkul, Livonia next began planning deliverance from Sweden altogether.

The net financial gain of the "reduktion" was an added fixed annual income to the state of 2,500,000 silver dalers, or approximately the equivalent to the purchasing power of 50,000,000 crowns at the present time. In Bremen and Verden the state secured an added income of 200,000 silver dalers, in Pomerania 66,500 dalers, in Ingria 188,000 dalers, in Esthonia 155,000 dalers, and in Livonia 543,000.

Effects of the "reduktion."—The effects of the "reduktion" were felt in every phase of Swedish national life. Most of the rich noble families were temporarily at least ruined financially, and many of the lower nobility were in time compelled to give up everything they owned. Gone forever was the political and economic supremacy of the noble class. Even the *bönder,* who found that their most profitable markets had been ruined by the impoverishment of their best customers, by no means escaped financial losses. While, no doubt, the growing power of the nobility had implied a menace to the nation, the services of the nobles to the state had admittedly been great. There was now no one to act as a check upon the king, since the lower Estates had neither the culture nor the leadership to do so. The practice of challenging all titles to noblemen's estates, with the king as the sole final arbiter, caused an uncertainty and a confusion that seriously retarded economic development and everywhere created intrigue, jealousies, and bitter hatreds.

On the credit side of the ledger may be entered the fact that the "reduktion" saved Sweden from oppressive dominion by an aristocracy which seemed well on its way to complete mastery. It thus was a potent factor in preserving the freedom and independence of the Swedish *bönder.* Sweden therefore escaped the violent revolutions which other progressive countries were compelled later to pass through in order to break the power of a selfish and powerful privileged class and equalize economic and social conditions. Finally, the "reduktion" enabled Charles to inaugurate measures for the national defence and the material development of the land which promised to give the country, as a whole, security and prosperity.

It was one of the serious weaknesses of the old régime that it was unable, mainly because of mismanagement, to procure sufficient revenue with which to pay adequate salaries to servants of the state. Partly as a result of this, it had become customary, in some cases, for men in office, high as well as low, to accept bribes. With the large and certain income now available, Charles could pay his officials definite salaries and in return demand that public servants render efficient and honest service. In no sphere was the reorganization and improvement inaugurated by him to proceed so far as in the army. Its officers were from now on to receive their regular pay from the rent of certain estates, while other estates were assigned to them for homes. Charles also extended and improved the military organization which Charles IX and Gustavus Adolphus had devised.

Strengthening the army.—Thus the country was divided into districts, each of which, in return for certain tax exemptions, was to furnish and equip one unit in the cavalry, in some cases more. In like manner the system by which the *bönder* of the different districts in certain provinces had been required to equip soldiers for the infantry was extended to the whole country. These soldiers were provided with small farms upon which they might live in times of peace. The standing army of Sweden now grew to 38,000 well-trained men. To the population along the coast-line, especially in the Stockholm archipelago, fell the duty of providing men for the navy. Mercenary soldiers were for the most part used for garrison duty in the conquered provinces; their number was 25,000. Under the able administration of Erik Dahlberg, the famous engineer who had made possible the march of the army of Charles X across the Belts, the country's fortresses were greatly strengthened. The remoteness of Stockholm from the principal ports of the Baltic and the prevalence of ice in its archipelago during certain seasons had proved it highly unsatisfactory as a naval base, hence work on an arsenal was begun at Karlskrona, in the province of Blekinge. Since experience had likewise taught Charles that control of the Swedish Baltic provinces could not be long maintained without control of the waters between them and the homeland, it seemed to him a prime necessity that his fleet should be strengthened. This task was entrusted to Hans Wachtmeister, the early champion of the king's confiscation policy, and so efficiently did he carry out his commission that at the end of the reign the navy counted 38 ships of the line and a large number of smaller naval vessels, which were manned by 11,000 men and armed with 2,648 guns.

Cultural life.—In the interest of order and justice the king also interfered in ecclesiastical affairs, sometimes, it is true, to the detriment of some of the traditional privileges of church and clergy. On more than one occasion he assumed the rôle of a dictator and even the bishops were made to feel their subserviency to him. He laid great stress on orthodoxy, and frowned on the religious movement known as Pietism, which at the time spread from Germany over into Sweden. Assemblies in private homes for worship were forbidden. Catechism, liturgy, and hymnbook in use in the churches were revised and a new translation of the Bible undertaken; this was not published, however, until the following reign. The clergy received new and more strict admonition and commands to care for the education of the young; on the cantor, or organist, in each parish devolved the duty of teaching the children to read, and in every parish the pastor was held responsible for the proper carrying out of these instructions. Two of the greatest men in the history of the national church of Sweden belong to this period and were the faithful co-labourers and guides of Charles in his ecclesiastical policies; namely, Hakvin Spegel, a great hymnologist and author of books of meditation, and Jesper Svedberg, also a great hymnologist and a mighty man of faith. He was bishop of the ancient diocese of Skara, and the spiritual welfare of the Swedish settlements in North America was entrusted to him. To his great credit may it be said that he was greatly interested in them and sought to promote faithfully their spiritual and cultural life.

While Charles had himself been denied the privileges of a good education, he showed a constant and live interest in the extension of scientific knowledge; consequently he befriended the great men of his reign like Olof Rudbeck and Urban Hjärne, whose active lives, filled with great scientific interests and investigations, fell partly in his reign. Christopher Polhem, a mechanical genius of the period, made a number of ingenious inventions, especially in connection with mining and the utilization of water-power; Nicodemus Tessin the Younger, like his father, Nicodemus Tessin the Elder, was a famous architect; Erik Dahlberg, the engineer, published a great work, *Suecia Antiqua et Hodierna* (Sweden past and present), in which a number of remarkable illustrations of Swedish cities, castles, and fine manor houses appear.

The reign of Charles saw great prosperity in some lines,

once the great wars had been brought to a close. The government strove constantly and energetically to develop industry. The taxes which had rested so heavily before upon the lower orders, and more particularly upon the *bönder,* were so greatly reduced that they almost reached the vanishing point—a new and strange sensation for the people—and prosperity increased

Christopher Polhem

among most groups. This applies particularly to mechanical industry and to mining, both profiting greatly by the large amount of material used in building the new fleet and arsenal at Karlskrona.

Humility of the Riksdag.—The king's power was in 1682 made absolute by legal sanction, as it before had been in practice. At a Riksdag meeting that year the four Estates joined in a common declaration that the king, as his predecessors before him, not only possessed legislative authority, but also had the right of interpreting and amending the common law. The Estates which in a multitude of Riksdag meetings ever since the time of Gustavus Vasa had played an extraordinary, and for the most part glorious, rôle in the nation's life, thus sank into impotency; they were still, as the "Estates of His Royal Majesty," summoned to meetings, but this was merely that they might affix their "rubber stamp" approval to the royal

Seventeenth century *bönder*

propositions, mainly appropriations. Their new humility and obeisance before the king was in strange contrast to the fearless and manly stand in evidence in earlier Riksdags; they now referred to the king as "an absolute, all-ordaining (*allom bjudande*) sovereign, who has the power, according to his own good pleasure, to rule his country." At best the Estates might humbly express their wishes. The new church ordinance of 1686 was sanctioned by the king just prior to a meeting of the Riksdag and the codification of a new law of the land was inaugurated and completed entirely on his initiative. Freed from the necessity of asking the Estates for advice or assistance in order to get adequate revenue, since the income from the confiscated property gave the crown an adequate income, the monarch was firmly entrenched. The last vestige of the Estates' influence was gone when they meekly agreed in advance to approve appropriations for war and assume responsibility for loans made by the king. "Ye Lords of the Diet, why hurry so? What ought to be done has already been done" was the derisive text which once greeted members of the Riksdag from placards conspicuously posted as they journeyed towards Stockholm. A great revolution had thus almost imperceptibly taken place in the land. Swedish absolutism was, however, modified considerably during the reign of Charles XI by a due regard for the known desires of the people. Under his son and successor, Charles XII, it became as complete as in France or Denmark, but the process by which the monarch became absolute was not the same in Sweden as in these other countries. The French kings had usurped power largely because of personal vanity and from a desire for self-aggrandizement, while in Denmark it had been achieved through a bold scheme concocted by the king and his advisers; in Sweden, on the other hand, the change had come through the peaceful acquiescence of people and Estates, who were ready to make almost any surrender to the king in order to manifest their appreciation of his splendid personality and heroic services. For the time being, the change was distinctly beneficial to the country, for it gave unity and concentration of power to the government, which, when directed by a patriotic and wise ruler like Charles, meant honest and efficient government and the wholesome respect of other nations. The evils of absolutism were, however, in time to appear here as well as elsewhere.

The guiding spirit of the government was the king himself, who ruled with a paternalistic regard for his people, even as Gustavus Vasa himself had not done. His working day often began, as before mentioned, at three or four o'clock in the morning and lasted until late at night. Even disease or accident were not permitted to interfere with his labours for the public good; once after having suffered a fracture of the leg while on a hunt, he was deep in consultation with one of his officials about a matter of state one hour after the accident. Even on his death-bed, almost to the last, he was engaged with his advisers in conferring about needed reforms. There was no surcease of labour for him; often he sat for hours poring over financial records in order to verify their accuracy; conferences with subordinates regarding phases of government work were legion. He would often go on long journeys through the land, preferring to travel incognito in order the better to observe the conduct of his officials, and innumerable are the stories which have been told of his drastic punishment of some royal bailiff or judge whom he found dishonest and incompetent. Absolute impartiality marked all his acts. The drastic execution of the "reduktion" hit some of his closest friends—de la Gardie was his brother-in-law—but their appeals for clemency were just as little availing as if they had come from a bitter enemy. As the process of confiscation went on his heart hardened, it is true, and, as in the case of Margaret of Denmark, the acquisition of property for the state became an obsession with him. During the latter part of his reign the machinery of confiscation was controlled by an exceedingly severe and reckless man, Jacob Gyllenborg, and intense suffering and bitterness ensued. Suffering among the higher and lower nobility alike became pitiable, and their hatred of the king was indescribably bitter. The knowledge that this was the case preyed heavily on the king's mind and more and more he sought solitude away from the capital. As much time as possible was spent on his estate, Kungsör, on Lake Mälaren, where in company with a few faithful companions he gave his spare moments to hunting and riding.

Foreign relations.—The last decades of the seventeenth century saw the intriguing and the self-seeking of several European rulers and statesmen more unscrupulous than the general run in their class, and for the smaller states the situation was, as a result, always full of perils. Louis XIV continued his policy of shameless aggression. His chief and uncompromising foe was now William III, Stadtholder of Holland and King of England. Frederick, the Elector of Brandenburg, who had succeeded his father, the Great Elector, in 1688, had his gaze fixed on the royal title and now sought to expand his dominions at the expense of Sweden and Poland. In Saxony the unprincipled and licentious Augustus the Strong, greedy for glory and power, no matter how or where they might be gained, was ruling. It was the age of "cabinet governments," an age in which principles of honesty and morality counted as little in diplomacy as perhaps at any time in the history of Europe. For the complicated game of international politics Charles had neither inclination nor understanding, and in his foreign policies he permitted himself to be guided by his close associates, to one of whom, Bengt Oxenstierna, diplomatic affairs were especially entrusted. Oxenstierna had represented Sweden with distinction in the peace congress of Nimeguen and had a wide experience in the diplomatic game, but he did not have the pliable mind necessary for adjusting his policies to the constantly shifting situations. Most of Sweden's envoys at the foreign courts were men of the plodding bureaucratic type, who, partly from lack of disinclination to enter it and partly from lack of the subtlety of mind necessary in order to follow its winding courses, kept aloof from the great mass of intrigue going on. They were, consequently, ignorant in a great degree of what was going on in the inner circles of diplomacy and often gave their king misleading information. One of the fixed ideas of Oxenstierna clashed completely with Gyllenstierna's noble policies regarding Denmark.

Revival of an anti-Danish policy.—Denmark, he firmly believed, could not be trusted and the anti-Danish attitude of earlier statesmen was therefore resumed. Unfortunately Oxenstierna found a strong ally in the king's mother, Hedwig Eleanora, who, as a member of the house of Holstein-Gottorp, shared the hereditary hostility of her family towards Denmark. Unfortunately, too, she wielded a greater influence over the king than did his gentle queen, Ulrika Eleanora. When therefore the King of Denmark threatened the independence of Holstein-Gottorp, Charles supported the latter, compelling the Danish king, at the Congress of Altona in 1689, to reinvest the Holstein-Gottorp duke with his former privileges. The old enmities now flared up anew, whereupon the Danish king made overtures to the Czar of Russia with a view to finding an ally against Sweden. It was a sinister situation, fraught with great danger to Sweden, but it was a situation for which her own statesmen were largely to blame.

Relations with France.—Oxenstierna also held firmly to the belief that France was an untrustworthy and dangerous friend and that Sweden's security for the future lay in an alliance with her enemies; namely, Holland, England, and the empire. When, therefore, fresh aggressions of Louis XIV stirred up a new war, known as the War of the Palatinate, Sweden assumed a friendly attitude towards his antagonists, but made no aggressive move. Louis made repeated attempts to attach his former ally to his side, but Charles's mistrust of the proud autocrat was so deep-rooted and intense that any change of policy was out of the question as long as he lived. During the ten years that the bitter war raged between Louis and his foes, Sweden was repeatedly on the point of being dragged into the vortex, but Charles held with steadfast hand to his policy of peace and neutrality. When finally all the belligerents were war-weary and utterly exhausted, he offered his services as mediator, and at the great peace Congress of Ryswick Sweden's representative wielded a deciding influence at the council-table. It was the last occasion on which she played the rôle of a great power.

Death of the king.—Before the Ryswick Congress adjourned, Charles's strenuous career had come to its end. His unceasing toil, numerous journeys over the country, the hardships endured during his campaigns, his utter disregard of the rules of health, and the anguish that sprang from the consciousness that curses and imprecations were uttered against him by those who had been impoverished by him, had early undermined his rugged health. In 1693 Ulrika Eleanora died, and from that time on he was a broken man. Not until a short time before she passed away did Charles come to a realization of the true nobility of her character, and the consciousness that he had been unjust and cruel to her made his grief at her passing the more poignant. Ulrika Eleanora's greatness of soul and her good deeds earned for her the almost worshipful love of her subjects, and she still lives in tradition as the embodiment of all queenly loveliness. As a biographer of her famous son, Charles XII, says, "To speak her name was to whisper a prayer, and the blessings of the people followed her wherever she went." [3] To add to his dismay and grief, an entire series of heavy calamities fell upon the stricken land; it seemed as though the mechanism of Nature herself had become totally disarranged. Such an intense cold visited the country in April 1692 that the ice froze to great thickness far out into the sea, and many people perished from the cold. In the fall the harvest was ruined by incessant rains. The following year, on the other hand, the crops were burned by a scorching sun. The year 1694 was a little better, but 1695 saw snow on the ground in June, and no warmth came at all that year to give a harvest. The year 1697 showed the worst disarrangement of the seasons, however, and brought the most intense suffering. Balmy weather came early and seed was put into the ground in February, but soon winter again set in and nothing could grow to maturity that season. The suffering caused by these successions of disasters was indescribable. The king bought what grain he could to distribute among the starving people, but the calamity was too overwhelming to permit of relief. More than 100,000 people died of starvation and whole parishes became depopulated. With the despairing cry of his dying people ringing in his ears, the king lay on his death-bed, stricken by cancer, labouring almost to the last hour to serve his country, until, his body frightfully ravaged by disease, and his mind anguished by the plight of his beloved country, he could endure no longer, and death came to him in April 1697. A son, Charles, then fifteen years of age, was now to succeed to the throne as soon as he reached his majority. The king was only forty-one years of age when the end came. Like the true hero that he was, he had borne his pains and his anguish of soul without a murmur of complaint. A post-mortem showed that the fatal malady had wrought fearful havoc with the internal organs and that his suffering must have been intense, but no words had ever come from his lips to give any intimation of this. Even as he closed his eyes in death, catastrophe pursued the nation and filled all minds with an unnamed fear that still more fearful things were impending. While the king's body lay in state in the royal palace, fire broke out which spread with great rapidity, and it

[3] Gade, J. A., *Charles XII*, Boston, 1917, p. 12.

was with the greatest difficulty that the royal remains could be saved from the flames. By destroying a great number of important documents bearing on the history of the country, the fire also brought an irreparable loss to Swedish historical research.

Chapter XVIII

THE STORM BREAKS OVER THE LAND

While the sudden illness of Charles X compelled him to make hurried arrangements for the government during his son's minority, arrangements that were ill-considered and unfortunate in many ways, Charles XI, on the other hand, had been given ample time in which to set his house in order. With the mistakes of his father and the consequent results in mind, the late king had endeavoured to provide against every contingency that possibly might arise, and to appoint as regents only persons well known for their intelligence and probity and among whom a spirit of co-operation for the nation's welfare could be expected. The new Council of Regency consisted of the young king's grandmother, the forceful Hedwig Eleanora, and the five chief officers of the state, among whom Bengt Oxenstierna occupied the foremost place. These were all individuals of the honourable, plodding, painstaking type, albeit without conspicuous ability, but sincerely determined to rule Sweden during the minority of their royal charge in conformity with the good traditions of his father's reign.

Boyhood of Charles XII.—The young king, Charles XII, was born in the castle of Stockholm on June 17, 1682. The constellation of the heavens at the time, according to the superstitious beliefs of that day, indicated that his life would be turbulent and filled with bloody strife. No efforts were spared in giving the boy such theoretical and practical training as his future high station demanded, as well as stability and high-minded purpose of mind and character. His parents themselves looked after his moral training, and to their admonitions and noble example, especially to that of his devout and loving mother, Charles, no doubt, owed those noble qualities—veracity, courtesy, piety, moral purity, and a never-failing sense of honour and fair play—which make his personality stand out in striking contrast to his corrupt and conscienceless contemporaries among kings and statesmen. His natural talents were brilliant. Under the able tutelage of wise teachers he acquired a thorough mastery of several languages and became well versed in several sciences, among which he showed a distinct predilection for mathematics. His memory was said to be so astounding that in interpreting ciphered dispatches later in life he often dispensed with a key. As the future ruler of the leading Protestant country, the young king had been carefully educated in the doctrines of the state church of Sweden, to whose faith he always clung with unswerving loyalty and whose admonitions that life should be lived on a high plane he constantly endeavoured to exemplify in his own life. The Bible was his constant companion, and amidst the hurry and distractions of camp-life he read a portion from it daily, no matter who happened to be present, be he the French ambassador or the famous Marlborough himself. The science of war had early entered into his curriculum, and for this subject he manifested a keen interest. Endowed with a robust body, he had in childhood and youth, through hunting, reviewing of troops, or in the strenuous and dangerous sham fights that his father loved to stage, been hardened to meet the most unusual tests of physical strength and endurance. Charles XI had found particular delight in observing the physical prowess of his son, who could ride a horse when he was four, and shot his first bear when he was eleven. For escapades in which the most reckless daring gave zest to the enterprise he had great fondness, and even after he became king he was not averse to the staging of some wild and startling game. This side of Charles's life has, however, been unduly emphasized. Disgruntled Swedes of his day both at home and abroad, but more especially those representatives of hostile powers at Stockholm, who in their reports to their respective governments dilated upon the prince's wild pranks and kept urging that now was the opportune time to attack Sweden, "since the country is now ruled by a madman," gave currency to these wild stories. The true facts in the case give a quite different picture of the young prince, especially as he appeared after his father's death. Although only a boy of fifteen at the time, Charles attended the

Charles XII

sessions of the regents regularly, and often took an active part in their deliberations. To all appearances, the government of Sweden was proceeding in the even tenor of its way, as it had done during the last years of Charles XI's reign, and would so continue. There were, it is true, some people who had the harrowing fear that great and catastrophic changes were impending, but certainly no one had a premonition how near these were or how suddenly and dramatically Sweden would be hurled from her high place into the utter depths of national disaster and despair.

Declared of age.—Events which were to have an important bearing upon the destinies of the nation soon began to happen. The careful provisions of Charles XI for a government by a Council of Regents during his son's minority were swept aside at the very first meeting of the Riksdag in the new reign. Being by this time reduced to almost complete helplessness and ruin by the merciless severity of the "reduktion," the nobles hoped and prayed that the new régime might mean a cessation of the attacks upon them, and in their anxiety to win their young king's favour they forthwith suggested that the Council of Regency be abolished and Charles at once declared of age and vested with the power of an absolute king. Either intentionally or through an oversight, Charles XI had strangely enough failed to specify at what age the minority of his son should cease and the regents relinquish their power. It might have been supposed that the regents themselves, either for selfish reasons or from a sense of duty, would have fought against this rash move by the nobles, but this they did not do; already they were weary of a commission which they felt would yield them neither material rewards nor gratitude, but instead was certain to bring bitter criticism and imprecations upon their heads. The fate that had befallen the members of the previous Council of Regency detracted considerably from the attractiveness of their new commission. If they now should oppose the move to declare the king of age, they might, they feared, incur his bitter displeasure, and this would be sure to place them in an unpleasant situation, in case their opposition were unavailing. After some years they must at all events relinquish their power, and the king, with the memory of how they had withheld power from him before, might make the situation unpleasant for them. In order therefore that the future autocrat should have no cause for grievance against them, the regents hastened to join the other nobles, and waited on Charles, offering to surrender their power. To this the prince answered that, although he realized the responsibility involved, he was ready to assume charge of the government. Not until the negotiations had reached this stage was the proposition laid before the other three orders, which speedily acquiesced also, although the clergy, seemingly the only ones to feel that this was a precipitate and dangerous move, made some objection. The *bönder*, always royalty-minded and mindful of the mismanagement of the previous Council of Regency, speedily agreed, saying that they would rather have one king than many. Thus, in a single day, all the careful provisions which Charles XI had made for a government by his trusty friends until such time as his son had reached sufficient maturity of judgment were swept aside. At the coronation, which soon thereafter took place, Charles failed to take the usual coronation oath, and at the ceremony he himself put the royal crown on his head, thereby indicating that in every detail the principles of absolutism had been accepted by him. None, however, of those who had hoped to win the king's favour profited by his obsequiousness, for Charles made blunt reply to the nobles' request for amelioration in the "reduktion" decrees that no slowing up in their execution could be considered. The unseemly haste with which the Estates vested the young king with absolute power has by many historians, especially those of the older school, been considered an important factor in unleashing the forces of jealousy and hatred which soon were to bring ruin upon the country, but the action very likely had little bearing upon the course of events. Already at the time when Charles XI lay on his death-bed the enemies of Sweden were well under way with secret and sinister plans for a concerted attack upon her. The whole situation was fraught with peril for the country. Its far-flung domains had increased enormously the difficulties of an effective defence, the seizure of large areas of foreign territory and the collection of tolls on the commerce that passed over the rivers of the foreign possessions, the rigid enforcement of the Swedish confiscation policy against the nobility in lands where interference with aristocratic privileges had before been unheard of and was looked upon as a heinous crime, and finally the unfortunate fact that the states which felt a grievance against Sweden were now ruled by utterly unscrupulous but able men—all these circumstances had a part in setting loose the storm which now broke over the land, sweeping away the most valued fruits of a hundred years of victories and leaving the nation desolate and paralyzed.

A general European war impending.—At the time when Charles XII assumed the reins of government, all Europe was tense with the expectation of war. The calm which followed upon the treaty of Ryswick was felt by every well-informed statesman as merely a temporary respite from bitter conflicts. France continued to be the principal disturbing factor. Louis XIV had secured the promise of the Spanish crown for his grandson as soon as the reigning King of Spain passed away, an event that was expected to happen at any time, since that monarch was old and decrepit. Austria, England, and Holland were all girding for a conflict against France in order to prevent such an enormous expansion of her power as the consummation of Louis' plans implied. The crafty diplomats of both the opposing camps were busy endeavouring to secure as many allies for their respective sides as possible, and Sweden's great prestige as a military power, and the well-known strength and efficiency of her army and navy, made her assistance an asset for which it was worth while to bid high. Charles XII and his advisers had, however, inherited the late king's bitter dislike of the French king, and their disinclination to enter into any alliance with France was strengthened still further by French unwillingness to support Sweden in her Holstein-Gottorp policy. On the other hand, Emperor Leopold I, one of the most inveterate foes of Louis XIV, was equally opposed to Sweden's Holstein-Gottorp policy, a policy to which unfortunately Sweden was strongly committed; under these circumstances it was natural that her statesmen decided to remain neutral in the impending conflict.

Denmark's fear of Sweden further aroused.—The plans of Johan Gyllenstierna, Griffenfeldt, and other wise statesmen on both sides of the Sound for a Swedish-Danish alliance had, as already intimated, proved but an evanescent dream and soon the mutual distrust and hostility on the part of the two nations was as strong and bitter as ever. For this the Swedish statesmen, through their support of the Holstein-Gottorp dukes against Denmark, no doubt were chiefly responsible. For the last twenty years it had been the fixed policy of Sweden thus to assist the princes of Holstein-Gottorp. Denmark was, however, convinced that her safety was in jeopardy as long as these districts adjoining her on the south were independent; in alliance with Sweden and with promise of its support the danger to her seemed to be increased manifold. This danger appeared to the Danes to assume most alarming dimensions when Frederick IV, Duke of Gottorp, married the sister of Charles XII and received a high command in the Swedish army. On the other hand, the Swedes possessed much concrete evidence that the Danes constantly harboured a bitter hatred against them and were ready to seize the first opportunity which might offer itself to get revenge. Because of this situation, Swedish statesmen considered Gottorp a most valuable Swedish base in Germany. Even as soon as it became known that Charles XI had been stricken with an incurable malady and that failure of crops and famine were sapping the strength of the nation, the Danish Government sent diplomatic agents to Russia to open negotiations for an alliance with that country against Sweden.

Czar Peter of Russia and Augustus of Saxony; Poland.—It was Sweden's tragic misfortune that the Muscovites were at the time ruled by Peter I, a man of clear vision regarding the needs of his semi-barbaric people, and an utterly unscrupulous but resourceful statesman; possessed of a dogged determination, he would never give up until he had gained whatever his mind desired. At this time his country was, however, engaged in a bitter war with Turks and Tatars, and Czar Peter was, furthermore, preparing to start on his historic Western journey just as Denmark made her first overtures; her suggestions for an alliance thus failed to bring any immediate results, but Czar Peter's intention had been directed to a field which offered him singular opportunities for expanding the limits of his country, and he kept the Danish proposal carefully in mind. In the Eastern area of Europe, other events had occurred which had a sinister portent for Sweden. Here Augustus, Elector of Saxony, had, by renouncing his Lutheran faith and judicially expending great sums of money for bribes, won the crown of Poland. This was a dissolute age, in which principles of right and justice were brazenly flouted, and the only commentary which need be made on Augustus's character and acts is the assertion that he, more than any other ruler of the day, typified the moral depravity of the period. It was inevitable that this unscrupulous and ambitious man and the King of Denmark should soon find themselves leagued together in a secret pact against the ancient enemy of their respective countries, now that this enemy appeared to be vulnerable. In deepest secrecy they joined in an alliance against Sweden in March 1698. The prime consideration of Christian V was to secure help in case Sweden undertook to support Gottorp, but over and above that the hope of settling old scores with the neighbour, and, if possible, win back the lost provinces weighed heavily with him. At the head of a well-disciplined and well-equipped standing army of 30,000 men, Augustus was in a formidable position to secure great advantage for himself from the chaotic situation that had developed.

At this time the Emperor Leopold had long been engaged in a war against the Turks, but the desire to be in readiness for the fray which the Spanish succession question made inevitable made him anxious to terminate this struggle. To both Augustus and Czar Peter, this desire on the emperor's part was very disquieting; to the former because the Turkish war had given him an excuse for keeping his army in Poland, where he sorely needed it for holding rebellious subjects in check, to the latter because he feared, with the emperor's withdrawal from the war against the Turks, he would be compelled single-handed to keep up the struggle against them. Having such mutual interests, the two rulers were not long in seeking each other's company. They met to discuss their common plans and aims for the Turkish war, but an eventual attack upon

Sweden seems also to have been one of the weighty matters touched upon. A harbour on the Baltic would, in the opinion of Peter, be just as great an asset to him and his country as fortresses in the Black Sea region, for the possession of which he had hitherto waged war, and a war on Sweden would afford Augustus the opportunity to keep his troops in the field and win military prestige, thus making his wobbly position in Poland more secure. Whether it was Peter or Augustus who first broached the question of a joint attack on Sweden is not known, but there is good reason for assuming that the idea was born in the latter's treacherous soul. At this psychological moment, when two minds were devising plans for an attack on her, another person, whose hatred of Sweden was like a consuming fire, appeared on the scene.

Patkul.—This was the Livonian nobleman, Patkul, who because of personal grievances was calling to high Heaven for revenge. Ten years earlier he had appeared in Stockholm at the head of a delegation of Livonian gentry to protest against the "reduktion" in their province, and had received courteous treatment by Charles XI, although the request for amelioration in the fiscal measures had not been granted. Later he sent a written document to Charles which was so offensive in tone that he was brought to trial on a charge of treason and sentenced to death, his property being confiscated. Having escaped from the country by flight, Patkul entered the service of Augustus and henceforth gave all his energies to the grim task of wreaking vengeance upon the nation which had interfered ruthlessly with aristocratic privileges in his land. To him an independent Livonia was out of the question, and therefore its transfer to Poland, would, he felt, be most desirable, for then neither law nor custom would place checks upon the cherished privileges of the nobles.

The conspiracy against Sweden.—Patkul now paid a visit to Augustus to urge an alliance of Saxony with Russia and Denmark against Sweden, at the same time promising him Livonia as a prize; Augustus was quick to give ear to such a proposal. Under an assumed name, Patkul then proceeded forthwith to Denmark, whose statesmen were already deep in plans for an alliance with both Augustus and Peter; naturally, matters were speeded up with the coming of the indefatigable Livonian. Christian immediately agreed to Patkul's plans, stipulating, however, that Russia should first enter into a definite alliance with him and that Poland must be a party to it. The marriage of the Duke of Gottorp to the sister of Charles XII, which had been celebrated shortly before, made the Danes more than ever anxious for action, and late in 1699 an offensive alliance between Denmark and Poland was formed, Augustus undertaking to invade Livonia while Frederick IV, the new King of Denmark—Christian V had died a few months earlier—agreed to attack Holstein-Gottorp and later Sweden proper by land and sea. Augustus in turn promised to secure Czar Peter's accession to the league, Patkul taking good care that this desirable ally would be securely bound to them. Proceeding to Russia, he soon had secured the signature of the czar.

The negotiations between the three countries had been conducted with all possible secrecy, and in order to still further lull the Swedes into a sense of security the three conspirators made a show of friendship, pretending that they were anxious to enter into an alliance with Charles. In the spring of 1699 Augustus sent an embassy to the Swedish king with the offer of a renewal of the treaty of Olivia, and the same year a Swedish embassy to Russia was almost overwhelmed by the peculiar brand of hospitality which Czar Peter affected. He also signed a treaty by which he bound himself to observe all former treaties with Sweden. A week earlier, however, he had signed a tripartite agreement for a joint attack upon her.

While the negotiations against Sweden had thus proceeded in deepest secrecy, the conspirators even endeavouring to deceive her statesmen into a sense of security by simulating friendship, Charles and his advisers gained some knowledge of what was going on, and the Swedish army and navy were rapidly put in fighting trim.

The storm breaks.—The stage thus being all set, the conspirators were by the beginning of the year 1700 ready to start the first act of the drama. This took the form of an invasion of Livonia by Augustus, his first objective being the capture of Riga by a surprise attack. This campaign ended in ignominious failure, however, thanks to the vigilance of the canny old veteran, Erik Dahlberg, who commanded the Swedish garrison in that city. Augustus's protestations of friendship had not deceived the doughty warrior, who had clung to his suspicions that mischief was afoot. These suspicions had finally been verified by reports which his spies brought him. Dahlberg had taken care, accordingly, to strengthen the defences of the city and place his forces in readiness for the expected attack. Simultaneously with Augustus's ill-starred attack on Riga, the Danish king launched an attack on Holstein-Gottorp. The news of these attacks did not appear in the least to ruffle Charles's composure; from now on until his death, eighteen years later, life became for him a grim struggle on the battle-field to save his country from dismemberment and ruin.

When Charles, now called upon to defend his country and its foreign possessions, left his fair capital, which he was never to set eyes on again, he entrusted the government to the Council and to the separate Colleges, reserving, however, the most important matters of state for his own decision. He also sent immediate reinforcements to Riga, and ratified pending treaties with England and Holland, at the same time calling on the emperor, France, and Brandenburg to enforce their guarantees of the treaty of Olivia. The only effect of this appeal was a mild and futile protest against the overt acts committed by Christian and Augustus against Sweden.

The Northern war came at a very inconvenient time for William III of England. In view of the impending conflict regarding the Spanish succession, and being anxious to localize and, if possible, end the struggle speedily, he sent a combined Anglo-Dutch fleet into the Baltic to co-operate with the Swedish fleet. It advanced very slowly, thus giving the Danish admiral an opportunity to place his fleet in such a position that it would prevent a junction between the Swedish and Anglo-Dutch naval forces.

War with Denmark.—Charles had swiftly formed his plans for meeting the Danish attack. He would land his troops on the island of Seeland and move directly upon the Danish capital, thus speedily bringing the Danes to their knees, exactly as his grandfather, by crossing the Belts, had done in 1658. Orders were therefore given his fleet to pass through a channel between the Swedish mainland and the Danish island Saltholmen, known as Flintrännan, which because of its shallowness and submerged breakers no fleet had ever before endeavoured to negotiate. The aged admiral of the Swedish fleet, who was none other than Hans Wachtmeister, the old champion of the "reduktion" and creator of the Swedish navy, protested vigorously against so foolhardy a venture, but gave the orders nevertheless. The manœuvre succeeded almost completely, the losses sustained being only insignificant. The Swedish men-of-war now joined the Anglo-Dutch fleet, the Sound was opened to them, and a Swedish force of 10,000 men could at once be transported to Seeland.

Denmark quickly beaten.—Frederick had concentrated his troops at other points, and was therefore utterly unprepared to protect Copenhagen, which now lay exposed to the enemy. The events of 1658 were repeated; the Danish capital was helpless in the face of the advancing Swedish army, and Frederick, as formerly his namesake, Frederick III, was forced to humble himself and at once sue for peace. By the treaty of Traventhal (August 8, 1700) he gave his sanction to the alliance between Sweden and Holstein-Gottorp, at the same time agreeing to leave the duke of the provinces in full possession of sovereignty, and promising to commence no hostilities against Sweden in the future. Only six weeks after she had begun the war, Denmark lay prostrate, and had suffered the mortification of a humiliating peace, dictated by the youthful King of Sweden.

Chastising the Muscovites; battle of Narva.—Soon came the news that Czar Peter had declared war and that his forces were already invading Ingria. With characteristic promptness, Charles had, after bringing the Danish business to a close, embarked with a small but well-disciplined force for Pernau, with the intention of advancing against the Saxons. On hearing, however, that they had already quit the environment of Riga and were retreating, he decided to go to the relief of Narva, where Czar Peter himself, with an army of 40,000 men, had appeared, thus placing the important stronghold in imminent danger. The story of the march of Charles's army of 8,000 men to the relief of the besieged city and of the battle which was fought outside its walls constitutes one of the most thrilling tales of Swedish history. The march led through vast stretches of waste land, where the heavy autumn rains had made the roads almost impassable, and since provisions failed the troops were forced to go practically without food for four days. The march was nevertheless made with remarkable speed, the soldiers being spurred on to almost superhuman efforts by the example of the king, who took the lead wherever danger or hardship threatened to block the way. On hearing of the approach of the Swedes, the cautious Czar Peter had precipitately deserted his army, leaving the command to the Duke of Croy, a Scotch adventurer who had entered his service.

When the Swedes, in the midst of a snowstorm, reached the city, they at once attacked with force, and before evening the Russian army had suffered an overwhelming defeat. The battle had in brilliant fashion revealed the superiority of the disciplined troops of Sweden over the Russian mob, but in so far as the easy victory helped to strengthen Charles's conviction that Russia was a far less dangerous foe than Poland, in fact that the Muscovite power held no serious threat against his country, the outcome cannot be viewed as wholly fortunate for the Swedes. Had Charles, after Narva, pressed his advantage over Czar Peter, the story of his reign and the subsequent history of Sweden would in all probability have been quite different to what they really are. Until quite recently historians and military writers have been in the habit of dilating at length upon Charles's colossal blunder in not following up his advantage at Narva by continuing his advance against Russia, but turning against Poland instead. The decision has been considered as quite conclusive proof that Charles had serious shortcomings as a military strategist, and that his course was determined by an insane and obstinate insistence upon wreaking vengeance upon one against whom he indeed had good reason for bitter hatred, but who by no means was his most dangerous foe. These accusations are now held by most authorities to be grossly unfair.

Reasons for the decision of Charles to continue war on Poland.—After Narva, Charles, indeed, intended to undertake a campaign into Russia, but was persuaded to abandon this plan by his generals, especially by Rehnsköld. The regions through which the march must be made had been laid waste by the Russians and the Swedish forces were entirely inadequate for a Russian invasion; furthermore, the danger was ever present that Augustus would, in case the Swedes entered on such a course, attack in the rear and thus cut off communication with the homeland. Charles's strong desire to square accounts with Augustus also seems a perfectly natural feeling. This ruler had been the arch-conspirator against Sweden, although he least of all had any just cause for making war on her, and he had showed the greatest duplicity. If Charles underestimated the strength of Russia, this cannot occasion surprise; other great military strategists both before and since have done the same. The sequel was to show that the Muscovites were by far the most dangerous foes of Sweden, but that was not due to the extent of Russian territory nor the size of the population of Russia at the time; it was because the autocrat who ruled the Muscovites with an iron hand was a singularly able, determined, and unscrupulous man. Neither Charles nor any of his contemporaries, even the shrewdest and most experienced among the statesmen, had, however, as yet had an opportunity to take the measure of the young Russian ruler. On the other hand, Poland was a great and populous nation with honourable traditions of military achievement, and now that this country was in alliance with Saxony it seemed to all contemporary statesmen to constitute one of the mighty kingdoms of Europe. Charles's decision to turn against this country first, rather than advance against Russia, was therefore but natural; for all that, it was a fatal blunder, one of those decisions that change the destinies of nations. A second alternative offered itself to Charles at this time which, if chosen, might have profoundly affected the course of Swedish history. When in the latter part of 1700 the decrepit Charles II of Spain died, having bequeathed his possessions to the grandson of Louis XIV, the latter immediately announced his intention to support his kinsman's claims, whereupon England, Holland, and Emperor

Leopold prepared for war. The assistance of Charles was eagerly desired and sought by both sides of the opposing groups, but contrary to the advice of his chancellor, Bengt Oxenstierna, the Swedish king announced categorically that he intended to proceed against Augustus and leave the Western powers to fight their battles without his aid.

After his victory at Narva, Charles went into winter quarters with his army near Dorpat. Hither came offers of mediation in the pending conflict, but the young king correctly perceived that these overtures were insincere. In the meantime Augustus and Czar Peter entered into a still closer compact for co-operation, while Denmark showed signs of intentions to ignore the obligations placed upon her by the treaty of Traventhal and again join the anti-Swedish forces.

In the spring of 1701 the Swedish army of 15,000 men advanced to Riga; here the Dvina River was crossed without difficulty, the enemy being completely outwitted by a ruse of the Swedes. A subsequent victory over the combined Saxon-Russian army—Augustus was making the war as Elector of Saxony and his army was Saxon, but the Polish nation indirectly supported him—led to the retreat of the Saxons into West Prussia, while the Russian contingent returned home. Courland was overrun by Charles. By December of the same year Swedish territory was completely cleared of the enemy, and Charles was ready to settle scores with Augustus in the latter's own lands.

Augustus's position had never been very secure in Poland, and after the discomfiture which he had suffered at Riga the opposition to him in Poland received new momentum. The Poles had no particular liking for Augustus's adventurous policies, which threatened to involve them in a ruinous war, and through their primate they sought to impress the fact upon Charles that their country was not at war with him; Augustus, they averred, had begun the war merely as Elector of Saxony, a sophistry which Charles met with the pointed query how it had happened that their country had been Augustus's base in organizing the attack as well as the haven in which he, after defeat, had found a refuge. Fearing further military defeats, with the probable loss of his cherished royal crown as an unwelcome consequence, Augustus now resorted to every possible argument and cajolery in order to prevail upon Charles to remain away from Poland. The latter, however, well aware that a large faction in Poland had from the beginning been opposed to Augustus and that this formidable opposition had made the king's position very insecure, now sent a demand to the Poles that they rid themselves of their ruler. It was an ingenious plan, and if successful would have given Charles the keenest satisfaction, since nothing could have been more humiliating to the haughty Augustus than to be unceremoniously driven out of the land by his own subjects. The move turned out to be a diplomatic blunder, however, and revealed not only Charles's inability to understand the psychology of the Polish people, but also the inability of his diplomatic agents to procure full and reliable information. The demand, bluntly made as it was, wounded the sensitive national pride of the inflammable Poles, and gave to Augustus the opportunity to present himself at the courts of Europe as a martyr to the evil machinations of a revolutionary demagogue. He could pose as the legitimate ruler of the kingdom of Poland, and to the kings and lords of Europe any attack upon "legitimacy" was, of course, a most heinous crime.

Charles wastes six years in Poland and Saxony.—Balked in his attempts to induce the Poles themselves to humiliate Augustus, Charles, in the spring of 1702, invaded Poland with his main army, and, now that the enemy stood at their very doors, large factions among her people became restless and loud in their denunciations of their king for having brought this calamity upon them; to save himself, Augustus made renewed and frantic efforts to prevail upon Charles to desist from carrying out his resolve to invade the country. First he sent his former mistress, the beautiful Aurora Königsmarck, and later a Saxon courtier, to Charles's headquarters to plead with him, but he refused to give them even an audience. It was an absolutely fixed idea with him that Augustus was merely playing for time.

The advance of the Swedish army into Poland was attended by an almost uninterrupted series of victories for the Swedish arms. The Polish capital, Warsaw, was captured, and soon thereafter Charles inflicted a crushing defeat upon Augustus in southern Poland, although the Polish army was numerically twice as large as his own. Cracow was next taken by a surprise attack. Other victories were won in 1703, and these, coupled with diplomatic pressure exerted by Charles, induced a part of the Polish nobility to organize a confederation for the purpose of restoring peace in the land. This confederation now elected a young Polish nobleman, Stanislav Lezczinski, a candidate of Charles, King of Poland. A high-minded man of considerable personal accomplishments, Stanislav was poorly endowed intellectually for the dangerous rôle which this election imposed upon him, and his social connections and prestige were not such as to win the support of the leading Polish families. A large party remained loyal to Augustus, who had the support of Czar Peter. The latter naturally wished to keep Charles entangled in the Polish meshes as long as possible in order that he himself might the more securely during this respite strengthen his hold on the Swedish Baltic provinces. In this scheme the czar was successful beyond his fondest hopes, for Charles remained in Poland for two years after the election of Stanislav, in order to overcome opposition and lay firm the foundation of his power. A treaty which Charles and the new government of Stanislav entered into in 1705 guaranteed freedom of religion to the Polish Protestants and promised Polish aid to the Swedes in a war against Russia. The following year Charles advanced into eastern Poland and cleared the land of the invading Russians. Convinced that only by an invasion of his native country, Saxony, could Augustus be brought to his knees, Charles next moved his army into this country.

Peace of Alt-Ranstadt.—About a month later Augustus was forced to sue for peace, which was concluded at Alt-Ranstadt (September 1706). By the terms of the treaty, Augustus surrendered the Polish crown, acknowledged Stanislav as king, renounced every anti-Swedish alliance, and agreed to surrender Patkul to Charles. To the very end Augustus played the part of the consummate liar. On the plea that if the terms of the treaty were revealed his own person would be in danger, he implored Charles to keep its provisions secret, but at the same time he himself transmitted the information to Peter, while assuring him of his undying devotion. Simultaneously he opened fresh negotiations at Berlin and Copenhagen for a new anti-Swedish alliance. Suspecting Augustus of duplicity, Charles now published the treaty and then compelled the shifty Saxon to sign it anew. Patkul was surrendered to Charles according to the agreement, and later was executed with all the brutal forms in which the age was adept. That Charles should wreak cruel vengeance upon the arch-conspirator was not to be wondered at, but that Augustus did not save him when it was in his power to do so was in line with his usual dishonourable conduct. Patkul had been arrested in Augustus's capital, Dresden, and kept in prison, and although it would have been easy for Augustus to save him he forthwith surrendered him to the vengeance of the Swedish king.

Charles remained in Saxony an entire year after Alt-Ranstadt, partly in order to insure an honest execution of the terms of the treaty, and partly to prepare for the campaign which he now contemplated against Russia. His stay in Saxony was also enlivened by a spirited tilt with the emperor, an episode which throws light upon the character of the Swedish king. The relations between Charles and the Emperor Joseph I had for some time been strained, especially since the latter, though nominally at peace with Sweden, had openly showed on different occasions that his sympathies were with her enemies. Charles now made a categorical demand upon the emperor that the Protestants of Silesia be given the rights of freedom of worship which had been guaranteed them by the treaty of Westphalia. This guarantee had not been respected, the Protestants having been deprived of the use of their churches and subjected to persecution, as a consequence of which they had appealed to Charles for help. This offered the young king an opportunity to play a rôle that was to his liking, and the emperor was not a little shocked by the boldness of his demand that his Protestant subjects be privileged to enjoy their rights. When the emperor tried to resort to all kinds of subterfuges, Charles cut the matter short by threatening forthwith to invade Silesia, and the proud Hapsburger soon found it expedient to yield. By the terms of an agreement between the Swedish king and the emperor, no less than one hundred and seventeen churches were restored to the Lutherans.

Charles's hostile attitude towards the emperor had filled the anti-French allies with fear that he was preparing to assume the rôle of mediator in behalf of France and, anxious to ascertain his intentions, they dispatched no less a person than Marlborough to the camp of the Swedish king in order to fathom his plans. Marlborough had no difficulty in getting the desired information; Charles made it plain that he had no intention whatsoever to turn aside from his fixed course until Augustus had been completely humbled. Incidentally Marlborough was profoundly impressed by the military genius of Charles and averred that he would like to go through a few campaigns with the young king in order to learn the science of war thoroughly.[1]

[1] Fåhræus, *Sveriges historia*, VIII, p. 391.

Chapter XIX

THE WRECK OF AN EMPIRE

Gains by Czar Peter.—Charles's victory over Joseph I, although salutary in some respects, was extremely costly to Sweden, for much precious time had been lost at the very time when Czar Peter was bending every energy to prepare for the Swedish attack which he knew was imminent. At the very moment when the Swedes were advancing from the west, Peter had been compelled to cope simultaneously with a serious Bashkir rebellion on the Volga and an uprising by the Cossacks on the Don. If Charles had come only a few months earlier than he did, Peter would have been placed in a desperate situation, but he was again given a respite and could therefore put his house in order. The six years which Charles had spent in Poland and Saxony had been used by Peter in organizing his military forces according to the most modern methods of the day and in overrunning the Swedish provinces, whose garrisons were entirely inadequate to stem the Muscovite inundations. Sweden was too poor and had by this time been so thoroughly drained of able-bodied men that she was not able to send sufficient troops to hold back the invaders. Already by 1703 the czar had advanced as far as the Gulf of Finland, where on the marshy islands at the mouth of the Neva River he laid the foundations of his future capital, the window, as he said, through which he could look out towards the west. The foundations of the city were laid in the face of incredible hardships, but the orders of the autocrat brought the required labourers and material, as well as tradesmen and artisans. The city was well protected by forts and a naval arsenal. With the foundations of the new city laid, Peter turned against Ingria, Esthonia, and Livonia, and captured Dorpat and Narva. In Courland, General Adam Ludwig Lewenhaupt commanded the Swedish forces, and he put up a vigorous and successful resistance to the Russian host, until he, too, was pressed back upon Riga where he defended himself with heroic determination.

Czar Peter looked, however, with apprehension to the coming of Charles, whose fame as a military genius had elicited the admiration and praise of Europe. The situation was rendered doubly serious for him not only by the revolutionary movement among his Cossack subjects along the Don, but also by the spirit of anger and rebellion in all parts of his dominions which the reforms that he had forced upon his unwilling subjects engendered. With the Swedish king approaching and threatening Russia itself, this smouldering discontent might easily flare up into an uncontrollable revolution, sweeping away the entire structure upon which he had so long and persistently laboured. He needed only time for carrying his great plans to execution, and hitherto the Fates had been propitious.

Peter tries to induce Charles to stay away from Russia.—Now, however, that the danger of a Swedish approach was imminent, Peter moved heaven and earth to induce Charles to refrain from invading his country. His emissaries laboured with the King of Denmark and with Augustus to prevail on them to threaten Charles from the rear, thus forcing him to turn his attention to other fields; but after their recent experience these rulers had become exceedingly wary. The anti-France allies were next offered 30,000 Russian troops for their campaigns if they would mediate a peace between him and Sweden, but these overtures proved fruitless. Next Peter had recourse to negotiations with Marlborough, who for a consideration did not seem averse to lending his good services to the czar. So anxious was Peter to avert the threatening Swedish attack that he gave Marlborough the choice of Kiev, Vladimir, and Siberia as possessions if he would intercede with Charles, and if he actually brought about peace with Sweden, 50,000 thalers as an annual pension and "a rock ruby such as no European potentate possesses." Nothing came of all these frantic appeals, and next Peter sought mediation through French intervention, but again to no avail. In his final effort he promised a reward of 100,000 thalers to the Prussian minister if he would undertake mediation and keep the Swedes away from the Russian land, but as in the former instances the desired help was not vouchsafed. Every one feared to offend Charles, and Peter was given up for lost. Swedish diplomatic agents had contributed to his discomfiture by bestirring themselves and reminding the Western powers that the Muscovite advance westward menaced all Europe. So isolated, apparently helpless, and despairing had Peter at last become that he offered Charles retrocession of all the territory that had been wrested from Sweden, except the mouth of the Neva River, including St. Petersburg and its fortresses. To Charles it was inconceivable why any Swedish territory at all should be ceded and least of all did he propose to give up the particular area which Peter desired to retain, since he realized fully its great strategic importance. To Charles it was perfectly clear that if the Muscovites were once given a foothold on the Baltic they would use this as a base and at the first favourable opportunity seize some more territory. Instead, therefore, of agreeing to Peter's terms, Charles demanded a return of all the Swedish territory which the Russian armies had overrun, and besides the payment of a considerable sum as war indemnity. The stubborn determination of Charles not to cede a foot of his rightful possessions was matched by Peter's indomitable resolve to derive some profit out of the venture, and since he had failed in all his efforts at mediation he determined to go through with the affair to the bitter end.

Peter's method of defence.—He therefore decided to fight according to his own peculiar style of warfare. His strategy for meeting the enemy was very simple and, as the sequel proved, most effective. Its first postulate was that the Russians should carefully abstain from meeting the Swedes in the open field, but instead retire before them, laying waste the country, thus preventing the invaders from subsisting on the land; in the second place they should offer resistance only at the river passages, hang on the enemy's flanks and in his rear, cut off detached groups whenever possible, and in general harass him constantly without coming to grips with him.

Many historians have been in the habit of speaking of Charles's invasion of Russia as a blind and reckless venture, undertaken without careful calculation and following no definite plan, but the verdict of military experts of our day, who have given special attention to this tragic episode in the king's life, is quite at variance with this traditional view. The researches of Stillé [1] and a detailed study of the whole question by experts of the Swedish Generals' Staff, which is presented in a two-volume work of more than a thousand pages,[2] seems to prove beyond a doubt that Charles had worked out a definite plan which, under the existing conditions, gave fair promise of bringing the war to a successful close. The fact that Charles never revealed what his plans for the Russian invasion were proves nothing, for he seldom, during all his campaigns, did make known his plans even to his closest advisers.

Charles's plans for the invasion.—So much appears certain that he intended a rapid advance upon Moscow, which, as he had every reason to believe, would compel Peter to sue for peace. Charles's own experience justified him in holding this belief, for Frederick IV of Denmark had been speedily humbled when the Swedish army advanced on Copenhagen, and it was only when this same army threatened Augustus's capital, Dresden, that this ruler had been compelled to call quits and submit to Charles's terms. Charles's line of march and his disposition of troops were chosen with due regard to the terrain. He was, indeed, deceived by Peter's unique strategy, but so was Napoleon a hundred years later, even though he might have been expected to profit by Charles's tragic experience. Another element which became one of the main factors in the disaster which overwhelmed Charles and his men—the unprecedented cold weather that set in unexpectedly early in the autumn—no one could, of course, calculate beforehand. When in the beginning of 1708 the king was ready to advance against Peter, he stood at the head of an army of 40,000 men, while a force of 8,000 men had been left in Poland. Lewenhaupt, one of Charles's trusted generals, who was at Riga with 14,000 men, had orders to join the main army with all dispatch, bringing with him a large supply of provisions. He was especially admonished not to engage the enemy in battle, if it could be avoided, or to yield to any temptation to pursue retreating detachments. With Swedish and Polish troops, Stanis-

[1] Stillé, A., *Karl XII's fälttågsplaner 1707-1709*, Lund, 1908.
[2] Generalstaben, *Karl den tolfte på slagfältet*, Stockholm, 1918-1919.

lav was to invade Russia from a point farther south and ultimately unite with the forces under Charles. The Swedish king likewise counted strongly on an uprising among the Cossacks in southern Russia as soon as he struck his blow at Peter and from the province of Ukraine aid could also be expected with reasonable certainty.

The world has seen few enterprises so persistently pursued by ill luck as Charles's expedition into Russia, and seldom has it witnessed such heroism, loyalty, and endurance as that which the Swedish army displayed on its dismal march into an ever-darkening world. Almost from the beginning, it was beset by difficulties and dangers of the most serious nature, some of which, at least, the most penetrating of human minds could not have foreseen or averted. The army crossed the Vistula on New Year's Day 1708 and began its march towards Moscow, the enemy making no determined effort to stop its advance until the Wabetsch River was reached. Here Peter had posted his army in an apparently impregnable position near the town of Holowczyn, but had made the mistake of stringing out his lines on too long a front, leaving gaps through which an alert foe could break. The experienced eye of Charles instantly detected this, and at once he hurled all his forces against the weak part of the line. After a bitter encounter, in which the Swedish soldiers, animated by the example of their king, who was in the thickest of the fray, displayed extraordinary courage, the Russians were routed.

Disasters.—This was the last important victory which Charles and his devoted army was destined to win; from this point on disaster lay in wait for them at every turn. King Stanislav was held in Poland by dangers of revolt and other serious internal troubles, and could render no aid. In accordance with prearranged plans, Peter cautiously retreated before the Swedes, taking care, however, that the region into which they advanced was first transformed into a charred wilderness. All grain and provisions were buried, the cattle driven into the forests, and towns and villages burned. After a time the Russians proceeded to attack the invaders, but they never offered the Swedes an opportunity to engage in a pitched battle. Small detachments who strayed away from the main divisions on foraging expeditions were intercepted and overwhelmed by superior numbers, and the rear and flanks of Charles's main army were constantly harassed by the enemy. The king therefore became increasingly anxious that Lewenhaupt, who had been ordered to come up with provisions at Holowczyn, should soon arrive. This general had, however, disobeyed the king's order not to engage in battles with the enemy, and had been seriously delayed on his march. It now became clear to Charles that Moscow could not be reached by the direct route which he had mapped out and two alternatives presented themselves to him: either to remain where he was and await the coming of Lewenhaupt with supplies, or to go southward into the Ukraine, with whose leader, the Hetman Mazepa, he had entered into an alliance. This old man of seventy, who was to play such a large and sinister part in the Swedish tragedy, was Polish by birth and a consummate intriguer from both predilection and necessity. He had previously won the confidence of Peter, whom he had rendered invaluable aid in keeping the Cossacks in check.[3] It was his ambition to make the Ukraine an independent state and in an alliance with Charles he now saw an opportunity to achieve this. The king was thoroughly deceived by the glib talk and calm assurance of the wily adventurer. Mazepa offered to place a large fighting force at his disposal and furnish ample provisions, the latter being a particularly strong inducement just then since food supplies in the Swedish army were, by reason of Lewenhaupt's blunder, running very low. For Charles it evidently was exceedingly difficult to make a choice. If he remained where he was and awaited Lewenhaupt's arrival, Mazepa would be in imminent danger of an enveloping movement by Peter's army, and thus in all probability would be prevented from giving any aid to the Swedish king; if, on the other hand, he joined Mazepa, Lewenhaupt would be in great danger of being intercepted and prevented from joining the main army. The king believed, in this dilemma, that it was the part of wisdom to proceed southward and join Mazepa, reasoning that in a serious situation Lewenhaupt would be more likely than the Ukrainian leader to extricate himself.

[3] Jensen, A., *Mazepa, Historiska bilder från Ukraina,* Lund, 1909.

The march into the Ukraine.—Charles's decision not to await Lewenhaupt was, no doubt, also due to the erroneous information which had reached him that Lewenhaupt was not far behind the main army. This decision, however, proved calamitous in every way. Lewenhaupt found himself sorely harassed by the Russians, who outnumbered his men four to one and doggedly hung on the rear and flanks of his forces, cutting down stragglers and smaller detachments, and putting the morale of the Swedish forces sorely to the test. To add to the seriousness of the situation, heavy rains fell, making the roads almost impassable and seriously retarding all progress. In order to save the remnant of his army, the distracted Lewenhaupt then decided to abandon all his stores, cannon, and ammunition, and in as hurried a march as was possible reach Charles's headquarters. When he at last reached this point his forces were more disconsolate and destitute than their comrades in the main division. "We had hoped," writes one of the soldiers, "that he would have brought us food, drink, and clothes, but he came empty-handed and utterly bewildered at the sudden change of fortune." Lewenhaupt's sacrifices had, however, been in vain. The force of 4,000 men which Charles had sent ahead under the command of General Lagercrona to seize the fort commanding the route to the Ukraine lost its way and this, coupled with a series of mistakes committed by Swedish generals, enabled Peter to anticipate Charles in seizing these strategic points. Mazepa's hopes of arousing his people to rally to the support of Charles had also failed, and when in November he appeared at the camp of the Swedish king it was as a ruined man at the head of a paltry 2,000 followers instead of the 40,000 which he had promised as auxiliaries to Charles. Peter now promptly prevailed upon the Ukrainians to depose Mazepa, seized his capital city, and came into possession of huge stores of grain, ammunition, and arms.

Weary and harassed, starving and disconsolate, seized by the feeling of an unnamed dread which their remoteness from the homeland and the constant sight of a desolate and miserable land accentuated, the Swedish soldiers were sustained only by the implicit confidence which they had in their hero king. Such implicit confidence was most natural, since during nine years Charles had gained victory after victory even when the odds had been overwhelmingly against him, and his men had come to believe that Fortune was always smiling on him and his country; it did not seem possible to them that the king would fail now. And was he not fighting a righteous war for his own land and against the most shameful treachery that the world had ever witnessed? While such reflections at first helped to sustain them, their courage and strength gradually, as fresh disaster came, reached a low ebb. Their cup of suffering and woe was not yet full. As early as the beginning of October, the cold began to grow severe, and from that time on there was no let-up in the intensity of the winter. It is claimed that the winter of 1708-1709 was the severest Europe had known in a century. Soldiers froze to death while sitting on their horses, and the army surgeons were kept constantly busy amputating arms and legs. Thousands froze to death in their tents, while others were crippled for life. When spring came, the once splendid Swedish army had dwindled from 30,000 fit soldiers to 20,000 haggard and ill-equipped men.

The disaster at Poltava, 1709.—The pillaging of the Russians and the dangers which lurked in the bitter enmity of the Muscovites forced the Swedes farther and farther southward, where Charles now proceeded to lay siege to the city of Poltava. What plan was in Charles's mind when he undertook this siege has been one of the most debated questions in connection with his campaigns. The best opinion inclines to the belief that it was his hope that Peter might be induced to offer battle with his entire army, in which event Charles felt confident of winning a victory. With a victory won, further military operations could be undertaken in this region, while reinforcements would have had time to arrive from Sweden and thus the Swedish army again be put in shape for effective action. In the beginning of June, Peter himself appeared on the scene and in person assumed command of the Russian forces. Soon thereafter Charles made a feint of crossing the Worskla River upon which Poltava is situated, and in the skirmish which ensued came the crowning disaster of the Swedes. The king's left foot was pierced by a bullet, which passed the whole length from heel to toes, crushing the bones and causing intense pain, and when soon a burning fever set in he was rendered incapable of directing the operations further. On being informed of this, Czar Peter immediately moved his entire army across the river to the side where the enemy was encamped and took up a strong position. In the confusion which the injury to the king had produced no efforts were made by the Swedes to prevent this movement. It had long been Charles's ardent hope that he might be permitted to measure strength with the Russian czar on the battlefield, but now that the opportunity had at last come he was rendered incompetent by excruciating pain and a burning fever to direct his devoted troops. Other factors contributed to add enormously to the disadvantages under which the Swedes entered the momentous battle which was imminent. Against their force of 20,000 men Peter could place 56,000, and these by no means constituted a rabble crowd like the one which had been so easily overwhelmed at Narva nine years before. With dogged persistence Peter had drilled his men into shape and had equipped them with the most up-to-date weapons that could be procured. Against this large and well-equipped army, holding a most advantageous position and protected by an artillery of seventy large cannon, the Swedish army advanced to battle on June 28th. The chief command of the Swedish forces had been entrusted to General Rehnsköld, an experienced fighter, but lacking entirely authority or the genius for strategy which had hitherto made Charles invincible. Their first attack against the Russian lines was successful, the battle proceeding according to the Swedish plans, but soon a serious mistake was made. Rehnsköld became hopelessly confused and further serious tactical blunders followed, with the result that a breach was made in the Swedish lines which the watchful eye of Peter immediately perceived, and rushing his battalions forward he succeeded in driving a wedge through the Swedish ranks and then enveloping the separate divisions with overwhelming masses of Russian troops. In the decisive encounter 4,000 Swedes had to meet the attack of 43,000 Russians, and no amount of heroic courage and desperate fighting could avail against such odds. The Swedes succeeded, however, in fighting their way through the encircling forces and retreating in good order, and their remarkable discipline enabled the remnants to reassemble near the battle-field. Five thousand men had been killed, wounded, and made prisoners, General Rehnsköld himself and Piper, the latter an especially trusted adviser of Charles, being among them. What the outcome of the uneven struggle would have been had Charles been in command in his usual vigour must, of course, always be

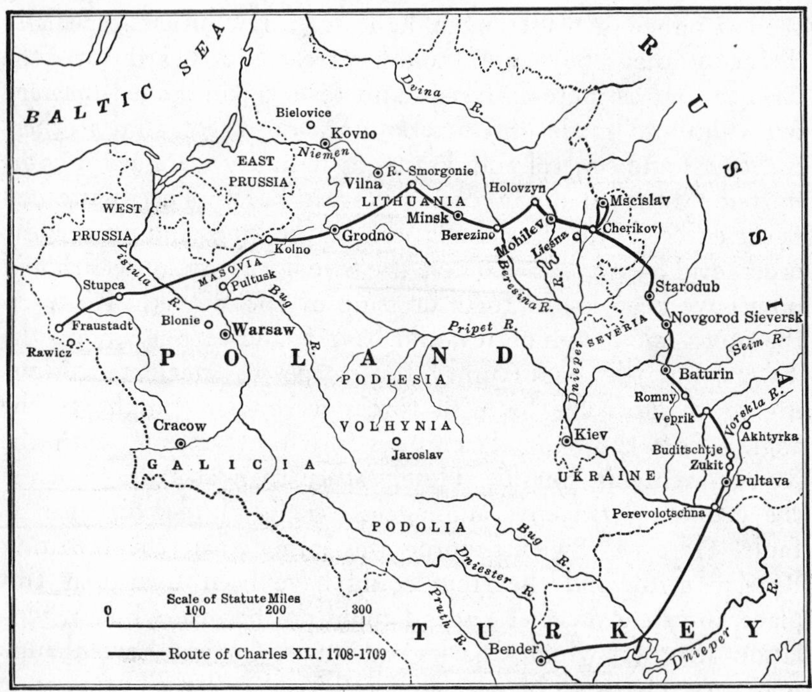

The march of Charles XII into Russia and Turkey

a matter of speculation, but certain it is that the tragic blunders to which the defeat can directly be attributed would in all certainty never have been committed. The exhaustive work of the Swedish Generals' Staff, to which allusion has been made (p. 495), gives a graphic account of the utter confusion and lack of co-ordination on the part of the Swedish generals in the battle, the chief blame evidently resting on Rehnsköld and next to him on Lewenhaupt, but generals of lesser rank also receiving their full measure of condemnation. The defeat, according to this authoritative work, was not primarily due to the smallness of the Swedish army, to lack of ammunition, or superiority of the Russian army in number of men and equipment, but to the blunders of the Swedish generals.

Resting on a litter borne between two horses, Charles had caused himself to be carried into the midst of the mêlée, and when his improvised bed was hit by bullets he mounted a horse and was one of the last to leave the battle-field. Summoning the last ounce of his strength, he issued a few orders, especially directing that the army should retreat southward into the Crimea, but as increasing pain and fever again gained mastery over him and made him utterly unfit to direct affairs others had to assume control and disastrous blunders were again committed. What to do in case a retreat became necessary had never entered into the calculations of the king, and no specific orders had been given. To save the Swedish army, orders should now have been issued for a crossing of the Worskla River on the other side of which it could have found refuge among the Tatars, but this opportunity for escape was neglected. Moving southward, the Swedish forces were soon caught at the angle where the Worskla empties into the Dnieper, with the Russian army in pursuit. Here, rather than at Poltava, came the crowning tragedy, and again Swedish leadership was at fault. Here the Swedish force was larger than the pursuing Russian army and the river could have been forded at this place, in case a successful stand could not be made, but in violation of orders which Charles had issued, General Lewenhaupt now surrendered all his men unconditionally to the enemy.

Surrender of Perewoloczna.—With this event, the surrender of Perewoloczna on June 30, 1709, the Swedish army became but a memory and the period of Sweden's greatness as a military and political power had definitely come to an end. With a couple of hundred followers, Charles escaped on a hastily constructed raft across the Dnieper into Turkish territory. In violation of the czar's promises that the captives of war, both officers and men, should receive humane treatment, the lives of the unfortunate Swedish soldiers were after this filled with unspeakable misery. Brought first to Moscow as exhibits at the czar's splendid festivities in celebration of the great victory, they were afterwards sent in scattered detachments to Siberia or to the mines of the Ural Mountain region. Few of them ever returned to Sweden.

The battle of Poltava and the subsequent surrender of the Swedish army meant a complete change in the alignment of northern Europe. Few statesmen realized, however, at the time, how portentous were to be the changes that this was to bring over Europe—to the great increase of her woes.

Already by the beginning of 1709 Sweden was groaning under the heavy burdens which the wars placed upon all classes. The enforced contributions of money for carrying on the war were impoverishing the people and the drain upon the man-power of the nation was terrible; units which originally were called upon to place one soldier in the field were now in many instances called on to furnish as many as five men. Industry was at a standstill, largely because the able-bodied men were consumed in war. There were mutterings of discontent among all classes, although the king personally was not held responsible for the misfortunes which had come over the land. The Council had frankly revealed to him the deplorable situation and had urged him to make peace with his enemies, but Charles had been deaf to all these appeals. It has been quite the custom of earlier historians to censure Charles severely for his attitude at this time, but later authorities generally take the view, and no doubt rightly so, that a peace then would have meant only a temporary respite; Sweden could enjoy no security until the issue had been fought to a finish with both Russia and Poland.

Ready to seize the spoils.—Even before news had reached the Western powers of the defeat at Poltava, it was well known to them that Charles was in terrible distress in a far-away region, and both Denmark and Poland made haste to return to their alliance with Peter and begin hostilities against Sweden. Stanislav's power in Poland now vanished as a dream. Apparently defenceless, Sweden was threatened with an invasion into the heart of the land itself. Eagerly Frederick IV sent an army of 15,000 Danes into Skåne, expecting to win an easy victory, since "nothing was now left to the Swedish lion but his claws." The world was, however, to learn that the nation still had fighting men and that it was not yet entirely prostrate. Fortunately for the country, there was one man who did not lose courage and who had the ability to drill a new army into shape. That man was Magnus Stenbock, who in a short time out of inexperienced country lads made an effective army with which he inflicted a crushing defeat upon the Danes at Hälsingborg and compelled them to return to their own country (February 10, 1710). While thus the Danes had gained nothing by their attack, they had done Peter a good turn by engaging the Swedish forces while he completed his conquest of the Swedish Baltic provinces, Riga, Pernau, Reval, and a large part of Finland now falling into his hands.

Charles in Turkey.—Charles remained in Turkey several years, and his failure to return to his own country has by many been taken as indisputable evidence of his recklessness and love of wild adventure. More than any other episode of his adventure-filled life, this has been seized upon as irrefutable evidence that he was indeed the "Madman of the North." He had, it is true, intended at first to remain among the Turks only until his health had been restored, but new opportunities seemed to open up to him through the aid which Turkish statesmen promised him in his fight against his enemy, who was also their arch-enemy, and this caused his stay to be prolonged. The Turks had been seriously alarmed by the Russian victory of Poltava, and now held out promises that a large military force would be placed at the disposal of the Swedish king. Charles now intended to return to Poland at the head of a Turkish army, and in this project he displayed a resourcefulness even in diplomacy which almost brought success. The Sultan Akmed was prevailed upon to renew the war on Peter—wars between Russia and Turkey were chronic affairs—and his grand vizier, Baltaji Mehemet Pasha, was sent against the czar with an army of 200,000 men. After having committed a number of serious tactical blunders, Peter found himself hemmed in between two Turkish armies and the Pruth River and was thus absolutely at the mercy of the enemy. As a last desperate attempt to escape, he resorted to diplomacy and bribes, offering the Turks the surrender of important territory and the payment of a large sum of money to the grand vizier, in return for which that worthy potentate should permit him to withdraw with his entire army. The grand vizier yielded to the temptation and Peter marched away with his army to the tune of lively music and with banners fluttering gayly in the air. So certain had Charles been that Peter could not escape the grip of his enemies that he had proceeded to the scene in order to witness the humiliation of his foe; instead he had the mortifying experience of learning, when he arrived, that peace had already been concluded and the Russian army was safely on its way. The punishment which subsequently was meted out to the grand vizier for his treason was small satisfaction to the Swedish king. Nothing daunted, however, by this set-back, Charles took a new start, and again he was able to prevail upon the sultan to declare war on Russia, but as the Turkish treasury was exhausted the new war was carried on in desultory fashion. In the meantime, Charles had taken up his headquarters at a small place called Bender. His prolonged stay in Turkey had now become a source of irritation, a party hostile to him having gathered strength, and these enemies sought to compel him to depart for home. Being aware of their deeply laid plot to fall upon him and make him a prisoner once he got started on his journey, and then to deliver him to either Czar Peter or to Augustus of Poland, he declined to budge from his quarters. Of all the deeds of daring and prowess which are associated with the name of Charles XII, the episode at Bender where, with a mere handful of trusty companions, he held 10,000 Turks at bay until the house which served him and his men as a fortress caught fire, is the best known. Finally taken captive, Charles was given kind and respectful treatment, for the Turks had been tremendously impressed by his heroic qualities.

Charles returns home.—Charles had ordered the Swedish Council to send an army under General Stenbock to Germany in order to advance upon Poland, where he would meet them. Stenbock did indeed manage to raise an army of 17,000 men with which he landed in Germany, but as the enemy in far superior numbers prevented him from advancing eastward he fell back into Mecklenburg. From every direction the enemy was now closing in on him.

He therefore decided to advance against the Danes, who again were decisively beaten in the battle of Gadebusch (December 9, 1712). Pursued by the allied armies, Stenbock now sought refuge in the fort of Tönningen, where he soon was hemmed in on every side, and with provisions gone no other course remained than to surrender himself and the entire army. Contrary to solemn promises, the heroic general was kept a prisoner and subjected to such cruel treatment that it soon broke his health and brought about his premature death. Next Stettin was lost, and before the end of 1714 all of Finland had been overrun by the Russians. With all outlying territory lost, and the enemy preparing to attack Sweden herself, the Swedish Council summoned a Riksdag, at the same time sending a full report of conditions to the king and even threatening to sue for peace on its own account. Finally Charles resolved to return home. In company with one lone companion he traversed the entire Continent through Hungary and southern and western Germany, part of it hostile territory, and after an incredibly rapid ride the two men appeared one dismal November night at the city gates of Stralsund, then a Swedish city, and demanded admission. Aften an absence of fourteen years Charles had at last returned to his kingdom. When he took his departure his realm was far-flung and prosperous, his country feared and respected, and he had left at the head of a splendid army. Now his people were bled white, all his foreign possessions with the exception of the little spot on which lay Stralsund lost to the enemy, and no Swedish army in existence anywhere. The wreck was complete. Like vultures waiting to seize upon carrion, the enemies were hovering about watching what was supposed to be the death agony of the mortally wounded prey. Eager to get a part of the plunder, Prussia and Hanover had joined the anti-Swedish alliance; the former because its king, Frederick William—Prussia and Brandenburg had become the kingdom of Prussia in 1701—wanted to keep Stettin, the latter because her elector, George I of England, cast greedy eyes on Bremen and Verden. As Charles obstinately refused to cede a foot of land, his many enemies continued their attacks upon his stricken nation. For over a year he defended Pomerania against overwhelming numbers of

Danes, Saxons, and Prussians, until the walls of Stralsund were in ruins; only then did he forsake the place, escaping to Sweden in a small boat.

The last heroic stand of Charles.—The magnetism of his personality again gave a spark of courage to the Swedes, and once more men rallied to the standard. The supreme faith which a Holstein adventurer, Baron George von Görtz, had expressed to Charles that Sweden was still able to throw off her enemies and emerge a victor from the fearful struggle, had completely won the king's confidence in him, and he now became all-powerful in the administration, even the Council and the old departments of state being henceforth ignored. Görtz was extremely resourceful, especially in financial matters, and he now proceeded to loan money on the security of the private property of citizens. One million in token money (copper coins to have the same value as silver coins) was also issued. With this money Charles was able to raise another army with which he invaded Norway, endeavouring in that way to strike at Denmark, but the expedition brought him no advantage. Czar Peter had in the meantime arrived at the Danish capital with 30,000 troops for an assault on Sweden proper, but after cruising along the coast of Skåne for a time he suddenly abandoned the project, partly because he had no liking for an encounter with Charles's forces on the latter's ground, and partly because he suspected his allies of designs to betray him. Charles had invaded Norway a second time, probably with the intention of taking possession of the country either to be kept as an integral part of Sweden or to be used for trading when the peace settlement eventually came. He was laying siege to Fredrikshall, when on November 30, 1718, his career was cut short by a bullet, probably from a fortress cannon which pierced both temples. The belief that Charles was killed by a bullet fired at close range and from his own camp has persisted down to our day. In order, if possible, to get data on the probable manner of the king's death, his sarcophagus in the Riddarholm Church in Stockholm has been opened by royal permission on three different occasions—namely, in 1746, 1859, and 1917—and the remains examined by scientists and technical experts. The examination made in 1917 was particularly thorough-going since use was made of Roentgen photography. The examination, besides showing conclusively that physically the king must have been a normal individual—strange tales on this point had been current—revealed that the fatal bullet had struck with remarkably great force as though fired at close range, but inasmuch as the trench in which the king was stationed at the time was only about six hundred feet from the enemy's position, this fact, it was held, does not prove anything. The manner of the king's death will, no doubt, always remain a mystery.

The body of Charles XII is carried back to his native land. From a painting by Gustaf Cederström

The body of the dead king was placed in a plain pine coffin and carried by members of his body-guard across the boundary into Sweden. It was indeed a sad funeral procession which slowly wended its way through the country towards Stockholm, where interment was made in Riddarholm Church, February 26, 1719. The ceremony took place at night by the light of torches in order that the poverty and simplicity which accompanied the rites should not be too apparent; so poverty-stricken had the nation become that it could not afford the display which befitted the memory of the fallen monarch.

The king was dead, and crumbled were all Swedish hopes

of power and prestige. In just about a hundred years, the nation, impelled by a remarkable spirit of unity and sacrifice, and inspired and guided by kings, statesmen, and generals of such commanding skill and daring that history can scarcely find a counterpart to this Swedish galaxy, had extended its domains to undreamed-of limits and had heroically set to work to plant its own civilization in the conquered parts. When Charles XII became king its treasury was rich and its army and navy were the best organized in Europe. And now, in the comparatively short period of eighteen years, the splendid structure had been laid in ruins, not a foot of foreign soil remained in Swedish possession, Swedish military prestige was a mere byword, money and man-power were gone, and six nations were arrayed against her, awaiting the opportunity to deliver the death-blow and divide the spoils. It was from such dizzy heights of power and glory down into the lowest depths of humiliation, abject poverty, and weakness that Sweden had fallen while Charles XII was king, and still, paradoxical as it may seem, he remains, next to Gustavus Adolphus, the great national hero of Sweden, and the anniversary of his death is still celebrated annually by students of the Swedish universities. When Sweden's greatest poet, Tegnér, hails him as "Svea's (poetic name for Sweden) greatest son," this tribute strikes a responsive chord in the hearts of Swedes everywhere.

Charles's place in Swedish history.—How is this seeming anomaly to be explained? He was first of all honourable; he fought with fair weapons; his sense of honour appears the more remarkable when viewed in contrast to the shameless lying and self-seeking of contemporary kings and statesmen. He despised the crooked ways of diplomacy, the oily tongue, the finesse of the professional diplomat. The closest study of his plans by military experts shows that these were wisely conceived and they failed because of a succession of events that no man could foresee. Fear was absolutely foreign to his soul and he never asked any man to take a risk that he would not gladly take himself. To the last he kept his soul untarnished by licentiousness and he remained constantly true to the fine ideals of godliness and purity which his mother had instilled into his mind. The judgment of the historian regarding Charles and his reign must also be tempered by the conviction that the areas which were lost to the Swedish state by him were by the very nature of the situation doomed to be lost some day anyway, through the irrepressible expansion of Germany and Russia, as their nationalism asserted itself. Charles knew that there was no use in compromising; if the enemy gained a strong foothold he would, on some pretext or other, soon reach out for more of the Swedish possessions.

Charles XII had with unyielding obstinacy refused to consider any proposal that Swedish territory be ceded to the enemy, unless recompense be made in the form of other territory, but now that he was gone the yearning for peace among soldiers as well as citizens asserted itself vigorously. It was no longer a question of the sacrifice of territory, but of how much could be saved out of the wreck. Those in control of Swedish affairs were willing to sacrifice the German possessions in the hope that they might thereby secure assistance against Russia and thus save the Baltic provinces.

The robbers secure their booty.—To this end they concluded peace first with Hanover-England, by which, in return for 1,000,000 riksdaler, Bremen and Verden were ceded to Hanover, next with Prussia which received Pomerania to the Peene River and the islands of Usedom and Wollin, in return for 2,000,000 riksdaler; finally, in a treaty with Denmark, Sweden relinquished her toll exemption in the Sound and agreed not to assist the Duke of Holstein-Gottorp further, and to acquiesce in a Danish military occupation of his provinces. These sacrifices had, however, been made in vain, for, with their booty securely tucked away, all these powers transferred their interests to other fields, leaving to the weak and stricken Sweden the uneven task of coping alone with the eastern giant. A plan for a grand coalition against Russia was indeed drawn up by Swedish, English, and French commissions. The plan failed mainly because the King of Prussia would do nothing after he had Stettin in his grasp, and privately he assured Peter of his neutrality. An English fleet did indeed join the Swedish fleet in the Baltic, but the commander was utterly indifferent to the whole project and sailed away. "The hope [for European intervention in behalf of Sweden] foundered in the first place on the selfishness of England and Prussia, or rather on the self-seeking duplicity and short-sightedness which invaded European politics after Utrecht (peace of Utrecht, 1713, at the conclusion of the War of the Spanish Succession) and opened up the golden age of cabinet diplomacy. The first vic-

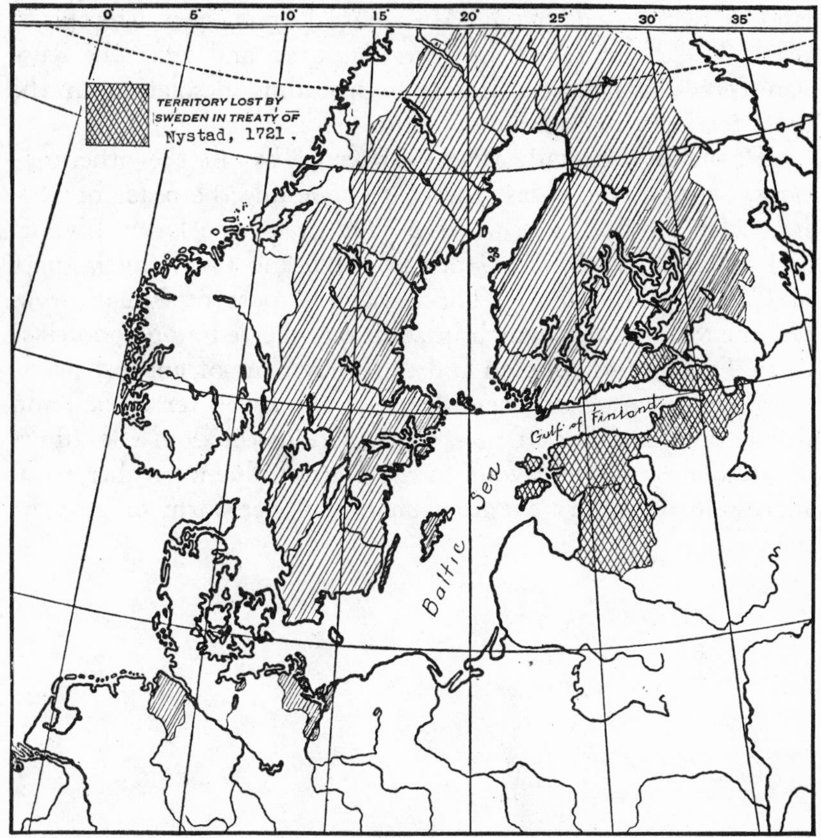

Territory lost by Sweden in the Peace of Nystad

tim of this faithless selfishness was Sweden. She was compelled to suffer and bleed in an unequal struggle, alone to meet the first great invasion into Western civilization of the Muscovite colossus, although the protection of the civilization of the Baltic lands was at least as much a European, and particularly a German, concern as it was Swedish."[4] The statesmen of

[4] Stavenow, L., *Sveriges historia,* Vol. IX, p. 58.

Europe sowed the wind in 1721 and Europe has often since reaped the whirlwind.

To speed up Swedish desires for peace and to show how futile was further opposition, Czar Peter in 1719 sent a fleet across the Baltic, Russian soldiers were landed in Sweden, and the coast districts of Uppland, Södermanland, and Östergötland were ravaged in true Muscovite fashion. An attempt to reach Stockholm failed, however. In 1720 and 1721 the Russian forces reappeared, this time spreading desolation in the coast territory of Norrland.

Peace of Nystad, 1721.—Deserted by all the other nations, Sweden was at last forced to conclude the peace of Nystad with Russia, by which she gave up to the latter Livonia and Esthonia, with the islands of Dagö and Ösel, Ingria, part of Carelia, and Viborg. The remaining part of Finland was returned to Sweden, which in addition received 2,000,000 riksdaler. Freedom of religion and the enjoyment of ancient privileges were guaranteed the citizens of the ceded territories, and Russia obligated herself not to interfere in the domestic affairs of Sweden or to endeavour to exert any influence in her royal succession or in any eventual change of her form of government.

Chapter XX

AN ATTEMPT AT POPULAR GOVERNMENT WHICH FAILED

Intrigues begin regarding the royal succession.—Charles XII had never married, nor had he made any provision for the succession. Nearest in line of succession after him were Karl Frederick of Holstein-Gottorp, son of Duke Frederick and Charles's sister, Hedwig Sophia, whose marriage had been one of the inciting motives for Denmark's readiness to join the conspiracy against Sweden, and the youngest sister of the late king, Ulrika Eleanora, who had married Frederick of Hesse. The latter acted with unseemly haste in order to secure the crown for his wife. At the moment when Charles's career was ended by the fatal bullet at Fredrikshall both Frederick and Karl Frederick were in Norway, and the former immediately sent a courier to notify Ulrika Eleanora of the tragedy, at the same time, on his own responsibility, causing Görtz to be arrested. Ulrika Eleanora had considerable ability, could make rapid decisions, and was endowed with the strong will-power so characteristic of the members of the Vasa family, and she in turn acted with great promptness. First she secured a decision by the vacillating Council upholding her right to the throne. Her husband was in the meantime busy cultivating the good-will of the army leaders, the 1,000,000 silver dalers which had just been received by him for the pay of officers being judiciously distributed where they would do him and his wife the most good. The army agreed to Ulrika Eleanora's elevation to the throne, but only temporarily, and on the express condition that absolutism would be abolished, and a Riksdag summoned to decide definitely regarding the succession and to formulate and adopt a new form of government. A limitation of royal power was very distasteful to Ulrika Eleanora, but, knowing the temper of the people, she dared not interpose any serious or strenuous objection. When the Riksdag met at Stockholm in the early part of 1719, she was compelled to approve a resolution declaring that neither she nor anyone else had a hereditary right to the crown; not until she had given these pledges and formally approved the new instrument of government was she formally elected queen.

The new plan of government.—After the nation's bitter experience, it was but natural that an uncompromising aversion was felt to royal absolutism, and a determination to get rid of the entire system, root and branch, existed. Those officials who had served and defended the system were hated and maligned. Görtz was speedily sent to the block for his many alleged crimes in conducting the government, the ordinary rights of defence procedure having been denied him, and some of his henchmen were sentenced to prison terms.

The provisions of the new instrument of government which the Riksdag next approved were determined mainly by the nation's desire to escape the defects of government which in the past, it was felt, had brought untold evil upon the land, and to avoid a repetition of these evils. Those periods in which lords, through the medium of the Council, had ruled the country had been cursed by a ruthless exploitation of the poor by the rich; these days had seen the reckless and shameful transfer of crown lands to a few grasping individuals, with widespread misery in consequence, and to save the nation from these abuses the "reduktion" had become a necessity. The absolute monarchy had sprung almost spontaneously from a common feeling of the masses that in it lay the surest safeguard against the predatory rule of the few. After much bitter experience, the evils of this form of government were now glaringly apparent, and the nation was ready to try a third expedient. The basic principle of the new régime was the vesting of supreme power in the Riksdag. This seemed the wise and patriotic course to follow. The Estates, so the proponents of the new scheme reasoned, represented all the people of the nation and hence must necessarily represent the popular will. Under such a rule the blunders of fallible autocrats and the selfishness and bickering of an oligarchy, as represented in the Council, would be avoided.

Desire to vest power in the people.—The underlying idea was, of course, the democratic notion that the people know best what is good for them. The new constitution was not based on any clearly thought-out theories of popular sovereignty, although foreign parliamentary experience, especially English, may have offered some suggestions.[1] It was almost entirely national and conservative. In the time of Gustavus Vasa, Gustavus Adolphus, and Charles X the Estates appeared to have had a determining voice in the government, but what escaped the eyes of the Swedish constitution makers in 1719 was the fact that this power had been more apparent than real. These kings had, after all, held the rudder firmly in their hands, but the early rulers of the new régime lacked almost wholly the ability and exalted purposes of the aforesaid monarchs. The vesting of power in the Estates, wise as this was in theory, held the possibility of great evil, since the Estates did not fully represent the nation, and the important agencies which are essential to the successful functioning of democracy were, furthermore, wanting. No publicity was given to the debates of the Estates, no check placed upon the members by an educated public opinion, and no system of election had been devised which could insure a real representation of the people. The three higher orders in the Riksdag were made up largely of officials who naturally supported bureaucratic interests; under such a condition, the Riksdag interfered largely in purely administrative details. The political conflict which ensued was therefore chiefly between parliamentarism of a democratic nature and bureaucracy. Still, if the Swedes had been left to themselves to work out their own political salvation, they might have struggled on with fair results, but other nations, unfortunately, found it to their interest to interfere in their domestic affairs. The political alignment in Europe at the time tempted both France and Russia to bid high for Swedish support, and both came, in time, to pour money by the barrelful into the country in order to control elections, thus sowing seeds of schism and playing havoc with the people's morale. Before long this was to result in bring-

[1] Hjärne, E., *Åmbetsmannaintressen och politiska doktriner på 1719 års riksdag* in *Historisk tidskrift*, 1916.

ing the nation nearer to the precipice of national dissolution than it had ever been before.

As already indicated, the new constitution of 1719 circumscribed royal power radically. The king had the power to make appointments to practically all positions, but with the limitation that the Council could reject those whose promotion conflicted with the stipulations of the constitution or jeopardized the welfare of citizens. For the important offices the Council was to recommend certain men from which group the king was to make his choice and in the case of less important offices departments were to make recommendations. The Riksdag was the final authority in matters of appointments and thus came to play an extremely important rôle. The king was indeed a member of the Council, but his only special prerogative lay in the right to cast two votes and to render a decision in case of a tie vote. In order, however, to preclude the possibility of an undue power by the Council, the new constitution stipulated that its members were to be appointed by the Estates; this assumption of power by the Estates was camouflaged by the stipulation that the king should make the appointments, but from a list furnished him by the Riksdag. The members of the Council were subject to removal by the Riksdag, thus offering it a further check upon this body; in practice this power came to be exercised largely for political ends, for they had in reality a very limited power. The great length to which the framers of the new constitution were willing to go, in their determination to deprive royalty of power, is seen in the provision which made it obligatory for the ruler to conform in his royal charter to the wishes of the Estates. Fearing that long intervals between Riksdag sessions would tempt Council and king to usurp power, the constitution makers stipulated that meetings must be held at least every three years.

Membership of the Riksdag.—In conformity with the traditional system of the land, the Riksdag was made up of representatives of the four orders—the nobility, the clergy, the burghers, and the *bönder*. In this period the first-named counted approximately 2,000 families, the head of each one of these being entitled to a seat in the Riksdag; in reality the group was never at any time represented by more than a few hundred. Its poorer members could ill afford to attend the usually prolonged sessions, no pay or mileage being provided; they found it more profitable to sell their proxies to others, generally to the highest bidder, a practice that naturally led to many abuses. The former schism in the noble group itself (p. 454) no longer existed, the controlling faction being now the lower nobility, consisting mainly of civil and military officials. The number of clergy in the Riksdag was relatively small, amounting to only about fifty. While the group was small, it came, by reason of superior education and ability on the part of its members, to exert an influence much out of proportion to its numerical strength. The burgher class consisted of merchants and traders and brought considerable practical experience into the deliberations. The number of representatives of this order in the Riksdag was generally about one hundred and twenty. The *bönder,* who in former days had stood as an unshakable bulwark against aristocratic encroachment and abuses, were now, because of their well-known predilection for royalty, pushed as far to the side as possible. They were excluded from the Council, as well as from the Secret Committee, a discrimination that was extremely significant and boded ill for the operation of the new government. To the Committee were referred such matters as foreign affairs, appropriations, administration, bank management, and defence. It was not an innovation in Swedish government, for similar committees had several times been appointed since the reign of Gustavus Adolphus, primarily for the purpose of considering questions of foreign relations. It was composed of fifty members from the nobility and twenty-five each from the clergy and the burgesses respectively, who were elected at the beginning of each session of the Riksdag. Under the "elastic clause" defining the scope of its power, and under the guidance of aggressive leadership, this body soon abrogated to itself most of the power which was vested in the Riksdag and thus became the real governing body, its chairman being the most powerful individual in the nation. The members were sworn to secrecy, and hence it was impossible to exercise any check upon the views and acts of individuals.

Frederick becomes king.—The election of her husband as king was Ulrika Eleanora's highest ambition. The personal popularity of the queen and the judicious bestowal of favours upon members of the Riksdag at last carried the day, and in 1720 Frederick was duly invested with royal power and dignity. The new ruler at first enjoyed considerable popularity, since he was generous and jovial, free and easy in his associations with his subjects, and not without talent. In the war of the Spanish Succession he had rendered honourable service on the side of the anti-French allies and later had accompanied Charles XII into Norway. On this venture he won the king's confidence to such an extent that he was appointed commander-in-chief of the Swedish armies, a position which meant little while Charles lived, but with the latter's death full opportunity came to him to exert a deciding influence upon Swedish affairs, an opportunity which he speedily and effectively used, as has been seen, to further his own and his wife's interests. There was much in the king's character and record that gave promise of wisdom and leadership in the new reign, but it soon became evident that an inherent weakness in his personality made him utterly unfit for his new rôle. After his first spurt of energy and ambition, he rapidly subsided into hopeless indolence and pleasure-seeking. A foreigner by birth and an adventurer by inclination, he had set out, as so many other princes of petty states in his day, to make his fortune, and having reached the beckoning goal, he seemed to feel that now the time had come for enjoying life to the limit. To him this meant licentious indulgence and freedom from every serious care.

Arvid Horn.—The sloth and moral turpitude of the king naturally served to increase the power and influence of the incumbent of the chancellor's office. Fortunately, the first chancellor under the new régime, Arvid Horn, who also held the office of "landtmarskalk" or president of the noble Estate and in this capacity presided at the sessions of the Riksdag, had such outstanding ability that he may be rated as standing next to Axel Oxenstierna and Johan Gyllenstierna among Swedish statesmen in point of ability and public service. Almost sixty years of age when circumstances laid upon him the responsibility of guiding the kingdom over the most hazardous road that it had ever been compelled to travel, Horn brought to his office a long and varied experience, honesty, sound in-

Arvid Horn

sight, tact, and fearlessness; these virtues set him quite apart from nearly all his contemporary statesmen and rulers. With great tact he had handled the negotiations which led to the election of Stanislav in Poland and later had returned home to Sweden, by order of Charles, to take an important part in the civil administration of the land. His independence and fearlessness had later incurred the ill-will of Charles, with the result that he had been relieved of all official duties, save that of the presidency of the Council. The same independence of mind and honest frankness of speech which had angered Charles had also bred ill-will towards him in Ulrika Eleanora, and through her influence he had also been excluded from membership in the Council. The Estates, however, later taking matters into their own hands, had elected him president and chancellor again. A kindly disposed man, of fine outward appearance and great dignity, Horn won the respect, if not the love, of all right-thinking people. Possessed of great wealth, he gave generously to the relief of suffering. In the routine of his daily life he observed all the practices of a Christian gentleman, whispered a prayer every time the church bells tolled, and never failed, even when foreign ministers or other distinguished dignitaries were visiting in his home, to lead in family evening prayers.

Horn's foreign policy.—Horn was the first Swedish statesman to abandon the traditional policy of Sweden that her interest and safety demanded the control of large areas of lands on the south and east side of the Baltic. He saw clearly that the days were gone forever when Sweden could play the rôle of a great military nation and hold extensive areas of land outside of her own natural boundaries. The preservation of Sweden as an independent state without pretensions to greatness, as measured by military power and political influence, but strong in the wealth which is acquired by the activities of peace, was his ideal, and for this he laboured with singular devotion and consummate skill. In this policy he was opposed by disgruntled individuals, political intriguers, and blatant chauvinists, and for many years his position was constantly imperilled by these forces of opposition. Patiently and wisely he laboured unceasingly to build up the resources of the country and with utmost difficulty he finally gained ascendancy over many opponents who tried to block his policies. The most formidable of these opponents were the partisans of Karl Frederick. This prince had been betrothed to the daughter of Czar Peter, who therefore was now interested in seeing Holstein, which the duke claimed as his principality, but which in the treaties following the wars of Charles XII had been ceded to

Denmark, returned to his prospective son-in-law. After the czar's death in 1725, his widow, Catherine I, pressed the marriage scheme with even greater energy than the czar had done, for being herself a child of the proletariat, the former wife of a Swedish officer, she had set her heart on marrying her daughter to a scion of one of the oldest among the European dynasties, in order thus to cover up the humbleness of her daughter's birth. In this ambition, the Swedish adherents saw dazzling possibilities for their country. The duke should, they reasoned, be elected heir to the Swedish throne, and from sheer gratitude for this great favour Catherine would help the Swedes regain the lost Baltic provinces. Sinister intrigues were thus going on with the object of bringing about an alliance between Sweden and Russia, and in these lay possibilities for incalculable evil. In order to thwart these activities and put a check on the Holstein party, Horn made approaches to England, for whose institutions he felt great admiration, with a view to bringing Sweden into the Hanoverian alliance which England, France, and Prussia had formed as a counter-force to the Spanish-Austrian entente. With assurance of the support of this league, the Swedish leader felt that his country could bid defiance to Russia, whose interference in Swedish affairs had become a brazen effrontery. Promises of Russian subsidies, as well as threats of a Russian attack upon Sweden, were equally ineffective in swaying Horn and his followers from their patriotic course. The Hanoverian alliance proposal was finally carried, but only by the narrow margin of the two votes which the king cast. Horn followed up his advantage by submitting certain documents to the Secret Committee which seriously compromised one of the leaders of the Holstein party, while others in the group were ordered to give an account of their part in the Russian intrigues. As a result, several of the plotters resigned from the Council and their places were filled by Horn's supporters. Convinced that the alliance with England, France, and Prussia would give him active support in case of need, Horn from now on pursued a firm and fearless policy towards the Muscovite power. A demand upon Catherine by the Swedish statesman that she must cease meddling in the affairs of his country aroused her bitter ire, but she found it the part of wisdom to heed the warning.

Ideals of peace.—Firmly entrenched at last in power, Horn turned his energy to the rehabilitation of his war-torn country, and Sweden was now to be privileged to enjoy a blissful period of peace and prosperity, the brightest aspect of which was a remarkable achievement by the nation in literature, science, and art. "In culture," says an authority, in discussing this phase of the nation's life, "this is in a certain sense our most glorious period. It is the early blossoming time of our young Swedish literature, our art, and our science. Neither before nor since has our country, nor many other countries, been able to show such an array of resplendent names. It seemed as though Sweden was on the way to regain in cultural achievement what during the wars of Charles XII she had lost in material wealth." [2] Just as the people's fortitude and spirit of sacrifice during the years of fearful warfare cause wonder, so their ability now to make good the losses of war and build up the nation's resources again must always elicit genuine admiration.

Horn's first objective was to put the nation's financial structure on a solid basis. The national debt at the end of the war was estimated at 60,000,000 silver dalers (190,000,000 crowns), about half of this sum being made up of the copper coins which Görtz had put into circulation with the dictum that they must be accepted as the equivalent of silver money. This part of the debt was materially reduced by a government decree that the coins would be redeemed at a figure far below their face value. A great saving was effected by drastic retrenchments in the expenditure for military defence. Extraordinary taxes in the form of "contributions" were levied until 1721, and by this time the debt had been so greatly reduced that special taxes were no longer deemed necessary.

Economic development.—In their economic policies, Horn and his aids, like all their contemporary statesmen, were guided wholly by the theories of the mercantilist school of economic thought. The government therefore sought to promote

[2] Warburg, K., *Svensk litteraturhistoria*, Stockholm, 1880, p. 60.

industry by liberal state subventions. By collecting and annually publishing a great amount of data regarding the economic situation in the land the officials proved themselves practical leaders and men of affairs. Regulations similar to the English Navigation Act were instituted for the extension of the nation's carrying trade. This resulted in a rapid increase in the merchant marine, and by 1736 the combined tonnage of native vessels lying in Swedish harbours exceeded the total of all foreign vessels in the same harbours. In that year no less than 1,844 Swedish ships with a combined tonnage of approximately 100,000 tons left the country, some sailing even to the distant Levant, carrying large quantities of the products of the rich iron mines of the country.

Treaties were made with the Barbary States and with Tunis, Tripoli, and Turkey for the purpose of securing protection against the Mediterranean corsairs. Swedish trade on the Mediterranean became so extensive that it was even found necessary to place Swedish consuls in places like Tunis and Smyrna. A new impetus was given the trade with India by the organization of the East India Company, with headquarters in Gothenburg. In order to give support to new industries in their competition with foreign merchants, a special fund was created, part of which was raised by government appropriations, part by assessment on all industries out of which subsidies were paid.

To this period belongs the introduction of the modern factory system into Sweden, with which event the name of Jonas Alströmer is indissolubly connected. Alströmer lived his boyhood days in great poverty. As a young man he had gone to London, where through diligence and keen business acumen he in time acquired a large fortune. His great love for his native land bred in him the resolve to establish at home the industrial system which he had discovered to be the real source of England's great prosperity. During extensive travels in England, Holland, and France, he familiarized himself thoroughly with the complicated manufacturing processes and factory organization of those countries. In order to be able to build a similar system in Sweden, importation thither of machines and experienced workmen was necessary, but serious obstacles were encountered as soon as he tried this, since the foreign governments, fearing competition to their own industries, vigorously guarded against any attempts to take men and equipment out of their lands. Alströmer managed, however, to get the parts of three looms, some material, and a few skilled labourers past the watchful customs officials of Holland, and with these precious assets he reached Sweden. In 1724 he received a charter for a manufacturing establishment in his native Alingsås, a town near Gothenburg. The enterprise prospered, capital flowed freely at first into the project, and soon a good beginning of a textile industry had been made. Alingsås became a sort of technical school for the entire nation, and the number of factories and workers grew rapidly. Between 1719-1739 no less than 149 new manufacturing plants were started for the production of woollen, silk, linen, paper, porcelain, iron, and steel wares. Other enterprises also began to flourish. An exchange office (*växelkontor*) was instituted in 1749 through the operation of which a lowering of exchange rates, which had risen unduly through an increased emission of paper money, would be effected. The government was at first very conservative in giving aid to new industries through subsidies and special trade privileges, and as long as this policy was adhered to progress was slow but safe; unfortunately, the pressure for all kinds of state aid in time broke down this conservatism, with the inevitable result that the business structure came to rest on an insecure foundation, speculation became rampant, and economic disaster followed in due time. Iron continued to be Sweden's most important export article, in value amounting to five-sevenths of the total of export trade. Copper and silver mining, which a hundred years earlier had been one of the main sources of the country's wealth, had now sunk into comparative insignificance. Agriculture continued to be carried on under very primitive conditions and was hampered by a number of restrictions against sale of land, and division of estates, and by limitation of the number of servants which a *bonde* might employ on his farm. Agricultural prosperity was also seriously hampered by miserable roads, which made access to markets exceedingly difficult. Sweden did not produce enough grain for domestic use and the necessity of importing large quantities was one of the most serious handicaps to the nation's economic progress. The shortage of grain was furthermore alarmingly accentuated by the increasing production of spirituous liquors. The Estates tried to put a check upon the privilege which the individual enjoyed to distil and brew for home consumption, but the restrictive laws which were passed were soon repealed out of deference to the *bönder,* who vociferously protested that such measures deprived them of their "sacred personal rights." Two new plants, potatoes and tobacco, were introduced in this period, and here also Alströmer took the initiative. The government encouraged the use of potatoes, and therefore caused instructions regarding their planting and use as food to be published and distributed, but in spite of these encouragements, such is human perversity, the wholesome tubers did not become popular as rapidly as tobacco.

Culture in Horn's time.—As was natural, the minds and energies of Horn and his co-labourers were far more engrossed with the problems of economic and industrial rehabilitation and development than with the purely cultural enrichment of the nation. It is to their everlasting credit, however, that they prepared the ground and bounteously sowed the seed which later in the Period of Freedom, as the era from 1718 to 1772 is generally called by Swedish historians, was to blossom forth in one of the most glorious cultural epochs in the history of the Swedish people. Utilitarianism was the watchword of the entire era. That which was judged practical and useful, and hence promised to increase the material well-being of the nation, was stressed. In view of the country's fearful losses by war, it behooved the Swedes more than any other people, so they seemed to feel, to give strict attention to material interests. The study of economics and natural sciences therefore came to be emphasized and pursued above all other branches of knowledge. Literature itself became a hand-maiden to the sciences, and morality as a practical factor in increasing the nation's productive power was stressed above orthodoxy in religion. All this was the expression of a healthy reaction against the fatuous ideas of dominion and military glory which before had ruled the nation.

Education.—The curricula of the schools, as well as their organization and teaching methods, were little in accord with these new ideals and their reform now became a crying need; changes were, however, slow and difficult. By an educational law of 1724, the appointment of rectors and professors was placed in the hands of the clergy, and since they, as a class, were more firmly fettered at this time by a most narrow and intolerant orthodoxy than at any other time, it was but natural that the schools should but inadequately reflect the new tendencies. Latin, Greek, logic, general history, and the Catechism were the subjects studied in the lower schools, to which were added Hebrew, Church history, rhetoric, arithmetic, and geometry in the gymnasia. No modern languages received attention. Demands became frequent that botany and geology be included in the curriculum, but the state-supported schools paid little attention to these appeals. Largely because of this inertia, private schools and tutors flourished. In Stockholm there were in the beginning of the century no less than eighteen such schools conducted by Germans, and 130 private tutors were listed.

Scientific studies.—Scientific studies were given prominence by these private institutions as well as by the tutors, and teachers and training methods were here far superior, as a rule, to what state schools had to offer. The situation was no better at the universities than in the more elementary schools. There were no scholastic prerequisites for admission to the university; the students who matriculated were immature, the professors were generally hidebound conservatives, and often lazy and dissolute. It is significant of conditions at the time that more than half of the entrants to the University of Uppsala in 1740 brought their own tutors with them. The Riksdag was consistently hostile to the university and interfered directly with matters of internal administration, even to the extent of appointing professors, with little regard to their scholarship, character, or teaching ability. While both elementary and advanced schools thus failed to emphasize the scientific and practical subjects as strongly as the spirit of the age demanded, some impetus was given to these studies by the learned societies which had their beginnings in this period.

Scientific societies had earlier been founded in London, Paris, and Berlin and the idea was now taken up in Sweden. The most enthusiastic promoter was Erik Benzelius, one of the rugged representatives of the period. He was born in Uppsala in 1675, and belonged to a prominent family. The father, Erik Benzelius the Elder, and three of his sons in succession held the archiepiscopal dignity. During a sojourn of three years at German, English, and Dutch universities, he had discovered a great number of important but forgotten classical manuscripts, and some of these he published. Benzelius's main service to scholarship came in connection with his position as chief librarian of the University of Uppsala. Most of the invaluable collections which this university had secured, many of them spoils of war, had up to this time not been arranged properly and catalogued, and were therefore inaccessible to scholars, but under the intelligent guidance of Benzelius this work was now carried forward. The Uppsala Library soon became known as one of the very best in Europe. A startling innovation was added to the curriculum when Benzelius began to lecture on the history of his own country in Swedish and to devote a great part of his lectures to a critical examination of sources. He assumed an attitude of scepticism towards the Rudbeckian theories.

During his sojourn abroad, Benzelius had visited the great German philosopher, Leibnitz, and it was probably from him that he first received the suggestion of a learned society in Sweden. A beginning to such an organization was made in 1710, a year made dismal by the disaster of Poltava and the outbreak of the bubonic plague. So paralyzed were all activities in that year that the University of Uppsala was compelled to close its doors, and in order to find some solace in their misery and anxiety a few of the professors, at the suggestion of Benzelius, banded themselves together for the purpose of pursuing scientific studies. While the organization was active only a few years, it aroused great interest in scientific investigations and was the precursor of a series of societies with similar aims.

Orthodoxy and Pietism.—Strict orthodoxy, which hitherto had been securely entrenched, was to become the object of persistent attacks in this period. By the fundamental law of 1719 all religions were tolerated in the land, except those of Jews, Mohammedans, and pagans, but dissenters, with the exception of foreign ministers and their servants, were prohibited from meeting publicly for worship. Foreigners in the land who wished to secure the right of citizenship for their children must educate them in the Lutheran faith, and apostasy on the part of church members was punished by exile, loss of property, and disallowance of the right of inheritance. As industry developed, the need of foreign workmen was more keenly felt, which resulted in demands that restrictions upon dissenters be modified. As a result, a greater degree of latitude was now permitted. The Lutheran Church in Sweden had by this time become almost wholly clerical in organization, since laymen had been almost entirely excluded from control. Impelled by a narrow-minded orthodoxy, the administration of the Church devoted a great deal of its time and energy to the enforcement of disciplinary measures. Failure to attend church on Sundays, tardiness at church services, or departure before the final benediction had been spoken, were alike punishable by fines. The royal guards were compelled to attend the sacrament of the Lord's Supper every other Sunday, and failure to appear was punished, in the case of the men, with stripes, in the case of the officers, with fines. Against this barren, cold, and oppressive religion the Pietists, who now made their appearance in the land, emphasized the importance of a warm and living faith. The soil had been well prepared for them in Sweden by the returned prisoners of war from Russia (p. 503); the terrible trials through which the nation had been compelled to pass had also made people more susceptible to religious influences. The leader of the Pietistic movement was Conrad Dippel, a radical thinker and zealous preacher, who in 1726 had come from Germany. He rejected, among other things, the doctrine of atonement, holding that God is not wroth against man, a doctrine of divine love which appealed with special force to the masses. Dippel was forced to leave the country because of his alleged heresy, but his influence remained. Fearless and warm-hearted leaders like Eric Tollstadius, Karl Michael Strokirch, and Sven Rosen, the latter dying as a missionary in America, continued to preach vigorously against the worldly-mindedness of the clergy, and to plead for tolerance. The dominant party in the Church was not slow in exercising its police power in order to check the Pietistic movement. The first Conventicle Act, passed in 1726, forbade meetings for devotional purposes except in churches and homes, and in the latter case only parents, children, and relatives who might be on a visit were to be permitted to attend. An effort was made to extend this privilege to other visiting friends, but was frustrated by the opposition of the ever-watchful shepherds of the flock. It was further ordained that no one should be excused from church attendance because he lived far from the place of worship. Attendance at proscribed religious meetings of worship was to be punished by a fine of 200 silver dalers for the first offence, 400 dalers, or two to three weeks' prison on bread and water for the second, and for the third, exile. This law remained on the statute-book until 1858, but it had long before this become, in the main, a dead letter. One of the leaders of the liberals, Tessin, had, in fact, in denouncing the Conventicle Act, before it was finally adopted, pointed out the absurdity of a situation which prohibited meetings of an edifying character and in the privacy of homes when at the same time people were permitted, as freely as they pleased, to congregate in grog-shops, give great banquets, and spend days and nights in wild carousing.

Censorship.—One of the agencies through which orthodoxy and the political party in control effectively checked free discussion was the censorship which had been inaugurated in the time of Charles XI. Under the régime of the absolute rulers, only the king could grant the privilege of publishing newspapers and books, but in case of religious books the decision in reality rested with the Church consistory and the censor. While this system continued as an institution under the new régime, the Riksdag itself at times insisted on its right to render the final verdict. It even happened that the members of the Riksdag insisted that entire manuscripts be read in their sessions, in order that they might themselves make sure of their contents, after which they voted approval or disapproval. According to new and detailed censorship enactments in 1719 and 1720 the censor was to supervise all book-shops, the dealers being required to furnish a list of all books which they wished to sell, and to scrutinize all the lists of works offered for sale at auctions; no book could be imported or published at home without the censor's approval. The censor during Horn's régime, Johan Rosenadler, interpreted his instructions in a very liberal spirit, and interfered as little as possible with authors, publishers, and booksellers, but delays were nevertheless most irritating, cases being known where an author was compelled to wait nine years before the censor's approval could be secured.

The struggle of the Caps and Hats; chauvinistic agitation.—That the memory of man ordinarily does not run back very far was strikingly illustrated by events in Sweden in this period. Soon the anguish and misery caused by the great wars of Charles XII were forgotten, and the clamour for military adventure became vociferous. Not that the rank and file felt any great urge towards warfare, but a constantly growing group of young noblemen, lacking in political wisdom and devoid of any deep sense of responsibility, began to raise its collective voice against the humiliating "piping times of peace," which Horn and his party had, through their policies, brought to the nation. As is generally the case with individuals who thus clamour for war, these men posed as the only simon-pure patriots in the land. As a result of this outcry the wise men who had rendered high-minded service in healing the nation's gaping wounds, and, in order to be able to do so, had kept firmly and courageously to the ways of peace, were derided as old dotards and called Night Caps, their traducers referring to themselves as Hats. The epithets, Caps and Hats, soon came into general use as party labels, the one designating the peace party, the other the war party. Relying upon the security which the alliance with France and England had brought to his country, Horn felt that friendly relations could now also be maintained with Russia, without incurring the risk that that country would take advantage of the situation and meddle in the purely domestic affairs of Sweden, but for this attitude he was by many bitterly denounced as a Russophile. When about this time war broke out between Russia and Turkey, it seemed to the Swedish chauvinists that the opportune time had come for their country to win back her lost provinces; the war party now began to grow rapidly in numbers and influence. The activity and tactics of these chauvinists in the elections of the 1738 Riksdag remind one of modern election methods at their worst. Money was spent profusely, the sinews of war being supplied to the Hats by the French ambassador, Casteja, bribery was common, political clubs were organized, and a regular deluge of scurrilous literature, directed against the party in power, descended upon the people. Against such tactics, Horn and his colleagues, worthy, aged, and honourable men, were pitifully helpless. In the consciousness that their services had been of inestimable value to the country, and in the belief that the majority of the people would have the wisdom to see this, these men met the attacks with equanimity and without attempting to deliver effective counter-blows. It was an uneven contest; the rabid appeals of the Hats to "patriotism" won constantly new recruits and effectively silenced those who urged caution. The election gave a decided majority to the Hats, who now elected their leader, Count Karl Gustaf Tessin, a brilliant man of great personal charm and one of the influential leaders in the Hat party, president of the aristocratic order. The Hats now also controlled the aristocratic contingent of the Secret Committee, through which they could assume control of foreign affairs.

The war spirit revived.—A young major in the Swedish army, Malcolm Sinclair, was now dispatched to Turkey to open negotiations for an alliance with that country, and an agreement was at the same time reached with France by which liberal subsidies were promised Sweden. Depressed in mind by the turn which events had taken, and convinced of the futility of keeping up any longer the struggle against the blind and blatant war party, Horn resigned his position as chancellor. The triumphant Hat majority had the decency to accept his resignation with expressions of gratitude for his valuable services, but six of his friends on the Secret Committee were incontinently dismissed and their places filled from the Hat ranks. Karl Gyllenborg, a shifty intriguer without the least spark of genius for statesmanship, was elevated to the responsible position left vacant by Horn's resignation. As Swedish ambassador in London, Gyllenborg had been involved in a political plot against George II, and had been arrested, an affront, in his opinion, which had made him violently anti-English. For the first time in her history, Sweden now had a parliamentary ministry—the Council and Secret Committee having been reorganized so as to carry out the majority will—and these now went recklessly ahead with their foreign policies. Those who had dared to raise their voices in protest against these policies were soon hushed completely by an event which occurred and at once stirred the fires of hate towards Russia to fever-heat. While travelling through Silesia, on his way to Turkey, Major Sinclair was murdered by Russian agents, and although Russia officially expressed regrets for the event, few in Sweden looked upon these as sincere. A stirring poem by Anders Odel, graphically depicting the scene when Sinclair entered heaven, met the famous Swedish warrior kings to whom he gave the details of the crime committed against him, and heard their expressions of indignation and call for vengeance, was soon on every one's lips, serving to inflame the public mind to the point of frenzy. In their anxiety to forestall a fatal plunge into a war for which they knew their country was ill prepared, the Caps now committed the colossal blunder, not to say crime, of admitting the Russian minister to Stockholm to their group as a sort of semi-official adviser; before long he was their real leader and the dispenser of their funds. This put a stigma upon the Cap party which has never been removed. The Hats, indeed, pursued an unwise policy in accepting counsel and financial help from France, but the worst which this course threatened to bring in its wake was a return to the humiliating subsidies of former days, when Sweden played the rôle of a satellite state revolving around France; the course which the Caps had entered upon led straight towards national annihilation.

Evils of the subsidy policy.—France had no sinister designs against the independence of Sweden; in fact it was the traditional view of French statesmen that Sweden ought to remain a strong nation in order the better to serve as a counterpoise to Russia in the North. Russia, on the other hand, was then working consciously and deliberately to break up and destroy three of her neighbours—Turkey, Poland, and Sweden. In associating themselves with the Russian emissaries, the Caps were therefore leading their nation directly towards the evil fate which later was to overtake Poland. After factional strife had culminated in civil war in Sweden, the Muscovites would find the opportunity convenient for interfering with armed forces, on the plea that the nation was unable to rule itself. The real culprits in the Cap party were, of course, the leaders. The rank and file in the group had little or no part in the fraternization with the Russians. To what lengths the leaders would go in giving consideration to Russia is revealed by the startling fact that they took counsel of the Russian ambassador in Stockholm as to who ought to be appointed to the Swedish Secret Committee, and who ought to be dropped.[3] Money was the main root of the evil. Members of the Riksdag found that by voting in accordance with the wishes of foreign agents, they could reap a money reward which made it unnecessary for them to worry about finances the rest of their lives. "The Swedes," wrote the French ambassador, "in general figure the income from a Riksdag meeting as others figure the income of their fields." Some, it should be noted, accepted money without permitting this to influence their votes. Thus Olof Håkansson, the chief of the *bonde* party, impartially accepted bribes from both French and Russians, but his votes were uniformly dictated by what he considered the welfare of his own land demanded. Others took the foreigners' money without the least compunction, on the theory that it would be folly not to pick up some good coins if others were fools enough to scatter them about with lavish hands. No doubt it was its demoralizing effect upon society, by undermining probity and the confidence of one man in the other, rather than any actual influence on momentous decisions, that constituted the real evil of the system.[4]

The Russian War.—What appeared to be an exceptionally good opportunity for taking advantage of an embarrassing Russian situation and win back at least part of the lost Baltic provinces came in 1740, when the czarina, Anna, died, leaving the succession to the Russian throne in doubt. One of the aspirants for the exalted office was Elizabeth, the youngest daughter of Czar Peter. With the connivance of the French ambassador at St. Petersburg, the Swedish minister to Russia

[3] Grimsberg, *Svenska folkets underbara öden,* VI, p. 568.

[4] Stavenow, *Sveriges historia,* IX, p. 468.

entered into an agreement with her, by virtue of which Sweden was to assist her in her aspirations, in return for proper territorial compensation when victory had been won. The excited and optimistic Hats thought that Carelia and St. Petersburg would be the least that she would offer as a reward for their help. Elizabeth took care, however, to make nothing but verbal promises.

In the face of the determined protests and opposition of the lower orders, especially the *bönder,* the triumphant Hats now decided to send a Swedish army into Russia. The venture was undertaken light-heartedly and from the most frivolous motives. Thus the licentious king cast his two votes for war, and thereby practically decided the issue, because of the assurance given him that if he did so his two illegitimate sons, and a mistress whom Horn had ordered removed from the capital, would be permitted to return. The expedition against Russia was a costly and humiliating venture from beginning to end. Success was contingent upon speedy action, but all Swedish movements were marked by hopeless dilatoriness. A Swedish detachment of 4,000 men was defeated by a force of 11,000 Russians at Villmanstrand in eastern Finland, before the chief commander, General Lewenhaupt, had had time to reach the scene of action (1741). Gradually 22,000 men were assembled under his banners, and with these Lewenhaupt finally, according to the secret understanding with Elizabeth, advanced into Russia. In the confusion which the Swedish advance created at the Russian capital, Elizabeth managed to seize the sceptre, whereupon she immediately sent word to Lewenhaupt that his aid was no longer needed. Instead of hurrying forward and bringing pressure to bear on Elizabeth for the payment of her obligations, Lewenhaupt now agreed to a truce. Soon the wily czarina repudiated even this agreement, and began hostilities against the Swedes, who, weakened by hunger, and their ranks decimated by disease, were forced to surrender. All Finland was now overrun by the Russians.

Humiliating end of the Russian war.—This, then, was the ignoble end to a war venture into which the dominant Hats had manœuvred their country and which they had entered light-heartedly and with such naïve expectations of easy revenge. Intense anger now naturally threatened to undo the Hats, but in averting the blow which was impending they displayed remarkable adroitness. Lewenhaupt and his subordinate officer, Buddenbrock, were charged with criminal negligence in the conduct of the war and arrested. In order to mollify Elizabeth and gain favourable peace terms, the Hats assured her that they would accept one of her distant relatives, Adolph Frederick of Holstein-Gottorp, as heir to the Swedish throne, Ulrika Eleanora having borne no children. This pleased Elizabeth and the agreement was made in conformity to which Adolph Frederick was duly elected. By the subsequent treaty of Åbo, 1743, the Swedes were let off by merely ceding to Russia the small part of Finland which lay beyond Kymmene River. The election of Adolph Frederick was, however, not to pass without serious disturbance. The anger of the Danish king, Christian VI, was aroused by the prospect of seeing a member of the feared and hated Holstein dynasty on the throne of Sweden, and he had, furthermore, set his heart on the selection of his eldest son, Crown Prince Frederick, for this honour, thus eventually uniting the Scandinavian North under one sceptre again. The *bönder* of Dalarna had especially been won for the candidacy of the Danish prince, whose agents were active among them in fomenting opposition to Adolph Frederick. A large force of these determined men of the soil marched upon Stockholm and encamped on Gustavus Adolphus Square, opposite the royal palace, for the purpose of intimidating the Riksdag. They were, however, soon dispersed. The fear of Danish intervention had, however, had the effect of forcing the Hats to invoke the aid of Russia, a friendly aid which Elizabeth most delightedly gave, sending a detachment of 12,000 Russian soldiers, who were encamped one entire winter near Stockholm. To such depths of humiliation had the Hats been compelled to descend; too weak, they feared, to defend their country against Denmark, if she made good her threat to attack, they had been compelled to invoke the assistance of the country which they had set out to chastise. When a peaceable settlement was finally reached with Denmark, the Russian troops still remained until Swedish protests against their further sojourn in the land led to their recall.

The new heir to the throne.—The new heir-apparent, Adolph Frederick, was distantly related to the old Vasa dynasty, but he had none of the strong personal qualities which were characteristic traits of the illustrious family. Rather dull of intellect and good-natured in disposition, he soon became little more than the humble flunky of his spirited wife, Louisa Ulrika, sister of Frederick the Great, a beautiful and talented woman, who, however, lacked the consistency of purpose and the political sagacity of her famous royal brother. While the queen thus failed to play the important rôle in government affairs to which she aspired, she nevertheless rendered her adopted country great service by her whole-hearted and generous support of its cultural activities. The favour and support of the royal couple now became the prize for which a bitter struggle between the two political parties ensued. Realizing the danger which an undue influence of the Russian court would create, the Hats sought to induce Adolph Frederick and Louisa Ulrika to pursue a pro-French policy, and the tactlessness of Elizabeth herself played into their hands. She wrote confidentially to the prince, warning him not to choose his friends from among the anti-Russian groups at the Swedish capital, and to give no heed to those who held out the prospects of an increase of power for royalty, an interference with his personal affairs that Adolph Frederick was man enough to resent vigorously. After this episode, the prince became quite susceptible to French influence and Louisa Ulrika's admiration for French culture made it so much the easier for him to align himself with the French party. Elizabeth was deeply chagrined at this outcome, and by no means willing to keep hands off in the future. Egged on by France on the one hand and by Russia on the other and financed by their gold, the Swedish parties now began an unrelentingly bitter struggle for control. Russia sent an especially resourceful and unprincipled man, Von Korff, as her minister to Stockholm, to assist in securing a Cap majority in the Riksdag and the overthrow of the existing government. The stream of Russian gold now flowed more freely than ever before, but in presenting a written demand upon Adolph Frederick that he remove Tessin and his friends from the court, the Russian czarina overreached herself. This high-handed interference in the affairs of a friendly state created a decided national reaction in Sweden which the Hats were quick to use in order to discredit the Caps. Their relations to the Russian agents made futile any attempts on their part to hold or regain power. Securely entrenched in power again, the Hats renewed their alliance with France and took measures for strengthening the defence of the country. The building of a strong fortress outside of Helsingfors, to be known as Sveaborg, was decided upon and the direction of the work entrusted to one of the most prominent of the Hat leaders, the engineer, Augustin Ehrensvärd.

Humiliation of royalty.—The worthless old king Frederick died in 1751 and soon Adolph Frederick and his queen were deep in a bitter struggle with the Council for the extension of royal privileges. Finally the matter was submitted to the Riksdag, which curtly informed the king that he was unconditionally bound by a majority vote of the Council; then, in order to make his discomfiture and humiliation entirely complete, the Estates authorized the councillors, in case the king refused his royal signature to their decisions, to use a seal with his name in official documents. In order to give still more point to the insult, a commission was next created for the special purpose of ferreting out and punishing all intriguing against the form of government as it then existed. The crowning insult came when the royal parents were denied the right to choose teachers for their children; the former tutors were thereupon summarily dismissed and others appointed who could be depended upon to inculcate only such political doctrines as were acceptable to the Council. Spurred on by the ambitious queen, the court party now planned a revolution, Louisa Ulrika procuring the necessary funds for the enterprise by pawning the crown jewels. The leaders of the Council and Riksdag were to be arrested, the Riksdag prorogued, and a new meeting of the Estates called. The plot soon became known to the ever-watchful Hat leaders, who quickly took measures to nip the incipient insurrection in the bud. Eight of the leaders were sent to the block, the queen herself was roundly scored by a deputation of clergymen, who did not mince matters in speaking of Her Majesty's delinquencies in religious matters, while the king was forced to listen to a lecture by the Estates, who curtly informed him that if he did not mend his ways his crown would be declared forfeited. The triumph of the Hat party was complete, but only for a time, as it soon fell, as will appear, before attacks which its own mistakes had done much to provoke.

Spurred on by French statesmen, the Hats next plunged their country into the Seven Years' War with no other results than that a large number of Swedish soldiers lost their lives and a huge sum of money was wasted. In Russia the unprincipled Catherine II had come into possession of supreme power, and now Muscovite meddling in Swedish affairs became more open and brazen than ever. In Catherine, Czar Peter's policies of heartless aggression were revived, but instead of making a direct attack on Sweden, she planned to destroy the morale of the nation first by fomenting class struggle and civil war; in due time she could then come forward and seize the spoils.

Subsidies and corruption.—The stream of gold from Russia into Sweden now began to flow wider and deeper than ever before. Prussia and Denmark were allies of the Muscovites and England, largely because of antagonism to France, generally supported them. Each nation had its special motive for keeping alive the party strife in Sweden and therefore supplied the sinews of war for the Caps. These received 3,000,000 silver dalers from Russia, Denmark, and England, whereas the Hats had to be content with 2,000,000 from France. In the Riksdag of 1765-1766, the Caps had a decided majority, and forthwith the day of reckoning came for the Hats. The senseless participation in the Seven Years' War, as well as the reckless waste in all departments by their government, had again placed debt burdens upon the nation as heavy as those which had weighed it down when the wars of Charles XII ended, and money had depreciated to half its former value. The extent to which officials had helped themselves from the public trough was, in the investigations which the Caps now instituted, found to have been perfectly scandalous. Directors of the exchange office had mulcted the state of 6,000,000 silver dalers.[5] Gratuities as large as 60,000 copper dalers had been given on most

[5] Grimberg, *Svenska folkets underbara öden*, VI, p. 552.

frivolous grounds. Other evidences of crooked deals were laid bare. For meals and collations for bank directors and other bank officers, 45,836 copper dalers had been recklessly spent. A dinner for the bank directors in 1739 had cost only 107 copper dalers, but standards and prices evidently had undergone a change, since three dinners of the same board in the Riksdag meetings of 1760-62 cost 21,536 copper dalers. Economy now became the watchword of the victorious Caps. In this they went so far that the Secret Committee objected to a small appropriation for defraying a contemplated trip of the crown prince to Uppsala. Numerous prohibitions against luxuries, tobacco, and extravagance in women's dress were imposed; even a tax of 200 silver dalers was levied on those who employed foreign governesses. The new economy program even stipulated that coffins were to be made of cheaper material than oak, and costly metal handles were tabooed. To guard against a recurrence of the reckless waste of money, which the secrecy that had surrounded every government transaction in the preceding régime had encouraged and made possible, a law guaranteeing freedom of the press was enacted in 1766. Free discussion was henceforth to be permitted in all matters, with the exception that the doctrine of the pure Evangelical Church and the fundamental law of the land must not be attacked; members of the royal family, public officials, and honourable citizens must not be made the objects of ridicule, honesty or civilized morality derided. Sweden was thus the first country after England to establish freedom of the press by legislation. The mischievous provisions of the existing government, the cause of most of the nation's ills, were, however, hedged about more securely than ever by a vote of the Riksdag to the effect that no change could ever be made in the fundamental law except by vote of two successive Riksdag meetings.

The Caps in control.—The complexion of the Cap party had changed materially since the days of Horn's leadership. He represented the aristocratic group, men who, on the whole, had been guided by high ideals of national independence, but now most of the leaders belonged to the lower orders, several among them being little better than puppets of Russia. They were clergymen and *bönder*, many of them indeed well meaning and patriotic, but deluded by Russian promises and influenced by their abhorrence of the corruption of the Hats to such an extent that they lost their ability to see clearly. At the request of Russia, work on Sveaborg was discontinued, and Crown Prince Gustavus prevailed upon, much against his will, to marry the Danish princess, Sophia Magdalena. Denmark, as usual, was at the time a close ally of the Muscovite power. This truckling to Russia carried with itself the doom of the Caps, but their ride towards retribution was speeded by their own economic mismanagement. They had some sound economic policies, such as insistence upon economy, the payment of the national debt, a rigid checking of accounts to prevent embezzlement and bribery; but, in stopping bank loans, they decided, in greatest secrecy, to redeem paper money, after ten years, at face value. The secret leaked out in spite of all precautions, with the result that every one hoarded money for the future, and a terrible economic crisis followed. People stopped buying, debtors were hard pressed for payment, no new loans could be made, factories were closed, and unemployment became general. As a result, farmers could not sell their products nor pay taxes and lands could hardly be given away. The Hats took full advantage of the Caps' law guaranteeing freedom of the press and subjected the bungling party in power to a terrific bombardment of criticism. The economic panic which the Caps brought on the land thus seemed to make the opportunity propitious for a determined attack upon them, in order to secure an increase of power for the king. Secretly, the leaders of the Hats, the French ambassador, and the young crown prince conferred earnestly about the matter. In accordance with plans thus agreed upon, the king, accompanied by the crown prince, appeared before the Council and urged it to summon an extraordinary meeting of the Riksdag as the surest expedient for relieving the national distress. This request was accompanied by the startling threat that unless the advice were heeded the king would abdicate. The members of the Council were utterly amazed at this manifestation of energy by their king; such decisiveness and courage by him were utter novelties. The explanation is found in the young crown prince's dynamic personality, which for the time being had vitalized the dull energies of the father into action. At the same time the crown prince tried to secure possession of the royal name-stamp but failed, whereupon he served notice that henceforth it must not be used any more. The Council, however, proceeded to issue orders as before, refusing obstinately to accede to the demand for a new Riksdag. True to his threat, Adolph Frederick now abdicated, thus leaving the country without a legal head. The demand for a Riksdag meeting now grew insistent, deputations of officials and large groups of people clamouring for the issuance of writs, but, egged on by the Russian and Danish ministers, the Council remained firm in its refusal to yield. Finally, however, when treasury officials declared they could no longer pay out any money as salaries, and the commotion among the people had assumed such proportions that personal violence against the Caps was threatened, the opposition gave way.

The election campaign which followed became notorious for the openly reckless manner in which both France and Russia poured out money. The Hats were furnished a war chest of 6,000,000 livres by the French ambassador, with the stipulation that, if they were victorious, the Swedish constitution would be changed so as to increase the king's power. The Russian ambassador, Osterman, was both the party manager and the treasurer of the Cap campaign. For this Riksdag Russia alone expended 2,000,000 silver dalers. The desperate Caps were so unbelievably blind to their own peril and so unmindful of the danger into which they were leading their country, that they had designated Norrköping, instead of Stockholm, as the meeting-place for the Riksdag, because the former place was accessible to the Russian fleet, which was ready to appear on the scene in case of need. Another reason for selecting Norrköping was the desire to get away from foreign ministers and office-holders at the capital. Russian diplomacy was cultivating the soil carefully and hoped soon to reap a rich harvest. The partition treaty regarding Poland, which had just previously been made, included a secret clause, put there at the instigation of Catherine, by which the contracting powers bound themselves to uphold, unchanged, the Swedish free constitution. This could have no other meaning than that the ruinous party strife in Sweden should go on and rend the country until Russia could find an excuse for interfering. Denmark was openly strengthening her military forces for the "protection of Swedish liberty."[6] During the election campaign, the Caps were in constant conferences with the Russian, English, and Prussian ambassadors; intimidation and bluffing were employed by both sides in the contest; but, in all the devious tricks of the unscrupulous politician, the Caps carried off the prize. In spite of all their desperate efforts, however, they were beaten in the election; the intelligent and patriotic citizens had proved themselves numerically the stronger and had recoiled at the treasonable actions of the Caps.

The Hats restored to power.—The Council was now reorganized by the appointment of dependable Hats and the meeting-place of the Riksdag changed to Stockholm. The joint note which the Russian, Prussian, and Danish ministers next presented to the Swedish Estates, warning them against any reprisals against the defeated Caps, simply made the discomfiture of these the more complete. The gain by the Hat victory was, however, inconsiderable. When, in accordance with their promise, the Hats faced the duty of changing the constitution, they lost their nerve; the old fetish, "the sacredness of the constitution," was brought out and it overawed the patriots. Vociferously the cry was raised, "The constitution is in danger," and such was the alarm felt at this cry that the "sacred" document was left unchanged. This failure to accomplish anything salutary was due largely to the influence of Pechlin, a leader of the Hats, who sold himself to Russia, and thereupon opposed all projects for an extension of royal power. It was not the last dastardly act of this consummate schemer, as the sequel will show. The future of Sweden looked more overcast than ever. A new alliance had, in December 1769, been formed between Denmark and Russia, by which these countries pledged themselves to attack Sweden at once if its constitution was changed on a single point; Denmark to retain all her conquests and in addition receive an indemnity.

[6] Stavenow, *Sveriges historia*, IX, p. 418.

This alliance constitutes the darkest stigma upon Denmark in her attitude towards Sweden since the time of Christian II.[7] Prussia also joined the alliance with Russia, with the same end in view as Denmark's. France was prevented from coming to the help of Sweden by her own trouble.

Crown Prince Gustavus.—After the Riksdag had adjourned, Crown Prince Gustavus set out on a long-projected trip to France, for whose culture he felt an unbounded enthusiasm. The journey was in reality undertaken in response to an invitation from the French foreign minister, Choiseul, who desired to confer with Gustavus regarding means for putting an end to anarchy in his land. Barely had the crown prince entered the gay social life of the French capital, and begun to confer with French statesmen regarding the situation in his own country, when the startling news reached him that his father had died suddenly (1771). Being by this time made a good deal wiser by the sage advice which freely had been given him in Paris, and his courage buttressed by the promise of further French subsidies, Gustavus hastened home by way of Berlin. Here his uncle, Frederick the Great, bluntly informed him that, in concert with Russia and Denmark, he had undertaken, by force of arms, if necessary, to prevent any change in the Swedish constitution.

With Gustavus's ascent to the throne, the Swedish nation was soon to discover that a man much after the fashion of its former great kings was again at the helm, able to guide the ship safely past the treacherous breakers.

The Hats made a sorry mess, indeed, when they plunged Sweden into war, and their ambitious endeavours to develop the economic and industrial resources of the country, although for the most part dictated by patriotic motives, brought scant glory to the party, but in one domain their intelligent interest and encouragement achieved so much good that the mistakes and failures in other fields may be judged charitably. Under their fostering care, science, literature, and art blossomed forth, until Sweden unquestionably for a time bid fair to occupy the most honoured place among the nations. This was particularly true in the scientific field.

[7] Stavenow, *Sveriges historia,* IX, p. 436.

Industrial measures of the Hats.—In the industrial and economic field, the Hats adhered to the principles advocated and followed by Horn, but impetuous as they were and impelled by a most naïve faith in their own insight and ability, they rushed ahead rashly where the aged statesman had proceeded slowly and with great caution. None had a more childlike faith in the mercantilist system than they, and subsidies were literally poured out in order to start new industries and enlarge old ones. As an initial measure for the promotion of domestic industry, the Riksdag in 1739 forbade the use of foreign-made cloth of any kind in the manufacture of clothes, violations by merchants, manufacturers, tailors, seamstresses, and apprentices being punished by heavy fines or imprisonment. The law was fairly effective and contributed largely to a rapid growth of the Swedish textile industry; not only did Sweden, in 1762, manufacture enough textiles for her home market, but she had a large surplus for export. In 1739 the government established the Bureau of Manufactures to serve as a buying and selling agency, as a clearing-house for information in all matters pertaining to manufactures, and as dispenser of subsidies and supervisor of the government machinery for the apprehension of violators of the industrial laws. Customs duties were raised materially and the Bureau was given extensive credits in the government bank for loans and subsidies, preferably to new industrial ventures. Free sites and material for new factories, certain exemptions from contributions by the employees, and abrogation of all import duties on raw material were guaranteed as a further inducement to industry to expand its activities. Special courts were instituted in the industrial centres to facilitate the adjustment of industrial conflicts and to supervise manufacturing processes and label the products. On a great number of articles, aside from textiles, which might possibly, if protected from foreign competition, be manufactured at home, heavy, in many cases prohibitive, customs duties were laid. As the years passed and according as the exigencies of the manufacturing industry seemed to demand, these provisions were supplemented by others, and Swedish industry grew by leaps and bounds. Just prior to the fall of the Hats from power, the annual value of the products of all Swedish factories was estimated at 6,000,000 silver dalers; the workers numbered 18,231, of whom more than 14,000 were engaged in the textile branch. No less than 142 textile factories were in operation. Iron continued to be the principal article of Swedish export and a special bureau was created for regulating and promoting its production. In connection with this bureau, a fund was created by imposing a tax on each quantity produced out of which mine owners might borrow on their supply up to seven-eighths of its value in case they wanted to hold it for better prices abroad. Under certain contingencies, the bureau even bought surplus stock in order to prevent price deflation in foreign markets. The iron industry was further aided by the introduction of improved methods of production as well as by the appointment of supervisors to watch over the manufacturing processes.

Agriculture.—While agriculture, under the influence of the mercantilist system, continued to be neglected, an important step towards its improvement was taken in 1757 when under the leadership of Jacob Faggot the consolidation of the numerous scattered patches which the different farmers of the villages had hitherto possessed was begun and each farmer given contiguous tracts. In order to encourage and benefit the farming class still more, special agents were appointed in the different districts, whose duty it was to give information regarding proper agricultural methods. Young people were, by the imposition of taxes, discouraged from leaving the farms and locating in the cities, and loans at a low rate of interest and on easy payment terms were made available to agricultural communities. High import duties were placed on grains, their importation in some cases being prohibited altogether. The question of intoxicants was a baffling problem for the Riksdag, and after various solutions had been suggested and partly tried, a sweeping prohibition against the sale and manufacture of these beverages was, in view of a threatening failure of crops, ordered for a period of years. All apparatus for gin-making was to be surrendered to state officials. The fact that 170,000 distilling vats and boilers were, as a consequence, delivered up conveys an idea of the extent to which the population had exercised their right to manufacture spirituous liquor.

The restriction was, however, abandoned, after four years' trial, largely because the *bönder* objected strenuously to this infringement on their alleged prerogatives.

Shipping.—Shipping was developed, until in 1762 the Swedish merchant marine numbered 572 ships, with more than 4,000 men engaged as sailors. The East India Company, chartered in 1731 and rechartered in 1746 with extended privileges, did a large and profitable importing business, mainly with the Orient. A considerable part of the imported goods were, however, re-exported. The Levant Company was formed at Stockholm to carry on trade with Oriental ports, its promoters hoping to secure prominence as a shipping centre for their city, just as Gothenburg had secured this through the East India Company. Under the stimulus of the various enterprises for extending trade, both the imports and exports trebled in value in a decade, the trade balance in 1760 being 3,000,000 copper dalers in favour of Sweden.

Mismanagement and failure of the economic program of the Hats.—The evils of the hot-house methods of the Hats for building up industry were not slow to appear. Gross irregularities were discovered in the making of loans. A typical case in point was that of the son of one of the prominent Hat chiefs, who secured a loan of 36,000 copper dalers for the building of a factory, but a year or two later his factory, machinery, and raw and finished products combined were valued at only 2,000 dalers. Another prominent Hat member had secured financial assistance to the extent of 30,000 dalers for the purchase of an improved breed of Spanish sheep, but three years later he had not bought a single sheep, the money being still in his possession and paying no interest. In many instances, the products of the Swedish factories were inferior to imported articles, either because the land had not the proper raw material or because absence of foreign competition made manufacturers indifferent. Many Swedish labourers, furthermore, lacked training and skill. Complaints against the kind of articles which were dumped on the market soon became loud and bitter, but party leaders tried to stifle all such outcries by counter-charges that the complainants were nothing but trouble-makers or even traitors against their country.

The constant expansion of trade increased the pressure on the bank for larger and easier loans, and as sufficient capital was not available, the Hats yielded to the inevitable temptation to secure added funds by issuing paper money. Since at the same time the coin reserves, through payment for purchases abroad, became depleted by constant drains, a rapid depreciation of the paper money forthwith set in. The government sought either by its fiat that the acceptance of paper money at less than face value was illegal—an expedient which, of course, was futile—or by increasing the export trade, by more and larger subsidies and premiums, to prevent this depreciation and the method was effective for a time, but, of course, it was only a palliative which in the end aggravated the malady, making the collapse, when it did come, the more serious. The careful economies of Horn had made possible the payment of a great part of the debt with which the many wars of the former régime had burdened the nation and the budget had virtually been balanced when this great administrator was compelled to relinquish his power. Through senseless wars, subsidies, premiums, and mismanagement the national debt had, however, grown, by 1760, under Hat administration, to the enormous dimensions which it had assumed in 1721 (p. 522). Paper money circulated at only half its face value and serious price fluctuations demoralized all business. It was the discontentment aroused by the Hats' mismanagement of the economic and fiscal interests of the country which soon brought bitter reproach upon them and restored power to the Caps. In justice to the Hats it should be said, however, that in the industrial fields not all of their enterprises were in vain, for industry made some gains under their fostering care which were not lost.

Cultural affairs.—While a recital of the economic measures of the Hats thus is a rather dreary story of mistakes and wreckage, their achievements in the purely cultural field were so important and salutary that one is readily disposed to forgive and forget their bungling endeavours to promote business and industry. Largely through their intelligent interest and generous support, Sweden, during several decades of the eighteenth century, held a leading rôle among the European nations in scientific research and progress. The leaders of the Hats were, as a rule, influenced by English scientific and philosophical thought, as typified in Newton and Locke, and by the social ideals of the French *illuminati,* and inasmuch as many of them were men of wealth and powerful political influence, they were able to give substantial encouragement to the scholars of their own land who, inspired largely by English and French thinkers, sought to unravel the mysteries of nature, and establish rules of equity and justice in human relations.

Learned societies.—The new cultural interest manifested itself, first of all, in the organization of a number of learned

Vignette to the first part of the Proceedings of the Swedish Scientific Society. Motto above: "For posterity."

societies, each in its place aiming to extend the boundaries of knowledge in its distinctive field. As an immediate successor to the scientific societies which earlier had been formed in Uppsala (p. 527), came, in 1739, the Academy of Science, with headquarters in Stockholm. The idea of a Swedish organization, similar in purpose and organization to English, French, and German scientific societies, seems to have been broached the first time by Linné. The encouragement of studies in mathematics and natural sciences was announced as its aims. It was the intention of the founders that the results of their investigations should primarily foster practical pursuits, especially agriculture and mechanical industries, and the practice of issuing the publications of the academy in Swedish in order that they might be accessible to as many as possible was therefore followed from the beginning. Soon after its organization, the academy secured sole right to publish an almanac which proved to be a very profitable concession, and made possible a number of stipends and loans for the encouragement of scientific studies. For the purpose of encouraging the study of history and antiquity, and establishing higher standards of literary excellence, an Academy of Letters (*Vitterhets Akademien*) was organized in 1753, mainly through the influence of the queen, Louisa Ulrika. At the beginning this was mainly an aristocratic clique which met in the Drottningholm Palace for discussion. Although this organization offered a number of stipends, and thus achieved some good in its field, it was entirely too exclusive in tone and organization to attain to an influence commensurate with that of the Academy of Science. Almost simultaneously came the organization of other societies, like the Swedish Linguistic Society (*Svenska tungomålgillet*), for the encouragement of the use of Swedish, the Academy of Arts, the Royal Swedish Opera, the Royal Academy of Music, the Society for Mental Stimulus (*Tankebyggar orden*), the special aim of the latter being the creation of higher ideals in literary production and increasing literary activity. *Utile Dulci* was an organization founded in honour of Dalin. Its members met frequently, on which occasions musical compositions and poems by members were presented. *Appolini Sacra,* in Uppsala, and Aurora, in Åbo, the two having practically the same aims and form of organization as *Utile Dulci,* also aimed to create cultural interests.

Language studies.—The patriotic Swedish sentiment, of which the scientific and literary societies and academies were an expression, resulted in an interest in the native language which was entirely new in the land. The great linguist of the period, Johan Ihre (1707-1780), who was perhaps the greatest scholar in the realm of Swedish philology, typified this aspect of national life in the period. He laid the foundation for a sound and scientific etymological investigation. His great work, *Glossarium Suigothicum,* or Swedish Glossary, published in 1769, gives a scientific account of the derivation of Swedish words and their relation to Icelandic, Gothic, and other kindred tongues. His study of Ulfilas' Gothic Bible led to important conclusions and greatly influenced subsequent investigation in this field. Ihre was a pioneer in Icelandic studies, his investigations causing him to reject many of the sagas which before had been accepted as authentic. He persistently urged that unnecessary foreign words be excluded from the native language and that the vernacular be used in university lectures, in scientific publications, as well as in elementary grade instruction. The first grammar in Swedish was published by Abraham Sahlstedt (1716-1776) about this time (1747). A new and enlarged work by him in the same field, published in 1769, served as the standard authority until well into the nineteenth century.

Historians.—Historical scholarship, which had been led astray by the fantastic theories of Rudbeck and his followers (p. 17), now established itself on the solid basis of investigation and criticism. While press censorship and the inaccessibility of government archives to scholars placed almost insurmountable obstacles in the way of trustworthy historical production, the period nevertheless was to produce a number of works in the historical field which had genuine merit and served to direct research into its proper channels. Eric Julius Björner (1696-1750) published the old Icelandic sagas in Swedish, a work which later was to supply Tegnér with much of the material for his great epic, *Frithiofs Saga;* Jacob Wilde wrote the first part of a history of the development of the Swedish state; in writing a history of Charles XII, Göran Nordberg (1677-1744) made careful and intelligent use of sources; Carl Gustaf Warmholtz (1713-1785) gave, in his *Bibliotheca Historica Sveogothica,* a ponderous work of fifteen volumes, so complete a bibliography of the historical writings in the Swedish field that it has been said that "No nation possesses a more thorough or more reliable inventory of its early book treasures than Sweden." Warmholtz was himself an inveterate collector of historical writings, his library at his death containing no less than 6,000 volumes. Olof von Dalin, the leading literary man of the period, "transferred Swedish history from the bookshelves to the hearts of the people." He was no eminent scholar or investigator, but he had a brilliant literary style and, more than anyone else, in this or the preceding periods, he made history a popular literature in the nation. In his historical authorship he was influenced strongly by the Frenchman, Charles Rollin, and sought in lucid and easy language to stress the moral principles which the records of the past have revealed. His principal work, *Svea Rikes historia,* in three volumes, carries the story of Sweden down to the reign of Gustavus Adolphus. Dalin is always sceptical of the trustworthiness of the ancient records, most of which he rejects as mere fables. As pointed out before, Dalin was the first who, on the basis of an observed fact, to which Swedenborg was the first to call attention, that the surface of Sweden was constantly rising, argued that the country could not possibly have been a habitat of man prior to the beginning of the Christian era. To those patriots who felt poignant grief at the prospect of being compelled to abandon the cherished belief that Sweden could boast at least as great an age as any land, Dalin held out the consolation that age in itself brings no glory to a nation. "Many," he said sarcastically, "do not know what happened in the time of Charles XI, but think they know all about the grandson of Japhet." By their rejection of many of the vagaries of earlier scholars, and by bringing a saner tone into historical writings, Dalin and his disciples performed a great service to historical scholarship in Sweden, but their rationalistic minds had no understanding of the value of sagas and legends; of early history, or of the great influence of religious movements, they had no intelligent comprehension.

A long stride forward was taken in historical research and production by Sven Lagerbring (1707-1787), who as professor at Lund created a new interest and new standards in the field. His *Svea Rikes historia,* in four volumes, was based upon a mass of source material which he examined critically. He wrote in pure and easy Swedish and to him history was not a mere recital of the deeds of kings, but above everything else an account of men's achievement in developing culture through agencies of education, working through the medium of literature, science, and art.

Economists.—Having a constant interest in so-called practical subjects, and being ready at all times to favour more extended studies of this kind, the Riksdag in 1739 ordered that the professorship in Swedish law be abolished and one in economics be established in its place. The first professor in the latter subject, Anders Berch, was appointed by the Riksdag directly. The instructions which it issued in connection with the appointment placed upon Berch the seemingly difficult task of lecturing on the following subjects: the history of industry from earliest times; advantages of manufacturing silk, woollen, cotton, linen, wood, horn, and leather articles; customs duties; maritime regulations of different lands; rights and duties of pilots; arrangement of beacon-lights; commercial treaties; mining and the use which may be made of ores; administration of the mining, forest, and manufacturing industries; production of coke; system of land titles; classes of estates and taxes; operation of mills; different judicial systems and courts of justice, and a variety of other subjects. In fact the incumbent had to be versed in economics and economic history, practical administration of all important industries, law, physics, and chemistry. It therefore occasions no surprise that Berch, although a remarkably versatile and able man, after a couple of years complained that his field was altogether too broad and varied. Almost simultaneously with Berch's appointment, the order of the nobles voted to abolish the professorship in poetry and use the money thus saved for a professorship in physics, but the other orders would not acquiesce in this program. It was not until more than a decade after Horn's retirement that professorships were established in both physics and chemistry; the professorships in poetry and Oriental languages were abolished to make this possible.

Statistics.—Per Wilhelm Wargentin (1717-1783), a famous astronomer, whose investigations of the movements of the moons of Jupiter were published in Swedish, French, and German scientific journals, was likewise a prominent statistician and the fact that Sweden became an early leader among European countries in gathering reliable statistics on population and mortality is due chiefly to him. The Tabulation Commission, established in 1756 at Stockholm, is said to have been the first statistical bureau in Europe.

Natural sciences.—The urge for the practical and the useful was, however, to achieve the greatest results in the field of the natural sciences, in which Swedish scholars, in this period, made epochal discoveries and brought unusual honour to their fatherland. First in the galaxy of Swedish scientists stands Carl Linnæus. (Later ennobled, he took the name von Linné.) "The story of his life," says Schück,[8] "is like an Aladdin tale of science. Easily and without effort he appears to attain new and entirely epoch-making scientific results, although, in fact, few of his contemporaries labour with the same tremendous energy as he. But this labour never weighs him down. There rest sunlight, spiritual health, and joy of labour over all his youthful years and he gives the impression of being a darling child of science (*ett vetenskapens söndagsbarn*)." He was a poet and a dreamer, but above everything else utilitarian and scientific.

Linné.—Linné's father was a clergyman and the son of a poor *bonde* in the province of Småland. When the future scientist was born in 1707 the father was curate (*kyrkoherde*) of a small parish in Stenbrohult in the same province. Somewhat contrary to the usual tales of the early life of great men, the records in this case emphasize the great influence which the father, rather than the mother, exerted on the boy in giving direction to his interests and energies. The elder Linnæus was a pious and tolerant minister, who indeed could infuse love of spiritual things into his children, as evidenced by the biblical tone and expression so common in the writings of his famous son, but his passionate love of flowers was, no doubt, of equal importance. His flower garden was said to be the finest in the entire province.

Linné's forbears on the side of both mother and father had served as curates of the Stenbrohult parish uninterruptedly for more than one hundred years, and when, therefore, young Carl informed his parents that he would not study theology but wished to devote himself to science, the news came to them as a shock, but again the wisdom and tolerance of the father

[8] Schück and Warburg, *Illustrerad svensk litteraturhistoria*, 3d Ed., III, p. 268.

stood revealed. He bestowed his blessing upon the son, the only thing he could afford to give. As a student at Lund and later at Uppsala, Linné was at one time so destitute that he had to stuff paper into his worn shoes to help keep out the wet and cold. He soon found influential friends, however, who relieved him of all anxiety for material wants and enabled him to devote all his time and energy to the study of his favourite objects, flowers. The first great experience of his early life came in 1732 when a stipend of the Scientific Society of Uppsala enabled him to undertake an exploring expedition to Lappland for the primary purpose of studying its flora and fauna. Later he made similar journeys to other parts of Sweden and not only did he collect an enormous amount of material and reach certain epochal conclusions, but he published voluminous accounts which touched upon all phases of life as he had witnessed them and were written in so fascinating a style that even today they charm the reader. The spectacle of a Swede travelling about in his own country merely for the purpose of studying its physical features, its animal and vegetable kingdoms, and the people, and then writing entertainingly and at the same time sanely about the things heard and seen, was indeed a great novelty. On a journey to Holland he won the degree of doctor of medicine, and as the candidate already possessed a good store of erudition, and the authorities were most accommodating, this business was disposed of in a week's time.

After this, Linné for some time continued his botanical studies in some famous Dutch gardens. Wealthy friends surrounded him everywhere and the temptation to cast his lot with the land of his benefactors was strong, but the love of his native Sweden—and the beckoning voice of the maiden whom he on his journey to Lappland had met in Dalarna and to whom he had plighted his troth—brought him back to Sweden, where he next spent some years in the practice of medicine in Stockholm. On becoming a professor in Uppsala in 1741, he entered upon a career of scientific research and production that was to earn for him the distinction of being one of the truly outstanding men among the leading scientists and benefactors of the ages. Already during his sojourn in Holland he published no less than fourteen books and treatises, almost every one of them of epoch-making importance.

That Linné was not by any means the first man who made a systematic study of the vegetable kingdom appears from the fact that he himself lists one thousand works on botany which he thinks should have a place in the library of anyone who aims to study the field thoroughly. Through his keen powers

Carl von Linné

of observation and his new principle of classification—based on the pistils and stamens as determining factors in organization—and through his creation of an ingenious nomenclature, he revolutionized the method not only of the botanical science but of related sciences as well. Zoölogy and geology were the two sciences which besides botany were especially enriched by his observations and system of classification. While Linné, through his works—the most important being *Species Plantarum* and *System Naturæ*—created a new science and gave direction and impetus to scientific research, the effect of which has been felt in all fields of scientic thought ever since he lived, his power of inspiring others with the same spirit of scientific pursuit and love of truth was an equally important service to mankind.

Disciples.—From the remote corners of the world, students flocked to Uppsala, and as many as two to three hundred disciples were in the habit of accompanying Linné on his many botanical expeditions. Many of his best students travelled far afield and penetrated hitherto inaccessible places to gather specimens, and Sweden became the great depository and clearing-house for the world of scientific material and information. Among these disciples were Hasselquist, who visited Smyrna, Egypt, Judea, Arabia, and Syria; Petrus Löfling, who journeyed to Spain and the Spanish possessions in South America to study their flora and collect a herbarium; Peter Forsskål, an explorer of Arabia; Pehr Kalm, a famous early explorer of the North American flora, and a trustworthy and interesting recounter of conditions there in the period just before the American War of Independence; Pehr Osbeck, explorer of Java, China, and the Ascension Islands; and, finally, Carl Thunberg, who visited Cape Colony, Java, and Japan. Others went to East India, Spitzbergen, and England and brought home an abundance of botanical specimens. Under the fostering care of Linné, the botanical garden in Uppsala became the foremost in Europe.

Other famous scientists.—A contemporary and colleague of Linné at Uppsala, Johan Gottschalk Wallerius (1709-1785), created a new era in scientific agriculture through his treatises on the chemical constituency of the soil. A. F. Cronstedt (1722-1765) was the discoverer of nickel, and T. O. Bergman (1735-1784), the successor of Wallerius at the University of Uppsala, developed the theory of chemical analysis and reaction, discovered new methods of analyzing insoluble substances, extended the use of the blow-pipe, formulated "affinity tables" to indicate degrees of chemical affinity in bodies, and demonstrated the acid properties of carbonic acid and its presence in air. Aside from his contributions to chemistry, Bergman deserved and won European fame by discoveries and publications in the field of geology, astronomy, and physics. Many of his treatises were published in the proceedings of the Scientific Society of London. His work, giving a physical description of the earth, was translated into most of the European languages, and established him as one of the great forerunners of Alexander Humboldt.

Scheele.—Among the galaxy of famous Swedish scientists, no one deserves greater encomium than Karl Wilhelm Scheele (1742-1783), whose remarkable career of scientific discoveries fell partly within this period. In the whole annals of the progress of knowledge it would be difficult to find a more heroic figure. "No one," says an authority,[9] "before nor since his day, has made so many important discoveries." Almost simultaneously with Priestley, the contemporary discoverer of oxygen, and Lavoisier, who is generally acclaimed the founder of modern chemistry, Scheele made discoveries in the field of natural sciences which revolutionized thought and scientific method. His achievements are the more extraordinary as he constantly laboured under difficulties which Priestley and Lavoisier never knew. The former had been able to pursue thorough studies under able teachers, and the possession of a competence enabled him to carry on his investigations without interruptions or worry; the latter was wealthy, had studied under the greatest masters of the age, and praise and encouragement had from the beginning made his path easy. Scheele, on the other hand, the son of a petty merchant in Stralsund, then a Swedish possession, had been compelled, at the age of fourteen, to leave home and become an apothecary's assistant in Gothenburg. To him was denied the privilege of ever going to school, or to study under capable masters, and not only was he always poverty-stricken, but his body was frail and ill-health was his constant lot. His library at his death contained twelve books. After being connected with apothecaries' shops in Gothenburg, Malmö, Stockholm, and Uppsala, he was enabled to get his own shop at Köping, an out-of-the-way place to which mail came only once a month. In the rear of this shop he fitted out an old shed as a laboratory and in these humble surroundings he made many of his epochal dis-

[9] Venable, F. P., *History of Chemistry*, Boston, 1903.

coveries. Many publications from his hand startled the scientific world, and despite his lack of academic training or university degrees he was elected to membership in the Swedish Academy of Science and offered a well-remunerated position by the Academy of Science in Berlin; from England came an offer which would have paid him £300 a year, offers which he declined, however, preferring to remain in his humble circumstances at Köping, for as he said, "I cannot eat more anyway than to satisfy my hunger, and so long as I can do this as well in Köping as anywhere else, why should I seek some other place?" Of the ninety fundamental substances known to science, Scheele discovered eight. His discovery of oxygen antedates that of Priestley, but through a delay on the part of Scheele's publisher, the latter's treatise on the subject was published first. Besides oxygen, he discovered tartaric, oxalic, malic, citric, gallic, molybdic, tungstic, and arsenic acids, besides manganese, chlorine, and glycerine. His discoveries laid the basis for modern photography and had a revolutionary effect upon all industry. Of almost greater importance than his discoveries, was his demonstration that truth in the domain of natural phenomena is attained not through the medium of abstract theories, but by actual experimentation.

Astronomy.—The study of astronomy yielded new results when Anders Celsius (1701-1744) founded an observatory at Uppsala and equipped it with instruments which made it the equal of any at the time. Celsius was the first to call attention to the influence of the Aurora Borealis on the magnetic needle, and he was also the founder of an international astronomical society. In the domain of physics, he made important observations on the intensity of light in relation to the remoteness of its source and was the first to construct the centigrade thermometer; this was later modified to its present form by Linné.

Swedenborg.—The outstanding enigma among the scientists of the period was Emanuel Swedenborg. Born at Stockholm in 1688, son of a scholarly and tolerant professor of theology at Uppsala and later Bishop of Skara, Jesper Svedberg, Swedenborg (this name was chosen when the family was raised to the rank of nobility) received the most thorough training in scientific knowledge that the age could give. At first he vacillated between the fantastic archæological and historical theories of Rudbeck and the sober truths of science, as taught him by Erik Benzelius. In the beginning, the latter's influence prevailed. Several years were spent by the young scholar in scientific study in England, where he probably made the personal acquaintance of Newton; at all events, he was the first Swede to embrace fully the great Englishman's theories. On his return to his native country, he founded a periodical *Daedalus Hyperboreus,* the first scientific journal in the land, and delved eagerly into the mysteries of nature. He evolved a cosmic theory which forms the basis for the later theories of Kant and Laplace. Appointed by Charles XII to be assessor extraordinary in charge of the College of Mines, he made important contributions to all the sciences which touched upon the mining and iron industry, mathematics, geology, astronomy, mechanics, and chemistry. One of the highest authorities in the field (Nathorst) says that Swedenborg's contributions to geology alone were sufficient to perpetuate his fame. A better understanding of his writings has made it evident that Swedenborg was far ahead of his time in practically every department of scientific activity. He stated new and surprisingly accurate theories regarding light and cosmic laws, cleared up many phenomena of phosphorescence, invented a method for determining longitude at sea by observing the moon and stars, invented an ear-trumpet for the deaf, improved the stove, suggested the decimal system for money and measures, suggested models for flying machines, submarines, steam-engines, and sluices, and worked out a detailed plan for a canal from Gothenburg through Lakes Vänern and Vättern to the Baltic. His anatomical investigations, especially on the brain, indicated correlation of brain centres and muscular activity.[10]

Swedenborg's religious speculations.—A problem which held a strong fascination for Swedenborg was the location of the soul in the body, and in the study of this baffling question he passed more and more into the realm of mysticism and

[10] A detailed and reliable account of Swedenborg's scientific contributions is found in Ramström's *Emanuel Swedenborg's Investigations in Natural Science,* published in commemoration of the two hundreth anniversary of the Royal Scientific Society of Uppsala in 1910.

metaphysics. Soon all his scientific interests were forsaken, and he became absorbed in speculations concerning the true nature of God and His relation to the universe. His new venture has well been compared to Rudbeck's bold speculations in another field, only Swedenborg's transcend these in boldness and grandeur. The hitherto sober scientist now began to imagine that he had communications with angels and the spirits of departed men from antiquity down through the Middle Ages. The alleged revelations became the basis for a new religion which today has adherents in many lands, especially in England and America.[11]

Medicine.—It remains but to be noted, in discussing scientific advancement in Sweden, that medicine was placed on a higher plane when Nils Rosen von Rosenstein (1706-1773) introduced a really scientific anatomical study at Uppsala, based on dissection of human bodies, and improved and extended clinical studies. Rosenstein was the first Swedish doctor to use Peruvian bark in the treatment of disease and to employ prophylactic grafting for smallpox, a system in vogue until Jenner's great discovery. He wrote a number of books and treatises on diseases and their cure; especially one work by him on children's diseases was translated into many foreign tongues and passed through no less than eight editions in Germany.

Literature.—The new interest in the studies and creations which men deemed of utilitarian value and the consequent remarkable extension of scientific knowledge, also gave new content and form to poetry and prose literature of an idealistic character. Always sensitive to exotic influence, Swedish literature became in this period largely a reflex of English, and especially of French, literary opinion and creations. In French and British writers the Swedes found an emphasis placed upon simplicity of style and upon moral content and practical values, which was entirely in accord with their own interests and ideals.

Dalin.—The leading representative of this new literature was Olof von Dalin, whose work on Swedish history has already been noted. Born in 1708, Dalin had studied at the University of Lund, where he came under the influence of An-

[11] The most impartial and penetrating study of Swedenborg's theosophy is Lamm, Martin, *Swedenborg, en studie öfver hans utveckling till mystiker och andeskådare*, Stockholm, 1915.

dreas Rydelius, the foremost Swedish philosopher at the time and a brilliant thinker, who emphasized reason as the reliable guide in man's search for truth. After moving to Stockholm, where he became a tutor in a rich nobleman's home, Dalin became the intellectual leader of a group of nobles who had literary interests. Before long he was *persona grata* at the court, whose dominant personality, Queen Louisa Ulrika, it will be recalled, was an enthusiastic admirer of contemporary French culture. While Dalin never became a sycophant of royalty, but always maintained a large measure of independence, the influence of the court could not fail to give direction to his energies. Of much more importance was the influence which Addison, Steele, Defoe, Swift, Holberg, and Voltaire exerted upon him. From these men he often borrowed ideas and models. His writings were, however, thoroughly Swedish in tone and sentiment, since he had an extraordinary ability to inject his own national and patriotic sentiments into the foreign material which he freely appropriated. The bitter diatribes of Voltaire against revealed religion were not re-echoed by him. In his writings he guarded himself so carefully against the admixture of foreign words that he set an entirely new standard of Swedish style and justly deserves to be called the originator of modern Swedish prose. A weekly periodical, *The Swedish Argus* (*Den svenska Argus*), edited and published anonymously by Dalin between the years 1632-1634, and modelled after *The Tatler, The Spectator,* and *Le Misanthrope,* came to exert a profound influence on Swedish thought, for here the author, in delightful and lucid language and with consummate wit, often in allegorical form, attacked stale orthodoxy and its ally, intolerance, and preached the new doctrine of practical utility. The periodical became so popular that Thursday, the day on which the week's issue appeared, came to be referred to as "Argus Day" and the discontinuation of the publication was looked upon as almost a national loss. His *Saga of the Horse* (*Sagan om hästen*), probably his best literary creation, gives in allegorical form a vivid and delightful characterization of the Swedish rulers and the events in their respective reigns from Gustavus Vasa to Charles XII. An allegorical poem, *The Swedish Liberty* (*Svenska friheten*), for half a century enjoyed such popularity that it could be rated as the national epic of Sweden. In stately, but rather cold, verse he depicts the vicissitudes of liberty in his native land to the time of Queen Ulrika Eleanora, who, realizing that her feminine power is inadequate for the difficult task of governing Sweden, delivers the sceptre to her husband. At the moment, however, when Light and Peace seem to have won a complete victory, Ambition, Malice, Selfishness, Pride, and Discord appear, sent by the father of evil, to wreck Sweden. Next the Goddess of Liberty appears before the queen and reveals to her how the forces of evil which threaten to engulf the land can best be mastered; namely, by increasing the power of royalty. While Dalin, in the bitter struggle between the parties and the royal power, was forced to walk circumspectly, his works leave no doubt as to his royalistic tendencies.

Nordenflycht.—New tendencies came to dominate literature about the middle of the century. The satirical and strictly formal writings of Dalin became wearisome to many who loved to give vent to their feelings and found delight in fresher colours and a warmer sentimentality. The leading representative of this tendency was Hedwig Charlotta Nordenflycht (1718-1763), the first writer in Sweden who used literary production as a means of livelihood. Her sentimentality was warm and glowing, her power of poetic expression was of a high order, and she gave masterpieces to her countrymen which in her day were dearly cherished. In time, however, she lost the fresh and tender tones of her early years and became wedded to the stale and formal style of the classicists. As the inspiring personality in a coterie of literary men and artists, who were accustomed to meet at her home, this writer also wielded a strong influence on other authors. The foremost among these were Gustav Philip Creutz (1734-1785), and Gustav Frederick Gyllenborg (1731-1808). The fine pastoral idyll, *Atis and Camilla,* by the former, was perhaps the best and most popular poetic production of the period. In no writer of the time is the influence of Rousseau and the British poet Thomson so strongly revealed as in Gyllenborg; here is found ecstatic love of nature, emphasis on virtue and morality, superabundant sentimentality, and love of country.

Chapter XXI

LIGHTS AND SHADOWS IN THE REIGN OF AN ENLIGHTENED MONARCH

Personality of Gustavus III.—Gustavus III, who by the sudden death of his father was summoned to take command of the badly storm-tossed and buffeted Swedish ship of state at the very time when it was fast approaching the most dangerous breakers, was twenty-five years of age when he ascended the throne. A number of discordant elements were intermingled in his personality. While quite superficial in his philosophy of life and ardently fond of pomp and theatrical display of every kind, he was in heart and soul a lover of his country, for whose illustrious past he felt unbounded admiration. Confident in his own ability, and with an imperious nature which brooked no opposition, he desired nothing so ardently as the heroic rôle of deliverer of his country from the evils which party strife and foreign intrigue had brought upon it, and which inevitably, as it seemed, would, if permitted to continue, result in the loss of national independence and sovereignty. Until the time of his accession, Gustavus had had scant opportunity to reveal his real designs or the sterling mettle of his personality. The bitter struggle which had raged between his parents and the Council, one unpleasant outcome of which had been the appointment by the latter of tutors who were extremely distasteful to both parents and child, had early taught him the art of dissimulation, in which he became a past master. He had shown full compliance with the demands of the Cap majority in the Council both when it insisted that he marry the Danish princess, Sophia Magdalena, for whom he personally felt great aversion, as well as when, without any apparent hesitation, he, prior to his accession, signed a royal charter, still further stripping royalty of power and dignity, which the Council laid before him. Endowed with a versatile and eager mind, Gustavus had in his youth given most of his attention to the study of the new French philosophy, as well as to art and literature. It was, however, more the frivolous and the gay, that which was spectacular, than the sombre truths, which appealed to his mind. His uncle, Frederick the Great of Prussia, appeared to him to be the ideal monarch, whose example he would emulate: the enlightened despot who, with unflinching determination, would use every opportunity which unrestricted royal power gave to defend his land against foreign aggression, labour for its internal development, abolish old abuses in administration, and permit freedom of religious thought. This was the ideal of most of the contemporary statesmen and rulers of Europe—even the coarse-grained and tyrannical Catherine of Russia essaying the rôle—and Gustavus aspired to a place of honour in the charmed circle.

Since it was absolutely clear to Gustavus that unless the shameful and demoralizing struggle of the parties could be ended through the transfer of broad powers to royalty, he would soon have no free country to rule, it became his first great objective to find a remedy for the grievous ills which afflicted the political life of Sweden and rapidly were destroying the moral fibre of the entire nation. In France he had been advised to assume a conciliatory attitude towards the Hats and Caps if he would win added prestige for his crown. Being by nature averse to harsh measures, and always sustained by confidence in his own powers of persuasion and leadership, this suggestion coincided with his desires and intentions.

Irreconcilable nature of the party strife.—A Riksdag having been convoked for June 1771, new elections were held which, as usual, were marked by bitterness and unscrupulous tactics on the part of both parties. Large sums of money were furnished by Russia to secure a Cap majority. At the opening session of the Riksdag, Gustavus delivered an impassioned and eloquent address in Swedish from the throne, the first time that the language of the land had been heard from this place for more than a century. The king's lofty sentiments won the hearty applause of the nation, but in the practical business of organizing the body they were soon forgotten amidst the bitterness of party feelings. New forces had now come to the fore to array the parties against each other more bitterly and more uncompromisingly than ever before. It was no longer merely a peace party arrayed against a war party, but the lower orders arrayed against the nobility. The old peace party, the Caps, which was now dominated by the lower orders, insisted that the special prerogatives in the appointment to office, which the nobles had secured for themselves, be repealed. A furious attack upon the nobility by the burghers and *bönder* therefore constituted the first episode of the session. The Caps had a majority in the two lower estates, but in the clerical order the parties were evenly balanced until they succeeded, for a sum of 50,000 copper dalers, in bribing three of the opposition to come over to their group. Finally the Caps managed to gain a majority even in the noble Estate.

Near the precipice.—Intoxicated by their victory, they now proceeded to launch such a violent attack upon their opponents that even the Russian ambassador endeavoured to restrain them, one of his measures to that end being a threat that the monthly Russian subsidy would no longer be paid unless the leaders changed their tactics. Feeling soon ran so high that even the former leaders lost control of the situation, and in violation of a previous compromise for the balancing of power in the Council between the two groups, the Caps proceeded to oust all the Hats. Disgusted and discouraged, the latter now withdrew in large numbers to their country estates. The lower orders now proceeded to break down practically all barriers which formerly had stood between the aristocracy and the commons. In trying to find a remedy for the great economic ills which afflicted the nation, they, however, failed utterly. As a final act in the humiliating drama, the Cap majority entered into negotiations with Russia, looking towards a compact between the two countries; among other provisions in this compact was a sanction by the Swedes to the partition of Poland. No formal treaty was, however, signed.

A revolution planned.—To Gustavus it was evident that only through a revolution could the Swedish royalty again be vested with sufficient power to enable it to put a check on the party strife which was wrecking the country, and in this opinion he had the support of the French ambassador at his court. In this dismal period of his career, when doubts and uncertainties were everywhere, a Finnish nobleman, Jacob Magnus Sprengtporten, a colonel in the army, who had shown himself especially reliable and resourceful, became the king's trusted counsellor. A young diplomat and soldier of fortune, John Christopher Toll, whose alert mind had clearly perceived that momentous decisions were impending at the capital, and that now his extraordinary talents could be put to good use, became, however, the leading spirit in a project for a revolution in order to secure changes in the constitution. According to plans agreed upon by Gustavus, Toll, and Sprengtporten, the latter was to start a revolt in Finland and then advance on Sweden, while Toll unfurled the banners of insurrection in southern Sweden and, simultaneously with Sprengtporten, advanced on the capital. The alert English agents at Paris had, however, some inkling of the secret Swedish plans, and they reported their suspicions to the Cap leaders, who promptly took measures for separating Sprengtporten from the king. This they achieved by ordering, on some pretext or other, that he proceed to Finland and join his regiment there—the very place he, above everything else, just then wished to go.

Neither of the king's friends, Toll or Sprengtporten, encountered any serious difficulty at the start of their enterprise. The former speedily won the garrison at Kristianstad to his side, and the Cap chief, Rudbeck, whom the Cap party had dispatched with all possible haste to the scene of trouble, found the gates of the city closed to him. Hurrying back to Stockholm, Rudbeck at once summoned the Council for a conference regarding the proper measures for dealing with the incipient revolution. Since Gustavus was suspected of being in league with the leaders of the revolution, the majority thought that he ought to be arrested, but inasmuch as there was no direct evidence of his connection with the plot, this suggestion was given up as involving too drastic and dangerous a procedure. In the meantime, the king was racked by doubts. After successfully staging his revolution in Finland, Sprengtporten had set sail for Stockholm, but contrary winds had held him back. Toll had not as yet had time to arrive from southern Sweden. Gustavus was therefore completely isolated. The Hat leaders, the only ones in whom he could put any trust, had left the capital in fear and disgust.

Gustavus acts promptly.—In this grave crisis when his throne and even his life were in jeopardy, the king acted with a promptness and a firmness which neither friend nor foe had thought the mild idealist capable of showing. On August 19, 1772, he summoned the officers of the royal guard to a room in the palace. Pale and labouring under deep emotion, he appeared here and at once proceeded to picture the seriousness of the situation, after which he unfolded his plans for forestalling the catastrophe. He ended with the appeal: "If you will follow me as your fathers followed Gustavus Vasa and Gustavus Adolphus, I will risk my life for yours, and for the salvation of our fatherland." Most of the officers were ready to agree to support him, and took the new oath of allegiance. A few moments later they were joined by the soldiers assembled in the courtyard, whereupon all the doors of the palace were closed and the members of the Council, just then considering measures for suppressing the brewing revolt, placed under arrest. Next came the turn of those members of the Riksdag who were considered most dangerous. These were placed under arrest, and the fleet, at the time lying at anchor in the harbour. was manned by trusted friends of the king, thus frustrating the attempts of the Russian and English ministers to stir up a counter-revolution. When soon thereafter the king in company with his immediate followers appeared on the streets of the city wearing the emblem of the revolutionists, a white handkerchief tied around the arm, the multitude hailed him with delight. Within an hour, the entire population had donned the insignia of the revolution. Gustavus was master of the situation. Victory had been won without the shedding of a single drop of blood.

Two days later the members of the Riksdag met by order of the king in their accustomed place, but instead of proceeding, as had been the custom before, in stately procession, each order by itself, the members now slunk into the hall by twos and threes, while determined-looking soldiers who lined the way, and guns planted at every point of vantage and trained on the Riksdag building, showed plainly that the king and his adherents proposed, for the time being, at least, to settle the momentous issues which long had plagued the nation by other means than parliamentary debates. Arrayed in the full regalia of his royal office, Gustavus now took his place on the throne, and delivered an address which still ranks as a classic of Swedish oratory. The full and ghastly extent of the fatherland's humiliation, the dangers which threatened it, and the causes of its woes were laid bare with incisive language, which by its very moderation must have cut deep into his hearers' hearts. The king carefully refrained from calling his listeners by any contemptuous names, but in the glare of the searchlight which he turned upon them only the most unregenerate could escape seeing that they had in the past been either knaves or dupes. The king thereupon presented a draft for a new form of government for their approval, and this was given with a loud shout. Next, the members took a solemn oath that they would faithfully observe the provisions of the new instrument of government, whereupon the king subscribed to a new coronation oath. Rising and removing his crown, he thereupon ordered the Te Deum to be sung as an expression of gratitude to Divine Providence for having brought king and people together again in friendly co-operation.

The new constitution.—With one single sweep, the new constitution abolished the vicious party system and restored large powers to the monarch. After this the Riksdag could assemble only on the call of the ruler, who likewise could prorogue it at any time that he saw fit. No new law could be adopted, no old law repealed, or offensive war begun, without the previous consent of the Estates. Only in case of attack by a foreign power could the king collect special levies. The members of the Council were to be appointed by the king. Moderation became the guiding principle of Gustavus after the revolution had completed its work. He insisted that there must be no reprisals for the past, able men were appointed to the Council and to important offices without regard to their past party alignments, and the old party names, Hats and Caps, were henceforth to be strictly tabooed.

The Swedish revolution and Sweden's enemies.—The news of the Swedish revolution shocked and enraged Catherine of Russia, for the prize which already had seemed secure in her grasp had suddenly been snatched from her. But although she fumed and sputtered prodigiously, her hands were for the moment tied by a war with Turkey and by a Polish imbroglio. Denmark and Prussia at once declared their willingness to take military action in conjunction with Russia against Gustavus, but the vigorous protest which the latter sent his royal uncle at Berlin made a deep impression and helped to stay his hand. Frederick also heard from his spirited sister, the mother of Gustavus, and she let him know, in plain terms, that she considered him an unregenerate scoundrel; he was in no particular mood to arouse her wrath any further. Against Denmark Gustavus staged a military demonstration which brought a declaration from that country that it had never had any intention of joining in any hostile move against him. More effective than any other influences in staying the hands of the enemies of Sweden, were, however, the enthusiastic unanimity with which the nation supported its king and a note from France to the courts at St. Petersburg, Berlin, and Copenhagen which plainly intimated that she was prepared to support Gustavus with a military force in case he were attacked.

Internal administration.—Heartened by the knowledge that the nation looked upon him as its saviour, and impelled by an ardent desire to bring security and prosperity to his people, Gustavus next threw himself with passionate energy into the work of rehabilitation for the wretched land. Unfortunately he was not fitted by nature to play the rôle of a great administrator, as Gustavus Vasa or Charles XI had been. His superficiality of mind, unsteadiness of purpose, inordinate frivolity, and love of pleasure made the routine of administration irksome to him, and lack of consistency made it impossible for him to win the hearty co-operation of his subordinate officials. In a crisis like that of the revolution of 1772, he could amaze his friends by his extraordinary courage and resoluteness, but with the excitement gone, he was prone to subside into utter indifference to public affairs, and give thought only to the gratification of his immoderate love of worldly pleasures. Since many of his acts were found to bring criticism, especially after the first enthusiasm caused by the revolution had passed, he began to fear that his popularity was waning and this made him bitter and peevish. In time he became haughty, held aloof from the people, and cared increasingly for ancient legal forms.

Disregarding his Council, in most instances, and taking counsel with only a few confidential personal friends, Gustavus first undertook the inauguration of two important reforms; namely, the reorganization of the state and communal administration, and the restoration of sound money. Royal officials throughout the land were called on to make an accounting of their stewardship and those who were found to have been venal and incompetent were dismissed, heavy fines in many cases being imposed for malfeasance, and new men appointed to their places. The knowledge that a strong man was again at the head of the government speedily served to energize the will of public servants everywhere. The misery caused by mismanagement and oppressive taxes had been intensified by a series of bad harvests, bringing in their wake one of the worst famines that the Swedish people ever had been compelled to suffer. The number of deaths from starvation had been exceedingly large. As a measure of relief, the government now forbade the distillation and sale of gin and purchased grain abroad for distribution among the people. In order the better to be able to control and limit the consumption of strong drink and at the same time increase the revenues of the state, the right of the individual to manufacture intoxicants was abolished and government distilleries were established instead. The government dealt firmly with all infractions of the laws, but nevertheless there was in evidence a sincere desire to right existing wrongs.

Economic reforms.—As was consistent with the ideals of the enlightened autocrat, Gustavus made special efforts to bring new activity into Swedish industry. The first requisite for a revival of industry and trade, a sound currency, was met by a decree that the paper money which had been in circulation at greatly reduced and constantly fluctuating values should be redeemed at half its face value. Silver was made the standard of coinage values, and silver money, long absent from circulation, was coined again. Credit for these salutary momentary reforms belongs to Johan Liljecrantz, a sound financier whom Gustavus put in charge of the national treasury. The tenets of the mercantile system were now being abandoned by the economic philosophers and statesmen of Europe, and instead the theory of the physiocrats, according to which agriculture is the main source of a nation's wealth, came to control economic thought and give new direction to government activities. A necessary step towards a better system of agriculture was the re-parcelling of the cultivated areas of the village communities. In the typical old village community the arable land was divided into a great number of patches, of which the individual *bonde* might own as many as sixty different ones, separated from one another by the scattered patches of other *bönder*. The individual strips were sometimes so narrow that a wagon could not be turned upon one of them. No fences were possible, and the tilling of the soil must be done simultaneously by all or several of the owners. The system was a source of endless disputes, and made a thriving agricultural industry impossible. Already about the middle of the century a beginning had been made towards a re-parcelling of the patches, for the purpose of enabling a *bonde* to secure contiguous tracts for his farm. Reforms along this line were now pushed with renewed energy. Progress was slow and difficult, owing to the deep-rooted conservatism and almost hopeless inertia of the *bönder,* but some advance towards a better order of things was now made. The *bönder* were likewise freed from restraints which had prevented them from selling their products in their own communities, and admission to the guilds was made easier for the labourers. With stabilized prices, business took on a new activity.

Humanitarian measures.—In full conformity with his humanitarian spirit, Gustavus abolished torture in judicial procedure, built orphanages, hospitals, and poor-houses, and instituted a system of free medical care for the poor in Stockholm. The humanitarianism of the age even extended to the dumb beasts and a veterinary school was established in the capital. Under the inspiring example of the king himself, it became quite the fashion for rich men to make liberal donations and bequests to charitable and cultural institutions. A great step towards toleration was taken by the law of 1781 permitting foreigners, who had taken up their abode in the country, to worship according to their own faith, build churches, and engage private teachers for the religious education of their children. The only restriction of importance placed upon dissenters was their disqualification to hold state office or membership in the Riksdag. These liberal laws affected principally the Jews, who now were given the right to take up their residence in Stockholm, Gothenburg, and Norrköping; here they were to enjoy freedom of religion, but in their political and social life they still remained under several restrictions. Liberty of the press was extended, and judicial procedure reformed. In order to honour those who had rendered valuable service in the development of industry and trade, and to give encouragement to greater efforts in these fields, the Order of Vasa was instituted, its insignia being bestowed by the king himself.

Manners.—Though Gustavus was guilty of many delinquencies in matters of administration, his enthusiastic efforts to enrich the culture of his people and bring greater refinement to their manners went a long way in making amends for these. Especially in the domain of literature did his reign become one of the most creative and brilliant eras in the nation's history. While levity and superficiality were much in evidence also in this phase of his interest and activity, there can be no doubt that a serious purpose was the main impelling force. A refinement and an intellectual wealth in the land which would place Sweden in the forefront of civilized nations—this was the cherished ideal of Gustavus and most of his literary protégés. They were thus thoroughly patriotic in sentiment, although they for the most part followed foreign, especially French and English, masters and imitated them. Whatever the source of their material might be, they sought in their own creations to give it a genuine Swedish character and colour. The king's enthusiastic admiration for everything French gave a decidedly new tone to court life in Stockholm, which to an almost ridiculous degree was made to resemble that at Versailles. There was the fulsome adulation of, and humble obeisance to, royalty, the array of noblemen as lackeys waiting on his Exalted Majesty; there were pageants, soirées, and receptions in endless procession and of startling magnificence. While the superficialities and the vagaries of contemporary French life thus protruded themselves most conspicuously, there was, after all, a solid gain derived from these contacts with French as well as English thought; many old superstitions were put to rout, freedom of thought was advanced, and manners were improved. To the charge that the admixture of so much foreign thought to Swedish life was unwholesome, Tegnér made the reply that barbarism alone is patriotic in the sense that it has nothing of the exotic. "What would we be if they had not lived?" he finally asked in his eloquent eulogy of the Gustavian era.

Culturally the period was a continuation of the preceding era when, under the beneficent rule of the Hats, science and literature had brought unusual honours to Sweden. Many of the scientists who had made the earlier period illustrious, as Linné, Lagerbring, Ihre, and Wargentin, continued their activities in the reign of Gustavus, although they had passed the zenith of their lives, while younger men like Bergman, Scheele, Chydenius, Botin, and many of the famous disciples of Linné were now in the heyday of their creative work. In Finland had also appeared a luminary in the person of Henrik Gabriel Porthan, professor at the University of Åbo, who may be rated the foremost representative of Swedish-Finnish culture before the nineteenth century. Another native of this country, Mathias Colonius, was reputed to be the foremost jurist of his generation.

Societies.—The reign saw a waning of interest in scientific investigation; literature came instead to hold pre-eminence. New vitality was injected into the already existing learned and literary societies and several new ones were founded. The Literary Society (*Vittra Sällskapet*) of Gothenburg was given the status of a royal institution in 1778, and Louisa Ulrika's creation, the Academy of Literature, which for some time had been defunct, was in 1786 quickened to life again, being now known, however, as the Royal Academy of Literature, History, and Antiquities (*Vitterhets, Historie och Antikvitetsakademien*). Perhaps the most valuable and greatest of Gustavus's services in behalf of the cultural progress of his people was rendered in connection with the founding of the Swedish Academy in 1786. The idea of such an institution in Sweden found an enthusiastic supporter in the king, who took a keen interest in the project. The famous French Academy served as a model and the number of members was fixed at eighteen. Of the original group Gustavus appointed thirteen. Vacancies caused by death are filled through election by the remaining members and an invitation to occupy a seat in the hall of these illustrious leaders of thought is rated the highest honour that can come to a Swede. To promote purity, strength, and nobility in the Swedish language is declared by the charter to be the primary aim of the academy; many and highly prized honours and stipends are bestowed upon authors of merit and financial aid is given towards the publication of meritorious works in the literary field. A substantial income was from the beginning provided the institution by the grant of a monopoly right for the publication of the official journal of the government, *Post och Inrikes Tidningar*. Today one of its most important functions and the one which attracts the greatest attention is the annual award of the Nobel Prize in Literature (p. 728). The Academy of Music, founded in 1771, always enjoyed the generous support of Gustavus, who likewise encouraged famous musical composers of other lands to take up their abode in Stockholm. The theatre was, however, his first and most abiding love, and a Swedish opera was through his initiative inaugurated in 1773. The Royal Dramatic Theatre was likewise founded about this time for the purpose of presenting Swedish plays, theatrical performances having, prior to this, been given almost entirely in French, German, or Italian.

The writers.—Literature was largely permeated by French thought, but English influence was also important. Rousseau and Voltaire were the masters who had devoted followers. Johan Gabriel Oxenstierna (1750-1808), a disciple in his early years of his countrymen, Creutz and Gyllenborg, showed a strong love of nature and of pastoral life. The influence of Rousseau and the British poets, Edward Young and James Thomson, also stand clearly revealed in his poems. His best poem, *Dagens stunder* (*The Periods of Day*), shows many points of resemblance to Thomson's *The Seasons*. Here Oxenstierna depicts the verdant and smiling scenes of a typical Swedish countryside in delightful episodes dealing with haymaking, folk dances, and other forms of innocent frolic. It is an idealized picture of the life of the country folks, as it appeared to those who saw it from the windows of a noblemen's mansion, as Schück has aptly remarked. The poem naturally has a decided physiocratic tendency. Gudmund Göran Adlerbeth (1751-1818) was influenced by Greek diction and he sought to bring into close harmony the poetic beauty of classic models and the robust virility and colorfulness of his own Northland heroes. Remarkable lyric power was revealed by Bengt Lidner (1757-1793), a man of many disharmonious elements. His *Året 1783* (The Year 1783) is remarkable among other things for its fine poetic tribute to George Washington and his American compatriots. *Spastaras död* (*The Death of Spastara*) which is based on an Italian tragedy, has so much of strength and elegance in dramatic presentation and shows such depth of genuine emotion and sympathy that it ranks as one of the masterpieces of Swedish literature. In *Medea* and *Yttersta domen* (*The Last Judgment*) Lidner gives free play to his love of the tragic and awe-inspiring.

Towering above his contemporaries in intellectual brilliance and biting persiflage stands Johan Henrik Kellgren (1751-1795), who more than any one else among his countrymen voiced the prevailing scorn of the past and admiration for the new. For him, reason, and not feeling and sentiment, was the trustworthy guide. He was thus a true disciple of Voltaire. Kellgren soon became the unquestioned leader of the literary group which enjoyed the king's friendship and patronage. His early writings reveal a decidedly sensuous philosophy, but his fundamentally serious and honest nature soon transformed him into an idealist of the purest dye. His unrelenting warfare on cant, hypocrisy, and injustice did not cease, however, although his philosophy of life was changed. The obscurantism of theological thought, the absurd teachings and practices of the various cults as spiritism, mesmerism, telepathy, and secret societies, which were the vogue—and a plague—in his day were the special objects of his piercing shafts of ridicule. *Våra villor*

(*Our Illusions*), and *Ljusets fiender* (*The Enemies of Light*) are typical of his iconoclastic tendency, while *Den Nya Skapelsen* (*The New Creation*) is a poetic tribute of surpassing beauty to love as the power which illuminates and gives meaning to an otherwise dark and meaningless world. His journal, *Stockholms Posten,* became during his period of editorship one of the leading moral forces of the nation. Kellgren collaborated with the king himself in writing operas with themes from Sweden's historic past, but he was too much of a man and too independent in character to permit the favours of the royal patron to determine his sentiments and expressions.

The Academicians, the group who followed prevailing French models and laid special stress upon forms of composition, found their completest incarnation in Karl Gustaf af Leopold (1756-1829), for whom virtue was the true religion. His poems are stately in form, but they lack warmth and feeling. The reaction against the frivolity and scepticism of Voltairism found its most vigorous champion in Thomas Thorild (1759-1808). He shared Rousseau's boundless enthusiasm for nature, which became the foundation upon which he built a pantheistic religion. Influenced profoundly as he was by writers like Macpherson, Milton, Shakespeare, Klopstock, and Goethe, Thorild rebelled vehemently against the rigid rules and formalism of the dominant French school; feeling and sentiment have their important place in literature and contents are more important than forms, according to his contentions. These views make him a forerunner of the Romantic movement in Sweden. His admiration for Rousseau did not embrace the latter's political theories, however. Instead of the Frenchman's democracy, he would have a government in which the wisest man is vested with absolute power. In his *Memorialet,* published in 1786, thus three years before the outbreak of the French Revolution he boldly advocates a world upheaval by which fools would be deposed and rogues stricken down. Since his fantastic plans for the regeneration of human society were neither understood nor appreciated in Sweden, Thorild went to England, the land of freedom *par excellence,* as he believed, where he would "associate himself with all excellent heads and hearts in order to break the fetters of thralldom everywhere on earth." The English manifested less interest in his theories than even his own obfuscated countrymen and he left their country a sadly disillusioned man. The excesses of the French Revolution made him recoil from the implications of his earlier revolutionary doctrines, and from this time on conservatism had no more steadfast adherent than Thorild.

The writer of the period whose popularity has been little dimmed by the passing of more than a century was Anna Maria Lenngren (1754-1817). An easy and attractive style in conjunction with unfailing good humour and homely, sound sense explains this endurance of her popularity. The arrogant and foolish pretensions of the somewhat decadent, but proud, gentry, and the humility, curtsying, and foot-scraping of the common folk in their august presence is ridiculed by her in genial fashion. The satisfaction and joy which spring from contentment and conscientious execution of duties found in her their warm-hearted panegyrist. Although Anna Maria Lenngren was never willing to carry on any propaganda for any woman's rights' cause, she may in a sense be looked upon as one of its early advocates.

The poetic genius of the period, the literary creations of which have become a heritage of the Swedish people, as in the case of no one else prior to the nineteenth century, was that odd and disharmonious soul, Karl Mikael Bellman (1740-1795), the man whom Tegnér eulogized as "the greatest singer that the Northland has ever produced." In the sense that no one has equalled him in rhythmical excellence, lyrical inspiration, and brilliant ability to combine words and music, the statement perhaps contains no exaggeration. Bellman grew up in a pietistic home and his early poems had a religious tone, but as he fell under the spell of the boisterous and devil-may-care life of the Stockholm wine-shops his literary effusions took on a decidedly different character: exuberant joys because of his new environment and scintillating, although sometimes vulgar—according to modern standards—stanzas. Bellman cannot justly be said, however, to have been a mere tippler, who liked to paint the pleasures of bibulous enterprises in lurid colours. Underlying his poetry is a serious and melancholy realization of the emptiness and vanity of all earthly joys. It therefore behooves the wise man to enjoy life while it may be enjoyed. While this was no exalted philosophy, Bellman's songs brought a distinct relief to a generation made utterly weary by vexing political questions and bitter party strife. Many distracted souls, taking their cue from him, began to ask, "Of what concern is the Polish affair to me?" (With this quaint remark Bellman evidently intended to say that there is no use in fretting about matters that one cannot help or solve anyway.) Bellman is the incomparable delineator of character, the brilliant painter of types and quaintly humourous situations. His ability to compose rhythmic songs and set them to music, generally borrowed from old French ballads and adapted to his own purpose was phenomenal.

Sergel.—The foremost representative of the plastic art in the history of Sweden, John Tobias Sergel (1740-1814), belongs partly to this period. All his creations are characterized by originality, gracefulness, and warmth of feeling. The most notable example of his art is the statue of Gustavus III near the royal palace in Stockholm.

Good-will to America.—In this period Swedish shipping suffered considerable losses through the activity of English and American privateers, and the country took the leading part in negotiations with Russia and Denmark which resulted in the declaration, "free ships make free goods." Sweden was the first of the European states to make the policy of armed neutrality a reality. Her protests against English depredations were, at least on one occasion, couched in such forceful language that they were practically tantamount to a declaration of war. No less than sixty-four Swedish officers joined the forces which were waging the fight for independence in America, chief among them being Axel von Fersen, first aide-de-camp to the French commander, Rochambeau. Fersen conducted many of the negotiations between his chief and General Washington and in these he displayed extraordinary tact. Fersen rendered conspicuous service in the campaign leading to Cornwallis's surrender at Yorktown, and at the end of the war he received the Order of the Cincinnati from Washington's hands.

The sympathies of the nation were entirely with the

American colonies. This was due not only to the old attachment for France, the ally of the colonists, and resentment against the English for their attacks on Swedish commerce, but also to a genuine belief that Washington and his people were fighting for a great human right. The Swedish Government gave unmistakable evidence of its friendly attitude towards the colonies. Sweden was the first neutral country to conclude a treaty of amity with the United States (April 3, 1783). In a letter to R. R. Livingston, the Secretary of Foreign Affairs for the colonies, under date of June 25, 1782, Benjamin Franklin, at that time representing the American colonies at Paris, relates that Count Creutz, the Swedish ambassador in the French capital, had suggested such a treaty. Creutz told Franklin that his king had so great an esteem for the American ambassador at Paris that it would be a particular pleasure to conduct such a transaction through him. He then added, according to Franklin's letter, that "it was a pleasure for him to think, and he hoped it would be remembered, that Sweden was the first power in Europe which had voluntarily offered its friendship to the United States without being solicited." [1] The cause of the American colonies became a popular theme for Swedish poets, who paid glowing tribute to the American leaders. Thus the passionate Bengt Lidner sang the praises of Washington in his lengthy poem *Året 1783*, Bishop Frans Mikael Franzen paid a fine tribute to Franklin in his "Song to Creutz" (*Sången till Gustaf Philip Creutz*), and Sweden's greatest hymnologist, Johan Olof Wallin, later extolled the greatness of "The first American" in his fine dithyrambic poem, "George Washington."

Laxity and disorganization return.—It was, as already intimated, Gustavus's great misfortune that he lacked the moral stamina and will-power requisite for the patient and consistent labour of a good administrator. By 1780, his inordinate love of pleasure had gained almost complete mastery over him; he grew increasingly tired of the monotonous and irksome duties imposed upon him by his exalted office, and he permitted himself to be drawn more and more deeply into the

[1] Wharton, T., *The Revolutionary Diplomatic Correspondence of the U. S.*, 1889, V, p. 512. Benson, A. B., *Sweden and the American Revolution*, New Haven, 1926, gives an illuminating account of these episodes.

quagmire of sensuous enjoyment. One after the other his old advisers stepped aside and adventure-loving individuals like Johan Kristoffer Toll, Gustav Mauritz Armfeldt, and Elis Schroederheim, sycophants all, whose main object in life, the winning of easy prosperity, they achieved by playing on the king's vanity and thereby gaining easy and lucrative favours, came on the scene. Reckless wastefulness now superseded economy and the country's financial status grew constantly worse. The king's delinquencies soon brought a relaxation of control all along the line; abuses such as nepotism, sale of offices, and graft of every kind began to eat as a canker at the very roots of the nation's life. The ruler himself took the lead in setting a bad example by rewarding worthless favourites, either by outright gifts or by diverting the income from lucrative offices, even important ecclesiastical benefices, to their spacious pockets. When the subsidies which the French had furnished did not suffice, and deficits occurred, these were covered by foreign loans. At the same time, a most alarming moral deterioration began to play havoc with the nation, for which the mistaken and disastrous government policy of dealing with the manufacture and sale of intoxicating drinks was mainly responsible. The system of state distilleries had proved an ignominious failure. The manufacturing of intoxicating drinks soon went on surreptitiously in almost every household, the sparsity of population in large areas of the country being particularly favourable to evasions of the law, and a flood of liquor engulfed the nation. A new excuse in addition to the many which before had been invented in justification or extenuation of the drinking habit, could now be advanced; the more liquor from the government distilleries one consumed, the more completely one fulfilled a patriotic duty to assist in providing the state with adequate revenue. Drunkenness increased at a fearful rate, and in its wake came all its attendant evils such as poverty, immorality, and disease. The dismal failure of the system caused bitter attacks to be made upon the government, but instead of trying to devise means for curing the evil, Gustavus merely issued orders which abrogated the right of free speech, thus stifling all criticism. As long as freedom of the press had meant that his own praise was sung, he had been satisfied with it, but when its searchlight was turned upon his own acts the thing no longer seemed so commendable to him.

Reckless foreign policy.—As the plaudits of the people, which once had tickled the ears of the vainglorious king, were turned to maledictions, he became extremely irritated and restless, and in order to regain his lost popularity he now entered upon a reckless foreign policy. This contemplated nothing less than a sudden attack upon Copenhagen and compelling Denmark to cede some of her territory to Sweden. Gustavus next made a journey to Russia, where, in a personal interview with Catherine, he sought her support for this scheme. The czarina, however, remained faithful to her ally, and, chagrined and disappointed, Gustavus now sought to establish new contacts in order to win support and thus strengthen his position. In 1783 he went on a grand tour which brought him as far as Rome. Anxious to convince the world that he was a rich and powerful monarch he was guilty of such reckless abandon in the expenditure of money on this journey that the financial situation of the country became worse than ever. His recklessness was the more reprehensible as dire famine was at the time sapping the strength of his people. The political gains of the trip were practically *nil,* the only gain being the promise of a slight increase in the French subsidies, and the transfer of one of the French islands in the West Indies, St. Barthelemy, to Sweden. By the time the king returned home, discontent was bitter and well organized. It had its stronghold among the noble families who, in spite of the king's efforts to bind them to him by generous favours and fulsome flattery, bitterly resented his absolutist tendencies, and with firmness opposed his adventurous foreign policies. It was in this atmosphere of discontent and suspicion, aggravated by misery caused by a serious failure of crops, that the Riksdag met in 1786 and proceeded to show that "Prince Charming" was no longer the great idol of the nation. Practically every royal proposition was rejected, and complaints against many of the king's measures, especially the crown distilleries and government encroachment upon the right of free speech, were numerous and emphatic. In this crisis the monarch did very little to abate the evils which had stirred up resentment in the nation. A curtailment of the practice of simony in ecclesiastical affairs and a royal permission to parishes to take over the distilling business on certain conditions, one of them being the payment of certain excise duties to the state, was all that was done to allay popular feeling. Rather than subject himself to the irksome and monotonous task of studying the situation of his country and grappling with the problem of how to remedy existing evils, he chose to resort to the favourite device of many an autocrat before him; namely, embroil his country in war with a foreign power, taking care, however, that this would have the appearance of a defensive war. Russia was the country with which Gustavus was now determined to have a war; this country having, it must be admitted, given him grievous provocations.

Catherine's meddling.—Ever since the revolution of 1772, Catherine had assumed an exceedingly overbearing and threatening attitude. In her instructions to her minister at Stockholm, the czarina had written these words with reference to Gustavus: "We have therefore decided that as soon as we find the time favourable we will without delay attack him and this so suddenly that his allies will not have time to come to his aid before everything is set in motion and the present government overthrown." At the same time she advised her agent how he could best win the Swedes who were hostile to their king to the Russian side. He was, among other things, to assure them that, in an eventual war between Russia and Sweden, she would know how to differentiate between friend and foe in the latter country.[2] The Russian minister lost no time in establishing contacts with certain Swedes who were disgruntled, with the object of reviving the former bitter factional strife in the land.

The arch-traitor.—The treason of Göran Magnus Sprengtporten had already created a serious situation in the land. This man, a brother of the hero of the revolution of 1772, had been appointed by Gustavus to a very important position in connection with the national defence in Finland, but when the king, who in various ways had tried to befriend him, found it impossible to grant his unreasonable requests for money, he entered

[2] Silfverstolpe, C., *Utdrag ur secreteraren hos kejsarinnan Katarina II A. V. Chropovitskys dagbok*, 1787-1792.

the Russian service. Sprengtporten now conceived the idea of an independent Finland under Russian suzerainty, and for this project he won a number of Finnish noblemen, with whom he kept up constant communication. At first, the adventurer had the noble ambition to become the George Washington of the "Republic of the United Provinces of Finland." He had once even sought the opportunity to join the forces under Washington in America,[3] but when he came to the court of Catherine and fell under the spell of her degrading influence, these ideals soon deserted him. Instead of becoming a warrior under Washington, he became a traitor to his own country. Catherine kept him at her capital. Gustavus was well informed of Sprengtporten's treasonable plans, and although he had faith in the loyalty of the Finnish people, he naturally was both angered and alarmed by the machinations of the Russian czarina.

War on Russia.—The right moment to strike at Russia seemed to Gustavus to have arrived in 1788 when war broke out between that country and Turkey. Gustavus had emphasized the need of strengthening the national defence and work on Sveaborg had been resumed. The fleet was strengthened by the addition of seven vessels of war. In this period he had a number of able statesmen as advisers, among them the aforementioned Johan Liljencrantz and Chancellor Ulrik Scheffer; the wisdom and integrity of the latter entitle him to an honoured place among Sweden's leading statesmen. Since he knew that many influential men in Denmark felt that their country's adhesion to the alliance with Russia was a national disgrace, Gustavus sought to come to an understanding with that country, but he was unable to prevail upon the leading Danish statesman of the day, Bernstorff, to cut loose from the old ally. Negotiations were likewise opened with England, Prussia, and Turkey, but these led to no results. Since by the provisions of the Swedish constitution the king could not begin an offensive war without the consent of the Riksdag, Gustavus took a fracas, in which Swedish and Russian troops along the boundary had become involved, as an excuse for declaring war and advancing with his army into Russia. While Catherine had left little un-

[3] Westrin, Th., *Om G.M. Sprengtportens tillämnade deltagande i Nordamerikanska frihetskriget,* in *Skrifter utgivna av Svenska litteratursällskapet i Finland,* IX.

done to give provocation to the Swedish king, she was nevertheless caught entirely unprepared. The haughty czarina was beside herself with rage. Deeply involved in the Turkish War, which likewise had come upon her unexpectedly, she sought with all possible speed to rally her forces for the defence of St. Petersburg. This seemed, however, a hopeless task, as her raw recruits could not possibly stand against the large and well-equipped Swedish army which was advancing.

The Anjala conspiracy.—From the humiliation of a surrender to the hated Swedish king she was saved by a mutiny which broke out among the officers of Gustavus and which completely paralyzed him. The ringleaders were young nobles who in the highest degree shared the resentment of their class against the king, and who had been carefully watching for an opportunity to humiliate him. His arbitrary and illegal act in starting a war without the approval of the Riksdag incensed them still further, and in this state of mind they became easily susceptible to the influence of some Finnish officers, friends of Sprengtporten. These officers now had the effrontery to write to Catherine directly, asking for terms of peace, and when Gustavus, to whom this strange and treasonable procedure became known, bitterly upbraided them for their conduct, they met at Anjala and signed a written justification of their conduct, at the same time urging their king to conclude a treaty of peace with Catherine; later they supplemented this with a demand that the Riksdag be convened. Among the officers themselves, one group insisted on a compliance with the provisions of the constitution of 1719, while another group went much farther and planned a complete separation of Finland from Sweden. Virtually a prisoner in his own camp and in immediate danger of death, Gustavus was in utter despair, but he was saved from his humiliating and perilous situation when Denmark, at the instigation of Russia, declared war.

Denmark declares war.—On receiving this news, he exclaimed, "We are saved," and at once hastened back to Sweden. His plan was soon ready in his mind. Precisely as the great national leaders of Sweden had done in the past, he would go to Dalarna and neighbouring provinces, and appeal directly to the people for assistance. On reaching Dalarna, he was everywhere met with enthusiasm and volunteers flocked to his standard. The good *bönder* and miners were stirred by bitter resentment against the traitorous officers, wherever Gustavus recited the tale of their dastardly conduct and laid bare the plight of the fatherland. "One God, one king, and God have mercy on all traitors," became their rallying cry. In the meantime, a Danish force had invaded Sweden by way of Norway, and was advancing on Gothenburg, which it had every prospect of taking, since its commander had become panic-stricken and was preparing for flight. In an incredibly hard ride, Gustavus hastened in advance of his army, reached Gothenburg, and, after assuming chief command, put fresh courage into the garrison. When his main army came up and the defences of the city had been strengthened, Gustavus could bid defiance to the Danish army. At the same time, England and Prussia, both alarmed at Russian machinations, as evidenced by her blunt orders to Denmark to begin war on Sweden, intervened and compelled the Danish commander to agree to a truce, by which the Danes speedily evacuated Sweden. Later this truce was made the basis for a treaty of peace which, however, involved no surrender of territory nor payment of indemnity. Gustavus now was certain that the indignation of his people against the conspirators of Anjala, and his own heroic conduct at the defence of Gothenburg, had caused public sentiment to swing around completely to his side, and therefore felt safe in summoning a meeting of the Riksdag. This convened in February 1789. The king's supporters, consisting mainly of the members of the lower orders, were overwhelmingly in the majority, but the nobility was still sullen and defiant. A new set of leaders now came forward, nearly all of them members of the lower orders. Foremost among them was the bold and resourceful Bishop Olof Vallquist. The king's request for a Secret Commission, with members from all the four Estates, to serve as adviser to him in the conduct of the war, was violently opposed by the aristocratic order. A joint meeting of all the Estates was addressed by the king, in the course of which he presented a demand upon the nobles that they apologize to their president for having insulted him at a previous meeting.

The king acts in a high-handed manner.—When this demand was met with angry cries of protest, Gustavus, in a fit of anger, ordered them from the room. The other orders, without much hesitation, voted the creation of the commission. The king now laid a draft for "an Act of Unity and Security" before them, by virtue of which the privileges of the nobility would be greatly curtailed. By this act initiative in legislation, control of the administrative machinery, and power to declare war and conclude treaties of peace were vested in the king. After some of the contumacious leaders of the opposition had been arrested, Gustavus again summoned the four Estates. The Act of Union and Security was presented and a vote on its acceptance or rejection demanded. The nobles, now made more than ever indignant and obstreperous by the arrest of their members, shouted a vociferous "No," but the burghers and *bönder* were just as emphatic in shouting "Aye." The clergy were divided. The king now calmly declared the motion passed, and the presidents of the lower Estates signed the act. Incidentally it may be noted that one important result of this measure was the passing into oblivion of the Royal Council which for six hundred years had existed as an important government organism. In the judicial domain, its functions were taken over by a new Supreme Court, while a special committee henceforth assumed its legislative and administrative duties. Reward came to the lower orders for their support of the king when he removed a number of restrictions that before had rested upon them. Before a secret committee, which he had requested and which now began to function, Gustavus was forced to admit that a public debt of 21,000,000 riksdaler had been contracted, without the knowledge or sanction of the Estates. These now guaranteed the payment of this huge debt, but on condition that they were henceforth to exercise control over finances through a specially created department. Appropriations for the pursuit of the war were voted by the lower Estates, the authorization to remain in effect until the next session of the Riksdag, which meant for an indefinite time. The nobility, on the other hand, insisted on a two-year limit, by which proviso they would be able to force the summoning of another Riksdag. In utter defiance of the vote of the nobles,

Gustavus, who himself went to their meeting-place in order to preside, declared that the motion approving the appropriations had been duly passed until the next Riksdag.

Some of the most prominent leaders of the Anjala conspiracy had in the meantime been arrested, while others had sought a safe haven in Russia. Only one of the traitors was later executed for his connection with the shameful affair; towards the others Gustavus showed great magnanimity and sought to again win their loyal support.

War against Russia resumed.—The war against Russia could now be resumed. On the whole the campaign was creditable to both army and navy. Gustavus had especially placed his reliance upon the latter, and when his fleet was bottled up by the stronger Russian fleet in the bay of Viborg, it seemed as if all these hopes would be frustrated. Since no help could be expected from the army, the situation became serious, and in desperation Gustavus ordered that an attempt be made to break through the Russian cordon. Through this manœuvre, known as the "gauntlet of Viborg," which was executed with skill and bravery, the fleet managed to escape, but with the loss of ten units. With a part of the fleet, Gustavus retired to Svensksund, and here he engaged the Russian fleet in an encounter which brought to the Swedish fleet the most glorious victory in its annals. The Russian fleet was shattered, one-third of its vessels being destroyed. Catherine had vowed that she would have sweet revenge on Gustavus, but sobered by the outcome at Svensksund, she was now willing to terminate the struggle.

Treaty of Värälä.—By the treaty of Värälä (1790), everything was restored to its former status. This might lead to the conclusion that the sacrifices of the Swedes had all been in vain, but some positive gains had been made; Russian meddling in Swedish internal affairs now ceased. The irreconcilable antagonism between the two countries remained, however, and was, before many decades had passed, to result in Sweden's worst disaster.

Gustavus and the French Revolution.—It was a strange coincidence that Sweden's transformation into a virtually absolute monarchy took place the very year that witnessed the outbreak of the French Revolution and the abolition of ancient aristocratic privileges in France. In Sweden the monarchy led the attack of the lower orders against the privileged class, while in France the king made common cause with the nobility, and paid the penalty with his life. Gustavus's vigorous espousal of the cause of the commons was, however, due more to peculiar political alignments in his country than to a real deep-rooted sympathy for the masses. The drastic acts of the revolutionists in France filled him with disgust and fear. Other considerations caused him to turn against the men who at the time controlled the destinies of France. He could not forget the splendour of French culture in the ancient régime, nor the friendship that France had, as a rule, evinced for his own country ever since the Thirty Years' War. The ideas of the French Revolution, so far as a strict censorship of the press permitted them to be known, were, however, generally applauded by the nation. The cultured classes, with a group of hot-headed aristocratic dreamers taking the lead, were especially conspicuous by their espousal of the revolutionary cause in France. Strangely enough, these nobles, who hated Gustavus with a most vindictive hatred because of his attacks upon their privileges, exalted as heroes the French leaders who ruthlessly attacked the same privileges. When Gustavus now gave evidence of his aspiration to become the leader of European royalty in a concerted attack upon the new French Republic, the maledictions of his nobles were poured out on him as never before.

In his endeavour to organize the opposition to action against the revolutionaries, Gustavus sought the assistance of Catherine II, his bitter antagonist of former days. An agreement was actually reached between the two which in effect made Sweden secure against a Russian attack and guaranteed to her the payment of annual Russian subsidies. The shrewd Catherine had, however, no intention of going any farther in her support of Swedish plans; by keeping Gustavus's mind occupied with French affairs she could postpone the execution of certain provisions of the treaty of Värälä regarding boundary adjustments which were not in Russia's favour. Gustavus's restless mind kept on forming new and fantastic plans in the execution of which he was to be the chief actor. He first sought the Polish crown, and again Catherine humoured him by certain promises of assistance, which she, however, took care not to make specific. These Polish plans miscarried completely and, egged on by Catherine, Gustavus now reverted to his earlier interest in the French Revolution. During a visit to Aix-la-Chapelle, in 1791, he gathered about him a number of French émigrés, who lost no opportunity to flatter his vanity by praising him as the coming saviour of France. His confidential friend, Count Axel von Fersen, served as the go-between in the negotiations between him and Louis XVI and Marie Antoinette. It was Fersen who laid the plans for the unsuccessful royal flight from Paris and who accompanied the unfortunate royal couple until they were taken prisoners. Gustavus contemplated the assembling of several armies, furnished by the crowned heads, under his general command, and a concerted advance on France. The other rulers, however, did not take him seriously.

While the king kept his mind busy with ambitious plans for foreign intervention, the administration of his country was sadly neglected. Economic distress and popular discontent, because of his chimerical schemes, compelled him to call another Riksdag meeting in 1792, which, contrary to all expectations, proceeded with its work in great harmony, the leaders of the nobility choosing not to resort to any obstructive tactics. Beneath the surface there simmered bitter hatred, however, and this was soon to lead to a dastardly act.

Conspiracy against the king; assassination.—In deepest secrecy a conspiracy was formed by the most implacable among the king's enemies, its sinister program including the assassination of the monarch and the staging of a revolution during the resulting confusion, with the purpose of securing a new constitution and a new government for the country. Leading the conspiracy was the cunning and unprincipled General Pechlin, who once before had acted a dastardly rôle (p. 542). Two young counts, Ribbing and Horn, both harbouring personal grievances against the king, were also in the group. The former was a cold and calculating individual, thoroughly selfish and utterly proud, the latter a crack-brained sentimentalist, who conceived it to be his patriotic duty to assist in ridding Sweden of its alleged tyrant. The man chosen to kill the king,

Jacob Johan Anckarström, was a former officer in the royal guards, a coarse and self-seeking individual, whose disapproval of Gustavus's war policies had grown to the intensity of a wild fanaticism. The conspirators chose a masquerade ball in the Royal Opera House, on the evening of March 16, 1792, as the most opportune time for carrying out their dastardly plans. Immediately prior to his departure from his apartments in the palace, the king was handed a warning note, but whatever failings otherwise might be charged to him, cowardice was not one of them, and the warning was disregarded; one of the conspirators, stricken by conscience, had tried to prevent the tragedy. A few minutes after having mingled with the crowd at the ball, Gustavus was shot from behind by Anckarström, after which the cry, "fire, fire," was immediately raised. This scheme to create confusion was frustrated by the calmness of friends of the king, who at once ordered all doors closed and the names of those present secured. Before long most of the conspirators were locked up in prison and the guilt of Anckarström established; the wily Pechlin had, however, managed to cover up his tracks so carefully that the evidence against him was insufficient to establish his guilt before a court. It was believed at first that Gustavus had not suffered any serious injury, but soon it became evident that the early diagnosis was wrong and that he was a doomed man. To the end the king maintained a remarkable fortitude, never complaining, never whimpering, and never giving utterance to any feeling of bitterness against his enemies; on the contrary, he begged that the perpetrators of the deed be treated with mercy. The dark shadows of his last days, during which he suffered excruciating pain, were dissolved, and his closing hours made bright by the gracious act of the members of the older nobility who came to his sick-room to express hope for his recovery and ask forgiveness for all the grief which they in the past had caused him. The end came to him thirteen days after the fatal shot had been fired (March 29, 1792); Gustavus was then only forty-six years of age.

Gustavus's place in Swedish history.—Concerning no Swedish king have the opinions of posterity been so divergent as in the case of Gustavus III. Just as his personality revealed the greatest contrasts in qualities, so his statesmanship was at times marked by genius and by a patriotism that was willing to make any sacrifice, at other times by pettiness and vainglory. His failings and mistakes may, however, be generously forgiven him, since, so far as any human mind can perceive, it was his unflinching courage and quick decision in the crucial test of 1772 that saved Sweden from anarchy and national annihilation. Aside from the tragedy of the manner of the king's passing, there was additional tragedy in the fact that his death came at about as inopportune a time as can be imagined and multiplied the dangers threatening the country. If there was any time when the land had need of a chief who had the wisdom of experience, it was just now when the assassin's bullet struck him down.

The premature death of Gustavus was the most serious calamity that could have befallen his country at the time. There was much in his life, in the years just before his death, which indicated that his character and ideals were undergoing a great change. His mind was being sobered by the stern realities of life, and he was settling down to the serious business of giving Sweden a good government. After the fantastic excursions into the realm of foreign affairs, he was ready, it seems, to bring the ship of state into channels which his illustrious predecessors had found the safest and most certain to lead to national security and prosperity. There were dangerous breakers ahead and Sweden had need of a calm and experienced helmsman at the wheel; instead, the destinies of the nation were now placed in the hands of inexperienced and foolish men.

Chapter XXII

THE CROWNING NATIONAL DISASTER

New leaders.—Gustavus III left only one son, Gustavus Adolphus, who was thirteen years of age when Anckarström's dastardly deed made him king. The brother of Gustavus, Duke Charles, became the head of the government during his royal nephew's minority. The regent was, on the whole, a well-meaning man, but pleasure-loving and indolent, and his inherent weakness of character made him easily susceptible to the influence of designing sycophants. His cherished hobbies were occultism and the vacuous speculations which were a part of the mysticism that flourished in the multitude of secret societies of the period. In his endeavours to delve deeply into the great secrets of existence, Duke Charles had come into contact with a kindred soul, Gustav Adolf Reuterholm, whose influence was such that he became the real head of the government. The record number of secret societies which he had managed to join and in whose cult and practices he had become an authority, constituted his main achievement up to that time. For statesmanship he lacked virtually every qualification, except those of industry and thrift. An enthusiastic follower of Rousseau, he had applauded the deeds of the French revolutionists, and naturally therefore had not shared the late king's sentiments regarding the great French upheaval. With unseemly haste he removed the faithful friends of Gustavus from government service, a procedure which gave no offence to Duke Charles, whose relations to the royal brother had most of the time been strained. Gustavus had indeed on his death-bed pleaded for mercy for his assassins, but Reuterholm and Duke Charles now took these admonitions so literally that the nation felt outraged by the consideration shown the regicides. Anckarström alone among the conspirators was made to suffer the extreme penalty.

Towards revolutionary France, Sweden now assumed a distinctly friendly attitude, and refused to join in the anti-Jacobin coalition which after the execution of Louis XVI had been formed by England, Holland, Spain, Austria, Prussia, and several of the smaller states. Instead she joined with Denmark and Russia in a union of armed neutrality for the protection of her trade. This political course, and certain vague insinuations which were circulated that Reuterholm and Duke Charles harboured sinister designs against the young king, caused uneasiness and bitter resentment.

Attempted revolt against the regents.—General Armfelt, a former favourite of Gustavus, now planned a coup, in which, with the aid of Russia, Reuterholm was to be removed from control. The canny Catherine hesitated, however, to give her support to the scheme, and the plot became known. Armfelt fled to Russia, and his associates, who were caught, were punished with a cruelty which seemed especially revolting in contrast to the leniency that had been shown the regicides. Among the conspirators was the fair Magdalena Rudensköld, Armfelt's mistress, who, to the intense disgust and indignation of the people, was pilloried on the public square of Stockholm. With good reason it was surmised that Duke Charles was bent on getting sweet revenge, because the young lady had previously rejected his amorous advances. The affair discredited the government beyond all repair.

Marriage plans.—Catherine II was very angry because she had been dragged into the affair at the trial of the conspirators, her anger growing more bitter still when, soon thereafter, Sweden formed an alliance with France. Incidentally, the latter move was financially very profitable to both Duke Charles and Reuterholm, whom France paid handsomely. For the purpose of placating the angry czarina, the worthy pair revived an earlier suggestion for a marriage between Gustavus Adolphus and Alexandra, a grandchild of Catherine. Since the French alliance had failed to give Sweden the expected security, it therefore became more than ever important that the haughty Russian ruler be speedily mollified. The young prince was induced to make a trip to St. Petersburg, his uncle accompanying him, but he made it a condition before leaving Stockholm that the question of a marriage between him and the fourteen-year-old princess should not be discussed. On meeting the princess and discovering that she was beautiful, he changed his mind on this point. A brilliant court assembly was arranged, it being understood that here the betrothal would be publicly announced. At the last moment, however, Catherine advanced the demand that the Swedish prince must give a written guarantee that Alexandra would be permitted to retain her old religion and form of worship in Sweden. As Gustavus Adolphus already had given a verbal promise not to coerce the princess in matters of religion, he looked upon this new demand as an aspersion upon his character and an insult, and refused point-blank to submit to it; the conviction that such a concession would be in violation of the fundamental law of his country also weighed heavily in the balance. With a firmness that neither cajolery nor threats could change, the prince held his ground, agreeing later, however, that he would yield if the Archbishop of Sweden and the Stockholm consistory would sanction a submission to Catherine's demands. Gustavus Adolphus soon returned to his native land, where he was acclaimed a hero because he had dared to defy the arrogant and treacherous Russian autocrat. Naturally the episode had no salutary effects upon the relations between the two nations, however. A few weeks later Catherine died, her death hastened, no doubt, by the mortification which the failure of the marriage plans had caused her.

Gustavus Adolphus takes the reins.—Two weeks after his return from the ill-fated journey to Russia, Gustavus Adolphus began to rule in his own right (November 1, 1796) under the name of Gustavus IV Adolphus, and Reuterholm was summarily dismissed. Before his dismissal the latter had still further incurred the ill-will of the nation by abrogating the right of free speech, a right which he had fondly cherished and boldly championed as long as its weapons were turned against his enemies, but which lost its virtue and became a serious menace, in his opinion, as soon as they were directed against his own person. One of his most unpopular acts was the closing of the Swedish Academy, on the frivolous charge that it had become a nursery for revolution, the real reason for his act being, that he felt bitter chagrin because he had not been elected a member. A riot in Stockholm aroused in him a mighty fear of revolutionary ideas and publishers were thereupon forbidden to print anything relating to the French Revolution, or to the Constitution of the United States of America. For the time being, Duke Charles also fades from the picture. His and Reuterholm's joint administration had not been entirely without merit, however. Strict economy had been practiced in the government business; the financial situation had therefore improved considerably; the administration machinery was now more effective, and plans for better means of communication had been formulated and partly carried out. The most important of these projects was a canal connecting Lake Vänern and the North Sea, actually completed in 1800 and known as the Trollhätte Canal.

Character of the young king.—Gustavus Adolphus began his reign under apparently auspicious circumstances. The exit of the hated Reuterholm and Duke Charles was hailed as good riddance. The friends of Gustavus III now came back and became his son's confidential advisers. Ever since the Russian episode he was a real hero in the eyes of the nation. The king was in all his measures actuated by a deep sense of duty, and the welfare of his people was the objective of his thoughts and desires. In spite of his good qualities and his early popularity, he was, however, a tragic figure from the very beginning of life to the end. Even his paternity had become the subject of cruel court gossip, one outcome of which was a bitterness between Gustavus and his mother that was most unseemly in its intensity and completely poisoned the court atmosphere. Evil tongues had busily but most surreptitiously spread the report that a certain handsome adventurer at the court was the father. The queen-mother gave credence to this insinuation, a fact which Gustavus never forgave. As the young king grew up, it became evident that he was sadly lacking in the qualities requisite for statesmanship; he had a ridiculously exalted idea of his royal dignity, and was utterly unable to grasp the significance of the new tendencies which were upsetting the old order of things. His country was still suffering from the wounds inflicted by the bitter party strife as well as the conflict between king and nobles, and abroad events which threw Europe into turmoil and threatened the stability of every nation were following each other in rapid succession; Gustavus Adolphus was too doctrinaire, too stubborn and unyielding, to be able to guide the ship safely in such perilous times.

Soon after Gustavus IV Adolphus had taken the reins of government into his own hands, dark and threatening clouds began to lower menacingly over the land. A series of bad harvests brought starvation and disease in its wake. Foreign trade, which the wars in America and on the European continent had stimulated into unprecedented activity, was now virtually ruined by the economic warfare waged between France and her enemies. Money had again depreciated greatly in value, causing further confusion and loss, and in order to get funds for the redemption of the paper money in circulation, the Swedish possession of Wismar was pawned to Mecklenburg-Schwerin for 5,000,000 crowns for a period of one hundred years, but on conditions which in reality precluded any possibility of its eventual return to Sweden.

Economic measures; the steam-engine.—Two innovations of epochal importance to the economic life of the nation were made in this period; namely, the enactment of the Enclosure Act of 1803, and the introduction of the steam-engine as motive power in industry. The vigorous and consistent advocate of the land reform was Rutger Maclean, a landed proprietor, who on his own extensive estate in Skåne had, in the face of almost unbelievable inertia and ignorance on the part of the *bönder*, set himself resolutely to the task of re-parcelling the land so that individuals might possess contiguous tracts. By the provisions of said act, a *bonde* or group of *bönder* could demand surveys and estimates of the value of the various patches which constituted the aggregate holdings of the villagers, in order that each individual might then get what he was entitled to in one tract. Promise was thus held out that the difficulties inherent in the old village system (p. 116) would soon disappear, but the reform made deplorably slow progress because the *bönder* did not understand its purpose. Suspicions and strife embittered rural life. Credit for bringing the steam-engine into Sweden belongs to the Englishman, Samuel Owen, who first came to the land for the purpose of installing some engines which a Swedish manufacturer had purchased in Great Britain. Since he found opportunities for an industrial development of this northern land most promising, he decided to remain. Endowed with great ability as an industrial leader,

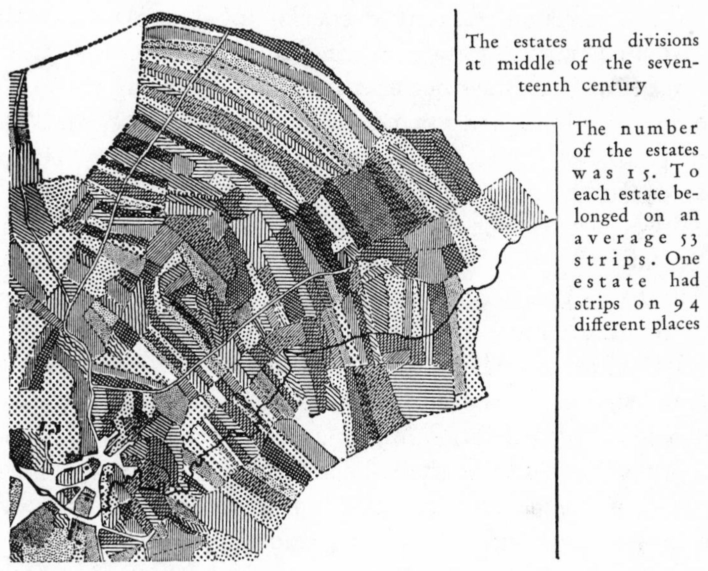

An old village community. Part of Bäcks village, Västergötland, in the middle of the seventeenth century.

Owen succeeded in building several factories, which became successful enterprises. He built the first Swedish steamboat, and because of his energy and leadership, Sweden soon advanced so far in inland-water transportation that only England surpassed her in this respect. In the opening years of the nineteenth century, the country was steadily advancing towards economic stability and a greater degree of material well-being. The population, which, at the death of Charles XII, numbered only 1,500,000 souls, had now grown to more than 3,200,000; the population of Finland had trebled. National wealth, while on the increase, was still comparatively insignificant. It has been estimated at approximately 1,000,000,000 crowns in 1805 or less than one-ninth of the figure a century later.

Foreign relations and war with Napoleon.—Swedish policies during the hectic years of the early Napoleonic wars were somewhat hesitant and shifting. In the bitter war which England, under the leadership of the younger Pitt, waged against the Corsican, the Scandinavian countries endeavored to maintain neutrality, and in 1800 a League of Armed Neutrality was formed between Paul of Russia, Gustavus IV Adolphus, Crown Prince Regent Frederick of Denmark, and the King of Prussia. Inasmuch as England, in order to prevent supplies being furnished her enemy, claimed the right to search all vessels, she looked upon this as a hostile league, and acted promptly to destroy it. A strong English fleet, under the command of Parker and Nelson, in the spring of 1801 attacked the Danish fleet outside of Copenhagen and although the Danes fought valiantly they were unable to drive the assailant back. Anxious to escape a bombardment of his capital, the Danish crown prince agreed to a truce, which virtually meant that Denmark deserted the League of Armed Neutrality. The English fleet then proceeded towards Karlskrona in order to attack the Swedish fleet, but just as an engagement was about to begin news came that the Russian czar had been assassinated, and that his successor had made peace with England. Left alone, Sweden had virtually no choice, and now reached an agreement with England which, in the main, implied considerable concessions by the proud mistress of the seas in the matter of Swedish trade. The supercilious attitude of England had, however, greatly irritated Gustavus Adolphus, and for a time he was inclined to cast in his lot with Napoleon, hoping, through his aid, to realize a fond ambition of his; namely, the merging of Norway and Sweden. Suddenly, however, the king had a complete change of heart, and from this time on Sweden swerved more and more to the camp of Napoleon's enemies. Political considerations lay back of this change of front. The agreement of 1803 with England in regard to Swedish trade and commerce had, after all, removed many of the early grievances and had given satisfaction to the nation. Napoleon's threats against Germany also served to jeopardize the still remaining Swedish possessions on the Continent (a part of Pomerania). The Russian menace also appeared the more threatening as the Muscovite power showed signs of a coming reapprochement between Russia and France. A rigid adherence to a policy of neutrality was perhaps possible even under existing conditions, but weighty considerations prompted Sweden to seek allies against Napoleon.[1] Gustavus Adolphus now stubbornly refused to recognize Napoleon as Emperor of France, and joined the league which Austria, Russia, and Prussia had formed against him (December 1804). Although without military experience and knowledge, deficient even in physical courage, Gustavus Adolphus now undertook to lead a Swedish army contingent in the field, but he soon became involved in useless controversies with the King of Prussia. When at last he was ready to advance with his army to the Rhine, the issue had already been decided by Napoleon's decisive victory over the Russians and Austrians at Austerlitz. During the campaign, Napoleon had sought to win Gustavus Adolphus to his side, but his overtures had brought nothing but insulting answers. When a French force thereupon invaded Swedish Pomerania, where the Swedish army was then quartered, Gustavus Adolphus left the command to General Toll and returned home. By display of great skill and tact, General Toll was able to induce the French general to sign a convention whereby the Swedish army was permitted to return to Sweden. After the French victories at Eylau and Friedland came the momentous treaty of Tilsit (1807) between Alexander I and Napoleon followed by an alliance between the two emperors. The Russian emperor thus deserted his former allies, and Napoleon was willing to leave Sweden to the tender mercies of the Russians. One point in their secret agreement specified that if England did not, within a certain time, accept Russia's offer of mediation and make peace with France, recognize the equality of all flags on the seas, and restore certain of her conquests, a demand should be made on Denmark, Sweden, Portugal, and Austria that they close their harbours to English goods and ships and declare war on England. Any country, it was further stipulated in their agreement, which refused to comply with these demands should be treated as an enemy.

[1] Lundh, Herberth, *Gustaf IV Adolf och Sveriges utrikespolitik 1801-1804*, Uppsala, 1927.

Sinister plots against Sweden.—For Sweden specifically it was agreed that if she refused to heed the demand, Denmark should be summoned to begin hostilities against her. It has been conjectured that Napoleon now orally expressed acquiescence in Russia's open designs to wrest Finland from Sweden. The French policy of friendship during one hundred and fifty years, a policy which had insured some degree of protection to Sweden, was thus completely reversed. The consequences of this unfortunate compact were soon to appear. England demanded that the entire Danish fleet be surrendered to her, on the plea that otherwise it would fall into the hands of Napoleon. Although prior to this Denmark was ready to ally herself with England, the arrogant and humiliating demand for the surrender of the fleet naturally aroused her bitter indignation and it was firmly rejected. Thereupon followed the bombardment of Copenhagen by the English and the seizure of the Danish fleet. This high-handed act naturally increased Danish bitterness enormously against the perpetrator and immediately brought the nation definitely to the French side. After completing its task at Copenhagen, the English fleet sailed home, leaving Sweden to her fate. Denmark now agreed to join France and Russia in an attack upon her. Alexander had carefully refrained from any overt act against Sweden as long as the English fleet was in the Baltic; in fact, he had wavered for a time between two courses: either he would invade Finland and add this province to his possessions, or he would turn against Turkey and make gains in that direction. It appears that the latter course appealed to him more strongly, but Napoleon, wishing to save Turkey from attack, now hastened to mediate a peace between that country and the czar. For a moment Alexander seemed to have given some serious thought to a break with Napoleon, since the alliance with him was very distasteful to the Russian people, and an attack upon Sweden was certain to leave a bad stain on his own honour; furthermore, a war in which England was likely to be arrayed against him involved serious risks. On the other hand, the czar had reason to fear that a break with Napoleon meant another war with France, and for this he just then had no desire, while Denmark's accession to the French-Russian alliance, making it necessary for Sweden to divide her forces, appeared to make the conquest of Finland a comparatively easy matter. These considerations led Alexander to reach the momentous decision to abide by the Tilsit agreement. In deepest secrecy, he now began preparations for an attack upon Finland. When finally Gustavus Adolphus realized the enormity of his danger there still remained a possible chance for him to save himself, but this would have meant a complete reversal of policy and an abject surrender to Napoleon. Political considerations as well as the king's stubborn nature precluded the possibility of such a course. Nothing, therefore, remained but to meet the attack as best he could. Besides his own meagre forces, he had only England's promise to send a fleet to assist his country, and the assurance of English subsidies, amounting to 100,000 crowns monthly. Gustavus Adolphus found it difficult to believe that Alexander, who was his brother-in-law—he had married a sister of the Swedish queen—and, as far as the Swedish king knew at the time, his ally, would attack Finland, and he neglected to make proper military preparations for meeting the threatening attack. This fatal neglect has been taken as conclusive evidence that Gustavus was utterly inefficient and derelict in his duty. The accounts of earlier historians regarding this phase of the sad episode have stated that the Swedish ambassador at St. Petersburg, Stedingk, repeatedly warned his royal master of Russia's sinister designs and that these warnings were given little heed at Stockholm. Material from the secret archives which later has come to light shows, on the contrary, that Stedingk was the man who permitted himself to be duped by Russian assurances, and that he advised the king to refrain from making military preparation in Finland, on the plea that this might provoke the Russians to begin war. Stedingk's correspondence, as published about the middle of the nineteenth century by his son-in-law, gives no inkling of these suggestions and warnings to the king, and the envoy has therefore until almost our own day been looked upon as a man of wisdom and acumen who, however, was mortified in finding that his advice was not taken *ad notam* at home. Certain gaps in Stedingk's documents, as published, aroused the suspicion of the Swedish historian Sam Clason and he proceeded to compare the published documents with the originals in the archives. He found that approximately one-third of the material, sometimes even entire documents, in other places merely sentences or phrases, had been omitted from the published documents, and that about one-half had been garbled in some manner; significantly enough, the omitted portions were just the ones which showed that Stedingk gave misleading information and unwise counsel, and at the same time proved that the king was in reality alive to the seriousness of the situation.[2] In this connection it must be remembered that the leaders of the revolution of 1809, which led to the deposition of Gustavus Adolphus, were very anxious to justify their act by putting the king in as bad a light as possible, and they were therefore ready to put the worst possible construction upon all his acts; even the falsification of official documents seemed to them justified.

On February 21, 1808, an ultimatum was handed Stedingk in St. Petersburg, demanding that Sweden join the allies in a war on England, or take the consequences. "His Majesty the King of Sweden," said the note, "can make a decision, which can keep the two nations in complete accord and in close alliance, but the decision must be made immediately." That very day the Russian forces marched across the boundary and opened hostilities.

The Russian attack.—The Russian invasion of Finland was followed by Denmark's declaration of war on Sweden. Denmark could derive no possible advantage from an increase of Russian power or extension of her territory in the north and the whole affair was evidently repugnant to both king and people. But Napoleon cracked the whip over them and they obeyed his orders. According to Napoleon's plans, 22,000 French and 14,000 Danish troops, under command of General Bernadotte, were to invade Skåne as soon as the Russians had reached Åbo. At the same time, a Norwegian army under Prince Christian August of Augustenburg was to invade Sweden from the west. A landing on the Swedish mainland was,

[2] Clason, Sam, *Gustaf IV Adolf och den europeiska krisen under Napoleon*, Stockholm, 1913.

however, frustrated by the arrival of an English fleet. For the disaster which now overwhelmed Sweden, the king must indeed bear a great deal of the responsibility, but he was by no means alone among his countrymen in showing reprehensible neglect. The heritage of old party strife, corruption, and treason hampered the ruler constantly. Utter dismay had seized the people; most fatal was this feeling to the army, whose commander-in-chief, Klingspor, a man of sixty-five, had neither the experience nor the ability requisite for his trying position. He was obsessed by the fatal notion that all attempts to save Finland must necessarily fail. Before departing for Finland to assume chief command, he had submitted a plan of campaign to the king, according to which part of the troops were to be assembled in the fortresses Svartholm and Sveaborg, while the others were to be withdrawn to the extreme northwestern part of the country. In this way, he believed, the forces would escape being surrounded by superior forces and enabled to save themselves from the necessity of surrendering. The king approved this plan, writing an instruction in the margin, however, that the army was to try as long as humanly possible to resist the invaders, and not retreat until this became absolutely necessary.

The military disasters in Finland.—This royal instruction Klingspor ignored completely, and as soon as he reached Finland the whole campaign—aside from brilliant victories by subordinate officers like von Döbeln, Sandels, and Adlercreutz—became one dismal series of retreats. The well-equipped and well-disciplined Russian army of 24,000 men, commanded by General Buxhövden, and accompanied on its march by the old Finnish renegade, Sprengtporten (p. 582)—the latter distributing pamphlets among the Finns which assured them of Russia's great love for them—was therefore able to spread out over the country until it had Åbo and the Åland Islands in its grasp and was ready to lay siege to Sveaborg, the impregnable fortress built in the reign of Gustavus III in the harbour of Helsingfors. The Russians now invested this fortress from every side, but as they had neither men nor necessary artillery for a successful siege, they resorted to bribery in order to gain their end.

Treason at Sveaborg.—Unfortunately, the commander of Sveaborg at the time, Karl Cronstedt, was a naval officer who lacked the training and experience requisite for organizing the defence of a fortified place. To add to his handicap, he was irresolute of character and easily influenced by minds stronger than his own; the additional fact that he harboured a personal grudge against the king detracted seriously from his efficiency as commander. The sinister influence of Sprengtporten was constantly directed towards breaking down the morale of the defenders. Several of the officers on whom Cronstedt leaned for support, the most energetic among them being Jägerhorn, a brother of the leader of the Anjala conspiracy, sold themselves outright for Russian gold. The prices ran high, but the Muscovite could in this matter well afford to be generous. These venal and traitorous officers now bent their energies to the task of convincing Cronstedt that resistance was utterly hopeless. They were aided by a number of officers' wives, who were most active in giving valuable information to the besiegers and in spreading reports within the fortress that the Russian forces outside were overwhelming in numbers. Further resistance, they insidiously whispered, was useless and would merely result in bringing down fearful vengeance on those who persisted in their resistance. Buxhövden reported to the Russian foreign minister that the wife of the commander of one of the series of fortresses within Sveaborg had evinced extraordinary zeal in behalf of Russia, and that in the name of the czar he had promised that after the war his master would provide handsomely for her and her family. Another feminine traitor afterwards received a life pension of 25,000 rubles annually until her death in 1860. The published communications of the French minister at St. Petersburg to Napoleon quotes the czar as saying in reference to the use of Russian gold at Sveaborg: "The showers of gold have had their effect during the duration of the truce, the garrison is thoroughly belaboured and, speaking confidentially, Admiral Cronstedt has a claim on the war treasury which I have obligated myself to pay." Cronstedt afterwards received a pension from the czar of 4,500 rubles annually, besides 50,000 riksdaler for a share which he held in a Swedish insurance company. No material reward could, however, counterbalance the hate and the scorn which his own people heaped upon him after the dastardly deed had been done. To what extent the traitors among the officers were sincere in their affirmation that they wanted to see Finland free, cannot well be determined.

Surrender of the fortress.—On April 6, 1808, Cronstedt was induced to sign a convention that if aid had not arrived from Sweden by May 3d, the fortress would be surrendered. Permission had been given the Swedish commandant to send messengers to Sweden to apprize his government of the situation and urge the sending of supplies and additional forces, but in violation of all these promises, the Russians put so many obstacles in the way of these messengers that they arrived in Stockholm simultaneously with the expiration of the convention. In the meantime, Cronstedt's nervousness and fears were excited to an ever-increasing tension by the Russians and their confederates among the Swedes, one of the clever and more effective details of their campaign being the printing of newspapers in Swedish, purporting to be editions of well-known Swedish weeklies, and giving startling information to the effect that revolution was sweeping over Sweden, her government had been overthrown, the Russians were already on the mainland, and further harrowing details. When no aid came by the fateful May 3d, Cronstedt, by this time utterly in despair and completely under the domination of the traitors in his camp, surrendered the fortress with large stores of ammunition, 100 naval ships which lay at anchor in the harbour, and a force of 7,000 men. The besieging force numbered only 6,500 men; and at Narva one Swede had put ten Russians to rout! The Finnish soldiers were permitted to go to their homes, but the Swedes were retained as prisoners of war. The surrender of Sveaborg sealed the fate of Finland. The subsequent victories in the field of the heroic soldiers under the equally heroic leaders, the aforesaid von Döbeln, Sandels, and Adlercreutz, did not matter much except as they gave glorious evidence that courage and patriotism still dwelt in the hearts of the soldiers. By November (1808) the Swedish-Finnish armies had been pressed back across the Kemi River, which north of the Gulf of Bothnia formed the boundary-line between Sweden and Finland. Alexander already looked upon the conquest of Finland as an accomplished fact and her leading men, in the hope that thereby they would receive better terms from the Russian autocrat, were ready to acquiesce quietly in her transfer to Russia. At a meeting at Borgå (March 1809), the czar in person received the homage of the people. Finland became a grand duchy under Russia and was guaranteed a great degree of autonomy and the retention of her old system of government and laws.

Military action on other fronts.—While this had happened to Finland, military action had languished on other fronts. In May 1808, an English force of 10,000 men arrived on board a fleet at Gothenburg to assist the Swedish king, but the latter and the English commander, Moore, could not agree on the place where the troops could best be employed and therefore the latter sailed away with his forces. The king next wasted valuable time in plans for an invasion of Norway, but soon this project was definitely abandoned. Enemies were ready to attack from every side and it seemed as if the country was doomed. In this tragic hour the stricken nation got some respite by the consideration which two of the leaders of the forces arrayed against it showed. General Bernadotte, who stood ready to attack with his French troops in Pomerania, refrained from attacking and similarly Christian August commanding the Danish and Norwegian forces on the Swedish-Norwegian border, abhorring the rôle which he was supposed to play in attacking a kindred people which, wounded and exhausted, was fighting for life, remained inactive. As the sequel will show, this consideration on the part of these two men was later, in a strange way, to be handsomely repaid by the Swedes.

The enemy on the eastern border which was ready to advance in order to administer the death-blow to the helpless antagonist would not, of that the Swedes could be certain, evince any such tender sensibilities as Bernadotte and Christian August had shown. The Russians were now preparing for an attack on Sweden proper at three points, north of the Gulf of Bothnia, across Kvarken (the narrowest part of the Gulf of Bothnia), and across the Åland Islands. The Swedes realized that their situation was desperate and the feeling was common among them that Gustavus Adolphus was utterly helpless and incapable of leading them out of the valley of despair. Loud and insistent demands for the summoning of a Riksdag were left unheeded. Finally one of the generals, George Adlersparre, moved his troops to Stockholm in order to arrest the king and force his abdication or deposition. Being duly warned of this move, Gustavus Adolphus prepared to escape to his army in Skåne. In order to frustrate this and thereby save Sweden from the further woes of civil war, another general, Adlercreutz, and six companions decided to act at once, and the king's room was therefore entered by soldiers and his person secured.

Gustavus deposed.—Not a hand was raised in defence of the unfortunate man, and the revolution proceeded without the shedding of a drop of blood. Gustavus Adolphus and his family were next declared to have forever forfeited their rights to the Swedish crown and a decree of exile followed. Switzerland was selected as a haven for them. As years passed, the night of insanity descended more and more darkly upon the unhappy king. Separated from his family, and after much aimless wandering about in Europe, he finally settled down to a peaceful life in St. Gallen, in Switzerland, where, under the assumed name of Colonel Gustavsson, he continued to live until 1837.

The new constitution.—Immediately after the arrest of Gustavus Adolphus, Duke Charles became regent and at once issued a call for a meeting of the Riksdag to be held in Stockholm. That radical changes in the government must now be made was quite generally admitted and a committee was at once appointed for the important task of framing a new constitution. Hans Järta, a young jurist who had become known as a fearless and radical opponent of autocracy and aristocratic privilege, became the guiding spirit of this committee. His earlier radicalism seemed to warrant the assumption that the new instrument of government would contain all the cherished radical principles of the liberals of that day; Järta could indeed discourse freely and even glibly about pure democracy as an abstract proposition, but he had a sound sense of realities and a deep appreciation of the significance and force of historical facts. When therefore the new constitution was laid before the Estates, they learned with some surprise that it bore the impress of wise compromises, most skilfully embodied in the document between conservative and radical demands. The fact that after almost one hundred and twenty-five years this constitution, although amended in some respects, still remains the organic law of the land testifies to the sound wisdom of its framers. It is the oldest written constitution now in force next to that of the United States.

The new constitution vested executive power in the king and this included the right to declare war and conclude peace. For his official acts he could not be held legally accountable. In all public matters he must, however, confer with his advisers, officially designated as the Council of State, and consisting of nine members—this was the ministry or cabinet; its approval was required to give legal validity to the royal decisions. While serving as the king's advisers, and as chiefs of departments, the councillors were held accountable to the Estates. A Supreme Court, whose judges were to hold office for life, continued, as before, to represent the highest judicial authority of the land. The legislative branch, or Estates, consisted as before of the four orders—nobles, clergy, burghers, and *bönder*—and in it was vested the sole authority to vote appropriations and levy taxes. The Estates might accept or reject propositions as they saw fit and, independent of the king, come forward with new motions. They also selected the special committees which were to take proposed legislation under consideration and formulate recommendations. The authority of the legislative branch extended to such matters as coinage, administration of justice, and fiscal administration. On most motions an affirmative vote of three orders was necessary to give them the status of laws, a unanimous sanction of the four orders being required, however, in the case of a proposed change in the fundamental law of the land or for granting special privileges. The constitution likewise guaranteed to all citizens security of life and property, liberty of conscience, and the right to publish newspapers and books without supervision of censor. In this latter provision lay the chief guarantee that laws and government orders would be obeyed. Supplementary legislation, as well as voluntary concessions by members of the aristocratic order, had the effect of reducing to a considerable degree the burdens which had rested upon the lower classes. The laws no longer placed any obstacles in the path of even the humblest citizen who dared to aspire to the highest office in the land below that of kingship itself.

The question of a successor to the throne.—Almost equal in importance to the framing and adoption of a new constitution was the question of a successor to the royal throne. Duke Charles, who, after the adoption of the constitution, had been elected king, and had assumed the name Charles XIII, was aged and childless and his failing health gave warning that some definite action ought to be taken without delay to designate his successor. In the days of a glorious past the nation had defended itself successfully and honourably against foreign enemies, had even won large areas of foreign soil through conquests, and had occupied an exalted place among the nations of Europe, but Sweden then had mighty rulers, kings of genius and courage to lead her, and the yearning for a leader of this type now became dominant again. Thinking men wanted a king who could arouse the nation from its lethargy and infuse new hope into its distressed soul; especially did they desire a strong military man who could win Finland back. The hope that out of the confusion and anguish might also come a union of Sweden and Norway likewise grew stronger in this period of dismay. Gustavus III had harboured the hope that such a union might be realized and Gustavus Adolphus had not been entirely a stranger to the project.

Christian August.—There was one prince who in full measure seemed to give promise of a realization of the hope that a good ruler would be secured and that Sweden and Norway might be brought together into a union and that was Christian August of Augustenburg, the Danish prince who, as commander of the Norwegian forces on the Swedish-Norwegian border, had shown such noble disinclination to press military action against the Swedes at the time when Russian attacks threatened the very existence of the nation (p. 606). Reminiscent of the old Kalmar Union days was the proposal, sponsored and supported by a considerable group in Sweden, that Frederick VI of Denmark be elected as successor to Charles XIII and thus unite the three northern countries again under one sceptre. The ancient national suspicions and animosities in Sweden and Denmark, coupled with Frederick's ineradicable dislike of liberal constitutions, soon shattered all hopes of establishing a Scandinavian union by this simple expedient. Sentiment in Sweden soon crystallized around Christian August. This prince had gained great popularity in Norway and his election to the throne of Sweden would, it was believed, aid effectively in realizing plans for a Swedish-Norwegian union, especially as a Norwegian group likewise favoured such a union. This group, of which Count Herman Wedel-Jarlsberg was the leader, had by this time come to believe firmly that a union of their country with the neighbour to the east was the best way out of the difficulties that then beset their country. The humiliation and suffering which the nation had been compelled to bear by reason of Denmark's stubborn adherence to the French alliance and the consequent merciless English attacks on the extensive Norwegian maritime trade had indeed created a strong desire for independence among the Norwegians, but many of the more conservative among them felt that the nation was too weak to stand alone; the idea of a union with Sweden therefore gained ground. King Charles having approved the candidacy of Christian August, the latter was now elected heir to the Swedish throne. The prince had a commission as general in the Danish army, however, and since his country at the time was engaged in war with Sweden, he was forbidden by his sense of honour to accept until peace had been established.

The plans for securing immediately a leader whom the nation could confidently follow having for the time being failed, the Swedish interim government had no alternative but to face the issue of peace with Russia and Denmark. It was not long in coming to the bitter realization that no help was to be expected from any foreign power. A new Swedish force that had been sent against the Russians in the hope that it could win some important victory and thus place the country in a more advantageous position when peace negotiations with the enemy were begun, failed utterly, mainly through the incompetency of the leaders themselves. Naïvely the Swedes had believed that in ridding themselves of Gustavus Adolphus they had earned the gratitude of Napoleon and that he would therefore befriend them now, but he continued to be cynically indifferent to their fate. No escape from further losses, humiliation, and misery therefore appeared except through an acceptance of Czar Alexander's hard and inexorable terms, and so the inevitable step had to be taken.

Finland is lost.—By the treaty of Frederikshamn (September 17, 1809), Sweden gave up her rights to Finland, the Åland Islands, part of the province of Västerbotten, and the Swedish Lappmark. About one-third of the Swedish dominion was thus lost and the strong ties which during six hundred years had bound the Swedes and the peoples of the ceded lands together were ruthlessly severed. The helplessness of Sweden and her humiliation had never been greater than now. Ancient thrones were falling everywhere in Europe, kingdoms were bestowed on Napoleon's favourites or obliterated altogether, and to many it seemed that also for Sweden the hour of dissolution had struck.

The new leader.—Sweden and Denmark being again at peace with each other, Christian August felt that he could now honourably accept the offer of the Swedish throne which some time before had come to him. On coming to Sweden, he assumed the name Charles August, the Danish name Christian, for obvious reasons, not having a pleasant ring in Swedish ears. A sincere and upright man of great modesty, who shunned all pomp and show and found his greatest delight in associating with the common people, Charles August soon won great popularity among his new subjects, a small group of snobbish aristocrats alone excepted. It is idle to conjecture what he would have been able to do, had he been permitted to live, for the realization of the many hopes that centred in him. Norway did not, on his account, as some had hoped, volunteer to join Sweden, but the memoirs of the brother of Charles August reveal that he hoped ultimately to be able to form a union of the three Scandinavian countries under a liberal constitution and with the royal Danish family at the head. If he failed in this project, the memoirs further reveal, he had some thought of adopting

Prince Gustaf, eldest son of the former Swedish king, as his own son, and in this way restoring the Swedish throne to the old royal line. Tragically and in a moment all the fond hopes of the nation were, however, shattered when, a few months after his arrival in Sweden, the prince died.

Death of Charles August.—As he one day was attending military manœuvres in Skåne, he was seen to reel in the saddle and fall to the ground, dying half an hour later. He had been in ill-health before, having had frequent attacks of vertigo, but the report became current and found ready acceptance in many quarters nevertheless that certain irreconcilable and unconscionable adherents of the old dynasty, the Gustavians, as they were called, had caused his death by poisoning. The excitement which these unfounded charges stirred up among the people was fanned by malicious demagogues until it grew into a wild frenzy. The most exalted personage to become an object of malicious suspicion was Count Axel von Fersen, the Swedish hero from the American War of Independence, who at this time held the office of Marshal of the Realm. A frenzied mob attacked him as he rode at the head of the funeral procession of the deceased prince and caused his death under the most revolting circumstances. This gruesome act seemed to give appalling proof that Sweden had reached the utter depths of impotency and shame. Soldiers had been present in sufficient numbers to control the mob, but the officers had permitted the bloody orgy to go on without making any move to protect the victim. King Charles, who never had liked his brother Gustavus or his friends, evinced a most indecent indifference to the whole affair. What had happened had revealed with startling clearness that the country's plight was terrible, for now anarchy was threatening to destroy that which had been salvaged from the wars. "Sweden lies in her death-throes and she should be permitted to die in peace," wrote a German statesman at the time. In this crisis, as never before, the hope that a strong man might be found who could save the nation was born anew.

The game of intrigue for a new heir to the throne.—Again intrigue began to play its brisk and subtle game. The election of the King of Denmark and a union of the three

Scandinavian countries under him was favoured by one party. King Charles and other influential men found another candidate in the person of Frederick Christian of Augustenburg, a brother of the late prince, but since he had the reputation of being a weak and less aggressive man than his deceased brother, this candidacy failed to satisfy the more thoughtful. The Danish king was anxious to prevent the prince's election and gave evasive answers to all Swedish inquiries regarding his feelings in the matter. Since his approval of Frederick Christian's election would be necessary, the prince being a member of the Danish royal family, no immediate action could be taken, and as negotiations dragged their weary course plenty of time was given the Swedes for considering other candidates. One of these was, in fact, the Danish king himself. He now, quite in contrast to his former attitude, manifested a decided willingness to accept the Swedish crown for himself and even sent emissaries to Sweden to work in his behalf. While thus discussions and negotiations went ceaselessly on, one man, acting with promptness and audacity, settled the whole vexing question with one masterly stroke, thereby giving an entirely unexpected turn to events; it is no exaggeration to say that his achievement constitutes the beginning of a new epoch in Swedish history.

Lieutenant Mörner's daring move.—This man was an obscure lieutenant, Baron Karl Otto Mörner by name, who at the time was stationed with his regiment at Uppsala. Immediately upon hearing of Charles August's death, Mörner hastened to Stockholm, and secured a commission from the Swedish Council to proceed to Paris as courier in order to sound out Napoleon regarding the candidacy of Frederick Christian. Having duly discharged this part of his duties, the young lieutenant proceeded to play the diplomatic game on his own account and with startling success. A military man himself, he was not satisfied with the rather innocuous Danish prince and therefore looked about for a likely candidate among the French generals. It did not take him long to come to the conclusion that Marshal Bernadotte, Prince of Ponte-Corvo, was the very man whom Sweden needed. His candidacy would, he reasoned, be certain to appeal to the Swedes, for not only had he proved himself a military genius, second only to Napoleon himself, but as governor of Hanover he had displayed exceptionally fine and humane qualities as an administrator. The Swedes had in addition a special reason for feeling kindly towards him, for as leader of the French troops in Swedish Pomerania he had shown their country most friendly consideration (p. 606).

Bernadotte is offered the crown.—After attending to the business which primarily had brought him to Paris, Mörner got in touch with Baron Wrede, the Swedish ambassador to France, and with the Swedish consul in Paris. They were won to the Bernadotte candidacy by Mörner's assurance that it had already been practically decided that Sweden would elect a Frenchman as heir-apparent to her throne. Through these men Mörner also managed to secure an audience with Bernadotte himself, in order to get his reaction to the project. Naturally the marshal was at first nonplussed by the extraordinary suggestion which Mörner made him; but very strange things were just then happening in Europe and royal crowns were being bestowed rather freely. He assured his interlocutor that the proposal interested him, and that if elected he would be willing to abjure his Catholic faith and become a Lutheran, thus meeting the requirement of the Swedish law relative to the religion of Swedish rulers. Later Baron Wrede waited upon the marshal who expressed willingness to accept the Swedish crown if it was offered him. At the same time he intimated that Napoleon would interpose no objection to his acceptance of the Swedish crown. With these assurances, and carrying with him a letter from Baron Wrede, Mörner returned post-haste to Sweden. In the meantime, assurances had reached Stockholm that Napoleon approved the Augustenburg candidacy and forthwith the Swedish Government had proceeded to offer the crown to the Danish prince. Two days after this had happened, Mörner arrived and hastened to inform the Council of his brilliant diplomatic exploits at Paris. The councillors felt utterly scandalized by what the young man had had the presumption to do, and forthwith ordered him to proceed to Uppsala and remain there, thus preventing him from attending the meeting of the Riksdag which had been summoned to meet at Örebro for the purpose of choosing an heir to the throne. When this meeting got under way, government leaders at first clung tenaciously to the Augustenburg candidacy, but the supporters of Bernadotte were by no means inactive and they soon won some accessions to their ranks. In order to facilitate the election project, the Estates created a special committee to consider the qualifications of the different candidates under consideration, and formulate recommendations. When this committee was ready to report, it urged the election of Christian Frederick, and then went out of its way to cite reasons why Bernadotte ought not to be elected. A decision was therefore near at hand, the confirmation of the committee report by the Riksdag alone remaining in order to insure the election of the Danish prince, but suddenly the situation was changed by the arrival of Fournier, a French merchant and former resident of Gothenburg. He claimed that he came as a representative of Bernadotte himself, but he had no credentials to prove this except a picture of the marshal's wife and son. Adroitly he let it be known, however, that a part of the Swedish debt would be paid if Bernadotte were elected, and this hint was not without its effect in influencing opinion. Fournier's arrival on the scene was taken by the Swedes as evidence that Napoleon was backing the candidacy of his famous general, while as a matter of fact the French emperor had by that time reached a decision to support the Augustenburg prince; no one in Sweden was, however, then aware of this. Support now swung immediately to Bernadotte and the trend was irresistible; amidst wild scenes of exultation he was unanimously, on August 21, 1810, elected heir to the Swedish throne and prince regent. "The royal election at Örebro is like a saga adventure and never did mere chance play a greater part in the disposal of a crown," are the words in which a Swedish historian has emphasized the unique character of this historic royal election.[3]

[3] Clason, S., *Sveriges historia,* XI, p. 176.

Chapter XXIII

THE NEW LEADER AND RECONSTRUCTION

Population and social conditions in the beginning of the century.—In the beginning of the nineteenth century Sweden was the second largest country in Europe, its aggregate territory embracing a little over 300,000 square miles, of which more than one-third belonged to Finland and the Åland Islands. In 1805 the population was estimated at 3,465,000, about 895,000 being credited to Finland. Although the population of Sweden proper was thus only a little more than a third of the present figure, it bore a larger ratio to the population of most of the other European states than is the case today. Thus the population of Great Britain and Ireland combined was then only five times that of Sweden, while now it is eight times, and Prussia, whose population in 1807 was only one-third larger than that of Sweden, now has almost six and a half times as many people. In density of population the country stood lowest in the scale, with the sole exception of Norway. The mortality rate was naturally much higher than now, being 26 per 1000 in 1805, as compared to 12.79 in 1922. In the former year the average duration of life was estimated as less than forty years, whereas in 1920 it was about fifty-six. In the period 1801-1810 approximately 19 per cent of the children born died within the first year, while in 1926 the corresponding figure was only 7 per cent. The population was almost entirely rural and agricultural, 78 per cent living outside the cities, and 85 per cent being engaged in agriculture. The metropolis, Stockholm, had in 1805 a population of 73,000, whereas the next in size, Gothenburg, counted only 12,000 souls, and cities like Malmö and Uppsala had not as yet reached the 5,000 mark. Agriculture still suffered under the handicap of the village system, and the extreme to which the division of land holdings had been carried is seen in the statement that twenty owners who are mentioned in one group had no less than 5,000 different patches. This subdivision of land imposed, as previously indicated, an enormous handicap on the tillers of the soil, as ploughing, seeding, and harvesting could usually not start until all owners were ready, and innumerable occasions for disputes arose (pp. 116, 596).

Agriculture.—Since 1805 the total area of the cultivated land in Sweden has been more than quadrupled and approximately doubled per capita, but the difference in favour of the present period is far greater than these ratios would indicate. Agricultural methods were crude a hundred years ago,[1] the greatest limitation to a reasonable yield arising from the general practice of letting half the fields lie fallow each year. In the beginning of the century a more rational method of cultivation gradually made itself felt and in time brought greater harvests. It was even hoped that the country, through enterprise and intelligent and energetic work, would become so important, not only industrially but also agriculturally, that the loss of Finland would be offset. This hope found bold and poetic expression in the admonition which Tegnér gave his countrymen in 1811: "Within the confines of Sweden win Finland back." As far as agriculture is concerned, the prophecy has been realized to the fullest degree. Aside from the increase in cultivated land already alluded to, changed agricultural methods have resulted in a tenfold increase in the wheat and oats crops over those of a hundred years ago and fourteenfold in the case of potatoes; at the end of the eighteenth century the Swedish cadets were served potatoes on holidays as a delicacy, but on other days they had to be content with rutabagas. If, then, the total production of grain in the beginning of the nineteenth century gave less rations per capita than now, it meant that even at the best hunger and want hovered very near. As a historian[2] says, in commenting on this point, "A century ago people had to be satisfied with much less than now, and they starved much more."

[1] The whole subject of the agricultural situation in Sweden from about 1750 to the present time has been investigated in masterly fashion and the exhaustive results presented in the late Professor Gustaf Sundbärg's monumental work, "*Emigrationsutredningen,*" in seven volumes, Stockholm, 1913.

[2] Clason, *Sveriges historia,* XI, p. 16.

Drunkenness.—While thus the margin between food supplies and actual needs was at the best always perilously and uncomfortably narrow, the nation wasted annually almost one-third of its crop in the manufacture of intoxicating liquors. Subsequent to the failure of the scheme of Gustavus III to make the manufacture of intoxicants a state monopoly, the privilege had been given everybody, on the payment of a certain tax, to erect a distillery and manufacture intoxicants for home consumption, and drunkenness had again increased at a fearful rate. It came, in fact, to be looked upon as a patriotic duty to consume generous quantities of gin since the state revenues were swelled by generous imbibing, and it must be said that the majority responded nobly to this call of duty. People drank most unseemly quantities, the per capita consumption being then, on the part of men, about five times that of the present time. It was to grow to even greater proportions and the attendant evils become still greater, before patriotic men began their effective campaign against the iniquity (p. 656).

Industry.—Aside from agriculture and the mining industry no occupation had by this time assumed any decided importance. In 1800 the enormous supply of fuel from her forests, the abundance of water-power, whose utilization had reached a remarkable development in Sweden, and the superiority of the quality of her ore had given to the country its supremacy in the iron trade; the value of the iron exported was 64 per cent of the total exports of the country. The lumber and sawmill industry, which now ranks as one of the most important, in 1800 employed only about 1,500 men and the number of men engaged in factories was only 10,293. Trade and commerce in general still suffered from the many restrictions which earlier economic theories had placed upon them. As a rule, women were not permitted to engage in trade, the widows of burghers being the only exception. In 1800 Sweden's export trade consisted almost entirely of iron, pitch, lumber, copper, and fish; no dairy products were as yet included in the list. The imported articles were mostly grain, salt, dyes, textiles, sugar, tobacco, and a miscellaneous variety of other articles, but one of the imports which figures prominently in the commerce of today, coal, is not mentioned. The consumption of coffee was insignificant, having increased eightfold in the land since the beginning of the last century.

In no field is the difference between a hundred years ago and now as striking as in the means of transportation. The obligation to furnish horses for travellers had at one time been one of the principal grievances of the *bönder* and while some relief had been given them, they still, at the beginning of the nineteenth century, might, in certain instances, as when the king or members of the court went travelling, troops or army provisions were to be transported, or the regular service by the inns did not suffice to take care of all the travellers, be called upon to supply horses and vehicles. That communication moved at a snail's pace is best illustrated by the time required for travelling between certain important cities. The ordinary time consumed in a journey between Stockholm and Malmö was five to six days; a courier could, at the best, reach St. Petersburg in seven days, Paris in twenty days, and Berlin was twelve days away. Sometimes extraordinary speed was made, as in the case of Bernadotte's election. A courier was dispatched from Örebro on August 21st to the marshal at Paris, and the latter's reply was received in Sweden on September 21st. A letter to England hardly ever reached its destination in less than ten days. During war-time, communication would occasionally, of course, be entirely cut off along certain lanes, and under these circumstances mail had to be sent by strange and devious routes. Thus the Swedish consul in Philadelphia in 1811, finding it impossible to send mail home by the ordinary route, dispatched it via Archangel. Mail from Austria sometimes was sent to Trieste, then to England, and finally to its destination in Sweden. An improvement in internal communication was made in 1800 when the Trollhätte Canal, connecting Lake Vänern and the Cattegat, was completed. As communication was slow, news likewise travelled slowly, and meagre indeed were the facilities for disseminating knowledge of contemporary events. In 1808 Stockholm had eight small newspapers, two of them dailies. Their contents consisted mainly of official or trade notices.

Cultural influences.—Already in 1723 the education of children had been made obligatory, but the law had not been generally observed. Some improvement can be noted in the latter part of the eighteenth century, when several parish schools were opened. The fact that only one parish out of ten had secured such a school shows, however, how inadequate, as yet, were the educational facilities. In places where no schools had been established, the children were taught at home by parents or by private tutors, the latter being generally nondescript individuals who were considered incapable of doing anything useful except teaching and training the young. The rural communities naturally felt the isolation most, and here also drunkenness was particularly common and demoralizing in its effects. Of spiritual influences there were practically none save what the Church was able to exert, which at this time was inconsiderable. An almost universal disregard of the teachings of Christianity was working havoc with the moral stamina of the nation. The nation which, impelled by an ardent religious zeal, had fought and made tremendous sacrifices for the safeguarding of the Protestant faith, had now become cold and indifferent in religious matters and a strict and narrow orthodoxy or sterile rationalism had stifled the faith which inspires good deeds. The eighteenth-century rationalism and deism of France had taken a particularly strong hold in Sweden, due largely to the enthusiasm with which Gustavus III and writers like Kellgren had embraced the new teachings. A naïve faith that, unaided, reason could lead them aright buoyed up the new generation, whose religion became largely a collection of platitudes regarding virtue and fraternity. Having cast aside the old beliefs of a life to come, with its rewards and punishments, men became mere opportunists; to the superficially minded there seemed no sense in living a life of sacrifice and loyal performance of heavy duties, when all the good a human being might ever enjoy must be sought during his brief earthly existence. This philosophy of life had a decidedly deleterious influence upon the moral stamina of the nation, and some of its ugly forms appeared in the callous and cowardly conduct of some of the Swedish subjects in the Russian-Finnish war. It is, of course, a truism to say that one of the tragic misfortunes of Gustavus IV was his lack of wisdom and strength to cope with the extraordinary difficulties which an unkind fate piled up in his path; equally tragic to him and the nation was the fact that unprincipled and shallow men, men for whom duty was not the "categorical imperative" of the public-spirited and honest man, held most of the positions of responsibility and trust.

Enthusiasm for liberal ideas.—The rationalism of the age was, it is true, liberalizing in tendency, and to a considerable degree it served to awaken dormant minds from the sleep into which strict orthodoxy and old tradition had lulled them, but in so far as it served to undermine the morale of the Swedish people at the time when there was more than ever need of courage and inspiring ideals, its immediate results were tragic. The far-reaching evil influence of Russian gold in the time of party strife, the drunkenness which, encouraged by state officials and even by certain men of the cloth, sapped the physical and moral strength of the people, a cynical atheism and a cold-blooded opportunism—these were the factors which contributed to the weakness of the nation. The fine but often fatuous ideals of internationalism and brotherly love, which became a sort of cult among the cultivated people of the period, to some extent dulled the old and bracing sense of duty to the fatherland. On the other hand, the picture has also its bright colours. Innumerable instances might be cited of sacrifice and heroic performance of duty on the part of men of both high and low estate; the gripping stories told in Runeberg's *FänrikStåls Sägner* (p. 689) emphasize this aspect of life in the period. Nor should it be forgotten that the rationalism and scepticism of the age resulted in the elimination of much superstition and many evil practices, and the more humane philosophy of the age tended strongly to make life more endurable.

In no country, perhaps, outside of France herself, did the ideals of the French Revolution, in the abstract, at least, find more enthusiastic reception than in Sweden. In his delightful memoirs, the historian Geijer has told how interesting the people of his native Värmland found the news from Paris which told of the bloody deeds of Robespierre and Danton. The gruesome details were, he says, enjoyed at the end of the meal like a delectable dessert. A quite general and deep-rooted indignation against the noble class, still enjoying many special privileges, accounts partly for this feeling. In the dismal period which saw Sweden sink to the lowest depths of helplessness and degradation, but also marked the coming of Bernadotte and the rebirth of a sustaining hope, there were already influences at work within the nation which gave promise of a new national spirit.

The new national awakening.—This movement had a most inconspicuous and modest beginning, but its effects were momentous; incidentally it gave to Sweden her Golden Age in literature. The genesis of the movement is to be found in a small group of talented and patriotic young men in Stockholm, most of them former comrades from their university days at Uppsala, and nearly all natives of the province of Värmland, who in 1811 organized the Gothic Society (*Götiska förbundet*) for the purpose of reviving the spirit of manhood, independence, and integrity of the old Goths, *i.e.* their forbears of the Viking period. These men had long pondered over the question why Sweden, a country once both feared and respected throughout Europe, had sunk so low in power and prestige in their generation, and they found the explanation in the unhappy circumstances that the nation had thoughtlessly abandoned the virile faith and simple virtues of the fathers, and instead had become flippant, pleasure-loving, and flabby of mind. A rebirth of the old and rugged virtue, these ardent patriots believed, could best be achieved through histories and poetical masterpieces which in vivid and appealing colours painted the rugged life and bracing ideals of the saga period.

Ling.—The most ardent apostle of these new national ideals was Per Henrik Ling (1776-1839), who, stirred by German and Danish romanticism, wanted to bring back the entire mode of thought of the earlier and more glorious past. For his ponderous poems he drew material from the old sagas—the quaint, the tender, the pure, as well as the coarse and crude. It was, however, not enough for Ling that the people be lifted to a higher plane of moral virility by mental training; their physical rehabilitation must receive attention as well. The hardy patriot therefore proceeded to work out a rational system of physical training, based on an intimate knowledge of the anatomy of the human body. As a poet, Ling was a dismal failure, for his long and heavy poems made little impression upon the few who had the patience to read them, and they have interested subsequent generations only as they served as specimens of a unique literary production, but his system of gymnastics, known as the Ling or Swedish system, has been adopted, complete or with modifications, in schools and army training camps in many of the countries of the world. It is perhaps no exaggeration to say that all modern systems of physical training are more or less adaptations of the Ling system.

Geijer.—Where Ling failed to give a fitting and appealing literary expression to the spirit of the saga period, Erik Gustaf Geijer succeeded much better. This versatile poet, historian, and philosopher was a native of Värmland and born in 1783. The virile spirit of the saga age—the men of simple faith who dared everything when duty called, and who lived contentedly though their work was hard and the harvest meagre—never found a better interpreter than Geijer in his masterly poems: "The Last of the Warriors" (*Den sista kämpen*), "The Last of the Poets (*Den sista skalden*), "The Freehold *Bonde*" (*Odalbonden*), and *Manhem*. The restless spirit of youth which seeks adventure, the stoicism of the hero who at twenty, without a whimper, meets death on the sea, has nowhere been better depicted than in his "The Viking" (*Vikingen*). As a historian, Geijer penetrated deeply into the life of his people in the heroic past, and by bringing profound scholarship and critical judgment into the field his works on Swedish history became epoch-making, while their delightful style made the reading of history a pleasant pastime even to laymen.

Tegnér.—The unrivalled leader in the national and literary revival in this period was, however, Esaias Tegnér, undoubtedly the most illustrious name in Swedish literature. Like Geijer, he was a native of Värmland, born in 1782, and educated at the University of Lund, where he, in 1814, became professor of Greek. Tegnér began to write poetry so early in life that he later affirmed that he could not remember at what age he first let his poetic fancy take flight, but it was in 1808 that he first attracted the attention of the nation by his stirring "Song of the Scania Reserves" (*Sång till skånska lantvärnet*), which rang with a tone of courage and defiance quite at variance with the tremulous voices heard around the Coun-

Esaias Tegnér

cil table. In his poem *Svea,* its first part written in stately and solemn Alexandrine verse, the last section in fluid dithyrambs, Tegnér epitomized in a gripping manner the despair and the hope of the nation; its vices and faults, the imbecile aping after foreign customs, the frivolous love of pleasure, the utter lack of enterprise and courage, are here scathingly denounced, but this having been done, the poet, with keen and almost prophetic insight, proceeds to exalt the resources of the land, pictures its forests, iron-ore, waterfalls, fertile soil, assets which, through enterprise and industry, can, he asserts, make a new and prosperous Sweden.

Religious awakening.—Under the stimulating influence of the great poets, the national awakening continued to foster new ideals and give fresh power to the nation to grapple with the serious problems confronting it. A wholesome religious awakening was likewise beginning which was destined to strengthen greatly the moral fibre of the people. Foremost in combatting rationalism and in preaching a faith which is inspired and guided by the revealed Word, was Henrik Schartau, an eloquent and devout pastor at Lund, whose influence as a preacher of righteousness and author of religious works of edification extended to practically all parts of the country and still survives as a wholesome force in the Swedish church.

Bernadotte's early career.—The man who in most dramatic fashion had been elected heir to the throne and now was expected to rehabilitate the practically bankrupt country, Jean Baptiste Bernadotte, was born in 1763 in Pau in southern France, his father, a lawyer, being a member of the bourgeois. The French Revolution had, by breaking down ancient social barriers, given opportunity to the lawyer's young son to employ his superior talents in military and administrative service and he had advanced rapidly from one important post to another. He in time won such influence and popularity that at one stage of his career he was looked upon as the chief rival of Napoleon for first place in the republic. Realizing the futility of further opposition to the First Consul, he became his ally and supporter. The French campaigns brought him great distinction, and although Napoleon never was quite able to free his mind of the suspicion that Bernadotte's support was grudgingly given, he rewarded him handsomely for his brilliant military achievements, climaxing the honours by creating him Marshal of France and Prince of Ponte-Corvo. His wife, Désirée Clary, was the daughter of a rich merchant of Marseilles and one son, Oscar, had been born to them. It was, indeed, a strange twist of fate which placed these French members of the bourgeois class upon the ancient throne of Sweden, the only ones, by the way, of the Napoleonic group of newly-created kings and queens to found a royal dynasty which has survived the vicissitudes of time.

Bernadotte's popularity in Sweden.—From the day when Bernadotte, who as Swedish crown prince assumed the

Bernadotte 1808

name Charles XIV John (*Karl XIV Johan*), in the fall of 1810, set foot on Swedish soil, he became the unquestioned leader of the Swedish nation. His exuberant energy and force were enough to give him a dominant influence under any circumstances, but his immediate assumption of almost absolute authority in his new fatherland reveals how utterly leaderless and helpless the Swedes had become. His own personal qualities as well as the political situation co-operated in winning instant popularity and support for him. His brilliant military career appealed with singular force to a nation so proud of its own traditions of glorious military exploits as the Swedes, and the fond hopes of the nation that his exceptional prowess, coupled with the aid of Napoleon, would restore Finland to Sweden, and remove the stigma of Sveaborg and Fredrikshamn, served to bring all classes and sections to his support. Bernadotte had, besides, almost every personal quality requisite for winning confidence and popularity. He possessed the superabundant vitality of a man in the prime of life, and his tall and erect body, raven-black locks, aquiline nose, piercing eyes, intensity of feeling and expression, unceasing activity, and last, but not least, an exuberant and unshakable faith that Sweden could be lifted out of the quagmire into which she had sunk and started on her way to new greatness, disarmed opposition completely. The weak and vain King Charles was, by gracious acts of respect and obeisance, won completely by the new ruler, and those who had feared that plebeian manners would immediately make their entry into the old court and shock the proud and finicky devotees of ancient forms were utterly disarmed by his affable and courtly manners.

Charles John breaks with Napoleon.—When Charles John arrived in Sweden he was bound by no promise to Napoleon regarding his future course of action, and he was fully determined on a policy which gave promise of greatest gain to his new fatherland. For the time being he found it expedient, however, to yield to a demand of the emperor and declare war on England, but privately the English were informed that this action had been taken under compulsion. Not a shot was fired by either belligerent and trade between the two countries went on very much as before. Napoleon then commenced to subject Sweden to most humiliating treatment, insisting upon placing his own customs officials at Gothenburg and finally sending troops into Swedish Pomerania. These high-handed acts failed to intimidate Charles John, but, on the contrary, they seemed to hasten the maturing of plans which had begun to take shape in his mind and which contemplated nothing less than a break with Napoleon and an alliance with the latter's enemies. This meant, of course, a complete abandonment of all the plans and purposes which had motivated his election in Sweden, but Charles John's influence and personality were now absolutely dominant in Swedish affairs and he knew the change of front could be made. He considered Finland irretrievably lost, for even if, by the aid of the French emperor, it might be wrested from Russia, it was an utterly forlorn hope, he believed, that Sweden could for any length of time retain the lost province. Another way out of the situation appeared to him more promising and more natural, a way which would assure compensation for the loss of Finland and at the same time create a new and powerful Swedish state, having the advantage of natural boundaries.

Plans for winning Norway.—Norway, he believed, ought to be united to Sweden. Swedish rulers and statesmen, it will be recalled, had more than once, and especially in the decades immediately preceding this period, shown a strong desire to achieve such a union, and on the Norwegian side was, as has been seen, a party of considerable size and influence which was disposed, on this question, to meet the Swedes at least halfway. A severance of Norway from Denmark could well be justified, so it was reasoned, by the latter's obstinate adherence to her alliance with Napoleon. That the Norwegians themselves might wish to be, or ought to be, consulted in this matter was a little detail which Charles John considered it wholly unnecessary to take into account; the desires and needs of weak nations mattered little to the typical statesmen and soldiers of that period. Regard for the wishes of the nation most vitally concerned seemed especially unnecessary and futile in this particular case. The statement that the Norwegians lacked a sense of national consciousness and pride may seem unbelievable and absurd to the present generation, which knows how assertive they now are in defending and exalting things Norwegian, but it is an incontrovertible fact that they had been extremely humble and submissive under Danish rule. Naturally it was assumed that in case they became subordinate to Sweden they would continue in the same docile frame of mind. What Charles John did not know, and his ignorance in the matter can readily be excused, for even old Swedish statesmen were equally uninformed on this point, was that a new national spirit had been born in Norway and that the majority of her people had begun to feel intensely that henceforth the nation not only ought but could take care of its own affairs.

Sweden joins the alliance against Napoleon.—Committed as they naturally were to the old anti-Russian and pro-French policy, the Swedish statesmen were greatly shocked by the suggestion of a complete reversal in this policy and made wry faces. An alliance with treacherous and detested Russia? Perish the thought! But in spite of all such scruples, Charles John had his way, and in April 1812 he made a compact with Czar Alexander whereby the latter promised, in return for military aid from Sweden in the event of an attack on Russia by Napoleon, to assist Sweden in winning Norway. The threads of European diplomacy now began to gather in the hands of the Swedish regent. At the very time when Napoleon stood ready to begin his ill-fated invasion of Russia, Charles John and the Russian autocrat met at Åbo to renew and ratify the aforesaid pact.

After the disaster to the French army in Russia, the enemies of the French emperor became feverishly active, and Sweden and England now entered into an agreement whereby the latter, in return for the aid of 30,000 Swedish soldiers in the campaign against the French, promised to pay the former a subsidy of 1,000,000 pounds sterling and to cede Guadeloupe, an island in the West Indies, to her. Simultaneously, England gave her sanction to Sweden's plans with reference to Norway; later Prussia followed with a similar sanction. In the gigantic struggle with Napoleon which ensued after his return from Russia, the allies were largely guided in their plans and manœuvres by the Swedish regent, whose intimate knowledge of the emperor's tactics enabled him to suggest a scheme of operation which was most likely to encompass his defeat. Being by no means a fledgling in the game of diplomacy, and deeply suspicious that the allies would gladly accept his aid when the need was great, but afterwards, when victory had been assured, forget to pay the stipulated price, Charles John was determined that his own army of Swedes should not be sent into the carnage and sacrificed. In case his allies failed him, he could then with his army of 30,000 men give considerable emphasis to his demands. He therefore took good care that his "precious Swedes" were not exposed too seriously to dangers at the battle of Leipsic, a precaution which aroused the ire of old Blücher and other allied leaders and brought bitter condemnation of his conduct. After Napoleon's defeat at Leipsic, Charles John turned against Denmark, whose sorely tried and distressed king was soon made to see the futility of further resistance, and by the treaty of Kiel (January 1814) he ceded Norway to Sweden.

Norwegian desire for independence.—The question of Norway's status in the new alignment was, however, not definitely settled by the Kiel treaty. The Norwegians believed that their wishes in the matter should be the determining factor in any arrangement pertaining to the future status of their country. During the long period of peace which Norway enjoyed in the eighteenth century, her maritime commerce had grown steadily, and with this had come wealth and a new spirit of independence and nationality. At the same time the newly formed *Selskabet for Norges Vel* (Society for the Welfare of Norway) was busily and effectively engaged in preparing the public mind for the idea of national sovereignty and a great religious movement, inaugurated and guided by that remarkable itinerant preacher, Hans Nielson Hauge, was bringing the people into closer unity. Through Denmark's adhesion to the French alliance, Norway became practically isolated from her, and when importation of food was completely cut off, a terrible famine afflicted the land, many dying of hunger. During these grim days the idea struck root that the country was deriving no benefit from the union with Denmark; that this could, in fact, give the Norwegians nothing but trouble and grief. A far greater degree of national security and contentment would be their lot, so the Norwegians reasoned, if they were independent as a nation. Symbolic of this sentiment, and a strong factor in stimulating the national awakening still further, was the establishment of a Norwegian national university at Oslo (Christiania) in 1811.

The Norwegians now refused to admit the right of the Danish king to give the nation away to another. The pro-Swedish party, with Wedel-Jarlsberg at the head, was indeed influential, but it represented only a minority of the people. The great majority, who desired an independent national existence, found a leader in the new governor, Prince Christian Frederick of Denmark, who, contrary to the instruction of the Danish king, encouraged the Norwegians to oppose the Swedish plans of annexation. Wedel-Jarlsberg was denounced as a traitor and Christian Frederick appeared as the undaunted protector of the nation's rights. After conferring with leaders of the national party, the prince issued a call to the Norwegian people to elect delegates to a legislative assembly, which was to be held at Eidsvold. This assembly passed a resolution declaring Norway to be an independent nation, framed and adopted a constitution (May 17, 1814), and elected Christian king. The "men of Eidsvold" had been in some haste to get their work completed, for they knew that Charles John, by no means disposed to relinquish the prize which he believed meant much to his country and for which great sacrifices had been made, was advancing against their country with an army. The approach of the Swedish force naturally stirred the national sentiment of Norway to fever-heat; the Swedes were painted as past masters in the art of oppressing the honest, hard-working *bönder*. Christian Frederick talked grandiloquently of his determination to resist the invader to the last ditch, and never forsake his beloved Norwegians, but he had neither the inclination nor the ability to lead a military enterprise. Although the Norwegian defenders were individually courageous and hardy, their leadership was hesitant and weak. The short campaign which resulted from Charles John's determination to force Norwegian acquiescence to the treaty of Kiel and the Norwegians' equally strong determination to resist him, was marked by no startling events and hostilities were terminated by the Convention of Moss (August 1814). In view of the disparity in population and resources, it is probable that if the war had gone on Sweden would have emerged the victor. Her population and resources were approximately double that of her neighbour and the difficulty for the invader in manœuvring in the mountainous land would hardly have outweighed this advantage. But Charles John had no liking for further fighting, which, if continued, must necessarily bring great losses in men and money and intensify national antagonisms; neither could the hazard of foreign intervention be ignored. By the Moss agreement, Christian Frederick agreed to summon the Norwegian Storthing, the legislative body created by the new Norwegian constitution, and surrender his crown to it, while Charles John, on his part, agreed that in the event that Norwegians agreed to a union with Sweden he would approve all the provisions of the Norwegian constitution not inconsistent with such a union. Undoubtedly he and his advisers thought that a closer amalgamation could be achieved later if only some kind of union could be made at the time. The haste with which the compact was made resulted in omissions and ambiguities which, in time, were to bring endless misunderstandings and bickering. England and Prussia showed plainly that they no longer felt any enthusiasm for the plans of Charles John, and Austria was openly opposed to the dismemberment of Denmark; Russia, however, remained steadfast in support of the Swedish regent, who must have felt that his own position in Sweden was still precarious and that caution was therefore necessary. The diplomats of Europe were, furthermore, soon to assemble at Vienna to adjust the many questions of boundaries and suzerainty which were an aftermath of the Napoleonic wars, and it behooved Charles John to get the union affair settled before they met. He was, therefore, willing to modify his original plan for making Norway a vassal state under Sweden and instead agree to a union which left the former in the enjoyment of her constitution and with her independence but moderately circumscribed.

Definite and final sanction to the provisions of the Kiel treaty was given by the Congress of Vienna, but it was not until many obstacles had been surmounted. Denmark was to have some compensation, it was agreed, and so the part of Pomerania which Sweden still held was ceded to Prussia in return for a sum of 7,500,000 crowns and the latter country, also as a part of the bargain, ceded the duchy of Lauenburg to Denmark. For the first time since the days of Birger Jarl, Sweden had now no longer any possessions on the other side of the Baltic; the civilization which she had given the conquered peoples was the only thing which endured from her period of conquest and heroic exertion. As a compensation, Norway had been united to her in a personal union.

Troubles of Charles John.—With consummate skill Charles John had succeeded in piloting the ship of state past the many breakers that often had threatened to wreck it, and he had won a tremendous popularity among his new subjects. He could now look to the future with courage and equanimity, certain that while the work of reconstruction involved tremendous labours, his ability would enable him to cope successfully with the task. The decrepit Charles XIII died in 1818, and now Charles John became king in name as he some years already had been in fact. With infinite care he sought to familiarize himself with the needs of the nation, and his astounding quickness of perception enabled him speedily to grasp a situation and decide on a course of action. Always ready to respond generously to every worthy appeal, he dispensed gifts with a lavish hand. Needy individuals and institutions alike became the recipients of his generosity. He was, however, compelled always to labour under a serious handicap. Never able to master the Swedish language, he to a great extent always remained a stranger to the people whose national life he so profoundly influenced. Many times his hot Southern temper clashed with the calm and deliberate minds of his Northern subjects, and, accustomed as he was, through military service, to expect implicit obedience, he at times found the independence and unruffled deliberation of officials and politicians most exasperating. Through a period of a thousand years or more, the Swedes had grown accustomed to have a hand in the management of their own affairs and they were incapable of showing abject servility to any ruler. Opposition irritated Charles John, and as the years passed he became increasingly suspicious and crotchety. The reaction following the fall of Napoleon which manifested itself in a panicky fear of free institutions held the Swedes as well as other nations in its clutches, and Charles John, the former republican, the man who had opposed Napoleon because he felt that he had betrayed the principles of the Revolution, himself became a suspicious and peevish reactionary. As time passed and liberal sentiment gathered strength, Charles John and his advisers came to be looked upon as the very personification of reaction and a violent attack was directed against them.

Economic confusion.—The years following immediately upon the Congress of Vienna saw exhaustion and desolation everywhere, but they also saw the beginning of reconstruction. The story of these years reads like a detached chapter from a history of the decade following the great World War. Disillusionment was the end of most hopes, and distrust ruled statesmen and masses alike. In the wake of the great Napoleonic conflict followed a wild orgy of speculation, upsetting of values, deflation, and financial ruin to hundreds of thousands. Sweden by no means escaped the woes which settled over the rest of Europe, and during the two decades following immediately upon 1815 the main efforts of Charles John and his advisers were devoted to the alleviation of the economic distress. At the Peace Congress of Vienna, Charles John sold the island of Guadeloupe to France and with the money derived from this sale he liquidated the country's national debt, the Estates at the same time agreeing to an appropriation of 300,000 crowns annually to him and his descendants. Sweden was thus one of the few countries which, at the end of the Napoleonic wars, had no foreign debt; this naturally tended to lighten the financial burden considerably. With the pressing needs for money which the military campaigns had created, the issue of bank notes had increased from 9,000,000 crowns in 1808 to 24,000,000 crowns in 1812 and other emissions had amounted to 27,000,000 crowns, while the coin money which was to redeem these notes totalled only 5,000,000 crowns. To the extent that confidence in the country's ability to redeem the bank notes was shaken, their value declined, and then came the inevitable price inflation and rampant speculation. Spendthrift habits were formed. The total imports which, in 1808, had amounted to 8,100,000 crowns, had, in 1815, increased to 29,260,000, or almost 12,000,000 more than the total exports, thus leaving a most unfavourable balance of trade. A serious aspect of this situation was the fact that a great part of the imports consisted of luxuries. The total value of the coffee imported had, in the five years before 1812, more than doubled, sugar had increased fivefold, wines and brandy trebled, and other non-essentials in somewhat the same ratio. Part of this import had, it is true, been re-exported, but the major part remained for home consumption. The expenditures for luxuries were so senseless and lavish that economic hardship was certain to follow in their wake. As speculation grew, prices naturally mounted rapidly, with the result that those who had fixed incomes in the form of salaries or investment dividends soon found themselves in misery. The borrowers could easily get money, with the result that speculation in land—considered the safest form of investment—became a wild orgy, and prices on farms shot skyward. The land-owner was, however, the first to be hit by the inevitable reaction and deflation. As borrowing and speculation ran their wild course, money interest rose steadily, finally mounting to 18 per cent, and then suddenly everyone wanted to sell. Prices of land fell in a short time to one-half the former level and on land products to two-thirds of the former scale. Industry and business, on the other hand, were able to shift from domestic to foreign trade and suffered far less than agriculture.

Remedies.—As a result of the plight in which the economic and financial crisis had left them, the *bönder* began to make insistent demands for state relief. These demands resulted in the appointment of a special commission by the Riksdag of 1815 to investigate the agricultural situation and suggest remedies for relief. When this commission was ready to report, it made suggestions which sound strangely familiar to a later generation that has seen similar economic distress. The suggestions included price fixing, protective tariffs and embargoes, sliding scales, subsidies, special institutions for making loans to the agricultural class on easy terms, removal of restrictions on trade in food products and government warehouses for storing grains. The helpful idea of co-operation does not, however, seem to have occurred to the men of the post-Napoleonic period. While the industrial and business interests were lukewarm, if not actually antagonistic, to these measures, the recommendations of the commission were, in the main, adopted by the Riksdag. The king was particularly interested in seeing relief brought to the agricultural class, but his clear insight and sound sense of fair play forbade him to favour unduly any class to the exclusion of others. He turned to administrative matters with the greatest eagerness, as he believed that they were his particular forte; he once remarked to his cabinet that there could, no doubt, be found in the land three hundred men who excelled him in military knowledge and strategy, but in the understanding of economic and fiscal matters he yielded second place to none. He was soon to discover, however, that the economic situation was most baffling and did not easily yield to the treatment he proposed. The greatest difficulty was encountered with exchange and discount rates, which he endeavoured to stabilize by large purchases of metal money out of his private funds, but this proved only a mild palliative. Inasmuch as the excess of imports over exports accelerated the decline of values in Swedish securities, he sought heroically, by legislation and royal orders, to curtail and limit the one and build up the other. An expansion of exports being possible only by the development of domestic industry and commerce, it became one of the cherished ideas of Charles John that factories must be built and new highways of communication provided.

Building of canals.—In line with plans to provide the country with better means of transportation, the building of canals was undertaken, thus realizing the dream of Bishop Brask three hundred years earlier (p. 253). The innumerable lakes and rivers with which Sweden has been blessed could, it was realized, be made to give the country an economical and convenient system of water-ways at relatively small expense. Already in the year 1800, the Trollhätte Canal, uniting Lake Vänern and the North Sea, had been completed, and the bolder project of building a canal to connect Lake Vänern, Lake Vättern, and the Baltic had been warmly advocated by a military man and state official of high rank, Baltzar von Platen. Von Platen had made thorough investigations into the feasibility of the project, and to the honour of the otherwise weak and irresolute leaders of 1808 and 1809, be it said that in the dismal day when the very existence of Sweden as a sovereign state seemed in doubt they resolutely decided to begin the great project. The first appropriation for the canal amounted to 2,400,000 riksdaler, but this sum soon proved entirely inadequate and new appropriations had to be made. The financing of the canal work became, in fact, one of the vexing problems which every Riksdag had to grapple with until the work was completed in 1832. Von Platen himself became the object of bitter criticism and heartless ridicule, but he stuck resolutely to his task, willing to make any sacrifice in order that the work might be completed. His own considerable fortune and part of his wife's were sacrificed in the venture. The most ridiculous arguments were advanced against the scheme, a characteristic instance being an objection to the withdrawal of so much land from cultivation as the digging of the canal would cause. In another instance the *bönder* stubbornly refused to sell land for the right of way. The representative of the canal company, however, finally secured their signature by intimating that they would certainly get their lands back. "Had anyone ever seen water run uphill?" he asked. None had. "Well, the crack-brained von Platen certainly cannot do it," the agent hinted, "and when the futility of the scheme becomes apparent you will get your land back." They sold the desired strips, but the expected return of the land never materialized. Von Platen did not see the completion of the project (Göta Canal), since he died shortly before the canal was opened to traffic. When completed, this had cost 13,714,000 riksdaler. In the meantime, the Södertälje Canal, connecting Lake Mälar and the Baltic, had been completed and thus freight and passenger boats could pass clear across the country via Lake Vänern from Stockholm to Gothenburg and vice versa. Many of the rivers of the country, especially those of the northern section, were made navigable over long stretches by dredging and clearing away of débris; this facilitated especially the shipment of fuel to the cities farther south.

Improvement in agriculture.—Vast areas of marshy land were drained and made arable, agricultural methods were improved, the old village system, with its inconvenient division of land patches, was gradually changed so as to give larger contiguous areas to the farmers, and so great was the improvement in agriculture by reason of these factors that from 1821 it became the rule that the country produced sufficient grain for its own needs. An Academy of Agriculture, with the king himself as honorary president, was founded as early as 1811. Its charter stressed the preponderating importance which agricultural pursuits held in a country like Sweden, and the purpose of the institute was declared to be the development of the industry through special investigations, subsidies, printed reports on agricultural methods, and the bestowing of honours upon those who had made noteworthy contributions to farm improvement. Later, in 1833, an Institute of Agriculture was chartered to give training in correct methods of farming; undertake investigations in the fields of agronomy and kindred subjects, and help to disseminate useful knowledge in everything pertaining to the cultivation of the soil.

The new idealism.—While military and political victories, administrative reforms and progress in the country's economic life, in themselves were sufficient to make the reign of Charles John a notable one, these interests loom small in contrast to the creations of the scholars and writers of the period. This was indeed the Golden Age of Swedish literature. The new ideals, born of the revivified national spirit which had inspired Geijer, Tegnér, and kindred souls to exalt the country's illustrious past in unrivalled literary masterpieces in order that the minds of their own generation might be filled with patriotic and serious purpose, continued to be a quickening and guiding force in the nation. The shallow and frivolous philosophy of the Gustavian period, with its emphasis on form rather than on content, and its glorification of a vague internationalism, gave way to a deeper sense of responsibility to God and country. It was no longer good form to scoff at religion or to ridicule the traditions of an honourable past. With its frivolous court life and its fondness for the theatre and for entertainments of every kind, Stockholm had formerly been the centre of the intellectual life of the nation. Now the university centres, Uppsala and Lund, became beacon-lights for the nation. The new intellectual leaders were serious-minded men and nearly all of them sprang from the sturdy *bonde* class or from the clergy. Their homes had been hearths where idealism had been fostered and they carried with them through life the influence of their early environment of home and province. Tegnér, Ling, and Geijer continued to be the leaders of the new romantic movement. Through his epic poem, *Frithiofs Saga,* generally accorded the distinction of being the greatest masterpiece of Swedish literature, Tegnér came to tower above all other Swedish writers. His brilliant and fertile mind gave to his people a number of other masterpieces, all breathing an ardent love of country and calling the nation to lofty thinking and heroic deeds. Through his exhaustive researches in early Swedish history and by a brilliant presentation of its salient facts, Geijer, in his historical work, *Svenska folkets historia* (to 1654), gave to his countrymen a new conception of their glorious traditions. In the third decade of the century came *Tales from Swedish History* (*Berättelser ur svenska historien*), by Anders Fryxell, which more than any other influence tended to popularize the reading of history. To this period also belongs Johan Olof Wallin, "the David's harp of the North," as Tegnér called him, who died an archbishop in 1839. Wallin was one of the foremost hymnologists of all times, the principal basis of his distinction in this field being the Swedish Hymn Book of 1819. Its poetic excellence and rich spiritual contents make it unsurpassed in its class, no matter what language or country may be considered. Besides the Gothic group (p. 622), there was another notable set of literary men, the Phosphorists, whose leading representative was P. D. A. Atterbom. Excelling the Goths in the ethical character of their program, they were like them in their vehement denunciation of the materialism and cold intellectuality of the preceding age. Sentiment, imagination, religious devotion became exalted notions in their minds. Their literary productions have an elegance that is truly charming, but their meaning is often vague. Almost coincident with the time of Charles John is the creative period of C. J. L. Almquist. This strange individual started as a romanticist, but soon became a bitter and brilliant critic of the institutions of his day. He was the first realist in Swedish literature.

Berzelius.—The reign of Charles John was also made illustrious by the work of great Swedish scientists whose contributions to knowledge were epochal. Pre-eminent among them was J. J. Berzelius, who, in continuing the remarkable work of Scheele, placed chemistry on a new foundation. Born in 1779, he had early been left an orphan and his childhood was full of privations and misery. In the face of great obstacles, he was able to pursue studies in natural sciences in which he felt an enthusiastic interest and in time he became professor at the Caroline Medical School at Stockholm. Before long he stood in the front rank of the scientists of his day. With infinite patience and care he for ten years conducted experiments to determine the constant of atomic and molecular weight of thousands of simple and compound bodies, and on the basis of this he completed the system of chemical nomenclature still in use. Innovations of far-reaching importance were made by him in laboratory methods, especially in the extended use of the blow-pipe. His literary production was enormous, there being no less than two hundred and fifty treatises on chemistry listed to his credit, and twenty-seven volumes of annual reports and text-books in chemistry, which were translated into many foreign tongues and used as standard works by scholars throughout the world, attest still further his commanding greatness in the scientific field. In his annual reports Berzelius brought together, explained, and elucidated the results of investigation in the chemical field in the different countries throughout the world, thus furnishing other scholars with an invaluable repository of special knowledge. Berzelius, it may be affirmed, held the same place in chemistry as Linné had once held in botany. An idea of his standing in the world of science is gained by the statement that when he died he had been elected a member of no less than eighty-one foreign scientific societies.

A contemporary of Berzelius was Anders Retzius, born in 1796, who in the study of anatomy introduced the dissecting-room instruction. In the study of races he introduced methods of exact observation and measurements (the cranial index), which lie at the foundation of the modern science of ethnology. In the field of archæology and zoölogy, Sven Nilsson (1787-1883), the son of a poor farmer, pushed the boundaries of knowledge far beyond their former limits. His invaluable service consisted in the introduction of the comparative methods of natural science into archæology. Nilsson is justly recognized as one of the foremost founders of this great science.

Education.—Coincident with this new interest in scientific

investigation and outstanding achievement in the field, was the remarkable interest which was taken in the subject of education. The Caroline Medical Institute, founded in Stockholm in 1810, the Technical High School, begun at the capital in 1827, but in reality a successor of the Swedish Institute of Mechanics, founded in 1798, thus only four years after the earliest technical school, the Ecole Polytechnique in Paris, the Chalmers Technical Institute in Gothenburg, founded in 1829, and the Institute of Forestry in 1828, all bear eloquent testimony to a genuine interest in scientific and special training. The desirability of providing all young people with at least some book knowledge was now felt more than ever. Popular education had ancient traditions in the land. The ecclesiastical law of Charles XI ordaining that the pastor of every congregation should diligently attend to the instruction of the young and teach the children to read, clearly reveals an early interest in popular education, but in the sparsely settled districts the education of the young had been poorly attended to. Few schools had been established and even in these the teachers had, in nearly all instances, been poor derelicts who were considered useless for any other occupation than that of teaching young children. Their remuneration was exceedingly meagre and shelter and food were provided them in turn by the parents of the children. Demands for a reform in the system and an extension of it so that children of all classes might receive at least the rudiments of knowledge became more and more insistent, and it is significant that this demand came mainly from the *bonde* class. The cultural leaders of the day, Wallin, Geijer, and Tegnér, especially after he became Bishop of Växiö, in 1824, had not only advocated a common-school system, but had formulated wise and practical general principles upon which this ought to be built. In accordance with the practice which now became common in the case of all important matters pressing for a decision, a special commission was appointed to investigate the situation and present plans for elementary schools. In conformity with the recommendation of this commission, a royal proposition was laid before the Riksdag in 1840-41. Its recommendation for a new educational system was motivated by the assertion that 1,211 out of the

2,308 parishes of the country were still lacking elementary schools. The proposition suggested a teachers' training school in every diocese to be supported by state funds, stipends for scholars, at least one properly trained and qualified teacher in every parish—except in the case of smaller ones which might merge for school purposes—a school board in every parish, ability to read and knowledge in the fundamentals of Christianity as a minimum requirement in the case of all children, and a minimum below which teachers' salaries must not fall. The debate on the question was extremely earnest and even turned to such complicated questions as co-education, maximum and minimum requirements in scholarship, and the like. The final decision, which was made in 1842, went even farther than the royal proposition had contemplated, for it stipulated that a school should be established in every pastorate—a Swedish parish may be divided into many congregations or pastorates—the minimum requirement was made to include writing and arithmetic, and the minimum for teachers' wages was raised. No other state had at this time advanced as far in providing opportunity for all to secure an elementary education as Sweden.

Growing opposition to the king.—The reign of Charles John inaugurated the period of peace which Sweden has enjoyed uninterruptedly since 1814. The king strove with all sincerity to keep aloof from all foreign conflicts and gain respect for his own land. His amicable relations with Russia, especially after Nicholas I had succeeded Alexander I, was very distasteful to his subjects and helped to undermine his popularity and influence at home, even though it was understood that his attitude had helped to ward off danger of an attack by her eastern neighbour. In fact the king found himself, as the years passed, confronted by an ever-increasing opposition. Liberal sentiment was growing apace, and when in 1830 Lars Johan Hierta began the publication of the ably edited and fearlessly liberal new paper, *Aftonbladet,* the forces arrayed against the ruler found a medium through which attacks could be launched effectively. Reverberations of the July Revolution in Paris were felt and heard in Sweden, where the keen and high-minded jurist, Johan Gabriel Richert, now became the leader of a constantly growing liberal group. A change in the organization of the Riksdag, whereby the old quadruple division of orders would be abolished and a representative body after the model of French or Norwegian systems substituted was the most insistent demand of its members. The absurdity and injustice of permitting the nobility and clergy to hold membership and wield a deciding influence in legislation merely because of their membership in the privileged orders had been apparent already to the framers of the constitution of 1809, but the time was not then opportune for making radical changes. This question was to agitate the public mind as no other during the remainder of Charles John's reign, and then pass on to his son and his grandson as a troublesome heritage. A discussion of the composition of the Riksdag was extremely distasteful to the king, a fact he did not conceal, and he naturally was severely criticized by the liberal group. He was, however, not the kind of man to endure attacks complacently; he struck back vigorously in public utterances, but the liberals were not to be silenced. The king then resorted to the dangerous expedient of suppressing the newspapers which had dared to attack him, but these showed a most remarkable tendency to emerge afterward as spirited and defiant as ever. *Aftonbladet* was suppressed no less than fourteen different times during these hectic days, but always appeared forthwith with a slight change in the title, as *Aftonbladet* the Fifth, the Sixth, and so on.

Charles John was also to discover that he had stirred up a hornet's nest when he united Norway and Sweden. His fond hopes that time would obliterate all misunderstandings and antipathies, and ultimately bring the two peoples into concord were soon found to be empty dreams. The first serious controversy arose when some Norwegian groups began to celebrate the seventeenth of May, the anniversary of the adoption of the Eidsvold Constitution, as a sort of national holiday. The Swedish governor in Norway at the time, Baltzar von Platen, who in his native country had won fame as a canal builder (p. 636), resented this, and finally tried by a show of force to dissuade the Norwegian patriots, with the natural result that these became more determined than ever to give appropriate utterance to their patriotic sentiments. The Norwegian Storthing next abolished nobility in their land, an action which aroused the ire of the king and he vetoed the law, only to have it repassed by a second Storthing, and then, according to the Norwegian interpretation of the agreement at Moss, passed the third time in spite of the royal veto. Since the fundamental law was found to be ambiguous in the matter of vetoes, the king suggested changes which would give him an absolute veto in certain vitally important matters, but every proposal in that direction was rejected by the Norwegian Storthing. The untoward results of the king's haste in drawing up the agreement at Moss (p. 631) were beginning to appear. While these controversies were going on, sentiment in Norway was still further aroused to opposition by patriotic national poets like Wergeland and Welhaven. It should have been apparent even to Charles John's generation that nothing short of dissolution of the union would ever satisfy the Norwegians. In the meantime, the king's popularity in Sweden waned steadily as the liberal opposition continued to attack him unmercifully. Long since had been forgotten the king's services to a kingdom which was fast sinking into the quagmire of helplessness and oblivion, when he came and lifted it from the depths. The liberal forces became jubilant and the conservatives proportionately dejected, when Geijer, the historian and the hitherto sound and safe conservative, confessed to a change of heart and joined the ranks of his former opponents. The forces opposed to the king at last made the impertinent suggestion that he ought to abdicate in favour of his son, Oscar, who was known to be in sympathy with the liberal program. Thus the opposing forces kept up the fray with increasing bitterness until towards the very end of the memorable career of Charles John; then the storms abated both in Norway and Sweden and in the closing days of his life the heart of the old warrior was gladdened by many tokens of his people's love and appreciation. He died in March 1844. His words as he lay dying, "No one has had a career like mine," best epitomize the unique course which his eventful life had run.

Chapter XXIV

LIBERALISM AND REFORM. MATERIAL PROGRESS, 1844-1872

Death of Charles John and the end of an era.—The passing of Charles John from the scene on which for more than three decades he had played the leading rôle definitely marked the end of an eventful period in the nation's history. New leaders and different ideals and policies were pressing forward to victory and in the era now beginning they were to become dominant. The period now coming to a close had been a time of reconstruction and convalescence, during which the havoc wrought by the disastrous wars in the early part of the century was, to a great extent, repaired and peace and growing prosperity brought a degree of well-being that the nation had not before been privileged to enjoy. The king, the former champion of the liberal ideas of the French Revolution, had, indeed, as the years passed forsaken his first love and become reactionary, thus incurring the bitter dislike of the growing liberal group in the land, but so firmly entrenched had been his personal influence and prestige that the citadels of conservatism successfully withstood all attacks during his reign. Now that he was gone, the struggle for reform and re-adjustment in conformity with the program of the forward-looking liberals in Sweden and elsewhere was taken up with renewed energy and with every prospect of ultimate success. Liberal thought was, at this time throughout Europe, making new and insistent demands for reforms, the forces of liberalism were gradually sweeping aside antiquated and mischievous laws and institutions and gaining new rights and privileges for the masses, mechanical improvements following one another in rapid succession, especially in England, changed not only standards of living but political ideals, and the Swedes, guided by courageous, sensible, and resourceful liberal leaders, were determined to keep pace with the procession towards a new order of things. In fact, they soon were marching near the head of the line.

Orderly process of reform.—It was the extraordinary good fortune of Sweden that the struggle for liberal reforms in her case was practically free from the mob spirit and excesses which, in other lands, caused severe losses and intensified class bitterness. Except for one or two occasions, when intemperate speech caused street crowds to bombard the homes of two conservative leaders, no howling mobs here endangered the program of progress and no bloody encounters between the populace and the police or military forces ever occurred. The reasons for this orderly process are to be found in the sense of order and reasonable conservatism which are innate in the Swedish mind, in their time-honoured traditions of self-government through deliberation and orderly adjustment, and in the possession of the institutions of free speech and a representative system, through which the popular will could make itself effective. In the possession of rights through which still greater rights could be acquired the nation was thus far in advance of most of the other European countries. The Riksdag, in which the four orders—the nobles, clergy, burghers, and *bönder*—met periodically, continued to be the medium through which the will of the nation could—with considerable difficulty, it is true—be transmuted into decisions designed to promote the common weal and the freedom of the press, as well as the immunity guaranteed to members of the Riksdag in their debates, not only helped to clarify the issues under discussion but served as a safety-valve for the pent-up fervour of the agitators. There were other factors which favoured an orderly and peaceful solution of important social and political problems. The country had no large masses of factory workers in congested cities and no proletariat in the ordinary sense; the overwhelming majority of the Swedish people still lived in rural communities and small towns, and while living conditions here were generally marked by poverty and self-denial, these people were not seriously menaced by the hazards of unemployment or subject to the evils of financial panics. Even the industrial communities that had been developed were relatively small and a close personal relationship between employer and employee still prevailed.

Shift in the position of the social classes.—By the middle of the fourth decade of the century, a considerable shifting of power and influence had taken place among the different social classes. While still proud, and claiming precedence everywhere because of an honoured name and a traditional superiority, the noble families were fast losing ground. Their economic power broken permanently by the "*reduktion*" of Charles XI (Chapter XVII), and their privileges shattered still further in the great social struggle in the reign of Gustavus III (Chapter XXI), they had never succeeded in regaining their former prestige. Relative to their number they still wielded considerable power, however, for an ancient and honoured name still counted for much, and superior intelligence and culture and a strong class consciousness gave many advantages to the group.

The clergy still remained intellectual leaders, but this position was more and more being challenged by able laymen, especially university and college (*gymnasia*) professors, journalists, and novel writers. The burghers had made the greatest advance. The business structure was gradually being transformed as industrial progress created wealth, and with it political influence had in constantly increasing measure been concentrated in the hands of manufacturers and business men. These naturally favoured the abolition of the many restraints which hampered trade and commerce. They, therefore, as a rule, became strong supporters of the liberal-reform program and their wealth placed them in a position where they could wield almost a preponderating influence. Believing that the numerical strength of the workers would be a material help to them, the burghers at first sought alliance with them, but co-operation between the groups could not continue long because of the radicalism which soon began to influence many of the leaders of the labouring class. The *bönder* had to a considerable degree recovered from the depression following the almost continuous wars, and they were gradually advancing towards greater wealth and enhanced political influence.

Hopes of reform under Oscar I.—The liberal group had good reason for welcoming with joyful anticipation a change in the incumbency of the royal throne. The new king, Oscar I, the only son of Bernadotte, was known to be fully in sympathy with its aspirations and program. Born in Paris in 1799, he was eleven years old when the strange twist of fate which brought his father to Sweden made the young prince heir-apparent in a land which up to this time must have had but a shadowy existence in his mind. He received a thorough Swedish training under most competent teachers, among whom were such brilliant lights as Atterbom, Berzelius, and Wallin. After an interval of several decades, the palace at Stockholm again became the hearth around which centred a delightful family group, thoroughly Swedish in speech and sentiment, and radiating joy and hopefulness. Oscar had in 1823 married Josephine, the amiable and gifted daughter of Eugène Beauharnais, Prince of Leuchtenberg, and to the royal couple were born several children, who, as they grew up, gave evidence not only of superior talents, but of noble, humanitarian sentiments and interests.

As crown prince, Oscar had clearly shown that he was in sympathy with liberal ideas and his conservative father had more than once been moved to express grave fears that the future held much evil in store both for him and the nation; the situation was similar to that of the time of Gustavus Vasa and Erik, or Gustavus III and Gustavus Adolphus IV, but fortunately the paternal fears were, in this case, needless. Even before his accession to the throne, Oscar had given tangible evidence of his humanitarian sentiments by publishing a pamphlet on "The Punishment of Crime and Penal Institutions" which was permeated by the spirit of humaneness and liberal thought. The cause of popular education had in him a staunch champion. He was unquestionably animated by the noblest resolves to be guided consistently in his acts by the principle enunciated in the motto he chose, "Justice and Truth."

Disappointment in Oscar.—The excesses which elsewhere marked the fight for reforms and the fiery and threatening demeanour of racial leaders among his people caused him, however, in time to waver and turn back from the course he had set out to travel, and the hopes of a great era of reform under his benign leadership were but partly fulfilled. Protracted periods of ill-health quite early in his reign cast over him a deep gloom and contributed to his failure at fulfilling expectations. Then, too, his chief interest was directed to foreign diplomacy, a field in which he believed himself especially competent to play an important rôle, a belief at least partly justified by achievement, and this detracted more and more from his attention to questions of internal improvement and development. When, therefore, after a comparatively brief reign of fifteen years, he died in 1859, the disappointment and disillusionment which embittered his last years were shared by those who had hoped for a great forward movement in his reign. It would, however, be an injustice to Oscar I to assert that he disappointed the friends of reform entirely; a number of liberal measures must be credited to his reign.

Character and ideals of Charles XV.—Charles XV, the eldest son of Oscar, who succeeded his father, had the latter's generous impulses. His artistic and poetic gifts were of high order. Personally ambitious and actuated by noble ideals, he was ardently anxious to lead his beloved nation to greater heights of power and prosperity. He enjoyed a tremendous personal popularity, especially in the beginning of his reign. The strict rules of court etiquette were ignored by him in a way that filled the strict devotees of the ancient formalism with consternation and poignant grief; he found his chief delight in mingling in a free and easy manner with the common folk. Innumerable are the stories, some based on actual facts, many, no doubt, apocryphal, of his visits to homes of humble citizens and of his delight in seeing the surprise and pleasure which attended the revelation of his identity and of his readiness to share any hardship with his people, especially with his soldiers. He was quick in repartee, but his personality was not harmonious; his mind was shallow rather than deep, his laxity in morals set an extremely bad example, and an unfortunate unsteadiness of purpose negatived many of his good intentions. Like Gustavus III, with whom he had many points of resemblance, he lacked the patience and the consistency requisite for the rôle of a good administrator. Like his father he was particularly interested in diplomacy and sought to play an important part in the settlement of some of the baffling international questions of the time. His impulsive and generous nature, his lack of insight, and his inability to foresee the ultimate consequences of his acts, made him poorly equipped, however, for the diplomat's rôle, and Sweden was to reap a goodly measure of ill-will and humiliation from his ventures into the diplomatic field. For the liberal reform measures which, in his reign, gained a formidable accession of supporters, and were somewhat advanced towards ultimate victory, he had very little liking at heart, but he craved popularity too much and was too good-natured to display any spirit of opposition.

The liberal leaders; Richert.—The great mentor and guide of the Swedish liberals was Johan Gabriel Richert, who, although he stoutly declined to accept the high offices which were proffered him, preferring to remain the incumbent of a judgeship in a rather obscure rural community in his native Västergötland, exerted a profound influence on the course of events in this entire period. The utilitarian principles of Jeremy Bentham and political doctrines of Immanuel Kant had early influenced him. Enthusiastically and with utter disregard for the tender feelings of the privileged classes, he had as a young lawyer championed the cause of the poor and the oppressed and was early listed as a dangerous Jacobin. As district judge he administered the law impartially and refused to truckle to the arrogant and imperious Adlersparre, leader of the revolution which cost Gustavus Adolphus IV his crown, and later governor of Richert's district, who believed that the young judge would, for the sake of his own welfare, be obsequious. In anger, the governor contrived to get Richert removed from office. So brilliant and convincing was his defence before the authorities at Stockholm, however, that he received a complete vindication, and in addition was honoured by appointment to the commission which previously had been created for revising the country's legal system. Absolutely incorruptible and fearless, clear-sighted and sober-minded, genuinely in sympathy with all efforts for the alleviation of suffering and eradication of injustice, Richert came to exert an influence more far-reaching than any member of Riksdag or ministry.

De Geer.—The man who on the arena of practical statesmanship was to lead the forces of reform to their most notable victories was Louis de Geer.[1] Despite the fact that he was a member of one of the most distinguished of Sweden's noble families, de Geer had early joined the liberals under the pro-

Louis de Geer. Marble bust by Per Hasselberg in the National Museum, Stockholm

found impression that the ancient aristocratic privileges were an anomaly in the new age. Increasing knowledge and wealth among the common people made it inevitable, he believed, that the rights which they asked must be granted them; not only was this a matter of expediency, but it was eternally right. Although not intellectually a brilliant man, de Geer had the

[1] De Geer's Memoirs, published in 1892, under the title *Minnen,* contain an authentic and interesting account of the most important phases of the great reform movements.

persistency and the resourcefulness essential to successful leadership. He looked upon defeats as mere temporary postponements, and stubborn opposition or mischievous intrigues never discouraged or embittered him. Rancour was never permitted to determine the tone of his public utterances and amidst the turmoil and bitterness of parliamentary debates he kept his mind serene. As chancellor of justice during a long and eventful period, he had in his advocacy of reforms the added advantage of official position.

Hierta.—Lars Johan Hierta, the fearless critic of Charles John and his policies, continued in the reign of his son to fight against special privilege and other forms of social injustice. Through his influential newspaper, *Aftonbladet,* he kept up the campaign of educating the nation to see the injustice and folly of many of the old laws and institutions, and to plead for reforms. As a member of the Riksdag over a long period, he took a leading part in the work of legislation. Perhaps more than any one else in the liberal group, he was anathematized by the conservatives and reactionaries, who looked upon him as the chief instigator of the social struggle under way; taunts, ridicule, and charges of timidity and vacillation came from the other camp where many could not, or would not, see, as Hierta saw, that permanent good can be achieved through reform only when this is based on justice and that discussion, delays, and compromises must precede great decisions. Finally Hierta grew tired of the fray and, in 1852, sold *Aftonbladet.* Until his death in 1872, he continued, however, as a publisher of liberal literature to wield a potent influence, not less than one thousand books and pamphlets having come from his presses.

Blanche.—An enthusiastic and popular champion of the liberal cause was the prolific writer, August Blanche (p. 684). The general tone of his stories served in a measure to discredit the pretensions of the aristocracy and to give self-consciousness to the common people. Blanche was always ready to plead the cause of oppressed peoples abroad. No popular demonstration voicing protests against injustice in Italy or Poland seemed complete without a speech by him.

Gripenstedt.—Another man of liberal ideas was J. A. Gripenstedt, who in 1848, although then only thirty-five years old, had been given a portfolio in the cabinet. In 1856 he was placed in charge of the department of finance. A man of absolute probity and moving eloquence, Gripenstedt exerted a profound influence, and he undoubtedly did more than anyone else to put the new principles of economic liberalism into practice.

The conservatives; Von Hartmansdorff.—Brains and character were by no means all on the side of the liberals in the great struggle of class interests. Foremost among the conservatives in the earlier part of the period in point of ability and influence stood August von Hartmansdorff. A parliamentarian of the first order, possessed of a phenomenal knowledge of detail regarding the administration, eloquent and fearlessly outspoken in his opposition to all novelties, Von Hartmansdorff received on his devoted head a full measure of the imprecations of liberals and radicals. He opposed reforms of the judiciary and the penal code, liberal trade regulations, abolition of ecclesiastical restrictions, extension of rights to the Jews, the decimal system, railroads, and simplifications of the system of direct taxes. On the other hand, he favoured reforms of administrative procedure, and was an ardent and consistent advocate of elementary schools for all the people and fearlessly joined in the fight that just then was launched against drunkenness and debauchery (p. 658).

Plan of the liberals.—In the endeavour to secure the enactment of their favourite measures, the liberals first of all sought to gain a majority in the two lower orders in the Riksdag. This goal having been reached, they would, by constant agitation, either win or coerce one of the other orders to their side. The right of any one of the orders to censure individual members of the cabinet, or all of them collectively, was found to be a most effective means for breaking down opposition. Few men could long endure standing against exposure to the persistent and often utterly unreasonable heckling and criticism of an aggressive order, and even if some more obdurate member was resolved to stick, the king generally found it expedient, in order to calm the storm, to contrive on some pretext or other to get rid of him. In the earlier part of the period, both the ministry, being dominated by the conservatives and the conservative group in the Riksdag, sought t maintain power unimpaired, and to guide royalty along a conservative course.

The Law Commission and reforms.—The accession of Oscar I was the signal for an advance by the liberals along the entire battle-front. The ministry was soon reorganized in a truly liberal spirit and already in 1845 a special commission was appointed with Richert as chairman and guiding spirit to formulate, in conformity with humanitarian ideas, a new Civil and Criminal Code and suggest such a new procedure in judicial trials that court processes would become cheaper and speedier. The erudition, wisdom, and humane spirit which were reflected in the final proposal of the commission are eloquent proofs of Richert's greatness of soul and mind. Inertia, ignorance, and selfishness raised serious obstacles in the way to the adoption of its main provisions, and many years were to elapse before the most important reforms suggested by Richert's commission could be adopted, but a good beginning towards judicial reforms was made. Many unnecessary courts were abolished, penalties were mitigated, flogging and many other brutalities, which before had been a part of prison life, were prohibited. The right of masters to inflict corporal punishment upon servants was abolished. In the face of strenuous opposition, especially by members of the noble order, a law was passed in 1845 which changed the ancient law of Birger Jarl, according to which daughters inherited only half the amount of parental estates that fell to sons; the new provision, which had the strong support of the king, made sons and daughters share equally in the distribution of their heritage. The spirited discussion started by Fredrika Bremer's novel *Hertha* (p. 683), was perhaps the main influence in securing legislation giving a legal status to woman at the age of twenty-five (1859). Prior to this she had always retained the status of a ward; married, under her husband; if unmarried, under father, brother, or other legal guardian. A new system of poor relief was adopted which scrapped many of the cruel and degrading features of the old system. Guilds were abolished and many ancient restrictions on the right of the individual to choose his trade or occupation were removed in 1846. Women still remained restricted to five occupations into which it had been deemed advisable to permit them to enter: they could sell fancy goods, pedlar's wares, or tobacco, conduct brokerage offices and hucksters' stands. By supplementary legislation in 1864, both women and men were given practically unlimited freedom in their choice of occupation. In 1859 women were admitted to the teaching profession and three years later they became eligible for service in the postal and telegraph departments.

Religious freedom extended; education improved.—The liberal spirit of the new age naturally was opposed to religious intolerance and coercion in matters of faith and worship; the obnoxious conventicle law (p. 529) went by the board in 1859, and the imposition of penalties for deserting the evangelical faith or exile for joining heretical faiths was discontinued. Under certain minor restrictions, members of other faiths than the Lutheran might henceforth organize their own congregations and enjoy complete religious freedom. The national education system was given the fundamental features which it still has and which have made Swedish schools and educational methods the equal of any in the world. One of the most ardent and effective supporters of the doctrine that all the people, rich and poor, high and low, should have the opportunity to attend school and receive instruction in the elementary branches, at least, was Oscar I. As chairman of the special commission created for the purpose of formulating plans for a common school system, he had taken a large and honourable part in the campaign which resulted in the adoption of the all-important educational law of 1842 (p. 642). As king he naturally evinced the same interest and gave hearty support to proposals for extending the elementary school system. One man especially deserves honourable mention for his unselfish and successful labours in establishing new schools and improving teaching methods; this was Torsten Rudenschöld. Although he boasted the proud title of earl and was in line for promotion and a brilliant career in the army, Rudenschöld nobly chose instead to devote his time and energies to the task of founding schools for children of the poor. He first opened a private school in which excellent teaching methods and a humane spirit were the distinct novelties and which therefore received so much favourable attention that parish after parish clamoured for similar schools. Before long the government gave Rudenschöld an official commission to travel through the country to inspect existing schools and assist in the establishment of new ones. Professor F. F. Carlson, a distinguished historian of the University of Uppsala, who twice held the portfolio of ecclesiastical affairs, the department under whose jurisdiction the educational system then operated, as it still does, also rendered conspicuous service in building up the Swedish schools, first of all by giving hearty support to Rudenschöld. Carlson worked out the comprehensive educational plan which, adopted in 1859, included primary grades, high schools, and gymnasia; his principles in the main still determine the organization and gradations of the Swedish educational system below the universities. His curriculum for the gymnasia followed two general lines, the classical and the modern or practical (*reallinien*), both preparing for admission to the university. Teaching methods were modernized and improved and new textbooks provided; some of the latter were exceptionally meritorious, and one, a text on natural sciences by N. J. Berlin, not only came into general use in all Swedish elementary and secondary schools, but in translation was used quite generally in the schools of several foreign countries. The national universities received new statutes in 1852, one important provision of which led to the abolition of the ancient academic jurisdiction over students in civil cases. The university jails now became an obsolete institution. Two professorships in Swedish and one in modern European literature were established. Technical high schools were opened in several towns. A school for the higher education of girls had been founded, through private initiative, in Stockholm as early as 1831, and in Gothenburg the following year, and in 1861 the state made provision for this phase of educational work by establishing the Higher Training College for women at the capital. Three years later a training school for prospective women teachers opened its doors.

The liquor problem.—The problem which now stirred up the greatest interest was the drink evil. This had assumed such alarming proportions that the physical and moral stamina of the entire nation was being destroyed. Drunkenness and its attendant evils had increased enormously as gin (*brännvin*), a distillation of potatoes or grain, and having a great alcoholic content, became a sort of national beverage. The Swedes first learned to know the vicious brew on their military campaigns in the sixteenth century and it was not long before it was distilled quite generally in their homeland. Already in his day, Laurentius Petri had found it necessary to warn his countryment against the drink evil. Again in the eighteenth century, Linné had scored the drink habit, saying that the moderate as well as the immoderate use of intoxicants ruined the drinkers' health and sent them headlong to their graves. In the eighteenth century the propensities of the Swedes for strong drink had become a by-word in all Europe, and Frederick the Great, in speaking of this national failing, remarked cynically that the people of Sweden had for hundreds of years sought their own destruction but strangely enough had not succeeded in their ghastly enterprise. The well-meant efforts of Gustavus III to curb the evil by state regulation had not, as has been seen (p. 580), improved a bad condition, but had, on the contrary, made it worse. The protests against Gustavus's system of state monopoly had resulted ultimately in restoring to the individual the right to have his private still. After the end of the wars in the beginning of the nineteenth century, the flood of gin which the innumerable stills poured over the land assumed the proportions of a devastating deluge. As a writer [2] grimly remarks, "the newly awakened spirit of liberty after the revolution of 1809 had won its greatest victory in securing to the individual the right to distill and consume *brännvin*." Excuses and arguments for liberal indulgence were elaborate and plentiful. Thus the *bönder* stoutly maintained that they must have the right to make gin in order that the products of their farms might be converted into marketable products, commanding a good price; the miserable conditions of the roads did, in fact, work a hardship on the agricultural class because of the difficulty in getting farm products to the markets. The majority convinced themselves that the chill and gloom of the long winter required a bracing and cheering beverage such as *brännvin;* likewise the transporting joys of the enchanting days and nights of the summer season could not find

[2] Wieselgren, S., *Peter Wieselgren,* Stockholm, 1907.

fitting expression except through bibulous exploits. Hospitality was an ancient virtue on which the Swedes prided themselves greatly, and not to offer the guest drinks came to be looked upon as a mean and shameful disregard of its obligations. Drinks should be taken at least morning, noon, and night to create a good appetite and promote digestion, and what was good for the system at these times, so it was reasoned, must likewise be salutary at intermediate hours. Both men and women servants customarily received part of their pay in regular allowances of *brännvin.* It was a common sight to see men and women carrying gin bottles with them to church and drinking openly and freely before and after divine service. Almost every gathering ended in disgusting brawls. Even small children were given the fiery stuff in the belief that it was good for their health. The deleterious effects were inescapable; one-half the children born died before the age of three. Certain years one-half of the army recruits were rejected because of physical impairment, in most cases attributable to drink. According to estimates, there were in 1830 no less than 170,000 stills operating in the country and the annual per capita consumption of *brännvin* was from thirty to forty quarts (approximately four and a half quarts per capita in 1927). In the wake of the drinking orgy naturally followed an appalling increase of pauperism, sickness, insanity, and crime.

Beginning of the fight against the drink evil.—Patriotic men, whose senses had not been dulled by drink, took alarm at the situation and began to raise their voices in warning against the doom that was impending unless the nation returned to sobriety. At first these were but voices crying in the wilderness. The abstemious Charles John, who more than once was appalled and disgusted by the drinking propensities of his new subjects, lost no opportunity in giving encouragement to the early temperance advocates. Stills were, however, in operation on the crown domains themselves, and the defenders of drink were in the habit of citing this fact for the purpose of squelching those who dared to attack the drink evil. Inasmuch as the king permitted these stills on his domain, said the liquor devotees, it was *lèse-majesté* to attack the system, as this, by implication, meant an attack on the king's own person; hence, an attack on stills was treason. A certain pompous individual, who took it upon himself to inform the king how this treason was committed, did not long remain in the royal presence, for the hot blood of the Frenchman boiled over when he heard how the existence of the royal stills was made to justify an evil. That same day orders were issued that such stills must be immediately closed. On this point the crown prince, Oscar, shared the feelings of his father and this he showed by proscribing gin altogether from his table. When later he became king, he gave steadfast encouragement and support to the advocates of temperance. Several men of learning and eloquence now entered the lists against the arch-enemy. In his statistical statement, published in 1832, Karl af Forsell made the startling claim that *brännvin* had brought more misery upon the Swedish nation than all the wars in which it had ever been engaged. About this same time a number of prominent men met at Forsell's home and formed a temperance society. The claim may, on good grounds, be made that this was the first society of its kind in any land. In that same year the government sent circular letters to all governors and consistories, urging them to work in behalf of temperance. Simultaneously, the Swedish Medical Society adopted resolutions condemning the drink habit and warning against its deleterious effects upon health. A total abstinence society was organized in 1833, with von Hartsmandorff as chairman, and about the same time the noted Berzelius published a series of articles in which the economic waste of strong drinks was succinctly stated.

Wieselgren.—In order that the temperance movement might become a mighty crusade and achieve a thorough national regeneration, there was, however, need of a man who was stirred by a burning indignation against the drink evil and was possessed of the fiery eloquence which could stir men's souls to their very depths, and this leader appeared in the person of Peter Wieselgren. No martial hero ever achieved greater victories for his people or displayed more physical and moral courage than this son of a *bonde* from the province of Småland. Born in 1800, he had in his childhood home been trained to walk the path of righteousness, and already as a student at Uppsala he had fearlessly defied iniquitous conventional customs such as hazing and student carousals. On becoming pastor of a rural parish in Skåne in 1833, he was appalled by the moral and economic havoc wrought by drink, which was in evidence everywhere, and he forthwith came to grips with the enemy. On his first Sunday in the parish, sixteen men and thirty women from his large congregation appeared at divine service in an intoxicated condition and the cantor lay in a drunken stupor in the sacristy; at his next meeting two drunken women began a fist fight below the pulpit in the middle of the sermon. Drunken men and women lay in rags in their homes, sodden and without hope. Children grew up like heathen. Wieselgren visited his parishioners in their homes to warn and encourage, exercise discipline, and to give a helping hand. From the pulpit and at special meetings, he denounced drink, and in words whose eloquence and touching appeal could not fail to stir even the most degraded, he painted the misery which it had heaped upon the community. The ghastly fallacy that stills were an economic advantage to the *bönder*, even essential to the marketing of their products, was completely riddled. His fearlessness aroused the bitter ire of many who felt hurt by his castigations or foresaw personal economic loss from the success of his campaign and several plots and attempts against his life were made, but they all failed, largely because of Wieselgren's alertness and unflinching courage. Soon

Peter Wieselgren

he came to wield an almost magical influence over friends and foes alike, and it was noticeable that the number of the former grew apace. In time his parish became a model of sobriety and prosperity. The number of stills in the parish fell in a few years from 200 to 31. In 1836 a total abstinence society was organized in one of his congregations with 80 members, but a year later the membership had swelled to 1,500, and a little later still, to 3,000.

The movement becomes nation-wide.—The movement started by Wieselgren in his parish soon spread to other localities. The transformation wrought among his parishioners held out a bright hope to others. Urgent appeals now came to him from all parts of the land asking for his assistance in the fight against drink and Wieselgren now became the great national crusader. In company with an American temperance advocate, Robert Baird, a native of Pennsylvania and a graduate of the theological department of Princeton University, who spent the greater part of his life in religious and philanthropic work in Europe, Wieselgren travelled through the central provinces and spoke to multitudes. By 1878, no less than 420 temperance organizations had been formed with a combined membership of more than 100,000. Meanwhile the printing-press was busy disseminating knowledge concerning the evils of strong drink. A distinguished physician, Magnus Huss, published a treatise on chronic alcoholism, which revealed the destructive influence of intoxicants on health, and a brochure by O. J. Hagelstam which was spread broadcast over the land, gave startling and convincing proofs of the economic losses caused by them. Hagelstam presented a rational system of control and taxation which, it was shown, would in fourteen years yield an income sufficient to pay for the construction of over two thousand miles of railroad. Demands for legislation to curb the drink evil now became insistent; to the Riksdag session of 1853 no less than 800 petitions were presented, urging that something be done which would strike at the root of the evil.

Temperance legislation.—The majority of the *bonde* estate, however, still clung to the fallacy that stills were necessary for the advantageous marketing of their goods, but in spite of the opposition of the order, this session passed laws providing for taxation and other restrictions on private stills which practically eliminated them. In the first year after this legislation took effect the number of such stills was decreased by more than 90 per cent. Economic and industrial factors at the same time came as allies to the advocates of temperance. The construction of railroads and the opening up of new markets for the products of the farms gave prices an upward trend, and the plea that without stills the *bönder* could not dispose of their grain and potatoes advantageously no longer carried weight.

Riksdag reform.—Opposition to the antiquated organization of the Riksdag had appeared in the latter part of the reign of Charles John, but he vigorously resented any suggestion that a change in the system of national representation was necessary, and none had come in his day. His successor on the throne was known to be in sympathy with proposals that the Riksdag be reorganized in such manner that it might become the medium through which the will of the nation could adequately express itself. No less than fifty proposals for reform were presented to the Riksdag prior to the final settlement of the question. A commission appointed in 1846 to study the matter and formulate legislation for reform in due time suggested a national assembly of two chambers, to which members should be chosen through a rather complicated system of elections. King Oscar and his ministers were indifferent to the matter; evidently many features of the liberal reform program no longer appeared wise to the ruler. He had, in fact, had a change of heart, caused mainly by the fear that royal power would suffer by a triumph of the Liberals. The extreme bitterness of the attacks which members of the liberal group next directed against the government, the king himself by no means escaping their shafts, naturally did not make him any better disposed towards their program. Interest in the question of a reorganization of the Riksdag therefore languished, but other important reform measures carried. After all, the Riksdag, as then organized, seemed to function so well that historians have seriously questioned whether some of the wise and beneficent legislation which can be cited to the credit of the period could have been passed under the reorganized system. The intelligent will to change and improve was, after all, more important than the machinery available for governing the land. The February revolution in France in 1848 stirred the liberals and radicals to new activity, and the question of the Riksdag reorganization again came to the fore. While the king himself, somewhat impressed for a time by the clamour for a change, was ready to urge a reform, his interest was again dampened by the March revolutions on the Continent and incipient riots in Stockholm. Egged on by the scandal press, the populace made a threatening demonstration before von Hartmansdorff's home in which some windows were broken, and while the mob spirit never led to any serious excesses, alarm naturally seized the more conservative. In spite of this, the king submitted a plan for reform which was so democratic in spirit that Richert himself approved it. The liberals as a group and the leading conservatives were, however, opposed to it, but for diametrically opposite reasons. Under these circumstances, it was naturally rejected. The exultation of the conservatives at this outcome was soon, however, turned to dismay when von Hartmansdorff, the hitherto undaunted and rock-ribbed opponent of the reform, published a book in which he expressed his conviction that new industrial and social conditions and the spirit of a new age made inevitable the doom of aristocratic privilege. Discussion went on intermittently, but by 1854 there was a lull in the storm which was to last well into the next decade. The general lines which must be followed in order to achieve a reform that would satisfy the nation had, however, been quite clearly marked.

De Geer assumes leadership.—Towards the end of the 1859-1860 session of the Riksdag, the two lower orders solemnly petitioned the king that a new proposition be prepared. This had the desired effect; de Geer, who was now the most influential member of the ministry, persuaded the king to accede to the request and himself took the leading part in preparing the new measure. It was presented to the 1862-1863 meeting of the Riksdag, but was held over, according to the provisions of the constitution, to the following session. This session began in 1865. An extraordinarily lively discussion in the press and in a multitude of brochures filled the interval.

Public opinion also gained utterance through an imposing array of petitions and public demonstrations.

The deciding debate, especially in the order of the nobility, presented a memorable and brilliant spectacle. De Geer was naturally the chief speaker in behalf of the measure. Changes in a liberal spirit were not only demanded, he claimed, by every consideration of justice, but the new spirit made them inevitable and wise, and experienced men ought therefore to guide the march of progress instead of blindly and stubbornly trying to stop it. His clear insight and honest reasoning, personal integrity, and absolute fairness toward friend and foe alike made de Geer an ideal leader in this crisis. Although at heart opposed to the reform measure, the king, who was now Charles XV, gave the measure his support. His good nature and love of the plaudits of the crowds made him recoil from opposition to a measure which he felt the majority of the nation ardently desired, but the status of his personal finances perhaps played a still greater part in determining his attitude. His financial troubles were chronic and the liberals had supported generous appropriations for his relief, thus placing him under obligation to support their pet reform measure. To de Geer, Charles was bound by a sense of deep gratitude for loyal service in saving royalty from a most embarrassing situation which had arisen in connection with the Norwegian governorship controversy (p. 705).

The final decision.—The support of the two lower orders for de Geer's program was a foregone conclusion. The clergy cautiously deferred action until the nobles had reached a decision and it was upon them therefore that the final decision rested. Their debate went on for four days and was replete with oratory and dramatic incidents. In his *Minnen,* de Geer expresses the belief that two-thirds of the nobles had come to the meeting with the firm resolve to vote against the measure. The opposition crumbled, however, before the masterful arguments of de Geer, Gripenstedt, and several of their eloquent compatriots. Tumults and violence were certain to follow if the measure failed, and as a majority of the nobles had now become convinced that a favourable decision could not be stayed for long anyway, they on December 7 voted, 361 against 294, to give their assent. This settled the matter also for the clergy, who, having now been granted the right of meeting every fifth year in a special conclave (*kyrkomöte*) to legislate in ecclesiastical affairs, were less disposed than before to oppose a change in the Riksdag organization.

The news that the nobles and the clergy had agreed to de Geer's reorganization scheme spread rapidly to all parts of the

Final session of the last Riksdag including the four orders. Meeting held on Gustavus Adolphus Square, Stockholm

country, and joy seemed boundless, especially in Stockholm. The millennium was at hand, the excited people believed, for now the popular will could always prevail, which, of course, was tantamount, according to the dominant thought of the day, to wise and just legislation for the welfare of the nation. True, there were men who predicted that the nation was headed for new troubles and that disappointment and disillusionment would follow close upon the exalted expectations of the moment, but these men were scowled at and ridiculed as disgruntled losers and hopeless pessimists. Charles XV is reported to have remarked, anent the decision: "The scheme will work somehow during my lifetime, but it means hell for Oscar's boys." (Meaning the sons of his brother, who was heir-apparent to the throne.)

The final session of the old Riksdag, held on June 22, 1866, was an impressive occasion. The noble and ecclesiastical orders, which had played so large a part in the affairs of the nation, especially during its most stirring times, now bade a last farewell to the national assembly. They had no longer a part in legislation as special and privileged orders. They had indeed on many occasions stood in the way of beneficial measures and had been too prone to look to the interests of their own group, but, on the other hand, their services had been many and glorious, and as they now with solemn ceremonies relinquished their ancient prerogatives, the populace, noisily exulting in the victory just won, was for the moment hushed.

The reorganized Riksdag.—De Geer's plan for the national legislature, still to be known as the Riksdag, provided for two chambers, instead of the former four orders, whose members were to be elected without any limitations as to birth and social status. Members of the first or upper chamber were to serve without pay. They were to be elected for terms of nine years by the provincial assemblies (*landsting*) or the councils of the principal cities, and must have attained to the age of thirty-five. Eligibility to the first chamber was contingent upon the possession of considerable property. Members of the second chamber were to be elected directly by legal voters, in the respective election districts, for three years. The franchise was to be granted every adult man having a minimum of 800 riksdaler (about $215) annual income or taxable property to the value of at least 1000 riksdaler. Members of this chamber received pay. The crown was given the power to prorogue Riksdags and call for new elections, and meetings must be held annually. Cabinet members were accorded the right to participate in the deliberations of the Riksdags, and, except in the case of money bills, taxation, and a few similar matters, where a majority vote of the two chambers in joint session decided, no laws would be valid unless they had been passed by a majority in both chambers.

Local self-government reorganized.—A reorganization of local self-government became a prime desideratum, as the old guilds and other antiquated trade units were abolished, and as population, industrial activity, and wealth increased in most communities. The changes brought new problems to the respective communities, and the local units could best grapple with them. It is an impressive fact that since time immemorial local self-government had always prevailed in the land, and that the freemen had themselves decided in matters pertaining to the villages, or counties. In course of time the central government had, however, extended its control over them until their autonomy had been greatly circumscribed. The new spirit of independence, as well as practical considerations, made a reversal of this policy desirable. A series of laws, enacted in 1862, definitely established the local districts and defined their rights and powers. Communal assemblies in the rural districts and councils or boards in the cities became the mediums through which legislation for local needs was effected. Proper checks were, however, placed upon them by the central government. Special governing bodies were created for ecclesiastical and educational affairs. These were the parish meetings, the vestry boards, and the school boards. There was a property qualification for all voters and gradations of wealth gave a corresponding number of votes. The districts (*län*), twenty-four in number, exclusive of Stockholm, into which the country is divided for administrative purposes, were given their own legislative assemblies (*landsting*), among whose duties was the election of members to the first chamber of the Riksdag.

Transportation difficulties.—The economic question, which in the fifth decade of the century held firmly the attention of the nation and provoked the most heated discussion in the Riksdag, as well as in the press, arose from proposals for railroad construction. Swedish industrial leaders had long believed that a great network of canals was the special need of the country, whose almost innumerable lakes and rivers made projects for a system of water transportation seem very feasible. The Göta and other canals had, however, not proved as valuable as their promoters had expected. They had been constructed too narrow and shallow, and the long winters made the working season too short. Transportation difficulties continued to cause great hardships and seriously retarded the industrial development of the country. On the comparatively short stretch which in our day is served by the Mora-Vänern railway, no less than fifteen lakes and eleven wagon roads had to be traversed between the terminal points in those days. Loading and unloading was a never-ending process.

Von Rosen's projects; opposition.—While Sweden had been lagging behind, other countries, especially England, had built railroads at a rapid pace. It now began gradually to dawn on the Swedish leaders that their country must do likewise if it was to attain to any great degree of material prosperity. Adolf von Rosen, an engineer who had gained wide experience, first as an expert employed in the reorganization of the naval defences of Greece, later as co-worker with his great countryman, John Ericsson, then residing in England and engaged principally in developing the screw propeller, became the first pioneer of railroad building in Sweden. Returning to his native Sweden after his sojourn in England, he was impelled by an ardent hope that he might be able to contribute effectively to the rapid material upbuilding of the homeland. To this end he enthusiastically launched projects for railroad construction to be financed by English capital. Von Rosen wrote and spoke eloquently in behalf of his pet scheme, but condescending pity or open derision met him almost everywhere. The wiseacres knew that it was the height of folly to try to build railroads in Sweden. The long winters and cold weather would make their operation impossible and in the vast uninhabited regions the rails would inevitably be removed and carried away by those who here saw an opportunity to get good steel gratis. Lakes, peat bogs, and morasses, furthermore, placed insuperable obstacles in the way, they believed. Innkeepers and *bönder,* who had the right to furnish horses to travellers and thus received extra income, took alarm and denounced von Rosen's project as a sinister scheme which would impoverish them. True, there were objections which rested on a more idealistic basis than these cited. Why, it was asked, must Swedes necessarily borrow newfangled notions and contrivances from others merely that they might have the opportunity to travel at breakneck speed from one place to another; with their predilection for pleasure and with their "wanderlust," the Swedes would in the enjoyment of new means of transportation become chronic travellers, flitting hither and thither as new opportunities for entertainment and excitement lured them on. One irreconcilable conservative dogmatically declared that railroads merely would serve to decrease human happiness and widen the cleft between rich and poor; his native country would, he hoped, be very slow in adopting this new contrivance for doing evil.

The state decides to build railway lines.—At the Riksdag session of 1847, von Rosen asked for a state subsidy for a stretch of road between Örebro and Hult. The proposition failed to carry among the *bönder,* whereas the three other orders were willing to support the project. Von Rosen failed, however, to get the required capital, the continued opposition of the *bönder* raised new obstacles, and he was never able to realize any part of his plans. He had merely shown the way by which others could advance to success. The Riksdag had in the meantime voted that the state itself should subsidize a line between Örebro and Nora, and this stretch was completed in 1856. In the debate on this and von Rosen's projects, Gripenstedt, who was now Minister of Finance, had emphatically maintained that all main lines ought to be built and maintained by the government, leaving the branch lines to private enterprise, and his opinion prevailed. In keeping with this reasoning, the Riksdag created a commission to study the situation and formulate recommendations for basic railway lines in the central and southern sections. In the face of opposition from the *bonde* estate, it was also voted that money for the project should be raised by the sale of state obligations.

Nils Ericson.—The dominant influence of the new commission was wielded by Nils Ericson, whose reputation for integrity and deep insight was such that almost every detail of his recommendations was in time accepted and he was given almost unlimited power in organizing and pushing forward construction work. A son of Värmland and brother of the famous inventor, John Ericsson,[3] Ericson had won distinction as an engineer under von Platen in the construction of the Göta Canal. Later he became chief engineer of this project and head of the road and canal construction department of the western district. Under his supervision and according to plans submitted by him, Trollhätte Canal was rebuilt to provide for boats of a deeper draught. In this enterprise the nation had had a most novel experience, and one which quite naturally attracted attention to the young genius who directed the work; the task was performed exceptionally well, yet it was completed prior to the date originally promised and the final cost fell considerably below the original estimate. The indefatigable and ever-watchful engineer took every precaution against dishonesty and inefficiency in the execution of the project. "Cost will be forgotten," he used to say, "but work that does not meet specifications or expectations will never be forgotten."

It was a fundamental idea in Ericson's mind that railroads should create trade and industry, and their builders need not therefore primarily take already prosperous communities into account. Hence the anomaly that the four oldest main lines in Sweden, aside from the termini, touched only eight of the country's ninety-four cities. Ericson proposed five main rail lines, and an appropriation of 103,000,000 riksdaler, to be raised mainly by floating obligations abroad, was voted for the project. Local interests, as well as honest differences of opinion on the part of those who had no selfish interest in the venture, precipitated many a bitter fight regarding the route to be followed by certain lines, but Ericson's recommendations prevailed in almost every detail. The stretch between Gothenburg and Stockholm was completed in 1862. Other main lines, like the one running south from Stockholm towards Malmö and another northwards from the capital towards Dalarna and Jämtland, were completed somewhat later. According to population, Sweden today has the largest railway mileage among the countries of Europe, and the character of the roadbeds and the high-grade equipment have evoked the unstinted praise of foreign engineers. The rich natural re-

[3] When he was raised to the rank of nobility in 1854, Nils dropped one "s" from the family name.

sources of the land have become available for industry, new markets have been won both at home and abroad, and places which before were practically uninhabited have been converted into prosperous communities. For this achievement the Swedish nation accords the fullest measure of praise to Nils Ericson.[4]

Telegraph and postal system; embargoes.—Other enterprises looking towards material betterment were undertaken. The first electric telegraph began operation between Stockholm and Uppsala in 1853. Two years later the postal department inaugurated uniform rates, irrespective of distances, and future expansion was made possible by a proviso that in the future the department could use its surplus for extension and improvement of the service. The decimal system of money was introduced (100 öre to a crown), but a simultaneous proposal to use the metric system for all measurements was rejected. (It was finally adopted in 1878, with the stipulation that it must be used to the exclusion of all other systems after 1889.) In the beginning of the century, embargo against importation rested on no less than three hundred articles of commerce and export embargoes upon fifty, the most important in the former category being pig-iron and iron-ore, silk cloth and certain kinds of woollen goods.

Abolition of trade restraints and growth of industry and commerce.—The tillers of the soil, as well as a majority of the factory owners, now began to feel that these restraints on trade were harmful to them and in accordance with these sentiments the Riksdag repealed most of these embargoes and lowered the tariff on many articles, especially raw materials and necessities. The taxing system was greatly simplified and its burdens materially lightened by the elimination from the tax lists of a multitude of articles which before had been included. With the founding of the Private Bank of Stockholm (*Stockholms Enskilda Bank*), on the initiative of A. C. Wallenberg, the first famous financier in a family which has become internationally known in banking and trade circles, a beginning was made towards giving the country a modern banking sys-

[3] Adelsköld, C., *Nils Ericson* in *Kungliga Vetenskapsakademiens handlingar,* Vol. II, 1878-1885, and Melin, Gustaf, *Statens järnvägar, 1856-1906,* Stockholm; both give a good account of Ericson and his work.

tem. The new bank emphasized the advantages which people of means derived from depositing their money with it and sought to encourage and support industry by loans. Foreign commerce was given a new impetus by trade agreements with China, Hawaiian Islands, and Persia; the abolition of all tolls in the Sound tended in the same direction. A hint of the growth which foreign commerce experienced under the new trade policy is given by the increase of custom duties; in spite of the lowering of many schedules and the inclusion of many articles on the free list, the annual sum collected rose from 3,600,000 riksdaler, in the beginning of the fourth decade, to 11,500,000 in the latter part of the fifth. In fact the foreign trade of the country increased in this decade as much as during the preceding one hundred years. The output of the manufacturing industry grew apace; in the aforesaid period the value of factory products rose 304 per cent, cotton yarn production rose from 220,000 pounds to 14,700,000 pounds, and cotton cloth from 587,000 pounds to 16,000,000 pounds annually. The value of manufactured broadcloth and woollen goods increased 300 per cent, sugar production 323 per cent, and the value of all the products of machine works approximately 930 per cent.

Steel and matches.—To this period belongs the perfection of the Bessemer process of steel production by the Swedish engineer, G. F. Göransson, who had co-operated with Bessemer in England and had bought a part interest in the Swedish rights to the new method. When he began production in his native land, Göransson found, however, that the new process was defective and not commercially profitable. With infinite patience, he therefore carried on new experiments and by 1858 he had perfected the process to the point where its commercial value was indisputable; steel production throughout the world was revolutionized by Göransson. Bessemer and his English associates, who were on the point of giving up, now availed themselves of his discoveries and English steel production began its enormous expansion. The Sandviken Iron Works, established in 1862, and reorganized in 1868, with Göransson as manager and directing genius, has ever since its beginning held a commanding position in quality steel production.

The Swedish enterprise which sells its products to a greater number of individuals in all parts of the world than any other concern and has made the names Sweden and Jönköping known in the remotest corners of the earth—namely, the match industry—also had its beginning in this period. In 1844, G. E. Patsch, a professor at the Caroline Medical Institute at Stockholm, secured a patent for safety matches. His process was later improved by Johan Lundström, known as "the father of the Swedish match industry." His ingenious contribution consisted of a preparation which made the match ignite only when struck against a specially prepared surface of the container. The first match factory was begun in Jönköping in 1845.

Improvement in agriculture.—While agriculture could not show the same progress as the manufacturing industry, certain innovations were made which, in time, were to transform Swedish farming methods so completely that the average yield per acre is now, in spite of the handicaps which nature imposes, approximately the same in Sweden as in the more favoured countries of the Continent. The reorganization of the village system of landholding was steadily carried forward, and this in itself marked a revolution in agricultural conditions. Simultaneously, many large estates were divided into smaller farms and sold to individual owners. Large and fertile tracts were drained and made tillable; the lowering of the water level of Lake Hjälmaren, begun in 1878, added approximately 40,000 acres of new fields, and in addition saved the surrounding communities from almost annually recurring inundations. Ditching and tiling were resorted to in all the agricultural sections and the resultant decrease of sogginess in the ground meant a large increase in the annual yield. Rotation of crops became the general rule and this made obsolete the old and wasteful system of letting a field lie fallow every second or third year. Provincial agricultural societies had been organized as early as the last decade of the eighteenth century and several more came into existence in the early part of the nineteenth; their number increased steadily in this period. They had a most salutary influence in arousing interest in farming and in disseminating information regarding new and improved methods. A national agricultural society met for the first time in Stockholm in 1846. The practice of offering substantial money prizes for agricultural achievement began a few years later. Institutions for higher agricultural education were founded at Ultuna, near Uppsala, in 1848 and at Alnarp, in the vicinity of Lund, in 1862. The making of loans on farm property was facilitated by new mortgage societies and in order to systematize their business and eliminate dangerous competition the General Mortgage Board was organized in 1861. A law of 1848 enabled stock companies to raise capital for industrial ventures more easily than before.

Forests.—As there was much ruthless cutting of timber, the problem of forest protection grew increasingly important. The problem was by no means a new one. Laws and ordinances limiting the right to cut trees had been enacted as early as the reign of Gustavus Vasa, and a law of 1647, supplemented by one of 1664, had instituted regulation by limiting the right of owners to cut and sell timber, prohibiting the practice of burning forest areas or individual trees, except in places where soil conditions made the cultivation of grain possible, and prescribing in certain cases that two young trees must be planted where one had been felled. A law of 1734 prescribed that *bönder* might cut timber on their lands for the market, "but so sparingly that the forest is not wasted and the estate ruined." In spite of all legislation, the timber situation was more serious than ever in the beginning of the nineteenth century, since the forests were wasted recklessly in supplying the mining industry with props and other timber materials, as well as in manufacturing charcoal; there was also an enormous waste of fuel in homes and industries. Failing utterly to foresee the importance and value of lumber, the government for a mere trifle sold one million acres of timber which became a field for private exploitation. As England lowered her import duties on lumber and steam sawmills increased enormously the profits derived from timber, forest denudation became more reckless and rampant than ever before. Lumber export alone more than doubled in the fifth decade of the century. Corporations sprang up everywhere in the central and northern regions which for ridiculously small sums purchased forest areas from *bönder* who at first had no conception of the value of their growing trees; their anger became thoroughly aroused when they learned that the purchaser by building mills and stripping the country bare of forests was reaping millions in profits. Forestry legislation in 1858 greatly curtailed the right of cutting on crown, county, and parish lands, and instituted an administration of forestry with wide powers to regulate the cutting of trees. This legislation has in a later period been supplemented by a number of forestry laws which have placed Sweden in the forefront with respect to a rational lumber conservation policy. So rational and effective is the control and so assiduously is replanting attended to that the enormous number of trees now felled for lumber and paper pulp annually is replaced by the natural growth of young timber. An interesting and pleasant feature of the reforestation work has been the large part which the school children have been called upon to take in planting young trees.

Emigration.—The era of peace enjoyed by Sweden after the close of the Napoleonic wars, an era characterized by the remarkable effort of government officials and private individuals to develop, through the utilization of new inventions and by abrogating old and harmful laws and customs, the natural resources of the country, naturally saw a marked increase of wealth and well-being. A series of laws, all in accord with the enlightened and humane spirit of the age, had, as has been seen, removed many evils against which the common people had justly complained. It may at first glance therefore seem like an anomaly that in this period of increasing prosperity and social justice an emigration movement was to set in on so large a scale that before the end of the century approximately 1,200,000 Swedes left for foreign lands, principally for the United States. Many factors played a part in starting and giving impetus to the great exodus. The innate love of travel and adventure which characterizes the Northern peoples lured them on and helped to obscure the dangers and difficulties that lay beyond the borders of the homeland. While living conditions, as measured by the availability of material goods, were considerably better at the middle of the century than in its beginning, new standards of living had been set, largely through the dissemination of knowledge by the common schools, and men were no longer satisfied with conditions which they before had borne patiently. In the decades following the Napoleonic wars the growth of population through an unprecedented birth-rate had increased the economic pressure. While in the decade 1801-1810 the birth-rate was only 2.04 per 1000 inhabitants, it rose to 11.02 in the period 1821-1830 and it stood at 8.32 in 1831-1840; in the following two decades the figures were respectively 10.39 and 10.36. As the children of the third and fourth decade grew to maturity and began to seek employment they found the labour marts uncomfortably crowded. A succession of bad crops in different parts of the country, especially in Småland, increased the misery and strengthened the resolve of many to emigrate. In the meantime the attention of the toilers was being directed towards the United States and its golden opportunities. There was not a decade in the first half of the century that did not see one or more Swedes return from America and publish accounts of its wealth and democracy.[5] The mighty tide of emigration from Ireland and Germany about the middle of the century naturally served to stir Swedes to a new interest in migration. Discontent was rampant in the land and this discontent had for the most part a social basis. Despite the independence which the common people, and especially the *bönder*, had enjoyed since time immemorial, class distinctions were an unpleasant reality, the upper class, so-called, assuming a very patronizing or supercilious attitude towards the common folk. Dissatisfaction with the formalism of the state church and worldliness of many of its ministers was quite common.[6] As the length of military service was extended and general conscription, according to the Prussian order, loomed in the offing, many sought escape from the irksome and unwelcome duty by emigration. The opportunity which the Homestead Act offered to the emigrant to get free land, the rivalry of states and railroads for settlers, the competition of steamship com-

[5] For an interesting account of such travellers and their publications see article by Roy W. Swanson, in *Swedish Historical Society Bulletin*, Vol. I, 1928.

[6] This and other causes of the Swedish emigration are discussed in George M. Stephenson's "Background of the Beginnings of Swedish Immigration," in *American Historical Review*, Vol. 31, 1926; and in A. A. Stomberg's *Den Svenska folkstammen i Amerika*, Olaus Petri Foundation lectures, University of Uppsala, Stockholm, 1928.

panies which led them to send numerous agents to Sweden to extol the greatness and wealth of America and help the emigrants on their way—all these factors were especially effective in giving impetus to the Swedish emigration movement. The peak of the movement was, however, not reached until the eighties, in which decade alone approximately 400,000 Swedes emigrated.

Early settlements.—The first Swedish settlement in America in the nineteenth century was founded by Gustaf Unonius at Pine Lake, Wisconsin, in 1841. Unonius had received a thorough education at Uppsala University, and, feeling discouraged about his future in Sweden, he resolved to emigrate to America. With his young bride, who like himself was unaccustomed to hard toil, he set out on the long and adventurous journey. In the belief that utterly primitive conditions prevailed in the new land, he took with him ploughs, harrows, and other bulky farm implements, not to mention an entire arsenal of guns, besides kitchen utensils and furniture. His settlement never prospered, mainly because most of the settlers who joined Unonius were of the gentry class, many of them having been failures at home, who believed that in the new Eldorado a comfortable existence could be had without effort. Unonius himself after some years became a preacher in the Episcopal Church and his colony disintegrated. Unonius was, however, a busy letter-writer, his epistles being published in various Swedish newspapers and serving to arouse in his native country a lively interest in America.

Practically the only instance where religion was a large factor in the emigration movement was the founding of the Bishop Hill colony near Galesburg, Illinois, in 1846. The name is a translation of *Biskops kulle,* the founder's native place in Sweden. Its founder was Erik Jansson, a *bonde* of northern Sweden, who entertained some strange religious notions, one of his vagaries being the doctrine that man through faith may at once attain a sin-free existence. Claiming that he was a prophet commissioned by God, he began to preach his new doctrines and soon gathered a considerable following. The disciples were strictly enjoined by Jansson from attending the divine services of the state church. Jansson was therefore arrested and later brought to trial, which naturally, in the eyes of his followers, placed the halo of martyrdom over his head. Escape from prison having been effected through the connivance of some of the faithful and resolute members of his sect, Jansson became a fugitive from justice, at times escaping detection by donning women's apparel. America as a land of freedom, where they could build an ideal community of the faithful, now began to beckon to Jansson and his followers, and after two of the group had preceded them to select a suitable site, the self-styled prophet and numerous members of his sect set sail for the land of freedom. Before long the Bishop Hill colony numbered more than 1,200 souls, among whom Jansson maintained a strictly communistic organization. The principal town in the settlement, Galva, received its name through a corruption of Gäfle, the name of an important city on the Gulf of Bothnia. Dissensions soon arose, Jansson met a violent death at the hands of an apostate member who resented the prophet's efforts to induce his wife to remain in the colony, and the organization disintegrated. The property fell into the hands of individual purchasers, after which the colony attained to considerable prosperity.

The first Swedish colony in the United States in the nineteenth century still existing, which was founded and developed to considerable proportions and wealth through the operation of the ordinary impelling forces of the emigration movement, was New Sweden, Iowa. It owes its beginning to Peter Cassel, a miller from Småland, who in 1845 led a party of his neighbours to the New World and settled in a region not far from the present city of Burlington. Like Unonius, Cassel was a prolific letter-writer and his epistles detailing his experiences in America and dilating in glowing terms on the golden opportunities which here were offered the poor man, must be reckoned an important factor in swelling the emigration tide from Sweden.[7] Realizing that emigration reduced enormously the labour co-efficient of the country and would result in higher wages, the upper classes in Sweden, as a rule, assumed a hostile attitude towards the emigrants. These were generally charged

[7] A number of "America Letters" and other early emigrant accounts have been published in the original and with English translations in the *Swedish Historical Society Year Book*, VII-XI.

with disloyalty and crass materialism; contemptuously it was alleged that their sole desire in life was to get a plentiful supply of bread and butter. The pictures that were drawn showing the dangers and hardships which the emigrant must encounter in America were terrifying enough, but neither charges of disloyalty to country nor spectres of evils to be met in the new land had any effect in cooling the ardour of those who had been infected by the emigration fever.

Chapter XXV

INTELLECTUAL PROGRESS. HOPES AND DISILLUSIONMENTS IN DIPLOMACY, 1844-1872

New literary tendencies.—Noteworthy literary and scientific contributions aided greatly in making illustrious the reigns of Oscar I and Charles XV. The men who had shed glory on the reign of Charles John passed away in the very beginning of the new era, Tegnér dying in 1846 and Geijer in 1847. Ling had died in 1839; Atterbom survived until 1855. Other writers, whose versatility and skill in depicting life were to win enthusiastic recognition far outside the realms of their own native land, were, however, already coming on the scene. Their writings reflected in a remarkable degree the spirit of the new age, since literature now became a vehicle by which liberal ideas were advanced. Having by this time developed a keen interest in its own life and in the many complicated problems which were inseparable from the new venture in the realms of democracy, it was natural that the nation should now develop the class of literature which especially adapts itself to discussion of social forces and progress—the Swedish novel was born.

Fredrika Bremer.—Fredrika Bremer (1801-1865), the first one to create novels in Swedish which technically conformed to the standards already established in England and France, was born in Finland, her father being a prosperous landowner whose home was one of culture. Foreseeing the rupture of the union of Finland and Sweden, and Russian dominion in the land, he sold his Finnish estates and the family settled in a new home not far from Stockholm. Fredrika's father was a stern and rather uncommunicative individual, and brooding over the fate of Finland cast a heavy gloom over his life. The mother was emotional, but firmly bound to conventionalities. One of her vagaries affected her young daughters most uncomfortably: she believed that girls should eat very little so as to be spiritually alert and thus escape dulness; they should be kept in ignorance of the world as long and as completely as possible, their education thus having as its prime aim the development of amiable society women, who in several languages could converse entertainingly about nothing in particular. The days of training must be governed by an absolutely rigid regimen: rise precisely at a given time, eat, study, do homage to the parents, likewise at definite strokes of the clock. Fredrika's entire life after she escaped from parental restraint was a frank negation of practically every detail of the mother's curriculum. She became the inveterate traveller who was determined to see as much of the world as possible, and no woman of her generation, it is safe to say, was on terms of personal friendship with more leaders of thought throughout the world than she. Her ideas of woman's place in society and of her proper education diverged about as far from her mother's as was possible. Largely for her own amusement and in order to give expression to the thoughts and emotions which stirred within her, Miss Bremer in 1828 wrote *Sketches of Everyday Life* (*Teckningar ur vardagslivet*) which won immediate popularity, for here was something new for Sweden, true and living pictures of ordinary Swedish folk, painted in pleasing colours and with real insight into their aspirations and their struggles, their foibles and their virtues. In one of her early works, *The President's Daughters* (*Presidentens döttrar*), she strongly pleads for woman's right to acquire a higher education and make her own career according as talents and inclinations seem to fit her. If she so chooses, she may remain unmarried without any stigma of unwomanliness or spinsterhood being attached to her and especially should she be free, if she prefers, to enter the professions of teaching and nursing. A delightful sketch of life in a Swedish country home, *The Neighbors* (*Grannarna*), is, no doubt, technically the best that Miss Bremer wrote. A dauntless and enthusiastic champion of woman's rights, Fredrika Bremer won many admirers and friends in America and England (many of her books were translated into English by Mary Howitt, and appeared in America almost simultaneously with the Swedish editions), for whom she became in many respects a leader. An irresistible desire to visit the young republic in the West and with her own eyes see the ideal conditions in a land which had accorded to woman the place in society which she was urging for the women of her homeland, led in 1849 to a trip to America which lasted two years. On this she reached points as far West

Fredrika Bremer, Portrait in "Brother Jonathan," 1851

and South as St. Paul, New Orleans, and Havana. In Boston she was warmly welcomed by the intellectual leaders, being a guest at the James Russell Lowell home for a fortnight, and when in company with Senator Charles Sumner she visited the state-house, the legislature adjourned to stage an impromptu reception in her honour. In Washington she was the guest of the President and with Webster and Clay she discussed leading questions of the day. Her discerning eyes saw in the young Minnesota territory, the chief executive of which,

Governor Ramsey, was her host during a two weeks' sojourn in St. Paul, an attractive place for her countrymen and she expressed the opinion that here a new Scandinavia might be built. Her observations gave her a very poor opinion of Indian males, whom she found selfish and lazy, but for the negroes of the South she conceived a great liking. While disillusionment and disappointment came when she saw that American women had not, in her judgment, risen to their opportunities, she was nevertheless generous in her praise of the American home and of the kindness and chivalry of American men. Her letters from America to her invalid sister were published after her return to Sweden, under the title, *Homes in the New World* (*Hemmen i Nya Världen*). The most interesting and valuable portions of the work have been published under the title, *America of the Fifties* by the American Scandinavian Foundation. The letters give a delightful and illuminating portrayal of America and most of her leading men and women at the middle of the century. In writing these letters, Miss Bremer had no thought of ever publishing them, and the frankness of expression which therefore characterizes them add to their charm and interest. Soon after her return to her native land Miss Bremer wrote *Hertha*, which bears the strong impress of her American experiences. It is a gripping and tragic account of paternal cruelty and injustice, which brings anguish and humiliation to a noble-minded and long-suffering daughter and leaves her penniless and alone, unable to marry the man she loves simply because of her father's legal right to prevent it. An eloquent plea is here made for legislation whereby unmarried women be free from guardianship at the age of twenty-five and receive the right to manage their own property and make their own decisions relative to the course of their lives. At that time these reasonable demands seemed dangerously revolutionary and a violent storm broke over the devoted head of the author. Victory was soon, however, won, largely because of the discussion which *Hertha* had provoked. While the storm was still raging, Miss Bremer left Sweden for another long journey, this time to southern Europe and the Orient, which lasted five years and forms the foundation of a new work, *Homes in the Old World* (*Hemmen i Gamla Världen*). Through her unfailing good-humour, deep human sympathies, dialectical skill, and enthusiastic and earnest championship of a cause in whose justice she believed with the faith of a crusader, Miss Bremer became one of the world's great leaders for the cause of her sex, revered as a leader not only in her native land but also in England and the United States.

Emelie Flygare Carlén.—The outstanding contemporary of Miss Bremer in the field of letters was Emelie Flygare Carlén (1804-1892), who also gained international recognition. Their training had been utterly dissimilar and in style and tendencies they were widely apart. Emelie Flygare Carlén was the daughter of a skipper on the west coast of Sweden and her early years were spent in regular tomboy fashion, free from every rigid schedule of study. On frequent trips along the picturesque and romantic western coast of Sweden, the scene of many a stirring drama of sea life, Emelie Flygare Carlén had become intimately acquainted with the life of fishermen and sailors and her memory was stored with a wealth of ancient legend and story. She becomes the story-teller par excellence. Her technique is greatly superior to Miss Bremer's, but unlike the latter she pleads no special cause. No less than fifty novels are credited to her. The best one, *The Rose on Thistle Island* (*Rosen på Tistelön*), gives a tragic story of a family on the west coast which is utterly destroyed by the crime of the father, a smuggler, who kills a customs officer. In keenness of psychological insight, vivid description of the impressive aspects of nature, clearness in detailing events as they occur, the book is undoubtedly worthy of being rated one of the greatest works of fiction of the period. The fame which this Swedish author attained is attested by the fact that the larger number of her novels were translated into most of the cultured languages of Europe, including English, soon after they appeared.

Blanche.—The democratic spirit of the age colours the writings of August Blanche (1811-1868), the handsome, witty, sentimental, and loquacious champion of the liberal cause (p. 652). An illegitimate son of an army chaplain and a poor maid-servant, Blanche in early life experienced all the bitterness and humiliation of poverty and ignoble birth, and this, no doubt, accounts for his abiding dislike of social inequalities and sympathy for all unfortunates. The love of his mother shed the only light and warmth that came into his early life. In spite of hardships, she provided him with an opportunity to secure a thorough education, and a pleasing detail of his biography relates how in after life, when fame, wealth, and friends had been won, his first thought was always of the devoted mother. A fair daughter of the nobility was willing to become his wife, but she made it a condition that his mother should not be invited to share their home. The answer of Blanche, so the story goes, left no doubt for a moment in the mind of the proud lady that in a choice between her and the mother Blanche proposed to remain loyal to the latter. The wedding did not materialize and Blanche never married. Although Blanche disliked the aristocrats, he was too kind by nature to bear malice against them or carry on any bitter warfare against the group. Aristocratic pretensions are, however, ridiculed in his stories and the feelings and aspirations of the lowly depicted with the skill of a master. He became the inimitable delineator of life in Stockholm in his day. Most of his short stories were collected in a number of volumes entitled *Sketches from Real Life* (*Teckningar ur verkligheten*); they give sympathetic accounts of life among the poor who were compelled to toil hard and forego every pleasure and comfort. Greatest interest attaches to Blanche's numerous comedies, in which field he still stands without a peer among his countrymen. Keen insight into human nature and rollicking good-humour have given him a lasting charm.

Mrs. Schwartz.—The new democracy found an ardent champion in Maria Sophia Schwartz (1819-1894), a most prolific novel writer, who enjoyed a remarkable vogue in her day both at home and abroad. Technically her works are very inferior to those of Carlén and Blanche and they reveal neither versatility nor deep understanding. She exalted the dignity of honest toil unceasingly, protested against the absurdity and iniquity of placing the workers on a socially inferior rung of the social ladder, and lost no opportunity to ridicule the preposterous and out-of-date claims of the gentry to special honours and prerogatives. To the masses, just bracing themselves for a mighty assault against the citadels of pride and privilege, Mrs. Schwartz's books were most pleasing literature. America is her fairyland, in which all good democratic virtues sprout and grow. Those of her characters who talk sense on the subjects of justice and democracy and make their deeds conform with their words have in almost every case visited America and become inspired by the fine ideals of that wonderful country. Most representative of her works are *The Man of Noble Birth and the Woman of the People* (*Mannen av börd och kvinnan av folket*), *Two Mothers* (*Tvenne familje mödrar*), and *Work Ennobles* (*Arbetet adlar mannen*). Mrs. Schwartz's works, which were widely read, most of them running through several editions, undoubtedly served to awaken among many the desire to emigrate to America and must therefore be rated as one of the influences which gave volume to the migration movement.[1]

Rydberg.—Near the middle of the century falls the early literary activity of the man who, after the death of Tegnér and before the advent of Strindberg and Selma Lagerlöf, held the most exalted place in Swedish literature; namely, Victor Rydberg (1828-1895). His career was a remarkable one, by reason both of the dominant position he won for himself in the realm of learning and creative activity in spite of early adversities, and of the wholesome influence he came to wield on the thoughts and ideals of his countrymen. Deprived of his mother through death when he was five, he was, as a boy, cared for by strangers and extreme poverty prevented him from acquiring a university education. His remarkable mental capacity and untiring industry brought him, however, through independent studies in time to the very front rank among scholars and creative writers. He gave to his countrymen some of the best novels and poetic masterpieces of which their language can boast, and his contributions to the literature on mythology, philology, history of art, and theology have an abiding value. As editorial writer in *Göteborgs Handels och*

[1] It has been surmised that Miss Bremer's *Homes in the New World* was a potent factor in awakening genuine interest in America and in directing the Swedes towards the Northwest, but her influence in starting the great movement was perhaps negligible: her works were not widely read in circles where interest in America was likely to result in a journey thither for the sake of founding new homes.

Sjöfarts Tidning, an influential newspaper of Gothenburg, during a period of twenty-one years, he wielded a unique influence on public opinion and always in the interest of justice and truth. His first novel, *The Journeying Students* (*De vandrande djäknarne*), gives delightful glimpses of the simple life of contented people in a rural community; poltroonery and the iniquitous right of masters to flog their servants are severely scored. The work is permeated by a warm spirit of idealism. His next story, entitled *The Freebooter on the Baltic* (*Fribytaren på Östersjön*), a skilful combination of adventurous details after the fashion of Balzac and Victor Hugo, and denunciations of hysteria and intolerance, is founded on the witchcraft delusion in the reign of Charles XI (p. 433). The black soul of the consummate hypocrite who, under the guise of religion, works dastardly evil in order to gratify his lust for power, is painted with unsparing colours in the *The Last Athenian* (*Den siste atenaren*), a voluminous and stirring account of the struggle between the Church and expiring Hellenism in the time of Julianus the Apostate. While the criticism justly can be directed against this work that it gives a false perspective, since, as has been pointed out,[2] it clothes the leading representative of the Church, the evil Bishop Petros, with all the unlovely attributes of paganism, and on the other hand invests the pagan philosopher, Chrysantemus, with many of the finest virtues of the true followers of Christ, it constitutes, withal, a ringing protest against formalism and hypocrisy in religion. Rydberg's style is characterized by remarkable clearness and vigour. His poems are marked by exalted idealism and stylistic excellence. Swedish idealism never rose to greater heights or found a nobler expression than in Rydberg's *Cantata* for the four hundredth anniversary of the University of Uppsala in 1877, when the author received the doctor's degree, *honoris causa.* His translations of Poe's *The Raven* and *The Bells* are done with admirable skill.

Poets of a high order near the middle of the century were Bernard Elis Malmström (1816-1865), Johan Nybom (1815-1889), K. V. A. Strandberg (1818-1877), and Gunnar Wennerberg (1817-1901). Common to them were stylistic purity

[2] Rudin, W., *Svenska Akademiens handlingar,* series 1886, XI.

and exalted patriotic sentiments. Wennerberg, the foremost of the group, gave to his countrymen a group of students' songs, *Gluntarne,* whose popularity remains undimmed. His *Songs of David* are among the finest in the realm of sacred compo-

Jenny Lind. Daguerreotype in the Academy of Art, Stockholm

sitions, and his patriotic songs, like *Harken to us, Svea* (*Hör oss Svea*) and *Stand Firm, Knightly Guards of Light* (*Stå stark du ljusets riddarvakt*) generally form a part of Swedish patriotic programs. Prince Gustaf, second son of Oscar I, who died in 1852 at the age of twenty-seven, composed songs of admirable purity and beauty, extolling the joys of student life and the glories of the Swedish land. Otto Lindblad aroused interest in, and developed students' song at, the University of Lund. J. A. Josephson, an unusually prolific composer of rare charm, gave new impetus to student song at Uppsala, which at the exposition at Paris in 1867 had already won unprecedented laurels by winning first prize in an international contest. In sculpture, Bengt Erland Fogelberg won international fame, especially by his statues representing characters from Scandinavian mythology and Swedish history; the best known of the latter are his statues of Birger Jarl and Charles John, in Stockholm, and of Gustavus Adolphus in Gothenburg. Æsthetically Sweden made her greatest contribution to the world in this period through the incomparable singing of Jenny Lind (1820-1887), a native of Stockholm. Her name connotes perfect soulful art and beautiful personality and her memory is cherished throughout a great part of the civilized world. Her influence in creating a new appreciation of song was especially strong in the United States. Christina Nilsson (1843-1921), a native of the province of Småland, enjoyed in this and the following period almost the same popularity as a singer as had come to Jenny Lind before her retirement.

Runeberg.—In Finland the Swedish element was in this period experiencing its golden age in literature. Its most brilliant incarnation, Johan Ludvig Runeberg (1804-1877) vies with Tegnér for the distinction of being the foremost of Swedish poets. The glorious memories of the country's past inspired the best of Runeberg's poetic creations as it had done in the case of Tegnér; the latter had gone to the Viking period whereas the former finds his heroes in the early part of the nineteenth century among those who fought and lost in the war against Russia. The manner of delineation is fundamentally dissimilar in the two men. The dominant influence of romanticism had caused Tegnér to idealize his characters. Runeberg pictures his heroes with realistic fidelity; they are men of flesh and blood in a very real world, eccentric, weak at times, but often displaying wonderful strength and loyalty to country. It would be difficult to find another land whose heroes have been paid so splendid a poetic tribute as those of Finland in Runeberg's *The Songs of Ensign Stål* (*Fänrik*

Ståls Sägner), the first part published in 1848, the second in 1860. They constitute the grand epic of a heroic race, in its tragic struggle against forces that threatened to destroy its independence and its culture. In the stately form of the Homeric poems, Runeberg has also given delightful pictures of the quiet and contented life of the Finnish countryside, as in *The Elkhunters* (*Älgskyttarna*) and *Christmas Eve* (*Julkvällen*). His tragedies based on Greek and Old Norse legends reveal great imagination and power.

Topelius.—A contemporary countryman of Runeberg, Zachris Topelius (1818-1898), like the former wrote his works in Swedish, but with him the purely Finnish element is strongly emphasized. Topelius was wholly under the spell of romanticism. His leading work, *Tales of the Army Surgeon* (*Fältskärns berättelser*), gives the story, embellished lavishly with romantic elements, of the stirring events of Swedish history from Gustavus Adolphus to Gustavus III. It remains to this day a favourite work with Swedish people everywhere. Topelius idealized the heroes of Finland and assigns to the Finnish people a rôle in the affairs of the land, especially in the period of the wars, considerably more important than historical facts justify. His poetry breathes the spirit of patriotism and virile hope and few writers have surpassed him in creating wholesome and engaging children's stories.

National sentiment aroused in Finland.—Strong impetus was, simultaneously with Topelius and Runeberg, given by other men to the movement which aimed to awaken the Finnish race to a fuller appreciation of their own cultural wealth. In 1844 J. V. Snellman (1806-1881) began the publication of a periodical in the Finnish language. In a Swedish journal, begun by him in the same year, he urged with force and great insistence that a fuller recognition should be given to the specific Finnish culture than had hitherto been done. Snellman enjoyed the friendship and confidence of Czar Alexander II and prevailed on him to issue an order in 1863 giving the Finnish language a more important place than previously in the affairs of the duchy.

This imperial edict was merely the first of a series of ukases aiming to place Swedish and Finnish on a basis of complete parity. Elias Lönnrot (1802-1882) was the first to reveal the real wealth of Finnish legend and poetry and more than anyone else he helped to lay the foundation for Finnish literature. With indefatigable energy he collected runes, songs, legends, and archæological remains. Living among the common people for long periods in order to learn from their lips the songs and stories which had survived from early times, he was able to reproduce in writing the noble national epic *Kalevala* and approximately 30,000 ballads, legends, and proverbs, which constitute the extraordinarily rich Finnish folklore. Most of the enthusiastic collectors of Finnish folklore and advocates of its serious study were men of Swedish extraction and the purest idealistic motives actuated them; the tragedy of the situation is that the sentiment of nationality which they wished to kindle in the hearts of the Finns was in time to flare into an almost fanatical adoration of their own culture and blind their eyes to the indispensable part which the Swedish element has played in their land.

Natural science.—In natural sciences the period continued the important work of men like Berzelius, who died in 1849. In botany, Elias Fries (1794-1878) supplemented and corrected some of the investigations and conclusions of Linné, and created a system of organization which in many essential details has since been adopted. The foremost man in the domain of science and invention in the period was unquestionably John Ericsson. Although he lived in the United States the greater part of his active life, his training was essentially Swedish. He rendered a monumental service to his adopted country in a great crisis by the invention of the ironclad *Monitor* whose successful conflict with the Confederate *Merrimac* had an important bearing upon the outcome of the Civil War. In England, where he sojourned for a time before coming to the United States, he built the locomotive *The Novelty* which competed with George Stephenson's *Rocket*. Sufficient time had not been permitted Ericsson for building his engine and testing it and defects in the flues took it out of the race, after it, on previous trials, had clearly demonstrated a superiority over its competitor. Contemporary accounts awarded the prize of victory to the young Swedish engineer, but officially Stephenson was the victor.[3] Among other notable inventions by Ericsson were the screw propeller, the steam fire engine, and the sun motor. Sounding apparatus for safeguarding at sea were perfected by him. When Ericsson died in 1889 on the anniversary of the battle between the *Monitor* and the *Merrimac*, his body was, in accordance with his wish that his remains might be permitted to rest in his native soil, conveyed to Sweden by the United States cruiser *Baltimore*. This is the only time that the United States has thus honoured one of her benefactors of foreign birth.

The religious situation.—Religious life was profoundly influenced by two of the greatest preachers in the history of the nation; namely, C. O. Rosenius (1816-1868) and Peter Fjellstedt (1802-1881). The former early fell under the influence of the ardently devout sentiments of the pietists in his native Norrland and he became a leader in conventicle meetings. An English Methodist minister, G. Scott, who had begun to preach righteousness in Stockholm in conformity with the doctrines and practices of his church, became a close associate of Rosenius, who, however, was far more influenced by the methods of his friend than by his doctrines. Scott was eventually forced to leave the country and Rosenius then became the leader of the new religious movement, which was spreading rapidly and turning men from worldliness and formalism to a warmer spiritual life. As editor of the widely read journals, *The Pietist* (*Pietisten*) and *The Mission Newspaper* (*Missionstidningen*), his influence extended to every part of the country. Next to Schartau, Rosenius was the greatest religious leader in Sweden during the nineteenth century. He always remained a member of the state Church, but after his death a separatist movement began under the leadership of P. P. Waldenström (1838-1917), Rosenius' successor as editor of *The Pietist*. The doctrine of atonement was the rock upon which religious unity foundered. Waldenström's followers, known as "Mission Friends," or "Waldenströmians," for short, became a separate church group in 1878. The members of this group rapidly grew in number until they reached about 300,000 and it remains decidedly the leading religious body outside of the state Church.

[3] Church, W. C., *Life of John Ericsson*, N. Y., 1911, p. 59.

Waldenström was an unusually versatile man and adroit debater, and as member of the Riksdag and prolific writer he exerted strong influence in behalf of national defence and temperance. In Fjellstdt, learning, piety, and eloquence were blended in a remarkable degree. His friend, Peter Wieselgren, asserted that he spoke twelve languages, wrote sixteen, and could understand thirty. His theological scholarship was profound, but his style of presentation clear and striking, and his commentaries on the Bible have undoubtedly exerted greater influence on the religious thought of his people than any book save the Bible, Luther's Catechism, and the Swedish hymn-book. Part of his earlier life was spent in missionary work in East India and Turkey and he travelled extensively through Switzerland, France, and Germany, preaching to multitudes in their native tongue. Fjellstedt's greatest service to his own people was rendered as head of "The Mission Institute" at Uppsala, a school for the training of pastors, which has laid special stress on a living faith and good deeds rather than on strict orthodoxy in Christian life.

Shift from Russia to the Western powers.—Charles John's consistent and successful endeavour to maintain friendly relations between his country and Russia had never been pleasing to the Swedish people, but the stern and stubborn old warrior had cared little for their feelings, absolutely certain as he was that his was the right and prudent course. Being far more susceptible to the influence of popular sentiment than Charles John in the beginning of his reign, and having a genuine admiration for liberal institutions, Oscar soon departed from the old course and instead aligned himself with Russia's great antagonists at the time, England and France. When the Crimean War broke out in 1853, the Swedish king issued a declaration of neutrality and through his influence and skilful negotiations Denmark issued a similar note. A request from the Russian cabinet that some modification be made in the interest of Russia was firmly refused and a subsequent personal note from the czar to Oscar, asking that Sweden give assurance that in no case would she attack his country, received the same firm and clear answer. Russia then accepted the Swedish declaration of neutrality as satisfactory, but the outcome had made her statesmen very bitter. Swedish distrust of Russia had been aroused earlier when the latter demanded that the right to fish on the ocean and in the fjords outside the Norwegian coast be guaranteed the people of certain districts in northern Finland and that a small area be ceded them on which they might legally remain over the winter season. Quite naturally the Norwegians feared this proposal as merely a Russian subterfuge for securing a foot-hold in their land, with a naval station and fortifications to follow in due time, and they rejected the Russian demands. Russia thereupon threatened to retaliate by closing her own harbours to the Norwegian Lapps who were in the habit at certain seasons to seek grazing for their herds in Russian territory. Whether or not Norwegian-Swedish suspicions of Russia were in this case justified is a controverted point; Russian statesmen and historians have maintained that their country harboured no sinister designs against their neighbours, but previous experience certainly gave Swedes and Norwegians every reason to be on their guard. In this attitude they were encouraged and supported by England and France. These powers now endeavoured to entice both the Scandinavian countries to join them in the war against Russia and prospects of winning Finland back were dangled before the eyes of the Swedes. King Oscar was willing enough to listen to these tempting proposals, but his native caution did not desert him; his co-operation with the anti-Russian alliance was made contingent on specific guarantees that military action on a large scale would be carried on against Russia in the Baltic and that no separate peace should be concluded until the common object had been attained. The king's caution was the more justified as the detachment of the allied fleets which had been sent to the Baltic for action against Russia had accomplished very little. After many negotiations with France and England, and after much pressure had been exerted on the Swedish-Norwegian government by these two powers, a treaty was finally signed which guaranteed the integrity of the united Scandinavian kingdoms, Oscar pledging himself not to cede any territory to Russia; in case the latter made any demands for such cession, the Swedish-Norwegian king was forthwith to inform his allies, who bound themselves to come to his assistance with sufficient forces for resisting the enemy. Coming quite unexpectedly, the news of this agreement provoked great bitterness in Russia. Evidently the Swedish king at this time stood ready to join in a military action against the ancient enemy, always provided, however, that proper guarantees were given by his allies, but the whole situation changed suddenly when the belligerents concluded a treaty of peace. It has been surmised that Sweden's evident intentions to join the Western powers strengthened the desire of the czar to terminate the war. It now only remained for Sweden to get some compensation at the peace conference. She sought to secure guarantees that Russian naval power in the Baltic should be reduced, the Åland Islands ceded to her, or else declared neutral territory under the joint protection of England, France, and Sweden-Norway, and Russia be compelled to agree not to build forts on the islands or on the Finnish coast west and north of Sveaborg. England evinced interest in the Swedish-Norwegian proposals and made some effort to force the desired guarantee from the Russians, but France, now dominated by peace sentiment, looked askance at any proposals which did not directly affect her, or which might obstruct the peace negotiations, and was therefore not willing to extend any support to the Northern kingdoms. The net result of the negotiation was a separate treaty between Russia on one hand and France and England on the other, in which the former bound herself not to fortify the Åland Islands nor establish and maintain any naval or military quarters there. This was the not inconsiderable gain to Sweden for her benevolent attitude to the Western powers. Russia respected her guarantee until the World War broke out, during which great struggle more than a dozen forts were built on the islands (p. 780).

Scandinavianism.—Overshadowing all other international questions in this period, so far as the North was concerned, was the Schleswig-Holstein imbroglio. Closely linked with this was the movement known as Scandinavianism. The bitterness against Sweden which the events of 1814 had engendered in Denmark lingered long, but by the end of the third decade it was decidedly on the wane. Before long a remarkable amity and sense of a community of interests were to bring the three

Northern peoples more closely together than an older generation ever could conceive as possible. The explanation of this salutary and wholly delightful change is found in the growing realization among them that, in a large sense, they must go up or go down together. In their blind endeavour in the past to serve their respective national interests, they had merely played into the hands of others. Consanguinity began to assert itself quite strongly. Scientists, literary men, and students of the universities were the first to see and feel this. The serious menace to Denmark which loomed in the Schleswig-Holstein difficulties served to quicken the sense of Scandinavian solidarity. Since mediæval times the two duchies had been linked up with Denmark in some kind of personal union. Holstein was almost entirely German, northern Schleswig Danish, and southern Schleswig about evenly divided between the two race elements. A strong national sentiment began to manifest itself, especially in the former duchy, soon after the end of the wars, and suggestions of its incorporation with the German states soon were given serious consideration. A large party in Denmark were especially anxious to save the Danish part of Schleswig for their nation. The question was complicated by uncertainties in regard to the hereditary rights of the Danish kings in the duchies. Indicative of the baffling nature of the controversy is a statement attributed to the English prime-minister, Lord Palmerston. Only three persons, he averred, had ever understood the Schleswig-Holstein controversy; one was dead, one crazy, and he himself, the third, had forgotten what it was all about.[4] It was but natural that the first steps towards a greater Scandinavian solidarity should be taken in Denmark and southern Sweden. These sections lay in close proximity to one another and their peoples were bound together by many ancient ties. In 1828 the first Danish steamboat entered the harbour of Malmö and now communication between Sweden and Denmark became easy and frequent. The next year there occurred an impressive scene in the cathedral of Lund when, in connection with the ceremony of bestowing the doctor's degree, Tegnér placed a laurel wreath on the head of the great Danish poet Oehlenschläger and spoke the words with

[4] Henderson, E. F., *Short History of Germany*, N. Y., 1927, II, p. 385.

reference to his own country and that of the distinguished visitor: "The era of division is at an end and it should never have existed in the free and boundless world of the spirit." Professors of the universities of Lund and Copenhagen now began to exchange visits and the first meeting of Scandinavian scientists was held in Gothenburg in 1839. That same year a group of Lund students paid a fraternal visit to the Copenhagen students. Other visits followed and the circumstance that Charles John frowned upon this growing fraternization by young men of the two countries had only the effect of stimulating interest in them. In a circular letter to the Swedish legations, the aged king condemned the movement and voiced the opinion that the existing status of the three Scandinavian countries ought not to be disturbed. Renewed and more bitter attacks on the finicky monarch because of his pro-Russian attitude was practically the only result of this royal expression.

Students' meetings.—Up to this time the students' meetings had had no political tinge, but the desire of the Danes to find allies in their fight against the nationalists of Holstein, who were pressing for complete separation from their country, and the fear of Prussia, which championed the Holstein cause, soon made political considerations pre-eminent. That the movement was no longer a delightful and purely inoffensive occasion for feasting and oratorical pyrotechnics by groups of harmless idealists became plainly evident at a meeting at Copenhagen in 1842 by Danish and Swedish students, the Lund group alone being represented among the latter. The liberal Norwegian constitution was here praised with great eloquence and the participants joined vociferously in singing Tegnér's "King Karl, the Young Hero," thereby voicing their determination to defy, as the hero king had done, the hordes of aggression, even though the number of the latter appeared overwhelming. A few weeks later at a similar meeting at Lund the sentiment that a wrong committed against one of the Scandinavian countries should be looked upon as an act of aggression against them all struck a responsive chord in the hearts of those present. The following year, students from Copenhagen journeyed to Uppsala and much grandiloquent talk concerning the community of Scandinavian interests was again heard. The Russian Government, fully in sympathy with Prussian diplomacy, always looking askance at liberal movements, and anxious to thwart any efforts towards Scandinavian unity, now took official cognizance of the movement and sent protests both to Stockholm and Copenhagen. The Swedish Government gave tactful answer in order to mollify the uneasy neighbour. Student feeling was aroused until it was on the point of breaking all restraint when Karl Plough, one of the Danish leaders and perhaps the most eloquent in the student groups, on his return home was arrested on a charge of sedition, his heinous crime consisting of the advocacy of an alliance between the three Scandinavian countries. Only with his acquittal was comparative calm restored. The high-water mark of the Scandinavian movement was reached at a meeting in the Danish capital in 1845 which was attended by students from all the Scandinavian universities. The Norwegians had heretofore kept aloof, presumably from fear that being young as a nation and inexperienced in political affairs they might be manœuvred out of a leading position by their eloquent and aggressive Swedish and Danish brethren.

Diplomatic efforts in behalf of Denmark.—Enthusiasm for the common Scandinavian cause became boundless when the eloquent Dane, Orla Lehman, in a fiery speech urged all his young confrères to rally to the cause of Scandinavian unity, in fact to perfect, as he pleaded, a union of brothers (*fosterbrödralag*) for their common defence. These were glorious days for the young students and their exuberant spirits were pitched to the highest degree of excitement. Here, asserted the most enthusiastic of the Swedish participants, the journalist, Oskar Patrick Sturzen-Becker, a new force in history could be discerned, the alliance of the peoples, a reality of flesh and blood, whereas the compacts of princes had never been anything but "scraps of paper." "O kings, kings," he exclaimed, "how much may you not learn from this assembly." The Swedish students had at this time nothing to fear from their government, since Charles John had now been gathered to his fathers and the new king sympathized with their aspirations. Before a group of students Oscar once gave expression to the memorable words, "Henceforth a war between Scandinavian brothers is an impossibility." To the extent that the cause was consistent with the safety of his own country, he endeavoured to give aid and comfort to the Danes. When, on the outbreak of war between Denmark and Holstein in 1848, the Danish king, Frederick VII, appealed to him for help, Oscar gave answer that he considered it a duty to send aid in the event that Denmark proper were attacked. An appropriation was simultaneously made by the Swedish Riksdag for auxiliary troops and Swedish volunteers in great numbers flocked to the Danish standards. The Swedish king held firmly, however, to his position that only if Denmark proper were in danger would he come to her assistance. He next devoted his energies to negotiations and the London Protocol of 1850, guaranteeing the integrity of Denmark and arranging for the Danish succession on the death of the childless Frederick, was consummated largely through his influence. This temporary pause in the seemingly interminable wrangling came as a distinct relief to the Swedish nation, which by this time had become decidedly lukewarm regarding the Danish interest. This attitude, it has been charged, frustrated an arrangement by which the Swedish crown prince would be adopted by the Danish king and thus in time bring the three crowns under one head again. If any such plans were ever seriously considered, they undoubtedly were vetoed by Russia and therefore discarded. Some years later the Danish minister of foreign affairs, the Holsteiner, von Scheele, issued a circular letter to the Danish embassies, probably at the instigation of Russia, in which "Scandinavianism" was condemned in so far as the movement aimed at a political union. Oscar then felt constrained in a letter to the Danish king to make clear his conception of the basis and character of an eventual alliance between the two countries: a binding guarantee that Sweden would support Denmark in her claim on Schleswig, moral support for her claim on Holstein, and 16,000 soldiers mobilized, when necessary, with which to back up Denmark. The Danish king answered that he could not approve this plan so long as it did not involve a binding guarantee regarding Holstein also. Oscar felt keenly hurt at this and inasmuch as his health was failing rapidly he ceased to be an active factor, save for occasional notes to foreign powers in behalf of Denmark.

Charles XV at first showed no inclination to continue and support his father's Danish policy, but since political considerations rather than personal feelings determined his early course he gave cautious support to the distracted neighbour. But as Prussia's aggressive support of the duchies increased Denmark's difficulties, he abandoned his policy of caution and had not his own ministers resolutely taken steps to restrain him he would have thrown his country into a venture in behalf of Denmark which, in all probability, would have ended in disaster. Several reasons impelled the king's desire to go the limit in championing Denmark's cause. His generous and impulsive nature revolted against the bullying tactics of powerful Prussia against a small nation, for the Danish king he felt a genuine personal friendship; finally, there was Victor Emmanuel's and Cavour's glorious achievements in uniting disunited Italy, and this had kindled in him an ardent desire to play a similar grand rôle in the Scandinavian North. In the controversy with Norway regarding the governorship he had blundered grievously (p. 704), and he now felt the need of doing something which might repair his shattered prestige. Historians have found it difficult to fathom the real intentions of the king. A union of the three Scandinavian countries, achieved either through his own election to the Danish throne, or through the election of his brother Oscar, who likewise some day would inherit the Swedish throne, the king having no heir, or, as a third possibility, through the marriage of his daughter to the eldest son of the Danish heir-apparent and the subsequent election of this royal pair to the Swedish throne—this was the grand scheme which evidently now stirred his volatile mind. Because of his habitual volubility of speech and changeableness of moods, it is difficult to follow his course or understand the means which he was prepared to employ, the more so as most of his negotiations were carried on through confidential friends rather than through responsible and accredited officials. Through Manderström, the cautious leader of Swedish foreign affairs at the time, Sweden was exerting herself through negotiations with different courts, especially at London and Paris, to find a solution to the Schleswig-Holstein question which would involve the least possible loss and humiliation to Denmark, but direct intervention was not contemplated, the more so as neither London nor Paris manifested any serious intention to aid her. As a crisis was nearing in their baffling affair, the Danes naturally more than ever desired Swedish support, and in 1860 their king, in company with his prime-minister, Hall, visited Charles at Ljungbyhed in southern Sweden and here the Danes submitted a draft for an alliance. Charles transmitted the document to Manderström, who concluded that its provisions gave all the advantages to Denmark and, pretending that he had never received it, he pigeon-holed it for over a year. In visits to Paris and London the following year, Charles endeavoured to gain the support of the Western powers for his Scandinavian plans, but with indifferent success. Napoleon III refrained from making any definite promises, but evidently gave some encouragement to the Swedish king, the importance of which the latter greatly overestimated. Lord Palmerston, at this time at the head of English foreign affairs, evidently was not deeply impressed by the eloquent discourses of Charles and his brother Oscar, who accompanied him, concerning the rights of nationalities. The prospect of a dynastic union of the Scandinavian countries was also alluded to. The English Government evidently felt that no serious objection could openly be raised against such a union, but it could not view without some concern that France was likely to secure an obedient ally in the Baltic. In March 1863, the Danish king took the momentous step of issuing the famous decree which in effect would establish a merely personal union between Denmark and Holstein and eventually incorporate Schleswig with the kingdom. The government of Sweden, having advance information of the contemplated move, had warned Denmark to proceed with caution, first making certain of the sanction of England and France. This sanction was, however, not sought by Denmark. Sweden was, therefore, not in any way responsible for the fateful step. As the Prussian attitude now became much more threatening, and war seemed imminent, Danish desire for a Swedish alliance became increasingly manifest. Charles and Manderström were agreed that Denmark ought not oppose a

Prussian-Austrian invasion of Holstein, but in the event Schleswig were invaded Sweden ought to form a defensive alliance with her distressed neighbour.

The king's promises.—Unfortunately Charles promised more than this in his conversations with his confidential friends, who in turn transmitted the information to the Danes. To add to the confusion inherent in Swedish foreign affairs at this time, all the Swedish cabinet ministers, except Manderström, were kept in ignorance of the king's plans. At a meeting at Skodsborg in Denmark in July 1863, between Charles and Frederick, the Swedish king, entirely carried away by his emotions and throwing all caution to the winds, urged the Danes not to oppose with military force any German action in Holstein but instead to blockade the German harbours, and in case this course were followed he would, even as soon as Holstein were invaded, come to the assistance of Denmark with 20,000 Swedish and Norwegian troops. This went beyond all previous promises and in case Denmark followed the suggestion Sweden would be irrevocably committed to war. The situation filled Hamilton, the Swedish minister at Copenhagen, with alarm and he tried as far as possible to have the terms of the projected alliance modified. In August Manderström authorized Hamilton to agree to an alliance whereby Sweden bound herself to assist in the defence of Denmark and Schleswig with 20,000 men. At this stage obstacles rose, however, which at once frustrated all plans for the projected alliance.

Opposition in Sweden.—At a historic encounter at the castle of Ulriksdal, near Stockholm, on September 8, between the king, Manderström, Hamilton, Gripenstedt, de Geer, and Sibbern, the latter a member of the Norwegian Council, the question of the Danish alliance was brought up. Fearlessly the men censured the king for his ill-advised actions in the Danish affair and especially for making promises which, if kept, would surely bring Sweden to disaster. Although they criticized the king for what he had done, Hamilton and Manderström looked upon the Swedish-Norwegian-Danish alliance as an accomplished fact, but Gripenstedt was irrevocably and uncompromisingly opposed to every alliance project. In the main, de Geer and Sibbern shared his opinions. With these influential ministers against him and with full knowledge of the popular support which they could at all times command, Charles dared not dismiss them or disregard their counsel, and the upshot of it all was a postponement of the alliance project until the Swedish government could have ascertained the intention of France and England. If one or both of these powers would guarantee assistance to Denmark, Sweden would do likewise. Neither England nor France were, however, willing to exert themselves in Denmark's behalf, and Sweden therefore also stood aloof when the attack on the little country came. For the Danes, Swedish failure to come to their assistance was naturally a bitter disappointment and caused much ill-feeling. For the fiasco of Swedish diplomacy in the matter neither the king nor his ministers were, however, wholly to blame. This was a transition period in the organization of the Swedish government itself and the limits which marked the king's and the ministers' power were as yet obscure. That the attitude of the men who blocked the king's fantastic and utterly hazardous plans was, from the Swedish viewpoint, the correct and patriotic one seemed to a later generation quite evident. An adherence to Charles's policies would inevitably have spelled disaster to Sweden. It would have been a sacrifice for another which, while splendidly magnanimous and heroic, went beyond what one nation reasonably may expect of another. As one historian [5] pointedly asks: "What would they have said and how would they have felt in Denmark if it had been a question of Danish assistance in winning back Finland, or merely the Åland Islands to Sweden?"

Swedish-Norwegian relations.—Negotiations regarding Swedish-Norwegian relations growing out of the union marked another failure for the diplomacy of Charles XV and brought great embarrassment to both him and his advisers. As has appeared, his father had pursued a very conciliatory policy towards the Norwegians in the hope that timely concessions would disarm opposition to the unfortunate union. In 1847 he consented to the creation of a national Norwegian Order, the St. Olaf, which gave him a temporary popularity in Norway. The Swedes, however, complained that in too many instances preference was given Norwegians in appointment to diplomatic

[5] Hallendorff, C., *Sveriges historia*, XII, p. 114.

and consular service and that Norway did not pay her reasonable share in the joint expenses, especially for defence. Regard for Norwegian sensibilities was again shown by the king in 1855 when he appointed the crown prince to serve as regent in Norway in place of the governor who had resigned. Some progress was made in fixing anew the principles which were to govern the co-ordination of the two countries. Consular affairs which affected both countries unitedly should, according to a proposal, be handled by the Minister of Foreign Affairs, while all consular matters which required consideration by the ministry should be laid before a joint ministerial group of Norwegians and Swedes. Swedish affairs should be handled by Swedish officials and those which concerned Norway exclusively by the Norwegian interior department. These arrangements did not, however, prevent a recurrence of the old troubles and soon the question of the governorship of Norway had opened wide the breach. The Norwegian Storthing had taken action during Oscar's reign to abolish this office which had never been popular in Norway, even though, ever since 1829, only Norwegians had been appointed to fill it. The king had then refused to approve the Storthing resolution and the matter remained quiescent for some years. With the coming to power of Birch-Reichenwald in Norway in 1858 the question was, however, brought to the fore again. Birch-Reichenwald was an ambitious and aggressive man, who shrewdly calculated that by gaining the favour of the king he would best be able to carry out his own policies in Norway. He had assured Charles, while the latter served as regent, that his popularity would be greatly enhanced in Norway if he would favour the move to abolish the governorship. Popularity was the very breath of life to Charles, and he was the more willing to acquiesce in the program as surface indications made it appear that the Swedes cared little one way or the other. Their general attitude towards the union at this time was that of indifference, but Charles failed to take into account that the spirit of opposition would surely be aroused the moment a challenge was hurled at them. From the beginning, the Swedish cabinet members, especially de Geer, Manderström, and Hamilton, felt no serious objection to the abolition of the office, but they vigorously insisted that the decision must be made a joint Swedish-Norwegian affair and not an exclusively Norwegian one. In December 1859 the Storthing almost unanimously passed the resolution abolishing the governorship office, and Birch-Reichenwald at the same time assured his colleagues that the king's sanction would be forthcoming. Money was voted for the new prime-minister who was to supersede the governor. Then obstacles began to pile up. Immediately vigorous assertions were made in the Swedish Riksdag that the issue involved a fundamental principle in the union and that the Swedish Government must have a voice in the matter. De Geer now came forward as the great pacifier. Emphasizing the many obscure provisions in the union act, he argued that differences of opinion were inevitable and that therefore hasty deductions of sinister designs on the part of anyone were unwarranted. Two months later the Swedes proposed that the Storthing and Riksdag should proceed to revise the Act of Union so as to secure definiteness in its provisions; the matter of the governorship should be held in abeyance until this had been done. In Norway this was looked upon as evidence of Swedish weakness, and the determination to go through with the Norwegian plan here became more fixed than ever. The ensuing discussion served mainly to irritate the people in both countries. The king, taking cognizance of the feeling in Sweden, refused his sanction to the Storthing's resolution and postponed action on the revision project to a later day. The Storthing next protested against the view that Sweden was in any way concerned about the governorship and rejected the proposal for a revision of the union act. The Norwegians were firmly wedded to the idea that the Swedes were bent on establishing an over-lordship in Norway, a suspicion which certainly at this time had no basis in fact. What the Swedes wanted was the perfecting of the union in a way that would give greater protection to both against other powers. Further negotiation in the reign of Charles proved fruitless, and when the Norwegians a year after his death again voted to abolish the governorship, the new king, Oscar II, and his cabinet acquiesced in this action.

Chapter XXVI

THE FRUITION OF PEACEFUL ENTERPRISE UNDER A SCHOLAR KING

Deep shadows gathered over Charles XV during the last years of his comparatively brief reign. The embarrassment and humiliation resulting from the fiasco of his Danish policy, the failure of his plans for a union of the three Scandinavian counties under his sceptre, and the awkward predicament to which he personally as well as his country had been brought by his blunders in the Norwegian governorship affair had left disappointment and anguish in their wake. Disease, bred and aggravated, no doubt, by an unwise mode of life, had early begun to sap his physical strength and before death came as a deliverer in 1872 he was but a shadow of his former self. Gone were the joviality, the exuberance of joy and good cheer, which his subjects had known so well and for which they had loved him so dearly. With the former boundless admiration for his talents and genial personality there was now mingled the sincerest pity and sympathy.

Oscar II.—The new king, Oscar II, had in youth not primarily been trained for the exacting duties of his exalted office. The third in order among the sons of Oscar I, it seemed a most remote possibility that the crown would come to him by right of heredity. Death had, however, claimed his elder brother, Prince Gustaf, in 1852, and his nephew, Charles Oscar, only son of Charles XV, in 1854, and he had therefore come to be looked upon as presumptive heir to the throne. Born in 1829, he had in 1857 married Sophia of Nassau, and as several sons were born to them the future of the Bernadotte dynasty became intimately bound up with his family.

In the long list of European kings it would be difficult to find one who ranks superior to Oscar II in natural endowments, wisdom, devotion to cultural interests, and noble and intelligent will to serve his people. The motto "The welfare of the brother peoples" (*Brödrafolkets väl*) which he chose as the guiding principle of his reign expressed the lofty ideal which determined his official acts. Tall of stature, standing more than six feet four inches in height, with finely formed and handsome features and walking erect and with elastic step, Oscar seemed in his prime a paragon of manly physical perfection. In youth his interests had been directed mainly to naval affairs in which he became an expert, and genuine merit brought him in 1859 to the exalted position of vice-admiral. The distinguished historian and cabinet member, F. F. Carlson, had been his chief tutor, and several terms at Uppsala University had widened and deepened his cultural interests. As an orator he was without a peer among his own countrymen, and his linguistic ability many a time astonished diplomats and foreign members of international organizations which, with increasing frequency, chose the fair Swedish capital as a meeting-place. A collection of poems by him have eminent merit; the fine rhythm and lofty sentiment of one of these poems, *The Baltic* (*Östersjön*) [1] entitles it to be ranked as one of the masterpieces of Swedish verse. Music was a passion with him, and as president of the

Oscar II

[1] This poem, as well as representative selections from other Swedish poems, has been translated into English and published in two small volumes under the title *Masterpieces of Swedish Literature* by Augustana Book Concern, Rock Island, Ill.

Swedish Academy of Music during many years he exercised a most beneficent and far-reaching influence in creating new interest in the exalted art. Scientists and scientific organizations found in him the Mæcenas whose generosity and interest made possible the realization of their worthy projects. A. E. Nordenskiöld, Fridtjof Nansen, and Sven Hedin, to mention only the most outstanding men, were in turn the beneficiaries of his enlightened and liberal support. He organized the Swedish Exhibition at Stockholm in 1866, as well as his country's section at the World's Fair in Paris in 1867, and the Swedish exhibit at the International Industrial and Arts Exhibition in London in 1872. Several extended journeys in Germany, France, England, and Holland had brought him into contact with a large number of the leading men and women of the period in every field of great endeavour. His extraordinary versatility, scholarship, and æsthetic instincts won for him by almost universal agreement the honourable appellation, "the most highly cultured monarch of Europe." As evidence of the high esteem in which King Oscar was held and of the confidence which his sagacity and honesty inspired, may be cited the fact that on more than one occasion he was called upon to act as arbitrator in complicated international affairs, notably in the Samoan question, in which the United States was one of the interested parties. Like his predecessor, he liked the plaudits of the crowd, but he never attained to the boundless popularity which his brother had enjoyed. His affability and good cheer never deserted him, however, and although he was in truth "every inch a king" and never was willing to relinquish an iota of royal dignity and prerogative, he showed withal a becoming humility and proper regard for the opinions of his subjects. Characteristic of his geniality and sense of humour is a pleasing anecdote of a visit which he once paid to the primary grade of a certain school. On taking upon himself the task of catechizing the children in Swedish history, he was told that Gustavus Adolphus and Charles XII were the great kings of the nation. A mite of a child, no doubt realizing that the polite thing ought to be said, added the name "Oscar II." "Tell me then," said the king to the little flatterer, "what Oscar II has done which has earned for him the right to be called great." Bursting into tears the poor child confessed that she did not know. Patting her on the head, the king said kindly, "Don't let that worry you, for, to tell the truth, neither do I know."

Lines of development in the Riksdag.—At the time of Oscar's accession, the lines of development in the Riksdag, as reorganized by the act of 1866, had been quite clearly marked. The trend had in many respects not run true to expectations. Most people had hoped, or feared, according as predilections and political ideas influenced them, that the system of English parliamentarism, based on a controlling majority in the second chamber, would be the inevitable outcome, but this had not come to pass. So far, de Geer was not disappointed in his handiwork, for he constantly desired to see in Sweden a powerful monarch in co-ordination with the legislative body. He wanted an extension of the parliamentary system, but in such manner that the composition of the ministry would be determined largely by both chambers and not by the second alone. Methods of elections and qualifications for membership had been, in the opinion of de Geer, so fixed for the respective chambers that they would be nearly on a par in authority and dignity. In both, the old burgher and *bonde* classes were expected to dominate.

The Agrarian Party.—Not many years were to pass, however, before the latter had won a decided majority in the second chamber and organized itself into a distinct political party, the Agrarian [2] (*lantmannapartiet*) which urgently and persistently began to press for legislation for the special benefit of the tillers of the soil. The question of legislative methods, whether strictly parliamentary or otherwise, concerned its leaders very little; the abolition of laws considered unjust to the *bönder,* and especially the removal of inequitable tax burdens, was to them of prime importance. Rigid economy was the watchword of the new party and it fought stubbornly, and at times blindly, against reforms or public enterprises. It cannot, however, in fairness be said that the *bönder* were lacking in patriotic sentiment, but their insistence on lower taxes was apt to take precedence of everything else. The foremost item

[2] A full and authentic account of the genesis, program, and leaders of the Agrarian Party is now available in Edward Thermaenius' scholarly work, *Lantmannapartiet,* doctoral dissertation, Uppsala, 1928.

on their program was the abolition of the old land taxes and the antiquated army organization (*indelningsverket*). Both had placed far heavier burdens, relatively, on the *bönder* than on the other classes. The circumstance that other and more favoured groups had fallen into the habit of speaking contemptuously of the *bönder,* as if these were socially inferior, was not calculated to temper their minds or make them less disposed to even up things now that they had the power; they were, in fact, determined to settle many an old score. True to their traditions, they felt, however, a deep sense of loyalty towards the king, which feeling also extended to his advisers, the members of the cabinet. The first chamber had come to include many of the leaders of the former order of nobility as well as industrial leaders from the erstwhile burgher group, and these quite naturally assumed an attitude of hostility to the particularistic program of the agrarians. The conflicting programs of the majorities in the respective chambers established an equilibrium of influence which had the effect of leaving the king free to choose his ministers very much as he pleased.

In their display of real qualities of leadership, the chiefs of the *bonde* party showed that their group had by no means degenerated since the heroic days of Gustavus Vasa and Charles XI. They rose to the occasion in remarkable fashion and real statesmanship was not lacking among them. True, the party at times, as intimated, was selfish and blind, but its members were not impervious to reason, and on the whole they showed as much capacity, sagacity, and tolerance as any group. This was the more remarkable since they, as a rule, had received little more than an elementary education; ever since the Reformation, elementary knowledge has been quite generally disseminated, however. For about two decades, Carl Ifvarsson, a courageous and resourceful *bonde* from the province of Halland, was recognized as the foremost leader of the group. He had a sound sense of realities, was always cautious and economical, and his unquestioned integrity always inspired respect. No one needed to have doubts regarding his position on public questions. At first Ifvarsson was fairly conservative, but he mellowed with age, became more liberal and disposed to acknowledge that other groups besides his own had rights, but he never lost sight of the interests of his own party. A sort of interloper among the agrarians was the nobleman, Arvid Posse, whose motives for joining this party have baffled the historian. He had been a strenuous opponent of de Geer's plan for the reorganization of the Riksdag and the most plausible explanation of his subsequent championing of the cause of the *bönder* in a most particularistic spirit and in most aggressive fashion is, no doubt, to be found in his chagrin at the defeat of the higher orders and his determination to utilize every opportunity for harassing de Geer and his confrères. He found his best opportunity for doing so through his leadership of a compact *bonde* party. Another member who held a high place in the party, both in the preliminary stages of its organization and subsequently as a leader in the Riksdag, was the idealist and liberal landed proprietor, Emil Key, father of Ellen Key.

Question of a military reorganization.—Practically all the members of the cabinet and first chamber, as well as a considerable contingent in the second chamber, had become convinced that *indelningsverket,* the army system which Charles IX had originated, a system that in its day had given Sweden a most efficient fighting force, was out of date and ill-suited to give the country the necessary defensive force. General conscription according to the Prussian plan seemed to many the only method which could provide the adequate land defence. The long period of peace which the country had enjoyed had, in fact, bred the belief that all danger of attack from without had definitely passed and both army and navy had therefore been permitted to sink into a state of almost complete inefficiency. As symptomatic of the prevailing indifference in military matters, may be cited the suggestion of a leader of the Liberal Party that military field-training for the men in the ranks be limited to four days a year instead of the customary twenty days. Guns were of the seventeenth-century type. Prior to the purchase of modern breech-loading cannon in the eighties, the Swedish artillery was reputed to be the most antiquated in Europe, and the few fortresses which the country had built were rated no better. The advocates of a modernized system of defences repeated with genuine relish a story to the effect that the famous Prussian general, Von Moltke, was seen to laugh only twice, once after his great victory at Sedan, the other when Vaxholm, near Stockholm, was pointed out to him as one of the Swedish fortresses. Many divisions of sharp-shooters had been organized after 1860, and many liberal leaders like Rydberg and Blanche cherished the hope that here was an adequate substitute for a standing army, but experience had already revealed that while enthusiasm for the organization was not lacking the system was practically useless in an emergency, unless, as Grimberg remarks, "enthusiasm could be relied upon to overcome an enemy." [3] Charles XV had several times urged that the defences be modernized and strengthened, but his adventurous foreign policy had bred deep suspicion that an improved military force would merely increase the risk of reckless war ventures. Even long after this king had passed away, the *bönder* reasoned that a small and inefficient army was the most effective means for holding all warlike propensities of royalty in check. Fear that a lengthened period for military service and general conscription would largely increase the number of able-bodied men who through emigration sought escape from the burdens was also a factor, as before intimated, in postponing military reforms. As one of the *bönder* pointedly once said: "If we extend the time of military service, we shall, indeed, have our officers here at home but our soldiers will be in the United States."

First steps to reorganization.—The need of a modern military organization became increasingly clear, however, to the nation, except to the most irreconcilable pacifists and unsophisticated optimists, who blandly cherished the belief that if danger threatened foreign powers would come to Sweden's rescue. The first serious step towards a rehabilitation of the decrepit military establishment was taken in 1873, when after many years of bitter contention a preliminary agreement was reached by the parties which implied that *indelningsverket* would be scrapped and a system of general conscription substituted. With this proposal was also coupled the proviso that the land taxes, against which the *bönder* were complaining, should be gradually eliminated. This "compromise," the designation which ever afterwards clung to the proposal, became the rally-

[3] Grimberg, *Svenska folkets underbara öden*, IX, p. 276.

ing-point around which fierce parliamentary battles were fought intermittently during nineteen hectic years. Ministry after ministry endeavoured to surmount the hurdles which the agrarian opposition to general conscription interposed, candidates for the Riksdag lost or won on the issue, and newspapers and pamphlets found it an issue of perennial interest. As the battle progressed, the *bönder* themselves came to realize more and more clearly that a reorganization of the army and navy must come, but their insistence that the cost must not be loaded onto them in disproportionate amounts, as formerly had been the case, became increasingly firm and articulate; the abolition or material reduction of land taxes hence became the inflexible condition for their acquiescence.[4]

Boström and the new military system.—Erik Gustaf Boström, the ablest and most resourceful statesman of the period, was the man who finally managed to bring the nation out of the wilderness of conflicting interests and interminable debates. He had become prime-minister in 1891 after Åkerhjelm, his predecessor, had been compelled to resign because of a serious indiscretion in speech; in a private interview with a member of the second chamber he had urged so large and efficient an army that "one might speak Swedish towards both East and West"; the remark becoming known to the public, it caused a mighty stir, as this was too evident and clumsy a threat against both Norway and Russia. On being proffered the portfolio, Boström pleaded that he be excused on the ground that he did not speak foreign languages, but Oscar good-naturedly brushed this objection aside by remarking: "Do like Åkerhjelm, speak Swedish." Boström was an adept at the game of politics. He knew how to play one party against the other, was most adroit in overcoming the objections of opponents by confidential talks, and he never hesitated to put up a good game of bluff if this appeared the surest means of gaining a desired advantage.

Rappe.—Throughout the country, societies for better national defence had sprung up and public opinion had been

[4] One should bear in mind that excise and custom duties, corporate, income, and personal property taxes, licences, and other sources of state revenue were proportionately insignificant in this and earlier periods, hence land taxes were looked upon as the chief source of income for state activities.

strongly influenced towards their proposals when Boström became prime-minister. He soon took the bold step of summoning the Riksdag to an extraordinary session, in order to bring the issue squarely before the nation. Another individual had by this time become conspicuous in the agitation for military reform. This was General Axel Rappe, a scion of a distinguished family with honourable traditions of military service. At the outbreak of the Franco-Prussian War in 1870 he had hastened to join the standard of France as a volunteer and had won the Cross of the Legion of Honour for extraordinary bravery in action. Later he took part in French expeditions against the Arabs in north Africa, but on hearing that a decision on the question of national defence was imminent in Sweden he hastened home, anxious that his observations and experience abroad might be put to the service of his beloved fatherland. With him it was a fixed conviction that the French defeat in 1871 had been due to military unpreparedness and he was ready to give the obstreperous Swedish *bönder* some harrowing details of the suffering and humiliation France, as a consequence, had been compelled to endure. Shortly after his return home, Rappe became major-general and chief of staff, and his sound knowledge of military affairs, wide experience, integrity, and evident disinterestedness soon won the respect even of the implacable enemies of the conscription system. Boström's shrewdness and skill in political manœuvring coupled with Rappe's authoritative knowledge and personal influence finally put the opponents of adequate defence to rout; a law passed at the extraordinary session in 1892 provided that all men between the ages of twenty-one to forty were subject to military service, the annual period of training being fixed at ninety days. As a compensation to the *bönder,* the land taxes were to be radically reduced through a series of years. The last vestige of the *indelningsverket* disappeared in 1901 when the time of training was fixed at eight months for infantry, ten for naval service, and twelve for special departments. The fleet was also strengthened and reorganized. In 1907 it consisted of twelve first-class and seven smaller battleships, all entirely modern. No doubt the possession of an efficient army and navy helped to give a respectful hearing to Swedish postulates in connection with the Norwegian secession from the union in 1905 and to her policy of neutrality in the World War.

Venture into free trade.—The program of the Liberals, as formulated by Richert, de Geer, and other leaders of the party, stressed free trade as the wise and practical policy for securing national prosperity as well as for maintaining amicable international relations. Foreign trade, unrestricted by embargoes or custom duties, was also a cardinal principle of Gripenstedt, and during his incumbency of the treasury portfolio practically all embargoes had been abolished and custom duties lifted from most farm products and many factory-made articles. Trade agreements with France, Spain, Prussia, and the German Customs Union had furthermore extended the free-trade policy until Sweden was virtually a free-trade country. By a trade agreement with Norway in 1874, reciprocal free trade in articles of domestic production was established between the united countries, except for grain shipped by water routes, which was to pay one-half of the customary duties.

In turning from the protective to the free-trade policy, Gripenstedt and the other liberal leaders had been influenced not only by the pet theories of the dominant economic and political thought of the day, but also by the course which England had chosen to pursue. She had adopted free trade as a national policy and her economic progress had been most astounding. Reasoning by analogy, the Swedish statesmen concluded that a similar course would lead to their country's prosperity and greatness. Their fond expectations were, however, not realized, which became painfully evident after a couple of decades. Now men everywhere in the land began to reason that a policy that was good for a great and aggressive nation like England, with vast capital at her disposal, possessed of colonies and markets in every part of the globe, and with a great industrial organization, might not be so wise for a comparatively poor and industrially backward country like Sweden. The experience of meeting unrestricted competition in the markets of the world had, indeed, at first quickened Swedish industry to new life, and had resulted in the introduction of more modern production methods, but the factory owners and workers were the chief beneficiaries of this. It was not only differences in wealth and political and industrial organization that made the analogy between England and Sweden misleading, but also differences in the distribution of occupations. Whereas in the former the agricultural class was small in comparison with the industrial worker, in Sweden, as late as 1880, it constituted two-thirds of the population.

Ruin wrought by free trade.—The inundation of the country by the products of the farms of Russia, Germany, Denmark, and America, made possible by the removal or decided lowering of duties and selling at prices which the Swedish farmers were unable to meet spelled economic ruin to them, and forced sales and foreclosures became a painfully common occurrence in the agricultural communities. One result was that the exodus to America assumed large proportions, reaching its highest level in the decade 1881-1890, during which 376,400 Swedes, 73 per cent of them being between the ages of fifteen to forty, left the country. The imminent bankruptcy of Swedish agriculture caused the cry for a return to the protective principle to become loud and insistent. The eloquent speeches of the free-traders that cheap food meant better living conditions to the nation as a whole and their gratuitous advice to the *bönder* that they turn to dairying and diversified agriculture failed to convince and quiet those who were tortured by a growing deficit. Other countries which had followed England on her free-trade venture had, moreover, returned to the protective tariff policy.

The party conflicts which for more than a decade raged in Sweden between free-traders and protectionists assumed a virulence which brings to mind the lamentable bickerings and deadlocks of the Hats and Caps in the eighteenth century. There were now, however, no foreign countries with sinister interests in the Swedish squabbles. The Agrarian Party became disrupted by the issue. Carl Ifvarsson shocked his former party comrades by abandoning the protective principle which he had formerly upheld and supporting free trade. In this he represented the small land-owners who had very little surplus grain to sell and therefore, as a rule, continued to support a policy of low tariffs or free trade. The large land-owners, on the other hand, insisted on protective duties.

New leaders.—The most picturesque and influential member of the second chamber now was Liss Olof Larsson, a typical son of the province of Dalarna. He had already at the early age of twenty-nine gained a seat in the Riksdag and his extensive knowledge in public affairs, adroitness in debate, fearlessness, and unswerving loyalty to a program of strict economy in government expenditures had early attracted attention. Scoffing at all dictums of conventionalized society, he wore the old-fashioned costume of his native province, whether he attended the Riksdag sessions or formal functions in the royal palace. Another picturesque and fearless representative of the *bönder* was A. P. Danielson, a native of Öland, a veritable giant in stature, who loved political frays dearly, and whose rectitude and frankness won the respect of even his opponents. Both Liss Olof Larsson and Danielson joined the ranks of the protectionists. In the election for an extraordinary session of the Riksdag in 1887, the free-traders won a decisive victory and in another election in the fall of that same year they again won, but with somewhat depleted ranks.

Protection re-established.—By reason of a most peculiar situation, power slipped from the free-traders, and the opposition lost no time in forcing the desired legislation through the Riksdag. One of the twenty-two members of the Stockholm delegation, all free-traders, it was discovered, had failed to pay his communal tax, a matter of 11.58 crowns (about $3) and therefore was declared ineligible. The courts ruling that all ballots on which the delinquent's name, as well as the names of his twenty-one party comrades, had appeared must be thrown out, the entire Stockholm delegation was unseated and protectionists took their places. While the famous Stockholm election case caused a furore of excitement and gave an earlier victory to the protectionists than had been anticipated, it in reality had little material bearing on the ultimate outcome; already in the election of 1888 the protectionists had a safe majority. Incidentally it may be recorded that the hapless individual whose delinquency had provoked such a furious storm was afterwards the object of so much hate and scorn by his party comrades that he found it expedient to leave Stockholm and ultimately emigrated to America. The tariff law of 1888

Liss Olof Larsson

laid heavy duties on many agricultural products, and a beginning was also made for a system of tariff protection of factory-made articles. Coffee was the only article which received a lower duty. A commission to prepare a comprehensive plan for an extension of the protective system was also created. Customs duties were again given a considerable boost in 1895.

Beginning of industrial conflict.—The growing industrialization brought the same kind of evils to Sweden as to other countries: uncertainty of employment; exploitation of the weak, especially women and children; misunderstanding and bickerings. There was, however, a difference in degree. The idealism and innate sense of justice and humaneness of the Swedish people served, in a degree, as a corrective. The very limitations imposed by Nature herself on the opportunities for rapid gains here helped to check exploitation. There were, however, enough of this to fill, even here, a long and gripping chapter on "man's inhumanity to man." The first industrial strike recorded in Sweden occurred in 1879 in the sawmill district of Sundsvall. Living conditions here were miserable, there being in one community thirty-three families confined to one room each. When a certain employer announced a decrease in wages, which already were wholly inadequate, the affected men marched to Sundsvall in order to lay their grievances before the governor. The latter, instead of listening sympathetically to their story and seeking to ameliorate their condition, ordered detachments of soldiers to surround them and six gun-boats lay in the harbour with cannon pointed at the strikers. After a night in the open in cold and rain, the men received a heartless answer to their protests; over one thousand men were ordered discharged and driven from their living quarters, several of the leaders were imprisoned, and the rest forced to return to work.

The Socialist Party is formed.—The first Swedish labour union was formed two years after the wretched Sundsvall strike. The initiative was taken by August Palm, whose burning indignation against the existing industrial system had been born of the hardships and indignities he in early life had been compelled to suffer. On a journey to Denmark and Germany he had become familiar with the doctrines of Socialism, which he embraced with a zeal akin to fanaticism. Returning to his native country, he travelled from place to place, proclaiming the new gospel of salvation from the alleged "economic slavery." With a humble capital of 108 crowns he started a journal, *The Social Democrat* (*Socialdemokraten*) in his home in Stockholm, in 1885. With so small a capital he was unable to publish the entire edition at once, so the editor himself went out on the streets to sell some copies in order to get money for printing the rest of the issue. In three decades this journal was to rise to the dignity of a government organ and become one of the most influential publications in the country.

Branting.—Palm was an uncouth, unlettered, and brutally tactless individual, and before long his few followers and partners in the newspaper enterprise bestowed the editorship as well as leadership of the party upon Hjalmar Branting, a man of entirely different type. For almost forty years he was to remain the great and unquestioned leader of the Socialists in Sweden and his integrity, fairness, and statesman-like qualities were to guide the Swedish workingman to a dominant place in the affairs of the nation. As for himself, he won universal recognition as one of the greatest among the statesmen of his generation.

As a labour leader Hjalmar Branting has had few equals. Branting was convinced that calm discussion and a wise exercise of the franchise were the only sure and safe means for attaining economic freedom and social recognition for the labouring class, and although his conservatism and reasonableness often brought down upon him the gibes and innuendoes of crack-brained fanatics and designing rascals he stuck resolutely to this conviction. A scion of a well-to-do family of the substantial middle class, his father being a professor at Stockholm, Branting had attended the University of Uppsala, sciences having been his major study. A position in the Stockholm astronomical observatory had opened to him the way to a distinguished career as an astronomer, but his deep sympathies for the common man and a burning indignation against his powerful exploiters caused him to throw these opportunities aside. In 1886 he became editor of the *Socialdemokraten* and some years later leader of the Socialist Party. A man of tremendous energy and aggressive impulses, he constantly kept himself and party under restraint, insisting rigorously, as stated, upon the principle that only through reason and exercise of their prerogative of the ballot-box could the labouring men win lasting influence and well-being.

Hjalmar Branting. From a painting by Richard Bergh

Labour legislation.—The separate groups of Socialists which had sprung up in the land were organized nationally in 1889. Meanwhile labouring men had organized themselves locally into sick-benefit associations and co-operative buying unions. The former began to receive state aid in 1891 and proper regulations were imposed on both by legislation. A law of 1881 against the employment of minors was supplemented by further legislation in 1900 which extended its protection also to women. Factory inspection was instituted in 1891, and protection was likewise assured workingmen in case of strikes. Accident liability insurance was inaugurated in 1901 and a government arbitration board for the settlement of labour disputes was instituted in 1906. An organization known as a "Society for the property rights of married women" was in 1896 merged with the "Fredrika Bremer Society," the latter founded in 1884 for the purpose of securing a better social and economic position for women through sound and peaceable development. Largely through the influence of this augmented society, a number of laws beneficial to women were passed.

Already in 1870 women had secured admission to the universities and in 1884 the Russian-born Sonja Kovalevsky was appointed professor of mathematics in Stockholm University, the first time in Europe, it is claimed, that a woman received this honour. In 1884 the legal age of unmarried women was lowered from twenty-five to twenty-one. A series of laws was likewise passed which guaranteed to married women a greater degree of financial independence. The right to vote in communal elections gave her a voice in the selection of members in the first chamber of the Riksdag. This was only indirectly, through her right to vote for members of the *landsting* or city councils, which in turn elected members of the first chamber. Her ambition was now directed to the right to vote for members also of the second chamber. Not until the next reign was she, however, to gain any further extension in her franchise rights.

The economic changes which took place in the reign of Oscar II, though not startlingly manifest, were revolutionary in character. These changes were associated with economic and social life in all civilized countries, but the traditional views of the limitations of natural resources and national lack of enterprise in Sweden make her extraordinary progress seem the more impressive.

Railroads and telephones.—Railroads were built to the iron-ore regions in Lappland and central Sweden, thus affording transportation facilities for their valuable products. The rich ore district of central Sweden was tapped by a private line, *Bergslagarnes järnväg,* built between the years 1875 and 1879. By 1902 the state railway line had been extended to the northern boundary of the country and thence to Narvik in Norway; whence shipments could proceed by steamer to any port. At an earlier date a line had been built to Luleå on the Gulf of Bothnia which carried most of the ore destined for the German market. The story of the building of these lines in the Far North constitutes one of the great epics of railroad enterprises. Direct railroad communication with Germany was inaugurated in 1897 by the establishment of a train-ferry between Trelleborg and Sassnitz. With the construction of railroads went the extension of telegraph and telephone lines. Through the inventive and organizing genius of H. T. Cedergren and L. M. Ericksson, Sweden became a leader not only in the completeness and efficiency of her telegraph and telephone service, where she long ranked first among the nations in point of instruments and mileage of wires, in proportion to population (only the United States and Denmark now take pre-eminence over her), but in the manufacture of telephone instruments for foreign export. By 1907 no less than 670,000 Swedish-made telephones had been exported. Despite the rapid growth of iron-ore exports, Sweden lost her relative rank as an exporter of iron, for while in the eighteenth century she supplied 38 per cent of the world's total of pig-iron, the corresponding figure in 1910 was only 0.9 per cent. Lumber production was given new impetus by the construction of railroads and changes in the industrial system. The value of Swedish lumber exported in 1871 was 84,739,000 crowns, but in 1910 it had risen to 155,000,000 crowns. In 1927 the figure was 817,113,000 for lumber and other wood products, including paper-pulp and paper. The annual output of matches at the end of Oscar's reign was approximately 16,000,000 crowns, whereas in 1928 the output of the Swedish match factories had mounted to 44,411,000 crowns, not counting the production of the subsidiaries of the Swedish Match Company in foreign lands.

The financing of the many industrial enterprises, especially of the privately owned railroads, was made possible by the growth and solidarity of various stock companies, whose operations were controlled by wise laws and rigid state supervision. Private banks grew rapidly in number and resources. Depositors in savings banks increased from 727,000 in 1876 to 1,500,000 in 1907, with aggregate deposits mounting from 143,000,000 crowns in the former year to 682,000,000 in the latter.

Growth of cities and emigration.—The construction of railroads and extension of the factory industry resulted in a rapid growth of cities. In 1850 Stockholm had 93,000 inhabitants, but by 1907 the number had increased to more than 300,000, while Gothenburg in the same period grew from 26,000 people to 160,000. A set of city ordinances from the year 1874, subsequently supplemented by legislation as the growth of urban centres created new problems, made the Swedish cities models of cleanliness, attractiveness, and safety. The locating of industries in hitherto unimportant communities meant rapid growth in population and wealth of these centres. The movement towards the cities and the drains resulting from emigration caused an actual decrease of population in some rural sections. Emigration, as before stated, was at high tide in the eighties, as agricultural depression, fear of military service, and the allurements of free or cheap land across the seas, the latter greatly augmented by the legion of agents representing American states, railway companies, and colonization associations who visited the land and indulged in their exuberant praises of the New World (pp. 676-677), combined to give impetus to the movement. While the early Swedish immigrants to the United States had settled mainly in the rural regions of the Mississippi Valley and had taken a prominent part in the process of converting this section into the leading agricultural district in the world,[5] a marked change in the trend of Swedish emigration was noticeable about the turn of the century. The emigrants were now mainly industrial workers who preferred to locate in the great cities and factory towns on the Atlantic border.

While the great outpouring of emigrants from Sweden suggests that the resources of the country were inadequate or not properly utilized for sustaining the growing population according to standards below which the Swedes shrank from descending, it also points to a remarkable spirit of enterprise and courage in the race. The trials of the journey to a new land and of early life in the wilderness tested their stamina to the limit. The tremendous burdens which they heroically carried in the work of clearing the wilderness to make place for fields, building railroads, and in developing factory industry affords incontestable proof of their virility and ambition. That those who remained at home were no less virile, intelligent, and progressive is amply proved by the remarkable intellectual and economic development which Sweden herself has experienced since the great exodus of her people. This development can unquestionably, in a measure, be ascribed to the

[5] It has been estimated that the total acreage of land which they have cleared for cultivation in the aggregate amounts to 10,000,000 acres. Johnson, Amandus, *Swedish Contributions to the United States,* N. Y., 1922.

influence of the transplanted kinsmen themselves. In the New World they were quick to adopt new and practical methods of work and to absorb its spirit of democracy, especially as this expressed itself in respect for any form of honest toil, and in casting aside of class distinctions. This experience has clearly reacted powerfully and in a beneficent manner on the homeland. Besides, the 10,000,000 crowns which the Swedes in America on an average have annually sent their kinsmen in the old country have assuredly not been an inconsequential item in improving living conditions there.[6] The widespread dissatisfaction with conditions in their own country which was bred of the fantastic and generally exaggerated statements regarding the ease with which wealth could be acquired in America, which emigrants sent home through countless letters, and the consequent confusion and unrest caused in Sweden, however, offset many of the blessings which the Swedes in America conferred on their native land. Here is to be found one of the main reasons why Swedish nationalism sank to its lowest ebb in the last decades of the century as reflected in the merciless castigation of the existing order in Sweden by Strindberg and other realists.

Since it had long been evident to thoughtful men that emigration had been a serious drain upon the country, the Swedes organized a movement for checking it. Its primary aim was to remove the incentive for emigration by creating favourable economic conditions at home. This could best be done by making land available to a greater number, and through the influence mainly of "the National Association Opposed to Emigration" which in 1912 had 12,000 members, legislation was adopted for opening up new areas for farming, dividing large estates, and making long-time loans possible to would-be farmers at a low rate of interest.

Better times.—Factory industry and emigration caused the relative numerical rank of the agricultural class to sink at

[6] In a measure at least these sums have offset the amounts of money which Swedish immigrants have carried with them into the United States. Dr. Babcock estimates that on an average each immigrant had $50 on arriving in the New World. On the debit side, from the viewpoint of the United States, should also be set the money which Sweden had spent in educating the immigrants who left her in their productive ages. Babcock, Kendric C., "The Scandinavian Element in the United States," University of Illinois, *Studies in Social Sciences*, Vol. 3, No. 3, 1914.

a rate which seemed alarming: in 1870 the tillers of the soil embraced 72 per cent of the population but in 1900 only 54.4 per cent. Aside from certain periods of depression, especially prior to the imposition of customs duties, the status of the *bönder* was materially improved during King Oscar's reign. Industry provided new and profitable markets, labour-saving machinery lightened the burdens on the farms, and increased production and sales of timber gave substantial incomes to many. The earlier era of lumber manufacturing was marked by shameless frauds upon unsophisticated *bönder,* who did not realize the value of their growing timber, by soulless corporations who sent oily-tongued agents among them who, in behalf of their principals, bought holdings worth millions for a mere pittance. Enlightenment and remedial legislation in time almost stopped this form of exploitation. Improvements in agricultural methods and an almost complete reorganization of the industry itself was, however, the chief factor in raising the level of rural prosperity. The epochal invention of the cream separator by the Swedish engineer, Gustaf de Laval, revolutionized the dairy industry throughout the world and for Sweden it meant a growth of exports of butter from 6,000,000 crowns in 1872 to 44,500,000 in 1896. The co-operative idea took rapid hold and co-operative buying and selling organizations sprang into existence everywhere. A new industry—namely, sugar production—assumed an unexpected importance. In the period 1871-1880 Swedish annual output of sugar had been about 1,000 tons, but in the period 1901-1905 it was annually more than 100,000 tons. The importation of sugar had in the latter period become an insignificant item.

The Church.—The status of the state Church had been greatly changed by the reorganization of the Riksdag in 1866. Deprived of the power and prestige which membership in the assembly and control of one of its four votes had conferred, the clergy no longer held a commanding place in the political affairs of the nation nor did it any longer hold a unique supremacy in the field of knowledge. Dissenters were free to join other groups or remain outside of religious associations, as they saw fit. It was inevitable that the new situation compelled the ancient and honoured institution to adjust itself to the new order of things. The leading men of the Church became more and more imbued with the idea that unselfish service for the religious and moral upbuilding of the nation, and not the exercise of political power or meddling with such mundane things as taxes, waterways, military preparedness, was the primary function of her servants. As leading exponents of this exalted conception, in the latter part of the former and the first part of the present century, may be mentioned the pious and learned professor of theology at Uppsala, Waldemar Rudin, the enthusiastic and eloquent Bishop of Karlstad, J. A. Eklund, the eloquent and courageous Frederick Fehr, a noted preacher of Stockholm. To an increasing degree the Church began to direct her attention to missionary activities and to the care of the sick and destitute. Missionaries were sent for the first time to India and South Africa in 1874, and the training of deaconesses and building and maintenance of hospitals were increasingly stressed.

Schools.—Impressive evidence of the growth of educational facilities during the period is offered by the statistical records showing that the number of primary schools (*folkskolor*) increased from 8,000 in 1870 to 14,000 in 1907, the teachers from 9,000 to 18,000, while annual state and local appropriations for education were in the latter year five times that of the former. The desire to afford opportunities for a more practical training and to create interest in the handicrafts art led in 1874 to the establishment of the famous Nääs Slöjd Institute by A. Abrahamson. This institution has ever since remained the world's foremost school for manual training, and its influence has been universal in extent. Students from more than forty countries have here been matriculated for longer or shorter periods. The annual appropriations for the national universities rose fivefold during the period, handsome buildings for class-room and administrative purposes were built both at Uppsala and Lund, new professorships were established, a salary scale adopted, and provision made for a generous retiring allowance for professors at the age of sixty-five. New institutions were established for training in pharmacy, forestry, and dentistry. The Stockholm High School and the Gothenburg High School, institutions of university rank, but having only the departments of science and jurisprudence, were founded.

The Nobel prizes.—A unique and highly distinguished position as promoter of scientific and literary achievement came to be held by Sweden through the inauguration of the Nobel prizes, made possible by the magnificent gift of 31,400,000 crowns by Alfred Nobel (1833-1896), a noted Swedish engineer, the inventor of dynamite and, in conjunction with two brothers, founder of the great oil industry at Baku on the Black Sea. From his great bequest 300,000 crowns were set aside for the Nobel Institute for Scientific Research and 900,000 crowns for a building and equipment for the Nobel Foundation in Stockholm. The interest on the remainder was, according to the will of the testator, to be paid annually in equal amounts to those who, during the immediately preceding year, had "conferred the greatest benefit on mankind." Five prizes of approximately 165,000 crowns each (approximately $45,000) have since the beginning of the Foundation been given annually with a few interruptions, *e.g.* during the World War, in physics, chemistry, medicine, literature, and for notable achievement in behalf of international peace. In the two first-named fields the award is made by the Swedish Academy of Science, the literature prize by the Swedish Academy, for medicine by the Carolina Medical Institute, and the peace prize by a committee of the Norwegian Storthing, the latter

Alfred Nobel

arrangement being due to Nobel's belief that the Norwegians were more pacific and less subject to international entanglements, and thus more competent to make decisions in this field without bias. The prizes awarded by the Swedish institutions are annually distributed at Stockholm on December 10, the anniversary of the death of Nobel, and the event each year attracts the attention of the civilized world. These prizes still remain the most substantial and honourable gifts bestowed by any country upon the great benefactors of mankind.

Explorers; Nordenskiöld.—Exploring expeditions of momentous importance, which were financed and led by Swedes, added great lustre to the reign of Oscar II. The king himself took keen interest in all enterprises for the extension of geographical knowledge and generously gave from his own private means to support them. He was one of the chief financial backers of Fridtjof Nansen's expedition in search of the North Pole in 1893-96 and the ill-fated venture of S. A. Andrée and his companions in 1897 to reach the Pole by balloon received his support. A. E. Nordenskiöld (1832-1901) and Sven Hedin (1865-), two of the outstanding men in the world's galaxy of explorers from the days of Marco Polo to the present time, could especially count on the king's generous support. The former was born in Finland, but had settled in Sweden after his irrepressible spirit of independence had made him *persona non grata* with the Russian officials of his native land. He had in youth received a thorough technical training, and practical experience had come to him in several expeditions to the Arctic Ocean. Ardent love of adventure and keen scientific interest were harmoniously blended in him. On his sturdy ship *Vega* he, together with twenty-nine companions, set out in 1878 on an expedition whose objective was the penetration of the Northeast Passage of the Polar Sea from west to east, during which the areas along the course were to be mapped and scientific observations made.[7] Preparations for the journey were made with scientific foresight, particular care being exer-

[7] Besides King Oscar, the wealthy Gothenburg merchant, Oscar Dickson, and the Russian, Alexander Sibiriakov, helped in financing the Vega expedition. The latter, now a man past seventy, lost his entire fortune in the Russian revolution, was exiled, and lived in dire want. The Swedish Riksdag then voted him a substantial annual pension in appreciation of the service he had, in his days of prosperity, rendered a Swedish enterprise.

cised in the selection of foods, and throughout the cruise scrupulous cleanliness was exercised in order to avoid the diseases which hitherto had been the scourge of polar expeditions.

Adolf Erik Nordenskiöld

According to the calculations of Nordenskiöld, open water would be found near the coast and he therefore selected his course near the mainland. His calculations proved correct and steady progress was made until a point only a few miles from Bering Strait was reached. Here progress was blocked by ice which held the *Vega* bound for almost a year; a few hours' earlier arrival at the point would have enabled them to proceed without delay. In July 1879 the extreme eastern point of Asia was passed and an enterprise that during centuries had beckoned the most intrepid of explorers was successfully completed. Nordenskiöld's journey from this point on, during which he touched Japan, China, India, and the Mediterranean lands, became a veritable triumphal procession, culminating in the magnificent ovations that met him and his men on their return to Stockholm in April 1880. Not only had the intrepid courage of Nordenskiöld and his men thrilled the world, and the ingenious organization on board the ship for insuring the safety of the men given most valuable object-lessons to subsequent explorers, but a vast amount of valuable scientific knowledge was gained as a result of the expedition.

Sven Hedin.—A glance at maps of Asia dating back four or five decades reveals vast white areas indicating that at the time these had not been explored and mapped. Modern maps, on the other hand, give names and location of rivers, mountain ranges, and communities. It is to Sven Hedin, more than to any other individual, that the world owes a debt of gratitude for making these hitherto uncharted regions known. In Thibet he discovered one of the largest inland seas on the globe and along the mighty Lop-nor River, which flows for a thousand miles through a desert region, buried Chinese cities were unearthed which revealed an ancient and remarkable culture. His most notable achievement was, however, the discovery of the sources of the Brahmaputra and Indus rivers and the mighty chain of mountains north of India to which the name Transhimalaya was given.

The lure of the unknown led another Swedish scientist of this period, Oscar Montelius (1843-1921), to explore a second field which was largely uncharted land when he began his epochal researches. The innumerable remains from remote ages which the earth has yielded held a strange fascination for him, and through his erudition, keen power of observation, and painstaking care the science of archæology was placed on a new plane. His genius wrested many secrets from the obscure past. As Swedish state antiquarian he spent a lifetime in unearthing, studying, and organizing archæological remains not only in his own country but in practically all the countries of Europe and in north Africa. By a careful comparison of types he was able to evolve a chronology for archæological epochs

Sven Hedin

which has since been accepted by practically all scholars in the field.

Gloom and criticism.—Many writers and artists added lustre to a reign made remarkable by great material and social progress and scientific achievements. The literary men and women of the period were, as a rule, coldly and severely critical of the existing order, which they found wrong in almost every respect, but on the other hand they were sustained by a naïve optimism that their attacks on the old and the proclamation of new truths would soon set right that which was awry. Dis-

Oscar Montelius

illusionments and disappointments had indeed been many. At an earlier day the poet Carl Snoilsky had joyfully sung:

I bring wine and roses
The young wine I pour;
On all paths, along all walks,
I beat the resounding tambourine;

but later, as the failure of society to realize the millennium which it was fondly believed the triumph of liberal thought would create, he exclaimed despairingly:

> "I, the restless heir to culture's treasure, natural son of an age in which Science invents new bombs."

The reasons for this attitude are apparent. Many of the conditions which bred a gloomy pessimism and reckless criticism of society were world-wide in extent, but some special factors served to augment and intensify disappointment and gloom in Sweden. Startling deductions of the great scientists of the period had caused many of the ancient and cherished beliefs to topple and other traditional beliefs and opinions were seriously threatened. The materialistic doctrines of Karl Marx sowed the seeds of discontent everywhere. Men no longer knew what to believe and this uncertainty was by no means conducive to a tranquillity of mind which ordinary human beings desire. The tragic ending of Denmark's struggle to preserve her integrity, the brutal attacks which two giants like Prussia and Austria made on the little nation, had filled with bitter anguish the minds of those who had hoped that justice and brotherly love would hold sway in a world in which liberal ideas had triumphed. Acclaiming France as the bearer of a great culture and of modern liberal ideas, and viewing Prussia as the embodiment of militarism and cold self-seeking, the Swedish liberals had been dismayed at the defeat of the former in the war of 1870-71. The constant and acrimonious bickerings growing out of the union with Norway, and the increasing conviction that this union was destined to end in failure, helped to fill the measure of Swedish woe to overflowing. It had become evident to the Swedes that the military and political advantages of the union were practically *nil*, but national honour forbade them to let go. When they yielded they were derided as timid and afflicted with a guilty conscience, and when, on the other hand, they made a show of firmness they were decried as reactionary oppressors of the weak. The Norwegians had become adept at garrulousness and innuendo and the Swedes were hurt to the quick by the constant attacks. The greatest disappointment came, however, from the failure of the new organization of the Riksdag to bring about the ideal condition that the majority had anticipated. To the idealists of the earlier decades everything had seemed perfectly simple and easy; given the mechanism through which the people could express their will, justice and concord would be immediately enthroned. Instead of this tranquil and happy situation, the nation had found the group interests asserting themselves as selfishly and aggressively as ever before; the Agrarian Party (p. 709), which at once was organized, following the reorganization act, had pressed for legislation solely, it was felt, in the interest of one class, and the social cleft appeared as wide as ever. Emigration was another factor in creating the general state of gloom and despondency which had gripped the nation. Their own cold and rock-bound land seemed miserable in comparison to America, and while at home class distinctions and mean selfishness seemed to have wrecked all concord and amity, multitudes of letters came from friends who had gone to the land of promise telling how there complete equality and a dominant spirit of friendship and helpfulness made life sweet and enjoyable. The habit of maligning the native country became common and expressed itself in very disagreeable ways. Meanwhile the tide of emigration flowed unceasingly on.

In this atmosphere of discontent and despondency the realistic literature of the eighties flourished abundantly; the bitter critics of society found plenty of material for their dismal tales and a public eager to listen. While one may deplore the unreasonableness of these critics, it is well to remember that there was much cause for complaint, that unquestionably their attacks, on the whole, aided in eradicating or mitigating many evils.

The titanic hate and brilliant powers of the man who became the very incarnation of the protests against the existing order gave a peculiarly acrid tone to the attack. This man was August Strindberg (1849-1912). Anyone who undertakes to summarize his opinions, as expressed in his works, will find the task a baffling one indeed. His productivity and versatility were unbelievably great. Keeping at the task steadily eight hours a day, a person reading aloud all of Strindberg's works would require two years to finish it.[8] His writings dealt with almost every imaginable subject. He was a poet and author of short stories, and Sweden has not yet seen his equal as a creator of imaginative plays and historical dramas. His thoughts and sentiments ran the gamut from the crassest materialism to the fervid mysticism of Swedenborgian speculation and Catholic theology. Amidst all vacillating and shifting opinion he always remained a severe critic of society and fearlessly frank in attacking what he believed to be fraud.

Early influences in the life of Strindberg.—Much of Strindberg's misanthropy had its genesis in the distressing experiences of childhood and youth, much of it had a pathological basis. In *The Bondwoman's Son* he has, with brutal frankness, laid bare all the sordid elements which entered into his early experiences. His home was far from affluent, the large family being crowded into squalid quarters, and the struggle of the parents to provide for all was hard and enervating. As a child, Strindberg was supersensitive, and harsh reprimands cut him to the quick. His mother's failure, as he imagined, to understand or sympathize with him gave him great anguish. His alert and rebellious mind reacted violently against dogmatic platitudes, as he considered almost everything to be which teachers in the elementary and secondary schools taught their pupils. The humility which acknowledges one's own shortcomings and tries to see some good in others was never one of Strindberg's outstanding virtues. Practically every view which he once held he abandoned, without deeming it necessary to give reasons for his change of heart, and he manifested the same degree of cock-sureness after every new shift. Poverty helped to intensify the bitterness which unsympathetic and pedantic professors had done their part to create, and he soon turned his back on the university which he attended a few terms. His early experiences in the tedious business of earning a living brought to his hypochondriac mind the conviction that the social order was badly out of joint and sadly in need of repair. First of all the old and time-worn must be scrapped.

The iconoclast.—The radical, the man who dared to make war on deceit and iniquity, to tear down everything, was in his

[8] Björkman, E., *Voices of To-morrow,* New York, 1913, p. 42.

eyes the hero. In his first great work, *Master Olof* (*Mäster Olof*), the reformer Olaus Petri fills this rôle. While floundering at times, and seeing with dim spiritual vision, his courage often failing him, Olaus Petri wills to break the power of entrenched evil and this makes him great. All Strindberg's concentrated hatred of society he poured forth in *The Red Room* (*Röda rummet*), with which literary realism rose to complete supremacy for a time in Sweden. It is a breezy and brilliant sketch of a group of carefree artists, vagabonds of Stockholm, who snapped their fingers in derision at all things respectable and conventional. In language that throughout scintillates with brilliant thrusts, he exposes the alleged fraud and hypocrisy of lazy and pompous officials, men of big business, journalists, and servants of the Church. The flashes of humour, the evident feeling of sympathy for the so-called failures of life, the brilliant style reveal unmistakable influences of both Dickens and Mark Twain.[9] This attack was soon followed by another broadside, *The New Kingdom* (*Det nya riket*), in which with bitter scorn he denounces the grandiloquent falsifications, as he considers them, of the teachings of Swedish history; he rakes, fore and aft, the small men who have been made heroes and the mediocrities who have been placed on pedestals of honour. The discussion which these works provoked became extremely bitter, made doubly so, no doubt, by the national propensity towards seriousness and extreme thoroughness in all things. The shocking brutality and unseemly intolerance of Strindberg, as manifested in these works, cannot obscure the brilliance of their style and the evident sincerity of the author. The provocations to anger were undoubtedly great and many. There can be no doubt that some good came from Strindberg's bitter tirades, but on the other hand one must not forget that the attacks were often most unjust, and their ruthlessness caused much dissension and anguish.

The woman question and Strindberg.—While Strindberg wrote the most bitter denunciations of certain perverted types of women and denounced the woman's emancipation movement of his day, the charge that he was the woman hater incarnate is hardly justified. He could claim that the best

[9] Björkman, *Voices of To-morrow,* p. 48.

friend is not the one who flatters and prattles glibly that all is well, but he who speaks frankly and fearlessly that which he believes to be the truth, and Strindberg, no doubt, honestly believed that certain modern tendencies in the relations of the sexes were evil and boded ill for the future of society. His soul revolted against the glorification of woman and emphasis of her right to seek selfishly her own happiness, even though it meant desertion of husband and children, which Ibsen's *Doll's House* had made a sort of cult. In Sweden, certain women writers had shortly before made malicious attacks on the male of the species; there was no type of deviltry which these women writers had not charged against him: brutality, selfishness, dishonesty, and lying being his most glaring faults. The most representative of this type of woman writers were Anna Charlotte Leffler (1849-1892) and Viktoria Benedictsson (1850-1888) (pseudonym, Ernst Ahlgren). Questions of love and marriage absorbed practically all their interests. Swedish society was still dominated by the view that woman as the weaker sex should refrain from entering professions which hitherto had been man's prerogative, that it was his right and his duty to exercise wardship over her, and all tendencies on her part to break down the old obstacles and enter new paths were supposed to be effectively checked by the charge of "unfeminine." The perversity of man was chiefly responsible, these women writers averred, for the failure of marriage to bring happiness to woman and the fact that after he had wrecked the peace and joy of married life he should deny to woman the right to enter into professional or business careers made his attitude doubly reprehensible. Typical of Anna Charlotte Leffler's books may be taken *A Summer Tale* (*En sommar saga*), in which the heroine, a woman with artistic talents, marries a man who is brusque, impulsive, and frank. Conflicts are inevitable and the young woman finally goes her own way. In *Money* (*Pengar*), Viktoria Benedictsson paints with lurid colours a man who deceives his invalid wife and adds to her humiliation by compelling her to witness his love-affairs with others.

Strindberg's reaction against these attacks found its violent expression mainly in three works, *Married* (*Giftas*), a collection of short stories, and the two short dramas, *The Father* (*Fadern*), and *Miss Julia* (*Fröken Julia*). Particularly the second part of *Married* is a brilliantly written but utterly coarse and heartless attack upon the marriage institution. Technically *The Father* is perhaps the most brilliant thing that Strindberg ever wrote, but it is hideous in its frank unfolding of the bitter struggle that goes on between the sexes. Laura, the mother, in her determination to thwart the will of her husband and in order to cause his undoing, insinuates that he is not the father of the child of the family, and the heartless struggle wrecks the man. In the struggle of the sexes, woman, according to Strindberg, when driven to extremes will sacrifice everything, and convention, customs, and dictates of chivalry give her a tremendous and undue advantage. From the discussion of the woman's question, Strindberg turned to the writing of fantastic symbolic plays which reveal how far he had now wandered into the land of the mystical and the occult. His historical plays remain, however, his greatest bequest to the Swedish people. In his portrayal, kings like Gustavus Vasa, Gustavus Adolphus, and Gustavus III become human beings, men of flesh and blood, weak at times and full of vagaries, it is true, but great nevertheless, because they willed to do great things.

Geijerstam; Levertin; Fröding.—One of the gloomiest realistic writers is Gustaf av Geijerstam (1859-1909), who, like Strindberg, is constantly on the war-path against traditional beliefs and institutions. In *Erik Grane*, a frank and realistic account of the experiences of a student at Uppsala who casts aside the ideals of early youth, the entire view of life which the university has been fostering is scathingly arraigned. In *Pastor Hallin*, the author deals with the problem of the student who enters the service of the Church out of gratitude to his parents who have sacrificed much for him, but feels inward doubt regarding the biblical and rational foundation of many of the tenets that he must subscribe to and promulgate. Hypocrisy in religion, affirmation of religious faith merely in order to ingratiate oneself with the simple-minded, and the use of the Church as a means for securing a livelihood are denounced. Geijerstam shows more psychological insight than any of his

Swedish contemporary writers, and his sympathies are always with the poverty-stricken and suffering.

The reaction against the merciless realists of the eighties was not long in arriving; the very vehemence of the attack soon wearied both the attackers and the attacked. The futility of trying to find a solution to all questions and to set everything aright at once became apparent; after all, this is not a perfect world and there is need of much mutual kindly consideration between sexes and classes. Oscar Levertin (1862-1906), the most versatile and sound literary critic of the period, protested against the eternal harping on the faults of woman, saying that woman hatred is equivalent to a hatred of one's own and of all life. Levertin must also be ranked as one of the prominent poets of Sweden and he wrote some novels of great merit. Gustaf Fröding (1860-1911), the incomparable lyricist, sang in genial mood of the trivial tribulations of home and married life; to their infinite relief, the Swedes discovered that they could laugh again. In Fröding appears the genial good-humor, keen appreciation of the ludicrous, dislike for cant, and phenomenal rhythmic power which have given Bellman his enduring popularity. That some unpleasant things must be borne patiently, that sacrifice and an unwavering determination to perform a given duty, even though this entails the surrender of happiness itself, is emphasized as the very essence of the heroic by Verner von Heidenstam (1859-), poet and novelist, recipient of the Nobel Prize in Literature, and member of the Swedish Academy.

Heidenstam.—Heidenstam belonged to an aristocratic and well-to-do family. As a youth he was frail in health and therefore was compelled to spend most of his time in the milder climes of south Europe and Asia Minor. His first collection of poems, *The Years of Pilgrimage and Wanderings* (*Vallfarts och vandrings år*), are warm with the sunshine and carefree moods of the Southland, and came as a happy elixir to a nation made fairly sick by discussion and fault-finding. The aristocratic youth, to whom in early years had been given the opportunity to dwell in the great cultural centres of Europe and in the sunny climes of the Southland, became the most eloquent interpreter of the heroic in the life of his own Northern land.

No man has sought more than he to rally his countrymen to a consciousness of their great traditions and of their solemn duty to achieve great things in science, art, and literature. His *Charles' men* (*Karolinerna*), gives a series of gripping sketches of the devoted followers of Charles XII, who, although they suffered incredible hardships, did not flinch nor whine, but bore with fortitude the evils which Providence permitted to come upon them. Warmth of feeling and abounding native humor have permeated the genial songs which E. A. Karlfeldt (1864-1931) has composed with motifs from his rustic native province, Dalarna. Per Hallström (1866-), while originally preparing himself for technical work, which in course of time gave him two years' sojourn in a factory in Chicago, a sore trial for his idealism, but not entirely destructive of it, ranks as one of the leading writers of the period. Genial characterization and brilliant portrayal of the striking aspects of nature in Norrland appear in his *The Dead Falls* (*Döda Fallet*), while his *Straying Birds* (*Vilsna fåglar*) sympathetically deals with the unfortunates who have not been able to attain to success, according to the commonly accepted meaning of the term, in this bewildering world. There is a sombre tone running through practically all of his later works.

Selma Lagerlöf.—It was, however, reserved for a woman, Selma Lagerlöf, to break completely the spell which stern realism had cast over the Swedes and again make literature a vehicle for cheering romanticism and the medium through which unbounded joy in contact with nature and with human beings could express itself freely. Born in 1858 in the idyllic homeland of poets, Värmland, Selma Lagerlöf had in childhood drunk her fill of the weird tales of bold cavaliers and fair women which have been born and have thrived in that picturesque land. As she reached maturity the resolve was born in her mind to write the story of these delightfully interesting people. In the belief that the matter-of-fact, cold, and analytical method of realism, then in vogue, must of necessity be followed, if she was to receive a hearing, she tortured her soul for years trying to write soberly and critically, but thoughts and words simply would not come. After some years she had completed only two chapters. A farewell visit to her beloved parental estate, Mårbacka, which had to be sold, since her father, who had died, had found greater delight in music, literature, and the comradeship of boon companions than in managing his estate, quickened her resolve to write as it pleased her to write, no matter whether anyone would care for her story or not. Now her pen fairly flew over the paper, and the story *Gösta Berling* was born. This reveals a cross-section of life in Värmland in the second decade of the nineteenth century and is aquiver with life and action. The frailties of poor mortals are depicted with a sympathetic touch. The delightful element which appears in all of Selma Lagerlöf's works and largely accounts for her popularity, is her irrepressible optimism. Her insight into the workings of the human mind has the directness and genius of intuition and the glories of nature stand revealed to her as to few mortals.

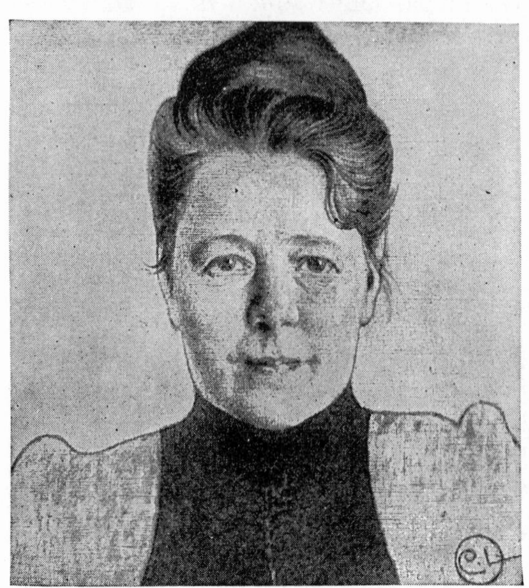

Selma Lagerlöf. From a painting by Carl Larsson

Her contribution to literature and life has been momentous, for she had again enthroned romanticism and idealism, but her characters are nevertheless as true to life as those of the most sombre realist. Her greatest work, *Jerusalem,* the grand epic of the God-fearing, hardy *bönder* of Dalarna who left their native home and emigrated to the Holy Land in the hope that there they could more easily than elsewhere "walk in His footsteps," must be conceded to be one of the most remarkable prose productions of recent decades. In other notable works like *The Story of a Manor* (*En herrgårdssägen*), *Invisible Links* (*Osynliga länkar*), *The Queens of Kungahälla* (*Drottningarne i Kungahälla*), *The*

Girl from the Marsh Croft (*Stormyrstösen*) the authoress has revealed her inimitable power of story-telling. *The Emperor of Portugallia* (*Kejsaren av Portugallien*) is a gripping story of parental love and cruel tragedy which comes from a child's ingratitude and waywardness. *The Outcast* (*Bannlyst*), appearing before a war-mad world in 1918, is an eloquent attack on war as an institution; *The Wonderful Story of Nils* (*Nils Holgerssons underbara resa*) is unique among books, for in the form of engaging allegory the author gives a description of the physical aspect of her own land and weaves into the story the delightful legends and tales which are a part of the nation's heritage. Unusual honours have come to Selma Lagerlöf, for in 1909 she received the Nobel Prize in Literature and five years later she became a member of the Swedish Academy, the only woman to attain this honour since the noble institution was founded almost one hundred and fifty years ago.

Ellen Key.—Extreme individualism was the ideal of Ellen Key (1849-1926), who gained an international reputation because of her radical views and able espousal of them. Her books have been translated into most of the European languages. Ellen Key championed the rights of woman vigorously, maintaining that she has the right to develop and exercise her individuality as freely as man. She maintained, however, that neither woman nor society in general can be benefitted by the exercise of woman's suffrage. By natural endowment woman is, she believes, restricted to certain spheres and these are found mainly in social and domestic activities. Miss Key's views on love, marriage, and the education of children were in many respects radical and aroused vehement opposition. Love, she asserted, is the only factor that can give sanctity to the marriage relation. In the education of the child she would discard strict discipline and instead permit its unfolding life to develop freely, except as guided by example and gentle precept.

Swedish art.—Swedish art, like the national literature, gave evidence in this era of a remarkable virility and originality. The thrilling memories of the nation's great past, the fascinating aspects of the Swedish landscape, and the innocent joys of home and family became its dominant motifs. The earlier masterpieces of the period reflect the moods which gave such a sombre tone to the realistic writers of the eighties. In such gripping pictures as "Erik XIV, Karin Månsdotter, and Göran Persson," and "Karin Månsdotter visiting Erik in Prison," Gustaf von Rosen (1843-1923), son of the early railroad builder, combines in masterly fashion the historical and the appealingly human elements into one. A portrait of the philosopher Pontus Vikner shows the furrowed countenance of a thinker, who restlessly searches for knowledge and whose soul is torn by suffering. His portraits of Charles XV and Oscar II show clearly the intellectuality of the two rulers. His weird painting, "The Sphinx," a finely moulded head of a woman, set upon the body of a wild beast, paints in unforgettable colours the sinister alliance of the fair and the inhuman. Julius·Kronberg's (1850-1921) work is resplendent with luscious colours and aglow with life. The chief representatives of his work are found in the ceiling decoration of the royal palace, as "Svea," "Aurora," and the "Ascension of the Soul." Nils Forsberg (1842-) emphasized historical scenes, the best known of his paintings being "A Hero's Death" and "Gustavus Adolphus before the Battle of Lützen." The despair that may grip a nation, the failure of earthly hopes, is nowhere more graphically revealed than in Gustaf Cederström's "The Funeral Procession of Charles XII." The sad procession of his few tattered and grim soldiers carrying the body of the dead king on a litter down the snowy path of a Norwegian mountainside is graphically symbolic of the end of Sweden's dream of political and military greatness. "The Sacking of Visby," a monumental canvas by Carl Gustaf Hellquist (1851-1890), depicts in vivid detail the dramatic incident when King Waldemar exacted heavy tribute from the proud Hanseatic city (p. 163).

The artists, like the writers, began towards the end of the eighth decade to feel the quickening impulses of new ideas. A group of painters called "The Opponents" drew inspiration from the throbbing life that lay revealed everywhere; fields and meadows, homes and factories, the stately forests and their bird and animal population, the glow of twilight, the mystic light of a summer night, were painted in delicate and alluring colours. The early leader of this group was Ernest

Josephson (1851-1906), whose innovations in Swedish art made his contributions epochal in influence. Golden tones, rich deep colours, romantic backgrounds, and modern restlessness are seen in his canvases. His "The Water Sprite" and "The Nix" are based upon ancient superstitions, but the irrepressible longing for the truth and ability to make it articulate reveal modern tones. Richard Bergh (1858-1919) was a profound thinker and the consummate artist stands revealed in his best production, "A Northern Summer Evening." The mystical light and shadows, complete stillness and unruffled happiness, are here traced with remarkable delicacy of touch and exquisite colouring. The weird light that faintly illumines the northern skies on summer nights, the mystic pagan feeling that still pulsates in the revival of ancient customs, the enchanting beauty that dwells in mountains and fields, have been charmingly portrayed by Karl Nordström (1855-1923). A notable group of Swedish painters includes such universally known and admired men as Carl Larsson (1855-1919), Anders Zorn (1860-1920), Bruno Liljefors (1860-), and Prince Eugène (1866-). An abounding joy of life, a keen perception of its innocent and humorous aspects, gives the paintings and sketches of Carl Larsson their special charm. Especially well known are his pictures of the delightful children of his own happy household. Carl Larsson is pre-eminently the painter of the home and he stands supreme as the painter of little folks. Romanticism always held him under its spell and he enriched the nation's art treasure by a number of monumental frescoes which are resplendent with colours. These portray notable events or great leaders in the nation's history. The best known among these is the "Entry of Gustavus Vasa into Stockholm." Bruno Liljefors has no peer anywhere as a painter of animal life. Close contact with nature is a passion with him and he has in remarkable fashion caught the form and the moods of the denizens of forests and lakes. Zorn was undoubtedly the master among painters in his day and generation. His astounding versatility in finding the essential in everything and ability to conjure upon the canvas individuals aglow with life and health are astonishing. Folk life in his own cherished Dalarna became one of his favourite motifs, and as a portrait painter he attained to an international prominence which perhaps no other man has held in recent decades. Prince Eugène shows a highly decorative quality in his art. He remains unsurpassed as the painter of the lyrical elements of that most enchanting aspect of nature, the northern summer night.

Further strain on the Swedish-Norwegian union.— The Swedish-Norwegian union continually provoked controversies during the reign of Oscar, and these assumed a more bitter character as years passed, until the weak bonds that held the two countries together were severed completely. The constant bickering and more particularly the final break caused the noble monarch the most poignant grief of his life. The inability and unwillingness of the two nations to understand each other's character and motives were driving the wedge deeper between them. The period was the heyday of Norwegian nationalism, while, on the contrary, Swedish national sentiment reached its nadir. Norwegian writers like Ibsen, Björnson, and Jonas Lie were past masters in the art of infusing enthusiastic appreciation of their country's greatness into the hearts of their countrymen. Ibsen, the giant among Norwegian dramatists, stressed the truth with all vigour that he is the strongest who stands alone and puts implicit trust in his own powers. The courage to strive towards a great achievement, no matter how weaker souls may fear and fret, was to him one of the great virtues. In his delightful tales of Norwegian country folks, Björnson pictured the sturdiness and the innate idealism of his countrymen, past and present, and gave to his nation a new conception of its dignity and its rights. Björnson was a born agitator, impulsive, reckless, eloquent, and he spent a good deal of time traveling about the country denouncing the union in unmeasured terms. Jonas Lie has had few equals as a story-teller. In his descriptions of the impressive aspects of nature in the Northland and portrayal of the innermost thoughts and emotions of his people, he brought into relief, as never before, the natural beauties of the country and the wealth of imagination and honest purpose of the nation.

The process of driving nails into the coffin which was to serve at the obsequies of the union thus went steadily on, although the separate blows might come at irregular intervals. In 1884, Sverdrup, leader of the Norwegian Left Party, forced the king to sanction the parliamentary system of government in Norway, whereby practically absolute power became vested in the Storthing. Some years afterwards, Norway voted to reduce the military force to be available for the common defence of the two countries to one-third of her total army. This was naturally resented in Sweden, which thus in eventualities would have to bear a disproportional part of the military burden.

The consular question.—The irreconcilable difference of opinion in the two countries regarding the control of foreign affairs was, however, the rock upon which the union ultimately foundered. According to the Act of Union, the two countries were to have a common department of foreign affairs. This placed Norway at a disadvantage, a fact which Sweden had admitted already in the reign of Charles John, and as early as 1839 a committee had been created to find a way to an equitable adjustment. Many committees later wrestled with the problem, but the inequality still existed. Instead of seeking an abrogation of the arrangement by which the two nations operated under a common foreign minister, the Norwegians next proceeded to gain their objective by a flank movement. This took the form of demands for a consular system, entirely free from Swedish interference or control. The arguments in favour of such an arrangement seemed reasonable, and Norway could, on this point, make out a strong case. Her merchant marine, to a great extent built and operated by English capital, had grown until the nation took a leading place, in point of shipping tonnage, among the nations of the world. Swedish shipping interests, on the contrary, were of little consequence, and it therefore seemed fair and consistent with national interests as well as national honour that Norway should have her own consuls. In reality, however, most of the consuls were Norwegians, and nothing has been adduced to prove that in cases where they were Swedes the interests of Norway suffered in any way.

Attempts at agreement.—No one could more ardently desire to find a basis for an amiable settlement of the entire controversy provoked by the union than Oscar II. He remained faithful to the motto which he had chosen at the beginning of his reign, "The welfare of the brother peoples." Mainly because of his interest and initiative, a joint Swedish-Norwegian commission was appointed in 1902 to study the feasibility of inaugurating separate consular service functioning under a common diplomatic control. This suggestion revealed a greater willingness on the part of the Swedes to make concessions than they evinced on former occasions when the matter had been discussed. One reason for this was the fact that Russia was at this time displaying a most sinister activity, her spies operating quite assiduously in the North, and both Swedes and Norwegians were sobered by the fear of Russian aggression. The commission reported in favour of separate consular services, the Swedish prime-minister, Boström himself apparently being in favour of this step, as he thought the Norwegians otherwise might force a complete rupture of the union. After private negotiations had taken place between three members of the Swedish cabinet, including Boström, and five Norwegian cabinet ministers, a joint communiqué was issued which stated that although the Swedish representatives had felt hesitation in sanctioning the proposal for separate consuls, they would not, in the interest of peace, limit the right of Norway to decide for herself on this phase of her foreign interests; only in case she decided to go beyond this and appoint her own minister of foreign affairs would this concession on the part of the Swedes cease. The ensuing debates on the question in the Swedish Riksdag revealed a strong sentiment in favour of conceding to the Norwegians the privilege which now had become the central point of their demands. An amicable separation, if mutual equality could not be attained, was the desideratum of a group which probably included a majority of the Swedish Riksdag. A severe financial stringency at the time in Norway inclined the Norwegians also to moderation and even the hitherto bellicose Björnson counselled moderation. Hagerup now became prime-minister of Norway and by his side stood the aggressive and not overly scrupulous Christian Michelsen. On May 28, 1904, the Hagerup ministry proposed the establishment of superior consular boards in the two countries.

Their relations to the minister of foreign affairs should, it was proposed, be limited to the transmission of information regarding their activity; only in a political crisis were consuls to communicate directly with the foreign office or with legations, but there was no guarantee in the plan that the consuls would abide by orders emanating from these sources. The Swedish ministry was a unit in rejecting this proposal. Boström made the counter-proposal that the foreign office should have a certain control over the consuls of both nations and the right to bring charges against offending consuls before the king; the right of the legations to suspend consuls was also included. The Norwegian ministry in turn rejected this proposal as contrary to the fundamental law of the land. Later it declared, in answer to another Swedish proposal, which went still farther than the former in taking cognizance of Norwegian sensitiveness, that if the Swedes insisted on any control whatsoever over Norwegian consuls all further negotiations would be futile. In its answer to this statement, issued on January 30 (1905), the Swedish ministry made clear the reasons why it could not yield entirely: unity in the control of foreign affairs must at all hazards be maintained; a friendly suggestion in the concluding paragraphs left the door open for further negotiations with a view toward modification of the terms. Immediately the Norwegians answered that they could not discuss the matter further. The king was therefore compelled to declare negotiations at an end, but at the same time he expressed the hope that the union would not be sacrificed. To this latter expression the Norwegian member of the joint Swedish-Norwegian ministry took exception. A wave of indignation was sweeping through Norway and agitators were busy. In vague terms and by innuendo, Boström was accused of breach of faith, no doubt unjustly.[10] "Out of the Union" now resounded throughout Norway. Sigurd Ibsen, the son of the dramatist, and calmer than most of his countrymen, urged that the Storthing decree the union dissolved and then ask Sweden to declare her acquiescence in this resolution. There is good reason for assuming that the Swedes would have agreed to this course, for they were

[10] Documents which might throw light upon some obscure phases of the controversy are still locked up in the state archives, safe from the historian's scrutiny.

heartily tired of the whole wretched affair. But the leaders among the Norwegians could not wait; the plan of Ibsen involved the holding of new elections to the Storthing and this would require time, which they could not afford to lose. Norwegian historians have since frankly admitted that their leaders were forcing the issue in order to get a decision while the good and peace-loving Oscar II was yet alive and before Sweden had had time to push her military preparedness much farther. The attention of the world was furthermore at this time focussed on the war of Russia and Japan. By a skilfully conducted propaganda campaign abroad, the Norwegians had won the opinion of the world to their side. The Swedes had up to this time almost completely neglected to carry on any propaganda in order to gain a favourable world opinion.

Michelsen now became prime-minister in Norway and events moved rapidly to their conclusion. Boström felt that his unpopularity in Norway made him useless for further negotiations, and he therefore resigned, giving way to J. O. Ramstedt, an honourable official but by no means a statesman of parts. It was, in fact, one of Sweden's misfortunes that in this crisis she had no large-calibred statesmen at the helm. In the meantime Crown Prince Gustav, who acted as regent during an illness of his father, asked the appointment of a secret committee to consider the entire situation. A new Swedish proposal that negotiations should again be taken up with the Norwegians on the entire question of the union followed. This suggested separate consular systems functioning under a common foreign minister, who might be either a Swede or a Norwegian. But all these efforts were rendered futile by the refusal of the Norwegians to enter into any new negotiation until a Norwegian consular system had been established. At the same time Norway negotiated a foreign loan of 40,000,000 crowns, which naturally aroused still further resentment and suspicion in Sweden. On May 18 and 20, the Storthing took the momentous step of voting the appointment of Norwegian consuls, but it did not define their relations to the foreign office. The suspensive veto of the king could, however, according to the Act of Union, set aside such an act until three successive Storthings, with intervening elections, had repassed it, but in this case the Storthing voted it should go into effect ten months after its passage. The king naturally refused to sanction the law and the entire Norwegian ministry resigned. It would not recede from its decision despite the king's refusal to accept the resignation on the ground that he could not then form a new government.

The union dissolved.—Ignoring the king's declaration that *at the moment* he could not form a new ministry, the Storthing on June 7 declared that the constitutional monarch no longer functioned and that the union was dissolved, the king no longer acting as ruler of Norway. The act was, of course, revolutionary in its procedure, a fact which the king solemnly emphasized in the protest which he at once issued.

The news of the drastic action taken by the Norwegian Storthing on June 7 provoked bitter indignation in Sweden, but the king steadfastly refused to resort to any measures of aggression and no mobilization orders were issued. The action of the Norwegian Storthing wounded King Oscar, aged and now infirm of body, to the quick. He suffered bitter anguish, but held nobly to the principle that if the "welfare of the brother peoples" was best served by their living their political lives apart, then let it be so. When an extraordinary meeting of the Riksdag met two weeks subsequent to the June resolution of the Storthing, the feeling was dominant in Sweden that the nation ought not to resort to arms in order to re-establish the union. This feeling was accompanied by an equally dominant sentiment that the union must end in a more proper and orderly manner and that Norway must first agree to conditions which were consistent with Swedish honour and safety.

Swedish conditions for separation.—The Riksdag at once took matters into its own hands, setting aside the weak Ramstedt ministry, and appointed a special committee with the clear-sighted and tactful Christian Lundeberg at its head, to formulate the Swedish terms. The committee suggested that as a prerequisite for a peaceful separation either a new Storthing or a Norwegian plebiscite must approve the resolution of June 7, after which Sweden would enter into negotiations with Norway regarding the terms upon which the separation would be sanctioned. As a *sine qua non*, the Swedes stipulated that all forts which Norway had built along the frontier must be razed within a certain belt, guarantees must be given that no new forts be built, trade and communication between the two countries to go on unmolested, and the Swedish nomadic Lapps be granted necessary grazing grounds in Norway. A loan of 100,000,000 crowns was voted the government by the Riksdag, but to allay fears that this might be provocative of war, it was stipulated that the Riksdag alone could determine the purposes for which the sum could be used. Simultaneously the Ramstedt ministry resigned and a strong coalition ministry, in which F. Wachtmeister, as minister of foreign affairs, Arvid Lindman, chief of the naval department, Hjalmar Hammarskjöld, and Karl Staaff were the outstanding leaders. The Norwegians agreed to the Swedish suggestions and the subsequent plebiscite was almost unanimously in favour of the dissolution of the union.

The Karlstad treaty.—A peace conference could, therefore, without much delay, begin its labours. This was held at Karlstad in Värmland. The Swedish commissioners were Lundeberg, Wachtmeister, Hammarskjöld, and Karl Staaff, the latter, like his colleagues, a commanding figure in contemporary Swedish politics and destined later to play a most important rôle in the enactment of liberal legislation. The leaders on the Norwegian side were Michelsen and J. Lövland. For the greater part of a month the deliberations were carried on behind closed doors, and anxiety was intense. All Europe was nervous. The French-German dispute in Morocco threatened to unleash the forces of war and to the great nations the prospect of a war in the North at this particularly inconvenient time was most disturbing. Norwegian propaganda had quite generally created the impression that Sweden was the aggressor, and if the negotiations dragged out Norway was in the most advantageous position to get encouragement and assistance from abroad. Germany was supposed to be friendly to Sweden, which caused England, after her accession to the Entente, to be more than ever friendly to Norway. Denmark was openly in sympathy with Norway, and while this gave the Swedes no alarm it was very irritating to them. The Swedish Government acted, however, with vigour and promptness to get its side of the controversy before the world. Her leading historian, Harald Hjärne, and the able naval officer, G. O. Wallenberg, were sent to London, and from this point of vantage they issued declarations which could not fail to impress foreign nations. Troops were sent by both nations to the boundary, the Swedish fleet, which was in a high state of efficiency, was made ready, and sent to the west coast, where it anchored not far from the Norwegian capital. The suggestion that the border fortresses must be razed was particularly distasteful to the Norwegians, who looked upon this as an insult to their national honour. On September 23 an agreement was, however, reached which in the main conformed to the stipulations laid down by the Swedish Riksdag. The suggestion of the Norwegians that territory of a certain width on either side of the boundary be declared a neutral zone, in which not only forts but all military equipment be proscribed, was incorporated in the treaty. Transit trade was to be governed by stipulations to be in force for thirty years and the regulation of water-courses flowing across the boundary was to be governed by an agreement to run for fifty years. A treaty of arbitration to run for ten years was also made a part of the general agreement. These important preliminaries having been agreed to by the Karlstad commissioners, the Swedish Riksdag in a second special session approved the Karlstad treaty and voted the abrogation of the Act of Union and Oscar relinquished the Norwegian crown. In their address to the king declaring the union dissolved, the Norwegians had asked his consent to the election of a prince of his family to the Norwegian throne. Sentiment was in Sweden almost unanimous against having one of their princes on the Norwegian throne, as it was feared that this would merely serve to keep Norwegian suspicion alive. The king had declared at the very beginning that he was opposed to the suggestion and would consider it in a favourable light only if the Riksdag urged it. Since this was the feeling of the Swedes, the Norwegians elected Charles of Denmark, grandson of Charles XV, who as king assumed the name Håkan VII.

Death of Oscar II, 1907.—Oscar II did not long survive the events which caused the greatest disappointment of his life. Broken in health even before the storm came, the aged monarch rapidly lost strength after this anguishing experience, and in December 1907 the end came. Despite the bitter disappointment of his life, his soul retained its magnanimity to the end. As the nurse stood by his bedside in the quiet hours of the night, when strength was fast ebbing, she heard him whisper a prayer to God for the welfare of the *two* kindred nations.

CHAPTER XXVII[1]

SINCE 1907

The years which have elapsed since Oscar II passed away and his eldest son ascended the throne as Gustav V have been crowded with so many events, some startling and dramatic, others transpiring in quiet tempo, but none the less of profound significance, that little more than a summary can be attempted here. An adequate evaluation of these events is, moreover, not possible until the passing of years has revealed their real significance.

General character of the period.—The dissolution of the union with Norway served to arouse the hitherto somnolent Swedish spirit of nationality, and proofs multiplied that the nation began to esteem its material and cultural resources far more highly than ever before. The drastic action of the Norwegians had, furthermore, given the Swedes a severe jolt which served the good purpose of hushing the voices of discord; a new sense of unity began to pervade the nation. The realization that they now stood alone also had a bracing effect upon them. Furthermore, they no longer had the uncomfortable feeling that they might at any time be called upon to yield to new demands by the Norwegians. A remarkable economic advancement, greatly accelerated by a number of ingenious Swedish inventions, but having its real source in a new realization of the possibilities created by the country's rich natural resources, has also helped to make the period noteworthy. Co-

[1] The literature on the period covered by this chapter is naturally voluminous. Two works have been especially drawn upon for data; namely, Karl Hildebrand, *Sveriges historia,* Vol. XIV, Stockholm, 1926, and Eli F. Heckscher, *Sveriges ekonomiska och sociala historia under och efter världskriget,* Stockholm, 1926. Hildebrand is a historian by profession, but has devoted the greater part of his active years to journalism and public service. He has been an influential member of the Riksdag and one of the important fiscal bureaus of the state. A staunch adherent of the moderative conservative group, he is nevertheless able to judge objectively and his account bears the stamp of impartiality and authenticity. The latter work, by one of the nation's foremost economists, is one of a series published by the Carnegie Foundation for International Peace. Valuable biographical data are also found in *Vem är det,* the Swedish *Who's Who.*

incident with this economic and industrial development, great progress has been made towards a true democracy. Bitter industrial and political struggles have indeed marked the march of progress, but no weapons have been used except those properly employed in orderly exercise of national self-government; discussion and the ballot have decided the issues. The World War and the readjustments after it have, of course, overshadowed all other matters in importance. For a country like Sweden, situated as she was in close proximity to the two belligerent groups, inevitably subject, as a neutral state, to suffer from overt acts by both, the great conflict was bound to involve risks and trials of incalculable dimensions.

Gustav V.—While the principles of democracy during this hectic period have come to be as dominant in Sweden as in any country, royalty has by no means been correspondingly stripped of power and influence. This seeming paradox, no doubt, finds its chief explanation in the personality of King Gustav. A deep sense of responsibility, insight, honesty, loyalty, energy, and firmness have inspired and guided his acts. His career as king has thus been truly consistent with his royal motto: "With the people for the fatherland." His announcement on assuming the royal dignity that no coronation ceremonies and attendant festivities would be staged to mark his accession to the throne, inasmuch as these necessitated useless outlay of money, is a typical expression of his sound sense and considerate regard for the spirit of the age. Gustav was born June 16, 1858, and received his early education in Sweden and Norway. Many journeys to foreign lands brought him into personal contact with a number of contemporary statesmen and enhanced his knowledge of European peoples and their culture. His father's illness had on different occasions placed the responsibilities of the royal office upon his shoulders while he was still crown prince, and he was thus neither untried nor unknown when he became king. He had married Victoria of Baden in 1881. Her deep interest in charity and her generous financial assistance to the leading Stockholm hospitals, as well as to other worthy causes, have served especially to arouse a genuine affection for her in the nation. Illness, unfortunately, afflicted her for many years. This made it necessary for

King Gustav V

her to spend a great deal of her time in the milder climes of Italy and south Germany.[2] Three sons were born to the royal couple. The eldest, Crown Prince Gustav Adolf, born in 1882, has shown a marked predilection for the life of the scholar, thus exemplifying the finest traditions of the Bernadotte family. His affability and serious and intelligent interest in literature, science, and art have won universal respect for him. As a speaker he ranks among the foremost in his country. His favourite study is archæology, and he counts his closest friends among the cultural leaders of the nation. All kinds of wholesome sports find in him their loyal patron. Few, if any, men of contemporary Sweden enjoy as much popularity as Crown Prince Gustav Adolf. The second son, Vilhelm, is a big-game hunter of note, a dramatist and novel writer, and brilliant author of hunting tales and travel accounts. A third son, Erik, died in his youth.

Crown Prince Gustaf Adolf

The great strike.—The most serious industrial conflict in the nation's history occurred in 1909. In proportion to the total number of industrial workers in the land, the labour unions of Sweden had a larger membership than was the case in any other country of Europe, and their power was commensurate with their numerical strength. In most instances, the employers had hitherto yielded to frequent demands for increase of

[2] Victoria died in Rome in 1930.

wages and improved working conditions. The right of the unions to act in behalf of the workingmen and the principle of collective bargaining had been quite generally recognized, but when the associations manifested an increasing tendency to interfere with matters which hitherto the employers had looked upon as coming solely within their own jurisdiction, as choice of foremen, dismissals of workers, methods of production, and the like, the latter began to balk. The stringency following the crisis of 1907 appeared to the employers, also by this time compactly organized into the Employers' Union, as a valid reason for refusing to grant the further wage increases that were demanded. Strikes thereupon broke out repeatedly in isolated industries or regions in 1908, some of which were attended by violence. The matter came to a head in the early summer of 1909, when the Employers' Union threatened a general lockout, if within a certain period the pending disagreements were not adjusted on terms that were acceptable to its members. The Central Committee of the National Labour Union accepted this challenge and ordered a general strike in all industries, excepting those involving care of the sick, supply of light, garbage disposal, and similar necessary activities. While many of the workers were loath to join in so hazardous a venture, their sense of solidarity ultimately brought them all into line. From July 26 to September 4 the wheels of industry did not move anywhere, except in the exempted occupations noted, but to the everlasting honour of the Swedish labourers it can be said that no acts of violence whatsoever were committed. In fact, the workingmen themselves organized companies for guard duty and property was carefully protected. The sale of intoxicants was prohibited during the duration of the strike, an action in which the nation quite readily acquiesced. Ultimately the workers agreed to return to work on practically the old terms, and economically considered the outcome of the strike therefore can be looked upon as a defeat for them, but their admirable calmness and reasonableness throughout the crisis were equivalent to a great moral victory. Many workers failed to get their former jobs back, as these had been filled by others. Undoubtedly, the outcome of the strike tended to weaken the unions for several years.

Pensions.—Proposals for a pension system of which all workers would be the beneficiaries had long engaged the attention of Swedish social workers, economists, and statesmen. Already in 1901 a workmen's compensation act had been adopted, which provided aid to practically all workers, except in shipping and agriculture, in case of disability through accident. The termination of the nation-wide strike of 1909 gave added impetus to the discussion of projects for the economic protection of the workers, and after a thorough ventilation of the problem a general pension system, covering both disability and old-age annuities, was adopted in 1913. This affected all subjects, both men and women, with the exception of such

Labour troubles and strikes. Left, as they manifest themselves in countries in the South of Europe; Right, as they appear in Sweden. Cartoon in *Söndagsnisse*, Swedish comic weekly

state officials as already enjoyed the protection of pensions. All prospective beneficiaries under the law, between the ages of sixteen and sixty-six, contribute, according to income, from five to thirty-three crowns annually. Since these contributions would be wholly inadequate to give reasonable annuities unless they were supplemented by additional sums, the communities and the state likewise pay certain fixed amounts. A large share of the state's part of the contribution is, in fact, derived from its interests in the rich iron mines of Lappland. The maximum amount which a man may receive in annuities after the age of sixty-six is 790 crowns; for women it is 660 crowns, the smaller sum in their case being justified by the fact that actuarians' figures had shown that their expectancy of life at sixty-six is a few years longer than that of men. Any individual may increase the above annuities by availing himself of a supplementary system in which membership is voluntary. Thus by depositing, after the age of fifteen, as little as thirty crowns annually in any postal station, an extra annual income in round numbers of 600 crowns for men and 500 crowns for women is assured at pension age, the state furnishing one-eighth of the money paid to beneficiaries under this supplementary system. The proper adjustment of pensions presented peculiar difficulties in Sweden, since here the relative number of individuals past the age of sixty-seven was found to be twice that of any other country. Investigations showed, further, that half of the men and five-sixths of the women who had reached the age of seventy did not have necessary means for their support, and the great majority of the people naturally looked upon the pension law as a great humanitarian act. The anguish and humiliation associated with life in the poor-houses were now for the most part eliminated; life can be lived far more pleasantly and with greater dignity in old people's homes than in the old institutions for the indigent. With pride the Swedes of our day are wont to boast that they no longer have any poor-houses in their land.

Threats from without.—Ominous signs of threatening storms coming from the east disturbed seriously the nation's peace of mind during the early years of the present century. The aggressive and relentless Russification process, which near the end of the previous century had been inaugurated in Finland by the reactionary forces in control of the Russian Government, and which aimed to uproot Swedish and Finnish culture alike, naturally caused the people of Sweden to feel the gravest concern about the future. They felt profound sympathy for the people with whom they had shared good and evil days for six hundred years, but this sympathy was accompanied by a decided anxiety regarding their own safety, since what was transpiring appeared to threaten Sweden's own independent existence.

Disturbing evidence of Russia's sinister designs seemed to become constantly more convincing and the feeling of alarm grew increasingly tense among the Swedes. When defeat of the Russians by the Japanese in 1904 thwarted their plans for extending their control to Pacific ports in Asia, it seemed but inevitable that this would stiffen Russian determination to get to the ocean by pressing forward in another direction. Here Sweden and Norway would be in her way. Signs were by no means wanting that Russia was preparing for a forward westward thrust in the North. The Russian railroad system was linked with the Finnish by a connecting-line and Russian military trains could henceforth move over the Finnish railroads, new railway lines were built to the Gulf of Bothnia, in northern Finland highways were constructed towards the Norwegian fjords, new military headquarters were established at several points in the duchy, Russian military forces strengthened in the land, and the Finnish pilot system was Russified. In the course of time the Russian espionage system reached out in brazen manner to Sweden herself. Itinerant Russians began to swarm over the land, posing especially as common labourers, with saw-filing as their specialty. Their apparently ready supply of cash and occasional slips of tongue, when off their guard, soon convinced the Swedes that foreign spies were abroad in the land; suspicions and fears, once aroused, naturally made it easy to see a foreign spy in every stranger. When in this period of nervous tension a Swedish daily published a Russian military guide which contained maps of Sweden, suggestions for eventual military operations in the land, a Russian-Swedish dictionary of military terms, and similar information, the proof of Russian hostile design seemed well-nigh complete.

The general European situation increased the precariousness of Sweden's position and caused genuine alarm. On the one side was the Triple Alliance, Germany, Austria, and Italy, and on the other the Triple Entente, France, England, and Russia. In an eventual conflict between these giants, only good fortune and sound wisdom could, so many thoughtful Swedes believed, save the nation from disaster, and sound wisdom seemed to demand that the military defences of the nation be strengthened and perfected.

Question of defences.—Elsewhere military preparations were being rushed forward with feverish haste and Sweden must not neglect her own defences. This feeling, shared by a large part of the population, resulted in 1908 in a decision to build one new armoured cruiser, larger and more effective than any earlier unit of the Swedish navy. The Social-Democrats and Liberals had, however, opposed this project violently, and the question of strengthened defences therefore became the great issue in the Riksdag elections of 1911. The two parties contended that the dangers of foreign attack were largely the creations of an excited imagination. The heavy tax increase which must inevitably result from entering upon the contemplated military program also was stressed vigorously. The Conservative, or Right, Party, which had sponsored the program of adequate defence, met defeat, Admiral Arvid Lindman, the indomitable and resourceful leader of the party and head of the ministry, resigned, and Karl Staaff, the leader of the Liberals, a man of genuine sincerity, great fearlessness, and strong devotion to the interests of the common people, formed a new ministry. He believed that no military system could be effective as a means of national defence unless it rested on the firm foundation of popular approval. Since the popular vote seemed to have proven conclusively that a majority disapproved of the proposal to increase the military forces, the ministry decided to disregard the earlier decision to build a new cruiser, and construction work which had already started was stopped.

Preparedness discussion.—The controversy which was aroused on the question, not only of the need of further military defence, but also regarding the right of a ministry to nullify a definite resolution of the Riksdag, was exceedingly bitter and stirred up great excitement. Later the ministry's action in the cruiser affair was approved by the Riksdag, but the excitement was by no means allayed thereby; on the contrary, it gave impetus to a unique national movement. A suggestion that the necessary funds for the new cruiser be raised by voluntary gifts at once won the enthusiastic support of all advocates of strengthened defence, and in a short time almost 17,000,000 crowns poured in for the purpose. A vigorous pamphlet written by the famous explorer, Dr. Sven Hedin, was very effective in arousing favourable interest in the project. In accusing and startling words he bared the aggressive and hostile policy of Russia. Regarding the sense of security and the indifference of his own countrymen, he wrote, "We live as though thought of war were a superstitious reminiscence of bygone barbaric days. Assuredly we have long enough trusted only in Providence. Before it is too late we ourselves must take hold with firm hands." Hedin's popularity at home, earned by phenomenal exploits, his genuine feeling of admiration for, and gratitude toward, the Russian nation, often voiced in his earlier travel accounts, and his admittedly intimate knowledge of Russian policies and leaders, gave special significance to his fiery words. Around Hedin and his message there soon raged a storm more violent than that which the question of a new cruiser had provoked. The famous explorer was bitterly denounced as an ingrate, ignoramus, and sword-brandishing chauvinist, while to another group he appeared as a dauntless patriot who had dared to speak the truth. After much contention and palavering, work was resumed on the new cruiser which received the name *Sverige* and in due time it was launched.

Karl Staaff

While the controversy regarding the new cruiser was going on, the government was conducting an investigation in order to ascertain what the military needs of the country actually were, and the probable cost of necessary improvements. Staaff and his colleagues admitted that the defences ought to be strengthened, but they were not willing to go as far in this direction as the leaders in the cause of preparedness desired. Meanwhile, new espionage plots came to light and important documents of the military department disappeared mysteriously. The popular mind grew more excited than ever. Staaff, in December 1913, finally made public the ministry's program; it stated that under existing conditions there could be no thought of a decrease in appropriations for national defence, but that, on the contrary, the nation must be prepared to bear some additional burdens. In important specific details, Staaff's plan was at variance, however, with the suggestions of military experts who had recommended a decidedly longer period for training of the infantry, while Staaff held that this part of the program must be put off until new elections could be held and the nation itself had spoken its mind on the question.

The demonstration in Stockholm: Bondetåget.—The ministry's announced program was very disquieting to the friends of preparedness, who saw serious risks in a postponement; the attack on the country, they feared, might come any day. Under the impelling force of this anxiety, the nation now staged a demonstration which the entire world beheld with astonishment. Even before the announcement of Staaff's program, a suggestion had been made that the *bönder* journey to Stockholm *en masse* and there make known their desire that the national military forces be augmented. This led to definite action when in December 1913 a number of *bönder* from the province of Uppland sent an invitation to their brethren in all parts of the country asking them to join them in a mass invasion of the capital. At once the nation was astir. Verner von Heidenstam, the great poet, voiced the sentiment of those sponsoring the movement in these words, "What is our desire? We do not want to sit crouching in a corner, whining and bickering, having no aim in life except that we may exist. We want to feel that, in the event that anyone approaches us too closely and in a threatening manner, we are able to answer him. We wish to be assured that the civilization on which we have laboured and built, generation after generation, and to which the best of our days have been devoted, shall not, perchance, be lost in the disasters of a few weeks. We want to be assured that our language never shall be hushed in the palatial school buildings which everywhere on the hillsides lie reflected in the sun; unitedly we vow that our ancient land shall never, even unto the very end of time, fall into the hands of barbarians." In response to the call, *bönder* flocked from the most remote sections of the land to Stockholm the following February (1914). After first attending services in various churches of the city, the visitors, marching in groups and numbering in all 30,000, assembled at the royal palace, February 6, where the king, together with other members of the royal family, received them. In assuring His Majesty that he represented not only the *bönder* who were present but 40,000 others who could not participate, the spokesman of the mighty host declared that they were willing and ready to contribute money for the army and navy "in whatever amount competent authorities have advised and the critical situation demands, so that everything that can and ought to be done is done immediately." A message from 70,000 other subjects, conveying the same assurances, was next presented.

In his most eloquent and solemn reply King Gustav stressed the fact that the nation had always been free, the people and the king labouring harmoniously together and making sacrifices for the welfare of their common country ever since the saga times. "Be assured," he continued, "that in the matter of wise and salutary measures for the safeguarding of the independence of our country I will never compromise with my conscience." In conclusion the king asserted that it was his conviction, and from this position he said he would not recede, that the Riksdag ought to vote such measures as the military experts had recommended. Later the *bönder* waited on Staaff and before him they repeated their demands for strengthened defence and reiterated their willingness to carry the burden.

Ministerial crisis.—For the ministry, much embarrassed by the demonstration, two courses now lay open: either it could yield to the demands of the *bönder,* or it could stick resolutely to its own program. It chose the latter course, at the same time raising a hue and cry that His Majesty, by expressing his own opinion in a vital government matter without first submitting his statement for approval to his ministers, had ignored the well-established rules and precedents of constitutional monarchy. In this attitude the Liberal ministry was warmly supported by the Social-Democrats. There were notes in the king's "sensational speech," said Branting, "which had a strange sound, and which the people did not recognize as consistent with the constitutional safeguards which constituted their heritage from past struggles against absolutistic tendencies."

Two days subsequently to the demonstration at the royal palace, a vast delegation of workingmen, also said to have numbered 30,000, waited on Staaff to protest against added military burdens.

On this occasion Branting, who acted as spokesman, urged that appropriations for military purposes, which he claimed already weighed too heavily on the people, ought to be reduced rather than increased; he warned against the danger of being swept off one's feet by the "senseless agitation for preparedness" which was under way. On February 10 the ministry tendered its resignation, giving as a reason that although the king had let it know beforehand that he intended in his address to the *bönder* to urge the adoption of the contemplated military reforms without delay and with the omission of no important detail, he had, in fact, spoken words which raised a doubt that he would in the future take such cognizance of the counsel of his ministry as the latter considered an indispensable prerequisite to constitutional government. To this the king replied that it had not been his intention to ignore his official advisers, but not having been informed of the provisions of their program he could naturally not reach a decision in this matter until he could meet the ministry at the council-table. The ministry found this answer unsatisfactory and next presented a categorical demand that His Majesty give an assurance that in the future he would, before voicing any opinion on matters of state policy, consult the prime-minister or other member of the ministry specially concerned. To this demand, orally presented, the king answered orally, "I will not deprive myself of the right freely to address myself to the people of Sweden." On a later occasion he did, however, declare that he had no intention of making declarations on questions touching upon state policies in disregard of the ministry. Having failed to derive adequate satisfaction from the king's statement, the ministry resigned.

The Hammarskjöld ministry.—Hjalmar Hammarskjöld, a scholarly and highly esteemed jurist, whose wisdom and probity had been revealed in many important official posts and whose pre-eminence as an authority on international law was recognized at home and abroad, was asked to form a new cabinet after Staaff. Besides serving as prime-minister, Hammarskjöld also at first held the portfolio of war under the new régime. The country's leading banker, K. A. Wallenberg, became minister of foreign affairs, and Dan Broström, Sweden's greatest promoter of shipping enterprises, served as minister of naval affairs. Uncertainty and anxiety now rested heavily over the nation. There was a general feeling that the new ministry would have to grapple with tremendously difficult problems, but neither its members nor anybody else, it may be safely assumed, had any conception whatever how stupendous and heartbreaking the task would be with which it must grapple, before many months had passed. The Hammarskjöld ministry was soon ready to announce its program of military reforms. Its most important provisions would extend the period of training for conscripts and provide for the construction of several new armoured cruisers. New elections were next ordered held for the second chamber, in order that the nation might have an opportunity to express approval or disapproval of the proposal. The subsequent election campaign was marked by unwonted activity and perhaps at no previous time in the nation's history had so much bitterness been engendered. The elections, in which an unprecedented number of votes were cast, gave the ministry increased strength in the Riksdag, but none of the parties had an absolute majority. The Conservatives won many new members, the Liberals lost heavily, and the Social-Democrats made great gains. The Liberals evinced

Hjalmar Hammarskjöld

an inclination to support the ministry's military program, but the Social-Democrats, under the leadership of Branting, continued tenaciously in their opposition, even reiterating that the military burdens were too heavy already, and ought to be made lighter. Debates on the military question raged furiously in the Riksdag and the press during the months of June and July (1914); then came the grim tragedy of Europe which hushed the discordant voices into silence.

Outbreak of the World War.—As they now stood in the presence of the grim reality of a general European war, consternation for a moment filled all souls in Sweden and threatened to unsettle everything. Measures were hastily taken for the defence of the country, in case it should be attacked; no one knew what might happen the next day, or even the next hour. In the shadow of threatening national calamity, perhaps even loss of national independence, the contending factions were ready, as intimated, to bury their differences and unite forces in behalf of the common fatherland. Everyone realized that the land was exposed to attacks by both of the belligerent groups. Church bells all over the land pealed out their dismal summons, calling the Landsturm to arms. Vessels remained in the harbours, their owners fearing to expose them to the risks which the war suddenly had created, and industry was at a standstill. In a few days multitudes of refugees, panic-stricken and often penniless, began to pour in from Russia and Germany; the care and comfort which the Swedes, without hesitation and at serious sacrifice of their own comforts, gave these unfortunates was but the prelude to the humane service which the nation later was to render in behalf of the war-stricken peoples.

Desire for neutrality.—The dominant sentiment of the vast majority of the nation from the very outbreak of the war favoured a policy of strict neutrality and a vigorous defence of the country's rights as a neutral state. The determination to remain outside of the conflict, unless forced into it, rested primarily upon a deep-rooted aversion to all war as a brutal, dehumanizing institution, entirely futile as a means for settling any great issues. For more than a century the nation had enjoyed the blessings of peace, having resolutely and with admirable calmness and wisdom refrained from drawing the sword when the situation seemed amply provoking; the utter folly of a war with Norway in 1905 had become increasingly clear as the years had passed. The nation had a clear understanding also of the national jealousies and spirit of selfishness which had precipitated the conflict. The hypocrisy of the claims and counterclaims of both the contending groups, the insincerity of the bombastic utterances of the leaders in the belligerent groups, were quite apparent to an intelligent people whose judgment was not perverted by nationalistic interests and chauvinistic clap-trap. The counterbalancing of feelings towards the nations at war, commercial relations with them all, and traditional association were other factors which had rooted deep the determination of the Swedes to remain outside of the conflict unless forced into it. As long as Russia was a leading member of the Entente group, it was naturally difficult for Sweden to feel any inclination to favour that side; about one-half of Sweden's former territory had been lost to Russia through ruthless wars, which the eastern neighbour had precipitated, and up to the very outbreak of the Great War this neighbour had appeared as a serious menace to Swedish independence and integrity. For France there was naturally a strong feeling of sympathy, born of admiration for her culture and quickened by memories of her traditional policy of friendship for Sweden. The splendid contributions to democratic and popular government by England were deeply appreciated, and few desired a military defeat or loss of prestige for that great country. On the other hand, there were many and strong ties, both sentimental and economical, which bound Sweden to Germany. Swedish theological thought, science, literature, art, industry, and social legislation had been enormously enriched by her. Sweden had been buying more goods from Germany than from any other country, and as buyer of Swedish wares Germany was outranked by Great Britain alone. The conservative element, especially the official and military classes, were, no doubt, as a group inclined to favour Germany as against her opponents in the great conflict, but workingmen as a class, on the other hand, sympathized with England and France; irrespective of such feelings, however, the vast majority desired, as stated, that their country pursue a strictly neutral course. A group known as the "activists," which in the beginning of the struggle clamoured for Swedish participation on the side of Germany, never had the support of any considerable part of the nation.

War exigency measures; meeting of the three kings.—Immediately upon the outbreak of the Great War, Sweden issued a declaration of neutrality, mobilized a part of her military forces, placed guards at public buildings and bridges, as well as at important points along the coast, and prohibited the exportation of several important commodities. An inventory of existing supplies of foods and other necessities, especially coal, was next undertaken, a moratorium law passed, and various commissions for directing and supporting industry and to provide against the expected unemployment began to function. Fortunately, the Riksdag was in session when the storm broke and important decisions could thus be reached speedily. Before this body, Wallenberg could already, on August 8, announce that Sweden and Norway had entered into a solemn agreement that no hostile action would be undertaken by the one against the other during the progress of the conflict. This assurance of solidarity was hailed with profound satisfaction. Perhaps even more auspicious and reassuring was the evidence of unity in the nation itself. As leaders of the Liberal and Social-Democratic parties, respectively, Staaff and Branting assured the Hammarskjöld ministry that it could count on the support of a united nation; this assurance extended also to the question of adequate defence. Soon thereafter the Riksdag voted approval of the ministry's military plans. The common distress and dangers had the salutary effect also of bringing about a better accord between the three Scandinavian countries than had ever existed before. On the initiative of the Swedish king, the monarchs of the three kingdoms, accompanied by their prime-ministers, met at Malmö late in 1914. It was the first time in several hundred years that the heads of the kindred peoples thus met in friendly conference. The meeting and the communiqués which later were issued, and which gave assurance that the three states would act unitedly in the common crisis, added appreciably to the feeling of security which gradually had come to supersede the earlier nervousness. Similar meetings were subsequently held, the most notable being the one at Oslo, Norway, November 1917, which city the Swedish king now visited for the first time since the disruption of the union in 1905. Here he spoke manly and noble words of reconciliation. The nations could now feel that henceforth the deep wounds inflicted by the dissolution of the union had been healed. This occasion was in reality the beginning of the very cordial relations which for more than a decade have existed between Swedes and Norwegians.

Rights of neutrals.—Sweden was soon to discover that in the life-and-death struggle of the great powers scant consideration would be given the small neutral states which happened to be in their way. International agreements regarding trade and commerce in time of war, no matter how solemnly they had formerly been approved, now availed little or nothing. Through the Paris Declaration of 1855, the Hague Agreement of 1907, and the London Compact of 1907, the rights of neutrals and restrictions upon belligerents had been defined. These acts stipulated, for instance, that goods may in time of war be exchanged between countries by every means and by all routes not prescribed by international law or in violation of trade practices. Enemies' goods on board neutral ships could be seized as contraband only in case they actually came under this classification; the same principle applied to non-contraband goods of neutrals on the ships of belligerents. Contraband and non-contraband goods had been defined. Cotton, wool, hides, ore, and fertilizers were not to be considered contraband; food supplies, clothes, shoes, feed, money, railway supplies, vessels, fuel, oils, and some other commodities were designated non-contraband; that is, they were articles which might be used in war or in peaceful industry, and hence their use for one or the other purpose determined their classification. Strictly contraband, *i.e.*, goods used primarily for war, included weapons, ammunition, military supplies, armour plate, war vessels, machines used in the manufacture of war supplies, and beasts of burden which could be used in war. International agreement made it unlawful for any belligerent state to proclaim a blockade of any coast or harbour unless the state making this declaration had an adequate military force to make it effective; neutral ships which defied such orders in case blockade was not effective were not subject to confiscation. A neutral ship within the blockaded zone, but destined to a port outside of this zone, should not be confiscated. Mines, when laid, must be so placed that they did not hinder neutral trade. Distinguished international lawyers and statesmen had solemnly declared that the right of neutrals to use the open sea and carry on legal trade took precedence over the claims of the belligerents to use the area for conflict, and that the rights of neutral states to trade with belligerents were restricted, but not so the rights of the subjects of such neutral states.

Sweden's insistence on her rights.—The rights of Sweden as a neutral state were therefore clear under the provisions of international law and these enactments had hitherto been respected by the countries which were now at war. According to these rules, the country had the legal right to import freely the things which she needed and to supply the civil population of belligerent countries with necessities. The Swedish ministry firmly insisted that these rules be now respected with reference to Sweden; yielding here and there, it was conceded, would bring the country certain temporary advantages, but these advantages, the ministry maintained, must be sacrificed for the sake of preserving the essential principles of justice. Had the war closed two years earlier, Sweden would undoubtedly have appeared in the eyes of the world as a dauntless champion of great moral and legal rights, but the insane hatred and the scrapping of all rules and precepts, which marked the final phases of the war, destroyed all earlier standards and warped all judgment. The belligerents would not, or could not, understand the motives of the Swedish statesmen who were bent on safeguarding the rights of the neutrals, and the Swedes, in turn, could not understand the desperation of those who were suffering untold woes and honestly believed that they were fighting for the very existence of their respective nations, and even for the preservation of civilization itself.

Violation of Sweden's rights as a neutral.—The Swedish statesmen were not long in discovering that the guarantees of international agreements meant little as protective measures. The case of cotton illustrates how inadequate these guarantees were. In the early part of the conflict the United States sent great quantities of this staple to German ports, but as risks increased much of it was sent to Scandinavian ports for transshipment to Germany. Much cotton was simultaneously shipped directly from the United States to Germany and this was considered a perfectly legal and proper enterprise on the part of the former. Then came the English Order in Council, declaring all goods directly or indirectly destined for the enemy subject to confiscation. By importing large quantities of cotton, or by having huge supplies of this staple on hand, Sweden now fell under suspicion as aiding Germany. English interference with her commerce became increasingly active as the war went on, and soon huge quantities of goods of every kind assigned for Sweden were held in England. The other belligerent group likewise dealt the country a serious blow when Germany declared all kinds of lumber to be contraband; this order was, however, later modified. England next declared all of the North Sea a military zone, designating merely certain lanes for neutral trade. Mines were laid in the North Sea and the Baltic by both fighting groups, and the hazards to Swedish shipping were enormously increased. Germany's next move was to declare the waters around the British Isles a military area, where neutral ships would run the risk of seizure and destruction. England's answer was another Order in Council declaring that she would seize and hold in her harbours vessels or cargoes assumed to be destined for a German port, although directly consigned to a neutral harbour. Mere suspicion that goods might find their way to the enemy now became sufficient reason for detaining them in England, or for appropriating them for her use. English censorship of telegrams and mail became extremely irritating, and trade spying and similar prying into the business of Swedish subjects aggravated the feeling of bitterness. Finally England declared that she had the right to stop all trade with her enemies which passed through neutral countries and that anyone among the latter which was not ready to acquiesce in this ruling would no longer be looked upon as neutral. This, in effect, meant that neutrals were henceforth subjected to a rationing system as far as goods from outside were concerned. The rule violated the plain provisions of international law and Sweden opposed it until the spectre of starvation, appearing towards the end of the conflict, and the creation of a new ministry which was friendly to the Entente, brought a change of policy.

Charge of Pro-Germanism.—Almost from the beginning of the war, the government of Sweden was suspected by the Entente countries and their sympathizers in neutral lands of decided pro-Germanism, and certain circumstances and occurrences seemed to give a basis for this suspicion. Its protests against Entente infringement of Sweden's rights as a neutral and its retaliatory measures were heralded abroad as evidence of its anxiety to help the Central Powers, but little was said when the Hammarskjöld ministry, in the same manner, protested against the overt acts of these same powers and sought to enforce the rules of international law against them also. Almost as a matter of course, it came to be believed in that part of the world where Entente propaganda was particularly active and effective that Sweden was giving aid to Germany by sending her supplies of food and other materials. Large quantities of food were, in fact, exported from Sweden to Germany in the early part of the conflict, before the government was able to check it. This trade was, however, carried on in accordance with the rules of international law as previously adopted and applied. Trade statistics for the period of the war indicate that Sweden showed no special favouritism towards the Central Powers. In the period 1914-1919 her excess of exports over imports in relation to the leading belligerent countries was as follows: England 601,000,000 crowns, Russia 303,000,000, France 205,000,000. Austria 125,000,000, Germany 97,000,000. Her imports of grains and other necessities from the United States prior to the entry of the latter into the war showed a considerable increase over the preceding years and this was taken as *prima facie* evidence that she was supplying the Germans with large quantities of necessities. This was, however, true only in part; Sweden was compelled to purchase more abroad to replenish her own supplies, dangerously depleted in the early part of the war. Furthermore, the other markets, where grain and other supplies had been bought before the war, were now closed to her and naturally she was compelled to buy more in the only markets open to her; namely, in the United States.

As the tightening of the allied blockade reduced seriously the supply of food in Sweden and rationing was resorted to in increasing degree, opposition to Hammarskjöld gathered force. It was felt that he was too doctrinaire and too stubborn in his opposition to the high-handed methods of England. As supplies dwindled still more and business interests found themselves in a worse situation than ever, the rumblings of discontent grew deeper and louder. Nor was the ministry itself united, Wallenberg, the minister of foreign affairs, favouring a larger degree of co-operation with England. The ministry therefore tendered its resignation in March 1917 and was succeeded by one headed by Carl Swartz, a moderate Conservative. Arvid Lindman, the resourceful statesman, whose ability had been demonstrated on many occasions, became minister of foreign affairs. Swartz was a practical statesman, who realized that concessions must be made to the Entente powers as well as to the Liberal groups at home. Charged by the Conservatives with too great a willingness to yield, and denounced by the opposition because he did not yield enough, Swartz quit office after his policies had failed to win the approval of the electorate in the fall of 1917, and he was succeeded by Professor Nils Edén, under whose incumbency of the prime-minister's office some momentous issues, as a trade agreement with England which assured the Swedes increased food supplies, the perplexing problems of the Åland Islands and the Finnish revolution, as well as the question of franchise reforms at home, also were settled.

The Luxburg affair.—Entente indignation against Sweden became most vociferous in the fall of 1917 when Mr. Lansing, the American secretary of state, published a copy of an intercepted dispatch from the German *chargé d'affaires*, Luxburg, at Buenos Aires to the German foreign office, which by permission of the Swedish Government had been sent in cipher as an official telegram from the Swedish minister in the Argentine capital to Stockholm for transmission to Berlin. The telegram asked that certain allied boats whose destinations and time of departure were given "should, if possible, be spared or else sunk so as to leave no trace (*spurlos versenkt*)." These disclosures raised a storm of angry criticism against Sweden in the allied nations, and the Swedish Liberal organs joined in the chorus by launching a vigorous attack upon their government. The contents of the Luxburg dispatch were, of course, unknown to the Swedish intermediaries, as was made plain by a government statement soon after the storm broke. This declaration further averred that the Swedish foreign office had on other occasions permitted the transmission of telegrams and letters between belligerent and neutral countries, on the same basis as *bona fide* Swedish communications; this had been done in the case of dispatches from the United States to Turkey, prior to the former's entry into the war; the promise of the Swedish Government in 1915 to prohibit such transmission, furthermore, applied only to Germany and the United States. The explanation appeared disingenuous and helped very little to allay feeling in the Entente world. Discussions continued for some time in the newspapers, but no formal action was ever taken by any government. The Swedish ministry had evidently not intended to commit an unneutral act, but the German officials had shamefully taken advantage of the trust which the Swedes reposed in them. That the storm provoked by the Lansing disclosure did not undermine confidence in Sweden's neutrality and policy of fair-dealing is amply attested by the fact that towards the end of that same year she had, at the solicitation of the different nations involved, assumed charge of the diplomatic and consular affairs of the United States, Belgium, and Serbia in Turkey, of Bulgaria and Turkey in Great Britain, of China in Belgium, Germany, Russia, and Egypt, and of Austria-Hungary in Great Britain and the United States.

Swedish impartiality.—As the war went on and its bitterness increased, the Entente regulations of trade imposed increasing hardships on neutral trade. Thus private traders in neutral countries were put under the necessity of giving guarantees that goods imported by them would not be resold to the enemy. The names of those who were found guilty, or were merely suspected of having violated these orders, were placed on the English black-list. New names were constantly being added to it. In order to obtain English coal, neutral ships must also agree to transport coal between English and French ports at low carrying charges. Inasmuch as Germany held that these vessels were in the service of her enemies, she felt no scruples against torpedoing them. Both belligerent groups were guilty of overt acts against Sweden in her own territorial waters. In very many instances, Swedish war-ships interfered when one of the belligerents attacked vessels or cruisers of the enemy in Swedish waters. Absolutely no partiality was shown in her attempt to enforce compliance with international rules regarding territorial waters. Interference with Swedish mail continued to create bitterness. When England seized Swedish mail to and from America, the Swedish Government retaliated by stopping the transportation of parcel post between the former country and Russia. A scheme which was next devised by a private individual, but undoubtedly with the backing of England, according to which English goods would be transported to Russia over Norway and Finland, was frustrated by the Swedish Government, which protested on the ground that this would constitute a rank discrimination against Swedish shippers and importers.

Swedish losses.—The hazards of shipping and the disinclination of ship-owners to face the risks involved in ocean trade, at first put an almost complete stop to the movement of Swedish merchant vessels, and the government therefore undertook to insure the owners against loss of ships and goods. Swedish ships now began to move freely again, but dangers were constantly lurking in their way and losses of both life and property were so great that the nation was appalled. By torpedoes and mines, the Swedes lost nearly 300 vessels, valued at 221,000,000 crowns and having a capacity of 291,549 tons. No less than 1,120 Swedish sailors and civilians lost their lives because of the hazards created by the naval warfare.

Rationing supplies.—With the entry of America into the war, and increasing destructiveness of the submarine warfare, the distress of the Swedish people became rapidly more serious. Government efforts to prevent profiteering, stop exports, and provide supplies from abroad were only partly effective. Almost from the beginning of the struggle, the government had fixed maximum prices for certain necessities and additions were constantly made to the list of these. The scheme undoubtedly served in a measure to control the sale and distribution of certain staple articles, thus helping to check hoarding and profiteering. The poorer classes especially, who could not afford to pay the higher prices, were to some extent protected against exploitation. Speculation, profiteering, and hoarding flourished, however, in spite of all efforts to curb them. The fuel situation became especially desperate, since only meagre quantities of coal could be procured. The state therefore entered upon a vast enterprise for cutting and distributing wood-fuel from the country's enormous forest resources. At the same time the building of power stations and the extension of the network of electrical cables for supplying towns as well as country districts with electricity was pressed energetically. Soon neither food nor fuel could be obtained except upon the presentation of coupons, issued by commissions and entitling the holder to certain daily, weekly, or monthly rations. The situation was most desperate in the winter of 1917-1918. Crops had been poor the previous season and the difficulties of getting supplies from abroad were well-nigh insuperable. The statement that the annual per capita consumption of grain had been 247 pounds in the period 1911-1913, and 253 pounds in the period 1914-1915, but fell to 120 pounds in the period 1917-1918, is mute testimony that the nation at one time was desperately near the point of actual starvation. All kinds of substitutions were resorted to. It seemed as though the pages of history were being turned back a few hundred years, for again it happened in certain localities that bark was mixed with the meagre quantities of meal in order to provide bread. Only such persons as were suffering from intestinal troubles could obtain wheat bread, and milk was reserved for children and invalids. Some relief came when Denmark sent considerable quantities of grain in exchange for ore and lumber. The government struggled heroically to mitigate the suffering, and although mistakes undoubtedly were made and bitter criticism often descended upon it, the wisdom of the statesmen in control of affairs during these anguish-filled years stands clearly revealed when seen through the perspective of the years.

Accord with England.—The spectre of starvation which month after month assumed increasingly appalling dimensions and grimness finally induced the government to come to an agreement with England, in order to get coal and food; professor Nils Edén was now head of the ministry. By this agreement, made in the fall of 1918, 400,000 deadweight tons of Swedish vessels were placed at the disposal of the Entente, in return for the right to import sufficient quantities of foods and other necessities. The negotiations were of a delicate nature, not the least because it was essential that the agreement should not give Germany cause for attacking Sweden. These breakers were successfully cleared and an understanding was even reached with Germany regarding the transport of Swedish ore to her ports. Sweden had thus managed to escape starvation and at the same time maintain her status as a neutral state. The margin between available supplies and actual hunger remained extremely narrow, however, and the belligerent nations themselves could hardly welcome peace with more fervent gratitude than did the Swedes. When news of the armistice was flashed to them it seemed as if there had finally come an awakening from a hideous dream.

The Åland Islands; Red menace.—By the Peace of Paris in 1856, Russia had pledged herself not to build any fortifications on the Åland Islands (p. 695) and England and France had both become guarantors of this agreement. Like so many other pledges which had at one time been solemnly made, this was violated during the great conflict. Huge fortifications, equipped with long-range guns, were erected by Russia, and two flying fields and a radio station established. Russia had also made arrangements for quartering twenty-six regiments on the islands. The Swedes naturally took alarm at this sinister move by their ancient foe and protested vigorously. This led to no results as long as the imperialistic régime lasted in Russia, but after the Bolshevik revolution the representatives of the new Russian Government agreed in the treaty of Brest-Litovsk to destroy all these forts. After further negotiations, these promises were carried out, the work of demolition having been completed in the latter part of 1919.

The feeling of inexpressible relief which, after the armistice, superseded fear and distress, was soon disturbed in Sweden by ominous events which were transpiring in Russia and Finland. The collapse of the czarist government had indeed seemed to

Professor Nils Edén

remove the danger of a military attack by the Muscovite colossus, a danger which before had always seemed imminent, but a new influence, insidious but no less dangerous, now had to be met and combatted. The Bolshevik propaganda and revolutionary advance to which the Swedes, because of their proximity to the headquarters of the aggressive and triumphant proletariat, was peculiarly exposed, created a new and serious menace. This soon showed its gruesome apparition in Finland.

Following the Russian revolution, an independent republic had been proclaimed in that country and as soon as Russia acquiesced in this action, Sweden, on January 4, 1918, gave formal recognition to the new state. That Finland was free from Muscovite domination seemed almost too good to be true, and among all classes in Sweden the outcome was hailed with unbounded enthusiasm.

Not many months were to pass before the question of the ownership of the Åland Islands projected itself into the foreground, however, and the Swedes learned with dismay that all was not yet well. Encouraged by the current talk of the self-determination of races, the people dwelling on the islands, 98 per cent of them being of Swedish extraction, voted almost unanimously for permission to join Sweden, as one of her integral parts. This move raised a storm of protest in Finland, where both the Swedish and the Finnish element objected to thus having her population decreased and a definite strategic advantage lost. By the same token, the people of Sweden were anxious to acquire the islands, not only because of a sentimental and racial attachment for their inhabitants and a desire to see the principle of self-determination honestly applied, but also because the possession of these islands by another power consituted a potential threat in case of future wars.

Sweden and the revolution in Finland.—For the time being, the Åland Islands question was relegated into the background by the sudden outbreak of revolution in Finland, an event which wrote a new chapter of blood in the history of this sorely harassed and much-suffering country. The Finnish communists, a peculiarly rabid band of radicals, in conjunction with numerous remnants of the Russian army which still remained in the land, set about to create a revolutionary government, deeds of violence were committed, Helsingfors was captured by the Reds, and the new Finnish senate dismissed. Soon all of southern Finland was in the hands of the aggressive revolutionary forces. Hastily the forces of law and order were organized under the leadership of General Mannerheim. The ensuing conflict became an intensely bitter class struggle. Naturally this new calamity was a matter of grave concern to the people of Sweden, but on the question of intervention in

Finland their ranks were split wide open. Many clamoured for the dispatch of Swedish troops immediately into the unhappy land. The Edén ministry, clearly realizing that such a move might plunge the country into war with Russia, proceeded with extreme caution. For this attitude it was vehemently denounced by the Conservative leaders, who maintained that sympathy for suffering Finland as well as the safety of Sweden herself urged a speedy intervention. While the Social-Democrats denounced the excesses of the revolutionists in Finland, they supported the ministry and strongly opposed intervention. The bitterness of the internal strife in Sweden which this question provoked is a distinctly unpleasant subject to dwell upon. The ministry stood firm in its refusal to send arms and ammunition belonging to the state, but was willing to permit shipments of war material from Germany to pass through Sweden. The government also sent some war vessels to Åland to protect its inhabitants against the excesses of the Russian soldiers. Individuals and groups from Sweden also proceeded to Finland to join the White Army, as the forces of law and order were called, and there contributed greatly to the ultimate suppression of the bloody insurrection and the restoration of an orderly government. It was, however, the timely intervention of Germany, more than anything else, that saved Finland from the Reds. To many Swedes it has ever since seemed that their country's failure to intervene in the social struggle in Finland showed a callous disregard for a neighbour in distress which was most unfortunate and must be viewed as a serious political blunder.

The Åland solution.—With affairs in Finland composed, attention was again directed to the question of the Åland Islands. Sweden ultimately resolved upon submitting the matter to the League of Nations for a decision. This body appointed a committee of three men to study the matter in all its bearings and formulate recommendations. The group finally ruled that the islands rightfully belong to Finland, and this, then, became the decision of the League. Although the committee's reasoning on the main points seemed quite illogical to the Swedes, they acquiesced in the decision with customary good grace. To them it was some consolation that the League declared that the islands should always be neutral territory and never be fortified by any power; the inhabitants were also guaranteed protection against encroachments on their right to speak Swedish and exercise local self-government.

Swedish war relief.—Perhaps in no land did the misery caused by the Great War stir human sympathy so deeply as in Sweden, and her labours and sacrifices for the alleviation of suffering among the stricken peoples stand out in bright and glorious contrast to the insane bitterness and bloody deeds which otherwise made the period one of gloom and despair. Almost as soon as the war began, the Swedes were ready to help in caring for its unfortunate victims. Most of this work was done on the initiative, and under the supervision, of the Swedish Red Cross, of which Prince Carl, the noble-hearted and popular brother of the king, was president and guiding spirit. As soon as prison camps in Russia and Germany began to fill, the Swedish Government and the Swedish Red Cross, acting jointly, succeeded in making arrangements for the repatriation of those prisoners who had been so badly injured that they could never again render military service. The transportation of these unfortunates to their homes proceeded through Sweden, the Russians coming by transports to Trelleborg, the southern terminus of the Swedish state railways, whence they proceeded by special hospital trains to Haparanda, at the Finnish border, north of the Gulf of Bothnia; the Germans were, of course, carried in the reverse direction. The army of unfortunates, mere wrecks of humanity, shell-shocked, insane, armless, legless, or blind, which passed through the land aroused the most profound sympathy, and the tender care given them en route through Sweden came as a sweet reminder to them that the spirit of charity had, after all, not entirely departed from the world. In all, 18,138 of these derelicts were returned to their homes through Swedish assistance. Supplies of food, clothing, and medicine, sufficient to fill 1,016 freight cars and having a monetary value of 100,000,000 crowns, were sent from Sweden to prison camps in Russia and Siberia, the Swedish Riksdag appropriating 1,500,000 crowns for relief work in the former country. The Swedes, furthermore, built hospitals in those countries, helped to modernize their sanitary conditions, established workshops, and provided the starving with food. Appeals by Prince Carl to both Germany and Russia resulted in the abolition of some of the worst evils of the prison camps. Elsa Brändström, talented and high-minded daughter of a former Swedish minister to the Russian imperial court, won the gratitude of multitudes by her heroic labours for the alleviation of suffering. Well did she deserve the title "the Angel of Siberia" which an admiring world bestowed upon her. After the armistice, the nation also sent 1,012 freight cars of food and clothing to Germany. Ambulances were sent to Finland and disinfecting stations established in Poland. The most beautiful and touching episodes in this noble enterprise were witnessed in connection with the bringing of approximately 20,000 starving German and Austrian children to Sweden, where they were distributed among rural and urban homes. Here they were fed and tenderly cared for until health and vitality were normal again, and they could return to their homes. It was this magnificent act of humanity which prompted the Austrian Government, as evidence of the profound gratitude which the Austrian people felt, to send the coat worn by Gustavus Adolphus at the battle of Lützen as a gift to the Swedish nation (p. 366). At one time there were so many German children cared for in Stockholm that two schools were opened especially for them. Swedish relief stations were established at Berlin, Cologne, Nürnberg, and Saarbrucken, and a hospital was built in Thuringia. At one time fifty Swedish kitchens fed daily 12,000 starving young people in Vienna. Tuberculosis hospitals were established in Rumania and France, and an orphanage opened in Thuringia. The suffering which followed in the wake of the revolution in Finland was largely relieved through Swedish charity, the Swedish Government assisting by an appropriation of 1,500,000 crowns. It was, however, in Russia that the Swedes made their greatest sacrifices in order to alleviate heart-breaking suffering. After the crop failure of 1921, conditions were there indescribably pitiable. In the Samara district the Swedes at one time fed 150,000 people daily; liberal assistance, coming from Holland and Czecho-Slovakia, enabled them to enlarge the scope of this enterprise. Of the 220,000,000 pounds of supplies which the world in this crisis poured into Russia, Sweden alone contributed one-sixth. It has been estimated that the food, clothes, medicine, and money which the Swedish Red Cross collected in Sweden and distributed among the stricken peoples abroad during the years 1919-1923 represented a monetary value of 36,430,000 crowns; to this should be added many other items, not least among them being the time which multitudes of workers gave freely in the good cause. In the light of the nation's own difficulties in the years after the war, in obtaining food and bringing about an adjustment of its own life, these figures appear as truly impressive.

Communistic agitation.—The sweep of revolutionary doctrines and overthrow of old dynasties during the fateful month of November 1918 galvanized the radical group in Sweden to new life. Branting declared that the masses would now think and act under the impression of the momentous events abroad. The Social-Democrats, acknowledging so wise and fair-minded a statesman as Branting as their leader, were, however, not contemplating anything drastic. There was, however, a group of communists which, taking its cue from abroad, staged noisy demonstrations, especially in Stockholm, at which the first chamber of the Riksdag was denounced as antiquated and as a bulwark of privileged wealth, and demands were made for the abolition of property qualifications in voting, as well as for the elimination of other alleged evils. The Swedish workingmen were next called upon to establish a new government to be directed by workers, soldiers, and *bönder;* as a first step towards this new régime, a republic ought to be proclaimed and a constitutional convention convened. Demands were also made that military training be at once discontinued, wages and salaries materially increased, the eight-hour working day established, workingmen vested with control of industry, and all land belonging to corporations, the state, or great land-owners transferred to the toilers. The workingmen were next advised to resort to a general strike in all industries in case drastic measures should be found necessary in order to impose this régime upon the nation. The voice of the Soviet revolutionistis could, of course, be clearly discerned in all this hue and cry.

Timely reforms.—The Social-Democrats, while opposed to so revolutionary a program, were ready enough to take advantage of the situation in order to get reforms for which they had long been clamouring. The Conservatives were naturally opposed to any subversive measures, but it was clearly evident to them that some concessions to the demands of the Liberal groups must be made. The ministry, of which Professor Nils Edén was still the head, was composed of seven Liberals and four Social-Democrats. Already on November 14 (1918) Edén was ready to announce his program for the crisis which the nation evidently was facing; in the main this provided that the voting privilege should be made the same for all adult males in communal elections and that the provision for forfeiture of the right to vote on failure to pay taxes should be stricken out. These reforms, urged the ministry, should become effective as soon as voted, whereupon new elections for the Landstings and Communal Councils should be held. In the following Riksdag, proposals would then be made that property qualifications for voting in general elections should be abolished and the franchise given to women. This program won the support not only of the Liberals but of the Social-Democrats. The Conservatives limited their objections mainly to a claim that as the Riksdag then in session was a special one, it could not properly act on this program, but must wait until the succeeding regular session. The Radicals naturally were in a rage, and denounced the proposals as utterly inadequate. The Riksdag was ready to vote on December 17, after some concessions had been made to the Conservatives, and the ministry's victory was decisive. Radical propaganda stirred up trouble and excitement everywhere in Europe, the air was surcharged with fears and suspicion, momentous interests were at stake, but the debates in the Swedish Riksdag on the radical changes proposed proceeded with admirable calmness and display of reason. In the following year the franchise reform was carried to completion in accordance with the program thus adopted, and the right to vote was thus extended to women also. While many felt that the changes were more drastic than had been necessary, the nation, as a whole, accepted them calmly and loyally. The leaders had acted wisely. The wind had been most effectually taken from the sails of the vociferous radicals who had shouted themselves hoarse that the common people enjoyed no rights in Sweden. Talk of revolution was, after this, merely idle prattle. The reasonableness of the victors allayed the fears of the Conservatives that they would now become the victims of exploitation. Especially significant was the eloquent declaration of Branting soon after the momentous vote. "The decision implies," he said, "that unitedly we shall strive and labour for the welfare of our common fatherland; we shall endeavour to bring those classes forward which hitherto have been held back, but this shall be done in such manner that no injustice is done to those who before this have held the sole power of decision." By these franchise reforms, the number of voters which in 1905 was 402,099 or 8.2 per cent of the population, in 1911, 1,066,200, or 19.3 per cent, was increased in 1921 to 3,222,917, or 54.3 per cent of the total. In sixteen years the number of those entitled to the franchise increased eightfold.

Late ministerial changes.—The Edén ministry suffered defeat in 1920, principally on the question of communal taxes, and Hjalmar Branting was asked to form a new ministry. This was the first instance in history of a purely Socialist ministry coming to power, as a logical result of a peaceable and orderly expression of the popular will. Failing to win desired support for its program of communal tax reform, the Branting ministry relinquished power after a few months. Since then ministerial changes have followed in rapid succession. Since no political party was now willing to assume the responsibility for a new ministry, a solution was reached by the creation of a ministry consisting of state officials, representing various departments. The head of the ministry was at first Louis de Geer, son of the great statesman of the Riksdag reorganization period, and later Oscar von Sydow took his place. His ministry, which held power for a few months, devoted itself particularly to the task of rehabilitating the country's demoralized industrial structure. Branting was in 1921 again called to head the government, after the elections in the fall of that year under the extended franchise had strongly approved the program of the Left, and the process of post-war adjustment was pushed with renewed vigour. The service rendered by the minister of finance, F. V.

Thorsson, or "Uncle Thorsson," as he was affectionately called, a man who started active life as a shoemaker, became a noisy agitator, but through native talent and industry advanced to a position of authority in the field of public finance, deserves special mention. Thorsson made short shift of a number of money-consuming commissions that had been organized during the war-time and still was functioning, some of them with a large personnel of chiefs and workers. Their interference with the affairs of citizens was often found to be rather irksome and irritating. About five-sixths of these commissions were now unceremoniously scrapped by the resolute minister of finance. The Branting ministry fell in 1923 on the question of aid for unemployment,[3] and Ernest Trygger, a noted jurist and financier, long a leader among the Conservatives, and very likely their most eloquent member, formed a new ministry. Its most notable achievement was the consummation of a trade agreement with Soviet Russia. Trygger endeavoured earnestly to allay discord and secure greater unity among the different political parties at home. The constant wrangling and bickering was, he believed, seriously retarding the progress of the country. The ministry favoured the continued maintenance of strong national defence and as a subsequent election went against it on this question, in fact supporting a decidedly anti-militaristic program, it relinquished power. In 1924, Branting again formed a ministry, his third within a period of four and a half years. Illness soon compelled the great statesman and party chief to retire and his place at the head of the ministry was taken by Rikard Sandler. Reaction against militarism, in conjunction with a desire to apply consistently the principles of international good-will and trust, now resulted in a decided reduction of the military forces of the country. After the drastic act had gone into effect, the Swedish army included only about one-third of its former units. Regiments, whose beginning could be traced back to the era of military greatness and whose exploits had written many a chapter of great military exploits, were ordered disbanded. The Sandler Socialistic ministry gave way to a Liberal coalition

[3] The Riksdag of 1922 had voted 100,000,000 crowns for this purpose, but the Socialist program for bestowing aid was rejected by a majority the following year as being too reckless.

ministry under C. G. Ekman, which in 1928 was superseded by a Conservative ministry under Arvid Lindman.

Post-war readjustment.—The course of financial and industrial readjustment has been a long and difficult one for the Swedish nation to travel, but there is perhaps no exaggeration in the statement that, on the whole, it has fared better than any of the other European peoples, with the possible exception of Switzerland and Holland. Profiteering and speculation were indeed rampant during and after the war, but the government never ceased to exercise a salutary control. Largely because of this, the country escaped the worst consequences of the abnormal world situation, and the Swedish crown, except for a brief period, maintained its parity with the United States dollar. No bank failures occurred to disarrange business and undermine confidence. The issue of paper money rose from 304,060,000 crowns in 1914 to 813,530,000 in 1918. Credits to foreign nations which in 1913 totaled 98,800,000 crowns had in 1918 reached the sum of 351,500,000 crowns. In the same period, state and communal loans increased to a total of 1,140,500,000 crowns. The figures of the state budget leaped from 273,700,000 crowns in 1914 to 1,645,600,000 crowns in 1918. Taxes naturally rose at an alarming rate; thus the revenue from income taxes which in 1913 amounted to 39,800,000 crowns had in 1918 mounted to 225,200,000 crowns. The profits of the national tobacco monopoly, tonnage tax, increased charges for postage, railway transportation, and other utilities helped to swell public revenues to such an extent that the year 1918 showed a surplus of 261,300,000 crowns. The state was naturally tempted to spend money recklessly. The national debt which in 1913 stood at 648,300,000 crowns, amounted in 1918 to 1,656,200,000 crowns, and in 1928 to 1,825,572,129 crowns. Offsetting this were assets of the state, as loan funds, railways, postal, telegraph and telephone systems, public domains, resources of the government bank, and many other items, in all amounting to 3,183,793,107 crowns, or almost twice the amount of the total national debt. Aside from a loan of $5,000,000 in the United States, the creditors of the Swedish state are, with few exceptions, Swedish subjects. Public works have been managed with conspicuous honesty and efficiency during the trying times of war and readjustment. Four men have especially distinguished themselves for their splendid management of public utilities; namely, J. Juhlin, postal department, Herman Rydin, telegraph, Axel Granholm, railways, and F. V. Hanson, waterfalls and power stations.

Special Swedish industries.—The lumber and mining industries have experienced considerable depression, and this has, since the war, furthermore been seriously aggravated by labour disputes, particularly in 1928. In spite of these untoward circumstances, these industries have remained a chief asset of the nation. To an increasing degree, quality production has come to characterize Swedish industry. Specialization has come to prevail, especially in fields where skilful workmanship, superior quality of material, and ingenuity in invention have enabled the nation to find a large sale in the markets of the world. Swedish matches have for decades been sold in practically every land of the globe, but it is only under the recent brilliant and daring leadership of the noted financial and industrial giant, Ivar Kreuger (1880-), that the Swedish match industry has managed to establish monopoly for its wares in practically all the principal countries of the world. The manufacture of Swedish self-adjusting ball-bearings, the invention of Sven Winquist (1876-), has grown into a large industry with branch factories in several foreign lands and representatives in practically every civilized country. What perhaps may be looked upon as the most ingenious of Swedish inventions in the last few decades is the sun-valve for beacon-lights, which, together with other equipment for lighthouses, is manufactured in a large plant near Stockholm, as well as in branch factories in the United States and France. The inventor of the sun-valve is Gustav Dalén (1869-), who, in spite of a tragic accident which many years ago deprived him of his eyesight, continues in active management of the Swedish beacon-light industry and even since the loss of his eyesight has placed other ingenious inventions to his credit. On the basis of the well-known physical law that dark objects absorb light and heat in larger degrees than light objects, and therefore have greater expansion, Dalén's sun-valve consists of a series of polished rods around a carbon rod; as the rays of the sun fall upon the mechanism, the latter rod expands in an almost imperceptible degree, but sufficiently to close the valve which supplies gas for the beacon-light. At the approach of darkness, this rod undergoes a contraction which by a geared mechanism opens the flow of gas, which, in turn, is lighted by a pilot-light. The mechanism can be arranged to send intermittent flashes at any desired intervals, thus giving an individual character to each beacon-light. Skippers equipped with the code of these lights can therefore always be certain of the identity of the particular beacon seen. This has greatly reduced the hazards of the sea. The consumption of gas has been cut to less than one-half of that formerly required and these beacon-lights will function unerringly for a year or more without the least attention. Dalén's lights have been installed along the Panama Canal and along the coast-lines in all parts of the world. Dalén has been rewarded by the Nobel Prize in Physics. The manufacture of telephone instruments and the building and operation of telephone systems by Swedish enterprise have assumed world-wide ramifications. Thus the L. M. Ericksson Telephone Company of Stockholm has installed exchanges in such large centres as Paris, Copenhagen, Amsterdam, Warsaw, Moscow, Singapore, Canton, Shanghai, Calcutta, Mexico City, and Johannesburg. In 1923 the company had branch factories in eight countries outside of Sweden. Other important products of Swedish industry which have a world market, largely because of special inventions and superior workmanship and material, are cream separators, precision gauges, gas-flame refrigerators, electrical machinery, and vacuum cleaners. Of the latter, it is claimed that Sweden produces approximately one-half of those sold in Europe.

Swedish electrical plants have installed equipment in distant parts of the world and large orders for Swedish locomotives have in recent years been filled from Russia and South America. Large power stations have been built by the state, especially at Trollhättan, near Gothenburg, at Älvkarleö, north of Stockholm, and at Porjus, north of the Polar Circle; especially in the construction and operation of the latter have the Swedish engineers encountered peculiar difficulties, caused by long winters, cold, snow, and ice, and in surmounting these they have shown a skill that has elicited the admiration of the great technical experts of the world. The railway between Boden and Riksgränsen in Lappland, a distance of 425 miles, and that between Gothenburg and Stockholm, 400 miles, have been electrified in recent years. The supply of abundant and cheap electricity, especially for illumination, made available to an increasing number, especially by state construction of power stations, has been particularly cheering and helpful to a people living in a land where nights are long throughout a great part of the year. Swedish shipping has lately reached out to all parts of the globe. The Swedish American Mexico line, the Nordstjernan, the Swedish East Asiatic Company, and the Swedish American Line are the principal maritime enterprises. Especially the latter concern, begun in 1915, has gained a remarkable prestige and volume of passenger business; it has been a leader in introducing palatial oil-burning passenger boats in the Atlantic trade, and two of its steamers, the *Gripsholm* and the *Kungsholm,* rank among the finest of the floating palaces that in our day facilitate travel between America and Europe.

Growth of wealth.—An index to the material growth of the nation is furnished by estimates of the increase of national wealth and annual income from all sources. The total of the former was, in 1885, computed at 7,207,000,000 crowns, and in 1920, the latest year for which data are available, 14,187,602,000 crowns. Annual income from real property, capital, and work, estimated in 1886-1890 at an average annually of 560,771,000 crowns, had for the year 1920 mounted to 6,015,260,000 crowns.

The liquor traffic.—A system of liquor control which eliminates private gain and aims to enforce the principle of rationing has been put into effect, and this, in conjunction with certain social and economic factors, has resulted in a decrease in the consumption of intoxicating drinks. The plan, as devised mainly by Dr. Ivar Bratt and following the principles of the earlier "Gothenburg system," provides for the retailing of liquors only through state-controlled stores which derive no profit from sales beyond a normal rate of interest on the capital invested. It furthermore permits the sale of alcohol and wines in hotels and restaurants only in connection with the serving of meals and limits the amount which each person may buy monthly in the designated stores. The maximum for the month, which is about four quarts, may be reduced by reason of poverty or misuse of the privilege. In certain instances the right to buy liquors is denied entirely by the authorities.

Cultural activities.—While the contemplation of the material progress of the nation in this period is a most engaging pursuit, the cultural progress that has been made is also worthy of attention. Writers who helped to give lustre to the reign of Oscar II, like Selma Lagerlöf, Heidenstam, Per Hallström, Fröding, and Karlfeldt, have continued to produce works of commanding merit also in this later era. There has, however, in the latter been evident no such originality and prolific production as in the former. The same subsidence of literary energy which has been noticeable in other lands has also been manifest in Sweden. The list of young writers who have produced works of genuine merit, especially novels, is, however, quite impressive and includes such names as Sigfrid Siwertz, Ernst Didring, Hildur Dixelius, Hjalmar Bergman, Anders Österling, and Hjalmar Söderberg. A notable literary achievement is a new history of Swedish literature in several volumes by Henrik Schück (1855-). There is perhaps no exaggeration in saying that no nation has a more scholarly, or brilliantly written, account of its literature than Schück here has given his native land. Another notable literary and scholarly achievement is the completion of a history of Sweden, *Svenska folkets underbara öden,* by Carl Grimberg (1875-). Its unerring sense of the historic value of events and persons and fascinating style has won for it an unusual popularity.

Of the great painters[4] who gave lustre to the preceding reign, Bruno Liljefors and Prince Eugène have survived to the present day, but naturally their period of great artistic creation is past, and no men of the same calibre have come forward to take their places. In the domain of sculpture and architecture, Swedes have in the last three decades evinced an originality and æsthetic taste that have attracted the attention

[4] An excellent survey of the field of Swedish art are the chapters by Carl Laurin, in *Scandinavian Art,* Publication of the American Scandinavian Foundation, New York, 1922.

of the world. Carl Milles (1875-) is, no doubt, one of the most generally acclaimed leaders of the guild of sculptors in the world today. His leadership rests mainly upon his striking conceptions of historic events and personages, and brilliant blending of classical and robust native elements. Recent Swedish architecture impresses by its massive proportions, rugged and yet æsthetic forms, fidelity to environment, and adaptation to practical use. Ferdinand Boberg (1860-) has especially embellished the capital, Stockholm, with many beautiful public and private buildings, typical examples of the former being the post-office building and the home of the greatest department store of Scandinavia, *Nordiska Kompaniet.* The splendid *Nordiska Museet,* completed in 1907, in Stockholm, is the work of Gustav Clason (1856-1930). The town hall of Stockholm, completed in 1923, at a cost of 20,000,000 crowns and designed by Ragnar Östberg (1866-), is generally acclaimed the most artistic modern building of Europe. The *Högalid* Church, the creation of the architect, Ivar Tengbom (1878-), which rises in stately grandeur on a lofty eminence across the bay from the town hall, has been said to have the finest interior among modern European temples.[5] The new concert hall in Stockholm and the new art gallery at Gothenburg have also been designed by Tengbom. The new buildings which have been erected for the Technical High School of Stockholm have been designed by Erik Lallerstedt (1864-). They impress by their splendid setting and symmetry as well as by utilitarian values.

Swedish song has continued to score exceptional triumphs and has maintained the glorious traditions inaugurated by the triumphs at Paris in 1867 (p. 689). The director of the Uppsala chorus, Oscar Arpi (1824-1890) was chiefly instrumental in giving freshness, melody, and idealistic expression to song by Swedish male choruses, especially at the national universities, qualities which have won admiration for their art in many lands. Hugo Alfvén (1872-), composer and musical director, has proved himself a worthy successor of Arpi.

Swedish scientists have been active and valuable discoveries

[5] Robert W. McLaughlin, Jr., "Swedish Architecture" in *American Scandinavian Review*, February, 1929.

can be cited to their credit. Svante Arrhenius (1859-1927), the greatest name on the honour list of Swedish scientists for several generations, and recipient of the Nobel Prize in 1903, did indeed originate his theory of electrolytic dissociation during the preceding reign, but to the present belong many of his greatest contributions to knowledge. Allvar Gullstrand (1862-1930), who received the Nobel Prize in Medicine in 1911, has made important contributions to the science of optics. The brilliant work of the geologist, Gerard de Geer (1868-), has already been noted in connection with the determination of the age of man in Sweden (p. 23). The chemist, Teodor Svedberg (1884-), and the physicist, Manne Siegbahn (1886-), both recipients of the Nobel Prize, the former in 1926 and the latter in 1925, are internationally known and attract men from all parts of the world who wish to work under their supervision in the University of Uppsala laboratories, E. F. W. Alexanderson (1878-), whose inventions have largely contributed to the present success of radio transmission, has indeed performed his great services while employed as a technical expert for an American firm, but he was born and educated in Sweden, being a graduate of the Royal Technical High School of Stockholm.

Archbishop Nathan Söderblom

World peace.—The world movement towards arbitration and international good-will has found whole-hearted support in Sweden. By agreeing to submit the question of the Åland Islands to the League of Nations and then loyally abiding by the results, the Swedes gave evidence of the sincerity of their peace sentiments. The Swedish delegates to the League of Nations have, in complete accord with the representatives of the other Scandinavian countries, been found steadfastly on the side of those who have counselled justice and moderation. One phase of the great effort to bring about a better understanding and closer co-operation between different groups has especially commended itself as exemplifying the Christian law of love. This movement, which has had Archbishop Nathan Söderblom (1866-1931) as its inspiring and resourceful leader, has resulted in several great religious conferences, most notable among them being the ecumenical assembly at Stockholm in 1925, at which representatives from thirty-five nations and all great religious bodies of the world, with the exception of the Catholic Church, were represented. No such ecclesiastical assembly, it has been asserted, has ever met since the meeting of Nicæa in 325 A. D.

When in June 1928 King Gustav had reached the age of threescore years and ten, the entire nation united in paying him loving tribute. The tangible evidence of its gratitude and esteem was a sum of money raised by donations, large and small, from all over the country and totalling more than 5,000,000 crowns. Following the noble precedent of his father, who in 1897 set aside a national gift to him for the fight against tuberculosis, Gustav announced that what he had received would be employed in combatting cancer. At these times of jubilee, king and nation could truly feel that the worst of the storms were past and that prosperity, peace, and national security again gave strength and hope to the nation.

INDEX